LORNE

SUSAN MORRISON

 RANDOM HOUSE   *New York*

THE MAN WHO INVENTED *SATURDAY NIGHT LIVE*

LORNE

Published in the United States by Random House, an imprint and division of Penguin Random House LLC, New York, 1745 Broadway, New York, NY 10119.

RANDOM HOUSE and the HOUSE colophon are registered trademarks of Penguin Random House LLC.

Photo credits appear on page 615.

Library of Congress Cataloging-in-Publication Data
Names: Morrison, Susan, author.
Title: Lorne / by Susan Morrison.
Description: First edition. | New York, NY: Random House, 2025. | Includes index.
Identifiers: LCCN 2024051268 (print) | LCCN 2024051269 (ebook) |
ISBN 9780812988871 (hardcover) | ISBN 9780812988888 (ebook)
Subjects: LCSH: Michaels, Lorne, 1944– | Television producers and directors—
United States—Biography. | Motion picture producers and directors—United States—
Biography. | Television writers—United States—Biography. | LCGFT: Biographies.
Classification: LCC PN1992.4.M5 Z75 2025 (print) | LCC PN1992.4.M5 (ebook) |
DDC 791.4502/32092 [B]—dc23/eng/20241028
LC record available at https://lccn.loc.gov/2024051268
LC ebook record available at https://lccn.loc.gov/2024051269

Printed in the United States of America on acid-free paper

randomhousebooks.com
penguinrandomhouse.com

2 4 6 8 9 7 5 3 1

First Edition

Book design by Debbie Glasserman

The authorized representative in the EU for product safety and compliance is Penguin Random House Ireland, Morrison Chambers, 32 Nassau Street, Dublin D02 YH68, Ireland, https://eu-contact.penguin.ie.

FOR NANCY AND HELEN HANDELMAN
AND IN MEMORY OF LILLIAN ROSS

THAT'S SHOWBIZ. IT'S NOT A GOOD TIME UNLESS SOMEONE GETS HURT.

—TOM DAVIS

CONTENTS

LORNE

PROLOGUE

Every week at *Saturday Night Live* is just like every other week. Every week is the same because it's always intense, fueled by insanely hard work, full of triumphs and failures and backstage explosions, and because it's built around a guest host—Jennifer Lopez or Lizzo or Elon Musk—who often has no idea what they are doing. It has been Lorne Michaels's job for the last fifty years to make it seem as if they do, and to corral the egos and the talents on his staff into getting the show on the air, live. Since he created the show, in 1975, he has periodically tweaked and fine-tuned it, paying attention to how the cultural winds are drifting. But the formula has essentially remained the same. Michaels compares it to a Snickers bar: viewers expect a certain amount of peanuts, a certain amount of caramel, and a certain amount of chocolate. ("There's a comfort level," he says.) The show has good years and bad years, like the New York Yankees, or the Dow, and the audience has come to feel something like ownership of it. Just about every person who has ever watched SNL believes that its funniest years were the ones when they were in high school. Michaels likes to say that everyone in the entertainment business has two jobs: their actual job and figuring out how to fix SNL. (When J. D. Salinger died, in 2010, letters surfaced in which even he griped about what was wrong with the show.)

The show's cast members and writers have speculated for years about the secret behind Michaels's extraordinary tenure. "It's him and Hitchcock," John Mulaney says. "No one else has had this kind of longevity." Half of them believe that Michaels has repeatedly been able to remake the show for a new audience because he's a once-in-a-lifetime talent, a producer nonpareil. The other half wonders whether Michaels, gnomic and almost comically elusive, is a blank screen onto which they've all projected a lifetime of hopes and fears and dark jokes; whether he, like the cramped stages in SNL's Studio 8H, is just a backdrop for the ever-shifting brilliance of the country's best comic minds.

PART ONE

MONDAY

Lorne Michaels's week started off with a tea party and a death threat. The death threat wasn't aimed at him, but at Jimmy Fallon, the host of *The Tonight Show,* which Michaels executive produces. The tea party was in honor of his friend the playwright Tom Stoppard. After that, in his office on the seventeenth floor of 30 Rockefeller Plaza, he would preside over the first meeting for that week's episode of *Saturday Night Live.*

"I was just at a lovely tea at the Lotos Club, for Tom Stoppard," Michaels said, standing in his office, addressing a handful of his senior producers and writers, who had gathered for a preliminary meeting to troubleshoot the coming week and take a moment to check in. "It was very civilized—in contrast to *this.*" He swiveled his head around to indicate present company, and gave a mild smirk. It was 5:45 on Monday, October 29, 2018, and in fifteen minutes the weekly Writers Meeting, the official kickoff to every episode of SNL, would start. (Monday, Michaels likes to say, is "a day of redemption," a fresh start after spending Sunday brooding over Saturday night's mistakes. On his tombstone, he says, will be the word UNEVEN.) Jonah Hill, the week's guest host, would soon be greeted by the show's twenty-seven writers and sixteen cast members, who would all squeeze into Lorne's office (everyone in the business refers to him by his first name, like Madonna, or Fidel) to pitch ideas for sketches. The goal is to make the host feel supported, like one of the gang. "At that point, you're more worried about them bolting than anything else," Michaels told me. The following six days would be punishing, physically and mentally, and would culminate in a live broadcast on Saturday night at 11:30, done with no net, before a worldwide audience of six million. Tina Fey, who worked on the show for a decade, says, "You don't say yes to that hosting job if you're not up for trying something insane." Over the years, performers have compared the experience of doing

SNL to jumping out of an airplane (Fey), serving in the marine corps (Jan Hooks), and being in a "comedy emergency room" (Amy Poehler). One of Michaels's most-repeated lines is "We don't go on because we're ready, we go on because it's eleven-thirty."

The tea party for Stoppard earlier that day, held at one of the city's more elegant private clubs, was the kind of café-society affair, with a highbrow sheen, that Michaels enjoys. A phrase he uses often is "the high end of smart," and he likes to say, "If I'm the smartest person in the room, I'm in the wrong room." The cucumber sandwiches and champagne with such guests as Tina Brown and Rupert Murdoch had been a reprieve from a savage couple of weeks. Just hours before the party, he'd huddled at 30 Rock with FBI agents, who had paid a visit to Jimmy Fallon's *Tonight Show* offices on the sixth floor because Fallon's name turned up on a list of targets of a Florida man arrested for mailing pipe bombs to a dozen people who had been critical of President Donald Trump. On top of the death threat, Fallon was being attacked for having performed in blackface on SNL decades earlier; Michaels advised him not to engage—doing so would only feed the internet trolls. Michaels had been blasted in the press, too: Taran Killam, a former cast member who used to play Donald Trump, had recently complained on a podcast that Michaels always insisted that he make Trump "likable," and the story wouldn't go away. (One of Michaels's core comedy tenets is that every impersonation should contain a speck of humanity or charm, to make the character relatable. Playing a character "from hate," he'll say, isn't funny; he often quotes Elaine May: "When in doubt, seduce.")

"I just want to go over where we are this week," Michaels, in a dress shirt and tie, said to the small group in his office, fifteen minutes before the Writers Meeting began. (This regular confab is known as the Topical Meeting.) "We're doing a show two days before the midterm elections." President Trump had been crisscrossing the country, holding rallies to whip up his base against the predicted "blue wave" of Democratic candidates. Since Trump's election, SNL had been on a high, getting the best ratings in years and winning eighteen Emmys (the show has collected 103 in its fifty-year history).

Alec Baldwin had become an unofficial cast member, regularly undergoing hours in the hair and makeup department in order to portray Trump as a lip-scrunching, slit-eyed scowl of aggrieved petulance. The impression was popular—people were stopping Baldwin on the street to thank him—and it provoked the president to spew unhinged Twitter rants, to the delight of everyone at SNL.

Viewers always expect politics in the show, but the news cycle was moving so quickly that it was impossible to say what stories would feel relevant by Saturday night. "Unless somebody has a foolproof idea now," Michaels said. "Trump is just going to keep going whirlwind."

Colin Jost, one of the show's two head writers and an anchor of the Weekend Update segment, wondered aloud whether Barack Obama had been out campaigning for Democrats.

"He was in Georgia with Stacey Abrams," Michaels said. "Will"—Ferrell—"was there too, knocking on doors."

A producer asked whether Alec Baldwin would be available. Michaels said that Baldwin had called to say that he would be sitting this show out. "He was in touch with the FBI too," Michaels said, referring to the pipe-bomber's target list. He chuckled and added, "These are dangerous times."

Michaels stands about five foot eight, but his posture and nonchalant confidence belie his actual height. His eyes are close-set and dark, with a glitter of mockery. Crinkles sprout from the corners. The attitude he projects is perhaps best captured by a phrase that A. J. Liebling used to describe a wine: "warm but dry, like an enthusiasm held under restraint." (His friend Paul McCartney says, "He always reminded me of Jack Benny.") His smile, when he summons one, is a straight line that bisects his face like a slash. His hair is silvery and frequently barbered; it frames his face in a brushy fringe, like a hedgehog, or a senator. A gleaming white asterisk—his Order of Canada rosette—is usually in his lapel; and on his right hand is a bulky gold signet ring, set with a square red stone engraved with Sufi characters, which he bought in the 1970s at a junk shop in Santa Monica. He has had replicas made for his wife and three grown children. "It was an old imam's sealing ring," he told me. "The guy I bought it from told me the inscription means 'With the luck of Ishmael.' And Ishmael had no luck whatsoever. So it's a joke, a Sufi joke. You could open with this in Persia."

Michaels has four chief deputies, each of whom embodies a different facet of his personality. Erik Kenward, a calm *Harvard Lampoon* alum with a neatly trimmed beard, has worked at the show since 2001 and has absorbed the boss's unflappable steadiness, with a tinge of the long-suffering. Colin Jost, who was also a *Harvard Lampoon* editor, is, like Michaels, demonstrably well-read and au courant about politics. He is married to Scarlett Johansson, which lends him a Hollywood shimmer that Michaels appreciates. Erin Doyle, whose family owned pubs in Philadelphia, rose through the ranks after starting as an intern and became one of Michaels's assistants. She has a palpable warmth and, like Michaels, a knack for dealing with high-strung famous people; she also produces shows for his production company, Broadway Video. Steve Higgins moonlights as Jimmy Fallon's announcer, egging on Fallon's boyish tendencies. He grew up in Des Moines, and had an early cable show with his brother in which they chain-smoked in a kitchen and watched comedy clips. He is a booster of silliness, a quality that Michaels considers essential to the show; and he is a reliable errand man when Michaels, known to avoid confrontation, has bad news to deliver.

In the Topical Meeting in Michaels's office, Doyle mentioned that Jim Downey had called with an idea for the cold open, the newsy sketch that starts every show and ends with a performer looking into the camera and shouting, "Live, from New York, it's Saturday Night!" Downey is a revered figure in these offices, a former head writer who was hired right out of Harvard in the show's second season, and stayed for thirty-three years. He has been responsible for many of SNL's most memorable political sketches. (The word "strategery," deployed by Will Ferrell's George W. Bush, was a Downey creation.) Downey and Michaels have always viewed the show's mandate as speaking truth to power, whoever that power might be. But in the age of Trump, many SNL staffers were finding that holding powerful liberals accountable was tough to stomach.

Doyle said, "Downey's idea was Chuck Schumer and Nancy Pelosi giving a press conference, and the point is that they're bummed out that no pipe bombs were mailed to *them*." Everyone laughed. But the bomber was last week's story—it would feel old by Saturday.

Michaels told the group that he planned to ask the cast to stay behind after the Writers Meeting. "I want to go through their various complaints," he said. Two of his star cast members were in revolt, and he planned to tap his patriarchal side to smooth things over. ("I think all comedy shows—this sounds a bit pretentious, but I am a bit pretentious—are based on family," he's said.) Cecily Strong, a dark-haired comedian who regularly killed with her impression of Melania Trump, was in a sulk about being asked to make fun of the Democratic Senator Dianne Feinstein in a sketch about the confirmation hearings for Trump's Supreme Court nominee Brett Kavanaugh. (Strong's Feinstein had barked, "We're back from lunch. I had *soup*," in a doddering drawl.) Leslie Jones, at fifty-one the oldest performer on the show, was becoming increasingly vocal about her conviction that the writers didn't know how to write for her. (Jones had been made a cast member in 2014, when Michaels, responding to criticism about the show's record on diversity, auditioned twenty-five Black women in the middle of the season. Two seasons later, Jones was nominated for an Emmy.) One more distraction: Pete Davidson, at twenty-four the youngest cast member, was being battered on social media after the pop star Ariana Grande called off their highly publicized quickie engagement.

Talking about the cast, Michaels continued, "I want to try to make them understand the distinction between their own political feelings and the script." There had been a lot of last-minute tinkering lately, with cast members wanting to adjust their lines just before air. At SNL, the writer is paramount, and sometimes the cast resents this. He continued, "If they think that they shouldn't be making fun of this person or that person, we have a problem." Michaels has been broadcasting political satire on the show since the seventies, when Chevy Chase played Gerald Ford as a bumbling klutz and Dan Aykroyd impersonated Jimmy Carter talking a caller down from a bad acid trip.

("Were [the pills] barrel-shaped?" he asks. "Okay, right, you did some Orange Sunshine.") He's accustomed to dealing with the ardent political sensitivities of millennials. "Also," he added, "there's nobody we ever *did* on the show who wasn't thrilled about it," he said. "See Anthony Scaramucci. Or Dick Cheney."

Michael Che, a Black comic who is Jost's co–head writer and Update anchor, said, "Really? Cheney liked it?"

Michaels made a half grin. "Oddly enough, we're not as menacing as you would think," he said. He learned years ago that politicians like to appear on the show, in order to look smarter by satirizing themselves.

Jonah Hill would soon arrive on the seventeenth floor. Before he came in for a ceremonial powwow with Michaels, the inner circle had a little more business to go over. Lindsay Shookus, the talent coordinator, mentioned that this would be Hill's fifth time hosting. That meant they could do a sketch about him joining the Five Timers Club, a pretend wood-paneled sanctum where veteran hosts (Steve Martin, Justin Timberlake, Melissa McCarthy, among others), drink brown liquor and wear smoking jackets emblazoned with a Five Timers crest.

"Yeah-yeah-yeah-yeah," Michaels said, the syllables tumbling out in a staccato rush. It's a verbal tic, along with "No-no-no-no, I know," which also indicates agreement. The longtime SNL writer Robert Smigel says that Michaels's "yeah-yeah-yeah-yeah" thing is the one bit of Jewishness still left in him.

"Do we *have* a jacket?" Michaels asked.

"We can have one made," Shookus said.

"So few things fit . . . ," Michaels mused, referring to Hill's recent weight loss. Mentally scrolling through Hill's previous four appearances on the show, he mentioned a sketch that Hill had done about a six-year-old at Benihana. "So he's here to do comedy?"

Shookus nodded. "He's sick of talking about vulnerability." Hill was fresh from promoting his directorial debut, a brooding independent movie about a suicidal teenager and skateboard culture, called *Mid90s.*

"All right," Michaels said. "Bring him in." The room emptied, and Jonah Hill strode in and stuck out his hand. He had on jeans, a black shirt buttoned up to the neck, and a trim khaki-colored jacket.

"Congratulations on the movie," Michaels said, as Hill took a seat in a chair across the desk. "Was Scott Rudin involved in it?"

"He produced it!" Hill said brightly, not realizing that Michaels was making an extremely deadpan joke, the kind that comedy people refer to as "dog whistle." Rudin is known for being an energetic promoter of his own projects, and had likely pushed for Hill's booking on SNL.

"Reaaaally?" Michaels said in mock surprise, making his joke clear.

Hill broke into nervous laughter. "Ha ha ha! That was very good! Your delivery was so dry that I literally didn't pick up on it."

Then Michaels indulged in a little insider talk, designed to draw Hill in and make him feel like he had a seat at the grown-ups' table. A message was embedded in the talk, as it often is when Michaels unspools a tale of Old Hollywood and drops a lot of names.

"I think Scott has turned into the best version of Scott Rudin," Michaels said. "He was more driven at the beginning." (Rudin is known for impetuously firing assistants and throwing staplers. A few years later he would be forced to step back from his businesses after former employees went to the press with these tales.)

Hill nodded. "I would hear all those bad things about him, but, as a director, I had nothing but the best experience," he said. "Do you recognize that sort of change happening with a lot of legendary people?"

"Oh, yeah-yeah-yeah-yeah," Michaels said. "Mike used to tell this story about when they were editing *Catch-22*." (He took it for granted that Hill knew he was referring to Mike Nichols. Sometimes he will pause after saying a famous friend's first name; then, as if realizing that his interlocutor is at a loss, he will supply the surname almost apologetically, in a clipped way. This results in a lot of sentences with a halting cadence: "Paul . . . *Simon* used to say . . ." Or "Jack . . . *Nicholson* told me." Colleagues refer to "Jack" and "Mick" and "Paul" as "Lorne's all-stars.") "Mike was walking on the beach with his editor, Sam O'Steen, and another friend. Sam said to the guy, 'You notice something different about Mike? He's not an asshole anymore.'"

Hill gave a huge laugh, elated at being included in this cozy conversational orbit with the late director of *The Graduate*.

"Because he'd *been* an asshole on his first two movies," Michaels clarified. "It's that thing of, when you start to *believe* in yourself, when you're not so frightened—"

Hill jumped in: "Then you don't have to be a psychopath!"

The cautionary tale dispensed, Michaels turned to business: "So, we're going to do a comedy show? The writers are going to come in, you're going to pretend to like their pitches."

Hill wagged his head up and down. "It's pure joy to be here," he said.

Michaels rules SNL with detached but absolute power. He harbors no illusions that his Canadian tendency toward self-deprecation is taken seriously by anyone. One talent agent routinely tells clients auditioning for Michaels to always remember that *he* is the real star of the show. He is the alpha in most of his employees' lives. To those people, and to the wider comedy world, he is, not accidentally, a mythic figure, a mysterious object of obsession. "He is aware of his own Lorne-ness," Mike Myers says. Conversations about him are peppered with comparisons: He is the Godfather (Chris Rock, Will Forte), Jay Gatsby (Bernie Brillstein), Obi-Wan Kenobi (Tracy Morgan), the Great and Powerful Oz (David Spade, Kate McKinnon), Charles Foster Kane (Jason Sudeikis), a cult leader (Victoria Jackson), Tom Ripley (Bill Hader), Machiavelli, and both the Robert Moses and the Darth Vader of comedy (Bruce McCall). Bob Odenkirk feels that Michaels "set himself up as some kind of very distant, strange Comedy God." "There's so many people who, their whole lives, have been trying to figure him out," Bill Hader says. Another colleague put it this way: "I feel about Lorne the way I feel about the ocean. It's huge and beautiful, but I'm afraid of it."

Michaels's office door opened, and Hill turned his chair to face the room, as thirty-some people filed in, most in jeans or sweatpants, several in slippers, many chewing gum. At least a few were fresh from talking about Michaels and the show in therapy sessions, Monday afternoon being the optimal therapy slot, given the week's ironclad schedule. As in elementary school, people sit in the same place each week: four across a velvet couch, a dozen on chairs placed against the walls, others standing in the doorway and wedged near Michaels's private bathroom (his Emmy statuettes are crammed in a corner by the sink), and around fifteen on the floor, their legs folded like grade-schoolers. The effect was of a young prince—Hill—on a throne, a throng of supplicants at his feet, the potentate behind him at the desk. (More than one staffer has heard their therapist say, "You start your week by *sitting on the floor?*") Tina Fey describes the Monday meeting, with its mandatory genuflecting, as "a church ritual."

Michaels, his back to a window framing the Empire State Building, put his feet on his desk. He's had it since 1975, when he first set up shop at NBC. "There were deer running through the halls of Rockefeller Center then," he told me. Of all the floors he was shown when picking out space for his new venture, he chose seventeen, because he was born on the seventeenth of November, and because it was serviced by a different elevator bank than the executive floor. He found the network-issued steel desks and shelves too corporate, so he hunted out some funkier wooden pieces in dusty NBC store-rooms. The network had initially put Michaels in temporary quarters, in the vacant office of a former programming executive. In the desk he found some old Maalox tablets and a desiccated ivy plant. As if trying to keep alive a connection to a swankier era of NBC—the age of Toscanini's NBC Symphony Orchestra and *The Tonight Show* with Steve Allen—he nursed the plant, faithfully hydrating it with a special mister. Today its vines of heart-shaped leaves climb the window frame and spread along the top of a pair of barrister's bookcases. The shelves hold hundreds of SNL episodes on VHS tapes.

Instead of the barren expanse that characterizes the average mo-gul's desk, Michaels's is cluttered with framed photos and kitschy totems—a bobblehead doll of Yankees outfielder Paul O'Neill; a Bokar Coffee can (it's the brand his mother drank) full of sharpened pencils, points up; a cut-glass canister of Tootsie Rolls (he once made a nice profit investing in the company); figurines of Bing Crosby and the Buddha; a green-shaded banker's lamp; and a promotional cardboard desk calendar for Broadway Video (its jagged-skyline design has not changed since 1979). The effect is part English club, part dorm room. Somewhere within reach of the desk is always a paper towel–lined basket full of freshly made popcorn, a habit picked up when he quit smoking in the eighties. The upholstered furniture is mostly refurbished Art Deco—all bulbous curves. A fish tank bubbles in a corner. On the wall are photographs by William Wegman, including a shot of one of his Weimaraners. A framed photo of a short man alongside a tall man in uniform, standing by a Lincoln Continental, commemorates the time in the eighties when Michaels and his friend Paul Simon got pulled over outside Memphis with a joint in the car, and the state trooper, a fan of *Graceland,* asked not for license and registration, but for an autograph. (Michaels stepped away from the vehicle to snap the photo.) Along one wall is a long bulletin board striped with columns of color-coded index cards. This is where the elements of each week's show get assembled and disassembled and assembled again. Above the board hangs an engraved plaque that Rosie Shuster, Michaels's first wife and a writer on SNL's early seasons, stumbled on in a West Village antiques shop in the seventies: THE CAPTAIN'S WORD IS LAW.

Once everyone settled, Michaels started the meeting: "This is Jonah Hill," he announced, and the supplicants applauded and whooped. Hill gave a small wave. A veteran, he wasn't cowed. (When you host the first time, Jon Hamm says, "you're assaulted by the history of the show.") Hill would not pitch any ideas that day, although hosts sometimes do. Christopher Walken had a memorable suggestion, in 2008: "Ape suits are funny," he told the room, in his flat Queens accent. After a pause, he added, "*Bears* as well."

"Beck!" Michaels barked, notifying Beck Bennett, a handsome cast member known for playing Mike Pence, that he would go first.

"Hi, Jonah," Bennett said from the arm of a couch. "Uh, how about if you're a guy who's into karate classes, but you don't have anyone to talk to about it? So you go to a doctor's waiting room and you pretend to fill out forms and you go, 'Hey, man, is your sensei riding your ass this week?'" Laughter in the room, including from Michaels. Good start.

Next he called on Aidy Bryant, a bubbly brunette with a daffy streak.

"*Hiii,*" she said. "So maybe we're in couples therapy, and the therapist is like, 'Why don't you both say why you fell in love with each other?' And I'm like, 'Because of his big heart.' And you go, 'Because of her feet.'" More laughs.

Kenward, the producer, was up: "HBO says all of its shows now have to have intimacy coordinators, sort of like animal trainers for sex scenes. So I thought you could be one of those."

Each pitch placed Hill at the center of a comic scene. But the exercise is largely ceremonial. It's rare for an idea floated on Monday to make it to air on Saturday night, or even to be written up as a script. If an idea were to elicit big laughs on Monday, it could lose its combustive force by Wednesday afternoon, when forty or so sketches are read aloud around a big table. The writers save their best stuff for the read-through. The Monday gathering is more like a session of speed stand-up, with the comics sitting down. The idea is to make the host laugh, to instill confidence that this roomful of the comedy-elect will provide a safety net.

Alex Moffat, a Chicago-born actor who was the show's Eric Trump, proposed a commercial parody pegged to the Red Sox's World Series victory the previous evening: celebratory boozing had created an epidemic of erectile dysfunction in Boston. The solution: "Jonah Hill's bonah pills." People groaned, and someone weakly said, "Well done." (Wordplay is viewed as a low-grade, if irresistible, form of humor.)

The pitches kept coming:

"Maybe you're a high-powered attorney in a big trial, but you keep accidentally calling the judge 'Mom.'"

"You play a guy who's really into pornography, but your one complaint is . . . *Why they gotta cuss?*"

"They say that Texas has gone from being a red state to a purple state. So you play a character called Walker, Texas Community Liaison."

"Maybe you're a vampire who's decided to go vegan."

Leslie Jones, the cast member whom Michaels was hoping to mollify, was next. "Okay, um," she said, with an unsteady bravado. "We're, like, friends, and we find out that we have the same therapist, and we compete with each other trying to be the best patient." Polite chuckles. Jones picked up the ambivalence and said, "Ugh."

A writer named Michael Koman came to her aid. "Maybe Leslie's a famous ventriloquist and you're her dummy," he said to Hill. "But it turns out that you're just a guy she got her hand stuck inside." The laughs (and some "ewwwwws") had a guttural edge, reserved for gross-out material.

Next up was Pete Davidson, whose long face and sleepy eyes, peeking out from under a hoodie, gave him a monastic look, if monks had blue hair. He told about opening the door to his hotel room recently to find a room-service waiter collapsed on the floor. "He wouldn't let me help him," Davidson said. "He just kept going, 'Mr. D! Your eggs are getting cold!'" It wasn't clear whether this was a sketch idea or a tidbit from Davidson's new life as a tabloid celebrity. He had recently moved out of the $16 million apartment that he had been sharing with Ariana Grande and a pet pig, and was now "homeless," he said. (A few people exchanged glances. "'Mr. D'? Is that a thing now?" someone murmured.)

Wedged behind a coffee table on the floor, Kate McKinnon, one of the show's stars, pushed aside a vase of hundreds of dollars' worth of peonies so that she could see Hill. "All right," she said in a sultry voice. "You're at a bar, hitting on people, and your line is 'I don't know if you know this . . . but I'm TSA-pre.'"

After everyone in the room had taken a turn, Michaels moved into his low-energy version of a coach's pep talk. "There's an election next Tuesday," he said. "People are going to be paying attention, so let's have some stuff about that. And then the rest of it will be some comedy. All right. Let's start." Everybody clapped, and Hill went off to confer with the publicity department, and to be measured for wigs.

Michaels asked the performers to stay put. Once the others had filed out, he gave the cast a rare talking-to, emphasizing that the show isn't a platform for their own political beliefs. "On whatever side, if there's idiocy, we go after it," he said. "We can't be the official organ of the Democratic Party." He urged the cast to respect the words the writers had written, and to remember that "we've got the whole country watching—all fifty states."

Michaels's first big job in network television was writing for *Laugh-In,* in the 1960s. He and his fellow writers worked out of a motel in Burbank, far from the NBC studio, entirely cut off from the production process, their scripts put through a sausage grinder. One of his fairly radical ideas, from the beginning of SNL, was that the writers should be elevated rather than marginalized. Though the boundaries between the cast and writers are fluid (most performers write sketches; many writers have stage experience), there can be competitive friction between the two groups. Michaels regards his job as "holding a group of people who don't agree about much together."

The meeting was brief and straightforward. Michaels believes in loose reins with creative people, and he reassured the actors that their input was valued. For instance, McKinnon, known for portraying Hillary Clinton, Kellyanne Conway, and Jeff Sessions (whom she zoomorphized into a possum), always contributed a lot to the writing of her characters. "So, if Kate wants to add a tail to her Jeff Sessions, I don't jump all over her and say, 'Well, he doesn't have a tail.' That's her idea," he told me later that evening. "If I think it's over the top, or distracting, then I might. It's the freest environment that way." He'd been worried about Cecily Strong, who'd objected to taking a jab at Feinstein. "Cecily didn't mind playing her, but she didn't want to do anything to possibly hurt her," he said, bewildered. "They care so deeply now. The women in particular feel so threatened." And Leslie Jones had been dropping hints about quitting. "It's a world made of eggshells, as my mother used to say." He concluded coolly, "In any event, in five years none of this will matter, and some of them will have careers and some won't."

ONE

TORONTO THE GOOD

WHEN LORNE LIPOWITZ WAS FIVE YEARS OLD, HE DECIDED TO RUN AWAY from home. His mother, Florence, played along, packing a little bag for him and walking him to the door of their house in the leafy Forest Hill neighborhood of Toronto. She asked him if he knew where he would be staying. "I'm going to live with a family that loves me," he told her. Lorne's little brother, Mark, who had been sitting on the stairs crying, looked up at his brother in the doorway. "What if they don't have a television?" he asked. It was 1950, and the Lipowitzes were one of the families on the block whose living room contained a TV set. Lorne paused at the threshold. He put the suitcase down.

Before television, there were the movies. For as long as Michaels can remember, his parents would sit around the kitchen table with his mother's parents and talk about Humphrey Bogart and Spencer Tracy and James Cagney. His maternal grandparents, Moishe and Sarah Becker, owned a movie theater, the College Playhouse, near the University of Toronto. (Florence had met her husband, Henry, whom she called "Lefty," when she was working in the box office.) Each week they went downtown to the film exchange to choose a new picture. Natural programmers, they had a feel for what their neighborhood audience would show up for. The family had passionate opinions about movie stars, and discussed them with an easy intimacy. "They would stick with Jimmy Cagney in a bad movie because, on some level, they didn't want to let him down," Michaels recalled. The movie-star talk was so fond and familiar that Lorne grew up assuming that his parents and grandparents were friends with Bogart and the rest.

After school, Lorne would often walk to the College Playhouse to be looked after by his grandmother. Some days he would do his homework in the lobby; sometimes he'd slip into the theater and watch a bit of whatever was on, maybe a Randolph Scott picture.

If Lorne's grandmother babysat the boys at night, she would turn on *The Colgate Comedy Hour* with Martin and Lewis, or Sid Caesar's *Your Show of Shows,* and explain how the people on the small black-and-white screen fit into the larger ecosystem of show business. Lorne listened as she described the almost Darwinian way the performers had adapted, as vaudeville gave way to radio, and radio to movies, and movies to television. "She'd explain that Jack Benny had been a handsome young vaudeville player, then became a gray-haired man in radio; then, for television, he dyed his hair black," Michaels remembers. His durable interest in the overlapping and interweaving of Hollywood generations began here.

Michaels and his friends went to the movies every Saturday afternoon, and whatever was playing is what they saw. He and Mark would ride their bikes to a theater on Eglinton Avenue. (Their sister, Barbara, nine years younger than Lorne, was too small for the movie outings.) Every so often, their father would drive them, a notable occasion for Lorne, who was always hungry for time with his dad. They saw westerns, Bowery Boys features, or adventure pictures, like *The Crimson Pirate* with Burt Lancaster. Lorne's favorite movies, *Casablanca* for example, were hard-boiled with a core of sweetness. He did not like scary movies and still doesn't. Like many kids, at four he was undone by *The Wizard of Oz.* "Nobody prepared me for the idea of pure evil," he told me. When the flying monkeys darkened the screen, he had to be carried out of the theater.

Henry Lipowitz's father, Aaron, had been a furrier who didn't have great business sense. As an adult, Henry took over the family fur concern and turned it around, becoming successful enough to put his brother Harold through medical school and to go into an early semi-retirement. Henry was quiet, Florence a talker. The marriage wasn't a great love affair, but Michaels remembers his parents as being close. Florence was an archetypal Jewish mother. "They had their way of dealing with each other," Michaels recalled. "If she was driving him crazy with her anxiety, he would go out for the late edition of *The Globe and Mail* at ten o'clock at night. She'd say, 'When will you be back?' He'd say, 'Soon.'"

Family friends describe Florence as having a "foghorn voice" and being "a real character." Paul Pape, a schoolmate of Lorne's, recalls her saying—for years on end—that a doctor had given her six months to live. "Comedy in that household was a defense," Lorne's cousin Neil Levy said. Rosie Shuster, a neighborhood girl who met Lorne when they were teenagers, said of Florence, "She would build Lorne up like he was a god amongst men. Unless he was there. Then she would tear him down." (When her son wasn't in earshot, Florence used to brag that he'd been so precocious, she used to throw magazines into his crib.)

"My mother was from a generation that kept the compliments in a tin box on a top shelf," Michaels said. "And there was a little bit of dust on it because it wasn't taken down very often. If you did really well, which I seldom did, she'd be on the phone, bragging about it. But she'd never say much to me. That was what I thought was normal." But around the neighborhood, Florence was known as a natural problem-solver. She'd open the door to her tidy kitchen to a troubled visitor and say, "Come into the mess." She'd put on a pot of coffee, light a cigarette, and listen. When Lorne came home from school, he often found a person sitting at the kitchen table with his mother, crying.

She was also a natural manipulator. As a girl, she'd loved playing the piano, pounding out the themes from *Ben-Hur* and other silent pictures, learned from the sheet music her parents brought home. When she married Henry, they didn't have a piano. Hoping to acquire one, she pestered young Lorne about whether he'd like to take piano lessons. "She later claimed that I told her that I just wanted to play baseball," Michaels recalled, suggesting an early guilt trip.

His memories of his father have a more wistful cast. He once took Lorne to a diner and encouraged him to order everything he wanted. Lorne couldn't finish the hotdog, hamburger, and french fries that he'd ordered, and his father told him, with some solemnity, "Your eyes are bigger than your stomach." It made an impression—Michaels goes so far as to call it "seminal"—and he links it with skills he'd later use as a producer ("You have to figure out what the right amount of something is"). It seems likelier that the novelty of having his father's undivided attention was as memorable as the platitude. "It was rare, and thrilling, that I went anywhere alone with my father," he said.

On the desk in Michaels's satellite office on the ninth floor of 30 Rock is a framed photograph of him as a toddler, nestled on the lap of his Aunt Joyce, Florence's youngest sister. Joyce had married a successful businessman named Morris Levy, known as Pep. The Levys were richer than the Lipowitzes and lived in a more stylish part of Forest Hill, in a mansion with an indoor swimming pool and a tennis court. (In 2020, the house was listed for sale at $18 million.) They also had a lakefront compound in Balfour Beach, a Jewish summer colony an hour north of Toronto. Joyce was a warm, imaginative woman with an easy laugh, less volatile than Florence, and she and Lorne were close. She had dreamed of directing and was a natural stage-mother; she and her husband attended every school play their nephew was in. Lorne was drawn, somewhat guiltily, toward this household of bright, attractive people, which functioned as the family seat, the locale of seders and celebrations. The Levys hugged; the Lipowitzes didn't.

"Everybody saw something special in Lorne," Neil Levy, who grew up in his cousin's shadow, said. The uncles and aunts curated his childhood witticisms, and he understood that much was expected of him. The population of Forest Hill was largely second-generation Jews, families who had arrived in Toronto, a Calvinist outpost of the British Empire, around the turn of the century. They had big dreams for their children. "This was a hothouse," Lorne's friend Paul Pape said. "Everybody was smart. Everybody was a super-achiever." The common goal among Lorne's schoolmates was getting into the University of Toronto and fulfilling their parents' plan for them to become professionals—lawyers or doctors.

The community achieved a blip of notoriety in 1956, when a group of social scientists published a government-funded study of Forest Hill's schools and culture. Thinly disguising the community with a pseudonym, "Crestwood Heights," the project's official goal was to improve Canada's mental health system, but the report caused a local furor and was picked up by American book reviewers. It described a "gilded ghetto" of status-obsessed strivers consumed with back-fence gossip about school placement and home decor. One researcher tsk-tsked the plastic slipcovers that protected upholstery from children who were banished to basement playrooms, adding that "broadloom is particularly incompatible with permissiveness in toilet training." The authors cited statistics suggesting that, owing to their parents' compulsions and the community's matriarchal tendencies, five to ten percent of Forest Hill's children were in need of psychiatric attention.

Crestwood Heights: A Study of the Culture of Suburban Life scandalized the parents of Forest Hill, who whispered defensively about it over bridge games. The supposedly neurotic children didn't notice. After school, they would ride bikes, and in the winter there was hockey on an ice rink improvised by flooding the playground. Afterward, Michaels said, "while you waited for dinner, you watched TV. And television was like a miracle." Television lifted the mood of the world he grew up in, still darkened by the gloom of the Second World War. Michaels remembers waiting for the broadcast day to begin, and then waiting again for the set to warm up. Early Canadian programming tended toward the worthy: Shakespeare, science shows, folk singers. By 1953, when Lorne was eight, the American channels arrived, and Canada, Michaels said, suddenly felt like "a branch plant economy."

He was immediately hooked on American television—particularly comedy programs like *The Phil Silvers Show.* He'd first noted the power of jokes in second grade, when he made a mean crack at the expense of a boisterous plump girl whom the teacher had threatened to shut inside a locker. Lorne blurted out, "She won't fit." More memorable than having his hand whacked with a ruler was the fact that he'd made his classmates laugh.

Everything about American television seemed more exciting than what the CBC offered. When Lorne and his friends watched their favorite shows, they were captivated by the ads for American candy bars. "And at the end they would say, 'Not available in Canada,'" he recalled. Whenever someone was going to Buffalo, a few hours away, they'd bring back Snickers bars, and later Levi's. The local Rowntree's and Cadbury candy bars were perfectly good, he said. "But they weren't advertised on television."

The candy bars gave way to rock and roll in 1957, with the advent of *American Bandstand* on ABC. That year, the rock promoter Irvin Feld brought his extravaganza, "The Biggest Show of Stars," to Toronto's Maple Leaf Gardens. Michaels had a ticket. The acts included the Everly Brothers, Frankie Lymon, Paul Anka, and the headliners Buddy Holly and the Crickets. "They only had three songs," Michaels said. After the Crickets performed, the audience refused to leave. "So they played 'That'll Be the Day' again." Michaels, a spellbound fanboy, remembers the scene as a "frenzy"; a local newspaper account described "an orderly crowd of teenagers."

Enthralled by the spectacle onstage, he daydreamed about various forms of show business—acting, writing, directing, even singing. As a thirteen-year-old at Camp Timberlane, in the highlands of Haliburton, Ontario, he explored his impresario side. "Your parents ship you off for eight weeks," he said. "And it's the best part of the year for you and the best part of the year for them." (It didn't always work that way. His mother kept one letter from an earlier summer, penciled in wobbly cursive on a sheet of camp stationery decorated with sailboats and ponies. It read: "Mom and dad I have not recieved one letter and I wrote 10 what happened gooby [sic].")

Most campers spent their days practicing archery among the white birches or rigging skiffs on Two Islands Lake, but for Lorne, putting on shows was the heart of the Timberlane experience. At thirteen, he was cast as Captain Hook in the recent Broadway hit *Peter Pan,* performing the hammy showstopper "Hook's Waltz" ("Who's the swiniest swine in the world? / Captain Hook! Captain Hook!"). His chief camp collaborator was Howard Shore, a precocious musician a couple of years younger, also from Forest Hill. Back home, the two boys used to listen to John Coltrane records in Shore's basement, Howard placing the LP on the turntable with a ceremonial slowness. As the cutting-edge jazz rose up the stairs, Shore's father would yell down, "Play the melody!" (Michaels still uses the phrase when he signs off on a phone call with Shore.) At camp, the two friends put on musicals, with Lorne directing and Howard playing piano and conducting a few woodwinds. But mostly they created freewheeling revues, part of a camp tradition called the "FAST Show," FAST being an acronym for the names of the four campers who had originated the show—"Something like Feinman, Abrams, Salter, and a kid whose last name began with *T,*" Shore said. Performed every week as the centerpiece of a camp-wide social, it was truly a fast piece of work, put together on the fly. They'd rehearse every afternoon at four, in wet bathing suits, and on Saturday night, after campers had worn themselves out on the dance floor, the FAST Show took over: comedy sketches, pantomime, lip-synching to records with choreography. "Anything you could think of to impress girls," Shore said.

Word of the FAST Shows spread on the camp circuit, with campers from Minnesota to northern Ontario hearing tales of the Timberlane whiz kid Lorne Lipowitz. For a teenager, he was a calm, commanding presence. He would stand in the middle of the room, and kids would scurry over, get their instructions, then rush off and execute them. Shore always felt that the seeds of SNL—quickly assembled live comedy and music on Saturday night—sprouted on the plywood stage at Timberlane.

ONE NIGHT, IN JANUARY 1959, A BIT MORE THAN A MONTH AFTER LORNE'S bar mitzvah, his father collapsed at home and was taken to a hospital, where he was kept in an oxygen tent for several weeks. The children were not allowed to visit. Their grandmother moved in, so that Florence could keep vigil at his bedside. Lorne, Mark, and Barbara were told only that their father was getting better and would be home soon. On one of these tense, peculiar days, Lorne squabbled with his grandmother and stalked off to the bedroom he shared with his brother. He heard a commotion downstairs. "At first I thought it was laughing," he said. "It turned out to be crying." Mark ran into the bedroom and said, "Daddy's dead." Henry Lipowitz was fifty. He died of a pulmonary embolism.

Lorne and his father had argued on the night of the collapse. He'd missed his curfew, and Florence had goaded her husband into disciplining him. "My mother was on him, like, 'You can't allow him to do this! He has to obey the rules!'" Michaels recalled. After the angry words that night, Lorne never saw his father again. For the rest of his life, he would make a point of knowing what was going on around him, and surrounding himself with people who kept him in the loop; he didn't want to be taken by surprise. He also became terrified of conflict. "At fourteen, you think that somehow you brought this all about," he said.

The family's ordeal was complicated by the fact that, when Henry died, the Lipowitzes were about to move into a new house. Florence had been excited about buying all new furniture—moving up in the world. "It was the future," Michaels said. They were living in a sparsely furnished rental, waiting for the new house to be ready. Florence fell into a depression. She had three children, the youngest five years old. She had to learn to drive. Lorne's home life hadn't been the warmest, but now it was shattered. "Even if the team is not a winning team, you're on a team," he said, referring to his parents' imperfect marriage. (Sports metaphors pepper all of his conversations.) With money tight, Florence gave up the new house and bought something more modest. Her husband had left debts, but she managed at last to buy herself a piano.

Michaels often invokes William Maxwell's novel *So Long, See You Tomorrow,* in which the narrator, reflecting on losing his mother as a child, says, "The worst that could happen had happened, and the shine went out of everything." He identifies with the way the young hero seeks solace in isolation. "It was just gloom," he said. "I was fourteen and I was the oldest. You don't know it at the time, but your childhood ends. The poles were uprooted." Ten months after his father's death, he wrote a poem called "Locust" on a sheet of notebook paper, which his mother saved. It read, in part:

> Clouds of doom, hiss and spit,
> Bearers of pestilence, dirt and grit;
> Reaping the harvest of tired men's toil.
> Searching, searching, for food to spoil.
> Millions of pillagers, winged and humming,
> Telling the victims ruin is coming,
> Musical death fills the air,
> Drowning out the farmer's despair.

The "bad year," as Michaels calls it, affected his schoolwork. He had just started at a new school, Forest Hill Collegiate Institute. Florence worried that he was becoming a juvenile delinquent. "There was talk of me having to repeat a grade, which would have been humiliating," he said. "Not that I thought I was so smart. Maybe it's just Canadian, but you always knew you weren't the exceptional one." He was embarrassed when people offered condolences, or if someone asked, "What does your father do?" The experience introduced a shade into his emotional palette—a watchful remoteness—that has never left. "You go, 'Well, he died.' And you're more worried about *their* discomfort than you are about the way you feel."

One of the things that helped him regain his academic footing was his decision to recite the Kaddish for a year. Every day after school he rushed to Beth Sholom, a nearby synagogue, by sundown, and prayed with a rabbi, helping, as he was told, to move his father's soul closer to heaven. "I was looking for something that you were *supposed* to do," he said. The Lipowitzes were not religious, but the routine created a kind of stability. He still failed his math exam, but passed the others.

Joyce and Pep Levy stepped in to try to dispel the desolation in the Lipowitz household. Joyce filled the deficit of maternal attention, and Pep handled practical financial matters. Pep ran a very successful company that dealt in used military equipment. During the Second World War, he and his siblings owned a scrapyard, and they became millionaires by selling metal and truck parts to governments around the world. Joyce and Pep made regular trips to Israel, bringing back rare Roman glass that they displayed in vitrines in their house. Rosie Shuster, who met Lorne a year after his father's death, remembers Pep as "a player, very dynamic, with an attractive, vital energy." She added, "There was something slightly mob-bossy about him. Lorne got a lot of his moxie from observing Pep."

Lorne liked to sleep in; Florence set all the clocks in the house ahead in an effort to get him to school on time. Pep went even further: On Saturdays, Lorne would be awakened early by Pep standing over his bed. "He'd say, 'Get dressed. We're going on a hike,'" Michaels recalled. "He was a giant force in my life. A powerful, strong man." During the weeks between school and camp, Pep put him to work in the auto-parts factory, doing dirty jobs in the paint shop. He'd hitchhike to the plant, punching in at seven-thirty. The job was designed to make him see what life might hold for a boy who failed his exams and didn't make it to university.

He devised ways to avoid going home after school, and hanging out at the Levys' was one. At their house, he felt more consequential and confident. "Lorne knew exactly what he wanted," Neil Levy said. "My father was part of the template. He'd take pieces of him and incorporate them into himself." He and Paul Pape spent hours in the Levys' basement, playing pool and ping-pong (their nerdy name for the game was "g-nip g-nop").

If Florence was giving Lorne a hard time, he retreated to his grandmother's apartment to do his homework. After his father died, he always gravitated toward older people—"they'd lived through stuff," he said. His grandmother had separated from her husband once their children had grown up. She kept a parakeet for company, and she would give Lorne tea and a slice of cake as he studied or chatted about the Jane Austen paper he was writing. They'd argue about W. C. Fields. He was a fan, but she thought that Fields was an anti-Semite. Lorne, having taken in hundreds of hours of television comedy, had a wider perspective. "I told her, I don't think that's what he is. I think he just didn't like *most* things—children, dogs, whatever."

As a refuge from the dreary atmosphere at home, he started writing funny items for the *Forest Hill Eye,* the school paper, and contributing comedy sketches to the school's Forest Hill Frolics. He'd also discovered that charm and persuasion could help him smooth over his academic troubles. A class photo in the 1959–60 school yearbook shows Lorne in the back, slightly apart, looking grave amid a group of smiling bobby-soxers. A caption next to the photo reads: "Lorne Lipowitz: Author of How to Win Friends and Influence Teachers."

Lorne's comedy studies got a colossal boost when he met Rosie Shuster. She and her family lived a few blocks over from him, in a modest brick house at 33 Ridelle Avenue. One afternoon she was playing in a construction site with a girlfriend, jumping up and down on boards and raising hell, and Lorne stopped to watch. Shuster, "an emotionally immature fourteen," as she put it, had skipped a grade, and sixteen-year-old Lorne was in the class above. "He followed me home," she said, "and he practically camped out there until after college."

Rosie was a petite girl with a mass of brunette hair, alert dark eyes, and a saucy smile. She met Lorne toward the end of his Kaddish year. "He was just looking up from that when he met a surrogate dad in my father," she said. Soon, Lorne was going straight to the Shusters' after school and staying until bedtime. The house had a cozy den, with an actual father in it, and Lorne spent hours and hours there being mentored.

Compared to his own house, the Shusters' was lively and welcoming. Rosie's mother was an autodidact who was immersed in the local arts scene. Her father, Frank, was half of the comic duo Wayne and Shuster, who performed more often on *The Ed Sullivan Show* than any other act (sixty-seven times) and specialized in a distinctly Canadian type of highbrow sketch comedy. In their signature piece, a Shakespearean baseball game, a player says to an umpire, "Get thee to an optometrist!" Another sketch flattered the audience for clocking a joke in Latin: "Hey, bartender—gimme a dry Martinus." "Don't you mean dry martini?" "When I want two, I'll ask for 'em!" Canadians were proud of the fact that Wayne and Shuster never gave in to the lure of Hollywood and stayed put in Toronto.

Frank Shuster was steeped in the lore of show business, and he passed it on to his daughter's young admirer. It was Shuster, rolling across the oyster-colored broadloom in his padded desk chair, who explained how S. J. Perelman's jokes worked, and why the Marx Brothers' first five movies, with Paramount, were much funnier than their later ones at MGM. He deconstructed Preston Sturges and rhapsodized about Chaplin's face at the end of *City Lights,* when the blind girl recognizes him by the touch of his hands. ("He'd say that that look had *everything* in it," Michaels recalled.) Many of the old studio-boss stories that Michaels would later tell and retell he first heard in Shuster's study, including the famous one about a drunk Herman Mankiewicz reassuring his host at a fancy dinner, after he had vomited on the tablecloth, not to worry because "the white wine came up with the fish."

Wayne and Shuster made regular trips to New York to do the Sullivan show, and Lorne would often walk over to their house on Sunday night to watch with his adoptive family. Later, he'd go over the beats of the show with Frank Shuster, who enjoyed explicating the fundamentals of television production. "How to shoot a sketch," Michaels recalled. "How to keep the reaction close to the joke. How to throw away a laugh. How to handle an entrance. How to cross-shoot. How to favor one person while keeping the other in profile. How to crop a wide shot to make it look like there are more people there." Shuster explained how jokes worked, including a trick picked up from Jack Benny. "It's a note I still give, which is: You pick up the cue, and then pause," Michaels said. "The audience has to know whose turn it is to talk and where they should be looking." Rosie has always felt that something essential about *Saturday Night Live* "came from inside my family."

"Lorne was an eager, avid sponge," she said. "He was looking for a dad and was hungry for show business. It was a match. It came up all cherries. My father's celebrity probably excited him too, although it took me many years to look at it that way. Lorne was good at metabolizing his fandom and turning it into a kind of intimacy. He was artful. He wasn't the kind of fan who asks for an autograph. He was the kind who showed a depth of awareness for a person's work, and that's seductive."

A vent in Rosie's bedroom connected to one in the den where her father and Johnny Wayne wrote. "The comedy rhythms would get in your blood," she said. When Lorne did his sketch shows at school and at Timberlane, where Rosie was also a camper, she pitched in jokes. "I used to whisper a lot of funny things in his ear," she said. "Then he would repeat them and get a huge laugh."

Meanwhile, the relationship between Lorne and Rosie resembled one of those Tudor engagements between a nobleman and a child princess. They were just chums until around the time of Rosie's sixteenth birthday. "Lorne was somehow patient," she said.

ONE OF LORNE'S TEACHERS, A MORDANT ENGLISHMAN, USED TO TELL HIS students, "Read till your eyes fall out of your head." And read they did—fat Victorian novels, the Romantic poets, Shakespeare, the newspaper. Lorne was drawn to culture. Continuing the course of self-improvement he was undergoing in the Shusters' living room, Lorne decided that he and Paul Pape should split a subscription to the O'Keefe Centre, a new performing arts venue. A lot of Broadway plays had runs there, and for thirty dollars a season, they could get seats in the second balcony. The first outing was the opening night of *Camelot,* in 1960, starring Julie Andrews, Richard Burton, and hometown boy Robert Goulet. Lorne was especially knocked out when

Nichols and May came to town, and, a few years later Beyond the Fringe, the seminal British comedy revue comprised of Peter Cook, Dudley Moore, Alan Bennett, and Jonathan Miller. These people were breaking all the rules—dousing comedy sketches in surrealism and boldly skewering authority figures. "They had the same effect on me that the Beatles would," he said.

In the winter of 1961, when Lorne was seventeen, he made his first trip to New York City, on an overnight bus. He went with his best friend, Michael Goldstein, and after a predawn stop in Albany for orange juice, they rolled into Manhattan at 8:00 A.M. They'd arranged to spend a few days staying with their friend Fred Reinglas— a drama director at a camp called Katonim, where Lorne had worked as a counselor—helping with productions of *H.M.S. Pinafore* and *South Pacific*. (Among those thanked in the typewritten program are "Mrs. P. Levy, furniture; Mrs. F. Lipowitz, bar; and Mrs. W. Pape, hula skirt.")

Reinglas was six years older than the two boys, working as a stage manager and living in Greenwich Village. When the boys got to his fifth-floor walk-up on Bleecker Street, they found that Reinglas had two actor friends crashing with him; it was the first time Lorne encountered an unmarried couple living together in the same room. He was agog, but enchanted. His school yearbook had published a screed against Beatniks, "the shabby and bearded men, the occasional sullen and pallid girls . . . who lounge in the doorways and cheap cafeterias of New York's Greenwich Village . . . Dirty people in sandals . . . they raise their voices against the world, particularly against Society, Mom, Dad, Politics, Marriage, the Savings Bank . . . to say nothing of the Cellophane-Wrapped Soda Cracker." Although Lorne was rattled by seeing bars on the windows, visiting Greenwich Village, he recalled, "couldn't have been more romantic."

Preternaturally skilled at using connections, he took in a lot of culture. He saw Neil Simon's first play, *Come Blow Your Horn,* about an innocent who moves in with his swinging bachelor brother in Manhattan. Lorne and his friend hobnobbed backstage, and one of the actors got them into a Paddy Chayefsky play called *The Tenth*

Man; they also sat through Henrik Ibsen's *Ghosts,* the show Reinglas was working on. The syphilitic storyline didn't do much for Lorne, but he was excited to learn that the lead actress had been married to George S. Kaufman, who'd written for the Marx Brothers. Another cast member was dating a writer on *The Tonight Show,* and soon the two boys were on their way to 30 Rockefeller Plaza to sit in the show's studio audience. They waited outside, beneath the famous Christmas tree, until their contact, a preppy young man named Dick Cavett, came down from the studio to give the boys their tickets to see Jack Paar. There was nothing in Toronto like the gleaming Art Deco lobby of 30 Rock, and the friends were dazzled. Sixty years later, Michaels could recall every detail of the show, including a guest named Betty White.

New York was a network of thrilling cultural touchstones. *Breakfast at Tiffany's* had just come out, so Lorne and Michael trekked over and gawped at the jewels. Lorne went to the White Horse Tavern—a Dylan Thomas pilgrimage. He was too afraid to order a beer, so he just gazed at Thomas's poem "Fern Hill" on the wall.

Green and carefree themselves, the boys one night got spruced up and headed to the Hotel Astor in Times Square, taking the subway. ("It was probably one of the last times I did," he told me.) Lorne had five dollars in his pocket, a sum that would last a weekend in Canada. As a waiter approached, intimidating in a cutaway tuxedo, Lorne panicked. He knew nothing about how to order a drink. "I said, 'I'd like a shrimp cocktail,' because I knew a cocktail was a drink," he recalled. The waiter returned with a plate of pallid shellfish. It was humiliating. Also, it ate up $3.75 of his five dollars. In Fred Reinglas's circle, Lorne became "the shrimp cocktail guy." The story followed him for years.

Before boarding the bus back to Toronto, he stopped in a record store and bought the latest Nichols and May album, and, for his mother, the live recording of Judy Garland's recent concert at Carnegie Hall. He also picked up a book by Jules Feiffer, the hipster *Village Voice* cartoonist, called *The Explainers.* (Among Feiffer's racy topics were "atomic-holocaust" ennui and postcoital discord in the

free-love era—"Put on your shoes—I'll walk you to the subway.")
And, though he didn't exactly know what it meant, he purchased a
button that read MARCEL PROUST IS A YENTA.

Margaret Atwood grew up in Toronto around the same time as
Michaels did, when the city was known as "Toronto the Good," a
reference to its Methodist-derived blue laws. "Toronto was where you
lived when you weren't having fun," Atwood wrote. But the safety and
dullness of the city provided a solid backdrop against which to develop a sense of humor; it "made you find ways to amuse yourself,"
Michaels said. During his final year at Forest Hill Collegiate Institute, Johnny Carson became host of *The Tonight Show,* and dissecting his monologues was a daily between-class pastime. Afternoons
were spent listening to Carl Reiner and Mel Brooks's *2000 Year Old
Man* LP on repeat. "People start to be funny early in their lives, when
they notice the difference between the official version and what their
eyes and ears tell them," he said. At school, Lorne wrote and directed
satiric revues, taking little jabs at the teachers; and he acted in plays
and co-edited the "Humour" section of the Forest Hill Collegiate *Eye.*
(Every cover showed a close-up photo of a teacher's eye, suggesting a
fledgling surrealist in the art director's chair.) A typical contribution,
co-authored by Lorne, was a Hollywood Bible satire using the high/
low formula of Wayne and Shuster:

> Okay, Moses sweetheart, baby, let's take it from the top. Do
> you want to climb up there, Moses—it's Moishe? . . . OK,
> Moe, Now you start reading the stuff on the tablets—oh,
> and listen, this scene is costing a fortune, so instead of all
> 613 just read the first ten— . . . You want what? Moe, no-
> body in the Bible has ever used a stunt man. It just isn't— . . .
> Josh, get Heston on the line.

An article in one issue complains that the school Christmas show
(a satire on Forest Hill life, directed by Lorne Lipowitz) should be
more inclusive; the show's writers, it said, "must not take it upon
themselves to select only those students who can give a polished per-

formance." Ignoring the plea, Lorne opened the 1962 Christmas show by having the cast sing "Comedy Tonight" from *A Funny Thing Happened on the Way to the Forum;* another bit was called "Guidance Department Blues." The last line of the "Musical Numbers" page in the program was a meta joke. It read: "Standing Ovation . . . . . . Audience." Michaels remembers being worried that the school employees he was making fun of would be mad, but they surprised him by laughing all the way through. He felt like he had found a voice.

AT THE UNIVERSITY OF TORONTO, MICHAELS RECEIVED WHAT HE CALLS "THE education of a Victorian gentleman," with "Love Me Do" as the soundtrack. He and his friends majored in English; Marshall McLuhan, Robertson Davies, and Northrop Frye were the reigning gods of the faculty. Frye gave an annual lecture on William Blake, which Lorne attended faithfully, drawn by the way Frye linked what he called "the nihilistic psychosis" of the Industrial Revolution, described in the poet's "Jerusalem," with the political tumult of the 1960s.

Like many UT students, Lorne lived at home, in the family house on Elm Ridge Drive. He'd bought himself a 1959 MG for $350 and changed around the taillights so it looked like a 1962 model (spiffier); the car was useful for the three-hour trips he and his friends would take to Buffalo, where the drinking age was eighteen. For gas money, he took a part-time job selling (and folding) sweaters at Eaton's department store, on Yonge Street. He slept late, and when his friends came by to see him, they'd gossip with his mother while waiting for him to get up, trying to provoke her into flashing her dour sense of humor. His brother, Mark, wasn't university-bound and instead went to work for Uncle Pep at the auto-parts company. He liked to shoot pool and crack jokes, and he had one thing on his big brother: "I'm the first Lipowitz to break six feet," Mark bragged.

At UT, University College was where most of the Jewish students ended up, including Lorne and his friends. The Great Hall in Hart House, a craggy Gothic Revival building, is lined with stained-glass windows, and around the walls winds a quotation from Milton's *Are-opagitica*: "Methinks I see in my mind a noble and puissant nation rousing herself like a strong man after sleep . . ." Lorne delighted in eating lunch there and reading in the wood-paneled library. The ideas of Mario Savio, the Berkeley student who had led the Free Speech Movement, were in the air. It was one of Savio's Berkeley comrades, Jack Weinberg, who came up with the slogan "Don't trust anyone over thirty." Michaels recalled, "McLuhan was telling us, 'We're leaving the Industrial Age. We're coming into the Information Age.' I had no idea what he was talking about then, but I would soon enough."

Lorne took it all in. In a political science course, he noticed how the teacher got a big laugh just by the way he pronounced the name of the unpopular Canadian prime minister, John Diefenbaker. The professor called him "DEEEF-enbaker." "I'd hear the laugh, and I'd think, 'But he didn't do anything funny,'" he recalled. "It was just that he'd made the students feel proud that they understood that he'd referred to our prime minister in an unflattering way." It was a lesson: people enjoy feeling like insiders; when they think they're in on the joke, they laugh.

He had followed in the footsteps of Frank Shuster by enrolling at University College, and in his second year he followed again, by co-writing and directing the U.C. Follies, the most well-regarded theatrical revue of the many on campus. (Shuster, né Shusterovich, had kicked off his act with Johnny Wayne, né Louis Weingarten, at the Follies.) Auditions were held in the cafeteria, with Lorne seated behind a table. A student named Earl Pomerantz showed up wearing glasses with lenses as thick as hockey pucks. Although he made the room laugh with his offstage shtick, he bombed in the audition. "I couldn't make that material funny," Earl recalled, of a Shakespeare pastiche Lorne had written. (One character was named "Handinbra.") The next day, Lorne got a call from Earl Pomerantz's big brother, Hart, a law student who wrote material for a professional revue called *Spring Thaw,* which featured Rich Little and Robert Goulet. Hart said that if Lorne cast his nearsighted little brother, he would let the Follies use some of his own comedy material. As a teaser, he sent over a skit he'd written about a nerdy guy asking a nun on a date; the punchline, when the nerd realizes his mistake, is: "Uh, Sister, do you have a sister?" Lorne snapped up the sketch and agreed to cast Earl Pomerantz as the nerd.

Frank Shuster dropped in at rehearsals and whispered notes to his protégé. Lorne brought in ringers from his high school shows, including Rosie Shuster, who was by then his girlfriend.

The 1964 U.C. Follies started with what might have been considered a daring self-referential wink. When the curtain went up, two dozen coeds wearing tights and T-shirts sang:

> We're not going to open the show with a dance,
> With girls in tight sweaters and boys in tight pants.
> It's a cheap stunt to get you caught up in the show.
> Like we said, we would never stoop so low!

"Lorne had a lot of ideas of what makes comedy work," a cast member named Leonard Wise recalled. Lorne had organizational skills, a grip on the technical aspects of mounting a show, a knack for spotting talent, and, at nineteen, a temperament that allowed people, even if they were pre-law wonks, to flourish creatively. "He never got mad," Wise said. "He could tell you when you were lousy in a *nice* way."

The revue ran for three sold-out nights, and Michaels regards it as his "first sort-of hit." (*The Toronto Telegram* published a rave, singling out Earl Pomerantz's original monologue—"My eyesight is so bad that my car has a prescription windshield.") The Follies gave him his first experience of an emotion—a resigned sort of ambivalence—that would come to define his life as a producer. "I never once felt that it went *well*," he said. "But when it worked, it worked." This would become a lifetime refrain. He learned that he was good at keeping the big picture in focus, and during the summer, he directed productions of *Bye Bye Birdie, Oliver!,* and *Guys and Dolls* as a counselor at Camp Timberlane. Getting onstage himself was holding less and less allure. He'd had a revelation while acting in a Hart House production of

Shelley's *The Cenci:* he looked into a fellow actor's eyes onstage and thought, *Oh, he's* really *that guy. That's what actors are.* He knew he wasn't one of them. Directing was more satisfying. "There wasn't a detail I wasn't on," he recalled. "It was all-consuming and I was *in* it."

The tendency toward catastrophic thinking sparked by his father's death was turning out to have a possible upside that served him well when he was in charge. If you're always afraid that life can devolve into chaos without warning, you become vigilant about order. You become a person with a clipboard, or a producer.

THE SUMMER AFTER THE U.C. FOLLIES TRIUMPH, LORNE TOOK HIS FIRST TRIP to Europe, staked by Uncle Pep. He flew to London on a chartered student flight full of other earnest Canadian kids with Eurail Passes. It was the first time he'd really been away, and he looked out the airplane window and marveled, "I'm on a *jet.*" He had a trippy insight that Joni Mitchell would soon articulate in a hit song: his was the first generation to see both sides of the clouds. But his plan to stay in pensiones and make friends along the way as he traveled fell flat. He was lonely and miserable. Missing Rosie, he'd walk through Leicester Square and watch the hip-looking young people holding hands. After a desolate week of having no one to charm with his gift for talk, he called his mother collect, just to hear her voice. The phone call is one of his warmest memories of her. "She just listened," he said. "She never mentioned that it was expensive."

When Lorne graduated from university a few years later, in 1966, Florence (with some help from Uncle Pep) gave him a blue Mustang convertible to mark the milestone. For the Forest Hill contingent, law school was practically a given, but Lorne and his mother had what he called "an understanding." Florence would like to have seen her son a barrister, but, since he had gotten through the rough period after his father's death without becoming a juvenile delinquent (to use her term), she didn't pressure him.

The understanding was that he could live a little. Instead of law school, he went back to England. He had concocted a job for himself with the father of his friend Michael Goldstein. Eddie Goldstein had an army-surplus store in Toronto, and he had branched out from camo jackets and rucksacks to open a business in the U.K. that bought and sold military vehicles. He'd gotten a deal on hundreds of used English army jeeps, called Austin Champs, which were in Nottingham. Remembering his lonesome Eurail trip, Lorne told Mr. Goldstein that young people like him "would kill for a car over there." He proposed that he take charge of unloading the jeeps, marketing them as "fun" cars to young people. Goldstein bankrolled the trip, and Lorne hired his old Camp Timberlane friend Howard Shore to come along as his assistant.

They rented a flat off of King's Road, in an imposing brick complex called Elm Park Mansions, and ran the jeep business out of a little office in Ealing, where the great old British comedies (*The Lady-killers*, *The Lavender Hill Mob*) had been filmed. For Lorne, there couldn't have been a more exciting time to be abroad. The Beatles' *Revolver* came out that summer, and *Time* magazine coined the phrase "Swinging London." Thinking about the throngs of travelers his age bopping around Carnaby Street, he had the idea to paint the jeeps pastel colors. "Kids paid three or four hundred dollars to rent one for the summer," Michaels said. "And they either returned them or they didn't."

"The project was kind of a disaster," Shore said, and not just because he and Lorne were having too much fun to get out to Ealing early every morning. The Austin Champs never worked properly, because the engines, made by Rolls-Royce, were too powerful for the bodies, made by Austin. Rosie visited the guys that summer in Chelsea and could see that the jeep project was a farce. "Lorne had big balls to try to unload them," she said. "Those rust buckets broke down all over Europe."

To goose business, Lorne decided to place ads in college newspapers. A middle-aged man responded with an invitation to meet him at his London club. The boys showed up to the stately building in Pall Mall, their T-shirts conspicuous in a sea of chalk-stripe suits. Their contact wasn't interested in jeeps. He wanted to buy military equipment. "He was an arms dealer trying to put together weapons for a coup in Cameroon," Shore said. No sale.

But the jeep business was secondary to having a good time. King's Road in London in 1966 was a world away from Toronto the Good, and Lorne didn't waste a moment. He went to the theater (Vanessa Redgrave was starring in *The Prime of Miss Jean Brodie*), he traveled to Spain, he saw a lot of bands. He glimpsed John Lennon at a Chelsea pub, and he spotted Paul McCartney at the Ad Lib Club, the wood-paneled SoHo sanctum where the Beatles had their own table (and where Lennon, Harrison, and Pattie Boyd once had an acid freak-out in the elevator). Lorne had been noodling around with a guitar, and he and Howard wrote some songs together, Lorne supplying the Dylan-derivative lyrics.

A ten-minute walk from Elm Park Mansions was a hipster haunt called Nick's Diner. Lorne befriended a taciturn waiter there, a British boulevardier type named John Head, who'd gone to school in Canada. Head lived with a pack of arty roommates in a rambling flat near Gloucester Road, and he brought his new Canadian friends home to meet them. On a cul-de-sac in Cornwall Gardens, the place felt like a nerve center for groovy London, overflowing with artists and actors and musicians. Melissa North, who would go on to become a muse to David Hockney and an interior designer, was a presiding tenant. She describes herself as a "wild sixties girl" from a posh background; she worked as a Gal Friday for a rock and roll agency. "Because there were six tenants, that meant that often twelve people lived there," she said. "Everybody was out of their minds and wearing these wild English clothes."

For Lorne, it was like happening upon a mod version of the Bloomsbury Group, with electric guitars and miniskirts and hash. These young people didn't necessarily have university degrees, but they were well-read and out in the world. They had jobs and earned money. "In Toronto you lived at home or you got married," he said. "All of that freedom was intoxicating."

With her Diana Rigg pageboy and bohemian wardrobe, North was a ringleader; she held a swirl of creative, like-minded people together.

She and Michaels have remained friends. For years he introduced her to people by saying that he'd smoked his first joint in her "mad flat." Head, who had worked on an investigative TV show called *World in Action,* soon moved out of the crowded crash pad to bunk with Lorne and Howard. Lorne was fascinated by him. Compared to the boisterous, pushy comedy types he knew back home, Head was a beetle-browed presence with a quiet sense of command; he was in no way a striver. "He had a world that was bigger than the one we were in," Michaels said. Head was cool. "John had a threadbare elegance, a feather-light footprint," Rosie Shuster said. "He was the very opposite of flashy, and he showed us the ropes in his quiet way." Head's low-key version of hipness became Lorne's lifelong touchstone.

TWO

TWO-MAN COMEDY

IN LATE 1966, BACK HOME IN TORONTO, LORNE TELEPHONED HART POMER-
antz, the comedy-writing law student whose nearsighted little brother
he'd cast in the U.C. Follies. "I want to go into show business," he
told Pomerantz. Lorne was just back from London. He'd stayed in the
flat off King's Road for seven months. It was the longest he had ever
been away from home, and although he reveled in the freedom, he
missed Rosie. He moved back in with his mother. "I was living at
home in the sense that I slept at home," he said. "But I was out in the
world."

To earn money, he took a job with Uncle Pep, writing ad copy for
Levy Industries, which now included CCM, a sporting goods brand
that sold bicycles and hockey equipment. (Sample ad: "Now a hockey
glove that *fits* like a glove!") After the hedonistic shimmer of London,
it was boring. He'd heard that Pomerantz had been down to New York
and had got his foot in the door of professional comedy. A newly
minted lawyer, Pomerantz spent his days processing real estate clos-
ings and doing stand-up at night. He'd done well at an open mic night
at the Bitter End, a Manhattan club that showcased young comedians, like Woody Allen. Jack Rollins, Allen's manager, saw his act and
called him in, and Pomerantz hit him with his best joke. "I went to a
second-rate medium," it went. "And all she could contact were the
critically injured." Rollins encouraged him to keep at it. "But doing

stand-up was too scary," Pomerantz said. "I wanted a partner. I wanted an audience up onstage *with* me."

Lorne knew that Rollins had launched Nichols and May, and if Pomerantz was in his sights, he wanted in. When Lorne called and asked, "Do you want to be my partner?" Pomerantz jumped at his invitation, and they formed a two-man comedy act. Pomerantz described their joke-writing method as "taped and typed": they'd improvise together, with Pomerantz preserving everything on a reel-to-reel machine; afterward, they'd refine the transcript into a routine. Lorne took the Frank Shuster role in the duo: he was the straight man, or, as he always put it, "the tall, good-looking one." Hart was what Rosie Shuster called the "shorter, funnier one." Referencing her father's act, she said, "Lorne was looking for his Johnny Wayne. He poured himself like pancake batter into the Wayne and Shuster mold."

As "Lipowitz and Pomerantz," they started doing their act in local clubs. One of these, a coffeehouse called the Bohemian Embassy, featured early sets by Gordon Lightfoot and readings by Margaret Atwood. "They had folk singers with long hair and black sweaters and depressing songs," Pomerantz said. "We brought comedy to it."

They did well enough that radio appearances on the CBC came next, with Howard Shore composing the music. The network gave Lipowitz and Pomerantz a fifteen-minute comedy segment every Wednesday on a radio show called *Five Nights a Week at This Time.* "We did political satire and thought we were bringing down the government of Canada," Michaels said. They were hired to write for *The Russ Thompson Show,* a weekday program done in front of a live audience. The host, Russ Thompson, the spokesman for General Motors of Canada, was a germophobe who put baby booties over the studio microphones. As part of the deal, the duo got to perform once a week. Rosie, still at university, was an usherette and acted in a few bits. Shore wrote a jingle for the Hart and Lorne segments that could have been an ad for the law firm that Florence Lipowitz had always dreamed of: a jaunty chorus, backed by an orchestra, sang, "We're Lipowitz and Pomerantz! We're Pomowitz and Liperantz!" Pomerantz viewed the song as a thumb in the eye to parochial Canadians. "It was traditional for Jewish comics to change their names," he said. "Using our real names bothered Canadians, and that's what I wanted to do."

In the act, Lorne would always interview a "zany" character, played by Pomerantz. His performances were solid if a bit effortful. He'd rush his lines in comparison to Pomerantz, who had a more natural comic cadence. In 1967, Canada was celebrating its centennial, and the team introduced its signature character, the Canadian Beaver, played by Hart as a bucktoothed rodent with an inferiority complex. Speaking to Lorne, the reporter, the Beaver aired his grievances, like being on the Canadian nickel while the Elk got to be on the quarter. But the Beaver's keenest jealousy was directed at the American Eagle, his aggressive and imperialistic neighbor to the south. An LP of their routines, called *The Comedy of Hart and Lorne,* was circulated to stations around Canada.

After a few months, Russ Thompson's producer called the two rookies into his office and told them that the show wasn't working. "We're not sure if it's you guys or Russ," he said. "So we thought we'd start with you guys." Hart and Lorne were fired.

They'd been at it for about a year, but already Lorne was starting to feel like the comedy act was too dopey, out of step with the culture. Pomerantz and Lipowitz were out of step with each other, too. Initially, they had bonded over the fact that each had lost his father at fourteen, but Hart was a full-time attorney with a wife and a baby, and Lorne wanted to steep himself in the counterculture. *The Graduate* came out that year, and it knocked Lorne's comedy aspirations right out of his head. Mike Nichols's dark fable of generational mistrust, the story of a promising young man trying to dodge graduate school, resonated. Suddenly directing movies looked like a much cooler and more relevant calling than doing corny bits on the radio.

At university, Lorne had befriended a fellow student named David Cronenberg, and, after the Russ Thompson radio gig ended, he started hanging out with Cronenberg at the New Cinema Club at Cinecity, an independent theater in a low-ceilinged former post office on Yonge Street. Backed by a Dutch lawyer and film buff, Michaels and Cronenberg—along with Ivan Reitman, an Englishman named Robert Fothergill, and others—set up the Canadian Filmmakers Distribution Centre, modeled on Jonas Mekas's Film-Makers' Cooperative in New York. The Dutch lawyer hoped to use the center as a front to get Canadian distribution rights for the films controlled by Mekas, who refused to participate in any commercial-leaning enterprise. He came up with the idea of mounting an around-the-clock film festival called Cinethon, to run from June 15 to 18, 1967. Lorne and Fothergill were put in charge of curating it. "It was one ticket for seventy-two hours," Michaels said. "You could come and go. It was what was then called underground." Fothergill remembered the two of them driving around Toronto in Michaels's Mustang, blasting Wilson Pickett, reveling in the ridiculous good fortune of being asked to organize a film festival, something neither was quite qualified to do. Michaels was to manage the finances while Fothergill flew down to New York to select films over at Mekas's co-op, running a tab at the Chelsea Hotel.

They embraced Mekas's motto: "We do not want rosy films. We want them the color of blood." Cinethon screened work that was considered "dangerous," like Andy Warhol's *Sleep,* a five-hour-plus film of a man doing just that. Also on the bill were Milos Forman's *The Firemen's Ball,* Alain Resnais's *La Guerre Est Finie,* and films by Shirley Clarke and Kenneth Anger. There was a live cinema event called "Bill's Hat" that combined a screening (footage of people, including Timothy Leary and Soupy Sales, wearing the same coonskin cap), strobe lights, two live bands, and a woman spread-eagled across a piano throughout, with the eponymous coonskin hat on her naked belly. Michaels said, "You watched it all, because you wanted to know what it was." A film called *The Hyacinth Child's Bedtime Story* (subtitle: *The horses are more important than the pig*) was accidentally projected upside down and backward. No one except the director noticed.

Cinethon was a financial disaster, but it succeeded in bringing the work of many experimental New York filmmakers north. The filmmakers came too, and Lorne Lipowitz got to schmooze with them, whetting his appetite for directing. A cinematographer he met urged him to buy a 35-millimeter camera and take a lot of pictures, to train his eye. He learned how to crop photographs and absorbed the rudiments of composition, skills he would later use when assessing camera angles on television shows. He wrote and started shooting a twenty-seven-minute surreal, Chaplinesque comedy short about the Green Hornets, as Canada's parking meter attendants were called. It was metaphysical physical comedy, with civil servants falling into manholes, and it was mentioned in an article in *The Toronto Daily Star* about the city's nascent film scene. "I'm going to make movies even if I have to hock my shoes," Lorne told the reporter. He then made clear that he would not have to do any such thing, and dropped Uncle Pep's name as a potential benefactor: "My family is involved in Levy Industries," he said.

Cinethon marked the period in Michaels's life that he pegs as "peak seriousness." But he was inhabiting a few different worlds at once: When he hobnobbed with Kenneth Anger at Cinecity, he was still writing ad copy about hockey sticks for gas money, and teaching an improv class at the New School of Art. The arty aspirations gave way to practical concerns, and the parking meter movie went unfinished. Hart Pomerantz had managed to get the William Morris Agency to sign him and Lorne as a writing team, with the aim of selling jokes to big-name comics south of the border. Their first agent, David Geffen, had just moved up from the mail room.

LORNE REALIZED THAT IF HE WAS GOING TO GIVE COMEDY A REAL GO AGAIN, he would have to break with the family business. Jobs were not easy to come by, and Pep Levy was an intimidating presence as well as an important father figure. Lorne didn't want to appear ungrateful, and he feared confrontation. Aunt Joyce sensed her nephew's agitation, and she suggested that he drive Pep to the airport, before a business trip to India, and break the news to him one-on-one. Driving through the stretch of the city that Atwood once described as "mile after mile of caution and utilitarianism," Lorne screwed up his courage and blurted, "I think I want to leave the company and try being in show business."

His uncle took a moment before responding. "I think you have to," Michaels recalls him saying. "Because if you don't find out whether you can, you won't be any good for us or for yourself." Lorne wasn't used to feeling that there was someone resolutely on his side; the sense of being given permission, the simple kindness, overwhelmed him. Before Pep got out of the car at the BOAC terminal, he assured his nephew that if things didn't work out, he could always come back to the auto-parts lot.

Frank Shuster had told him to forget comedy and go to law school. ("Anybody who's actually in show business never advises anybody to go into it," Michaels told me.) Lorne ignored that advice, but he did internalize one lesson from Frank Shuster's career. Wayne and Shuster hadn't stayed put in Canada because they were timid, but because they wanted to raise their families there, away from the Hollywood hubbub; they prioritized quality of life over their careers.

Being in the William Morris stable was thrilling, but it was Pomerantz, and not an agent, who made most of Hart and Lorne's key professional connections. Pomerantz was fearless about approaching people; he reconnected with Jack Rollins, who was looking for writers to help with material for Woody Allen, his client. Allen was on a speeding upward trajectory, having just released *What's Up, Tiger Lily?* and with the Bond spoof *Casino Royale* about to come out. His play *Don't Drink the Water* was on Broadway, and his schedule was crammed with TV gigs, including hosting an episode of *Kraft Music Hall* and an upcoming CBS special. He needed more jokes.

Rollins flew Hart and Lorne down to New York to meet Allen. "I had them over to my house, which would have been unusual," Allen recalled. "But Jack had spoken highly of them." They were booked to do their act that night at Budd Friedman's Improvisation, the club on West Forty-fourth Street that popularized the brick wall as stage backdrop. They were put up at the Hotel Albert, a bohemian establishment on University Place that fit Lorne's romantic notions of showbiz. (Anaïs Nin, who stayed there in the sixties, remembered it as "full of students, all-night saxophones, bathroom down the hall.") Still intimidated by New York, Lorne was awestruck, anticipating his big break, as he stood with Hart outside Allen's East Side townhouse and rang the bell.

Inside, Allen brought out a plate of tuna sandwiches, and the three got to work in the living room. Allen wanted to flesh out a setup he'd been tinkering with, one that involved a lobster in a tank. Hart liked to work with his tape recorder, but Lorne thought that would be embarrassing, so a briefcase was rigged with a hidden reel-to-reel apparatus. Listening to the two-hour tape today, it's clear that the two younger men were trying hard to not blow it.

ALLEN: Let's make a story about a lobster, or a sturgeon.

POMERANTZ: Fine.

LIPOWITZ: Do you know that lobsters have many, many legs?

ALLEN: Yes. So what?

LIPOWITZ: Maybe something with the legs?

ALLEN: [*pauses*] What would our story be? Maybe he gets caught?

POMERANTZ: How about if he finds out that he's died?

ALLEN: Yeah, but something's wrong with him in terms of . . .

LIPOWITZ: . . . something that would lower him in the eyes of the others in the tank, the ones he's been snubbing. What if he has to go to a clam for help? Like, if his antennas get caught under a rock. And he needs to go begging to the clam for help.

POMERANTZ: And he says, "Clam, will you help me?" And the clam says, "No, blah blah blah. Remember what you did to me?"

LIPOWITZ: No, the clam should help him, and then the lobster reverts back to his old ways. That's the joke.

ALLEN: Well, sure. That would be okay.

[*Long silence.*]

ALLEN: Legs, antennae, stuck in a tiny little tank in a seafood store. Living with four other lobsters in a little tank. What the hell happens to him?

LIPOWITZ: Is he cramped?

ALLEN: What if they serve the lobster stuffed with crabmeat? A crab that he shunned years ago?

LIPOWITZ: I know! They do this with snails: they take the snails out of the shell, and save the shell. Because they have to import snails from France, it's cheaper to ship them without their shells. Restaurants use the same shells night after night when they serve them.

ALLEN: [*very long pause*] Mm-hmm.

POMERANTZ: Our problem is doing anything with animals. It's hard to be funny.

ALLEN: I find this problem with all jokes, all the time. It takes me ages to get great jokes. It's really a terrific pain in the ass.

POMERANTZ: [*trying to sound upbeat*] I know but we enjoy it, providing—

LIPOWITZ: Providing we can get there. And we *have* done it.

ALLEN: I do it because I have to do it.

POMERANTZ: Well, we like it, really, because it's a great thrill to come up with a joke, a great one.

ALLEN: Yes, it's fun, but then you have to get on to the next joke and the next joke—

POMERANTZ: That's why, if you're rich, you hire writers!

[*A long silence, broken by a phone ringing in the background.*]

ALLEN: Should we move on to . . . fish?

A successful lobster joke never coalesced, and the session didn't yield anything usable. Lorne tried out a gag about an eye doctor who only treats Cyclopes, which seemed to have the right combination of premise and erudition, but Allen explained to him that *he*—Woody Allen—was his own premise. He just needed solid gags, like any comic. His delivery and persona would imbue a joke with the convoluted intellectualizing that defined his style. As for the mirth-free afternoon at his house, Allen said, "There's not a lot of laughter in writers' rooms. I've written in rooms with Larry Gelbart and Mel Brooks, and really, you're just struggling to find the lines."

"There was no synergy there," Pomerantz recalled of the writing session. "Woody was a disciplined, scientific writer. Bending, twisting, seeing if a joke could work." Instead of stopping when they hit on a decent punchline, he'd say, "But what if—?" "Lorne had a way of dealing with Woody," he said. "He tried to dominate him a little bit." For his part, Michaels had noticed how ruthless Allen was with material. "I was impressed by the quality of his garbage," he said. "Most comedians could make a whole act out of what Woody was throwing away." Allen paid the pair $1,000 for their efforts.

Hart and Lorne were due onstage at the Improv later that evening, but before they left Allen's house, Lorne suggested that he and Hart show him their act. They did their set in the living room, while Allen sat on a sofa. "Woody was polite," Pomerantz said, embarrassed at the memory. "He said, 'I think they'll like it.'"

A week after the unfruitful meeting, Lorne came up with a joke that he thought would be perfect for Allen—it was what he called "a bright joke"—one for smart people. He telephoned Allen from Toronto and pitched it: A man is obsessed with the idea that there's no such thing as an original thought—that somewhere in the world, another guy is thinking the exact same thoughts as he is, at the exact same time. Eager to meet this mental doppelgänger, he somehow finally gets the other guy's phone number. He dials the number . . . and the line is busy.

Allen didn't use that joke either, but he did tell Lorne that it was very funny. The compliment meant a lot to a guy who was writing slogans for hockey gear. "Woody saved my life with that," Michaels said. "It kept me going for about a year."

Back in Toronto, Hart and Lorne continued to send jokes to

American comedians through William Morris, earning ten dollars for every one that got used. There were more trips to New York, including one to meet with Joan Rivers and her husband, Edgar, in their Upper East Side apartment. She was pregnant and hoped to work the birth into her act. Lorne and Hart came up with the following: "I had my baby in Larchmont, New York, and it's a very small town. The hospital is called Fred's Hospital and Grill." Rivers told the joke at a club called Upstairs at the Downstairs, in a set that was released as an LP. The pair earned $150.

They flew down to New York another time to meet with Dick Cavett, who was hiring for a new talk show that he was hosting, set to launch in 1968. He took Hart and Lorne to lunch at the Russian Tea Room. Lorne felt out of his depth among the shiny red banquettes and bottle-green walls of the room, the glow from the gold-leaf ceiling and the liquid butter pooling under chicken Kiev—"It couldn't have been more glamorous," he recalled. Eating in restaurants was a novelty, and he was beguiled by Cavett's preppiness and Yale pedigree. But Hart's refusal to check his bulky briefcase mortified him. "Hart would bring the tape recorder to every lunch," he said. "He taped everything." They didn't get the job.

On one trip to New York, Lorne caught a young comic named Richard Pryor at the Improv. He remembered being captivated seeing him on *The Ed Sullivan Show* a year or two earlier, a polite, gangly young man playing all the parts in a gentle theater piece about an elementary school class's production of "Rumpelstiltskin." This time the material was harsher. Pryor did a fifteen-minute one-man tour de force about a group of liberal New York actors bringing a play about interracial romance to a prison in the South. The warden keeps saying, "I was told there'd be a dead n—— on this stage." This was a new turn in comedy—devastating and brave—and Lorne knew that he wanted to follow it. His Cinethon seriousness started to inform his thinking about jokes. "I believed it should be of *use*," he said, referring to comedy. He recalls being "messianic about it."

———

AS IF FULFILLING A PACT MADE IN ADOLESCENCE, LORNE AND ROSIE WERE married in November 1967, just before his twenty-third birthday. But first, Lorne dropped the name "Lipowitz." He had consulted his rabbis, Frank Shuster and Uncle Pep, for advice on the matter. They told him that if he wanted to go professional, he should change his name. (Rosie's mother, Ruth, was also in favor of a change; she didn't want the daughter she had named for Shakespeare's heroine to go through life as Rosalind Lipowitz.) It was traditional for Jewish comics: Jack Benny was born Benjamin Kubelsky; George Burns was Nathan Birnbaum; Milton Berle was Mendel Berlinger. Even Russ Thompson had been born Boris Wegeruk. Lorne's father, Henry, had been the only one of his siblings to stick with Lipowitz; the others had truncated the name to Lipton or Linton. But Lorne didn't want to shorten it, and he disliked the initials L.L. He'd met a guy on a train to Zurich, during his Eurail trip, who told him that Lipowitz was a forest in a beautiful part of Poland, and he considered naming himself some variation on "Wood" or "Forest." But a connection to the ancestral homeland felt forced. Rosie floated some jokey possibilities: Lorne Ranger and Lorne Zwelk.

Shuster believes the name he landed on was inspired by a fondness for Wordsworth's "Michael," a pastoral poem about a noble shepherd who loses his only son to the corruptions of city life. Lorne says he picked the name to honor his oldest friend, Michael Goldstein.

He wanted to get the name business out of the way before he encountered any real professional success (and perhaps to distance himself from the Pomerantz-Lipowitz jingle on the CBC). Pomerantz handled the legal filings for his partner's name change, and, in the way that comedians do, turned it into a bit: "I said, 'Your Honor, my client's name is Lipowitz and he wants to change it to Michaels.' 'No reason needed,' the judge said. So I said, 'Thank you, Judge Lipschitz.'"

The speeches after Lorne and Rosie's wedding, held at the Holy Blossom Temple before 350 guests, had a Friars Club flavor. Frank Shuster welcomed his longtime apprentice into the family: "The only man happier than me tonight is the florist!" he said. Lorne's toast used Florence as fodder: "The second thing my mother always said when she met you was 'How do you do?' The first thing was 'What am I going to do about my Lornie?'"

Marriage finally got him out from under his mother's roof; the newlyweds set up house in an apartment ten minutes from their childhood homes. For a while, John Head lived with them, a restrained presence among their wisecracking friends, who came around to play the pinball machine that Shuster had given her new husband. But she got restless soon after the wedding, attuned to the early rattlings of feminism. She wanted to distance herself from the family comedy business, and she'd started going to art school, trying to find her own direction. Margaret Atwood was about to publish her first novel, *The Edible Woman,* about a character who feels that her engagement is literally devouring her identity. "I took Lorne's name for ten minutes," Shuster said. "Then I went back to being Rosie Shuster really fast." It was dawning on her that she'd never been on her own, and she'd never dated anyone but Lorne. She'd been his sidekick since age fourteen; then she'd followed him to UT, where she inherited his textbooks. He'd guided her in her selection of classes, and they fought over whether she should study psychology or, as he suggested, political science. "He was trying to produce me," she said.

Now that they were married, she felt trapped. "This was a time of sex and drugs and rock and roll, and at some point I discovered pot. It was major, epic," she recalled. "I wasn't the conventional little bourgeois wife that I was supposed to be."

Florence, her anxious mother-in-law, was aghast. "Is *this* a marriage?" she'd say to relatives. Michaels, too, had ideas about how a wife was supposed to behave. For a person who was au courant about culture, Shuster said, "there was something in terms of a wife where he still was on the old software." She took refuge in hanging out with her painting teachers in taverns after class.

Michaels was always looking to re-create the intact family unit he'd lost, and the wobbliness of his new marriage was painful. Shuster made it clear that she needed space, so it was a relief to them both when Michaels got an opportunity to leave town for a while. A Hollywood TV producer named Bernie Orenstein, originally from Toronto, reached out to Pomerantz about coming to L.A. He was putting together a variety show that would star Phyllis Diller, a bid by NBC to siphon some viewers from CBS's *The Carol Burnett Show,* which had premiered in 1967. Orenstein needed writers with experience crafting jokes for women. Diller, who had made her name in New York clubs, specialized in disparaging her own looks (she wore a frizzy wig and had a cackling laugh) and her slovenly husband. She had been sent a packet of the jokes that Hart and Lorne wrote for Joan Rivers and was impressed. Orenstein offered Pomerantz a job, and when Pomerantz insisted on bringing along his partner, saying that they'd work cheap, the deal was sealed. In the summer of 1968, Hart and Lorne were headed to Hollywood to be junior writers on *The Beautiful Phyllis Diller Show.*

Michaels always intended to follow the Wayne and Shuster template and make a show business career in Toronto. They'd turned down the Canadian Dream, he knew—to *not* be working in Canada. But with his marriage fraying, getting some time away seemed sensible. L.A. could be a new start, and the fractiousness with Rosie might settle down. Before leaving, he got some showbiz wisdom from an old friend of Frank Shuster's, an MCA agent named Berle Adams. "Out in Hollywood, they're like space cadets," he told Michaels. "They get to go up in space, and while they're up there, they only talk to other space cadets. After a while, they forget the Earth language. So when they come back down, they have to relearn how to talk to Earthlings. Once they're down, very few ever go back up." Michaels wasn't sure whether to be excited or spooked.

THREE

ON THE ASSEMBLY LINE

HAVING BEEN INFUSED WITH THE ROMANCE OF HOLLYWOOD SINCE CHILD-hood, when his grandparents' movie talk dominated the household, Michaels arrived in Los Angeles at a peculiar time. The week before he left Canada, the California mood—flower children slouching through the Summer of Love—shifted abruptly; Robert Kennedy was shot at L.A.'s Ambassador Hotel. "I literally watched it on TV in Toronto and then went to L.A., where it happened," Michaels said. But when he landed, the sun glinting against the purple hills steadied his nerves, and William Morris had put him and Pomerantz up in a cool hotel—the Continental Hyatt House, just down Sunset Boulevard from the Whisky a Go Go, where the Doors had been the house band. The hotel was known as the Riot House, and would become famous as the place where Keith Moon and Keith Richards tossed TV sets out the window, and Robert Plant proclaimed "I am a golden god" from a balcony. Pomerantz nervously checked in with his wife and baby, but Michaels arrived solo, ready for anything.

The Beautiful Phyllis Diller Show's writers' room was a trailer on the NBC lot in Burbank. Michaels arrived for his first day with his long hair encircled by a hippie headband. He was surprised to find that his new colleagues were in their fifties and sixties, men who'd started in radio and whose Ban-Lon-sheathed paunches hung over their belts. The work itself seemed outdated, too. "The first assignment we were given was to write fifty fag jokes and fifty mother-in-law jokes," Michaels said. (The comedian Rip Taylor played Diller's effeminate hairdresser, Paul of Pasadena.) He worried that he had made a terrible mistake. "I was twenty-four, and at that age you think every decision is momentous: Now your life is ruined," he said. Had he traveled twenty-five hundred miles just to end up back in the creaky vaudevillian precincts of Russ Thompson? Sometimes Diller would accompany her musical guests on the soprano saxophone. Every episode of the show ended with a big production number saluting a "forgotten American," like James Knox Polk, or the inventor of the sewing machine.

The show premiered on September 15, 1968, against Barbra Streisand's live concert, *A Happening in Central Park,* on CBS. *Funny Girl* was in theaters, and Streisand was a huge star. "I thought, 'We're dead,'" Michaels recalled. But Streisand did a 19 share, and Diller did a 34 share. "That's when I woke up to the fact that I was in America now," he said. "I realized, 'So, television is different than Toronto or Broadway or the movies.'" The TV audience was vastly larger, and more mainstream. A few months earlier, the newspaper columnist Joseph Kraft had coined the term "Middle America," and as Michaels spent more time in network TV, he would learn to keep that demographic in his sights.

The strong start didn't last. Guests on the Diller premiere included Johnny Carson, Sonny and Cher, and Dan Rowan and Dick Martin, of the hit show *Laugh-In,* but after that the A-list guests disappeared, and so did the ratings. The director had the radical notion that the studio audience should sit in movable hydraulic bleachers that would follow the show's action around a soundstage. Michaels was amazed by the technology, until the seating module got stuck in the middle of the show. At one taping, stagehands were pushing the bleachers full of captive audience members around the studio at three o'clock in the morning.

The *Los Angeles Times* deemed the first episode "not too successful," and in its list of the show's writers, it misspelled Michaels's name ("Loren Michaels"). He had been so excited about working at an

American network—with his own parking space!—that it was hard for him to see how weak the show was. Diller warmed up the audience before the tapings with some jokes. Her opening was: "What's brown and has holes in it? Swiss shit." The second joke: "What has hair and hangs from a wall? Humpty Cunt." Michaels would call Rosie in Toronto, and describe his day at work. She was the one who told him that the show was garbage. "This was a profound lesson, my first—how easily, in television, you can be seduced," he said. "This was the beginning of the realization that I had to pay very close attention."

Despite following *Bonanza* in the evening lineup, the ratings kept dropping. NBC sent over some testing information indicating that viewers couldn't relate to Diller. "She was too hard-edged," Michaels said. To make her seem more human, a segment was added in which Diller, as herself, sat and interviewed a famous person. Carol Burnett's producers had solved a similar problem—the problem of viewers being uncomfortable watching a woman in charge—by having Burnett take questions from the audience, generating a warm, den-motherly feeling. Michaels and Pomerantz were dispatched to pre-interview Diller's guests and then type up questions. Their subjects included such sixties icons as Hugh Hefner, Vidal Sassoon, and Rudi Gernreich, the designer of the topless bathing suit.

For Michaels, who liked to talk to people—particularly people who had achieved some distinction—working on the "chat spot" was a high point. Sassoon had become famous for giving pixie cuts like the one Mia Farrow wore in *Rosemary's Baby*. "Sassoon said this thing that had tremendous influence on me," Michaels recalled. "We were talking about his career, and he said, 'There's only so much you can do with a head of hair.' And I thought, 'Absolutely!' It was such a relief to be talking to somebody who was not pretentious. I mean, it's not late-period Picasso. It's just, 'I cut hair.'"

Michaels worked hard to make the interview segments fizzy, but they'd be cut to shreds in the editing room. "It was the beginning of my realizing you were in a big machine and you were just a small part of it," he said. Orenstein, the co-producer, felt that, of the two Canadians, Pomerantz was the born comedy writer. Michaels's talent, he felt, was more curatorial. "He knew what was funny," he said. "But he couldn't come up with it himself."

A bright spot was Diller herself. She'd regularly take the writers to lunch or have them home for dinner. She'd always have on a bald cap that fastened under her chin with a strap, because she wore wigs onstage. Before eating, she would take her bridgework of false teeth out of her mouth and stow them inside a big, flashy diamond ring she wore, with a hinged compartment. Michaels liked that she didn't pretend.

He also discovered that his paunchy radio-days colleagues had a lot to offer. They included Bob Schiller and Bob Weiskopf, who wrote for *I Love Lucy* (the classic grape-stomping episode was theirs); Keith Fowler, who'd written for W. C. Fields and Jackie Gleason; and George Balzer, who worked for Jack Benny for twenty-five years. The old-timers would take the two apprentices to lunch at an air-conditioned deli called Kosherama, where they'd bump into other NBC employees, like the guys writing Dean Martin's variety show. The war stories they told are ones that Michaels still repeats. Balzer gave Michaels stacks of old Jack Benny radio scripts to study. They were deceptively short, "because they were all pauses," Michaels said. "So I began to see what a joke looked like on the page. It was like knowing how to prepare a dish. Like: 'To start with, the eggs go here.'"

This dynamic was familiar; Michaels always felt a pull toward father figures. His colleagues' expertise galvanized him, but even as he was drinking in the comedy dogma, he was uneasy. "Television was still being written by people from radio," he said. "They'd been doing it forever—writing jokes for *Duffy's Tavern* or Fred Allen. There was no one my age in television." He was more interested in what his peers were doing—rock and roll, independent cinema, cool restaurants. He started to get what Marshall McLuhan had been talking about back at UT—the idea that whenever there is a new mass medium, like television, it frees up the medium that came before it, allowing it to innovate and blossom. "Television becoming so powerful liberated movies, so that movies no longer had the burden of being mass," Michaels said. That's why, as groundbreaking filmmakers like Stanley Kubrick, Roman Polanski, and John Cassavetes appeared on the scene, Michaels often wished he was writing his own version of *The Graduate*, and not shopworn gags for a bitchy hairdresser character. "Everything *but* television was changing," he said. "Everything happening outside the show seemed more interesting." His conception of his own talents was undoubtedly loftier than the Phyllis Diller job demanded, but he was learning that he had bigger dreams for himself than writing jokes.

In August, he went to see Simon and Garfunkel in concert at the Hollywood Bowl. They opened with "Mrs. Robinson" from the soundtrack to *The Graduate*, Michaels's north star. Later in the set they sang "And I know I'm fakin' it / I'm not really makin' it." Sitting in the dry night air, taking in the skunky smells of pot and meadow rue, he couldn't help but reflect: People his age were rejuvenating the culture. And he was at home reading Jack Benny radio scripts. "I wasn't *in* what was happening," he said.

The agonizing over whether to quit his job was cut short when, one day, he pulled into the Burbank lot and found that his parking place had been reassigned. *Beautiful Phyllis Diller* had been canceled. He didn't come out of the experience empty-handed. He'd learned the ropes and made contacts, including a father figure who would shape his career for decades. On one of the nights when the rolling bleachers were on the fritz, Michaels started talking to a bearish man in the hallway. It was Bernie Brillstein, a manager who represented Norm Crosby, an old malaprop comic, who was the Diller show's announcer. Brillstein also had a hand in creating the smiling platoon of folksingers known as the Doodletown Pipers (whom Roger Miller used to introduce on his show as "the Poodletown Diapers"). In his gravelly voice, Brillstein asked Michaels to show him some material, and he promptly signed the two young Canadians. "I wouldn't say Bernie was on the edge when it came to young talent," Michaels said. Veterans in the business spent Sundays at Brillstein's house watching football and drinking beer. Not yet forty, he was nonetheless regularly described as a Jewish Santa—beloved, but a bit of a bullshit artist. Like Geffen, he started in the William Morris mail room, but he'd had an uncle in vaudeville, and he was steeped in the kind of old-time show business lore that Michaels loved.

Lorne had also caught the eye of Bob Finkel, the Diller show's producer, a variety-TV eminence who'd recently produced the highest-rated special of the year, Elvis Presley's comeback concert. Bob Schiller, the middle-aged *Lucy* writer, had also become a close friend. Michaels memorized the comedy rules Schiller dispensed: In every script, there has to be a joke every three lines. Also: The audience has to see a performer's eyes. Schiller invited Michaels home to meet his curly-headed son Tom, who had dreams of directing art films, having recently returned from Europe, where he'd hung around with Buckminster Fuller and Henry Miller. Bob Schiller thought that Michaels, who dressed like a hippie but was sophisticated beyond his years, might have some advice that would help his dreamy son focus. Like Michaels, Tom Schiller had grown up around people who parsed jokes like sections of the Talmud. "I was pulled out of bed at age seven, on a school night, if a sketch was going well on *Your Show of Shows*," Schiller said.

Michaels came over one afternoon and took a long walk with Tom around Pacific Palisades, asking him, in an avuncular way, what he wanted to do with his life. Neither knew that their professional paths would soon converge. Schiller couldn't quite figure out Michaels; his dad had described him as someone who knew every good restaurant in L.A. "Lorne seemed kind of mild-mannered, a little nebbishy," Schiller recalled. But then he lit a joint in Tom's bedroom, which Schiller found strangely bold.

While Michaels was occupied with building his West Coast network, Pomerantz felt licked. He was ready to take his family back to Canada, but they couldn't get out of the lease on the split-level house they'd rented. (Michaels had relocated to the Landmark Motor Hotel, another rock and roll haven; a couple of years later, Janis Joplin would be found dead there.) So, stuck in L.A. and newly unemployed, the partners looked for another job as a writing team. A packet of jokes was sent to Dan Rowan and Dick Martin, at *Laugh-In*, NBC's loopy, high-octane sketch show. (*Laugh-In* is one of the few topics about which the word "zany" can be legitimately used.) Rowan and Martin had started as a Vegas club act, and they thought the Canadians could be a good fit to write jokes for their opening monologue, which had a more conventional tone than the blackouts and other loopy skits that filled the hour. The show was a William Morris package, so the agency slotted them in as junior writers.

Laugh-In gave Michaels a much wider window into the workings of "professional show business," as he has always called it. Like many variety series, *Laugh-In*—a pun on "love-in"—had originated as a special. It was the brainchild of George Schlatter, a Barnumesque charmer who'd gotten his start booking comics into Ciro's in Los Angeles. Schlatter envisioned *Laugh-In* as wildly anarchic and freeform, but Timex, the show's sponsor, wanted a conventional host. So NBC installed Rowan and Martin, who had a deal with the network, and retitled the program *Rowan & Martin's Laugh-In*. Older than the rest of the cast (both were forty-five), they were not Schlatter's choice, and from the start there was tension over exactly who was in charge.

When Schlatter screened the pilot for NBC, the executives were put off by the lightning-quick cuts, the staccato quips about the Pill and pot-smoking ricocheting off the kaleidoscopic set. They almost pulled the plug. Thinking fast, Schlatter explained that his program was informed by the latest thing in Europe, "Comedy vérité." He would tell the anxious executives that Goldie Hawn writhing in a bikini with suggestive slogans painted all over her body (HANDLE WITH CARE, DANGEROUS CURVES AHEAD) was a European art trend called "Ep Art" (short for epidermal art). The network bought it.

Laugh-In debuted as a series in January 1968, and it was hailed as something radical, TV's first collusion with the counterculture. The comedy bits derived from pie-in-the-face burlesque, but what distinguished the show was the frenetic pacing, which Schlatter took from *Hellzapoppin'*, a fourth-wall-breaking Broadway revue from the thirties. Each show opened with Rowan and Martin doing a monologue—Martin the goofy, girl-chasing rascal, and Rowan the exasperated straight man. They'd wrap it up by saying, "Let's go to the *party.*" That would be the Cocktail Party, a frantic montage of blackouts, quick jokes, and snippets of girls frugging. There was the Joke Wall segment, in which performers poked their heads out of holes in a spin-art wall, like cuckoos emerging from a clock, and spouted one-liners ("What goes 'Ho ho thump'? Santa Claus laughing his head off"). Schlatter compared the show to a pinball machine.

On the door to Schlatter's office was a sign reading IF YOU DON'T HAVE A PUNCHLINE, DON'T COME IN. Michaels and Pomerantz were more sedate than their colleagues. In charge of the writers' room was Allan Manings, a "devout anarchist," in Schlatter's words. "And for balance, we had Paul Keyes, who was a fascist, and close to Richard Nixon." (After Nixon was trounced by JFK in a 1960 debate, he hired a group of young advisers to help with his TV persona. Keyes was among them, and so was Roger Ailes.) Then there was Digby Wolfe, a warm-up comic for the Beatles, who had bit parts doing posh-Brit roles on the Monkees' TV show and *The Munsters.* Schlatter gathered interesting performers, too. He hired Lily Tomlin after seeing an audition tape of her doing a barefoot tap dance with metal taps taped onto her feet.

Michaels and Pomerantz arrived at the start of *Laugh-In*'s second season, with twenty-six episodes to write; they quickly became known as the young guys with the tape recorder. "We went from the lowest-rated show to the highest-rated show," Pomerantz said. The writers worked out of the Toluca Capri Motel, two to a room, a few miles from NBC's Burbank studio. Appearing "with it" was *Laugh-In*'s brief, but most of the writers were pushing forty. The one who made the biggest impression on Michaels was David Panich, who'd written for Woody Allen. Panich had taught math in Bed-Stuy, Brooklyn, and legend had it that he had carved the lion's head into the scroll of Charles Mingus's bass. In Hollywood, Panich had started out writing for *The Monkees* (an unusual incubator of talent), and Schlatter teamed him with a guy named Marc London. Panich was a pothead, and London was a drinker. Panich talked in Elizabethan dialect, punctuating sentences with phrases like "prithee, sire," but Michaels found him funnier than anyone there. Michaels came up with a bit based on a news item about how a Russian scientist had grafted the head of a dog onto another dog. "It was a page-eight story about this two-headed dog, and about how they could feed one dog without the other dog knowing," he said. As the table of writers mulled a punchline, Panich said, "It's really a long way to go to fool a dog." Michaels recalled fondly, "He was *that* kind of writer."

One Monday morning, the writers arrived at the motel to find that Panich, in a stoned fog, had scrawled jokes all over the walls. His colleagues told him that Schlatter would be furious, and they warned him that he must not write on the walls. The following Monday, the writers showed up to find that Panich had scribbled "I must not write on the walls" on all of the doors. "It was a big playpen for adult children," Schlatter said. One day the police came to the motel after the writers taped up a sign in a window. It read HELP! I'M BEING HELD CAPTIVE IN THE LAUGH-IN WRITERS' ROOM!

Schlatter noted that Michaels had an "aroma of respectability," unusual on that staff. He was nice, he was polite, and he listened. The veterans in the motel liked him. "Lorne is one of the great schmoozers of all time," Schlatter said. "He could talk his way out of a life sentence."

Schlatter would shoot huge, two-hundred-page scripts and end up with seven hours of material per hour-long show. A producer named Carolyn Raskin supervised the editing, and Michaels marveled at the way she'd single-handedly create the show in the editing room. Michaels and Pomerantz mainly wrote topical jokes for Rowan and Martin, who wouldn't see them until the taping, where they sight-read them off of cue cards. Rosie had arrived in Los Angeles by this time, for a trial reconciliation, and she hung with the writers at the Toluca Capri. Under the radar, she wrote some jokes that got used. "I didn't get credit, and I didn't get paid," she said. "I was such a guilty twit in those days, I thought I was getting away with something!"

Michaels recalled one of his wife's bits, a dialog between Rowan and Martin, about a hot date:

"I went out with Siamese twins last night."

"Siamese twins? How did that go?"

"Uh, yes and no."

In her autobiography, Judy Carne, the Carnaby Street pixie who was one of the cast's breakout stars, quoted Allan Manings comparing writing for *Laugh-In* to shoveling coal on an ocean liner while a wild party was taking place on deck. That was certainly how it felt to Michaels, who was never once in the studio. The writers never saw a taping and never met the talent. Even during the table reads, they remained penned up in the Toluca Capri. At the motel, Manings would sit at a typewriter as writers pitched jokes for the Cocktail Party. He'd type them in his own words, and then Keyes would put the jokes on index cards and post them on a bulletin board. Then Keyes rewrote the jokes. Even if a writer's notion made it through, he got no credit for it. The gags went into the maw, and they would change right up to the last minute.

"I was at a number one show and a cool show," Michaels said. "But we were not part of the process." The only way the writers knew if any of their jokes had made it was to tune in on Monday night. They watched together in the motel room, listening for glimmers of their hard-won ideas. Although the show's writers were nominated for an Emmy Award that season, Michaels took little pride in the honor. "I felt like I was standing next to the guy who gets shot and you both get the Purple Heart," he said.

For Michaels, perhaps more galling than having no control over his work was missing out on all the glamour. Every Wednesday, a marathon taping session took place in the studio; a portable bar was rolled in and celebrities showed up to tape cameos. It was a free-wheeling Hollywood party, with lots of raucous ad-libbing. Johnny Carson, Harry Belafonte, Joey Bishop, the Smothers Brothers, Bob Newhart, and—most painfully for Michaels—Jack Benny all stopped by to do one-liners from the Joke Wall.

Laugh-In looked and sounded like a product of the counterculture, but politically it was toothless. Paul Keyes engineered the famous September 1968 cameo by Nixon, who, as the GOP presidential candidate, looked into the camera and said one of the show's catchphrases, "Sock it to *me?*" Jokes about homosexuality and women's lib gave the show a sheen of irreverence, but Keyes made sure that it avoided topics like the Vietnam War, which the Smothers Brothers, over on CBS, were hammering regularly. (After President Johnson placed an angry call to network chairman Bill Paley, the Smothers Brothers invited Pete Seeger on to sing "Waist Deep in the Big Muddy.") *Laugh-In*'s approach was a bit with Goldie Hawn biting her lip and saying, "I don't like the Viet Cong because in the movie he nearly wrecked the Empire State Building."

Michaels was frustrated that he couldn't get any Nixon jokes on the air. He envied the writers on *The Smothers Brothers Comedy Hour,* who were a decade younger than his *Laugh-In* colleagues—part of his generation. Like Michaels, Tommy Smothers used the phrase "what was happening in the streets" to describe the kind of material he wanted. The staffs of the two shows played touch football against each other; at one of these games, Michaels made the acquaintance of two of the *Smothers* writers, Rob Reiner and Steve Martin. He felt that he was stuck on the wrong team, the uncool one.

Ever since he was a kid watching Sid Caesar on TV with his grandmother, he had paid attention to when "the music changed," to use a pet expression of his, and it was changing now. He'd arrived in Hollywood in the middle of an unusual style shift. He knew that, in some decades, hemlines and hair lengths rise or fall slowly, and one cultural era fades smoothly into the next. The sixties, for a while, were an outpost of the fifties. But the second half of the decade bumped along in a series of brash collisions: Sansabelt slacks with a peasant top, love beads over a Savile Row suit, Hush Puppies poking out from under a daishiki. When the Beatles visited the Whisky, they brought Jayne Mansfield along. The generational mismatching was all over the place: the young fogies who booed Dylan for going electric vied in awkwardness with the spectacle of squares who tried to be hip, as when Sinatra recorded "Mrs. Robinson" (*"Jilly* loves you more than you can know!"). On *Laugh-In,* Goldie Hawn wriggled in psychedelic body paint, but Rowan and Martin wore tuxedoes, as if beamed in from the Eisenhower era.

Just because *Laugh-In* was a trendy show didn't mean that all of America was watching. Studying the ratings, Michaels was reminded of his surprise at seeing Phyllis Diller get a bigger share than Streisand. *Laugh-In* often tied in its Monday-night timeslot with *Here's Lucy,* one of Lucille Ball's weaker sitcoms, which appealed to what was then known as the housewife demographic. In other words, hip didn't necessarily beat humdrum. "I realized: there were two different audiences," he said. "There's always been two countries." Succeeding meant appealing to both.

Many who knew Michaels on his way up can't resist trying to find *Saturday Night Live's* origin story in one of his earlier enterprises. Schlatter believes *Laugh-In* was the blueprint: "When I first saw SNL, I realized, a lot of it was *Laugh-In,*" he told me. *Laugh-In* started with a monologue; repeating characters spawned catchphrases ("Here come da judge," "*Verrrrry* interesting," "Sock it to me!"); it had a news segment and short films (Ruth Buzzi's old lady yelling "Masher!" while swatting a man with her purse). Schlatter also booked non-showbiz figures, like Billy Graham, Martha Mitchell, and William F. Buckley. (Buckley responded to the invitation, "Not only do I refuse to appear, I resent having been asked." He relented after Schlatter offered to fly him to Burbank "on a plane with two right wings.")

Another way *Laugh-In* prefigured SNL was in the energy Schlatter spent getting around the censors in NBC's Broadcast Standards Department. He instructed the writers to devise a series of "freedom words," nonsense utterances—*bippy, nurdle*—that viewers understood as stand-ins for something naughtier. One catchphrase that the clueless censors didn't catch was "Look that up in your Funk and Wagnalls!" with the first two words blurted as *Funkin'.*

Michaels got a lesson in audience dynamics when he and Pomerantz were asked to write material for Rowan and Martin to use in a *Laugh-In* touring revue. "We went to a hockey arena in San Diego, and when Rowan and Martin came on, I'd never heard laughs that big in my life," Michaels said. It made him understand the huge power that television has to ratify taste. "Dick Martin told me that they'd been doing the same act for sixteen years, and for fifteen years it wasn't funny," he said. "Television sells things. Once you'd been told that Rowan and Martin knew what they were doing, you were there to laugh."

But working on a number one show, it turned out, was no better an experience than working on a failure. Despite the success, Michaels was nagged by a mental picture of what his career should be: "My romantic idea, my magic notion, would have been closer to George S. Kaufman—out of town opening a show, staying up late and drinking a lot of coffee and fixing the second act, or coming up with jokes with the Marx Brothers." He felt like he'd washed up in a cul-de-sac.

Hart and Lorne were fired from *Laugh-In* after one season; they were told that it wasn't cost-effective to have two writers who did only monologue jokes. Rowan and Martin weren't around to protect them; they were off filming a horror-movie satire, *The Maltese Bippy*. Losing the *Laugh-In* job was not a cataclysm for Michaels. It was tougher for Pomerantz, who, Michaels thought, always needed to be the funniest person in the room. Michaels didn't feel that pressure to make people laugh. "I was more a fan of it," he said. "It's a different way of being funny." But Hart's wife was unhappy in L.A. and Shuster was feeling unmoored. She'd enrolled in some courses at UCLA, still trying to distance herself from the family business.

Michaels was the only one of them who liked California, but he agreed to move back home to Toronto. The Emmy nomination would be a useful professional calling card. (*Laugh-In* lost in the writing category to the Smothers Brothers, whose show had just been canceled, months after Nixon took office.) Hart and Lorne had performed their comedy act a few times in L.A., editing out the beaver bit, and in their off-hours they'd taped a spot as guest comics on a Dean Martin Golddiggers TV special, sharing the bill with Frank Sinatra Jr., Joey Heatherton, Albert Brooks, and Paul Lynde.

Back home in Toronto, they found that having left Canada once, they were desirable properties upon their return. When the head of the CBC's entertainment division, Doug Nixon, called to lure them back to the network with an offer, Michaels didn't mention that he and Pomerantz had been let go from *Laugh-In*. His confidence had been bolstered by his time in the sun, and he had a clearer idea of what he wanted out of show business. He worked out a deal with the CBC. "I told them that we wanted 'creative freedom,'" he said.

RETREAT

Old joke: A restaurant has two tanks of lobsters, one with a lid, one without.
The chef explains: "The first tank is for American lobsters. Without a lid
they'll escape. The second one is full of Canadian lobsters. It doesn't need a
lid: every time one tries to climb out, the others pull him back down."

THE CANADIAN HOMECOMING OF MICHAELS AND POMERANTZ HAD A TINGE
of Preston Sturges's *Hail the Conquering Hero* to it. "No one ever
comes back unless you're in a box," Pomerantz said. "2 *Laugh-In* Men
to CBC," read a July 18, 1969, headline in the *Toronto Star*. The network, mandated by the government to beef up Canadian-created
content, had announced a "new look" in entertainment. The press
started referring to Pomerantz and Michaels as "the Whiz Kids" and
"the CBC's resident wunderkinder." They were hired to write, produce, and star in four television specials spoofing Canadian mores.
The "unprecedented contract," as the papers called it, also included
a pilot for a sitcom on a "youth theme." Michaels was determined
that the shows reflect the turmoil of the times, even if what passed
for turmoil in Canada was Quebec separatism and a cabinet minister's affair with an East German prostitute.

He had spent his time in L.A. watching and learning how the le-
vers of power worked, and he took the lead dealing with the CBC.
"Lorne has a great social IQ, particularly when it comes to powerful
people," Pomerantz said. "He can be quite hypnotic in his methods."
His social IQ, however, was not as finely calibrated when speaking to
the press. The *Toronto Star* quoted him sounding cocky and defensive
about the budget he'd negotiated, which provided for a huge staff of

ten writers and twenty-eight performers. "Why shouldn't we get this kind of deal?" he asked the reporter. "Sure, there are a lot of CBC variety producers sitting around not producing anything. But we were nominated for Emmys." He went on, "We're looking for young writers and young new talent. Make sure you get *that* into the paper." The "new" talent they recruited was mostly old friends from the U.C. Follies, including Rosie Shuster, who would help out, uncredited, once again. "Lorne likes rabbits' feet," Earl Pomerantz, who joined the staff, said. "He likes familiar people around, a comfort zone."

Determined not to be a mere cog in a machine again, Michaels envisioned setting up his own comedy commonwealth: he negotiated for a share of his show's foreign sales, should any materialize. Also, the contract included a provision that he and Pomerantz would conduct improv workshops, to stuff the CBC pipeline with homegrown talent, and they planned to open their own club to train comedians. "But first we have these shows to do," Michaels told the *Star*. "And we live or die on them. We'll have no one else to blame but ourselves if they bomb."

The hero's welcome engendered some skepticism among the show business establishment: the CBC had blown its budget on two unknown kids. A veteran *Toronto Star* columnist named Patrick Scott sneeringly referred to Hart and Lorne as the "repatriate comedy writers," and broke the news that *Laugh-In* had fired them.

Michaels wanted the atmosphere of the new show to be more collaborative than the joke-factory isolation of *Laugh-In*. He promptly set up camp in a CBC office above a bar on Yonge Street and convened a staff-wide brainstorming meeting. Among those in the packed room were Andrea Martin, Victor Garber, Alan Thicke, and Dan Aykroyd, a teenager who'd come with his comedy partner from Catholic school, Valri Bromfield. (The two of them had brought in a demo reel earlier, and the grizzled CBC producer who looked at it sent them directly to Michaels.) Aykroyd remembers Michaels's "Fu Manchu mustache," and also his erudition: "He was massively well-referenced, as an English Literature student." This was the first of many bull sessions, one of which started with the prompt "Let's think about what the world would be like without string." Among the resulting punch-lines: yo-yos thrown on the ground, wayward kites.

"I was twenty-five, and this was the first time I was a grown-up producer," Michaels said. "I remember sitting down at the end of a long, long table for a read-through, and everyone else was older than I was. But we started, and, miraculously, everyone just listened to what I had to say. I thought, 'Oh, they just see the job. They don't see *me*.' It's that line from *King Lear*—'Even a dog's obeyed in office.'"

For the first special, called *That's Canada for You* (Michaels's title), the CBC assembled 160 young people to watch the filming of the monologue and the musical acts; the sketches and blackouts were taped separately. They ended up with twenty-five hours of material; Michaels was counting on finding the show in the editing room, the way Carolyn Raskin had done at *Laugh-In*. "We're looking at it, and I'm totally depressed, because it all seems flat and dead and lifeless," he said. "And, as always, I thought I would never work again." A CBC editor named Ron Meraska took him in hand, sitting beside him at the console and teaching him to notice things like continuity. "It was as if we hadn't been watching the same footage," Michaels said. "I'd been watching the performances and the writing. And he'd been watching the composition and how it looked." Meraska taught him how to choose shots. "Like, if you pick *this* shot, you have *this* person's profile, but you see *that* person full-on, so the joke's happening *there*," he said.

A few days before the initial special aired, in September 1969, the papers carried a publicity photo of a model shivering in a bikini, while an "Eskimo" carves her curves into a totem pole. The doltish caption, provided by CBC PR, reads "Frigid? Here's one model who's REALLY frigid." Hart and Lorne opened the show with a dual monologue, like Rowan and Martin's. There was a sketch about the chairman of the Royal Commission on Canadian Apathy reading his report to an audience of two; a Canadian version of a nude shower scene (with clothes); and a chat with a filmmaker named Cecil B. Canuck about his biblical epic. Nothing in the show was as funny as the weird hair on Hart and Lorne. Lorne had a droopy Zapata mustache and a sprayed-stiff Prince Valiant hairdo; sideburns like strips of Astroturf frame both of their faces. The show also offered an inventory of late-mod looks, including wide flowered neckties, long pointy shirt collars, and knotted neckerchiefs in a wallpaper showroom's worth of far-out patterns.

Patrick Scott, at the *Star,* pounced in his next column. The special was "campus-juvenile," he wrote, "and lacked even the wit to be embarrassed by its own embarrassment." Others piled on: "A complete waste of viewing time and taxpayers' money—trivial juvenile junk" (*Vancouver Sun*). Some were more positive. *The Ottawa Citizen* called the show "Proof that Canadians can be fun. Even when they're working in Canada." A few reviewers stirred up Oedipal issues that must have created awkwardness at home. *The Edmonton Journal* wrote, "*That's Canada for You* was a refreshing contrast to the tired Wayne and Shuster comedy specials the CBC has been pushing for so many years."

The second special, *Today Makes Me Nervous,* aired in February 1970. A press release described it as a program that "zeroes in on some of the things that make modern life so disconcerting, disturbing and funny—from the clothing revolution to office politics to the doctor/patient relationship, from groupies and hippies to the continuing war between men and women." (The PR photo was no less cringey: a CBC publicity shot showed two young women with no clothes on, holding a strategically placed banner reading NUDE AUDITIONS.) The reviews this time were better. "The CBC appears to be on the verge of breaking the shackles of variety mediocrity," said the *Ottawa Journal*. "Given a little time, Canada could compete with the good humour men south of the border."

That's Show Biz, the third installment, billed as "a zany spoof of the entertainment industry," aired in March and presumably drew on Michaels and Pomerantz's sojourn in Hollywood. In the team's signature sketch, Michaels, as a trenchcoated reporter, interviews the Canadian Beaver, just back from a visit to the coast and full of disdain for his Hollywood co-stars, Gentle Ben and Lassie. The final show, in

May, *I Am Curious (Maple)* (titled, again, by Michaels, who loved foreign films), did well enough that the CBC's new entertainment director, Thom Benson, signed them up for four more.

A lot of show business is driven by the fear of missing out. In a circular kind of logic, Hart and Lorne got press in Canada (where they'd been fired) because they'd given up Hollywood (where they'd been fired) for the homeland; and this made people in Hollywood take notice. Sandy Wernick, a young talent agent in L.A., flew up to Toronto to see if he could sign Michaels and his partner as clients. Wernick took them for drinks at Michaels's favorite aspirational meeting spot, the Windsor Arms Hotel, a 1920s neo-Gothic edifice. Wernick was impressed. "Lorne had the greatest gift for gab that I had ever heard in a guy in his twenties," he said. "He had theories of what comedy was all about. He knew exactly where the comedy of that era was going to go." Pomerantz, he recalled, "was always trying to make a joke. Lorne was never making jokes. He was a hundred percent serious."

Michaels told Wernick that his goal was to be Thom Benson, the elegant CBC executive who always walked around with a bouton-niere in his lapel. Wernick thought that was aiming high for an un-proven guy still in his twenties. But he made a case that he could help Hart and Lorne with their careers. He represented Bob Finkel, the Diller show executive producer, and he said that Finkel was eager to work with Michaels again. Michaels had never been courted before. Before Wernick headed back to L.A., he signed the pair.

Lorne and Rosie took a vacation to France the summer after the first season wrapped, and while they were away, Pomerantz rumi-nated about ways to make the show better. "We weren't becoming stars," he said. The hosts of other variety shows—Glen Campbell, the Smothers Brothers—were household names. He suggested that they retitle their program *The Hart and Lorne Terrific Hour*. It put their names out there, and, Pomerantz said, "the word 'terrific' would be in every review." It was a splashy, un-Canadian innovation, and Mi-chaels went for it. They also added a horn-filled theme song written by Howard Shore, an announcer with a booming voice, and a mod animated title sequence. Against a psychedelic background, cartoons of Hart and Lorne cavort as superheroes in tights, as the reporter interviewing the Canadian Beaver, and as dudes riding two-up on a motorcycle down a rainbow highway. The aesthetic was a blend of *Yellow Submarine* and the opening credits of a British show that had just begun airing in Canada and was high on Michaels's list of influences, *Monty Python's Flying Circus.*

For their second season, the two partners took turns producing—booking musical guests, writing sketches, organizing scenery and costumes—reflecting their diverging comedic tastes and talents. While promoting the *Terrific Hour* on a local talk show, Pomerantz did shtick ("It's been our philosophy that if we've made one person laugh in the world"—beat—"we'll be out of business!"), while Michaels talked in a pedagogical way about the psychological underpinnings of humor. "Mel Brooks once defined comedy as polite hostility," he said, loftily explaining that comedians must never shy away from difficult topics. If you start to say, "You can't do jokes on *that,*" he went on, "you're ineffective as a comedian." Pomerantz objected to a sketch on one of Michaels's episodes in which an actor dressed as Hitler sings "My Way." "It made me very upset," he said. "I worry about Jews getting killed still. That's the job of being Jewish." Michaels kept the bit.

He continued to spend long hours in the editing room with Ron Meraska; performing interested him less and less. When he stood onstage, before the cameras rolled for a sketch, he realized that he was more engaged in checking that the lights were positioned correctly than he was in delivering his lines. Pomerantz felt that he wasn't pulling his weight. "My brother, like every comedian, thinks the straight man is a freeloader," Earl Pomerantz recalled. "Hart was the unpredictable, funny one and Lorne was the bank president one, which resulted in my brother losing his producer co-equalness."

Hart felt sidelined. It annoyed him that Michaels never seemed to be writing anything. ("But he had a producer's eye for light bulbs," Pomerantz said.) He felt embarrassed showing up in court for his day job as a lawyer, when he'd been on TV the night before dressed in the beaver suit. Michaels strenuously avoided looking ridiculous.

There were only three years between them, but they were from different generations. "Lorne liked music and Lorne liked marijuana," Earl Pomerantz said. "Lorne partied and my brother went home." Hart was mystified when Michaels started using the word "groovy." "Lorne is Mr. Zeitgeist. It was cartoonish to me," he said. "I had a mortgage." *Laugh-In* had made Michaels realize that he was through being a gag writer. The CBC show made him see that he didn't care about getting applause. He was a big-picture guy. As Aykroyd put it, "He saw skills and abilities in people. He'd say, 'You can pull this off. You can sing this song.' He could put it all together, and it would coalesce into something with impact." He compared Michaels early on to "the great impresarios, like P. T. Barnum. They see the talent. They can blend it and turn it into a fabric that is very finely woven, and impermeable."

He was becoming skilled at managing creative egos. When a costume designer created an ornate ensemble with elaborately painted boots for a minor gypsy character who'd be shown only above the neck, he had to be diplomatic when he explained that that level of detail wasn't needed. He realized that everyone always sees the enterprise through the prism of his or her job. The producer's role, he was learning, is helping people feel that their contributions are valued, while making them understand that no one will ever get it all their own way. In a similar way, he took pains to get the old guys on the CBC stage crew excited about the show. "As long as you estimated your carpentry hours correctly, the CBC was happy," he said.

Determined to make the show hipper, Michaels doubled down on scouting cutting-edge music acts. He and Howard Shore found Randy Newman playing in a Toronto basement club called Grumbles. ("It was so hot in there that you had to take salt tablets to play," Newman said.) Michaels renewed his acquaintance with David Geffen, by then running Asylum Records, to help recruit the right pop stars. He'd check which big artists were coming to Massey Hall and book them when they were in town. Neil Young was on the show, and Melanie and Cat Stevens. Pomerantz said, "We'd hold back the music till the end of the taping so the audience would stay."

One of the episodes that Michaels produced featured James Taylor at the height of his "Fire and Rain" fame. A gear shifted in Michaels's fledgling producer's brain when he had the idea, during "Sweet Baby James," of making the stage lights green and blue as Taylor sang the line "deep greens and blues are the colors I choose."

But any aspirations to coolness were thwarted by the Taylor episode's opening monologue, which contained this Friars Club–worthy groaner:

LORNE: A lot of people are concerned about the flora and fauna of Africa. Is it still the virgin territory it once was?

HART: Well I would say Flora was, but Fauna I can't vouch for.

When a critic knocked the show for being juvenile, Michaels had a ready retort: "We made a conscious decision to go after an audience of ages one to thirty-five."

In early 1971, the CBC announced plans to launch a late-night talk show targeting a young demographic. Michaels, who anchored a parody newscast called "The Lorne Report" on the *Terrific Hour,* was in the running to host it, and he was asked to tape a tryout show. *TV Guide* ran a story about the search for "Canada's Cavett," which quoted Michaels describing his vision: "The show will be freaky and very loose; simple yet eloquent." Critics were gunning for the twenty-six-year-old whiz kid, who, one noted, had "never been accused of excessive modesty."

On Michaels's audition show, he, as host, sits at the head of a table dotted with ashtrays, surrounded by a pack of guests, including Pomerantz and a local ingenue named Margot Kidder. The meandering conversation lands on the films of Ingmar Bergman, and feeble topless jokes are cracked (Pomerantz: "I saw her back there . . . then I saw her *front* there"). Michaels is loose and giggly; he says "um" a lot. Kidder tries to keep things moving. Someone muses, "How do they kill kosher cows?" Pomerantz, fed up, and probably a little envious, answers: "They bring them on talk shows like this and bore them to death." After viewing the episode, Patrick Scott wrote, "Michaels, whose show hit the all-time rock bottom, may well go down as the only talk-show host in history to stare blankly at his clipboard and mumble haplessly: 'Gee, I, wish I could think of a question.'"

He didn't get the gig, and a month later he and Pomerantz shot the pilot for a "youth-themed" CBC sitcom called *The Students Are Coming! The Students Are Coming!* Their producers were Bob Finkel and Jackie Cooper, the former child star who had grown up to run Screen Gems, the sixties sitcom factory; Wernick put the deal together. It was a collegiate comedy featuring Victor Garber, who was about to star in what would be a breakthrough Toronto production of *Godspell*. Other *Godspell* newcomers whom Michaels then met were Eugene Levy, Dave Thomas, Martin Short, and Gilda Radner—all future rabbits' feet. A young pianist named Paul Shaffer was the musical director.

The Students Are Coming! wasn't picked up (the network told Michaels it was "too smart" for the audience), but it left Michaels with a formative memory. Jackie Cooper, whom Michaels couldn't help but invest with paternal authority, told him a long story one night. Michaels likes to tell it himself, as if still trying to square his own unresolved feelings about his father, who didn't live to see his son's success.

"After shooting, we finished every night by drinking," Michaels said. "Jackie drank perfect Rob Roys, one after another, and one night he told me the greatest story ever, if you have 'dad issues,' as I did. He was a child actor. His mother's mother lived with them, in Hollywood. His father was a piano player, and the mother-in-law didn't approve of him, and didn't think he worked hard enough, or whatever. One day when Jackie was two, the father went out for cigarettes and never came back—he couldn't take it anymore. The grandmother would take Jackie around to wait in line for extra work in the movies. And Jackie's career rose, and he was eventually paired with Wallace Beery and became a star. He invited Wallace Beery to, like, his eighth birthday party, and Wallace Beery didn't come. You know? Anyway, by seventeen or eighteen he's washed-up. He has money, but he has no work. So he goes to New York to audition for Broadway. He ends up in London, playing Ensign Pulver in *Mister Roberts*. And at the end of the run, he buys himself a Jaguar convertible. And he ships it back home, and then is gonna drive across the country. And he's driving, and driving, and driving, and he's in the middle of the country, somewhere—Kansas. It's early in the morning, and the convertible's top flies off. So he has to stop. He pulls into a gas station and a guy starts working on the car. After a while, the guy looks at him and says, 'You Jackie Cooper?' He says, 'Yeah.' The guy goes, 'Your dad lives right down the street.'

"In the bar in Toronto, now, it's two in the morning, and there's been an enormous amount of alcohol already—and I go, *'Yeah?'* And, Cooper goes, 'I waited until the guy fixed the roof, then I got in the car, and I just drove off.' I said, 'So, you didn't want to see what your father looked like? You didn't want to talk to him?' He said, 'He was never there for me. And I needed him.' And I'm, you know, I lost my dad suddenly, and that was the defining thing in my life. I go, 'So, you were *right there,* and you didn't even want to see what he was like, or hear his side of it?' 'Nope.' Yeah."

THE HIGH POINT OF *THE HART AND LORNE TERRIFIC HOUR* WAS A FILMED piece called "The Puck Crisis." It was a mockumentary about an invasive species that spread "Dutch Puck Disease" and devastated the crops of Canada's hockey puck farmers. Over grim footage of lab-coated scientists examining shriveled pucks drooping from branches, a dead-serious voiceover explains the blight's origins: "Puck pests, or *puctococci,* were accidently carried over on the sticks of a touring Dutch hockey team." Michaels, in trenchcoat mode, plays a newscaster interviewing citizens in the street about the disaster. Hart's brother Earl wrote the script, and Michaels cut in clips of real Canadian hockey stars Derek Sanderson and Bob Baun playing along. (Baun: "Without pucks, I'm just a guy who skates backwards.") Pomerantz recalled, *"That's* producing. I wasn't good at that."

"The Puck Crisis," more than anything Michaels had done, embodied the kind of subtle conceptual humor he wanted to create. It had the flat sheen of a news segment and no overt gag lines; the joke was wonderfully underplayed. A critic in *Maclean's* called it a media breakthrough that could only have been produced by people raised on television, young enough "to think instinctively in its language."

Although the show was on a roll, with two million viewers, or 10 percent of the population, tuning in, the CBC abruptly canceled it, with no explanation. Michaels blamed the decision on a Canadian mixture of self-loathing and bureaucracy. "In Canada, every time you get an opportunity, you're denying it to six others," he said. "Canada is a wait-your-turn kind of country. It's all about fairness."

The show over, he took a moment to reassess where he was in his life. All the hours he'd spent in editing rooms and drinking into the night with colleagues over the past several years hadn't helped his marriage. He and Rosie lived in a big pink house that became a communal party scene. John Head crashed there often, as did Aykroyd, and the many members of the free-floating creative family who came through referred to it as Hormone House, for the number of liaisons it fostered. Then, in a bid for stability, the couple bought a tall semi-detached Victorian house at 307 Carlton Street in Cabbagetown, a gentrifying neighborhood in the east end of Toronto. Paul Pape said, "I'm not sure what Florence Lipowitz thought, but my mother was upset when I moved to that neighborhood."

Rosie was still casting about for a calling, taking courses in assorted creative disciplines, even traveling solo to the Middle East. She joined a feminist consciousness-raising group where Atwood was a guest speaker. "Atwood said, 'Forget all the rest of it: economic independence is what you want to go for,'" Shuster recalled. All the work she did on the *Terrific Hour* had been under the radar, as usual. "Lorne was old-style in those days," she said. "He was very controlling." But they kept working at the marriage.

Meanwhile, Sandy Wernick had been relaying job offers from Hollywood, and Michaels had been turning them down. The latest was a writing gig on a variety show—an ABC summer-replacement series hosted by Jack Burns and Avery Schreiber, an Irish-Jewish comedy duo. Wernick was getting frustrated with his picky new client. "It wasn't an automatic," he said. But Michaels stubbornly clung to the Wayne and Shuster formula; he wanted to raise a family in Canada, and to buck the showbiz trend of moving to the States.

Undeterred by the CBC canceling the *Terrific Hour*, he came right back at them with some fresh pitches—quasi-experimental ideas that carried a whiff of his "peak seriousness" period. With Aykroyd and Valri Bromfield, he made a pilot called *The Clesson E. Goodhue Show*, hosted by an elderly character actor whom Michaels picked at random out of a Canadian headshot book. "We built the show around him as if he were a superstar," Aykroyd said. It was a not-quite-successful meta exercise—a comedy show that aimed to deconstruct what makes something funny. Another high-concept pilot was in the works with Victor Garber and Gilda Radner: *Jack: A Flash Fantasy* was a rock opera that would explore "all the iterations of Jack," Michaels said, through the four jacks in a deck of cards. The plan was for the CBC to tape it in February 1973. But the project dearest to Michaels was an eggheady idea he pitched based on *They Became What They Beheld,* an au courant book of photographs by the anthropologist Edmund Snow Carpenter, a loose collaboration with Marshall McLuhan. The book explores, rather ponderously, the difference between "observing" the world and being "involved" in the world.

Around this time, Michaels ran into McLuhan himself, at a UT student hangout called Fran's, beloved by Glenn Gould. Michaels was surprised when McLuhan knew who he was, and he was even more surprised when he pitched him a TV idea: Why not make a mock-heroic epic about Toronto? Although Michaels didn't take the suggestion ("That wasn't a genre that was happening back then," he said), the idea that the philosopher of the moment considered Toronto somehow ridiculous, a worthy topic for satire, struck a chord.

Michaels got a firm no on the pretentious Edmund Carpenter project and became newly discouraged. "Whenever I saw something really good, like a movie, I'd have this pain—like, *I've done nothing with my life,*" he recalled. "But I didn't want to close any doors." Swiveling back to the movie dream, he wangled a meeting with a venerable Canadian programmer named Sydney Newman, who had just returned from a long stint at the BBC (developing *The Avengers* and *Doctor Who*) and was running the National Film Board. Newman couldn't understand why Michaels would want to stick around in Canada. ("A deeply Canadian attitude," Michaels said.) He urged Michaels to do as he himself had done, and get out. But Michaels still hoped that he could make a real career in Canada, as Frank Shuster had done.

It's what the Canadian Beaver had been moaning about all along: "You're never really appreciated in your own country."

Michaels had hoped that his might be the first generation of Canadians who stayed put. "But I didn't have a wide shot on it then," he said. "I didn't know that there just wasn't enough going on in Canada to sustain a whole industry." He flew to London and took some meetings at the BBC that Newman had kindly set up. No offer was forthcoming, but he did sit in on a few tapings, including one for an episode of *Monty Python*. He was riveted by the group's mixed media approach (combining animation with live-action), and their even more radical solution to the problem of ending sketches: simply announcing, "And now for something completely different." It hadn't occurred to him that a show could have characters recur in unrelated sketches ("Nobody expects the Spanish Inquisition!"), and make fun of its own techniques (Eric Idle, in a police uniform, citing "offences against the Getting Out of Sketches Without Using a Proper Punchline Act," threatens to place "this entire show" under arrest). Mainly, he admired the way the troupe didn't pander.

He also watched a rehearsal for a program by Spike Milligan, the former star of BBC Radio's *The Goon Show*, and a particular hero. "Spike, being a comedian—and good—had one eye on the monitor," he said. "And he saw that the cameraman was framing the shot in such a way that it stepped on the joke." Milligan asked to stop the scene, and explained the problem to the director, who became defensive. "You could see Spike going *down*," Michaels said. A break was called, and Milligan, who suffered from bipolar disorder, took a seat in the audience. Michaels, sitting nearby, heard him murmur to himself, "Sometimes I have to go away for a while." He internalized the idea that talent needs to be protected. "I saw that the whole point was to let *him*—the center, the genius—do his thing," he said. "But crews will kill you; directors will kill you."

Back in Toronto, he talked things over with Rosie and took stock of his options. He'd learned a lot about producing at the CBC, but he felt that he'd flatlined. The Burns and Schreiber job Wernick was dangling in L.A. was thirteen shows in ten weeks, and a good paycheck. It wouldn't be groundbreaking, but it could cement some relationships—to Wernick, to Brillstein.

There was no question of Hart Pomerantz going to L.A. After the CBC show, the partnership had stalled, and the gap in their cultural tastes widened. Pomerantz said, "I always felt I was too old, even at twenty-eight." The friends had a final dinner together at the Balkan Restaurant, a cheerless place on Elm Street. "Lorne let me know that his career was going in a different direction," Pomerantz said. He saw that Michaels wanted to produce, to make his mark on a bigger stage. He understood that being a straight man wasn't a life, and there was no acrimony. He continued his legal practice, and he was a panelist on a game show about Canada's funniest laws. The shelves in his living room in a Toronto suburb are lined with whimsical clay heads that he's sculpted, a surrogate audience. "I'm a small footnote in Lorne's life," he said.

PART TWO

TUESDAY

On Tuesday evening at around seven, after walking from his apartment on Central Park West to 30 Rock, Lorne Michaels stepped off the elevator and turned left toward his office, down a long hall lined with cast headshots from over the decades. He handed his Fitbit to an assistant. Now, after an unpleasant dentist appointment and an afternoon dealing with business from home, he was beginning his official workday. On his way upstairs, he had stopped in at *The Tonight Show* to see how Fallon was weathering the death-threat situation, and to check in on the fallout from another muddle: A few weeks earlier, one of Fallon's producers had abruptly canceled an appearance by Norm Macdonald, the SNL veteran known for his ferocious deadpan, and for getting fired from the show for his unrelenting jokes about O. J. Simpson. A flip Macdonald comment about the #MeToo movement had inflamed Twitter, and a *Tonight* producer, instead of seeing it as an opportunity for a newsmaking TV bit between host and guest—a Hugh Grant moment—had bumped him. The producer was promptly sidelined. The whole incident exasperated Michaels. "It's generational," he said of the overreaction. "Just have Jimmy say to Norm, 'That was idiotic, the thing you said.'" Michaels stops in at *Tonight* regularly, but he keeps more of a distance from the other projects he produces, which include *Late Night with Seth Meyers,* an array of comedy series, movies, Broadway shows, and an agricultural operation in Maine that sells goat cheese and wild blueberries. His other shows, a mix of hits and misses, include *30 Rock, Portlandia, Documentary Now!, Up All Night, The Awesomes, The Maya Rudolph Show, Man Seeking Woman, Detroiters, A.P. Bio, Miracle Workers, Shrill, Kenan, Schmigadoon!, Mapleworth Murders, Los Espookys, Bupkis,* and *That Damn Michael Che.* But SNL has always been his primary focus.

Outside his office is a row of desks. Willa Slaughter, his "first assistant," sat at the one nearest his door, with two others manning the rest. When he arrives, an assistant always follows him into his office. Waiting on his desk: a fresh legal pad, three sharpened pencils arranged on the left, and a basket of warm popcorn. In many offices, the job of assistant has changed, as people reach each other directly on cell phones rather than on a landline. But in Michaels's world, the assistant-as-gatekeeper model still holds, and the assistants, who used to be known around the show as "Lornettes," are always on the phone, answering calls, rolling calls, or placing calls to make restaurant reservations, or to check that flower or gift deliveries are on schedule.

There is often a visitor in the waiting area outside his office. Everyone has a waiting-for-Lorne story. ("It's the least original story in L.A.," the writer and director David Mandel says.) The first time Mike Myers met Michaels, he sat waiting through lunch and dinner (he dashed down to the concourse level for a sandwich, and then, later, went down again). The seating—a couch so deep that the feet of anyone sitting on it dangle above the floor—contributes to the sense of discombobulation. The waiting is a marker of the odd dynamic that Michaels has created around time—his own and other people's. He thinks nothing of scheduling a meeting at 1:30 A.M. on a Wednesday. (Asked about his habit of keeping people waiting, he'll cite triage: "The problem in front of me is always the one I'm going to go to.") But friends who vacation with him, kept waiting for a long stretch in a hotel lobby, have banged on his door to find him lolling in the bathtub wearing headphones. On the other hand, his friend Randy Newman recalled, "You'd go into a restaurant with him and his Caesar salad is already there. I'd say, 'Lorne, what the fuck is this?'" An assistant had pre-ordered for him to save time.

This Tuesday, after Slaughter went over Michaels's messages with him, she updated him on the guest list for the upcoming American Museum of Natural History gala. Michaels, a board member, had been chairing the event for years with his wife, Alice Barry, and had bought several tables. (In 2012, an AMNH scientist identified a new species of daddy longlegs and named it *Stylocellus lornei* in his honor.)

Slaughter's job was to make sure that his tables were packed with celebrities. Steve Martin and Martin Short were unavailable, she noted, but Tina Fey—another gala co-chair—was inviting people. At some point Erik Kenward, one of the show's senior producers, walked into Michaels's office and said, "Leslie is still being Leslie." Michaels sighed.

The first piece of actual business on a Tuesday is the host dinner, which is held in the back room of an Italian restaurant on West Forty-sixth Street called Lattanzi. The meal is phase two of breaking in the host and an opportunity for Michaels to take the host's measure in a roomful of people who have an almost compulsive need to make the others laugh. "I'm heading toward Saturday, so I have to know what I'm dealing with," he told me. "And the more the hosts see that these people are on their side, the less they'll panic." As he put on his jacket to walk the five blocks to the restaurant, a producer named Caroline Maroney (a former assistant) was at his heels, briefing him in the elevator on plans for the Macy's Thanksgiving Day Parade. The stars of *Mean Girls,* the Broadway musical he'd produced with Fey, based on her hit 2004 movie, were slated to perform a number in front of the reviewing stand.

Out on the street, he went into what people call his "Lornewalk" mode. Since the seventies, long before anyone counted their steps, he has made sure to schedule time for a substantial walk every day, usually in Gucci loafers. Walking reflects his medium-cool temperament; breaking a sweat would be out of the question. "It's how I think," he said. It also provides a private setting for discussion; Michaels was saying "Walk with me" to underlings decades before Aaron Sorkin ever dreamed of *The West Wing.* Fallon estimates that, when he travels in the summer with Michaels to London, they walk seven miles a day. Familiar routes—New York side streets, stretches of country lane or beach (St. Barts or Amagansett), the curvy grid of the Beverly Hills Flats—affect his brain like a lit-up switchboard of conversational possibilities.

"This is where we buried Chris Farley," Michaels said, walking along West Forty-ninth Street and nodding toward St. Malachy's, a

Catholic church where Farley used to volunteer. A little farther along, on Eighth Avenue, he pointed at a construction site; there used to be a liquor store there, where he'd bought a birthday present—"a decanter of bourbon in the shape of a blue Cadillac"—for Phil Hartman, another cast member who died too soon.

The dynamic between fathers and sons is often on Michaels's mind. Walking west, through the theater crowds, he mused on *First Man,* the movie about the Apollo 11 moon landing. He was skeptical of the way the film linked Neil Armstrong's taciturn personality to the death of his young daughter, which felt to him like a pop-psychology overlay. "I had a father, and that's what they were like back then," he said. "World War Two, John Wayne." He'd seen the movie with Pete Davidson, who lost his father, a Staten Island firefighter, on 9/11, when Pete was seven; and who, Michaels felt, needed a dose of paternal TLC. He sympathized with the way Davidson, all his life, likely heard "I know you'll make your father proud." Every Father's Day, Michaels gets messages from dozens of surrogate sons, ranging from Davidson to Ted Sarandos to the pitcher David Wells.

When he reached Lattanzi, the SNL squad was already seated around a big table. The group included his top deputies and a few select cast members. The dinner is a coveted invitation, and not being included can cripple a person's confidence for the week. "When you first get there," Will Ferrell said, "you're marking down who got invited to the host dinner and who didn't."

Jonah Hill arrived last and sat down by Michaels, to a round of applause. "I'm very grateful to be here," he told the group, with a certain formality. "It never ceases to amaze me how you create something like this every week." He was feeling nostalgic, he said. "So I want to tell you a little story about my first time hosting, ten years ago. Between dress and air that night I got broken up with over the phone. I was hysterically crying, still dressed from the last sketch—as White Madea. Full grandma. Eye makeup was running down my face. Total sad clown. It was one of the top five most cinematic moments in my life."

"Whoah!" Colin Jost said. "No one is actually in clown makeup when they get broken up with."

Plates of bucatini arrived, and a big steak for Kate McKinnon. As soon as Michaels sat, a Belvedere on the rocks had been put in front of him, with a dainty cordial glass of cranberry juice on the side, to dose the drink. A few others ordered single glasses of wine; they would have to go back to the office later and write all night, in preparation for the Wednesday read-through. The conversation bounced around between the news—the choice of a recent event to use for the cold open looms all week—and show business. Whitey Bulger, the eighty-nine-year-old Boston mob boss turned informant, had been murdered in his prison cell that day.

"Such a cinematic moment," Hill said. The murder weapon, someone said, was a lock in a sock.

"It sounds like a failed Dr. Seuss book," Jost said. In any gathering of comedy writers, there's a joke echo effect: a straight remark will be followed by a knowing riposte by a fellow comic, the conversational equivalent of a rim shot.

"Didn't Sinéad O'Connor become Muslim this week?" Michaels asked the table, hopping to a news story that was, in a roundabout way, deeply interwoven with SNL. O'Connor often turns up on lists of the defining moments in the show's history because of an incident in 1990, when she tore up a photo of Pope John Paul II on camera and shouted, "Fight the real enemy!" NBC got hundreds of calls from angry Catholic viewers, but what bothered Michaels about the incident was not that it was inflammatory, but that it was unscripted. In a live show, surprises throw off the camera people and the timing, the near-military precision required to make the show go.

"She called that priest stuff early," Steve Higgins said.

"Which is why I did not chastise her," Michaels said. "I thought that whatever she was doing was completely sincere. Frank Sinatra thought it was a publicity stunt." Not long after O'Connor tore up the photo, Sinatra announced that he wanted to "kick her ass." SNL satirized the ongoing feud in a sketch called "The Sinatra Group" (a send-up of the political show *The McLaughlin Group*), with Phil Hartman playing a snarly Sinatra brawling with O'Connor (Jan Hooks)—he refers to her as Sinbad, and "the bald chick."

When Michaels is surrounded by a group of young acolytes, like Don Corleone in a back room or Jesus at the Last Supper, he likes to hold forth, dispensing stories as if from an internal jukebox. He once joked that a doctor told him that he has "thirty-five percent more lung capacity than the average." Although he speaks at a low volume, with the calm precision of a man announcing a golf tournament, words flow out of him in torrents. "I have this incredible faith in conversation," he once said. The talk can start with a cascade on a mainstream subject, like politics. Then it will swerve into another channel—early show business, say, or how to fish for pickerel in Maine. Friends describe Michaels's conversation as if it were a continuous stream that one drops in and out of, hearing scraps of stories that, over time, cohere into complete narratives, the way years of flipping channels and landing on Turner Classic Movies will eventually give you an idea of the plot of *Double Indemnity*. It will meander along, sweeping up bits of historical gossip and asides on current bigshots, and then flow back to its original subject. The segues are heralded by a few interchangeable phrases: *The thing of it is, All I'm getting at is, My point with it is, It's that thing of, like . . .*

"It all rolls out of him, like jazz," Dana Carvey said. Disciples obsessively dissect the well-thumbed stories for nuggets of wisdom. Sometimes they're merely puzzling, like the gnomic koans Michaels regularly dispenses, but often they're the showbiz equivalent of *When the water rises, go up to the hills*—i.e., "If this happened to Lew Wasserman, it could happen to you," Higgins said. The flow of talk also functions as a cloak; when Michaels warms to a topic, it shields him from questions he might not want to answer.

People who spend a lot of time around him seem happy to sit through a story they've heard before, the way a churchgoer won't bristle at hearing the Twenty-third Psalm on repeat. The sage status took time to achieve. In the eighties, Buck Henry, a regular SNL host, walked out of a restaurant after Michaels launched into a *Laugh-In* motel chestnut that he'd heard once too often. ("That fucking does it," Henry said.) Usually the listeners keep listening, alert to the privilege of being one-on-one with the boss. When Bill Hader took his first private jet trip with Michaels, a red-eye to the Emmys, Seth Meyers, an old hand, offered "Why don't *you* sit with Lorne?" Hader was delighted, at first. He recalled, "Lorne would be going, 'And that guy, of course, was Chevy Chase,' and I would fall asleep for a bit and then I'd open my eyes and hear 'And Ray Charles said, "You know, they all still owe me money"' and then my eyes would close and next time I open them he's saying, 'And that's how you grow blueberries in Maine.' For five hours he never stopped speaking."

Many of the stories have a when-giants-walked-the-earth feel, and there is usually a moment in these tales, like a key change in a song, when the giant's life intersects with Michaels's. With a regal nonchalance, he downplays the connection, making it seem like the most natural thing in the world, but his eyes brighten slightly. At the Lattanzi dinner, he described the time his friend Penny (. . . Marshall) brought him to a mob restaurant on the East Side, where Joe Pesci was working between movies. Pesci walked them around and introduced them to the mafiosi. "I only remember the rings gleaming in the dimness of the booths," he said. From organized crime, he segued into another sort of family saga, the life and times of Pamela Harriman. He is a student of the way different social worlds intersect, and he often interrupts his own story to sketch in lineage. Hill and Jost leaned in to hear how Pamela Digby—the wife of Randolph Churchill; confidante of her father-in-law, Winston Churchill; mistress of Gianni Agnelli; wife to Leland Hayward and W. Averell Harriman— became a formidable Democratic Party fundraiser and handpicked Bill Clinton as the candidate in 1992. Michaels admired her ability to identify stars early on, and he was delighted when she asked him to produce a fundraiser for the Democrats in 1990. Paul Simon had been the go-between, and he'd told Michaels that Digby, at seventy, was sexy. Seated in her flower-filled Georgetown living room, a Van Gogh over the fireplace, he understood why. "Power and femininity," Michaels said. "There's no one like that now." The fundraiser that he put together, with Crosby, Stills & Nash, Gladys Knight, and Dana Carvey, "was a nice night in show business," as he likes to say.

While Michaels can always be counted on to tell stories about famous people, his employees can always be counted on to talk about him. "Whenever I'm sitting around a table with anyone in the comedy world, there's a gravitational pull to talk about Lorne," Conan O'Brien told me. The tone is a mixture of affection, reverence, fear, and sometimes a lick of derision. The people he's hired are grateful for the opportunities he's given them, but his encouragement can turn to aloofness overnight. He lives a mogul's life, and the power he wields is intimidating. Jim Downey talks about the "Kim Jong Un–like deification process" that, over the years, has helped protect the show from network meddling and has also rendered Michaels more and more inscrutable. O'Brien continued, "In my experience, all conversations, no matter how they begin, inexorably become about Lorne. You could ask me, Stephen Hawking, Ziggy Marley, and former Prime Minister Theresa May our opinions on the single-payer healthcare plan, and within six minutes we'd be riffing on Lorne trying to buy flip-flops on St. Barts." Will Ferrell speaks of having to apologize to non-SNL people at dinner parties: "Sorry we just spent twenty minutes on Lorne." Hader recalled, "The number of 'Does Lorne hate me?' conversations I've had . . ." The obsessiveness extends to minutiae. Andy Samberg and John Mulaney each bought a forty-dollar Hermès Terre deodorant stick, relying on intelligence from one of Michaels's assistants, so that they could smell like him. It turned out to be the wrong scent.

The riffing about Lorne is usually funny, deconstructing one of his quirks. For instance, the way he drops names. He's always done it, just like he's always had a predisposition to befriend celebrities. The names are dropped casually, without a resounding clang, but the habit has generated a subgenre of shtick among the people who work for him. Cast members have been refining their Lorne impressions for years; Fred Armisen does Japanese Lorne and German Lorne. Hader does an impersonation (it has what Alec Baldwin calls "all the Lornian beats") of him dropping the names of serial killers: "You know, John-Wayne Gacy—he killed, but he killed in that way, in his basement, which is so Midwest, you know." Another writers' room bit: Lorne name-dropping superheroes. ("I was with Green . . . oh, Green *Lantern*.") Hader has observed that when Michaels name-drops, he wearily rubs his eyes, "like he's really put out by the amount of famous people he knows." Conan O'Brien invented a private game called "Which Paul?" The joke setup would be Michaels asking, "Will you join me for dinner with Paul?" O'Brien explained, "And you'd want to figure out, is it Paul Simon or Paul McCartney?"

At Lattanzi, the talk eventually turned to books and movies, including *Giant,* the 1956 James Dean film. "Dean had been a model, and he knew how to find the light in a scene," Michaels said, explaining that stars used to stick with the same lighting director for their whole career, a practice he has largely followed with the tech people on SNL. Hill, who was listening avidly, had clearly been steeping himself in the literature of Hollywood; his dinner conversation was studded with references to showbiz gods. ("As Lew Wasserman used to say, 'Dress British, think Yiddish.'") He had just read a memoir by Michael Ovitz, the Hollywood player who, in the 1980s, transformed the agenting business by packaging agency talent together in movies. Michaels jumped in with a relevant story: Ovitz had asked to be introduced to Bill Murray during SNL's second season, hoping to lure him to his new firm, Creative Artists Agency. When Michaels declined, wanting to keep Murray focused, Ovitz got tickets to the show, sidled up to Murray, and signed him anyway.

When Michaels tells stories about the original Not Ready for Prime Time Players, a patch of pink appears in the center of each of his cheeks, giving him a toddlerish look. Most of his charges listen with their eyes wide. The longest-serving among them had heard these founding-fathers tales hundreds of times. At Lattanzi, he told one about the day in 1976 when he took Chevy Chase, John Belushi, and Dan Aykroyd to the White House, where Gerald Ford's press secretary was to give them a private tour.

"We drove up to the gate, which went up and down like a studio gate," Michaels said. "A guy asks us for ID. I'm Canadian, so I hand over my license. But Belushi had no ID. I'm like, 'John, how the fuck do you come to the White House with no ID?' The guard says, 'I know who he is,' and he waves us through." The clean-living young people at the table basked in their connection, by proxy, to this glamorous, dead forebear. (Dan Aykroyd told me, "There will always be a new comedy army ready to serve Lorne.")

Sometime after ten, the waiter brought cannoli and espresso. McKinnon leaned toward Michaels and thanked him for the pep talk the day before. A fierce Hillary Clinton supporter, she had been especially devastated by Trump's election. Having steered the show through nine presidents, Michaels sees it as his job to provide perspective. "When Nixon was elected, he seemed to us as bad as Trump," he told McKinnon. On top of Watergate, he said, "he'd denounced Charlie Chaplin on the Senate floor as being a menace to young girls." Desecrating a comedy god rates with high crimes and misdemeanors.

Trump had hosted SNL in November 2015, a year before his election. Afterward, Michaels was attacked for sleeping with the enemy in the name of ratings, and the staff was unhappy. At Lattanzi, Jost crowed about how they'd talked Trump into doing a sketch about being endorsed by a pair of porn stars. Lindsay Shookus, the talent booker, said, "I remember him asking, 'Is this presidential?'" He'd shown up at 30 Rock with only a security guard and no media handlers to vet material. The guard had shaken his head no, but the writers prevailed.

Michaels lifted his eyebrows. He still seemed to feel a need to justify having Trump host: "We were alerting the audience that *this guy* is actually going to be the candidate."

Jost reminisced about some Trump bloopers. They'd written a sketch in which he visited Disneyland's Hall of Presidents with Ivanka. It ended with Trump saying the line "Told you." Then he was supposed to yell, *"Turkey legs!"* (as in, "Let's eat some turkey legs!") But he'd run the lines together, saying to Ivanka, "Told you, Turkey Legs," as if it were her nickname.

Michael Che chimed in. "The Giving Tree one was probably the best," he said. In that sketch, Trump played a tree standing next to the Giving Tree, the character from the beloved Shel Silverstein children's book, who gives and gives of himself until he is reduced, by degrees, to a stump. The Trump tree calls the Giving Tree a sucker. In the end, Trump refused to do the piece not because it portrayed him as heartless, but because of a wardrobe issue; he thought that having his face poke out of a hole in the tree costume made him look like a loser.

Out on the sidewalk after dinner, a cluster of professional autograph hustlers with 8x10s of Jonah Hill had gathered. Hill signed a few and hopped into an SUV to be driven back to 30 Rock. Everyone else set off on foot, through the theater district. Michaels likes not being recognizable. He's never had what he calls "that thing of, 'I want to be famous,'" he told me, adding, "I think all the people who have to know about me already know about me, and I get to walk to work. Jimmy"—Fallon—"can't walk up to Nobu."

Looking at the marquees in the West Forties, Michaels mentioned that he'd arranged tickets to *Mean Girls* that evening for his old friend Margaret Trudeau. He was displeased that an understudy had gone on in place of one of the leads. "Her dog ate glue and she had to rush it to the hospital," he said of the actress, rolling his eyes. "It's a millennial thing. If it was Patti LuPone's dog, it'd be dead."

A few blocks along, he sidled up to Michael Che and asked him if he would emcee the museum gala. "I'm afraid of the whale!" Che said, referring to the huge fiberglass model that hangs from the ceiling of the Hall of Ocean Life, the site of the party. What about Jost or Higgins, he suggested.

Higgins said, "*Use* your fear of the whale."

Jost, who hosted the gala the previous year, peeled off from the group as it approached 30 Rock. He has a superstition about the building's entrances: he avoids the Forty-ninth Street doors, and instead loops around the block and goes in from Fiftieth Street. (The show breeds compulsion; Tina Fey, who doesn't consider herself superstitious, said, "When I worked there, I'd think, 'If I get off the B train and go to the right of the pole, my day is going to go well.' The show can make you neurotic.") Michaels accommodates this magical thinking. He has his own superstitious side, clinging to outmoded methods at the show, like using cue cards instead of teleprompters and insisting that script revisions be done on paper. When the SNL offices were renovated in 2017, he ordered that no detail be altered. "Mike Myers wouldn't walk down the hallway when he came to my office," he said. "He had to cut through the design department."

Higgins said, "He also had to touch a special thing when he was in the studio."

Michaels: "Farley would touch things, too." Several times during my week there, he made reference to the number of people at the show who are "on the spectrum."

Waiting for the elevator on the ninth floor, where the group switched to another elevator bank, Michaels nodded at a vitrine full of NBC memorabilia. A monitor inside the case showed a clip from *The Dean Martin Show,* the wolfishly grinning star gripping a glass of whiskey. "Biggest star of his time," Michaels said, in crisp admiration. He values longevity, a performer's ability to go the long haul, reinventing himself to keep pace with the times. After years as Jerry Lewis's partner, as a movie star, and as a maker of hit records, Martin hosted a popular variety show for nine years, and, at his death, is said to have been the single largest minority shareholder of RCA stock. His showbiz persona as a lush was a put-on, down to his vanity license plate, which read DRUNKY.

The display case also contained a *Laugh-In* trash can and an original puppet of Triumph the Insult Comic Dog, a brilliant regular on *Late Night with Conan O'Brien,* which Michaels executive produced. O'Brien was once one of Michaels's fair-haired boys, handpicked from the SNL writers' ranks to become a star and, for a flash, the fifth host of *The Tonight Show.* These days he and Michaels don't speak as much. In the NBC Guest Services lobby, screens flash montages of the network's stars. The *Tonight Show* array includes shots of Steve Allen, Jack Paar, Johnny Carson, Jay Leno, and Jimmy Fallon, but none of Conan O'Brien.

Back on the seventeenth floor, around 11:00 P.M., Michaels

glanced at a few potential new cell phone models that his second assistant, Grace Godvin, was holding out, and went into his office to go over ticket requests for Saturday's dress rehearsal and live show. Demand was higher than usual. "It might be Jonah, or maybe it's the election," he said. It didn't seem to occur to him that the draw might be the week's musical guest, Maggie Rogers, a twenty-four-year-old singer-songwriter. She had not yet released her first album, but she already had a following among young women.

Next was a meeting with the producers and senior writers, setting the table for the following day's read-through. It was 11:30, and some of them were full of Italian food, trying to clear their heads to settle in for a long night. Over the years, writers have questioned the wisdom of scheduling the dinner on the same evening as the writing all-nighter. But, embracing an if-it-ain't-broke logic, Michaels won't tamper with tradition. "I like to say, fatigue is your friend," he said. "Fatigue wears down the critical faculties, the inner editor. If you're tired, it's easier to go, 'How about this?'" He himself is resolutely nocturnal, and he has nurtured the habit into a philosophy. "People are too focused in the morning," he said. "Also, the comedy is going to have to work around this time at night, on the show." In the first year, he had everyone come in at noon on Monday and watch Saturday's show, "to see what we could learn from it," he said. "It was always awful. It wasn't meant to be watched at noon."

There's an old joke that Michaels tells to illustrate how comedy writers work. He credits it to a comic he knew in the sixties named Stanley Myron Handelman, and it's a riff on the Infinite Monkey Theorem, which posits that if you put a thousand monkeys in a roomful of typewriters, one of them will eventually write *Hamlet*. Handelman's joke, as Michaels tells it, ends: "I looked in on the roomful of monkeys, and you know something? They were just fooling around." Michaels explained: "The joke illustrates perfectly what we do at the show. It means things are healthy and it's going well. People always think that if the process was better organized, it would work better. They don't realize that there's more invention in disorder." He told the monkey joke from the podium the first time SNL won a Peabody Award, in 1990. ("It got no reaction whatsoever," he said.) He probably tells it once a week.

In the seventies, the fooling around involved more partying. "People would drink, people would smoke a joint," he said. "But it was never as interesting as any of the books made it seem." These days, the cast hoards Ozempic.

The group of lieutenants in the office was upbeat. Jonah Hill had been deemed "very collaborative." One producer reported, about Leslie Jones, "Leslie is very mad, in a very consistent way."

Michaels, mellow from two vodkas, conducted the meeting in a quiet, deliberate way, as if trying to conserve energy for later in the week. A political idea for the cold open was the first priority. He wanted to talk about the caravan of immigrants on its way from Central America that Trump had been fulminating about, threatening to send in the military.

"What is the operation called?" Erik Kenward asked. "Trusty Patriot?" Everyone laughed, and someone corrected him: Faithful Patriot.

Kenward reported that Hill was writing a parody trailer for a movie called *Late90s*, a fake sequel to *Mid90s*, the movie he'd just directed.

Michaels frowned: "How many people have seen *Mid90s*?"

"Uh, maybe in the mid-nineties," Kenward answered, and described another idea that Hill was working on, about an annoying waiter in a movie theater where you can order dinner from your seat.

In meetings with his top people, Michaels often raises concerns and then waits for someone to talk him out of them. "We did Jonah's kid at Benihana three times?" he asked. "Did it get worse each time?"

"I think it peaked the second time, like most of those things do," Kenward said.

Other ideas were floated: Kenan Thompson, the cast darling who had been on the show for fifteen seasons, was planning to reprise his popular impression of David "Big Papi" Ortiz, the former Red Sox first baseman and inveterate product pitchman, to riff on the team's World Series victory. Shookus had been in touch with the Red Sox to see if any of its players would do a cameo. But Michaels worried that the timing was off; by Saturday the Sox would be last week's news. He asked about the midterm polls. He prides himself on having an inside track on politics. "People are going to be looking at what we do on this election," he said. "Any ideas? The stories keep coming so fast." Poker-faced, he added, "Kanye stepped out of the running."

"Turns out he didn't know a lot about politics," Che said.

Michaels, matching Che's dryness, said, "He was pretty convincing when he was here." A few weeks earlier, West had been the musical guest and had hijacked the Goodnights, the segment at the end of the show when the performers gather onstage and hug and wave to the audience. With the embarrassed cast cowering behind him, West delivered an incoherent pro-Trump rant. (The cameras had stopped rolling before he got too far.)

Michaels turned to Shookus and asked what other celebrities were floating around who could potentially do cameos. In the past few seasons, the show had been drafting movie stars to play recurring roles. (They make news and drive up the YouTube numbers.) Baldwin's Trump started that way, a move that was a painful surprise to Darrell Hammond, the master impressionist who had been doing Trump on the show since 1995. Hammond now announces the SNL opening credits, having succeeded its original announcer, Don Pardo, in 2014. Trump's circle was filled out by Melissa McCarthy (Sean Spicer), Ben Stiller (Michael Cohen), Matt Damon (Brett Kavanaugh), and Jost's wife, Scarlett Johansson (Ivanka Trump). Audiences love the surprise guests, but cast members can resent losing choice parts to interlopers.

Shookus said that the only outsiders under discussion for that week were Five Timers Club members. There was an idea about doing a Five Timers Lounge sketch with a #MeToo angle, using only women Five Timers—Tina Fey, Candice Bergen, Drew Barrymore, Melissa McCarthy, and Scarlett Johansson. Not picking up on the no-boys-allowed premise, Michaels barked some names. "Steve? Hanks? Five Timers was his idea to begin with," he said. "Justin"—Timberlake—"is here but he's lost his voice." Timberlake was to be on *The Tonight Show* that week, and bruised vocal cords had required Fallon's writers to come up with a no-talking approach to a talk show. This is what Michaels calls "a Tuesday problem," not as dire as "a Friday problem." (By the same logic, "a summer problem" isn't anything to lose sleep over.)

Next, the group ran through the cast to make sure everyone would have enough to do. "Cecily?" Michaels asked. "She needs a really strong show." Kenward, who oversees the pre-taped material, said that she was covered. He added, "And Pete is writing a film piece with Jonah about his breakup with Ariana. Ripped from the headlines!"

Michaels absently said, "I'd rather *not* do *Mid90s*. I don't want to promote a movie that's in two theaters." (In the early years, he found it tacky if a guest wanted to plug a new project. Now SNL is a regular stop on the studio publicity circuit.) Finally he asked, "What about Leslie?"

Someone said that there was a piece for her to do about black Ted Cruz supporters, and they were planning to reprise a gospel-brunch idea. Michaels frowned. "What's she punishing everybody over?"

"She says no one will write for her," Erin Doyle answered.

"She thought the meeting yesterday was all about her," Michaels said, and sighed. "I told them they have to work *with* the writers." One story he brings out often is how Gilda Radner used to bake cookies and bring them to the writers on the Tuesday all-nighters; she knew how to make alliances. He said that he and Jones had been emailing. "I told her, 'You're overheated.'" He read her response from his phone's screen: "I'm not overheated; I'm disappointed. And I'm done being upset at this job."

Normally, Michaels sticks around for part of writing night, conferring about pieces in progress. Cast and writers know it's a good time to approach him—before the pressure of the week kicks in, and while he's a little loose from the vodkas. But this week most of the trouble-shooting had been taken care of, so he was done for the day. A lot of his time in the office is spent tending to people, smoothing things over. "It's not unlike being a doctor or a shrink," he said. "You learn to put up boundaries. Belushi would be in my building at three A.M." Chris Rock compares Michaels to a coach. "This guy's been thousands of people's boss, and he's watched them go from nothing to something," he said. "It doesn't make you quite a psychiatrist, but it gets you close to that level."

Michaels felt that his current cast was a good group. But the competitive nature of the show—everyone is always fighting for airtime—pushes people to re-create their own family dynamics. "I used to say that I could tell how everybody here felt about their father," he told me. "If you trusted your parents, you won't have any problem here. But if you were the sibling that wasn't getting enough attention, you come in with that." He went on, drolly, "I'm not quite Prometheus—the one who brought them fire—but it's not far from that."

At around 1:00 A.M., as the writers and producers settled in for the long haul, Michaels headed for home.

FIVE

THE COAST

Television is a medium, so called because it is neither rare nor well-done.

—ATTRIBUTED VARIOUSLY TO ERNIE KOVACS,
FRED WARING, AND *CATHOLIC DIGEST*

WHEN MICHAELS RETURNED TO L.A. IN THE SPRING OF 1973, TO TAKE THE job on the Burns and Schreiber show, he arrived without a writing partner or a wife. He and Rosie had decided to separate again. She'd grown up as "Frank Shuster's daughter," and she didn't want to spend her life being "Lorne Michaels's wife." "I'd come to the end of things in Canada," Michaels said. "Between a failed marriage and a career that had run out of gas, I was starting over."

Disoriented and lonely, he drove his rental car up and down Pacific Coast Highway and tried to recapture the feeling that he'd had about the city a few years earlier, when it was brand-new to him. But the pace on the job he'd come for—writing on the Burns and Schreiber summer-replacement show—distracted and energized him. It was thirteen shows in ten weeks; he had to churn stuff out. There wasn't time to overthink or get too precious. "I realized that to get better, you've got to get up to bat," he said. The show was hammy, the sketches ticking along to Catskills rhythms; Teri Garr was a regular, just before her breakout role in *Young Frankenstein*. The pay was $500 a week.

When that wrapped, Wernick got him hired as a writer on Perry Como's annual Christmas special. Wernick's agency represented Como, and he hoped that Michaels would help the sixty-one-year-old singer find a younger audience. (For a 1968 Como special, Wernick had booked Jefferson Airplane. When Como walked into dress rehearsal, Wernick recalled, "Perry turned to me and said, 'Get rid of them. I ain't working with those dirty-looking people.'") For *The Perry Como Winter Show*'s 1973 edition, a vocal group of young people called The Establishment provided backup; grinning in bright, tight turtleneck sweaters, with long, center-parted hair, they looked like a scrubbed-up version of the Manson Family. The show opens with Como driving a snow-covered El Camino through sunny L.A., a Christmas tree in the cargo bed, crooning a song about "tinseltime in Tinseltown." A magic elevator transports him to a rustic Vermont lodge with a lime-green color scheme that matches the fat-yarn bows in The Establishment girls' pigtails. Como goofs with the youngsters (he makes "get a haircut" jokes), and Sally Struthers, another guest star, does a faux-burlesque number set in "Club Igloo," where a seal balances a champagne glass on its snout.

The special was nothing that Michaels could feel proud of, but it reunited him with the producer Bob Finkel, from the Phyllis Diller show, and Finkel helped him see what Perry Como did that made him a TV star. It was a kind of minimalism. "Como was very good at two things," Michaels said. "One was walking. He could walk out onto the stage singing for sixteen bars. He walked really well." The second thing was subtler. "He'd tell the director, 'If you cut to me during the bridge, you'll see this little twinkle in my eye.'" On TV, the tiniest things make a performance; a brass-band approach ("the Ethel Merman of it all," as Michaels put it) feels like an assault. He'd already noticed how, "when 'hot' comedians—guys who performed at clubs—went on *The Ed Sullivan Show*, it never worked, particularly in the middle of the country." They were pushing too hard; they were "sweaty." It made people uncomfortable, while Como made people relaxed.

One of Michaels's colleagues in the writers' room was Bob Wells, who, as a young man, had co-written the holiday chestnut about chestnuts, "The Christmas Song," with Mel Tormé. The notion that one good idea could set you up for life made an impression.

He was in Hollywood again, and he was working in TV and picking up the craft, but a familiar feeling soon overtook him—it was as if he were moving backward. He was writing gags for a square in a cardigan who'd started as a singing barber. Meanwhile his old agent, David Geffen, was producing Joni Mitchell and the Eagles. "Warren Beatty was making *Shampoo*," he said. "There was Vietnam. There was a lot more ferment in movies and music than there was in television. The music had completely changed."

After the Como special he hit a dry spell, with no work. To stay on in L.A., he had to borrow $1,000 from his little sister, Barbara, who had a paper route back home. His emotions were so ragged that he cried watching an episode of *The Mary Tyler Moore Show*. At one point, he found himself in bed with the flu, sweating and fretting, alone. He woke up in the middle of the night and thought to himself, *I don't really live here. I should just go home and go to law school.*

When he told people that he wrote for TV, they'd sniff and say that they didn't even own a set—they read books. "Television was embarrassing," he said. "It was vulgar. It had money. It was like what people in the theater probably felt about the movies, in the twenties and thirties." With the arrival of Norman Lear and shows like *Mary Tyler Moore,* sitcoms were making a leap forward, but TV was still largely seen as the boob tube, Newton Minow's vast wasteland. If clamoring to be part of it made Michaels feel lame and conventional, not being able to get a job in it made him feel even worse.

His generation was the first to have grown up on television, and he was eager to subvert its old formats, which seemed exhausted. Steve Allen referred to the TV-variety era of the early seventies—Como, Glen Campbell, Donny and Marie, Helen Reddy, Johnny Cash, Sonny and Cher—as "the period of Singers Horsing Around." Scrambling to stay relevant after canceling the Smothers Brothers, CBS had ordered up a show called *Subject to Change,* basically cinema verité footage of countercultural happenings shot by a collective called the Videofreex. A profanity-heavy rough cut about Fred Hampton and the Black Panthers frightened the network's executives into scrapping it; they opted for *Hee Haw,* which Bernie Brillstein had pitched as a way to merge *Laugh-In* with the rural Hooterville sitcoms that were topping the ratings.

The hinges between eras had always fascinated Michaels, and Hollywood provided plenty of case studies. The summer he returned, he got an up-close look at one, sitting in the audience for a Bobby Darin comeback show in Las Vegas. After a successful career as a teen idol, actor, and top-selling lounge singer ("Dream Lover," "Beyond the Sea"), Darin had, in the sixties, taken a countercultural swerve, putting his cover of Tim Hardin's earnest ballad "If I Were a Carpenter" in the top ten and working for Bobby Kennedy's campaign. After the assassination, he retreated to a trailer in Big Sur. (Along the way, he divorced Sandra Dee.) When performing his new, folky material, he billed himself as "Bob Darin" (more Dylanesque), and switched out his tuxedo and toupee for denim and a harmonica rack. But he found himself playing to half-empty houses, so he reverted to his slick persona and went back to the Vegas Strip.

It was this comeback show that Michaels saw, on his first trip to Las Vegas. The casino buffet cost $1.85, and the in-house movie theater was showing a "multi-sensory" spectacle called *Bing Crosby's Hawaii Experience* that involved many screens and a bubble machine. Watching Darin snap his fingers as he belted "Mack the Knife," Michaels could see how the singer had misjudged the moment when he'd "dropped out" and lost his audience. Flower power was already over by then. "So he's wearing the toupee, he's in the old tux," Michaels said. "It's just economics. It's what the audience wanted to see. But it was a cultural confusion." Onstage in Vegas, Darin was defensive about his Rat Pack relapse. He waved off complaints that he'd ripped off "If I Were a Carpenter," enumerating the royalties Tim Hardin earned from the cover version. "He's explaining publishing to a Vegas audience on opening night," Michaels recalled. "And people in the crowd are yelling, 'Splish Splash!'" Having filed the details away in his mental log of lessons—chiefly, *stay relevant*—Michaels recalls the peculiar evening as "a nice night in show business."

The TV business seemed to be in a cultural confusion too, and he was despairing of getting the kind of unconventional comedy he liked on the air. But it was taking hold on a smaller scale, off-screen, and Michaels was tracking it. In addition to Richard Pryor, comics like Lily Tomlin, Steve Martin, and Albert Brooks were beguiling club audiences with raw new material that rarely made it onto Carson. The common ground was a casual worldliness about the drug culture and sex, and skepticism about politics and corporate America. Show business—the hacky, sentimental kind—was a target, too. Regional comedy troupes were doing the same. There was the Committee in San Francisco, and its L.A. spin-off, the Groundlings. Chicago had Second City. In print, there was *National Lampoon*—a *Mad* magazine for post-adolescents—spun off from *The Harvard Lampoon* in 1970 by Doug Kenney and Henry Beard. At Yale, Garry Trudeau had needled the Nixon administration with his comic strip, *Doonesbury,* which, in 1970, went into national syndication.

Albert Brooks had crossed Michaels's path when Hart and Lorne did their act on the Dean Martin Golddiggers special in 1969. Like Michaels, Brooks dreamed of bringing what he called "my comedy" to television. In 1972, CBS gave Brooks a deal for a summer variety show and the network invited him to perform at a private gala honoring Carol Burnett. "I did this bit about how the most precious word for a comedian is 'shit,' and how, if used correctly, in some parts of the country, it can literally save your life," he said. "Like, if you're in Texas, and your act isn't going well, you take a deep breath, you say '*Shiiiit!*' And they build statues of you and you become a hero." Burnett loved it, but Bill Paley ordered "that foul-mouthed young man" to be banned from the network. Brooks was losing faith in TV too.

While Michaels looked for the next gig, he was crashing at a ramshackle beach house in Malibu that John Head, his soigné friend from London, shared with a young American named Joe Boyd. Boyd had been part of the scene around Melissa North's London flat, and had had some success in the music business, producing Nick Drake and Fairport Convention. Mo Ostin, the Warner Bros. Records executive, had hired Boyd and Head to make a documentary about Jimi Hendrix—just the kind of hip cultural project that Michaels felt was passing him by. The house, just across Pacific Coast Highway from Carbon Beach, was a bland 1950s structure—"petroleum-byproduct carpets, a lot of ants in the basement, a carport, succulents in the front yard, and cheap rent," Boyd recalled. Michaels slept on the couch. In Malibu, he set about looking for the next job and tried to get into the rhythms of California life. "He'd do his hustle, get in touch with his contacts," Boyd said. "He would cold-call people."

Their neighbor was a dark-haired British actress named Barbara Steele, a bona fide B-movie star. A little bit older than the boys next door, she was known as "the Queen of all Scream Queens" for her work in Italian horror movies. She remembers Michaels as "very cerebral and buttoned-down," but the atmosphere in their neighborhood was fervid, experimental. "It was that period where all the men decided to be girls, and they all wore caftans," she said. "And if they didn't wear caftans, they wore these itsy-bitsy teeny-weeny bikinis, and they'd trot down the beach with their mega-tans. Everybody went bananas." Geffen lived on the other side of Steele, and down the road were some of the Mamas and the Papas, Jane Fonda and Jerry Brown, and the director John Schlesinger, who "was always cooking up a storm," she said. "It was a cauldron of famous people."

Larry Hagman, in a career lull between *I Dream of Jeannie* and *Dallas,* was a self-appointed community chieftain, headquartered in a pink bungalow. Every evening, he led a ragtag procession down the beach. "He turned into a pied piper with a flute, and he would pass out these handmade flags," Steele said. "And a band of children and stray dogs would follow him." Sometimes he wore a gorilla suit. "Usually Larry would have a joint the size of a cigar in his mouth," she said. To her, Michaels seemed out of place in that scene. "He was too smart, too caustic, too ironic for the blinding, delirious light of Malibu," she said. "Everybody else was into doing their own exotic dance and smoking ninety joints an hour, but he was more introverted. He was almost wearing an invisible necktie."

When he was solvent enough, he moved into a room at the Chateau Marmont, the imposing but seedy Sunset Boulevard hotel designed as a mishmash of Moorish and Norman styles, redolent of Old

Hollywood. He also paid Steele fifty dollars a month to crash in her spare room on weekends. Boyd remembers it as a bunk bed in a hallway, but the place looked out at a blinding blue slash of ocean. John Head was renting Steele's garage as a studio, which he furnished with an enormous slab of foam covered in red felt.

"I don't think anyone had any money, or any specific direction," Steele said. "It was one of those special moments in time, like finding yourself in Paris in the late twenties." Drugs were everywhere, but beyond smoking pot, Michaels wasn't into them. But being the boarder of a fading movie siren fueled his Hollywood fantasia. (Her take: "I was the landlady who was trying to sweep up the sand.")

Head had a friend named Gary Weis, who'd grown up as a cool beach kid in Santa Monica. Weis had done a few years at UCLA film school, but spent more time surfing and dropping acid. One day in 1970, in a scene right out of an Eagles song, he got picked up hitchhiking by Sam Peckinpah's daughter Sharon. She brought him home to her father, who fell for him too. Peckinpah was shooting *The Ballad of Cable Hogue,* and when Warner Bros. wanted a behind-the-scenes featurette about the filming, he hired Weis, who'd been a cameraman at Altamont.

Weis had a fluffy Afro and a goofily seductive smile, and he lived in a warehouse in Santa Monica, on the corner of Pico and Main. The space was spare, a bed on the floor and a few cushions, and he screened his featurette against a wall for Boyd and Head. They asked him to join them on the Hendrix project. "Gary was the social hub," Boyd said. "He was a walking party." People said that he'd smoked a joint with Charles Manson. Michaels and his roommates always checked in with Weis at the end of the day to get their marching orders—a gallery opening, an outré Mexican restaurant. Jobless, Michaels tagged along with them to the Warner Bros. commissary, or for dinner at Dan Tana's. Across the courtyard from Weis, the photographer William Wegman lived with his Weimaraner, Man Ray. Michaels would join Head and the others for ping-pong tournaments there, Man Ray chasing the balls. They hung out with the painters Ed Ruscha and his brother, Paul, who once picked up Michaels for a Halloween party wearing silver contact lenses.

If Weis was the social director, Head was the arbiter of what was cool. He was discerning about movies, music, and restaurants. He smoothed the rough edges off Michaels, demonstrating how to say more by saying less, and tutoring him about clothes, including the offhand effect of pairing a sport jacket with jeans.

Head had a friend named Penelope Spheeris, who was a film student at UCLA. She'd answered an ad that he and Boyd posted on a bulletin board, looking for a typist and transcriber. When they found out that she'd worked with Richard Pryor on the first film he starred in, *Uncle Tom's Fairy Tales*, they hired her for the Hendrix movie. Spheeris, petite with a whorl of dark hair, had a little girl at home in Venice; being embraced by the houseful of glamorous beach bums was an "eye-opening, life-changing experience," with nonstop partying. "They were the coolest guys around," she said. "I was the trashy chick that was kind of cute that could type fast." She'd cook omelets for everyone while Michaels sat in a corner and read *The New York Times*. "He had such an imposing, 'I got it all covered' personality," she said.

Michaels may have been absorbing a lot about discernment, but he didn't feel like he had anything covered. He was unemployed, anxious about his next move. Every afternoon, while his friends were at work, he went to Topanga Beach. He didn't go into the ocean, but he would sit on the sand and read. One day he read a piece in the *L.A. Times* about stressful life events that can lead to fatal disease. At the end of the article was a quiz you could take to calculate your risk: Divorce was 3 points. Moving was 3 points. Changing jobs was 3. Michaels stared out at the ocean and thought he was a goner. "The level of dislocation was overwhelming," he said.

He leaned on Wernick and Brillstein to find him writing gigs, and finally they delivered two offers: a Jackie Gleason special, and a special starring Cass Elliot, who'd gone solo after the Mamas and the Papas broke up. Each was twelve or fifteen weeks of work, for around

$15,000. Michaels was broke, but two unrelated developments inclined him toward turning the jobs down. The CBC wanted him to come back to Toronto to produce *Jack: A Flash Fantasy,* with Victor Garber. And he'd met Lily Tomlin.

TOMLIN HAD ARRIVED AT *LAUGH-IN* IN THE THIRD SEASON, JUST MISSING Hart and Lorne, and became a star almost despite herself, having always viewed TV as selling out. She grew up in Detroit, the daughter of a factory worker, and she viewed comedy as a vehicle for revolution and subversion. On *Laugh-In,* she'd performed characters that she created herself (and negotiated to own), such as Edith Ann, a precocious little girl in a giant rocking chair; and Ernestine, a supercilious, snorting telephone operator. Tomlin was horrified when the real telephone company offered her a contract to do commercials as Ernestine. She wanted to enlighten people, not help monopolies sweep up profits.

After *Laugh-In,* she'd released a Grammy-winning comedy record (*This Is a Recording*) and went on tour, selling out venues around the country. CBS hoped that a Lily Tomlin special could spawn a hit variety series. She and Jane Wagner, her partner in work and in life, heard about Michaels through a mutual friend. In July 1973, Tomlin invited him to come to her agents' offices at CMA to discuss the special. After their meeting, they took the conversation down the street to Nibblers, a coffee shop on Wilshire, and spent seven hours in a booth drinking coffee and communing. The connection was immediate, electric. Tomlin had done one special already for CBS, with Richard Pryor as a guest; it was the first of what would be several extraordinary collaborations between the two, even though the network had cut her favorite sketches. Michaels was excited to hear that Pryor was on board for the second one, too. He and Tomlin bonded over their ambivalence about TV, and the way it lagged cheesily behind the rest of the culture. It drove him crazy, he told her, when there was a sketch about marijuana on a Bob Hope special, and the "stoned" performers would just act drunk.

Michaels showed her the "Puck Crisis" film and other bits from the CBC show he'd done with Hart Pomerantz. He was anxious during their early conversations; trying to act producer-ish, he would offer Tomlin critiques of her work, and she'd have only compliments for his. Her graciousness was daunting. Nonetheless, he got an offer to be a writer on the upcoming special, which would tape in early November. Michaels called the CBC and told them that he was taking a one-off job in L.A. and that he would fly to Toronto in November to prepare for the February taping of *Jack*. The CBC said they needed him there sooner.

Two scary decisions loomed. Should he go back to the familiarity of the CBC, or stay in L.A.? And if he stayed, should he take the Gleason and Mama Cass specials, or the one that Tomlin was making? He remembered how bracing the pace of the Burns and Schreiber gig had been: thirteen shows in ten weeks. The job in Canada was six months' work for one hour of television. Also, on the phone, the CBC executive had asked him that old self-loathing Canadian question: "If you're that good, why do you want to be *here*?"

Michaels always appreciated Brillstein's brashness about business and his middlebrow taste, an antidote to his own high seriousness. "Bernie knew the good stuff from the bad stuff, but it didn't stop him from dealing with either," he said. "Whereas I thought if I was involved with anything bad, it would destroy my life." The decision paralyzed Michaels. Brillstein pushed the Gleason and Cass Elliot jobs hard. The Tomlin special would be ten weeks of work for $3,500, a quarter of what the other jobs paid, but enough to cover the Chateau Marmont rent. It wasn't a simple decision; as a kid, Michaels had watched *The Honeymooners* religiously. But Tomlin was on his wavelength. When the two first met, Michaels had a beard. He and Shuster had recently split; he had no money, and he felt like he was just one of a million Hollywood hopefuls wearing sunglasses on the freeway. Tomlin asked him, "How long have you had that beard?" Seven or eight months, he told her. She said, "When I want to hide, I just grow bangs." Her perceptiveness startled him, and he shaved the next day.

Still, he agonized. One Sunday night he met Weis and Head for dinner at a restaurant called Tonga Lei. It was a tiki-hut joint near the Malibu pier, with a volcano bowl on the menu and framed photos of Jayne Mansfield behind the bar. Brillstein expected a decision on Monday morning, and Michaels was a wreck of nerves. When the fortune cookies came after dinner, he pulled the slip of paper from his and read: "You will not know truth until you've experienced the beauty of the lily." He decided to go with Tomlin. Feeling that he really might be an Angeleno, he turned in his rented Pinto and bought a red convertible Volkswagen Beetle.

Tomlin and Wagner hoped that Michaels would help them by running interference with the suits. On the first special they did for CBS, the network had installed Bob Precht, Ed Sullivan's son-in-law, as co-producer. "He was like a babysitter," Tomlin said. Precht functioned as an informer with the network executives, who were nervous about Richard Pryor. "I was mad for Pryor," Tomlin said. When she was courting him to be on the special, Pryor, who grew up in a brothel in Peoria, had put her through what she called a "white-girl test," to make sure she was hip enough. One night, when they were both high, she said, "he took me to a blind pig"—an unlicensed saloon—"in the hood to see how I'd fare." She held her own, and even tried to organize the working girls.

On the first special, Tomlin had personally guaranteed the CBS men that Pryor would behave. He showed up in the studio with his hair in cornrows threaded with pale leather laces. When the network people objected, he told them that the laces were strips of white people's skin. He grudgingly covered the braids with a hat. But CBS nixed plenty of sketches that it considered incendiary. "The script came back all red-lined," Tomlin said. She was devastated to lose a long, cerebral piece by Wagner, almost a one-act play, in which Pryor plays a junkie named Juke who has a tender friendship with a greasy-spoon proprietor, Opal, played by Tomlin. The network was expecting to get an hour of Ernestine and Edith Ann, but Tomlin and Wagner had grander ambitions; they wanted to reflect what was going on in the world—racism, income inequality, injustice, drugs. They were after what Hilton Als, in an essay about Pryor, called "the human untidiness" of everyday life. Tomlin sought to capture "essences of people," and she redeemed her darker subjects with glimmers of hope.

The network also vetoed a sketch in which Tomlin plays a prim housewife, Mrs. Beasley, calling her son in from the backyard, which is an actual war zone, ablaze with exploding mortar shells. "Billy!" she yells. "Where's your leg? You think legs grow on trees? Come on, leg or no leg, supper's on the table." Afterward, she told *The New York Times*, "The networks feel certain things don't belong on a variety show; but what I've always hated about variety shows is that they have no variety."

The first special came in on budget and got strong ratings, a 45 share overall. It was nominated for a writing Emmy, and CBS, still wavering on a series commitment, signed up Tomlin for another try. She and Wagner thought carefully about how to leverage their ratings to retain more creative control. Michaels would be a buffer; he could hold his own with suits, but at the same time he smoked pot and saw the absolute necessity of having Richard Pryor on the show. "Lorne had a lot of showbiz savvy," Tomlin said. "And he was hip, and that's what we valued. People from Canada are kind of on the outside. They're like the great Southern writers who feel a little displaced by the Civil War. Canadians feel displaced by being second to America. So they're alert to America, and they're going to make fun of it."

To prevent another Bob Precht incursion, they brought in their own co-producer, Herb Sargent, a charismatic fifty-year-old New Yorker who had written on the original *Tonight Show* with Steve Allen. Michaels was smitten; he'd found another father figure and guide to the good life. He loved that Sargent lived in a bungalow at the Beverly Hills Hotel and had been married three times. Born Herbert Supowitz near Philadelphia, he had reinvented himself much in the way Lorne Lipowitz did. "Herb was the opposite of the comedy writer who's always on," Michaels said. When friends talk about Sargent, they often repeat the line "If only Herb could talk, what stories he would tell."

Three months had been budgeted for pre-production, and an of-fice culture quickly developed. With Tomlin, Michaels finally felt in-vested in the way he had during the Hart and Lorne show. "I was kind of in love with Lily," he said. "I thought, 'She's an artist; she only cares about being good.' When technical people said, 'You can't do that because we can't shoot it right,' she'd ask, 'Why?'" After years of feel-ing like he was limping along at the end of a race that had already been run, he felt in step with the culture.

Within a few weeks, though, things got bumpy. Tomlin was an-noyed that Michaels never showed up before noon, and found him pretentious. He liked to sit cross-legged on the floor and hold forth on theories of comedy. "He was hard to handle when he first came on, because he wasn't used to being on a staff," Tomlin said. Or maybe, she thought, he was unaccustomed to working for two women. (He hadn't picked up that they were a couple.) "I saw him behaving badly—just protecting his place," Tomlin said. "He would make kind of cutting remarks." He had a way of consolidating power by keeping colleagues a little off-kilter. "I went to Jane, and I said, 'I think we should fire him. He's a pain in the neck,'" Tomlin recalled. Wagner was more circumspect. "Jane would say, 'You've got to be more sup-portive of Lorne. He's used to being a star up in Canada. You've got to *exclaim* over him.'"

Irene Pinn, another producer, called Michaels in for a talk about his work habits. She told him that Tomlin wasn't happy and that he would have to work harder. Taken aback, he marshaled his gift for persuasion and, over several hours, emphasizing his experience with networks, talked his way back into his superiors' good graces. The working relationship got back on track, and Michaels found writing on the special more rewarding than anything he'd done in his career so far. Tomlin never stopped inspiring him.

The *Lily* specials featured long, character-driven sketches, with Tomlin addressing the audience in between. As he'd done for Rowan and Martin, Michaels mainly worked on these monologues. "Lorne can add to stuff, but he's not necessarily, like, a really diligent writer," Tomlin said. He was better at shaping ideas than filling up sheets of paper. He paid close attention to Tomlin's sketch style. Tomlin, he later told *The New York Times,* was responsible for creating a "comedian's lib"—freeing the form from punchlines, allowing it to have a psychological dimension. "Male comedy is punchy, broad, aggressive; it assaults you," he said. "Men shy away from the 'moment' and go for the joke. They get nervous if they don't hear laughs immediately." He went on, "Lily, by refusing to be hostile, by making herself vulnerable, is breaking the mold." He compared her to a genre painter who scrupulously depicts daily life without idealizing it.

While they were writing the special, Tomlin would try out the new material at the Ice House, a club in Pasadena. Michaels remembers an especially brilliant piece: Tomlin's Mrs. Beasley, a prim housewife character, summoning a kitchen onto the bare stage by the sheer force of her physical comedy. At the end, "she walks over and she closes the door to an imaginary cupboard," he said. "It was that level of commitment and detail."

The opening of *Lily,* which aired on November 2, 1973, had Tomlin getting off a bus at CBS Television City, where she runs onstage past a man pounding a timpani in the wings, whom sharp-eyed viewers would recognize as Richard Pryor. The show had a feminist slant. At a time when female comics were still doing jokes about burning the meatloaf, Tomlin made housewifery a fixed target. In one monologue she says to the viewers, "You're watching television when you could be doing something constructive, like putting your spice rack in order alphabetically."

The one sketch that Michaels wrote had a wistful, conservative bent. It was based on his failing marriage. Tomlin and her guest star Alan Alda (fresh from the first season of *M*A*S*H*) play a couple who have separated and run into each other at a restaurant, each with a new date; they gaze across the room and secretly pine for each other. Using an editing trick, a second Alda, transparent like a ghost, stands up and converses with corporeal Alda, who remains seated. A spectral duplicate of Tomlin does the same, and the two alter egos end up in each other's arms.

A CBS executive named Perry Lafferty had repeatedly warned

Tomlin not to get too arty, telling her, "Remember Podunk!" The net-work made her cut the Mrs. Beasley anti-war sketch, but the Juke and Opal diner piece stayed in, running at an unheard-of ten min-utes. The piece opens on Tomlin, as Opal, watching Julia Child on TV in her café. Pryor, as Juke, enters, pulling up his collar against the cold. Juke has been down at the job training center. "I always used to think those training programs was mainly to provide jobs for the peo-ple doing the training," Opal says. They make fun of two white do-gooders who come in to do a welfare survey, and Juke spooks the pair into leaving. "You got a black car?" he asks them. "A family just moved into it." The piece ends on a hopeful note. Juke gives Opal back the ten-dollar bill he'd cadged to score drugs, and, heading out into the cold, tells her, lovingly, "I'll be glad when it's spring."

It made it in, but just barely. When Lafferty and Fred Silverman, a top executive at CBS, saw an early cut of the special, they were furious. For one thing, it was over budget. Worse: Tomlin kissed Pryor in "Juke and Opal." Silverman called the show a "three-hundred-and-sixty-thousand-dollar jerk-off," and he said he wouldn't air it. Tomlin persuaded Alda to have lunch with Silverman and talk him down. The network agreed to air the special, but only if a laugh track was added. Also, "Juke and Opal" had to run last, so it wouldn't spoil the ratings when viewers changed the channel.

"It failed," Silverman later said of the special, calling it "too eso-teric for a general audience." Critics felt otherwise. *Variety* described the show as "something important . . . wise and picking at the dark edges of truth . . . it was what the public has asked for for some time." *Lily* won two Emmy Awards, one for writing, and one for best Comedy-Variety, Variety or Music Special. After his rocky L.A. start, Michaels was overjoyed to be taking home an award. Onstage, Ginger Rogers handed the trophy to Tomlin, who had on a spangly, 1940s-inspired ensemble. "But this is not the greatest moment of my life," she said, after dispensing the usual thanks. "Because on Friday I had a really great baked potato at Nibblers on Wilshire." After all the battles and compromises, she was over television, at least for a while. Her next project would bring her an Oscar nomination.

———

A MONTH AFTER THE TRIUMPHANT RECEPTION OF *LILY*, CBS AIRED THE *PERRY Como Winter Show*, and Michaels had been embarrassed to see his name in the credits. It was a reminder of where most of the television business still languished. Making his misgivings about TV even more acute, the director Robert Altman had just cast Tomlin in a lead role in his next movie, *Nashville*. Altman was one of the people revolutionizing the film industry (*McCabe & Mrs. Miller, The Long Goodbye*), and Michaels, once again, felt left behind and out of sync. (Weren't the movies supposed to be *his* dream?) Genuinely good and innovative television shows, the kind that he and his friends wanted to watch, were still a rarity. He thought about what the Smothers Brothers had tried to do with their TV show, back in the sixties, and what it had cost them.

Earlier that year, in March 1974, he'd gone to the opening night of the Smothers' comeback show at the Troubadour. They had kept a low profile in the five years since CBS canceled them over their antiwar material, and the club was packed with disciples who saw them as First Amendment heroes. Also in the audience was John Lennon, a friend of Tom Smothers. Lennon—who had come with his girlfriend May Pang, the singer-songwriter Harry Nilsson, and Peter Lawford—was already drunk, and Nilsson ordered Brandy Alexanders all around. During the show, Lennon started heckling, loudly calling the Smothers "fuckers."

"He wasn't making witty remarks; he was just a drunk," Michaels recalled. Tom Smothers stopped and said, from the stage, "John, honestly." The brothers' manager finally shushed Lennon, who responded by punching him in the jaw and flipping the table, sending sticky glasses of brandy and milk flying, before security hauled him out.

Michaels was horrified, and he thought about that evening many times in the coming years, whenever he found himself in a difficult spot with the network. "I never got tempted by the idea of being a martyr," he said. "One of the things I taught myself is, you have to stay on the air. It's not worth it to blow yourself up for principle in a community that will sell you out." He went on, "I realized, okay, you can take it to the brink, but if you give up your power, you've done nobody any good."

He knew he didn't want to end up like Tom and Dick Smothers. Could he keep on trying to make television relevant and, at the same time, "remember Podunk!" as Perry Lafferty, the CBS exec, had put it? A lifeline suddenly appeared. A young executive named Barry Diller was running ABC, with his number two, Michael Eisner, and they were fans of Tomlin's CBS specials. Diller believed that Tomlin could be a TV star, and he signed her up to produce and star in two variety specials at ABC, to be made after *Nashville* wrapped. Tomlin wanted Michaels on board again, and he decided that he wanted to work on the specials, even if it meant waiting around. "Lily, at a low point in my life, said, 'I appreciate you,'" he recalled. "She was probably *the* formative influence on me."

SIX

THE MUSIC CHANGED

MICHAELS HAD SOME TIME TO FILL BEFORE THE NEXT TOMLIN SPECIAL. BUT now that he had an Emmy, the offers poured in, including one to write for a Shirley MacLaine special, which he turned down. More in line with his view of himself was an inquiry, from the producer Earl McGrath, about helping with a special celebrating *Rolling Stone* magazine. Michaels took Gary Weis, his most rock-and-roll friend, along to the meeting, and as the man from *Rolling Stone* detailed their idea for a comedy-inflected musical hour, Weis, unaccustomed to the corporate setting, whispered, "This guy is breathing carbon monoxide in our direction." Michaels, who didn't like the promotional vibe either, recalled, "We were, like, 'Must flee.'"

Ever since the CBC canceled the *Terrific Hour,* Michaels had nurtured dreams of launching his own comedy-variety show modeled on it. Wernick set up meeting after meeting for Michaels to pitch the idea to executives who said they were looking for something like *Laugh-In;* they always seemed to mention *Hellzapoppin'* ("a show no one in the seventies had ever seen," Michaels said). At one meeting, with an NBC programmer named Larry White, Wernick also brought in Bob Finkel, Michaels's old mentor from the Phyllis Diller show. Finkel had a deal with NBC and was close to Robert "Bobbie" Sarnoff, the chairman of RCA, the network's parent company. "Lorne needed to be shepherded by a godfather," Wernick said. "They're not going to turn a show over to a young kid from Canada." In a Burbank screening room, Michaels showed clips from his CBC show, including the Puck Crisis film, and bits of Monty Python. Larry White took a phone call while the footage played. The show Michaels pitched him was a mixture of filmed pieces, rock music, and sketches performed by a group of young players. He did his "when the music changes" spiel. White didn't go for it, saying that it wasn't "an NBC-type show." He might have remembered that, when Python appeared on *The Tonight Show* a year earlier, they bombed.

"I didn't understand how things were sold then," Michaels said. "You couldn't just sell an *idea*." Variety shows were expensive star vehicles. Michaels's pitch wasn't solving any problems for NBC—like helping a star fulfill her contract—so it didn't register. For money, he took a job writing a special hosted by John Davidson, a bland and twinkly singer around his own age, called *The Hollywood Palladium*. To prepare, he drove his Beetle to Reno to check out Davidson's act. The singer, dripping with turquoise jewelry, ended his show with "God Bless America" as patriotic streamers dropped from the ceiling. To help write, Michaels brought in his old friend Earl Pomerantz, whose hockey puck film he had been using as a calling card. The Davidson show was a typical variety grab bag—Sly Stone, a trapeze artist named Arturo, a poetry reading by Richard (John-Boy Walton) Thomas. Remembering the finished product, Michaels said with a grimace, "It was in the round."

As he tried to figure out where he fit in, he kept noting uncomfortable collisions between the Hollywood old guard and the new. He was queasily fascinated by how one's moment could pass in a flash. One Sunday in 1974, he was delighted to meet Robert Bolt, the legendary English screenwriter of *Lawrence of Arabia* and *A Man for All Seasons*, at a gathering at Margot Kidder's place on Leo Carrillo Beach. (She liked to tease Michaels by introducing him as the Canadian Johnny Carson.) Bolt, who was about fifty then, was in L.A. to visit his estranged, much younger wife, the actress Sarah Miles. He was out of place. "I remember him being too dressed up for Sunday in Malibu," Michaels said. "He was smoking Player's Navy Cut and drinking whiskey, while everyone else was smoking pot." At one point a cry went up that whales had been spotted offshore. The barefoot youngsters—including Miles's new boyfriend, Bruce Davison, who had just starred in the movie *Willard* as the rat-loving youth—scampered off to look, but Bolt refused to budge. Michaels, the only one there who understood who Bolt was, stayed and kept him company. "He finally walked over to look at the whales, but he said, 'I don't see them.' He rejected this new time, and this new generation," Michaels said. "He'd lost his wife to all that." Michaels drove him home. "Bolt was a master, and I thought, 'It must be terrible to outlive your time.'"

EVERY NIGHT, WHEN MICHAELS RETURNED TO THE CHATEAU MARMONT, HE could tell from fifty feet away whether there were any pink message slips for him in his cubbyhole behind the reception desk. Before handing over messages, the reception clerk, Mrs. Volte, would always ask, "What room?" He'd answer, and she would say, "Ah—that was Dorothy Parker's old room." She'd name a different famous resident every time, but it was still intoxicating.

The Chateau Marmont was one of the only constants in Michaels's life. Anyone who called the hotel in those years liked to imitate the voice that picked up—a deep, quaalude-inflected whisper, like Lurch in *The Addams Family*, saying "Cha-teauuuuuu." Despite the brownish-orange shag carpet and the shabby furnishings, the turreted Chateau was a kind of Disneyland for Michaels, who was as much an old showbiz buff as he was a young man in a hurry. There was no restaurant, no bar, and no room service, but there was lore: Jean Harlow carried on an affair with Clark Gable in 38C; Marilyn Monroe stayed there while shooting *Bus Stop*; Paul Newman bumped into Joanne Woodward in the elevator; Boris Karloff lived in the penthouse; Dustin Hoffman slummed at the hotel, collecting unemployment, between the filming and the opening of *The Graduate*.

Michaels bounced between different rooms depending on his economic situation. When he was tapped out, $220 a month would get him a bed and a bathroom; when he was riding high, he'd pay $580 for a parlor, kitchen, and bedroom. The flexibility allowed him to be fussy about the writing jobs he took. (Laraine Newman, who met him around this time, remembered a hotplate and popcorn dinners.) By late 1974, after about a year, he'd zeroed in on the perfect room, 7F. It had rose-colored glass in the panel that separated the bedroom and living room, a small kitchen, and two little balconies. One looked south toward Melrose Avenue, the other faced the Hollywood Hills. He had taught himself how to make omelets. "I kind of liked who I was," he said. A lot of people refer to the hotel as "the Chateau," but Michaels calls it "the Marmont," using a tone that suggests that that's what insiders say, and pronouncing it the way a high-school French student would: "Mar-*mone*."

The hotel attracted 1960s survivors, people who wanted to hang out and act out or at least to have a good time. Rosie Shuster relocated from Canada, even though the relationship was "getting ragged," as she put it. "We were together some of the time, and then not," she said. "It was an amazing time at the Chateau, with a revolving group of fascinating people talking about movies and music. It was Lorne's own salon." Michaels was an Anglophile, and there were plenty of Brits in residence. He'd reconnected with Bob Schiller's arty son Tom, who felt that "the nucleus of the *Saturday Night* idea was starting to form in an ectoplasmic way there." Dan Aykroyd crashed in Michaels's room, having driven from Toronto in a '63 Chevy Bel Air, with stops in New Orleans and Tijuana. "That's when he first told me that he was hoping to be able to re-create *The Colgate Comedy Hour* and the Sid Caesar show," Aykroyd recalled. "I said, 'Call me.'"

When the time came to start on the next Tomlin special, Michaels was more surefooted. Tomlin's vote of confidence was as important as Woody Allen's had been years earlier. This time, Tomlin asked him to co-produce with Jane Wagner, and Brillstein negotiated a fee of $30,000. Although Tomlin valued Michaels's professionalism and competence, she again noticed his knack for political maneuvering and remembers him "pontificating" about comedy. (Staffers began imitating him in private.) "He knows where the weight is in an office," she said, "and he will seek it out."

When Tomlin interviewed potential writers, she would ask them about their personalities and their astrological signs; she gave every new hire a plant. Michaels had a different style—"orderly, intellectual, low-key," the writer Marilyn Suzanne Miller, who came from *The Mary Tyler Moore Show,* said. With a thirteen-week pre-production period, writing sessions were long and unstructured. Michaels liked to hear Miller, a brassy fast talker, describe how, at *Mary Tyler Moore,* the showrunner Jim Brooks would hold three-day story meetings, urging the writers to "dig down into the sub-amygdala of Rhoda's and Mary's brains." One day in May, they all watched on the office TV as federal agents stormed the house where the Symbionese Liberation Army was thought to be holding Patty Hearst hostage. "There was gunfire, and they killed people," Michaels said. "And we were watching Watergate every day. So you couldn't go out and just do big, dumb comedy."

Tomlin hired Laraine Newman as a supporting player, after she and Michaels saw her do a new kind of character—a Valley Girl—at the Groundlings. Newman had never met a Canadian, and she remembers finding Michaels "so cute, so good-looking," with his tousled pop-star hair. He radiated a high-wattage confidence for someone his age, but Newman picked up a lonely-guy vibe. He told her about how, at night, he'd look at the Marmont switchboard lit up with incoming calls and wish that one of them were for him. He didn't mean work calls, Newman said: "He meant human contact, a personal connection with someone."

His romance with Shuster was over, but they remained connected. Michaels brought her on to the writing staff of the Tomlin special, although she insisted on using a pseudonym. "In my grand and largely successful self-effacement project," she said, "I impulsively used 'Rosie Ruthchild' as a credit on *Lily*—to try to convince my mother, Ruth, that I didn't hate her." (Other times she wrote under the name Sue Denim.) Michaels was happy to have her there. She could help him navigate the "enclave of woman power," as Newman described the office. If he'd had a tense day at work, clashing with his female superiors, he would drive out to Topanga Beach and watch the sun set, "to calm down, and to get in touch with some notion of light," he recalled.

Lily, on ABC, opens with Tomlin backstage, amid hokey showbiz razzle-dazzle; showgirls in plumed headdresses mill idly, along with a nun, a swami in a turban, and a man dressed like Abraham Lincoln. (Years later, on SNL, Michaels would take this noble sight gag and run with it.) The sounds of tap shoes can be heard. Variety television, the scene suggests, is a hoary anachronism, but Tomlin is going to do her best to try and redeem it.

One sketch has Tomlin as an uptight sorority sister, who keeps repeating a proto–Valley Girl catchphrase: "I could just barf." A fake news report covers a local bylaw making it a crime to be overweight in Beverly Hills, "where perfect bodies are ordinary and ordinary bodies are a civic disgrace." (Husky-sized Bernie Brillstein plays an offender, who protests, "I'm just big-boned.") Michaels came up with a feminist-leaning sketch about a one-night stand: the girl (Tomlin) is blasé, the guy so bowled over that the next morning he brings his parents over to meet the girl, who brushes them off as she gets ready for work. The hour ends with an *I Love Lucy* parody: a boss-coming-to-dinner, wife-burning-the-roast fable, with a subplot about a pet goldfish.

Hours and hours of material were taped, and the show was frantically stitched together in the editing room, way after ABC's deadline. This gave rise to a philosophical debate. Wagner thought they should have done the show live. It would have felt hipper and rougher that way, she argued, and it would have prevented the network from adding a laugh track. Michaels, Tomlin recalled, countered that live television was over; editing tape was the way of the future. But when Michaels and Tomlin sat down together at the editing console, they fiddled and fiddled, overthinking every single cut. Their perfectionist tendencies turned the sessions into marathons, and the show went drastically over budget.

Michaels had had an epiphany about editing after seeing a rough cut of *Nashville* that was more than six hours long. "I kept wondering how Altman was going to cut it down," he said. "He would take what should be a thirty-five-second link scene and have the actors improvise. And it's brilliant—but now it's seven minutes long. In the editing room, keeping the thread is almost impossible." It affirmed his belief in the importance of the script in comedy. "The way I work, you do all your work beforehand, and you write down the dialogue that you've actually chosen," he said. With improv, "what you gain in originality you lose, because it degrades the writing." His models were auteurs like Billy Wilder and Preston Sturges, writer-directors who expected their actors to respect the script. Comedy, he increasingly believed, was about precision.

After granting several deadline extensions, the ABC executives, Barry Diller and Michael Eisner, were scheduled to see the finished product on a Friday night. Michaels stayed up for forty-eight hours and got it where he wanted it. Diller and Eisner arrived and waited patiently for the final tweaks to be made, and when they watched the cut, they were happy. They locked the show. But the next day, Tomlin went back into the editing room on her own and made more changes.

"We were doing so much coke. We were just coked out," Tomlin recalled, adding that she considered the final product "a complete disaster." The narrative of the *Lucy* parody got inadvertently mutilated in the editing frenzy. The payoff was supposed to be that "the boss, Mr. Fitzdithers, comes over for dinner, and I serve him the goldfish," she recalled. "But we'd got rid of the fish in editing before I could cook it."

Michaels believed that the eleventh-hour re-editing made them seem flaky to ABC; part of making a pilot was proving to the network that you were disciplined enough to handle doing a weekly show. ABC didn't give the special an air date, but Diller and Eisner still believed in Tomlin, last-minute editing notwithstanding, and they were up for financing another special. Diller remembers the working relationship as "good chaos." He said, "Jane and Lily worked in a completely different way than Lorne did. That made them jump back and forth endlessly between choices. It was never final until it was too late to do anything else."

Wagner, who had an apartment in New York, went to see *Lemmings*, the *National Lampoon*'s musical parody of Woodstock culture. John Belushi and Chevy Chase (as Joe Cocker and John Denver) had been getting good notices in it, but Wagner singled out a different bright spot: Christopher Guest, who did killer takeoffs of Bob Dylan and James Taylor. Michaels was intrigued; he liked *The National Lampoon Radio Hour*, which he listened to every Sunday night in his car, as he made his weekly trip to the health food store. But he'd never been a fan of the *Lampoon* itself, which he considered sophomoric and "reeking of privilege." He said, "It always seemed to have three breasts on the cover."

Tomlin hired Guest to write and perform on her next special. "Chris was his own man," she said. "He had his own sensibility." He and Michaels were not the coziest of colleagues. If Michaels gave Guest a note he didn't like, Guest would just take the matter directly to Tomlin. "I thought Chris had a strong commitment to his own aesthetic," Michaels said, adding, "He probably knew his better than I knew mine." Michaels, a natural politician, viewed Guest as having a similar aptitude. "Chris understood how things work more than I did," he said. "He knew where the power was." A talented musician, Guest wrote two songs for the special. Michaels had an idea for an opening, in which four men in suits present Tomlin with a plaque from the Detroit chamber of commerce—an intentionally dull premise. Just as the audience is glazing over, the men do a synchronized pivot and break into a Motown song written by Guest and Earl Pomerantz, "Detroit City," twirling like The Temptations. "The moment of the reveal—when the guys start singing—is a giant hard laugh," Michaels said. To choreograph it, he hired Hermes Pan, who had created dances for Fred Astaire and Ginger Rogers.

Guest wrote another song, for a sketch based on a film Pomerantz had made at the CBC, about a couple who are horrified when the wife gives birth to a baby clown with a big red nose and giant shoes. Michaels asked Pomerantz, whom he'd hired as a writer, to adapt the sketch for Tomlin. In it, she plays Lorraine "Bobo" Jones, the outcast clown child, rejected by her parents and neighbors, who are repelled by her seltzer-squirting ways. When grown-up Lorraine finally meets another clown, he brings her to a rip-roaring secret gathering of fellow outcasts ("a special kind of party that respectable people in Dull City never knew existed"). At the party, Guest strums a guitar and croons, in a Sweet Baby James drawl, "Been looked at and laughed at and kicked at and thrown out of town . . . Oh, I'm a clown, and proud to *beeee* . . ." Even before the police raid the place, in a scene that evokes the Stonewall riots, a gay subtext is clear. Lorraine ends up in jail, undergoing conversion therapy meant to crush the pie-throwing out of her. It was one of Tomlin's favorite pieces in the show.

When they showed a cut to ABC, Eisner didn't like the clown piece, which ran more than ten minutes. He kept trying to kill it or trim it. Diller, who had remained silent while Eisner voiced his concerns, finally said, "Michael, don't be a moron. It's a fable. It has a beginning, middle, and end—and a moral. You can't cut a part of it." Michaels and Tomlin exchanged glances. "We thought to ourselves, 'Did he just say *moron?*'" Michaels recalled. The clown film aired at full length.

The editing on the special was again tortured, but the result was solid and funny. If it went to series, Michaels thought, it could be exactly the show that Sandy Wernick had been helping him pitch for years. But ABC didn't quite see it. The network didn't seem to have any plans to schedule the special; the earlier one hadn't aired either. Michaels couldn't understand why ABC would squander such good work. It made him nuts. Years later, Herb Schlosser, then the president of NBC, told him a TV-business joke that circulated in the seventies: "If you want to end the Vietnam War, put it on ABC."

WHILE MICHAELS HAD BEEN FINISHING UP THE FIRST TOMLIN PROJECT, Wernick got an offer for him to produce a special for Flip Wilson on NBC. Wilson had had a variety show on the network for four years. His character Geraldine Jones had launched two catchphrases: "The

Devil made me do it!" and "What you see is what you get!" In 1972, *Time* magazine named him "TV's first black superstar." Two years later, his ratings slipping, he quit—having done nearly a hundred episodes, just enough for a lucrative syndication deal—and agreed to finish his contract by hosting four specials. Wilson's manager, Monte Kay, wanted Michaels to help make his client relevant again. "Because he had been so popular in the middle of the country," Michaels said, "he'd lost the coasts."

After working with Tomlin and Pryor, Michaels was feeling choosy. He wasn't sure he wanted to be the guy people turned to in order to make middlebrow performers seem cool. Kay invited Michaels to a party he was hosting for Wilson, so that the two men could spend some time together. It was the same night that Eisner and Diller saw the cut of their first Tomlin special, after days of coke-fueled editing. When the special was locked, Michaels drove to Kay's house, where he met the guest of honor. Flip Wilson eyed him warily and asked, "So, what are we doing?" Michaels hadn't slept in days, and mouthed some vague assurances. Wilson looked skeptical. He was expecting a little more tap dancing. "Well, I guess you're just going to have to trust me," Michaels said, with a mixture of cockiness and apprehension. Kay and a few guests laughed nervously.

The introduction accomplished, Michaels said his goodbyes, ready for a long sleep in room 7F. Wilson walked him out. In the driveway, they stopped at Wilson's sky blue Rolls-Royce Corniche convertible. The license plate read KILLER. The glove compartment always contained a vial of coke and a handful of joints. Wilson said, "Get in." Michaels paused. He asked where they were going. He'd learned one California rule of thumb: Never leave a party without your car.

"Come on, get in," Wilson persisted. Michaels reluctantly opened the door of the Rolls and asked again, "Where are we going?" Wilson just smiled. "I guess you're just going to have to trust me," he said.

He said "Trust me" several more times over the next thirty-six hours, including once when he handed his passenger a tiny square of paper that looked like a Sen-Sen breath mint. Michaels wasn't used to psychedelics; an acid trip in the late sixties had been distinctly un-fun. To regain his grip that time, he'd turned on *The Tonight Show*; hearing Ed McMahon laugh at Carson's jokes calmed him down. But this time, a compelling job offer was on the line; Brillstein had let him know that he'd get $100,000 for the four Wilson specials, more money than he'd ever been paid in his life.

When Michaels finally stumbled back to the Marmont a couple of days later, having collected his Beetle at Monte Kay's, he learned that Tomlin had returned to the editing room to tinker. Disheartened, he sensed that, as good as Tomlin and the special were, the network would never give them a series. But now he had Flip Wilson to think about. After the wild weekend, he'd agreed to take the job.

On set, Wilson comported himself like a star. He'd grown up one of fourteen children and was in foster care at seven; he told Michaels that as a kid, he'd slept in the bathroom, because it was the warmest room in the house. As an adult, Wilson always had a frosted layer cake under a glass dome on his kitchen counter. It was to remind him of all the times, as a child, when he'd been in a diner looking hungrily at a cake on display, but couldn't afford a slice. The cake under glass meant that he'd made it.

Michaels booked the first special with four cutting-edge guests—"everybody that I wanted to work with," he said. These were: Tomlin, Pryor, Peter Sellers, and Martha Reeves. For the writing staff he brought on two of his rabbits' feet, Earl Pomerantz and John Head. Gary Weis was enlisted to shoot an opening montage of clips of Black neighborhoods set to Martha Reeves singing Van Morrison's "Wild Night." Michaels had a big conceptual idea for the structure of the show, which was titled *Flip Wilson . . . Of Course*. Each of the four stars would play the lead in one sketch and be background characters in three others. "It was the last phase of my idealistic period," Michaels said. "It was a rep company idea."

Things went wrong right away. At the first rehearsal, Pryor eagerly approached Sellers, who was one of his heroes, and blurted out, "You were a poor kid too, weren't you?" Sellers, who was rushing off to a gallery opening of photographs by Lord Snowdon, was put off by Pryor's familiarity. The next day, word came down that Sellers would not participate in any sketches with the other guest stars. His solo piece was a brief blackout in which he is Napoleon and speaks one line. Two lieutenants jabber at him in French over a battlefield map; Sellers responds, in a Cockney accent: "I'm sorry, I can't speak a word of French."

Michaels's grand concept was beginning to fall apart. The sketch featuring Tomlin ran into trouble too. She and Wilson played a couple; the people from Budweiser, the show's sponsor, didn't like that; interracial relationships were taboo. An NBC executive brought the Budweiser reps into the editing room to look at some footage over a few beers. After viewing the sketch, the exec said to Michaels, "Do you think that's funny? Because we don't think it's funny." Michaels recalled, "And I'm explaining, in my Canadian way, why it works, that it's a *mood* piece." The executive cut him off: "They want it out. They don't want a Black and white couple."

Michaels looked down and saw that his finger was bleeding; he'd been gripping a Budweiser can so tightly that he had cut himself on the sharp metal of the opening. He was able to edit the sketch to eliminate all traces of a romance, but he was angry. Budweiser's meddling seemed to confirm that television was still a hopeless backwater. He'd been trying to hang on to the belief "that there was a revolution coming in the field of entertainment. And we kept looking to the left, and it didn't come." Painful as it was to give up all that money, he told Monte Kay that he wasn't going to produce the remaining three shows. When *Flip Wilson . . . Of Course* aired, Michaels was amazed to see it get a 46 share. If the show made Wilson seem hip again, any cred he gained was lost the following summer, when, dressed as Geraldine, he wished Gerald Ford a happy birthday at the president's surprise sixty-second birthday party.

A MONTH AFTER THE WILSON SPECIAL AIRED, MICHAELS DECIDED TO THROW himself a thirtieth birthday party at the Marmont. He was still waiting for ABC to schedule the Tomlin specials, and, in his usual way, he was caught between feeling like he was going places and panicking that he had dead-ended. He wangled permission from Tor Olsen, a fuss-budgety Norwegian who was the hotel's manager, to invite friends over and hire someone to play the piano in the lobby. For refreshments, he'd get a few snacks and some jugs of Inglenook wine.

Drawing up the guest list was easy. He'd schmoozed a lot of people in his travels on the variety-special circuit, and he'd acquired a group of friends—powerful, glamorous, useful, creative, idiosyncratic people. Brillstein and his date arrived ten minutes before the appointed hour. The lobby was empty, so a desk clerk called up to Michaels, who was just getting out of the shower. "Your guests are here," the clerk said. Michaels threw on some clothes and took the elevator down to the lobby, where he sat with the middle-aged early birds for fifteen minutes, beneath the heavy ceiling beams, in the weak glow of the Spanish sconces. Brillstein felt awful, thinking that no one else would show up. When Michaels excused himself to go upstairs and finish dressing, Brillstein stuck around. People started drifting in—Richard Pryor, Lily Tomlin, George Carlin, the handsome trio from Malibu, and dozens of other happening young people. "I discovered that, right under my nose, Lorne Michaels was really somebody," Brillstein wrote in his memoir. "Every young person who would make television or movie history in the next twenty years was there."

The party went late. Michaels spent forty-five minutes talking to a bearded guy with long, side-parted hair, about Dylan Thomas. They were discussing "Poem in October," with its repeating line, "There could I marvel my birthday away." Tor Olsen showed up drunk and accidentally knocked over the lobby's glass water cooler, which shattered on the tiled floor. As Olsen surveyed the damage, he blurted, "Don't say Tor did it!"

The next day, a notice was slipped under every door in the hotel announcing that henceforth there would be no more parties in the lobby. Michaels's Marmont neighbor, the screenwriter Carole Eastman, had a batch of T-shirts made, printed with the words DON'T SAY TOR DID IT. Michaels discovered that the guy he'd been talking poetry with was Graham Nash, a fellow Chateau resident. For days, the opening line from Dylan Thomas's ode to the rhythms of life rang in his head: "It was my thirtieth year to heaven."

TOMLIN WAS AS VEXED AS MICHAELS THAT ABC WAS SITTING ON HER SPE-cials. Like Michaels, she was hoping that the network would turn them into a regular series that they could work on together. But in the months after Michaels's birthday party, Tomlin kept spotting him when she stopped to pick up coffee at Nibblers, where the two had first bonded. He was always hunched in a booth across from a young man with a Prince Valiant haircut and an air of intense self-assurance. She was irked. She thought that he was set on doing a show with *her,* and he hadn't mentioned any meetings. She said to Wagner, "Don't you think that's sort of odd?" Later, she learned that the man was Dick Ebersol, a young NBC executive. He and Michaels were plot-ting a new show without her.

The work that Michaels did with Tomlin had come closer to his comedy ideal than anything he'd done so far, but he also sensed that she was never going to break through in network television. "Lily was an artist pure and simple," he said. "But this was the wrong medium for it. Prime-time television was about: How do you hold forty million people?"

He had to keep pitching the show that he had in his head. Meet-ing Ebersol was a new start. "For the first time in my life, I knew who I was," he said. "I could've been persuasive, or possibly charming, at other times in my life, but this time I was very clear on what I wanted to do." His gift was for seizing the main chance.

Describing Michaels's noiseless momentum, a Tomlin associate remembered a line about a certain kind of striver, "a man who enters a revolving door behind you and comes out ahead of you." Tomlin was hurt by Michaels's desertion. "I mean, I wasn't getting any bids to do a show," she said. She never confronted him about it, but she had the uncomfortable sense, more common in Hollywood perhaps than in other cities, that she had been used as a stepping stone—that feeling, as she put it, "when protégés float over you."

SEVEN

NEW WINE IN OLD BOTTLES

Before my grandfather came to America, he was told that the streets
were paved with gold. And when he got to America he found out three
things. One, that the streets were not paved with gold. Two, that the
streets were not paved. Three, that he was gonna be the guy paving them.

—SHELLEY BERMAN, QUOTED BY MICHAELS IN *COMEDIANS IN CARS GETTING COFFEE*

IN THE 1970S, TELEVISION VIEWERS WHO COULDN'T SLEEP WERE USED TO
seeing a rainbow-striped test pattern on their screens, accompanied
by a flutey sine tone. At 1:00 A.M., the networks signed off. Weekend
nights were particularly barren of original programming after the
eleven o'clock news. NBC's affiliate stations were offered a rerun of
The Tonight Show for that slot, but in 1974, Johnny Carson decided
that he wanted his weekend repeats off the air. He wanted to use the
reruns to lighten his own weekly workload: Soon he would negotiate
a new contract that had him taping just three shows a week; Monday's *Tonight Show* would have a guest host, and on Tuesdays, NBC
would put on a Carson rerun.

Carson was NBC's biggest star, and Herb Schlosser, the president
of NBC, had an interest in keeping him happy. But Schlosser knew
that if he took the weekend Carson reruns off the air, the affiliates
might take back the 11:30 slot and put on a late movie. If NBC gave
the stations new programming that they wanted to air, NBC would
get the ad revenue, and it would be a way of shoring up control over
the affiliates.

Flying across the country one day in 1974, Schlosser found himself sitting next to a twenty-six-year-old man who introduced himself as Dick Ebersol, of ABC Sports. Ebersol was a protégé of Roone
Arledge, the legendary ABC programmer who helped turn sports into

entertainment. Ebersol had grown up in the WASP hub of Litchfield County, Connecticut, and had graduated from Yale. He veered toward flamboyant country club plumage—madras plaids, shiny buttons, color-blocked sweaters (often with American flags on them)—and he wore his hair in the kind of feathered sweep that Farrah Fawcett would soon make famous.

Schlosser didn't know it, but Ebersol had had his plane ticket changed so that they'd be sitting together. At ABC, Arledge had promised to promote Ebersol and another young sports staffer, Don Ohlmeyer, but the promotions had never materialized, and Ebersol was auditioning. Schlosser was taken with the chatty young man, and he invited him out to his house on Fire Island for the July Fourth weekend. Ebersol arrived wearing a pair of pants with one red leg and one green, and Schlosser impetuously offered him a job revamping the network's weekend late-night schedule. Although Ebersol had no experience in entertainment, he accepted. He packed up his desk at ABC on August 9, the day that Nixon was helicoptered off the White House lawn.

Schlosser, an Atlantic City native who graduated from Princeton and Yale Law School, had joined NBC in 1960, starting out in business affairs. It was Schlosser who negotiated the deals between the network and its stars, including Carson, who in 1962 had been poached from ABC, where he hosted a quiz show called *Who Do You Trust?* Schlosser had also made a mark by championing Black artists at NBC, supporting such shows as *Julia,* with Diahann Carroll as a Vietnam War widow and single mother; *Sanford and Son;* and *The Flip Wilson Show.* At the top of his to-do list as the new network president was sprucing up the weekend schedule to pull in a younger demographic.

The network had had success with what Schlosser called "time-of-day" shows—*The Tonight Show* and *Today,* created by Pat Weaver in the fifties. In 1970, Congress banned cigarette advertising on television, and to make up the lost revenue, NBC extended its broadcast day by an hour. By 1973, it had put on two new time-of-day shows after Carson: a rock music showcase called *The Midnight Special*

(1:00 A.M. on Saturday night), and *Tomorrow* (1:00 A.M. on Tuesday through Friday). *Tomorrow* was hosted by Tom Snyder, whose comb-over flopped across his scalp like a pelt. His barking demeanor, the late hour, and his unusual bookings (his guests included John Lennon, Ken Kesey, Charles Manson, Ayn Rand, James Baldwin, and Sex Pistols frontman John Lydon) made him essential watching for viewers who were home getting high.

Tomorrow and *The Midnight Special* were working, so Schlosser thought, why not create a show called *Saturday Night*? He held a meeting in his Art Deco boardroom at 30 Rockefeller Plaza, then known as the RCA Building, and instructed Ebersol and his programming staff to come up with a replacement for the Carson reruns. Ebersol began fiddling with an idea based on ABC's *Wide World of Sports,* a showcase of sports coverage that changed week to week. He wanted to bring that concept to NBC, commissioning thirty or forty different entertainment specials that would air on Saturday nights at 11:30. These could replace the Carson reruns, and they might also secure Ebersol's future. "Dick was wildly ambitious," Michaels said. "He thought, 'I can use that slot to do pilots.'" If some of them became prime-time series, Ebersol would be on his way to becoming the head of programming.

Figuring that he'd be spending half his time in L.A., Ebersol got a room at the Beverly Hills Hotel and filled the closet with his flashy clothes. Among the first people he talked to was his fellow Arledge protégé, Don Ohlmeyer. Another was Sandy Wernick. Ebersol's line was that he was looking to create a "wheel" of pilots for Saturday night, shows that would appeal to the eighteen- to twenty-four-year-olds who didn't watch TV. "He said 'I'm going to come out and meet a bunch of guys,'" Wernick recalled. "I told him, 'Well, I don't have a bunch of guys. I have one.'"

Wernick set up a 10:00 A.M. meeting one December morning for Ebersol and Michaels at his office on Sunset Boulevard. Still basking in the glow of his birthday bash, Michaels was feeling like he was somebody. "I put Lorne and Dick together in the room, and stayed ten minutes," Wernick said. "I left and let them fall in love." He came back after lunch and found them still absorbed in conversation. Michaels had laid out all the beats: his show would have a repertory company, rock music, films, what Wernick called "young appeal." The pitch was practiced, but Michaels avoided coming off like a salesman. "Lorne is deliberate," Wernick said. "He thinks very carefully about what he's going to say. Then he spews it."

Ebersol immediately saw that Michaels had two important things going for him. He'd done his time churning out workaday TV comedy, and he had a more cerebral, ambitious notion of what television could be. The prevailing wisdom was that the TV generation held the medium in contempt. As Steve Martin had put it, in a line he wrote for the Smothers Brothers, "It has been proven that more Americans watch television than any other appliance." (Martin credits his friend Gary Mule Deer for the joke.) To this generation, TV was *The Flying Nun* and Lawrence Welk. Michaels wanted to recapture this disaffected group—his cohort—by satirizing the way TV saturated people's thinking and shrink-wrapped the culture. Ebersol liked what he heard. Michaels kept the words flowing as he maneuvered the conversation out of Wernick's office and over to Nibblers, where he and Ebersol carried on for several more hours. Before the afternoon ended, Ebersol had asked him to produce one of his pilots.

Ebersol was preternaturally ambitious and confident, like Michaels, but in a more blustery, toothy way. "Every shirt had epaulets," recalled Michaels, whose uniform was jeans, a Hawaiian shirt, and sneakers. "But Dick liked what I was talking about," he said. "So I thought I'd probably get the chance to do one of his pilots." He didn't hold his breath.

Ebersol was taking meetings all over L.A., trying to round up talented people to make pilots. But Schlosser, back in New York, was losing patience with the wheel concept. It was too complicated, and doing a series of one-offs wouldn't build viewer loyalty. Schlosser wanted *one* show, and he had a lot of specific ideas about what it should be. Most important, it should be based in New York, to bring some life back to the RCA Building. On February 11, he dictated a long, detailed memo to NBC executives. "I would like a thoroughgoing analysis done on a new program concept called 'Saturday Night,'" it began. He described a show that would be broadcast out of the RCA Building, either in the old *Tonight Show* studio or in Studio 8H, which, since the days in the 1940s when Arturo Toscanini broadcast his NBC radio symphonies there, had been little used. "It should be young and bright," Schlosser wrote. "It should have a distinctive look, a distinctive set, and a distinctive sound." He wanted the show "to develop new television personalities" that might feed the prime-time schedule. He envisioned using rotating hosts, and he mentioned, as potential hosts, two stars who had recently signed deals with NBC: the quarterback Joe Namath (the network often hired sports stars because executives liked to golf with them) and Rich Little, a tame impressionist known for his jowl-juddering Nixon. The most radical idea in Schlosser's memo was that the show be broadcast live.

Schlosser instructed his staff to figure out if the show he was describing could be made for between $85,000 and $125,000 an episode. In closing he said, "'Saturday Night' can become a major show in television that people will talk about. It can carve out its own audience and increase sets in use if we do a good job on it." Schlosser's memo torpedoed Ebersol's wheel-of-pilots concept. But Ebersol figured that if he was going to get to do only one show, he wanted to do it either with Lorne Michaels or with his old ABC Sports friend Ohlmeyer.

One night in February, Michaels walked into the dim lobby of the Marmont. It was after two. A pink message slip was waiting for him, from Ebersol. It said to be at the Polo Lounge at the Beverly Hills Hotel at seven-thirty the next morning. Some NBC executives were in town from New York and wanted to hear about the show he had in mind. Michaels was famous, even then, for staying up all hours and sleeping in, and the ungodly-early time of the meeting would become one of the well-worn stories in the lore of *Saturday Night Live*. He somehow made it to the hotel in time and slid into a booth, hoping that the greenish glow from the restaurant's walls and striped circus-tent ceiling might make his hangover less noticeable. Ebersol was already there, as was Marvin Antonowsky, NBC's vice president of programming, and Dave Tebet, NBC's talent czar. Antonowsky and Tebet were quite a bit older than their two breakfast guests, whose hair grazed their collars (although Antonowsky's sideburns signaled a furry plea for relevance), and the meeting was not of great consequence to them. NBC had bigger problems to solve than weekend late nights, and neither took Schlosser's pet project too seriously. The network had long been number two in the ratings, struggling in vain to unseat CBS; suddenly it looked like it could slip into third place.

Michaels didn't know that Schlosser had vetoed Ebersol's wheel concept and that he was pitching the executives a regular series rather than a one-off. Despite having worked in the business for six years, he had never had a meeting like the one at the Polo Lounge. He didn't know the room, nor its powerful inhabitants. He was slightly jaded about his idea's prospects. "I'd already been a wunderkind and then a failure," he said. But to Ebersol he was a smooth, smart guy, a couple of years older, who had been around. Like Hart Pomerantz had, Ebersol sized up Michaels as good partner material. Michaels viewed Ebersol as a useful, if somewhat bumptious, advocate, trapped in a company full of men twice his age. And if the pilot did get made, he figured that they were likely to have some freedom, because the stakes were so low in late night.

Bolstered with coffee, Michaels launched into his spiel, taking care not to come off as a firebrand. Tebet and Antonowsky didn't listen that closely; every time a Hollywood player walked by, they interrupted Michaels's pitch so that they could schmooze. They didn't act alarmed when he said that he wanted the show to look like a bunch of kids crept into the studio and took over after the adults went home.

Antonowsky was a research guy—all about numbers. Tebet, with his tinted aviator glasses, Acapulco tan, and gray crew cut, was a force in an older generation of Hollywood, a legend of the fifties. He'd started as a cigarette-voiced press agent with a boxer's rough edges and worked his way up to being a consigliere for the Sarnoffs. He was tight with Carson, and he had been married to the actress Nanette Fabray. In L.A., he lived at the Beverly Hills Hotel; in New

York he had a suite at the Dorset, and in London he had one at the Dorchester. Tebet was known as "Mr. Talent"; he took care of the network's biggest stars and kept their scrapes out of the papers. He gave away RCA color TV sets by the dozen and lied about his age. His Rockefeller Center office had no desk; it was a dark lounge full of Asian art, including a Samurai sword over the door; he was known to keep a list of the Chinese dynasties in his wallet. David Letterman, who would encounter him in the early 1980s, once said that Tebet was "a talent liaison, in the same way that Al Capone was a beverage distributor."

When Michaels mentioned that he'd worked with Richard Pryor and hoped to get him on the show, Tebet and Antonowsky flinched. Pryor had just been banned from the Burbank lot for punching an NBC page on the set of Flip Wilson's special. (Cher, frightened, had locked herself in her dressing room.) Tebet said that if Michaels wanted unconventional guests, how about the USC Trojan Marching Band? Michaels knew enough to nod politely.

After breakfast, Ebersol gave Michaels a thumbs-up and scurried off to join his bosses at the valet stand. Michaels headed back to the Chateau to sleep. Over the next weeks, Ebersol joined him there often, staying up all night hashing out ideas, with Michaels's cool friends drifting through.

Schlosser was in Fire Island one weekend, thinking about the two potential producers that Ebersol had described to him for his new show: Lorne Michaels and Don Ohlmeyer. "Normally I wouldn't be involved in who produced a show," Schlosser said. "But I had a real interest in getting this on the air." Barry Diller called Schlosser to put in a word for Michaels. "He's the real deal," Diller said. "He's the only one you want." Michaels was surprised to hear, decades later, that he'd been in competition with Ohlmeyer, who would show up in his life twenty years later as a different kind of adversary. He was just as surprised to hear about Diller's invisible assistance. "There's no one in show business who does that kind of favor and doesn't mention it," he said.

When Ebersol called Michaels and told him that NBC wanted

him to come to New York to produce a regular series at 11:30 on Saturday nights, however, he wasn't completely overjoyed. The show in his head had gone from being one of the spokes on Ebersol's wheel to being the wheel itself, but he was ambivalent. The sudden green light, after so many years of hearing "No," had caught him off guard, and he did not say yes right away. He was in the bottom of the trough in his latest burned-out-on-television cycle. The week Ebersol had started his job at NBC, Michaels had winced to see his name on the credits for the limp John Davidson special (*Variety*'s review: "Writing was zilch and originality absent"). Even his role models, the Pythons, had chucked television for the movies. Swayed by the fumes of Shalimar and pot smoke wafting through the halls of the Marmont, he couldn't shake the dream of working in the film business. "I'd decided that all I wanted to do was direct movies," he said.

Out of the blue, there'd been an opening. A young writer from one of the Tomlin specials, Ken Shapiro, had lucked into a development job at Paramount Pictures, and he'd asked Michaels to collaborate on a script. Shapiro had had a surprise hit earlier that year with an indie film called *The Groove Tube*. Like Michaels, he felt that TV was an untapped source of satire, and he shared Michaels's fascination with the tawdry detritus of showbiz culture. Shapiro's father had made a killing selling coonskin caps to Davy Crockett–obsessed kids in the 1950s, and Shapiro himself had appeared with Milton Berle on *Texaco Star Theater* as the "kid" who is repeatedly told, "Get away from me, kid. You bother me."

The Groove Tube parodied TV tropes: toothpaste ads, kids' shows (Koko the clown tells the children at home to shoo the big people out of the room for "make-believe time," then reads aloud dirty passages from *Fanny Hill*), live sports coverage (a play-by-play of grainy footage of a German couple competing in the thirty-fourth annual International Sex Games), and a fake newscast, which concludes with the phrase "Good night, and have a pleasant tomorrow." A spoof of variety-show hokum featured a handsome guy in a barbershop quartet getup—Shapiro's friend Chevy Chase, a Bard College classmate. But Chase's funniest contribution to *The Groove Tube* utilized his talents only from the waist down. It was a public service announce-ment about venereal disease narrated by a flesh-colored puppet called Safety Sam; as the camera zooms in, it's apparent that Sam's doughy eyeballs and prominent nose, which jiggles as he talks, are a man's inverted genitals—and the man is Chase. (Reader, this is hard to picture; you can find the footage on YouTube.)

The film, bankrolled by ten Long Island dentists as a tax shelter, was an improbable success, earning more than $20 million. Para-mount wanted Shapiro to make a sequel and bring in other hip scripts. He tapped Michaels to write a screenplay based on the story of a real L.A. teenager who was the king of "phone phreaking," a forerunner to computer hacking. The kid had built an electronic device called a Blue Box that would mimic tones of particular frequencies into a phone receiver in order to patch into distant networks and mainframe computers. Using the ruse, he siphoned thousands of dollars from the phone company. (Another Blue Box adept was Steve Wozniak, who turned his friend Steve Jobs on to it.)

"It was a fantastic story," Michaels said. "This kid was living with his parents. Meanwhile he had his own house up on Mulholland, and he was living this other life." He threw wild parties up at his house, and during the day he'd be studying for the SATs in his telephone van. Michaels hung out with the kid to research the details, then wrote a draft of the script. "There was no style or spin to it," he said. "I wouldn't have known how to do that." But he was elated; he could tell himself that he was writing a movie at Paramount. It's all he'd ever wanted.

So even though NBC had offered to let him produce the show he'd been dreaming of for years, his focus was on the big screen, and the romance of the Paramount lot. The Marx Brothers filmed there. Billy Wilder had shot parts of *Sunset Boulevard* there—Norma Des-mond, the faded silent star, drives up to the studio's iconic Bronson Gate. Shapiro was getting offices and a secretary. Dick Ebersol, in New York, didn't even have a secretary—he'd forgotten to ask for one when he negotiated his deal. And Michaels wasn't so sure he wanted to throw in with Ebersol anyway. The qualities that made him an attractive partner—his huge ambition and his Eddie Haskell-ish facility with higher-ups—made him difficult to take day to day. Around town Ebersol was known as "the WASP Sammy Glick." He didn't fit in with Michaels's languid Chateau salon, part of an L.A. scene that the writer Eve Babitz compared to a "drifting, opulent barge." Also, *Saturday Night* was NBC's idea, which meant that it would be owned by the network, and not by Michaels and a production company, as had been the plan when he'd pitched his idea earlier with Bob Finkel. For the third time since he'd left Canada, he found himself asking: Was television a dead end?

Another factor in his ambivalence: he'd grown attached to the L.A. lifestyle. New York City in the mid-seventies did not seem inviting to him. Travelers arriving at JFK were greeted by police officers, who, protesting layoffs, handed out pamphlets with a skull on the cover under the headline "Welcome to Fear City." Murders had doubled in the past decade. The city was on the brink of bankruptcy. The New York movies of the period told the story: *Taxi Driver, The French Connection, Escape from New York, Death Wish.* That kind of florid decay was useful for nurturing punk rock and a cadre of artists like Andy Warhol and Robert Mapplethorpe, but it did nothing for Michaels. Even in his cinéaste period, he hadn't been susceptible to the glamour of decline and squalor. It's an argument he still has with young writers who want their work to have a gritty "indie" vibe.

"New York had that level of superiority to it that seemed so corny," he said. "Very judgmental. New York was the Ramones; L.A. was the Eagles, Neil Young, Jackson Browne." Culturally, Southern California seemed more vital. "The New York approach was to think that everyone in L.A. is an idiot, and that they all say 'Have a nice day.' That wasn't true."

In California, he'd come to love the desert and the beach. New York was buried under a foot of snow that February. In the Mojave, seven dollars a night would get him a room at the Joshua Tree Inn, the motel where Gram Parsons had overdosed. Michaels had been spending a lot of time there, doing mushrooms with Gary Weis and Tom Schiller. (Even on mushrooms, Schiller noted, Michaels maintained his high level of matter-of-fact competence.) There was an ice dispenser and a cigarette machine, and Michaels would drive half a mile to Safeway for groceries. But mostly he would chill out in the Monument, more than a thousand square miles of stark, serene desert.

The difference between the coasts was related to the way he thought about television. "California invented fun as a value not to be ashamed of," he said. "We don't think of Germans as doing anything just because it'd be fun. In California, you can like books, and you can like an Elvis movie, too. It doesn't mean you're not serious." The idea that leisure is not a self-indulgence stayed with him.

EBERSOL NEEDED TO TELL HERB SCHLOSSER WHO WAS GOING TO PRODUCE his show on Saturday night. But Michaels was still waffling. This time there was no fortune cookie to make up his mind for him. At the end of February, ABC finally aired the first of the two Lily Tomlin specials. The critics were enraptured and didn't seem to notice the coke-fueled editing. In his review, *The New York Times*'s John J. O'Connor called Tomlin "deceptively matter-of-fact about ordinary insanities . . . it might be disturbing if she weren't so funny." The warm reception to the special made something snap in Michaels's brain. Maybe television wasn't a lost cause. Maybe embracing TV was embracing the undervalued aesthetic of fun. As for his network fears, of the big three, NBC felt like the safest bet. "There is a DNA to these networks," he said. "CBS always had great sitcoms. But all of those variety shows from early television, that's all NBC."

Urged on by Brillstein and Wernick, he finally decided that the chance to do the show that had been brewing in his mind for years was too good to pass up. He told Ken Shapiro that he would have to finish the phone-phreaking movie on his own. (Shapiro replaced Michaels with two other aspiring auteurs, Tom Schiller and Gus Van Sant, but the film never got made.)

At first, Michaels was thrown by Schlosser's mandate that the show be live. In live television, as Steve Martin once put it, "anything that went wrong stayed wrong." Michaels was used to polishing and re-polishing in the editing room. But he began to see it as a positive. For one thing, a live show would not require a pilot. Doing a pilot, he realized, "makes all your most conservative instincts come out. You end up doing what you *think* will get you on the air." With no pilot, there'd be no audience research reports and no notes from executives or advertisers. "With a live show, I could get directly through to the audience," he said. "The network and the viewers would see it at the same time." Broadcasting live also appealed to his sense of nostalgia. He remembered the exhilaration he felt, in 1969, watching the moon landing on TV at Uncle Pep's lake house, and knowing that everyone around the world was watching too.

Brillstein and Wernick negotiated a deal. Michaels's salary, the first season, would be $115,000, not much more than what he'd turned down for four Flip Wilson specials. If the show had a second season, the salary would rise to $145,000, and if it stayed on for three seasons, $175,000. Brillstein insisted that his client be paid for seventeen shows even if NBC canceled the program earlier. The deal was signed on April Fool's Day, which Michaels found ominous.

The next step was to get Michaels to New York, a place he associated with anxiety. But NBC put him up at the Plaza, and when he was checking in, the hotel's airy Palm Court at his back, the city's crud and crime momentarily vanished from his mind. It brought him back to the day when he and Michael Goldstein had visited Tiffany's. That trip down on the night bus from Toronto was the only other time he'd seen the glorious Deco interior of the RCA Building. Returning now, he had a vivid (if fleeting) sense that the show could be a success. Just walking into the lobby, he thought, would put audiences in a good mood. But once he got past reception, the place was desolate.

His wardrobe of Hawaiian shirts wouldn't do for New York City, so he walked across the street to Saks to purchase a sweater and a green corduroy blazer—corduroy being a fabric that, in the 1970s, a renegade could wear without appearing to capitulate to the Man. Arriving at Ebersol's tiny office in his new oxblood V-neck, for the meeting to present the show to NBC executives, he was miffed to find that he wasn't going to be included. Ebersol had just been informed that only NBC employees could attend; Michaels was a freelance producer.

Up till then, Michaels's charm had done a lot to mask the vagueness of the proposed show. But Ebersol, on his own, nervously walked a tableful of older executives through the idea in broad strokes—rep company, guest hosts, films, rock music. Schlosser arrived at the meeting late, and even though it was his memo that had got the *Saturday Night* ball rolling, his men sat through Ebersol's presentation in resigned silence.

More corporate meetings followed, with Michaels now doing the talking. After years working alongside radio veterans, he was at ease around older men. He told them that his show would be "new wine in old bottles," and promised that it would take shape organically over time. "We will always be experimenting on the air and responding to our own mistakes," he said. "I know what the ingredients are, but not the recipe." Some of the men thought that Michaels, with his flowing hair and Sufi ring, came across as an over-caffeinated hippie; others noted the pedantic seriousness with which he discussed comedy. Another protested that the young audience Michaels wanted would never be home at 11:30 on Saturday night.

But Schlosser waved away the objections of his people. He beamed through Michaels's spiel, and when he interrupted to suggest that seventy-one-year-old Bob Hope might be a good host for the first show, Michaels didn't break stride. He told the group that he reckoned the show would figure itself out by the tenth week. "I'll watch show ten," Schlosser said with a smile.

The network put Michaels in a temporary office on the fourth floor, the executive precinct, not far from Tebet's smoky lair. It had been recently vacated by Larry White, the programming executive who, a year earlier, had told Michaels that his idea was a dud. If that wasn't unnerving enough, Michaels, susceptible to portents, opened a drawer of the desk and found a couple of forlorn artifacts: an old *Racing Form* and a handful of Maalox tablets.

EIGHT

GOING ON BOARD THE ARK

THE NEW YORK TRIP WAS A CORPORATE EDUCATION. MICHAELS AND EBER-
sol first met with the budget department, which was led by a Harvard
MBA named Don Carswell who kept a sign on his desk reading THE
ANSWER IS NO. They laid out what they thought they would need in
terms of talent, staff, cameras, and sets, and Carswell came back
with a budget figure of $180,000 per show—higher than the number
mentioned in Schlosser's memo. That figure soon got revised down to
$134,600. Michaels was puzzled. He innocently assumed that the
budget would be calculated according to the needs of the show. It
was only much later that he learned that the budget was reverse-
engineered: Carswell guessed how much the show might generate in
ad revenue, and he used that figure to calculate production expenses.
The sales guys predicted that the show would lose money. Michaels
took the opportunity to pitch the ad department a pet idea of his own:
Since they were going back to live TV, which was rooted in the 1950s,
why not run the actual commercials that aired in the fifties? The sales
people just stared at him.

Schlosser was eager to get started, so in April a vague press release
was thrown together about the still-vague "Saturday Night" (it errone-
ously described Michaels as a writer for Monty Python), so that by
the time NBC's 219 affiliates gathered for their annual meeting in
May, they would know that a new program was in the offing. The af-

filiates' receptiveness would be key to the show's success. The press dutifully reacted, *The New York Times* reporting that "a zany, irreverent program that can spin off ideas and talent into primetime" would originate from the "Toscanini Studio" in New York; it called the show "a big risk."

In May, Michaels and Ebersol were to present the show to the affiliates, so they scurried to make their idea more concrete. Michaels had always envisioned a rep company, but he hadn't considered having different hosts every week, as Schlosser wanted. He finally warmed to the idea after Brillstein pointed out that *The Hollywood Palace,* a long-running variety show, had rotating hosts, which brought in a new audience every week. It wasn't a good show (guests ranged from gorilla acts to Don Ho), but having fresh faces expanded its reach. "Writing for the same people every week leads to 'What will Sonny say to Cher when they come out?'" Michaels said.

Albert Brooks also suggested the revolving host idea. One day, Michaels and Ebersol found themselves stopped next to Brooks at an intersection in L.A. They were both fans. (The previous summer, Ebersol had tried, and failed, to get Brooks to commit to creating one of his wheel of pilots.) They hollered at him to pull over, and urged him to be part of *their* show. Brooks told them that he wasn't interested in working live. Also, he hated staying up late. Even playing at clubs, he'd peak at 8:00 P.M. and then be listless for the second and third shows. "I'd literally come out and tell the midnight audience, 'Go find the people who were at the early show; they'll tell you what was good.' Don't make me do this again." But he offered Michaels and Ebersol a countersuggestion: revolving hosts. "This was not a eureka moment," he said. "I was just making excuses for turning them down." (The origin story of *Saturday Night Live* has many authors. George Schlatter thought the show was *Laugh-In;* Howard Shore thought it was the FAST Show; Hart Pomerantz viewed *The Hart and Lorne Terrific Hour* as its beta version; Rosie Shuster felt that it sprang from her father's den; Earl McGrath, who'd wooed Michaels for the *Rolling Stone* special, believed that his idea had been stolen. "I felt kind of used," McGrath told Joe Hagan, the biographer of *Rolling Stone* founder Jann Wenner.)

Before Brooks drove off that day, Michaels asked whether there was anything at all that he might want to do for their show. Actually, Brooks said, there was something: short films. He had just made a little movie—a fake infomercial—for PBS, called "The Famous School for Comedians." In the film, Brooks plays the dean of a comedy college, where students take classes on how to do a spit take and how to time jokes to a rim shot. Brooks had enjoyed the process, so he made a deal with Ebersol and Michaels to direct six short films, and he would stay in California. To produce the films, Michaels hired his friend from the Malibu days, Penelope Spheeris.

Albert Brooks was the only big name that Ebersol and Michaels had wrangled, but soon Brillstein came through with another, offbeat one. Since 1960, Brillstein had been representing Jim Henson, the creator of the Muppets. They were chiefly known as cuddly characters on *Sesame Street,* but Brillstein assured Michaels that he saw something "hip and slightly dark" in Henson. Michaels liked the Muppets fine, and, more important, as regulars on *Ed Sullivan,* they were household names. They had a "variety element" that appealed to him. Henson, eager to escape the children's television gulch, envisioned a troupe of what he called "Muppet Night Creatures." He tossed around potential universes for them to inhabit, including a TV game show, a rock group, and a therapy session. Michaels was sold.

He had asked the network for three months to find his people, and then three more months for them to get to know each other. He knew that the show was bound to have grueling hours, so he said he was looking for "people you could drive cross-country with and not kill." One of his hiring mantras was that comedy, as a humanizing force, is too important to be left to the professionals. He was looking for "enlightened amateurs," people with little or no TV experience. He hadn't considered that many of the talented people in that category had little or no TV experience because they had little or no interest in TV.

He started with some rabbits' feet: his old Canadian cohort. First he called Gilda Radner, from *Godspell,* but she told him she had taken a role on a David Steinberg sitcom; Michaels enlisted Brillstein to persuade her to defect. (Brillstein performed this kind of service frequently, a role he attributed to Michaels's "fear of rejection," and need to have "clean hands.") He also put out a feeler to Aykroyd, and he recruited his old camp friend Howard Shore as musical director. From L.A., he wanted Laraine Newman, who'd brought her Valley Girl character to the Tomlin specials (he described the show to her as a cross between *Sixty Minutes* and Monty Python; she pretended she had heard of the latter), and he wanted his old Malibu guides, Gary Weis and John Head (who'd helped Michaels hone his pitch to NBC). Weis would make short films, and Head would book musical acts. "I wanted a level of style and a level of cool," Michaels said. "Its identity shouldn't only be comedy. And it shouldn't look like a comedy show that was trying hard to please."

With Ebersol, he scouted comedy clubs and spent more late nights kibitzing at the Marmont. One evening, Earl Pomerantz— a funny writer but, with his Coke-bottle glasses, definitely not cool— wandered in while Michaels was making tea for a roomful of friends. He heard Ebersol tell someone that he had hired Michaels because of his hockey puck film. Pomerantz looked up and said, "I wrote that." The room went silent. A job offer on the writing staff was extended to Pomerantz, but New York City spooked him. Michaels said that he made the same offer to Hart Pomerantz, although Hart doesn't recall being asked and has long told himself that SNL was "not my kind of comedy."

In L.A., Michaels asked Tom Schiller to come aboard as his assistant. Schiller thought TV was junk, but Michaels wooed him by bringing him to Joshua Tree, where he held forth about the show day and night in a way that Schiller recalled as "monomaniacal." Michaels evangelized: "Now is the time to enter television. *We* now have the airwaves." When he wasn't talking, he was taking calls from New York, steady even when tripping on mushrooms. "He never becomes noticeably different under any circumstances," Schiller said. "You can't get through the glaze of brown eyes."

In the motel in the desert, Schiller threw the I Ching to help him decide. The message came back: "abundance." He wrote in his journal: "All my dreams of power, wealth and TV glory seem to crystallize in images . . . The RCA Building at 30 Rockefeller Plaza looms like neon magnets of the mind. Banks of gleaming Art Deco elevators ready to whisk me to the studio and offices of my choice." He took the job.

Around this time, Michaels went to a midnight showing of *Monty Python and the Holy Grail* in L.A. with Rob Reiner, who'd been a writer for the Smothers Brothers. While waiting on line, they bumped into Chevy Chase, whom Reiner knew. Chase got Michaels's attention the way he often got attention, by doing an elaborate pratfall. Michaels had admired his John Denver send-up in *Lemmings*. Chase had just written on a tepid Alan King special (he had a cameo as a streaker) and was living with Christopher Guest. He was on unemployment. Charmed, Michaels invited him to come by the Marmont. When Chase dropped in, a marathon talking session swallowed the afternoon, and he became Michaels's wingman as he met with potential writers. "I knew instantly that Lorne was a funny guy," Chase said. "He wasn't an initiator of humor as much as a believer in humor."

Michaels offered Chase a spot on the writing staff. But Chase wanted to perform, so he passed. He'd taken a role in a summer stock play called *Stop, Thief, Stop!* opposite Paul Lynde, the character actor known for his role as Uncle Arthur, the campy and sarcastic warlock on *Bewitched* ("campy and sarcastic" defined the roles that closeted gay actors played in that era). Chase had gotten the part after Lynde picked him up hitchhiking.

Describing his vision for the show with job applicants was good practice for Michaels's upcoming presentation to the affiliates, at L.A.'s Century Plaza. Doormen in Beefeater costumes welcomed the hundreds of station managers to the hotel, whose distinctive semicircular facade Diane Keaton would, years later, try to save from the wrecking ball, comparing its curvy contours to "a sexy woman surrounded by ogling men, like Sophia Loren in the nineteen-sixties." The conventioneers dutifully sat through Ebersol's thin presentation of the new *Saturday Night* show. He emphasized the involvement of Albert Brooks and Jim Henson. Then he vamped, listing guests that the show *hoped* to book, like the Rolling Stones and Stevie Wonder. He talked vaguely about a "comedy breakthrough" that would address what was happening out in the world. Saigon had fallen weeks earlier, but the managers were restive, more focused on their afternoon golf games than on topical satire.

Michaels's role was to meet the station managers individually and try to pitch them on the show. Brooks had been persuaded to help out. Each station had a hotel room decorated with props and motifs from its home city. The managers of the Miami station, for instance, held court amidst palm trees and plastic flamingos. When Brooks and Michaels walked in, the station managers said, "Hi, Albert! Welcome to Miami!" They ignored Michaels. Brooks recalled, "Every stop was: 'Albert, what's your new show gonna be?' I'd say, 'I don't know. Ask this guy. I'm just making some films.'" Brooks believes that his biggest contribution to SNL was getting the show on the affiliates' radar that day. "I provided a service," he said. "I always said that I was like the Saturn 5 rocket of that show."

The station managers may have shown little interest, but Michaels's new show had become an object of concern over in Burbank. During the convention at the Century Plaza, Dave Tebet grabbed Ebersol and told him that Johnny Carson and his producer Fred de Cordova wanted to see him and Michaels right away. The summons provoked mixed emotions: Michaels was going to meet his hero. Had he offended the great man?

The next day, waiting in Carson's outer office, they felt like they'd been called in to see the principal. They were nervous, but tried to keep their cool. After all, Carson was another generation; they knew that young comedians dismissed *The Tonight Show* with the line "You can smell the polyester." When Carson's secretary announced them, they heard his voice, through the crackly intercom, say, "Send the kids in." (After that, Ebersol signed memos to Michaels as "The Kid.") It was midafternoon, and Carson was wearing a denim work shirt. He had just done a run-through of his monologue. "I remember there were sweat rings under the arms," Michaels said. "I thought, 'Wow, he's been on the air twenty years, and he still cares enough to be nervous.'" Carson was avuncular, but he wanted to make sure that the new show wouldn't infringe on his turf. De Cordova, who was spiffed-out in a suit and tie and had big rectangular spectacles and a leathery perma-tan, told the young visitors that they had to stay away from the comedians that appeared on *The Tonight Show*. Michaels, thinking about the people that Carson featured—the Don Rickles and Rich Little set—said that wouldn't be a problem.

The meeting lasted thirty minutes. In parting, Carson grinned and said, "So, the show you boys are doing is ninety minutes, *one* night a week?" "There was a twinkle when he said it," Michaels recalled. Carson wished them well and got back to work.

Relieved, Michaels resumed assembling his team. He was buoyed when, a couple of weeks later, Chevy Chase called from a pay phone at the summer stock theater. After one rehearsal, he'd bailed on the Paul Lynde project. He asked if the writing job was still available.

Lynde inadvertently almost derailed another *Saturday Night* hire. One night at Catch a Rising Star, in New York, Michaels saw a set by a tall guy with a short neck and big shoulders named Alan Zweibel. Zweibel was living with his parents in Woodmere, Long Island, and slicing cold cuts in a Queens deli for $2.75 an hour; in his spare time he wrote jokes, at seven dollars a pop, for Catskill Comics. His biggest score was selling a joke to Rodney Dangerfield. ("Even as an infant I didn't get any respect. My mother wouldn't breastfeed me. She said she liked me as a friend.") Zweibel took the jokes the old guys wouldn't buy and used them in his own act. His set didn't knock Michaels out, but something about the torrent of one-liners got his attention.

Zweibel, Michaels thought, might be a good voice to add to the mix. He figured that he already had hipness and cleverness covered. He'd recently signed up Andy Kaufman, after seeing him at the same club and being entranced by his arty, conceptual material—Foreign Man, an Elvis impersonation; Gary Weis was there that night, and told Michaels, "Man, that should've been at the Guggenheim." Now Michaels wanted to make sure that his show would have hard laughs. (A hard laugh, he says, makes you feel like you're nine years old, and "reminds you of a happier time in your life.") He asked Zweibel to submit some material, and Zweibel pulled two all-nighters typing up eleven hundred jokes. He clipped the pages into a loose-leaf binder and took the train into Manhattan to put the book into Michaels's hands personally. To look sharp for the interview, he wore a maroon leisure suit that he borrowed from his dad.

Michaels, in his room at the Plaza, opened the binder and read the first joke: "The postal service is issuing a new stamp commemorating prostitution. It's a ten-cent stamp, but if you want to lick it, it's a quarter." Michaels liked it. It had the cadence and payoff of a classic hard laugh, but it had an edge. Michaels kept the binder and brought it back to L.A. to show Shuster, who was helping him vet writers. She approved.

Shuster always assumed that she would be on the writing staff. The marriage had effectively petered out, but she and Michaels continued to share a blurry bond. "I knew I wanted to be part of it, from my gut," she said. "It felt like a birthright." Michaels liked having her there, despite the awkwardness. "The deal was that my job was not contingent on us being together," she said. "In return, I wouldn't lead any feminist insurrections against him."

When Zweibel finally got an offer to be an apprentice writer on *Saturday Night,* he was on the verge of taking a job on *The Hollywood Squares,* in prime time. He'd been asked to write the joke answers for the occupant of the center square—Paul Lynde. Michaels's show paid less, and, given its time slot, Zweibel told himself, "The only people who are going to watch it are people who are not getting laid." And yet, because Michaels was masterful at making his experiment seem like the chance of a lifetime, Zweibel signed on.

HAUNTED BY THE *LAUGH-IN* ASSEMBLY-LINE METHOD, IN WHICH EVERY writer's jokes went into the maw, Michaels envisioned a show in which a sketch's author would be recognizable from its style. He wanted the show to feel like an issue of *The New Yorker.* He tried to hire Marilyn Miller, from the Tomlin specials, but she wanted to stay in L.A. and urged him to consider her friend Michael O'Donoghue. He had recently left *National Lampoon* in solidarity with his girlfriend, Anne Beatts, who'd quit when she learned that she was being paid less than her male colleagues. Michaels was a bit dismissive of the *Lampoon*, which he associated with "a kind of male-ego sweatsocks attitude," and O'Donoghue was famous for being difficult, but Miller insisted that Michaels would appreciate him. O'Donoghue was thirty-five and a literary snob: before the *Lampoon*, he'd contributed to the *Evergreen Review*. A high-strung perfectionist, he liked comedy that veered in a direction more nihilistic than the *Lampoon*, which leaned toward kegs and horny teenagers. For the *Lampoon*, he'd written "The Vietnamese Baby Book," a keepsake album noting such milestones as "Baby's first napalm burn" and "Baby's first word: medic." (Beatts's work was unflinching too; Volkswagen sued the *Lampoon* over a parody ad she'd written showing a Beetle floating in water over the line "If Ted Kennedy drove a Volkswagen, he'd be President today.") Michaels called O'Donoghue to propose a meeting.

Since storming out of the *Lampoon*, O'Donoghue and Beatts had been barely scraping by. A job Beatts got them reviewing restaurants for *The Village Voice* had ended abruptly, after O'Donoghue turned in a piece about Lüchow's, the German stalwart near Union Square. Of the restaurant's large Christmas tree, he wrote, "It looks like the last thing the folks at Nagasaki saw before they turned into tuna melts." When Michaels called, O'Donoghue suggested that they meet at the Oyster Bar, in Grand Central Terminal.

"Michael and Anne showed up wearing antique clothing," he recalled. In their thirties regalia, they reminded him of Scott and Zelda Fitzgerald. They were part of a demimonde living a highly curated life, what Beatts called a "style-based existence." Their parlor-floor apartment on West Sixteenth Street, which their crowd referred to as the Winter Palace, had marble fireplaces and mirrored French doors, every surface crammed with collections of morbid kitsch. O'Donoghue, with his thin brown More cigarettes and his wide-brimmed fedoras, and Beatts, in veiled hats and shoulder pads, oozing reflexive sarcasm, made him realize that New Yorkers were susceptible to the same level of fantasy and reinvention as the people he gravitated toward in California. It was part bullshit, part commitment.

Michaels himself had a handful of uniforms: jeans, sneakers, Hawaiian shirt, and the corduroy jacket, across whose lapel marched a mother duck and three ducklings on a vintage silver brooch that he'd picked up in Santa Monica; a Nordic reindeer sweater was also a staple. Michaels's Canadian surfer-dude getup did nothing to impress O'Donoghue and Beatts, but they listened to his patter beneath the vaulted Guastavino arches. It was a free meal, after all. O'Donoghue told Michaels that he regarded television as a lava lamp with better sound, and Beatts critiqued the *Lily* specials, which she considered more feminist than funny; she said she preferred the unabashed camp of Cher. There was no immediate electric connection the way there had been with Tomlin or Chase, but Michaels sensed that the couple had a level of savage savoir faire that could be useful. For his part, O'Donoghue was put off by what he called Michaels's "kindergarten comedy theories," and hinted that his own humor might be too subversive for NBC.

Intrigued nonetheless, the couple invited Michaels to visit them at the Winter Palace, correctly assuming that he would be impressed by their distinctive mise-en-scène. Michaels brought along Tom Schiller, and the two silently marveled at the JFK dinnerware, serial-killer souvenirs, and the stuffed panda bear strapped into a toy electric chair. Michaels felt a prick of recognition in the way O'Donoghue, out of sheer will, had engendered in himself a sense of entitlement; he knew what he liked, and he liked nothing more than being the center of a glamorous scene.

Michaels picked up in O'Donoghue's conversation persistent notes of aggrievement and spite. "Every story Michael told was about someone fucking him over," he said. "And I, in my naivete, was determined that, if I hired him, that would not happen to me. I wouldn't be the guy who fucked him over; I would always protect him."

The courtship continued, O'Donoghue projecting ambivalence and Michaels affecting a cool distance from the corporate aspect of his project. He promised that, at his show, the writer would be king, and assured O'Donoghue and Beatts that in late night they'd have artistic freedom. O'Donoghue, desperate for income, said yes immediately. Beatts hesitated, having a contract for a book of women's humor, called *Titters*. But Michaels persuaded her, making the preposterous promise that the show wouldn't be all-consuming. Later, she concluded that he liked the idea of hiring couples because they were less likely to chafe at the brutal hours. It was "like going on board the ark," she said. "Once you were on, you couldn't get off."

O'Donoghue was one of the people, along with Gilda Radner, who, early on, pushed Michaels to hire John Belushi. An Albanian American from Chicago's Second City, Belushi was then starring, with Radner, in *The National Lampoon Show*, a follow-up to *Lemmings*. Although Michaels was focused on finding writers first, he invited Belushi to come in and talk, and the interview was a bust. It was a point of pride for Belushi to proclaim his hatred of television. When he arrived in Michaels's office, he'd declared, "My television has spit all over it."

Michaels had been listening to people trash TV for a decade. "I was done with it—the snobbery of people who say, 'I only do *important* work,'" he said. "It was a cliché." Belushi had shown up in an old T-shirt and with a wild beard, wanting to look like a bad-boy artiste; he smirked when Michaels said that *Saturday Night* was going to be dangerous. But Michaels wasn't about to do a sell job. "I don't want you to do anything that you don't want to do," he told Belushi, and the conversation seemed to be over. Startled, Belushi shot back, "Yeah, but everybody says you're doing something *different*." Michaels paused. "Well, it's still going to be on television," he said. He wished Belushi well and said that, if he was still interested, he could come to the open auditions in August. He also suggested that Belushi shave.

Michaels generally trusted the recommendations of other performers, and he doted on Radner. But with Belushi, he hesitated. He wanted to make sure there was enough warmth in the show, and he already had a big ration of *Lampoon* snark. Radner insisted that Belushi had a sweet side, but Michaels worried that he was "anti-audience." He said, "After that bad first meeting, I thought, 'This guy is trouble.'"

AS MICHAELS WAS GOING OVER LISTS OF POTENTIAL WRITERS, HE GOT A call one day from Herb Sargent, the many-times-married *Tonight Show* veteran who'd mentored him during his first Tomlin special. The next night, Sargent initiated him into the hierarchical world of Elaine's, the Italian restaurant in Yorkville that no one went to for the food. It was a hangout of Woody Allen's and an assortment of New York literary types, including Norman Mailer, George Plimpton, and Gay Talese. Sargent was a favorite of Elaine Kaufman, the theatrical, somewhat frowsy proprietor, and he appeared in a number of the framed photos on the red walls. Michaels, who loved a clubhouse, was captivated. As nobodies jostled at the bar for vodka and tonics, Sargent sheepishly described his latest project—an Alan King special called *Energy Crisis*. Michaels outlined his plans for *Saturday Night*, straining to sound like he knew what he was doing.

The next day, Sargent showed up to see Michaels unannounced. "I want to do your show," he declared. Michaels was touched but wary. *Saturday Night* was about giving the reins to the young people. Michaels, stalling, explained that the top salary for writers was $700 a week. "I can't afford you," he said. Sargent said that sum was fine. "And then, of course, I didn't have a choice," Michaels said. He hired him. He'd come to view Sargent, a gentle presence, as a father figure. A real New Yorker, Sargent also would become a crucial guide to the city for Michaels and the other transplants on the staff. He absolutely hated L.A., and would tell people that, when he died, his ashes were to be dropped into any body of water that did not flow into the Pacific Ocean.

Michaels knew he wanted to have a Black writer on staff, and he put out a feeler to the Writers Guild. A friend there sent over a play by a thirty-eight-year-old Juilliard-trained playwright and actor named Garrett Morris, who'd also worked as a schoolteacher. Michaels liked what he read, and he hired Morris, telling him that he hoped that in addition to writing, Morris could recruit Black performers to audition for the cast, in August.

For the last writing slot, he wanted a duo—two writers for one salary, according to Writers Guild rules. Schiller had been wading through submissions, and among them was a packet by two young guys who'd moved to L.A. from Minnesota. Al Franken and Tom Davis had been trying to make a living doing stand-up, augmented by gigs playing Santa Claus and Winnie the Pooh at Sears. Their fourteen pages caught Schiller's attention: it read like a blueprint for what Michaels wanted. There was a fake commercial, a parody of *The Sonny and Cher Show*, a newscast about World War III, and a script for a conceptual taped piece. "The film piece was supposed to be security-camera footage from a robbery at 7-Eleven," Franken said. "But the security camera keeps moving and missing what's happening. At one point you hear gunfire and then you see a can of V8 start spurting red. As soon as the camera moves one way, the robber goes in the other direction."

Michaels thought that Franken and Davis could cover the college-kid demographic. When they got the call, they were outside playing basketball. They had tickets to see the Rolling Stones a few days later in L.A., but they blew off the concert and jumped on a plane. Franken—prickly and adamant—and Davis—gentle and spacey—were the only writers Michaels signed without a meeting. Later, everyone joked that if Michaels had actually met them, he never would have hired them.

MICHAELS KEPT HIS BASE AT THE MARMONT, FLYING TO NEW YORK EVERY couple of weeks, as he continued to look for writers and a production team. A facilities manager named Dan Sullivan showed him and Ebersol possible office space in Manhattan. There was a lot to choose from, including a suite attached to Radio City Music Hall, some raw space in the Exxon Building, and a spread on the twenty-second floor of the RCA Building that had been Nelson Rockefeller's headquarters: one huge executive chamber and a lot of tiny offices. "I knew that I couldn't be *that* person," he said. He settled on the eastern half of the seventeenth floor. One window in Michaels's corner office framed an arresting view of the Empire State Building, like an advertisement for New York City. Windows on another wall overlooked the Rockefeller Center skating rink, ringed with the flapping flags of two hundred nations. The Prometheus statue gleamed over it brightly, having been regilded that spring. Michaels's office felt big to him, so he had a second desk moved in for Tom Schiller, his assistant.

Besides Michaels's office, the space was basically an open bullpen. There was no budget for furnishings, and the decor came together willy-nilly, much the way the staff did. "We were all used to buying stuff in thrift shops," Michaels said. "None of us had ever been to a furniture showroom." Also appealing to Michaels was the fact that the seventeenth floor was serviced by a different elevator bank than the executive floor, so the *Saturday Night* staff wouldn't bump into the adults.

When it came to the look of the show, he also wanted to go against the grain. The typical variety-show set was a wide shiny floor and a cyclorama wall—a seamless stretch of nothingness—decorated with a few props. There were "suggestions of sets": a lone lamppost, or a window frame. Michaels wanted what he calls "hard-wall reality"—actual rooms with doors and furniture that wouldn't compete with the comedy. He'd seen Hal Prince's new production of *Candide,* with sets by the husband-and-wife team of Eugene and Franne Lee. Franne also did costumes, and when the show swept the Tony Awards, the Lees each took one home. Michaels was dazzled by the set, an interlocking series of platforms that required no scene changes.

He invited the Lees over to his room at the Plaza. They were skeptical, and didn't want to relocate from Providence, Rhode Island, where they were living on a fifty-foot sailboat. Franne had sewn costumes for Jimi Hendrix and Janis Joplin at Woodstock; Eugene had a long hippie beard, and even being in the Plaza felt weird to him. "No one from television had ever talked to people like that before," Michaels said. "But I wanted people who didn't know what couldn't be done." Michaels stretched out on his hotel bed in his socks and wore them down. He assured them that he'd always had one foot in the theater and explained how a live show, late at night, wouldn't feel that different from Off-Broadway. And he promised that they could commute from Rhode Island. He invited Eugene to come on a scouting mission to a comedy club with him later, and the next day brought him to the RCA Building to show him the vast, empty Toscanini Studio, which could be his canvas. Michaels, Lee said, "could talk the peel off a grape." He and Franne quickly came on board.

Michaels soon moved into a furnished sublet in a stately old building on Fifty-seventh Street called the Osborne. The imposing lobby had mosaic-tiled walls and Tiffany glass, and Michaels's apartment was small but similarly ornate, with a framed letter from George Bernard Shaw on the wall. He loved that the Osborne, like the Chateau Marmont, was a magnet for show business types (Leonard Bernstein, Imogene Coca, Bobby Short, Gig Young). He'd sublet the place from a friend of a friend, a producer named Michael Mindlin, who'd worked for the Broadway impresario David Merrick. (From a 1959 classified ad in *Billboard*: "GYPSY is looking for a two-man cow act. Please contact Michael Mindlin, Jr.") Michaels would have grapefruit juice in the apartment and then he'd go downstairs to Chock full o'Nuts for coffee and a whole-wheat donut before walking the six blocks to work. He'd left the red VW in L.A., and he would keep his room at the Marmont for a year, not being sure whether this new life would pan out. Howard Shore, also wanting to walk to work (a priority that he called "very Canadian"), sublet a place in Hell's Kitchen from a missionary who was in Africa. The walls were covered with photographs taken by the missionary's late common-law husband, pictures that Shore found unsettling. Years later, he learned that the photographer was Weegee.

To assemble a band, Shore cold-called session musicians he'd heard on records. Michaels was promising NBC that Randy Newman would compose an opening theme. (He touted Newman as the composer of the Dr. Pepper theme song.) In the end, Shore composed the show's bluesy opener, as well as the closing theme, "Waltz in A." With those pieces, Shore created a musical personality for the show, and, fifty years later, Stax-style blues with a saxophone is still the dominant sound of comedy. "You instantly know how it makes you feel," Shore said. One of the first musicians he hired was Paul Shaffer, who had conducted the Toronto *Godspell* and was playing keyboards in the Broadway orchestra for *The Magic Show*. Shaffer showed up at the RCA Building and found Michaels looking at an institutional coffee maker with two pots of coffee brewing. To no one in particular, Michaels asked, "Which of these coffees is the fresher?" It sounded funny to Shaffer's ear—an ironic musical cadence. "Lorne seemed to speak in comedic pentameter," he said.

IN JUNE, MICHAELS SENT A THREE-PAGE MAILGRAM TO EBERSOL, DESCRIBing his progress so far. He always avoided committing himself in writing, and the memo was written under duress, to reassure the network. It is a rambling, sometimes funny list of possible show elements:

1. Rotating guest host ("The requisite quality I am looking for is spontaneity. Fame and talent would not hurt.")

2. Musical guests: two per show, coordinated by John Head

3. A five-minute film by Albert Brooks ("Albert has already talked to such diverse talent as Peter Boyle and John Lennon about the possibility of cameo appearances . . . All indications point to high human expectations.")

4. Muppets ("Jim Hanson [sic] has agreed to create a totally new group of Muppets . . . These will be adult puppets so there will be no problems about their staying up late. As to what these Muppets will do or say, I really have not much of an idea.")

5. Repertory cast of three men and three women, whom Michaels would work with "improvisationally throughout the preproduction period so that, hopefully, a family feeling will exist by the time of the first show"

6. A five-minute documentary, "light in tone" and "offbeat," "under the direction of award-losing filmmaker Gary Weis" ("example: 'The Midgets of Massachusetts'")

7. Live remotes

8. Pre-taped commercial parodies ("enormously helpful in pacing a live show")

9. A period instructional film, or "found humor" ("At the Los Angeles Public Library a resourceful Tom Schiller has uncovered a short training film on proper conduct during the coffee break")

10. Three new talent acts

11. Mock documentary along the lines of "The Puck Crisis"; under consideration: "The Bermuda Triangle—intersection in Bermuda, Ohio—and aphrodesiacs [sic]"

What's interesting about this rundown is the marginalization of the repertory players, who seem to have been conceived as background characters. Michaels refrained from spelling out for the network what he would later articulate as his countercultural comedy code: "knowing drug references, casual profanity, a permissive attitude toward sex, a deep disdain for show business convention, blistering political satire, and bitter distrust of corporate power." Nor did he say that he wanted to target "a book and movie audience." This was on purpose; he knew what the network wanted to hear. Craig Kellem, a CMA agent whom he'd hired to help book talent, studied Michaels in meetings and told him, "You're the only person I know who could be president of the United States." Michaels demurred (the Canadian thing), but recalls, "I didn't think I wasn't qualified. And it wasn't arrogance; it was just that I could speak about what I knew confidently." Kellem thought it was something more essential: "People wanted to be around him."

NINE

"A CRYPTO-BALLSY GUY"

ONE FRIDAY NIGHT IN THE OFFICE, DURING PRE-PRODUCTION, MICHAELS turned to Tom Schiller and asked if he had ever heard of a place called Bridgehampton. Edie Baskin, an L.A. friend whom he'd hired to be the show's staff photographer, was dating Paul Simon, and the couple had invited him to spend the weekend at a house Simon was renting. Michaels had asked how he should get there, and had been told, "Get a limo." Schiller looked up "limousines" in the Yellow Pages and ordered one.

At eleven that night, Michaels set off in the hired car with Schiller as his wingman. They arrived in Bridgehampton at around two. Simon had waited up. He and Michaels smoked a joint and spent the whole night talking. "The next day, I woke up and looked out the window, and there was the ocean," Michaels said. He hadn't expected beachfront; he had no idea what the Hamptons were, and had assumed, incorrectly, that it must be where Gatsby lived. Like Fitzgerald's outsider, Michaels increasingly seemed to possess what the author called a "heightened sensitivity to the promises of life."

Baskin had introduced Michaels to Simon, and they'd quickly bonded, one of the spontaneous mind melds that Michaels seemed to generate at will. He had been a fan of Simon and Garfunkel even before *The Graduate,* and Simon's solo record *There Goes Rhymin' Simon* was in heavy rotation on his turntable that year. Simon was a huge star, but the two men had a lot in common. Both had grown up in middle-class Jewish communities and had dodged their families' expectations of law school. They saw something karmic in the fact that Michaels grew up in Forest Hill, Toronto, and Simon grew up next to Forest Hills, Queens. Both were competitive and high-achieving in the way that men with low centers of gravity can be. Their first dinner together, at Chin-Ya, in an SRO called the Hotel Woodward, concluded in a classic New York moment: On the way out, they had to step around the police's chalk outline of a body on the lobby floor. Then, while walking home, Simon showed Michaels some baseball cards he had bought for his son Harper. They discovered that, as kids, they'd both played the game Farthies, tossing baseball cards on the sidewalk, trying to get their cards as close to the wall as possible. They stopped on West Fifty-seventh Street, divvied up the cards, and started tossing. There was an immediate ease between them. Simon had been going through a depression, and that summer, getting to know Michaels, who didn't treat him like a famous person, helped lift him out of it. Simon has always believed that he and Michaels communicate on a private comic wavelength.

Michaels's few off-hours that summer were spent in the studio where Simon was recording *Still Crazy After All These Years,* and he added, to his growing trove of showbiz stories, the one about how his friend Paul took the title of his song "Mother and Child Reunion" from the name of a chicken-and-egg dish on a Chinese menu.

He also added to his collection of celebrity friends. As well as sharing Michaels's office, Tom Schiller was sharing his apartment at the Osborne, sleeping on the sofa. Simon would drop by at all hours to talk or smoke a joint, and so would Mick Jagger, whom Michaels had somehow befriended. Schiller, who'd grown up around famous people in Hollywood, said, "I kept praying that Mick Jagger would leave so I could go to sleep on that couch."

When Michaels traveled to Ontario to see Uncle Pep and Aunt Joyce at their lake house, he brought Paul Simon along. He wanted to show off his new famous friend and also to tell the Levys about his new job in person. They sat on the porch and listened, and Pep gave the project his blessing. ("Pep was a teacher about family for him," Simon recalled. "And money and money management.") During the visit, Michaels took his twenty-year-old cousin Neil aside on the dock. They had a bond: neither wanted to work in the family auto-parts company. Neil's show-business experience consisted of having once brought a telephone to Ethel Merman at the '21' Club, where he'd worked in the coat check. But Michaels offered him $175 a week to come to New York and help with the show. In one sense he was repaying the Levys for the care they'd given him when he was young, and also paying it forward, setting in motion a pattern that would characterize his hiring practices for decades.

Neil ditched art school and took up residence on the sofa that Tom Schiller had recently vacated at the Osborne. Now it was his turn to be kept up at night, waiting for Mick Jagger to stop talking and smoking pot and go home; he remembers the singer holding forth about architecture. He recalled asking himself, "How does a guy like Lorne, with okay credits, but not famous—a nobody—how does he pick up with Mick Jagger and suddenly be friends?" The answer, he figured, was a combination of charisma and an ability to intuit what a person wants to talk about. "He always had an innate intelligence in terms of reading people and guessing right," he said. As Rosie Shuster put it, "He was more comfortable with celebrities than with regular people."

By this time Michaels had also befriended Candice Bergen, a bona fide movie star with a legendary showbiz father, Edgar Bergen, and a wooden showbiz brother, Charlie McCarthy. Michaels ad-judged her a perfect amalgam of Old and New Hollywood; her father had done radio broadcasts out of Studio 8H. Bergen had attended Truman Capote's Black and White Ball wearing a mink bunny mask by Halston, and, with her boyfriend Bert Schneider, the producer of *Easy Rider,* she'd been arrested for lying down in the Senate chamber to protest the Vietnam War. Thinking that she'd be an ideal guest host for his show, Michaels set up a meeting in her agent's office and ar-rived with a Betamax tape, a brand-new technology then. "He put the tape in the Betamax player, which he could barely work," Bergen said.

She hadn't heard about *Saturday Night,* but when she saw his magic reel (the calling-card clips of Python, "The Puck Crisis"), she was all in. "I'll do anything you want," she told him. She pegged him as "a crypto-ballsy guy; stealth ballsy."

Besides agreeing to host one of the first season's shows, Bergen widened Michaels's social circle. She introduced him to Buck Henry, the writer of *The Graduate, Catch-22,* and the TV show *Get Smart.* Michaels took Henry to the Russian Tea Room and did his spiel about the new program. It was unusual to book a mere writer on a variety show, but he asked Henry to host an episode. A well-read Ivy League graduate (Dartmouth), with a vinegary sense of humor and sterling comedy credentials (Mel Brooks, Mike Nichols, Steve Allen), Henry checked a lot of Michaels's aspirational boxes and would become an important adviser. Michaels marveled that Henry, with his seen-it-all sprezzatura, read several newspapers a day. "You could make a whole world out of what I didn't know back then," he said.

It didn't look that way to Neil Levy, now posted at Schiller's little assistant desk in his cousin's office. (Schiller had been promoted to the writing staff.) He'd listen as Michaels talked people into things over the phone. "He'd look at me to see if I was listening," Levy said. "He laughs easily, and he feeds you lines. So you feel good when you've made him laugh. People get off the phone feeling good."

TEN

SKETCHES, NOT SKITS

ON MONDAY, JULY 7, 1975, JUST OFF THE PLANE FROM L.A., AL FRANKEN and Tom Davis found themselves in the lobby of the RCA Building, a couple of stoners cowed by guards in uniforms trimmed with gilt braid. Waiting in line at reception, they heard a tall guy in front of them ask how to get to the seventeenth floor. It was Chevy Chase, also reporting for duty. They were headed to the show's first official staff meeting. When they got upstairs, they found a mishmash of writer types, plus Gilda Radner and Andy Kaufman. (He had been asked to be part of the enterprise in a vague way, and had taken to hanging around the office, unnerving staffers who weren't sure who the twitchy guy with acne was.) As the group that Michaels had spent three months assembling shuffled into his corner office, they did what comedy writers always do—they riffed on a news story. Ruffian, a champion racehorse, had been injured the day before in a race against the Kentucky Derby winner, Foolish Pleasure, and had been euthanized. A "second-bullet theory" was floated.

Michaels's manner was as loose as his agenda. "We've got to figure out what we're going to do here," he told his new staff. His only credo: "Let's make each other laugh, and if we do, we'll put it on television and maybe other people will find it funny." Chase got the first big laugh by standing behind Michaels's chair, pretending to sneeze loudly, and spraying the boss's neck with his plant mister.

Florence Lipowitz used to say that her son liked to bring home strays—whether it was an animal, a kid at school, or Rosie Shuster. The group he'd assembled bore that out. He'd been thinking of the show as similar to a magazine, a collection of distinct voices, and his writers covered the bases: one Westchester preppy, two avant-gardists, a pair of goofy collegiate types, a Borscht Belt tummler, and a venerated legend. Balancing it out was the arty California trio of Weis, Head, and Schiller. Anne Beatts said that Michaels's decision to hire the writers before the cast was a good sign—and an unusual thing in television. "I became a producer to protect my writing, which was being fucked over by producers," Michaels told them.

If he didn't have too many specifics about the show to share, he did have his comedy rules of thumb. He made it clear that performers would be expected to respect the writing, and that he wouldn't tolerate them ad-libbing—or, worse, cracking up or breaking character—onstage. That was the kind of unprofessional self-indulgence—milking the gag—that you'd see on *Carol Burnett,* a show that would become shorthand for things to avoid. There was an important matter of terminology, too: *Saturday Night* would feature "sketches," not "skits." Skits are one-joke bits done in grade school or by guys at the Rotary Club. A sketch is more complex; it's a vignette, with a beginning, middle, and end. Michaels also declaimed his views about realism in comedy. He explained that realistic sets and costumes, unlike silly, over-the-top ones, don't compete with the writing. And funny names—Walter Crankcase, Dan I'd-Rather-Not—would have no place in his show.

He brought up one matter of immediate practical business. The show wouldn't start airing for three months, but commercial parodies could be filmed early and banked. Zweibel raised his hand and asked if, besides parody ads, they could write sketches that were parodies of specific TV shows. Sure, Michaels said. One of his operating principles, he explained, was that his generation grew up being as familiar with television as French kids were with wine: any aspect of the medium was fair game.

O'Donoghue reeled off a list of notions that he'd been working on, including the high-concept visual idea of a bullet being fired from the inside of the television set and cracking the screen, leaving the image viewers saw fractured for the duration of the show. Many of his sketch ideas had to do with sea monkeys, or with badgers or wolverines, two species that he found especially funny. Other of his ideas were one-liners: "Cutting the Zen Master in Half," "Oven Mitts of the Gods." As ideas were pitched, Neil Levy scribbled them on colored index cards and pinned them to a bulletin board. Michaels, fussy about aesthetics, made him redo them in neater penmanship.

Ebersol attended the kickoff meeting too, wearing a Lacoste sport coat (alligator buttons), a pink shirt, and the only necktie in the room. He looked like a suit, and he talked like a suit. In a short address, he let everyone know that NBC would not tolerate any bad behavior. The writers assumed that this meant drugs, but the halls were already fragrant with weed. They ignored him.

As work got underway in the following weeks, the writers would drift into the office throughout the afternoon, forming little clumps and collaborating on sketches, which would be brought in and out of Michaels's office. He'd upended his habitual nocturnal schedule, arriving before noon to handle what he called "right-brain stuff"—the network—until the writers came in. He had a theory that writers automatically keep writing their last hit—the last successful thing they've done—until they're actively discouraged from doing so. "I thought, let everybody just keep writing that way," he said. "And then, out of boredom, or my prodding, gradually something will emerge that isn't what's already been done." He scribbled comments on script pages and suggested new pairings of writers. "Cross-fertilization started," he said. "And the people who were the most formed, like O'Donoghue—whose style had already become somewhat rigid—evolved."

Michaels was guided by what he regards as the Canadian idea of assembling a group where there is no rank. (He often references his Canadian-ness, but he also likes to say that it's hard to know what's uniquely Canadian, because Canadians talk about what's uniquely Canadian more than any other group.) "The people from design, the people from music, the people from film—no one would be more important than another," he said.

He didn't anoint a head writer, although Chase and O'Donoghue each claimed the title at times. At around seven each evening, the three of them, a self-appointed brain trust, would congregate in the corner office and write together. Michaels contributed not by dreaming up premises and punchlines, but by considering how a joke could be performed and how a sketch was paced—where the laughs were on the page, and how many there were. "I never saw Lorne writing," Chase said. "But I could hear it coming out of his mouth. He knew what was funny and why." The first time Chase lit a joint in this setting, Michaels looked up uneasily, caught between the feelings of being the boss and being one of the guys. "You can't smoke pot at Rockefeller Center," he said. Chase smirked and opened a window. O'Donoghue laughed and said, "Sure you can."

Michaels would always credit Chase and O'Donoghue with helping to create the show, emphasizing that it was not a "full-blown-from-Zeus sort of thing." Toward the other writers, each could project high-handedness that bordered on disdain. Michaels internalized a version of this quality that alternated between benign and aloof. His conception of the comedy he liked was similar to the way he conceived of himself: underplayed, with a light touch, never "sweaty" or trying too hard.

He instinctively sought the approval of O'Donoghue, both because of his literary pedigree and his ruthless devotion to a dangerous comic vision. And he looked up to Chase the way you would to a cool older brother. Chase had a breezy, athletic nonchalance. He grew up in New York and Massachusetts, in a family that had a listing in the Social Register and a country club membership. It went the other way, too. Colleagues noticed Chase starting to dress like Michaels, in Hawaiian shirts; he also signed with the boss's manager, Bernie Brillstein. O'Donoghue regarded Chase warily, even though he'd admired Chase's work on *The Lampoon Radio Hour*. "Chevy came from a preppy background, without so much ambition," Michaels said. "He had long hair and carried a purse—a leather satchel thing. He didn't have to care how he looked, but he was handsome. For Michael, it was very important how he looked. Chevy wouldn't have ever considered that he wouldn't be welcome somewhere. Michael, from upstate, had to invent a persona."

Dan Aykroyd, who hadn't been officially hired yet, dropped by the office wearing leather motorcycle gear; O'Donoghue looked him up and down and declared that he looked like "rough trade." (Aykroyd remembers the assessment in more detail: "Michael said, 'Aykroyd, you look like the biggest, ugliest leather queen I've seen since Rondo Hatton tried to fuck Montgomery Clift.'") O'Donoghue liked to figuratively brandish what he called "The Rod of Ridicule," a reference to a Zen master's *keisaku,* used to poke fidgety meditators. When he learned that Franken and Davis were splitting a salary of $350 a week, he told them, "That's what I spend every week to shine my cat's shoes."

Michaels had a more professorial style. He would listen to an idea and immediately have a critique. If a pitch was too elaborate, he would say "Premise overload." Once, when Schiller described an idea, he said, "Well, I like it for three reasons and I don't like it for four reasons." He conferred authority by talking.

Shuster described the months of preparation as an incubation period in which "everybody was kind of falling in love, and trying to crack each other up." Differences in class and style faded as people began to mesh. "That was the thing that I was smartest about," Michaels said. The writers figured out how to play off of each other, like jazz musicians.

But people had different ideas about what constituted collaboration. Early on, Garrett Morris came up with an idea for a sketch about liberal guilt, based on one of his plays, and ran it by Tom Schiller. Before he knew it, Franken had written up his idea as a piece called "White Guilt Relief Fund." Furious at being neither consulted nor credited, Morris determined to confront Franken. "I knew he would whup my ass," he said. (Franken had wrestled in high school.) "But I was going to make sure he remembered the fight." Heading off a physical confrontation, Michaels called Morris into his office and told him how much he had enjoyed his performance in *Cooley High*, a new film that Morris was in. He suggested that maybe Morris would prefer to be part of the cast, and not merely a writer, and urged him to audition in August, effectively kicking the conflict down the road.

During the summer, NBC haphazardly subdivided the big space on seventeen, and writers no longer had to share desks or sit on the floor. Like teenagers, they called the new spaces "rooms," not offices. O'Donoghue had his own room, which he kept fastidiously neat. He decorated his walls with a framed photo of the mass murderer Richard Speck and pinups from a niche porn magazine for amputee fetishists called *Stump Love*. He had his own bulletin board, with tidy rows of index cards, like the one in Michaels's office. Over a few weeks, Shuster and Schiller moved the cards a half inch to the right every night, so that, over time, they migrated off of the board and onto the wall. It drove O'Donoghue to distraction. Practical jokes were part of the culture: things were set on fire on colleagues' desks, and someone once removed all of the furniture from Franken and Davis's little office in the middle of the night. When they arrived the next day, they found a note that scared them silly; it read "See me. —Lorne." The joke hit two targets: the other was Herb Sargent, into whose office the stolen furniture had been crammed. Another time, when Michaels was talking to a reporter, Chase strolled into his office and pantomimed unzipping his fly and peeing on the desk.

As this kind of silliness was going on, Michaels spent most of his time in his orderly office. It exasperated him when his writers put out their cigarettes in his plants, but he thought the chaos outside his door was fertile chaos. Although he had envisioned a community without rank, everyone was driven to win his approval. The plaque declaring THE CAPTAIN'S WORD IS LAW was only partly a joke. Making him laugh was to earn a gold star. "You learned early on to distinguish Lorne's real laugh from his fake laugh," Laraine Newman said. "The fake laugh would be 'gasp gasp,' a kind of inhale. The real laugh would be his face totally crinkled up, his teeth bared, and a kind of a wheeze." Penelope Spheeris remembers a day when a group had gathered to watch a tape on a VCR, at that time a wondrous technology. People scrambled around on their knees, futzing with the tangle of wires at Michaels's feet until Gary Weis finally got the machine to function. "It was almost like he enjoyed us groveling," she said. "And that's the source of it all: everybody trying to please Lorne."

In the midst of the preparations, ABC finally aired the last of the Lily Tomlin specials that Michaels produced, the one with the clown film and the "Detroit City" opening. Reviewers were ecstatic. John J. O'Connor, in *The New York Times,* wrote, "I consider Miss Tomlin the most wonderful woman, bar none, on television. Her carefully rational treatments of all that is not rational, or all that is even insane in our various worlds, are unusual—often hilarious, sometimes sad, not infrequently both." A young critic at *The Washington Post,* Tom Shales, called it "one of the best comedy specials of the year," and chided ABC for sitting on it. The response bolstered Michaels's conviction that the world really might be ready for the new show that was slowly taking shape under his watch.

ELEVEN

NOT READY FOR PRIME TIME

AS MICHAELS PREPARED TO HOLD AUDITIONS FOR HIS REP COMPANY—THE final piece of preparatory business—he was feeling like he had things under control. The 11:30 P.M. Saturday time slot had always made him feel that he had a measure of safety. "It was literally a vacant lot on the edge of town," he said. The network wouldn't pay much attention or meddle, he figured, and the only competition at that hour was late-show movies. So it was demoralizing when, a few days after the first writers' meeting, he read in the *Times* that ABC had scheduled its own live variety series on Saturday nights, hosted by the sportscaster Howard Cosell. Michaels had heard rumblings about the ABC show, which would be broadcast in prime time and was being produced by Ebersol's mentor Roone Arledge with his old colleague Don Ohlmeyer. But he hadn't known that it was to be called *Saturday Night Live,* which is what he had been thinking of calling his own show. He kept his head down and got back to work, resolved to go with *Saturday Night,* Schlosser's original title.

The ABC show would compete with Michaels for talent, too, and Cosell had already nabbed a director that Michaels had his eye on. Then Brillstein pointed out that in live television, directing is mostly logistics: getting the show on and off the air on time. So they zeroed in on the best assistant director in town, Davy Wilson, whom Brillstein knew from a Muppets special. Wilson, forty-two, came in for an interview wearing a suit; when he saw Michaels's long hair and DRACULA SUCKS T-shirt, he thought he was sunk. A summer camp association (always a meaningful touchstone for Michaels) saved him. Wilson mentioned that the comedian (and potential host) George Carlin had been his bunkmate at camp, and he got the job.

The last task was to fill out the cast, and here Michaels again found that he was in competition with Cosell. NBC had given him a budget for six performers. So far, Michaels had only Radner, but he was fairly sure he was going to hire Newman and Aykroyd. Auditions for the other three slots were held on two sweltering days in August, at the top of the Steinway Tower on Fifty-seventh Street. More than two hundred applicants milled in the lobby next to the showroom full of grand pianos.

"Lorne was very buttoned-up and in control," Schiller recalled. When people came in, he said, "Welcome. What do you have for us?" Aykroyd, who still wasn't sure if he had been hired, showed up dressed like a British banker, with bowler hat and umbrella. Seeing the throng in the lobby, he headed straight up to the audition room, to say hi. He did a manic five minutes in the guise of an affronted gent ("I'm not going to wait anymore! I'm going to miss my plane!"). Bill Murray, a Second City alum who'd stood out on *The National Lampoon Radio Hour*, auditioned by doing a character that he called Honker, a lovable bum who talks out of one side of his mouth. Then he burst into song as a cheesy lounge singer. Murray had also tried out for the Cosell show, as had Jane Curtin, an all-American blonde, who auditioned for Michaels doing a bit about a cheerful housewife discussing domestic preparations for a tornado. And Garrett Morris, the writer who'd clashed with Franken, mesmerized the room, improvising a scene as a cab driver picking up Radner at JFK and driving her all over creation, jacking up the fare.

On the second day, Michaels received word from the crowded lobby that a guy was swinging a big stick around and scaring people. It was Belushi, who was irate at having to audition with the gang of hopefuls clutching copies of *Backstage*. (One of them was Meat Loaf.) But despite his antipathy for TV, he was determined to be on

Saturday Night. Four hours later, Belushi stomped into the audition room with his hair tied up in a topknot, and performed a character that he'd done at Second City, a Samurai billiard player. He brandished a wooden closet rod, emitting unintelligible grunts, rubbing his chin sagely and wagging his eyebrows. Every time it looked like he was going to erupt into violence, he'd swing the pole down and mime a difficult billiards shot. He had the room in hysterics. Michaels decided that anyone who could create such a stir in a television audition room couldn't be all that ambivalent about television.

Back at the Osborne after the second day of auditions, Michaels and his people discussed what they had seen. Belushi was a definite yes. O'Donoghue and Beatts pushed for Murray, but Ebersol wasn't sold. Although Michaels definitely wanted Aykroyd, somehow Aykroyd never got the signal that he was in (unclear signals would become a hallmark of Michaels's management style), and so, after the audition, thinking he'd failed, he drove across the country with John Candy and took a job with Second City in Pasadena. For the third woman, O'Donoghue and Beatts favored a dark-haired comedian named Mimi Kennedy, who'd sung a parody of Helen Reddy's "I Am Woman." (Hers was "I Am Dog.") Ebersol preferred Jane Curtin, whose fresh-faced Waspiness was a foil to Radner's Jewishness and Newman's more Bohemian style. "Jane looked like she belonged on television," Michaels said. "She had a face built for parody." He hired Garrett Morris, too. Besides a receptionist, Morris would be the only Black person working in the *Saturday Night* offices that season.

With his cast set, Michaels spent a few weeks leading them in improv workshops, hoping that they'd bond the way the writers had. The sessions didn't really jell, but one improv scene, about a group of befuddled aliens, would resurface later.

The cast and writers kept college-student hours. Michaels suspected that they stayed all night at the RCA Building because the office was nicer than their apartments. Schiller compared those months to living on a submarine. Others said a dorm, an army base, a huge "anti-NBC" playpen. The smell of pot mingled with the odors of the deli food that arrived in soggy Styrofoam containers at all hours from Pastrami 'n Things in the concourse downstairs. Neil Levy walked around doing magic tricks. Writers were known to pee in the kitchen sink, since the men's room was half a city block down the hall. As a foil to the anarchy and a bridge to the corporate side, Michaels hired Kathy Minkowsky, who had been Herb Schlosser's secretary, to work in his office. She found the air of misrule baffling.

Michaels likes to quote a psychiatrist who once told him, "Like neuroses vibrate together." It was not a coincidence, he believed, that several people in his original group had experienced the early death of a parent. Like him, Radner lost her father when she was fourteen; Bill Murray, who joined in Season Two, was seventeen when his father died; Chase lived with an erratic mother and difficult stepfather in a household where money was tight. "There's something about being stuck in the defiance of adolescence," Michaels said. "You're challenging authority."

He had produced shows before, but he'd never been the boss of a group of peers. "It was a family in formation," he said. "I made sure that everybody tried to be nice to each other." Although Michaels would become famous as a father figure, Anne Beatts considered his management style maternal; if he saw talent in people, he created the conditions for them to flourish. His businesslike calm was a counterbalance to the whirling egos and animosities that drove his employees. When he held forth about the principles of comedy, some found him mesmerizing, but some merely tolerated it. "I never really thought *he* was funny," Curtin said, "but I could sort of glean what he *thought* was funny, which was very wry, dry—not anything that you laugh out loud at." She pegged him as the type of comedy professional who, instead of laughing, "says, with a completely straight face, 'Hysterical.'"

SIX WEEKS BEFORE THE PREMIERE, MICHAELS STILL DIDN'T KNOW QUITE how he would fill sixty-six minutes every week (twenty-four minutes would be commercials). A fake newscast had always been part of his vision, and at the start, he expected to play the newscaster himself, the way he'd done on *The Hart and Lorne Terrific Hour.* He even screen-tested himself doing it. As the air date approached, he changed his mind. It would be awkward to cut other people's material while leaving himself in. That, he said, would be "a little too Orson Welles, even for me." And it would have required being vulnerable in front of his staff. "You have your hat in your hand when you're a performer," Newman said. "And that seems to be the thing that Lorne would want the very least in his life."

Chevy Chase was the one who was making Michaels laugh the most around the office, so, even though he'd been hired as a writer, Michaels tapped him to be the anchor of Weekend Update, as the segment would be called. Chase had made sure that everyone saw how funny he was. He fell down a lot, contriving ludicrous pratfalls almost daily. Michaels got Ebersol to push NBC to approve adding Chase to the cast, putting the number at seven. (Chase somehow avoided signing a contract as a performer, which would have consequences later.)

Herb Sargent, who had worked at the British show *That Was the Week That Was,* became Weekend Update's de facto head counselor. People would go into his office and ask, "Herb, where's Vietnam?" (Franken and Davis were the exceptions; they had a TV in their office, and they'd shush anyone who dared interrupt the news.) Sargent also showed the young writers such TV fundamentals as what a script should look like on the page—stage directions in single-spaced boldface caps, music and effects cues in all-caps on the left. The formatting was a challenge for O'Donoghue, whose sketches always had paragraphs-long blocks of stage directions that served the purpose of controlling all aspects of his pieces.

The first scripts to be ready were the commercial parodies, which were filmed during a hot week in late August in the suburbs north of the city. Michaels wrote two of them. One was a military recruitment ad, parodying a real spot made by the U.S. Marine Corps. Garrett Morris, in a dress uniform, walks down the street in search of, as a voiceover says, "a few good men." It's a gay joke. Schiller, in a flannel shirt, ambles by and takes the marine up on his pitch. They stroll away arm in arm, mugging salaciously. A fake luxury car ad was also shot, in which a mohel circumcises a baby in the back seat, proof of the vehicle's smooth ride. (Mercury had done a similar commercial with a diamond cutter.)

The outing felt like the kind of camp field trip that Michaels loved; he even took his shirt off in the heat. But filming the parodies was expensive; Don Carswell's budget had been ignored. Everything involving the show was turning out to cost more than expected. Even though the writers were being paid scale, Michaels had hired more of them than NBC anticipated. The executives continued to view the show as "Schlosser's Folly."

The budgets of NBC shows were overseen by unit managers, who reported to a vice president named Stephen Weston. A man with a military bent who kept a riding crop in his office, he was exasperated at the ways Michaels and his people refused to learn the procedures for filing expense reports or getting overages approved. Barbara Gallagher, a mild-mannered associate producer whom Michaels had hired (she was said to be the model for *The Mary Tyler Moore Show*'s Mary Richards), bore the brunt of the anger, and soon resigned. In protest, Michaels and his people stopped interacting with Weston's department altogether. That became Ebersol's role.

Several shows' worth of commercials shot on location were in the can, but Michaels was itching to get his people into Studio 8H. There were obstacles here as well. Michaels's designer, Eugene Lee, had been drawing up plans to renovate the space, which had been built in the 1930s as a radio studio to broadcast Toscanini's NBC Symphony Orchestra. After television basically moved west in the sixties, 8H had been a white elephant, used for game shows—including a *Name That Tune* rip-off hosted by Gene Rayburn called *Dough Re Mi*—and coverage of space launches. The studio was a strange oblong shape, which Lee compared to a shoebox. He wanted to build stages against the long side of the rectangle, across from a deep balcony; Michaels liked this idea, because it put the audience closer to the action. "With comedy," he said, remembering one of Bob Schiller's rules, "it's real important that there be that eye contact."

Everyone who walked into the RCA Building felt a reverence for its Deco splendor, but Lee's vision for the sets paid homage to a different aspect of the city. He wanted a "home base" stage that evoked a dingy Greenwich Village basement nightclub, an idea that jibed with Michaels's affinity for realism. Variety shows had for years been shot on vast stages with glossy floors and cyclorama walls. "They called it the Infinity Look," Michaels said. "But in '75 you had brownouts, paint peeling. The city was in a state of collapse." The New York that he wanted to evoke should have "the feeling of an old shoe." Lee called the look he was going for "urban decay." When Michaels saw what he had come up with, he was thrilled. "We weren't doing glamour," he said. "We weren't doing Fred and Ginger."

The NBC union crew was shocked when Lee ordered old bricks and planks of solid oak to build his home base. He wanted some swivel seats scattered on the studio floor, which would be movable to allow pathways for five cameras to shoot sketches on eight different stages. In the wide balcony he installed folding stadium seats, extras sourced from Yankee Stadium, which was in the process of replacing its old wood seats with ones made of fiberglass. Michaels worried that the bleachers, as they came to be called, might be uncomfortable to sit in, but their hometown provenance won him over.

Turning the raw cavity of 8H into Lee's vision caused the first impasse with NBC. Don Carswell balked at the cost, estimated to be almost $300,000. If 8H was good enough for Toscanini, he thought, it was good enough for this ragged bunch. Michaels took the matter to Herb Schlosser—a card he didn't play often. "I just thought, 'He wants this to be good. I want this to be good,'" he recalled. He and Ebersol and Lee lugged a four-foot-long model of the set down to Schlosser's office and plopped it onto his desk. Schlosser looked at it and said, "Well, what's the problem?" Michaels amazed Lee by talking Schlosser through the design as if he were a real estate agent, explaining how things interconnected, where the host would stand, etc. Schlosser was delighted. "You've got it!" he said. (The experiment ratified a lesson that Michaels has passed on to generations of employees: If you need to solve a problem, always talk to the highest-level person you can.)

Lee's designs called for elevated stages, like in the theater. It was important psychologically, Michaels felt, that performers be situated *above* the audience. The director, Davy Wilson, couldn't understand how that would work. Television cameras were hunks of heavy equipment that sat, immobile, on pedestals on the floor, with stools beside them for cameramen. With Lee's elevated stages, Wilson complained, he would have to be "shooting up." Michaels told him to figure it out. A McLuhan idea he liked ran through his thoughts: "You can't change something just by changing the contents of it. You have to change the shape."

Wilson's resistance reflected a divide between the talent and the crew. At the craft services table, the actors and writers nibbled crudités; the crew ate doughnuts. The backstage guys were older, from another time. From the start, Michaels had told NBC that he wanted everyone assigned to the show—lawyers, publicists, graphic designers, accountants—to be under thirty, but that demand wasn't practicable when it came to the 8H crew members, many of whom regarded Michaels's people as a bunch of stoners and high-handed amateurs. According to Doug Hill and Jeff Weingrad's 1986 book, *Saturday Night: A Backstage History of Saturday Night Live,* some old-timers started referring to the show as "The Children's Television Workshop." When rehearsals started, crew members were offended by the material; booing could be heard from the wings. Joe Dicso, the stage manager, later said that if crew members told Michaels that something was too difficult to execute, he wouldn't engage. "Lorne was full of 'exactlys' and 'ahhs' and 'of courses,'" Dicso told Hill and Weingrad. "'Ahh' meant he'd made a mistake. There were no apologies."

Michaels's young charges, however, soon came to realize that the old guys knew their way around. "When we saw the crew kick into action, it was a whole different thing," he said. "A crane was flying around the studio, cameras were moving. The 8H crew was the only one in New York that could do that."

Links to the studio's past surrounded them. When Howard Shore showed up for his first band rehearsal, he asked if there was a music stand anywhere, and an old-timer went into the props department and brought out Toscanini's elaborately carved podium. And Michaels looked to provenance when he hired an announcer for the show; he chose Don Pardo, who was pushing sixty and had been at NBC for thirty years.

Updating the Toscanini-era sound system for the kind of rock and roll bands that Michaels wanted provoked another skirmish. When Elvis Presley appeared on *Ed Sullivan,* he sang under a suspended microphone. "You couldn't have the music of our generation with just a boom mic," Michaels said. The network balked at the price of upgrading the technology to art-rock standards. "Because live television didn't have a reputation for good-quality sound, a lot of musical acts that we wanted to book were wary about doing the show," Shore said. "We were creating a new sound for live TV." Like the hosts, the musical guests were intended to be an index of cool. Rather than Top 40 stars like the Bee Gees or Barry Manilow, Michaels and Shore wanted FM radio darlings—Leon Redbone, Keith Jarrett, Sun Ra. Michaels also worried that, with an antiquated sound system, the studio audience wouldn't hear the sketches clearly and so wouldn't laugh, making the show look like a flop to the viewers at home. After some tussling, he got the sound upgrade approved.

NBC found Michaels to be a micromanager when it came to the studio audience, too. An internal memo between executives described Michaels's exacting yet vague directions for how to fill the seats with college kids: "Lorne cautioned against having too many students from one school as this might result in an imbalance of studio audience reaction." He insisted on "the 'right' kind" of audience, and he wanted a mechanism to deny tickets to people who were not "suitable."

ON SEPTEMBER 17, AS ELABORATE RENOVATIONS WERE UNDERWAY IN 8H, Michaels gathered his cast in a midtown studio to tape a series of screen tests. They had been horsing around on the seventeenth floor, but, astonishingly, he didn't have any idea of what they would look like on-screen. He taped the players individually, improvising or doing characters. Also in front of the camera were Andy Kaufman and Bill Murray; Michaels was still hoping to hire Murray, if Carswell could be persuaded to increase the budget.

In the tests, the cast members come off as a bit lost, unsure of where to look. Newman, in a blond wig, does her Valley Girl character, complaining about her Jewish boyfriend's parents: "I, like, made a peach cobbler, and I heard them say, 'Well, look. The shiksa made us a Presbyterian pie.'" A mustachioed Aykroyd demonstrates variations on his pitchman persona, one hawking "Lloyd Manganaro Deltoid Spray." (Michaels is heard off-screen, saying "Cleaner look," a facial-hair directive. He'd cut his own hair short by then.) Belushi does a suite of Brando impressions, including Don Corleone, achieved by stuffing his cheeks with toilet paper. Curtin offers a One A Day Plus Iron commercial as a woman who is worried that getting her vitamins through food could make her fat. Radner is the least assured of all, futzing in her seat before she finally announces, "I'm not going to talk about food." She then does what she called her "only character," a dimwit named Colleen, who, in every situation—at the ballet, losing her virginity—just stares blankly. Michaels, in the background, yells, "Gilda, that was great!"

Chase is the most at home in front of the camera. Wearing a polo shirt with the collar popped, he launches right into his cocky anchorman persona, delivering a report about a rare baby sandpiper just hatched at a zoo and then stomped by a baby rhino. He closes with a line cadged from *The Groove Tube,* "Good night, and have a pleasant tomorrow."

In his test, Andy Kaufman sits at a desk, wide-eyed and skittish, and recites "MacArthur Park," the AM-radio hit whose lyrics rival those of "Stairway to Heaven" in their rococo inanity. He closes his eyes as he intones, "Someone left the cake out in the rain. I don't think that I can make it. 'Cause it took so long to bake it. And I'll never have that recipe again. Oh—no." Michaels knew he wanted

Kaufman's radical novelty in the show. "It was as beautiful a thing as you could witness," he said. "He wasn't enmeshed in the show business of it—show business being that it was simply an act. There seemed to be some other commitment, something very pure and more personal about what he was doing. And it was simply arresting." Bill Murray was filmed crooning "Hey There" from *The Pajama Game* while playing air piano.

Off camera, Michaels can be heard telling the performers not to smile so much ("Less teeth!"). He wanted a level of naturalism that undercut standard show-business crowd-pleasing.

The screen tests reassured Michaels that his people would be funny on television, but all summer, as he worked out what he'd be putting on the air, he had been shadowed by a mysterious doppelgänger—the other variety show, hosted by Cosell, that had made off with his title. He thought of it as "the expensive version of what we were trying to do." He acted unconcerned, but it gnawed at him. Cosell, he'd heard, was desperate to bring the Beatles together for a reunion, and had even pitched the idea to John Lennon at the '21' Club.

A few days after the screen tests, *Saturday Night Live with Howard Cosell* debuted at 8:00 P.M. on ABC, and Al Franken and his girlfriend, Franni, threw a party in their rent-controlled apartment (formerly Al's grandmother's) on West Eighty-sixth Street to watch it with their new colleagues. Despite having just done a screen test for Michaels, Bill Murray had accepted a job in Cosell's rep company, which was called the Prime Time Players, along with his brother Brian Doyle-Murray, and Christopher Guest. (If the gig on Michaels's show came through, Murray was prepared to quit Cosell in a flash.) Any competitive feelings vanished the night of the premiere. Cosell's show was schlock, and it demonstrated one of Michaels's mantras: the music had changed.

Despite the talent in Cosell's cast, the performers were sidelined by a jumble of cornball acts simulcast live from around the world via satellite, all lashed together by Cosell's stiff, nasal introductions, beamed from the Ed Sullivan Theater. The episode's unfortunate guests included Frank Sinatra, Paul Anka, Shirley Bassey, the tennis pro Jimmy Connors (singing), the Bay City Rollers, Siegfried and Roy, and the cast of *The Wiz*. Don Mischer, the director, later called the show "one of the greatest disasters in the history of television."

Uptown at the Frankens', relief flooded the room, and everyone doubled down on their partying. Bill Murray, still hopeful, headed up to the party after he wrapped, and Franken greeted him by blurting his condolences for not making the cut on *their* show. Murray was crushed; he hadn't officially heard that news.

Cosell had made off with Michaels's title, but *Saturday Night* got its revenge. Chase wisecracked that Michaels should call his show *Saturday Night Live Without Howard Cosell*. But another in-joke stuck. At a meeting in Michaels's office to brainstorm names for the show's repertory company, ideas ranged from arty (the Group) to arch (the Saturday Night Repertory Theater Company). Herb Sargent never said much in meetings (O'Donoghue nicknamed him "the Boo Radley of comedy"), but that day he scribbled something on a pad that became the winner: "The Not Ready for Prime Time Players." Besides jabbing Cosell, it encapsulated the Canadian self-effacement that was Michaels's trademark.

MICHAELS'S PLAYERS WEREN'T QUITE READY FOR LATE NIGHT YET EITHER, but on October 4, a week before *Saturday Night*'s premiere, NBC filled the empty 11:30 Saturday slot with a special edition of *Tomorrow*. Tom Snyder started the show with a long interview with Jerry Lewis, and then devoted the final fifteen minutes to introducing Lorne Michaels and his cast. Ebersol, under pressure from NBC to get some promotion going, had insisted that the group participate. The result was an apt encapsulation of the cultural changing of the guard that was about to occur: Lewis, who had closed his recent muscular dystrophy telethon by dropping his tuxedo pants, represented everything about show business that Michaels hated: the bathos of fake sincerity.

"Before we start, I just want to say that I thought Jerry was *won-*

derful," Michaels tells Snyder, as the segment begins. There's a disingenuous glint of mischief in his eye, and his cast, around him, snorts in agreement. They sit, fidgeting, in a circle of chairs. Chase is loose, looking like the guy who invented manspreading. Michaels, wearing his reindeer sweater and Stan Smiths, does most of the talking. In his practiced way, he dodges questions about what the show will be. "What shall we look for?" Snyder asks. Michaels answers, "Anxiety." After he introduces the players, he undersells them, to quasi-comic effect: "We've got eight"—perhaps he was counting himself?—"and we're hoping for two to really work."

"I clearly had something to prove," he said later of the segment, "but I went back and forth, as I normally do, between 'I think it's gonna be great' and 'Oh my God, it's gonna be awful.'"

Concerned about ratcheting up expectations, he had resisted doing advance publicity. When NBC placed a newspaper ad that claimed "This is a big one! Don't miss the exciting premiere of a new series that's a whole new dimension for TV!" Michaels picked up the phone and got the publicist on the show reassigned.

But the network wasn't about to let the show premiere with no fanfare. To drum up interest, Michaels was pressured to publicly announce his first seven hosts. At a boardroom meeting (still an alien environment for him), he told a table full of programming people who he had lined up: George Carlin, Paul Simon, Rob Reiner, Candice Bergen, Robert Klein, Lily Tomlin, and Richard Pryor. Dave Tebet had continued to offer blandly conventional host suggestions, and Michaels continued nodding politely, in a manner that Bergen described as "silky." He was protective of his picks, who'd gamely signed on to an unknown entity. The executives pushed back hard on Pryor, who had a reputation for being an unpredictable cokehead. (The NBC page he'd tussled with on the Flip Wilson set had sued.)

"First it was 'You can't have him. He's going to say "fuck" on the air,'" Michaels recalled. He assured them that Pryor was a friend, that he knew the rules and what was at stake. The network dug in. "Then I said, 'Well, I'm not doing the show. I can't do a contemporary comedy show without Richard Pryor.' It elevated the importance of what we were doing in comedy." (In retrospect, he said, "I can't believe how deadly serious I was then.") After some backroom lobbying by Ebersol, the network relented, and Michaels agreed to its demand that the Pryor show be aired with a ten-second tape delay, so that if he said something obscene, it could be bleeped.

Michaels sleepwalked through much of the mandated promotion. In a press release explaining why he'd asked George Carlin to host the first show, he took a swipe at corporate ideology: "He's punctual and he fills out forms well." But Carlin was not his first choice. Carlin, Michaels later said, "was slightly older than us, a little more jazz-influenced, a little different music." Tom Smothers was the person he wanted as the inaugural host, but Smothers had said no; he was still too angry at TV. Paul Simon would seem to have been the natural choice, but Michaels felt that asking his new friend to carry the premiere was out of the question. He is a believer in the first-pancake theory. "I thought it might be a disaster," he said. "And it's always been a strategy of mine to try to make the second show 'hotter' than the first, because you want the ratings and the word of mouth to go up, and I thought Paul could do that."

Several days before the premiere, Herb Schlosser took the elevator up to 8H to see how his pet project was coming along. He looked at Eugene Lee's central stage—home base—which featured a flight of rickety wooden stairs, a corroded pressed-tin ceiling, a sign from the old BMT subway line, doors covered with peeling paint, and a ratty Oriental rug. He was flummoxed. Perhaps he hadn't examined the architectural model carefully enough. "Is the work still in progress?" he asked. Michaels calmly explained that the set looked that way on purpose—the idea was urban decay. "That's what cost the money," he said. Schlosser, maintaining a genial "kids today" attitude, took it in stride.

PART THREE

WEDNESDAY

"Rounding! Rounding!" It was 4:15 P.M., and the young women seated at the row of assistants' desks outside Michaels's office were urgently repeating the word into their phones. In the SNL lexicon, "rounding" is the signal that read-through is about to begin. The call went out to every department—writers, talent, music, design, wardrobe, makeup—to assemble in the writers' room. Wednesday is the day when the contours of the week's show emerge; from a lot of amorphous goofing around, sketches materialize.

Until read-through, the seventeenth floor is quiet on Wednesdays. The writers and cast are home napping and showering, having stayed overnight at the office finishing sketches. Many of them find the all-nighter tradition stupid, a vestige of a distant coke-fueled era. (Will Ferrell thought there was a logic to it at first; since the show is on at 11:30, "maybe it just gets you on a late-night schedule, so you're not tired," he said. "Then someone told me, 'No. It's just completely arbitrary.'") The stress gets most intense at around 7:00 A.M., when the exhausted writers hear the *Today* show's audience cheering on the sidewalk below, triggering deadline anxiety. Soon they have to hand over their scripts. The rest of the staff is conserving energy for the big push to come, the stepping-on-an-accelerator sensation that happens right after the read-through.

For most of Wednesday, Michaels takes calls from home, and he arrives at the office around three. That day, several cartons were stacked by his door with labels reading BUDD SHIRTMAKERS, from Piccadilly Arcade in London. The shop, which specializes in cotton batiste pajamas, at 345 pounds a pair, is a regular stop for Michaels and Jimmy Fallon, who make a regular pilgrimage to Wimbledon together in July. "I ordered pink pajamas from Budd for the *Mean Girls'* Broadway cast," Michaels explained. The pajamas were a custom order, and the tailors had got some detail wrong, so the boxes were heading back across the Atlantic.

Michaels has developed something close to a theology of gift-giving. (Getting cut from the gift list is like excommunication.) On birthdays and holidays, cast and favored employees receive carefully curated luxuries that are designed to up their games, to usher them into the good life. "Lorne has this level of personal taste that really sets him apart from other people," Conan O'Brien told me. "It was an education." For their first birthday on the payroll, an upper-level employee might get crystal glasses from Simon Pearce; the next year might be an Apple Watch or a Fitbit. Then there are Pratesi sheets; T. Anthony luggage; Sulka silk pajamas (he sent a pair to the writer Tom Davis as a wedding gift, with caviar, a bottle of Cristal, and a note reading: "Dear Tom—Now, more than ever, it's important to look good in bed"), K2 skis, high-end gadgets such as Roombas, and rare printings of Mark Twain; for Mike Nichols's birthday, a first edition of *Howards End*; one year, Fallon got bespoke shoes from a London cobbler. There are Yankees tickets, Knicks tickets, tickets to Rolling Stones concerts. (O'Brien said, "He'd never give you the Bose headset that everybody gets everybody.") The presents Michaels gives his protégés can have a lordly whiff of tutelage, but his latest stock holiday gift—wild blueberries and jam from his property in Maine—is the ideal thing to give fellow plutocrats, who can buy all the Pratesi sheets they want. Gifts are accompanied by a card with a carefully composed message, typed by an assistant. The writer Paula Pell can recite the note that accompanied the flowers Michaels sent after her knee-replacement surgery: "Can't wait for you to be on your knees again soon." John Mulaney cherishes a birthday email from Michaels that ended with the words "I appreciate you." Mulaney said, "I thought, 'That's all I ever wanted.'" Thank-you notes count for a lot. Michaels's files contain one from Mick Jagger, reading, "Dear Lorne, Just a note to thank you for the wonderful birthday gift of the thermometer."

———

DOZENS OF STAFFERS STREAMED INTO THE WRITERS' ROOM FOR READ-through. A large space, it was dominated by a gray formica expanse of four big tables pushed together. Microphones hung from the ceiling, to amplify the performers' voices. The table appeared to be set for a large dinner party, but instead of plates and cutlery, at each place was a thick slab of scripts bound by a rubber band, one for each cast member. Trays of sandwiches, platters of salad, cookies, and bottles of water covered the table, fuel to get the group through the next three-plus hours of a forced comedy march. (New people don't touch the snacks. Kristen Wiig said she "didn't eat a morsel of food at read-through for the first few months.")

Lined up on the east side of the room were rows of chairs, a fat script packet on each one. As at the Monday writers' meeting, seats are assigned. By 4:30, the room was jammed, quiet but for the sound of script pages being riffled. The host and cast had had about an hour to familiarize themselves with the sketches before the read-through—time to work up a Slovakian accent, say, or an impersonation of Howie Mandel. The music people had pulled together snatches of canned music and sound effects, according to cues in the scripts. From the back of a door a toy basketball hoop dangled. Jonah Hill arrived and sat at the head of the table, toting a large iced coffee and a gallon-sized plastic water jug. Read-through is a strain on the bladder.

Michaels arrived last and quietly took his seat beside Hill, with Steve Higgins to his left. Kenan Thompson, the cast's elder states-man, sat, per tradition, on the other side of the host. As soon as Michaels sat, he began to read aloud the title and stage directions of the first sketch. This is his read-through role. He does it in a businesslike way, mumbling, impatient to get to the performances. Often as he reads, his mouth is full of edamame or Doritos. There is no commenting as the group works through the packet of scripts. "My favorite Lorne is read-through Lorne," Seth Meyers told me, noting that it's the one time of the week when Michaels is completely open. "I've been to plenty of them where he sat stony faced for the full four hours. But when he's surprised, he has one of the great laughs, a real head-back, mouth-open thing."

The first script, for the cold open, had four writers' initials at the top. It was a Fox News report about Barack Obama making a surprise appearance at a rally for the Black congresswoman Maxine Waters. Michaels read:

(CUT TO: RALLY STAGE. EXTRAS WEARING BLUE HATS AND HOLDING SIGNS STAND BEHIND A PODIUM. IT LOOKS LIKE A TRUMP RALLY EXCEPT FOR THE BLUE. LESLIE AS MAXINE WATERS STANDS OFF TO THE SIDE. CHRIS AS BARACK OBAMA IS AT THE PODIUM. HE LOOKS DISHEVELED, WITH A LOOSENED TIE, MESSY HAIR AND A STAINED SHIRT.)

The premise is that Obama is trying to beat Trump at his own game, acting unhinged and spewing lies to whip up voters. *"People are saying that Republicans are building a T-shirt cannon that shoots immigrant babies!"* Chris Redd, as Obama, shouted. *"When an immigrant baby is born, they want to put it in this cannon and—whomp!—shoot that baby back across the border."*

The piece got a few laughs, but everyone knew that, by Saturday, it would be replaced with something timelier. Michaels refers to this ongoing process of tweaking day by day as "making rolling decisions." A high-energy cold open is important to him, and he often has the writers start from scratch on Friday or even Saturday. The idea is, if you begin the show with a home run, then momentum will carry through the next ninety minutes.

Next came Jonah Hill's host monologue, his induction into the Five Timers Club. They'd gone with the women-only conceit. The male Five Timers have been banished—a #MeToo joke. The script has Scarlett Johansson greeting Hill by using a little gun to implant an electronic chip behind his ear. "Ow, what was that?" he asks. "That chip is a tracking device in case the show needs you for a political impression," she explains. Hill asks what the women talk about in the lounge—"Equal pay?" *"Bo-ring,"* Johansson says, and explains that they make prank phone calls. Then Tina Fey calls Kyle Mooney, pretending to be Lorne with an idea. "Let's meet in your favorite place," Fey, in a Lorne voice, says. "Your mama's *big old ass.*" Mooney pauses then shouts, "Oh my God, Tina. Stop!" When Hill finally gets his Five Timers jacket, it's a girly sequined bolero. The reaction in the room was positive.

There were thirty-eight sketches to read. The first one to get a big laugh came ten minutes in—"Benihana," the fourth installment of Hill as a precocious six-year-old bothering fellow diners at a hibachi grill. Leslie Jones, as his babysitter, shrieked when he read the line "I like my coffee like I like my nannies, black and bitter." When Hill, as the little boy, says, "You know why divorce costs so much? Because it's worth it!" Michaels, who has been married three times, cracked up. ("When Lorne laughs, he looks like he's in pain," Amy Poehler says. "Which I enjoy.")

At read-through, Michaels laughed at almost everything Kenan Thompson did. A TV show parody called "America's Got Talent: Wait For It!" featured colossally unpromising contestants who then turn on a dime and suddenly wow the judges. Thompson is a man in a coma who, when he hears the opening bars of "Ain't No Mountain High Enough," tears off his hospital gown and belts. At the table, the way Thompson made his eyes pop to simulate waking provoked the most coveted Michaels reaction: he removed his glasses, shoulders heaving, and put his head down on the table in surrender.

The writers had delivered on the request for election material. One high-concept sketch by Jost centered on a right winger (Hill) dressed for Halloween in a big map of America made out of foam. It had some funny lines, but felt didactic, like a political cartoon. A parody commercial for a sleeping pill took a shot at Trump's press secretary, Sarah Huckabee Sanders, answering the question: How does she sleep at night? When Aidy Bryant, as Sanders, delivered the line "Before Tylenol Huckastrength PM, my brain was full of dreams, like me sittin' in a hot tub smoking cigars with the devil," the room exploded in laughter. Bryant was also at the center of another pre-tape script, an ad for an amateur political musical created by self-important drama students. "We don't have to do a thing, but *siiiing!*" she trilled.

Late90s, the promised sequel trailer to Jonah Hill's *Mid90s,* came up. It was basically a list of goofy pop culture references to the end of that decade: Heelys sneakers, Sisqó, glowsticks, the Y2K bug, Craig Kilborn, Tamagotchi. It got a few laughs, but Michaels, who was a teenager in the late fifties, did not react.

Weekend Update jokes are written on Friday and Saturday, but a few Update features (character monologues) are usually prepared for Wednesday's read-through. These are guest slots, sometimes filled by recurring characters, like Gilda Radner's Roseanne Roseannadanna in the early seasons, or David Spade's "Hollywood Minute" guy or Bill Hader's hypersexed and coked-up nightclub reviewer, Stefon. Appearing on Update, Michaels tells new cast members, can be a way to forge a connection with the audience, in part because they look directly into the camera and often say their own names. Adam Sandler broke out this way when he started performing silly guitar songs on Update. (The first one, "The Thanksgiving Song," went: "Turkey with the gravy and cranberry / Can't believe the Mets traded Darryl Strawberry / Turkey for you and turkey for me / Can't believe Tyson gave that girl V.D.")

At this read-through, there was a weak Update feature with Kate McKinnon as Benjamin Franklin back from the grave, wondering whether the Republic will survive Donald Trump. Michaels had hoped that she'd reprise her impression of Angela Merkel, who had just announced that she was stepping down, but McKinnon, who plays the chancellor as a peppy schoolmarm in a bowl cut ("In America you call it the Alt Right; in Germany we call it why Grandpapa lives in Argentina now"), considered the occasion too sad to joke about.

Thompson did his Big Papi to raucous glee. Michaels barked with pleasure when Papi described the ad he does for vaping pens: "*Juul*: if you walk around sucking on a vape pen, *Juul* look like an idiot!" The read-through's most successful Update feature was by Melissa Villaseñor, who, in Michaels's estimation, "had not popped yet." Her character this week was "Every Teen Girl Murder Suspect on *Law and Order*."

Twenty sketches in, there was a fifteen-minute bathroom break.

Back at the table, the second half kicked off with a self-referential sketch called "Pete's Heart," about Pete Davidson's personal life. He got a big laugh with the opening line, "I don't know if you know, but I was engaged to Ariana Grande." Davidson's voice emanated from a voluminous hoodie. The gag was that Davidson unburdens himself to Jonah Hill about how he and Grande rushed into things—and then he and Hill fall instantly in love. They get matching tattoos, marry, and adopt an African village and an elephant, who mauls Davidson after the marriage goes south. Cut to Pete doing physical therapy and bumping his walker into Betty White's; the final shot is Davidson and White making out. The people in the room liked it.

The idea about the ventriloquist with his hand stuck inside someone—the only pitch from the Monday writers' meeting that made it to read-through—died at the table, despite a committed performance by Leslie Jones. She was extraordinary in a sketch about a dinner-party host who argues with a guest over which of Weezer's albums is the best. Her performance "took it off the page"—a phrase Michaels learned from Bob Schiller, the *I Love Lucy* writer. "Bob used to say that about Lucy," he said. "She'd make the script so much funnier."

As the read-through reached the three-hour mark, laughs began to morph into yawns. (Anxious writers call this stretch of the afternoon Death Row.) Listening to thirty-eight sketches in one go, it becomes apparent that the show leans on a handful of tropes. There were two dinner-party sketches, two about theater, two based on TV news shows. One, called "KCR News," had Hill as a loser barging into the TV station where his girlfriend, Cecily Strong, is a weather girl. The other, "Live Interview," was a *Dateline*-style show where Bryant interviews a murder suspect distracted by two audience members who look exactly like Beavis and Butt-Head. As for ad parodies, besides the sleep-aid piece, there was an infomercial for a boutique that sells wigs for pet pugs. And two sketches were set in classrooms. One, called "Teacher Fell Down," was the first piece submitted by a new writer named Alison Gates. In the sketch, a slow mood piece, McKinnon played a teacher who has fallen on the floor and turns philosopher before her skeptical pupils ("Teacher's on the ground, everything's different; are we okay?" she asks, dreamy as a Tennessee Williams heroine.) The room gave its attention to the rookie writer's work, and McKinnon nailed it.

Close watchers of SNL know that the final sketch of the show—known as the "ten-to-one sketch"—is often a weird, even avant-garde piece. (Some writers call it the "Jack Handey slot," in honor of the former writer whose contributions, including "Deep Thoughts," were underpinned with a silly surrealism.) The ten-to-one slot is likely where the sketch most admired by a comedy purist will go. But if a sketch is put last (or even late) in the running, the odds increase that it will be cut during the live broadcast, as the show inevitably "spreads" and segments run longer than anticipated. (That's why writers in some eras referred to the ten-to-one slot as "Death Valley.") "Teacher Fell Down" had the experimental feel of a ten-to-one sketch.

Also vying for that slot at read-through was "Montreal Motorcycle Club," a lark about five weekend warriors waxing metaphysical in Quebecois accents while riding their choppers to see fall foliage. A sketch called "Craigslist Sale" provoked a collective gasp because it ventured into edgy territory: a car-shopping couple meets a guy selling a used white van covered in hate-speech placards—the very same van that had turned up on the news as belonging to the guy who was sending pipe bombs around. Alex Moffat read the part of the guy selling the van with skeezy exactitude.

When all the sketches had been read aloud, four hours and fifty-two minutes later, people shouted "Good table!" Overall, Hill had a solid read-through. His idea about a movie theater that served pretentious cuisine got a few laughs. ("The chef is doing a butter-poached halibut with a side of Sour Patch Kids, if that sounds scrummy to you.")

The room emptied and the carpet was slippery with pages from discarded scripts—almost forty thousand sheets of paper. Some of the production assistants who'd had seats on the fringes timidly approached the table to cadge scraps of leftovers.

It was after nine o'clock. Michaels went to his office and picked at a takeout dinner of shrimp and rice that an assistant had arranged on a china plate. His core group—Erin Doyle, Caroline Maroney, Erik Kenward, Steve Higgins, some senior writers—drifted in to assess what they had just heard. This is the meeting at which Michaels "picks the show," in SNL jargon. As his people settled, Michaels told a story about the time he and Paul Simon took their sons trick-or-treating and had gotten dressed up themselves—as Batman and Robin ("Don't think I've ever been as famous in my life").

The post-read-through culling session is one of the two most crucial meetings of the week. It's when Michaels says no to more than two-thirds of the material his staff has generated. The reaction around the table counts for a lot. "That's an honest room," Dana Carvey has said, of read-through. (In the late-eighties, in an attempt to neutralize perceived favoritism, the writer Robert Smigel lobbied to remove writers' initials from read-through scripts. Michaels tried it out, but reverted to the old way. Smigel, he felt, had "no poker face," and writers, he knows, want the credit.) The bulletin board on his wall is divided into three columns, with the headers 11:30, 12:00, and 12:30. Thirty-eight index cards were pinned up along the side. Most were blue, but ideas for pre-taped pieces were on yellow cards. The musical act's two songs are on pink cards, and eight white cards labeled COMMERCIAL are scattered amid the columns. The core group goes through the sketches one by one, while the laughs are still fresh. The winnowing process is repeated several times over the course of an hour, until around a dozen blue and yellow cards are left on the board.

The sketches that make it are not necessarily the funniest. Other factors inform the choices: What will make the host happy? What group of pieces will work within the physical constraints of Studio 8H? Does everyone in the cast have something to do? Are there "tonnage" issues? (Too much scatalogical humor? Too much Trump?) Are there enough sketches that will play in all fifty states? Is there enough topical material? Michaels has said that, in the culling meeting, he is always trying "to find enough colors to make a rainbow."

He stood and looked at the board. "There's a lot of stuff," he said, approvingly. Some weeks, he struggles to assemble a show; his staff has been hearing him complain, "I don't have a fucking first act!" for five decades. If things are still bleak toward the end of the week, he'll ask writers if they've been saving any good stuff for an upcoming host, telling them, "Sometimes you have to burn the furniture."

Going in order, he started on the cards. "I thought the Obama rally could play," he said, but added that he didn't have faith in Chris Redd's untested Obama impression. "If we had Jordan Peele doing Obama, it'd be great." He moved on to Hill's Five Timers monologue, which he pronounced "mostly there." He said, "There are beats," meaning serviceable jokes.

"Jonah loved Five Timers," Lindsay Shookus, the talent coordinator, said, adding that he had a couple of suggestions to fine-tune "his voice." "Can I go ahead and try to get the women? Tina, Scarlett, Candice, Drew?" she asked, and added that Melissa McCarthy was in Chicago visiting her parents.

Michaels dinged the next card, a sketch about a royalty-obsessed news show. "Although the accents were slightly better than the French Canadian motorcyclists' were," he said.

Everyone laughed, and Jost asked, "Can they take *away* your Order of Canada?" Michaels received the Order, an honor akin to a knighthood, in 2002. His Canadian-ness is an ongoing source of wisecracks. Jost was parroting a familiar Michaels put-down. When a sketch is going badly on air, Michaels will often look at its writer and say, with weary derision, "Can they take *away* the Emmy?"

Next. "Benihana we're doing," Michaels said. "God, he's funny doing that." Next: "America's Got Talent made me laugh. Anyone else?" "Yeahs" all around. Next: America Map. "It was elaborate and smart in a certain kind of way." Michaels went on, speaking more diplomatically than usual. "But I don't know whether it competes at the level of the other pieces in play." He paused. "Whose sketch is it?"

It seemed likely that he knew that the writer was Colin Jost, one of his pets. Jost said, with only a touch of defensiveness, "Me." He wasn't going to argue for his piece. (Pushing for your own sketch is "not part of our code," Michaels says.) The card went in the trash.

When it comes to pieces about the news, Michaels often says, "Clever is overrated. It's better to be good than clever."

"How are you all on Political Musical?" Michaels asked, eyeing the board. Kenward worried that it was too close to a black box theater sketch they'd done recently. Michaels said, "I like how dumb it was."

Kenward said, "We should talk about it"—standard code to express doubt.

"It made me laugh," Michaels said firmly, pinning the card to the board.

Hill was waiting outside the door to join the meeting, but first Michaels wanted to discuss *Late90s*. "It had style, but I just don't know," Michaels said. "The movie's in, like, three theaters?"

"The sketch is up its own ass a little bit," Shookus said.

Hearing his doubts echoed so bluntly, Michaels retreated. "Well, it *is* a freestanding piece," he said. "And all those references are funny."

Part of every week's calculation is determining how far to go in servicing the host. In Amy Poehler's first season, the host wanted to play a role that Poehler had written for herself. "Lorne called me into his office and asked me what I thought," she said. "My sketch was on the bubble. I remember thinking: 'Is this a test? Should I stand up for myself?'" She realized that if the host didn't get to be funny, she probably wouldn't push for the sketch. "I learned that picking battles is important here," Poehler said. "And that the show is a marathon, not a sprint." She rewrote the piece so that both she and the host got to be funny. When David Spade was new, he had an excruciating phone call with the host David Bowie, one of his idols; Bowie wanted to play Spade's regular role as Dick Clark's receptionist in a recurring sketch, rather than be the straight man. Spade pushed back and Bowie hung up on him. Lesson: "Don't give the host nothing," Spade said.

At this point, Jonah Hill joined the others in Michaels's office, carrying a takeout container. "That was the most *joyous* experience ever!" he said. Michaels waved him to a chair and turned back to the board.

"What's 'Dinner Party'?" Michaels asked. When he has to be re-minded what a sketch is, it usually doesn't get picked. Dinner Party wasn't. "Craigslist Sale?"

"I like that!" Jost said. There was discussion about how to handle the reveal of the white van covered with hate-speech stickers.

Kent Sublette, a writer, was worried. "Is it too *chilling* to see the van? Don't you think people will go, 'Yecch'?"

"If it doesn't work, the audience will let us know," Higgins said, meaning that, during dress rehearsal, they'd determine whether the piece "chilled" the audience.

"It's really funny," Michaels said. "I'm slightly worried that Alec"—he meant Baldwin, who was on the pipe bomber's list—"might freak out." But the card stayed.

Next was "Teacher Fell Down." Everyone liked the combination of McKinnon's bravura performance and the chance to showcase their new writer, Alison Gates. It stayed.

"Pete's Heart" was next, and Hill raised his hand, a serious look on his face. "Can I say something about that?" he asked. "I understand the super value of the joke that Pete posts about our relationship right away. But the part about us kissing and becoming a couple—I don't know." The first time Hill hosted SNL, in 2008, he was in a digital short called "Dating Andy's Dad," in which he falls for Andy Sam-berg's father, played by the fifty-six-year-old writer Jim Downey. The piece, which shows the pair snuggling on a pier and sloppily snog-ging, went viral. But this time, Hill didn't want to make out with Pete Davidson. Wouldn't it be just as funny if Davidson merely overre-acted to his new friendship—"He's posting, 'Jonah is the rock of my life!' And I'm like, 'Dude, I hardly know you.'"

Jost jumped in. "But if you go only as far as *friendship,* will it read? Versus going to *making out* right away." Kenward agreed: "It only works if it's, like, marriage."

Hill spelled out his objection. "To me, the joke that we're two straight guys being gay doesn't seem that tight right now," he said. "I mean, how *funny* is that, really? *'We're gay!'*"

The mood shifted; no one in the room wanted to get into a debate about wokeness. Michaels said, "There's only so many filmed pieces that we can do, so let's move on." The sketch was dropped. A piece about touchy-feely French guys was nixed (accent tonnage). Michaels preferred the Quebecois motorcycle gang, even though it presented technical challenges. Part of the joke was that the riders keep changing formation as Hill gets splattered with maple sap and jumped by a wolf.

Hill chimed in to critique how the writers had executed his idea about movie-theater dining: "The joke that it's *world-class food* needs to come in sooner. Like it's an Alice Waters restaurant."

Michaels barreled on. "'Dog Infomercial'?" he asked. Tom Broecker, the costume designer, said he thought they could come up with better celebrities to base the dogs' wigs on. "The less words the better," Higgins said. "All you want is the pugs in wigs."

Michaels asked Erin Doyle how she felt about the piece. She sometimes functions as the group's conscience, flagging jokes that the audience could find offensive. "It might be problematic," she said, suggesting that viewers might think that the dogs were being mistreated.

The others scoffed and piled on. Jost said, "Well, you'd have to *staple* the wigs onto their heads." Someone else said that they'd "have to use a hammer and nails." Jost went one better: "We can just buy dead pugs and then move them around on sticks! No one could complain, because they'd already be dead!"

Doyle giggled, and the piece was safe. Michaels looked at the board. Live Interview, the Beavis and Butt-Head sketch, was next. The card stayed. "Sleep-Aid Ad made me really laugh," he said. "Just people saying to the press secretary, 'How do you sleep at night?'" He suggested rewriting it without using the brand name Tylenol (a potential advertising conflict). When Michaels gets to a sketch that he doesn't like, he'll say, "Anybody?" The next three cards went in the trash. But he was high on Melissa Villaseñor's Update feature, the teen murder suspect. "What could go wrong?" he said.

"Straight to air," Doyle added, a line reserved for the rare piece that looks like a shoo-in.

The group, some of whom had been up for thirty-six hours, was losing steam. Three more sketches were quickly rejected. "What's 'Neighbors'?" Michaels asked.

Several excited voices answered at once: "Weezer!" Hill said, "Leslie screaming about Weezer was super funny." Michaels wasn't having it. He felt that it was in the same outlier category as Montreal Motorcycle Club. "We have to pick just *one* of those," he said. Hill voted for Motorcycle. The others were not prepared to let the Weezer piece go so easily. Kenward said, strategically, "Leslie loves it, FYI."

The cards having been run through once, the next phase of the discussion concerned how well the sketches still standing served the individual players, and whether anyone was "light" in the show. Hill, as a Five Timer, knew that pleasing the host was part of the mandate; he spoke up for his *Late90s* idea. Michaels gently explained the conundrum: "How do you make it work as *not* dependent on people knowing that it is a sequel to your movie?"

"Yeah," Hill said, reading the room. "If it doesn't work, then fuck it."

Michaels turned from the board and said, "Shall we bring the others in now?" Maroney opened the office door and a dozen more people filed in—music, design, wardrobe, script supervisors, and Janine DeVito, an associate producer who had used a stopwatch to time each sketch as it was read. This was their opportunity to see what technical obstacles the proposed rundown might present. Sometimes the cards on the board add up to what is called, in SNL shorthand, "too much show." Everyone studied the board, and Michaels continued mulling the choices. "There's certainly something edgy about Craigslist," he said.

As the tech people scribbled notes, issues were raised in overlapping conversations. Was the Five Timers script ready to show to Tina Fey? Design issues were hashed out: For the Craigslist piece, maybe they could get away with having only the *side* of a van in the studio? Hill was asked how he visualized Movie Theater. He answered by making another pitch for "more, like, farm to table, eccentric foods."

And he made a final appeal that any sketch he did with Pete David-son *not* be a gay joke.

Michaels went around the room asking everyone to name their top three picks. Movie Theater, Pugs, Motorcycle, and Weezer got the most votes. Michaels said he liked "the dumbness" of the motor-cycle sketch. "Montreal more than Weezer?" he asked a writer named Fran Gillespie, a former improv performer.

When she indicated the former, he smiled and asked, "And would you help them with their French accents?"

DeVito reported that, with the cards left on the board, the show was running twenty-eight minutes and sixteen seconds over. Ken-ward said that everything would come down in rewrite. "There are a lot of thirteen-pagers in there."

"You always say that," DeVito said brightly.

Michaels frowned. "What does Leslie have?" he asked, scanning the cards. He was relieved that she'd had a good read-through, which put her on track to have a calmer week. ("It's a very intimate process," he said later, of the culling. "That's the part that no cast member knows." Will Ferrell once told him, "You never understand the show when you work here; you only understand it when you come back to host and get to sit in these meetings. I hated having a hand in the fate of people losing their stuff.")

There were only a few decisions left to hash out, and Michaels asked everybody but the writers and producers and Hill to leave. He ran through the undecideds. Kenward pushed for doing both Motor-cycle and Weezer, even though both were, as he put it, "luxury items."

Michaels squinted at the board. "America's Got Talent is solid comedy. The Five Timers monologue is, too. Benihana is hard com-edy. Beavis and Butt-Head is hard. Movie Theater, too." He worried about overlap in KCR News and a piece called Inner Child, "because they're both about a guy going after a girl and being a dick."

He swiveled around. "All right, then let's go with Montreal Motor-cycle, and hold Weezer and Inner Child." He turned to Hill and asked, "Anything not there that you're missing?"

"I mean, Weezer," Hill said. "If you'd be okay with doing two punk crazy ones."

To appease Hill, Michaels asked his deputies, "Is it going to be a nightmare staging Motorcycles?"

"It should be a fun nightmare!" Higgins, the staff cheerleader, said.

The lineup settled, Michaels returned to the cold open. "Shall we just keep floating?" he asked. "Again, if we had Jordan Peele, I'd buy the Obama one." Jost said he had a problem "presentationally" with the idea: Why should an Obama rally be on Fox News? Maybe better to just simplify the premise: What if Obama did a rally the way Trump did?

Che agreed: "Especially if you have a Jordan Peele, you just bring him out there and let him go."

"Well, first he has to say yes," Michaels responded. He always encourages taking big swings when it comes to asking a star to appear. Tina Fey remembers wondering whether her sitcom *30 Rock* should approach Matt Damon about doing a guest shot once. "Lorne would say, 'You never offend someone by offering them a job,'" she recalled. The obverse of that is what Michaels mutters about actors (Geraldo Rivera, Tony Danza) who are almost too eager to be asked: "He's circling the building." When he hears that some B-lister is dying to host, he will look over his glasses and ask, "And what is his body of work exactly?"

Still pondering the cold open, Michaels made the longshot suggestion that maybe Dave Chappelle could play Obama. (When Chappelle hosted five days after the 2016 election, it was the culmination of an elaborate, lengthy courting process.) "But is the piece funny enough?" he wondered aloud. "When I see Obama now, because he's thinner and grayer, it doesn't look like him at full power. And because Trump is such a cartoon version of a human, Obama doing beat-for-beat Trump doesn't work."

"Didn't Jordan Peele retire from acting?" Hill asked. "I don't trust anyone who says he's retiring. They always come back. Look at Jay-Z—"

"Or Kanye," Michaels said.

"I guarantee it," Hill said. "Daniel Day Lewis is gonna move to Malibu and do *There Will Be Blood 2*."

"*There's* Still *Blood*," Jost said.

After everyone had left, Michaels took a few bites of cold shrimp and reflected on how much of his job is managing touchy talent. "In the end you just have to figure it out for yourself," he said. "If you're thinking that the system should be fair, as opposed to that each talent is its own special thing, it's not going to fly."

There was a knock at the door, and a PA came in and wrote down the titles of the sketches still pinned to the bulletin board. She then walked down the hall and posted the lineup on the wall of the writers' room. The exhausted writers and performers crowded around, like kids looking to see who had been cast in the school play. Body language (high-fives, slumped shoulders) telegraphed the reactions. Physically posting the lineup is one of the many SNL folkways that Michaels long resisted updating; the information could just as easily be communicated by email, sparing staffers the humiliating scrum. (Within a few years, they *would* switch to emailing the lineup.) For the cast and writers, this moment determines whether they have a good week or a bad one.

It was almost 10:00 P.M., and on a normal Wednesday, Michaels might meet someone for a drink. But this night, he went directly home, puzzling more than usual over the cold open. At 2:00 A.M. he'd watch Brian Williams's late newscast and keep thinking. Heading out the door, he said, "If we could only get Chappelle . . ."

After he had gone, the writers whose pieces were picked huddled with the design teams, discussing sets and costumes. (The wardrobe department employs fifty-five people.) The designers would sketch all night so that they could get the plans to the carpentry shop in the Brooklyn Navy Yard by morning. The music people would start sourcing clips and composing riffs. Kenward would assign directors and preliminary locations for the pre-tapes. The heavy machinery had been switched on, and it would not stop running until early Sunday morning.

TWELVE

LIVE FROM NEW YORK

ONE OF MICHAELS'S EARLY TALKING POINTS WITH EXECUTIVES WAS THAT *Saturday Night* should look like the adults left the studio and the kids took over. The week of the premiere, in 1975, that's exactly what happened. NBC was broadcasting the World Series that year, and Game One was at Fenway Park on October 11, the night of Michaels's first show. The network higher-ups, including Dave Tebet and Herb Schlosser, flew to Boston for the game.

The week leading up to the show was hellish, and Michaels's face broke out from the stress. Tebet had summoned him to his office to insist that George Carlin, the inaugural host, cut his hair and wear a suit. The Standards people had been shielded from the knowledge that Carlin was flying on cocaine all week, but they were still anxious; his most famous club bit was a riff on the seven words you can't say on TV ("shit," "piss," "fuck," "cunt," "cocksucker," "motherfucker," and "tits"). Concerned that he might let fly with one of the seven words, the censors were threatening to broadcast the show with a seven-second delay. At a read-through on Wednesday in Michaels's office, Jim Henson and his team showed off their Muppet Night Creatures to the cast for the first time, and the sensibilities did not mesh. The brickwork at home base was still being noisily installed, and when Howard Shore and his musicians rehearsed, the sound wasn't right; the 8H engineers were still trying to understand the instruction manual that came with the new audio equipment Dick Ebersol had procured. NBC lawyers were agitated that Chevy Chase and John Belushi still hadn't signed contracts. "Lorne plowed through all the difficulties," Tom Schiller said. "You could see he was holding on for dear life." But he had a way of remaining stoic. People instinctively rallied around him.

The mood in the studio swung between cockiness and dread. Michaels walked around assuring his performers that they were going to be stars. He told Jane Curtin, the only married person in the cast, that she would be so famous that her marriage wouldn't withstand it. In the next breath he said brightly, "On the other hand, none of us may ever work again."

Friday night at 8:30, they did a wobbly run-through. No one had thought about spectators, and at the last minute, NBC pages were sent out to Sixth Avenue to recruit pedestrians, so that Michaels could see how an audience reacted. The show was more than twice as long as it should be. The lighting director had vanished, and the sound was so muddy that the dialogue was hard to hear. The run-through went so late that Andy Kaufman, who still hovered in limbo between cast and guest, almost didn't get to do his segment— lip-synching to a record of the Mighty Mouse theme. Michaels convinced him to miss the last train home to Great Neck. Billy Crystal, another guest comic, did his monologue for the first time that night as well, after hanging around all week waiting. It was a six-minute story about going on safari, the sound of footsteps in the brush simulated by Don Pardo crunching handfuls of potato chips. As chaos swirled, Michaels half-joked that NBC should get a late movie lined up in case the whole thing combusted.

In the wee hours of Saturday morning, Michaels sat on a stool in front of the whole staff and gave detailed notes on every segment of the run-through. "We're doing a show tomorrow night," he said, as if to reassure those who doubted it. "And it will go smoothly." Ebersol called around trying to find a lighting director and a working sound system. The cast and writers headed downtown, to a party that Belushi threw.

On Saturday afternoon, there was another run-through and another notes session, and, at 7:30, a full dress rehearsal. The biggest challenge was getting the show to time. On the Tomlin specials, Michaels had sat for days on end at an editing console, cocaine-fueled, fussily shaving minutes and seconds. At *Saturday Night,* the deadline was real. Everything was up for grabs in Michaels's mind, and, in the hour before airtime, he all but started over.

He had too many ingredients, but no recipe. Michaels had wanted Stevie Wonder and Carole King for his first musical acts. He ended up with Billy Preston and Janis Ian. Carlin had only agreed to host because he had a new album to promote, and although he was instructed to bring fresh material, he used his three stand-up slots to recite cuts from his record. With Ebersol running interference, a compromise was reached on the wardrobe crisis: Carlin would wear a three-piece suit over a T-shirt.

Remembering how Phyllis Diller's interview segments had made her seem warmer to viewers, Michaels wanted his hosts to begin by addressing the audience. For a stand-up like Carlin, a monologue was easy. Sketches were hard. After rehearsing all week, he bailed on the only sketch he was in, an O'Donoghue piece about Alexander the Great attending his high school reunion (the gag: his classmates still treat him like a loser). Carlin later admitted that he'd been so high on cocaine that he was visibly grinding his jaw onstage.

Losing Alexander the Great saved some minutes, but a lot more needed to go. Janis Ian's hit, "At Seventeen," clocked in at four untrimmable minutes. It was impossible to cut from Albert Brooks's film, a fake newsreel of weirdo clips (a blind New York cab driver; a press conference announcing that the state of Georgia and the country of Israel would change places; the Georgian says, "I know that my entire state is looking forward to heat without humidity"). There were three guest stand-ups—Crystal, Kaufman, and Valri Bromfield, from Canada. Michaels asked Bromfield to cut a chunk from her monologue about a school volleyball player, and told Crystal that he'd have to edit his safari routine down to two minutes.

As the audience for dress rehearsal was settling into the Yankees seats, Michaels was studying a rundown annotated with numbers of seconds, still trying to make the math work. He was interrupted by Billy Crystal's manager, a Rollins-Joffe partner named Buddy Morra, who was in a rage. Morra announced that his client would not cut his piece, and he advised Michaels to instead ax Andy Kaufman, whose act contained several long, uncomfortable stretches of silence. Michaels wasn't about to do that; Kaufman telegraphed the show's arty, even surrealist, ambitions. Morra moved on to Bromfield. "She's not funny," he said. "Get rid of her." At that point, Bernie Brillstein, who always stood near Michaels when confrontation loomed, said, "Fuck you, Buddy." Morra stormed out, and Crystal found himself on a Long Island Rail Road train heading home. Michaels added two minutes back to his lineup.

The Morra face-off was a collision of old showbiz and Michaels's underground vision, another version of the doughnuts vs. crudités divide. The culture clash showed up in other ways. Just before dress, Brillstein ran up to Michaels, alarmed: Why hadn't the band changed into their tuxedoes yet? He didn't get it. And Belushi was still refusing to sign his NBC contract, worried about selling out to "the man." Just before airtime, Brillstein persuaded Belushi to sign by offering to represent him.

Meanwhile, Kaufman had locked himself in Herb Sargent's office. He'd taped a note to the door: "Please do not disturb me while I meditate—Andy Kaufman."

A traditional variety show would have opened with the guest star. But Michaels wanted viewers to know immediately that his show was, in Monty Python's phrase, something completely different. He would open cold—jumping right into the comedy, with no glitzy preamble. (The origin of the phrase "cold open" is murky. "I'm not looking for credit," Michaels told me. "But I made that phrase up.") The first thing viewers would see in his first show would be a Dada-ish sketch in a minor key, written by O'Donoghue. The piece is unconventional in many ways: The first two people on-screen, Belushi and O'Donoghue, are far from the show's most attractive, and one is a mere writer (and terrified). They are seated in armchairs on a set that recalls *The Honeymooners* in its spareness. O'Donoghue, in a suit, begins to give an English lesson to Belushi, whose schlubby bomber hat and sack of groceries peg him as an immigrant. The professor has the student repeat a series of phrases, starting with "I would like." In a thick accent, Belushi repeats, "I would like." Then: "To feed your fingertips." Belushi says, "To feed your fingertips." O'Donoghue goes on: "To the wolverines." The audience erupts into startled laughter, the show's first. Other sentences about wolverines follow, and one involving a badger. Suddenly, O'Donoghue clutches his heart, gasps, and falls to the floor. Belushi takes a beat, working the eyebrows, then grunts and tumbles to the floor as well. After a pause, Chase enters, in jeans and a stage manager's headset, and takes in the scene. He turns to the camera, flashing his tennis-pro smile and says, "Live, from New York, it's Saturday Night!"

The sketch brings together a lot of Michaels's preoccupations: a twist on an old joke ("Repeat after me," a variant of "Walk this way"); not relying on big stars; an unsettling, mordant flavor; the abrupt, Pythonesque ending; a self-conscious meta element, with the "stage-hand" calling attention to the process of the show itself. It's only a bit of a stretch to see O'Donoghue's professor as a stand-in for Michaels, offering American viewers a beginner's lesson in subversive comedy.

Don Pardo, the announcer, flubbed the opening, introducing the cast as "The Not for Ready Prime Time Players." But after that, the show unspooled with relative smoothness. One unwelcome surprise: Carlin swapped in a new cut from his record for the one that had been rehearsed. "That fucker," Michaels muttered in the control room, mindful of how this could mess up the timing. Between live music, Carlin, Muppets, Bromfield, Kaufman (whose twitchy naivete enraptured the audience), and Brooks's film, there wasn't a lot of time for sketches featuring the cast. But Chase, who at Michaels's urging introduced himself by his real name as the Weekend Update anchor, made an impression. A parody of a Lark cigarette ad, called "Show Us Your Guns," got laughs, as did a fake ad for a newfangled three-bladed razor: "The Triple-Track—because you'll believe anything."

Right away, Michaels discovered that there would be something in every show to make a member of his team unhappy. O'Donoghue was mad about losing Alexander the Great. Brooks was annoyed that Michaels had held the (too long) introductory film he'd made specially for the premiere and had run his second film first. Franken was disappointed in a corny jury sketch; Belushi, as a juror, gives a lascivious eyebrow wag when he misapprehends a piece of evidence—a note reading "Will you sleep with me?" "It was an old-fashioned blackout," Franken said. "I went, 'Umm, I didn't think that's what we're doing here.'"

One piece, written by Rosie Shuster, signaled the direction that the show's humor would take. "Bee Hospital" opened with soap-opera organ music in a maternity-ward waiting room. Expectant insect fathers buzz and pace, and a nurse comes out at intervals and says, "It's a drone." "It's a drone." "It's a worker." It was staged in a corner, where the untried PA system didn't work well. (Over the years, the cast came to refer to that corner as Shitcan Alley.) "It went totally into the toilet," Zweibel remembered. "Even Fellini would have to take acid for this fucking thing." But the sketch's low-tech silliness appealed to Michaels. Franne Lee had painted stripes on thermal long johns for the costumes, and her father, a tool-and-die maker, fashioned metal springs into antennae tipped with Styrofoam balls. Belushi found the rig undignified. "He was like a macho man in this fruity-ass bee costume," Shuster said, crediting the sketch with getting their relationship off to a bad start. ("SNL Killer Bee Costume" remains a big seller at HalloweenHallway.com.)

When the credits rolled, over Howard Shore's bluesy "Waltz in A," Michaels exhaled. (He grimaced, though, when Carlin held up a copy of his new LP as he said good night from the stage.) Earlier that day, Michaels had gone over the credit list in the control room. Still looking for ways to make his show distinctive, he'd ordered that "Bud" be inserted between the first and last names of everyone on the roll. There was Lorne "Bud" Michaels, John "Bud" Belushi, Jane "Bud" Curtin, etc. The last name on the crawl was Dick "Bud" Ebersol, who was listed as "executive producer for NBC." It was unorthodox at the network to credit an executive this way. Ebersol had run his EP credit by Michaels earlier in the week, and although it undercut Michaels's vision of the show as non-hierarchical, he had okayed it.

Ebersol's aptitude for self-promotion could grate, but his facility with the corporate types smoothed Michaels's path. Ebersol would excel at cutting through red tape, figuring out how to get NBC to build more dressing rooms, or to pay for the cases of white wine that made it possible for Michaels to walk around the studio floor holding a glass, one of his methods of projecting nonchalance. (The wine cost ended up hidden in the props budget.) And after the dismal Friday run-through, Ebersol had found a new sound system overnight; Rick Wakeman, from the progressive rock band Yes, was at Madison Square Garden that week, doing a solo tour dressed up as King Arthur; Ebersol persuaded the techies breaking down the equipment to bring it fifteen blocks north and reassemble it in 8H.

Up in Boston, the Red Sox beat the Cincinnati Reds 6–0, and afterward Schlosser and his wife, Judith, invited the baseball commissioner Bowie Kuhn and his wife up to their suite at the Ritz to watch the premiere of *Saturday Night*. The commissioner, who was a sobersided man, sat expressionless through the Wolverines sketch, but, during Carlin's opening monologue, about the difference between football and baseball, he started to laugh. During another Carlin monologue, positing that God is really only a "semi-Supreme being" ("He's had billions of years to work on this stuff. And everything He has ever made died!"), the phone rang in Schlosser's suite. It was an irate Dave Tebet. "Herb," he said, "how can you put a show like that on?" Schlosser didn't mention the Tebet tirade when he placed his own call to Michaels later; he said he had liked the show very much—particularly Chevy Chase.

Tebet had made another call that night, to Ebersol. He angrily relayed that outraged viewers were jamming the NBC switchboard with complaints about Carlin—including the archbishop of New York. (That call turned out to be a hoax.) He also said that Ebersol's executive producer credit violated NBC policy and forbade it going forward; Ebersol said that Michaels had suggested it.

Three thousand miles away, Michaels's old Malibu roommate Joe

Boyd watched the show in a rented house in Stinson Beach, with his brother and a gang of friends. There was no TV in the place, so he'd found a 16-inch set to rent, so as not to miss his friends' big moment. After some fiddling with rabbit ears, he sat on the floor with the group to watch. Everyone loved the Wolverines opening. "And then, after eleven-forty-five, there were no more laughs," Boyd said. "The show started laying an egg. People tiptoed out." When the credits rolled, Boyd was alone. He remembers thinking that no one he knew "had ever had such a calamity happen to them as this. The show was a catastrophe."

Steve Martin, whose stand-up career was ramping up, watched the premiere in Aspen. He was shook. "I felt like *I* was the avant-garde. *I* was the one doing the new comedy," he said. "I thought: 'Oh fuck; they did it.' They had gotten there first. They had captured the zeitgeist on national television."

A lot of critics agreed with Tebet and Boyd. *The Hollywood Reporter* called the show "lackluster." *Variety* wrote, "Many of the ideas seemed funny enough at the beginning. But execution was mostly a tedious failure." (A few days later, the *L.A. Times* weighed in, calling the show "bright and bouncy.") The network was jittery. Where was Rich Little or the Marines' marching band, they wanted to know? Michaels wasn't worried. "There was a bad reaction to the first show within the network, but not with the audience," he said. "NBC was expecting Up with People." He had the bad reviews posted on a bulletin board outside his office and walked around saying, "I guess we're a hit."

MICHAELS HAD BEEN NOODLING WITH THE FIRST SHOW FOR SIX MONTHS. Now he had to do it all over again in six days. The Not Ready for Prime Time Players had had only about seventeen minutes of screen time in the premiere. They would barely appear at all in the second show, which, due to haphazard planning, was mostly music. Michaels had Paul Simon lined up to host that one. Art Garfunkel came on, too, reuniting with his estranged partner. They were joined by Randy

Newman, whose darkly satiric *Good Old Boys* was on the charts; and Phoebe Snow. In all, there were eleven musical numbers.

The only specific note from the NBC executives after the first show was that they hated Bee Hospital. Piqued, Michaels had an idea that both obeyed and disobeyed the network, and established who was in control. When the Not Ready for Prime Time Players made their one brief appearance in the second show, they were all dressed as bees. They show up at home base around the host Paul Simon, who, looking uncomfortable, tells them, "I'm really sorry. The Bees number is cut." The downcast bees exit to laughs.

With the on-air kiss-off of the bees (and the network), Michaels conjured the peek-behind-the-curtain feeling that he was after. It set up a posture of combativeness between the corporate overlords and the onstage underdogs. Although the cold opening was straight— Simon on a stool, wearing immoderately flared jeans with a knife-edge crease, and singing "Still Crazy After All These Years"—it concluded with Chase crossing the stage and taking one of his falls, shouting, "Live from New York, it's Saturday Night!" The only other comedy was performed by celebrity guests: the real Jerry Rubin, of the Chicago Seven, hawking a line of pre-graffitied "Up against the wallpaper"; and tiny Paul Simon playing one-on-one basketball with the former Harlem Globetrotter Connie Hawkins (a sight gag that was Simon's idea), with commentary by the sportscaster Marv Albert. (The only glitch: Simon, concerned that his bald spot might show, kept looking over at the monitor instead of into the camera.)

Viewers couldn't be faulted for thinking that what they had just watched was a music special, and that's just what the *New York Times* critic John J. O'Connor concluded, referring to the show in his review as a "Simon and Garfunkel reunion." "The reunion was, it should be stressed, nice while it lasted," he wrote. "The same cannot be said, unfortunately, for the rest of 'Saturday Night,'" which he appraised as "dreadfully uneven comedy efforts." He complained that he couldn't tell the parody ads from the real ones, and singled out as "thoroughly tasteless and insensitive" a fake ad for batteries that used old people with pacemakers as test subjects.

What made the review especially irksome is that O'Connor had missed a chunk of the show: "An unusually good dinner on Long Island and a steady rain during the 100-mile drive back to the city thwarted thoroughly noble intentions," he wrote, cementing his standing as an old fogy. Television critics were used to seeing shows early, on videocassettes; many were put out by having to sit in front of the set at 11:30 P.M. Michaels tacked the review to the bulletin board, just another thing to laugh at.

O'Connor would not have understood that his fussing about the fake ads looking too real was, in fact, a compliment. The TV generation was used to the firehose of phony sincerity that gushed from the screen; commercials were a big part of that. Sick of the transactional logrolling that underlay most of show business, Michaels didn't want hosts who would use the show to hawk their new projects, or even hosts who were part of mainstream TV. When Rob Reiner, a star of *All in the Family,* hosted the third show, he passed muster presumably because his role as Meathead, Archie Bunker's hippie son-in-law, lent him some countercultural cred. Michaels had spent a day in L.A. cajoling Reiner to do the show, a display that made Reiner's wife, Penny Marshall, tell him, "You're the most manipulative human being I've ever met, and you do it beautifully."

But on the night of the show, Reiner holed up in his dressing room after dress rehearsal and announced that he was not going on. He'd already complained that his dressing room was too close to a public hallway. Now he was hysterical. "I can't do it. I can't do it," he said, near tears. Michaels used some calm, adagio talk to bring him around. Reiner was terrified that he was going to bomb, and given how the week had gone, Michaels might have suspected he was right. After O'Connor's review, the writers were eager to step up the comedy, and Reiner had brought a few of his own ideas. He had written a monologue for himself in the guise of a cheeseball lounge singer, an idea that Michaels found unfresh; his generation's approach to comedy, he said, was a reaction "against the neediness of performers." But Reiner got his way, and in the actual show, his flopsweat evident, he took the stage wearing a tux with a ruffled-pastel shirt and greeted the "beautiful human beings" in the audience. "This is the way I look *live*, ladies and gentlemen," he said. "This is the *real* me, *thank-you-very-much*." He then invoked his "close personal friend . . . the late, great Mr. Bob Dylan." A whisper from offstage advised him that Dylan was still alive, and he launched into a Muzaky "Blowin' in the Wind," punctuated with finger-snapping: "How many times must those cannonballs fly, before they're forever banned? And speaking of *bands*, ladies and gentlemen, how about Howard Shore and his orchestra!"

Reiner wanted viewers to think that the slick Vegas character was the real Rob Reiner, completely removed from his Meathead character. "That was a common style in the seventies," Michaels said. "The 'my character is really an asshole' thing. That's your joke. That you're not really an asshole. I didn't want the staleness of it." He called it "the low end of smart, as opposed to the high end, like Nichols and May." Bill Murray tapped a similar vein with his own lounge-singer shtick. "But this wasn't Billy doing the Vegas guy," Michaels said. "It was Rob Reiner." All week Michaels tried to tell Reiner that he didn't think the bit was working. On the air it was flat.

He also found himself in the middle of two other power struggles: Dave Tebet sent a memo arguing that the show should abandon broadcasting live and instead "go to tape." And Ebersol weighed in with a critique of the Reiner show's script. He hated the lounge-singer monologue, too, putting Michaels in the uncomfortable position of wanting to defend it. He was affronted that someone he regarded as a suit thought he had a say.

Michaels had always gravitated toward performers who were not professionally packaged entertainers, but people who felt like everybody's funny friends: mischievous, sarcastic, a little fed up. This attitude didn't preclude genuine feeling. Since the fifties, sincerity had been gradually leeched out of show business, replaced by a slickness as shiny and blank as a cyclorama wall. Michaels hated the way somebody on a TV show would say, "Give a warm welcome to my very, very best friend" about some guest he had been introduced to twenty minutes earlier by a William Morris agent. So he was delighted when, a few weeks after the Reiner show, *The New Yorker's*

TV critic, Michael Arlen, zeroed in on this quality. The grammar of modern TV, Arlen wrote, was "that strange fantasy language of celebrity public relations . . . formalized as a kind of national version of a modern courtier style." He recognized that Michaels wanted to start fresh. "What is attractive and unusual about [*Saturday Night*] is that it is an attempt, finally, to provide entertainment on television in a recognizable, human, non-celebrity voice—and in a voice, too, that tries to deal with the morass of media-induced show-business culture that increasingly pervades American life." Arlen noted that *Saturday Night* "seems to speak out of the real, non-show-business world that most people inhabit," investing comedy with the power to affect our "basic ways of trying to view and organize experience." Michaels told his people to use their own lives as inspiration, to put their own personal concerns onstage. A sketch shouldn't be a joke delivery system, but a way to communicate something interior and real.

Giving viewers a sense of being behind-the-scenes accomplished something similar. The Reiner show ended with a sketch that broke the fourth wall in two ways. As Reiner notices Bees appearing around him, he breaks character and shouts, "I was told when I came on the show that I would not have to work with the Bees!" Belushi, a bee in Brando mode, stands up to him. "We didn't ask to be bees," Belushi declares. In a withering tone, he calls Reiner "Mr. Hollywood, California number-one-show big shot," and says, "You've got Norman Lear and a first-rate writing staff. But *this* is all they came up with for us."

In three episodes, the show had developed in-jokes that viewers could feel cool for noticing. And being cool was Michaels's true north. The Bees would make thirteen more appearances, each time signaling that a meta disruption of the show was in store. Another way Michaels brought viewers inside the show's charmed circle was by cutting to shots of audience members, superimposing a screen caption: LEONARD BERNSTEIN'S CATERER; SURVIVOR OF OFFICE SNUFF PARTY; A GOOD FRIEND OF DAVID EISENHOWER. The people in these bumpers looked thrilled, lucky guests at a VIP party.

In the fourth episode, Chase introduced his Update newscast

with the line "I'm Chevy Chase and you're not." "By then, we'd found the show that resembles the show today," Michaels said. The host was a proper movie star, Candice Bergen, and she performed seamlessly with the cast. In a sketch called "Jaws II," a dumb land shark (Chase, in a foam rubber shark head), tries to get into the apartments of dumb young women, claiming to be a deliveryman, a plumber, a Candygram guy. The episode also introduced Chase's non-impression of Gerald Ford, in a cold open that portrayed the president as a klutzy oaf. Chase wore no special makeup as Ford, and his impression was inspired by a random news clip of the president tripping as he descended the stairs from *Air Force One*. Ford was an athlete at the University of Michigan, a man of some physical grace, yet Chase's impersonation would define his single term—a man who not only tumbled down stairs, but stumbled into the presidency.

Michaels loved the off-center characterization because it defied expectations. Rather than eviscerate Ford, it made him human; it let the audience in. When Chase played Ford, he was being himself—and showcasing himself, as he started to turn into the show's leading man. It was the opposite of what Dan Aykroyd did as a performer—nailing dialects from all over the planet and vanishing inside the characters he played. The theater scholar Matt Fotis wrote that Chase's performance of Ford embodied a "Brechtian technique of presenting both the actor and the character." Ford's one-off flub also gave Chase opportunities to flaunt his gift for falling down.

The Bergen show also marked the first time that the cast gathered onstage with the host to say good night; each handed her a rose. (The Goodnights often revealed how the performers really felt about each other; warmth, and occasional tension, were evident.) Bergen called Michaels the "show coach." "He gave you the illusion that, as the host, you had a measure of input," she said. But the pace shocked her: "People wheel you around, because you are just in a fugue state." Michaels told her that when she came out to do her monologue, she looked "like Patty Hearst opening the door to find the SLA."

———

BERGEN DIDN'T KNOW IT, BUT RIGHT AFTER HER MONOLOGUE, MICHAELS had quit. An engineer at a New York affiliate had mistaken one of the show's parody ads—about the "Ambassador Training Institute," a send-up of how rich political donors are rewarded with glamorous diplomatic postings—for a real ad and had put on a local commercial instead. Michaels flew into a rage at Ebersol, who, as the network's man, should have been on top of such things. He said that he'd stay until the show was over, out of deference to Bergen, but then he was walking.

On Monday, Brillstein called Ebersol and announced that Michaels wasn't coming back. The commercial screwup was the final straw; Ebersol had been interfering more and more on the creative side and dropping the ball on important things—like finding a new lighting director. "I was highly strung," Michaels recalled. "I felt I had to fight for the show." Although exhausted, he'd been feeling more confident, and he believed he had some leverage. A week earlier, a glowing piece in *New York* magazine had come out, and the writer, Jeff Greenfield, had parroted all of Michaels's regular talking points. He referenced the TV generation and praised the show's "explicitly hip, cynical outlook," calling it "the sharpest departure from the TV-comedy norm since the debut of 'Laugh-In.'" Another auspicious sign: Herb Schlosser's teenage son, Eric, was a fan, and he often turned up at 8H with friends from the Dalton School on Saturday night.

Michaels's vision ratified, he was ready to declare a bit more independence from the network. "We had begun to see which people didn't quite fit our culture," he said. Chief among those people was Dick Ebersol. It wasn't just the clothes. For the fifth show, hosted by the comedian Robert Klein, John Head had booked the singer-songwriter Loudon Wainwright III, whose wry anti-love songs were perfectly in sync with the show's sensibility; for the second musical act, Ebersol insisted on ABBA, the Swedish pop quartet with a string of bubblegum AM-radio hits. "Dick *was* ABBA," Michaels said.

Staffers had begun to notice that when Ebersol talked to reporters, he sometimes failed to even mention Michaels, and took a lot of creative credit for the show. (Schlosser noted a joke that went around in those years: "Whenever someone in the world tells a lie, Dick Ebersol gets a royalty.") Michaels wanted Ebersol to steer clear of the comedy and focus on solving technical problems.

But Ebersol had been getting pushier with his opinions, sending memos about camera angles and scripts; he defended a suggestion made by an executive that all the ad parodies be lumped together in a "commercial corner." One week, when Michaels was scrambling to find a host, Ebersol pushed Jo Ann Pflug, an actress pal and game show stalwart who'd been on *Love, American Style.* Ebersol wrote in a memo to Michaels, "I don't think that in any way you can look at me as a typical Network Executive who is either fearful of his bosses or trying to push his friends on to his shows. With that as a lead-in, please don't look at Pflug as my friend."

Michaels had threatened to quit before, and Ebersol didn't take his walkout seriously. At the office, the week's host, Robert Klein, was told that Michaels was sick in bed. Unsure of what to do, the writers hastily convened a meeting; then word came from the Osborne that the show must go on without him. With Michaels absent, a lot of hours were spent that week debating whether ABBA's two female singers were wearing underwear.

Stewing in his apartment, Michaels put in a call to Toronto, to discuss the standoff with Uncle Pep, who could always be counted on to gauge whether a battle was worth fighting. Brillstein did what Michaels was paying him for: he got confrontational. After an unsatisfactory conversation with Ebersol, Brillstein called an NBC vice president named Myron "Mike" Weinblatt, who had become a kind of guardian angel to *Saturday Night.* Weinblatt listened to the complaints, including how the show needed to feel more love from NBC.

Going to the brink was risky. Even though the reviews and word of mouth were improving, Michaels wasn't operating from a position of strength. Don Carswell hadn't been far off with his revenue predictions. The budget had been set at $134,600 per show, and from the start they were spending closer to $200,000. "All I knew was that if it was a hit, I'd be okay, and if it wasn't a hit I wouldn't," Michaels said. The weak ad sales were partly why he'd agreed to have Bergen do a live real commercial on the show for the Polaroid SX-70, dressed as a bee.

But NBC may not have been paying attention to the ad revenues or the good reviews. For the first time, the network had fallen into third place; the executives' attention was on its prime-time schedule. "If it had been a typical fall season," Ebersol said, "I could see us not having made it."

Michaels didn't know it when he walked off the Robert Klein show, but an important business development was about to strengthen his case. The Monday that he stayed home, the A.C. Nielsen company sent a report to NBC showing that more than three-quarters of the people watching *Saturday Night* were between the ages of eighteen and forty-nine. This demographic, which all three networks had been chasing, would theoretically make it easier for NBC's ad salesmen to do their jobs. Ebersol was ecstatic when he saw the report, and he sent a staffwide memo about the "fantastically incredible" news. So he was surprised when, that Wednesday, he was effectively removed from the show. Weinblatt and Schlosser had taken Brillstein's complaints seriously. To get Ebersol out of Michaels's hair, they decided to make him vice president of late-night programs. The new job was technically a promotion, but his involvement in *Saturday Night* would be minimal. Ebersol was crushed, but being able to brag that he was the youngest vice president in NBC history took some of the sting out of it.

Michaels was back in his office the same Wednesday, in plenty of time to produce the Robert Klein show, which contained flashes of newfound autonomy. The writers had contrived to position ABBA as the band on the *Titanic*. Toward the end of the song "Waterloo," the camera careens wildly, and buckets of water are sloshed across the stage. "We tried to drown them," Howard Shore said. Michaels had been horrified to hear that the band did not intend to actually sing; he insisted that a chyron appear on-screen reading RIGHT NOW ABBA IS LIP-SYNCHING.

On Update, Chase took a moment to wish a happy birthday to the beleaguered boss, "Lorne Michaels, executive producer of the *Saturday Night* show and functioning schizophrenic." He went on, "The show will soon be replaced by the network with their new series *Hilarious Test Patterns of the Sixties.*"

THIRTEEN

THE FRIENDSHIP ECONOMY

THE WEEK BEFORE THE CANDICE BERGEN SHOW, THE FRONT PAGE OF THE New York *Daily News* read "Ford to City: Drop Dead." New York was nearly bankrupt, and the president had rejected a federal bailout. But Michaels, whose life was not affected by cutbacks in city services, had found himself liking New York. He viewed the city as "the knowledge capital," and he appreciated that, unlike L.A., a one-industry town, New York had the theater, politics, publishing, art, and finance. It thrilled him to see Philip Roth sitting at a table across a restaurant. One night over dinner, Candice Bergen told Michaels that he was "like Little Mike." Big Mike was Nichols, who had directed her in *Carnal Knowledge.* She soon introduced the two. Each had the wide view of an impresario and an unpushy charm that made them agreeable to people who were in no particular need of new friends—famous, rich, or very talented people. They had similarly unglamorous backgrounds. Nichols was born Igor Peschkowsky, in Berlin, and he had a difficult Jewish mother just like Michaels did. Both men viewed the world as a series of social and professional peaks to be scaled. They intuitively gravitated toward the brightest in the hierarchy, and they were active if discreet brokers in the friendship economy. Michaels recalled Nichols encapsulating this value system once by posing the question "Who, on opening night, is the person you put in the aisle seat? Who's that person whose high regard you want?"

Nichols recognized that Michaels's show was reconfiguring what television could be, and he quickly became one of Michaels's rabbis. Michaels told Nichols's biographer Mark Harris about hearing Nichols say, of a man he had just canceled dinner with, "He lives the same life we live—he'll understand." Michaels said, "It was the first time I put it all together—that this is *a life,* and that the small group of people who live it are different from Hollywood people. I started to see what it looked like to be nourished by being around people who are bright and funny."

Michaels's secretary Kathy Minkowsky pinned on the bulletin board the notes that he received from famous people. Many made an effort to be funny, inviting smirks from the tough crowd on seventeen. After Steve Lawrence and Eydie Gormé turned up in an audience bumper caption, on a list of PEOPLE WHO DOLPHINS ARE DEFINITELY MORE INTELLIGENT THAN, the married singers wrote to suggest other animals who were smarter than them: "whales, barracudas, snakes, and the rest of the country." Fred Rogers sent a note expressing delight about a sketch called "Dr. Jekyll and Mister Rogers." Letters from intellectuals were especially prized, including notes from Joseph Heller, Ken Kesey, and Senator Daniel Patrick Moynihan. One hand-scrawled card concluded, "Thanks for making TV fun again—Rod McKuen." After a sketch about the Manson girls weaving pot holders from human hair, a spooky letter arrived saying that "Charlie" had watched it and didn't like it. Michaels quipped that he was just happy that someone was watching.

As the show took off, the need for the celebrity rocket boosters that had helped at the beginning fell away. For the fifth show, during the opening, Don Pardo said with a flourish, "*No* film by Albert Brooks!" But the Brooks films were popular; one, called "NBC's Super Season," was a reel of promos for fake midseason replacement shows, including a series of Bicentennial specials "guaranteed to make you feel two hundred years old"; one was *Black Vet,* about an African American man back from Vietnam who opens a veterinary practice. But the hierarchy of fame within the show was already shifting. "The films were great, but the focus was supposed to be the host," Michaels said. "Then the focus became the cast."

Brooks felt that he'd been used as comedy bait. Gradually, his films were treated as if they were "this virus, this foreign thing that arrived in the pouch each week, an intruder," as he put it. After nine weeks, he and Michaels decided not to continue the arrangement.

The other star whose name had initially helped placate NBC was Jim Henson. Michaels had thought of the Muppets as a congenial variety act, and when Henson announced his plan to create *new* Muppets for the show, his "heart sank a little bit." The Muppets-after-dark that Henson came up with, inhabitants of the Land of Gorch, were neither cuddly nor cutting-edge. Compared to the Crayola-colored *Sesame Street* regulars, they were drab and lumpy, with warts, bloodshot green eyes, and in one case, furry cleavage. The Gorch Muppets had late-night vices, too, including drinking, drugs, and fornication. It was as if Michaels had signed up Vegas Bobby Darin and got Big Sur Bob Darin instead.

The collaboration was troubled from the start. Writers Guild rules stipulated that the Muppet scripts be the work of the show's writers, and Michaels had to implore them to pitch in. O'Donoghue declared, "I don't write for felt." He referred to the puppets as "little hairy face-cloths" and once strung up a toy Big Bird on the cords of Michaels's Venetian blinds. (He did turn in one script, called "The Day of the Muppets," in which the Gorch dwellers become evil mutants after an atomic bomb blast, and devour Henson.)

Before the end of the first season, Michaels decided to pull the plug on Henson's creatures. The new Muppets introduced a problem that would also come up with hosts: performers "who are known for one thing and want to show range," as Michaels put it. Henson had hoped his new critters would result in a career "thunderclap." But he was almost a decade older than Michaels—enough, in that era, to constitute a yawning generation gap. "They were from a more Bohemian past," Michaels said of the Muppet crew, citing their "leather-pants aesthetic." Their earnestness grated. Muppets talking about being horny was embarrassing, in the way that the scratchy instructional drawings of hairy intertwined bodies were in the 1972 best-seller *The Joy of Sex*. "It was so sincere, and we were much more savage," Michaels said. Also, the tops of the puppeteers' heads sometimes showed.

One of the handful of successful Muppet appearances was with Lily Tomlin, who, when she hosted the sixth show, sang "I Got You Babe," with Scred, the only Gorch Muppet that, to Michaels's mind, had some "sweetness." The source of Michaels's biggest success, Tomlin fit the culture of the show perfectly. He'd always liked the way she reached for emotional truthfulness. There had been sprinklings of it in the show already—for instance, a monologue called "What Gilda Ate," in which Radner simply listed what she'd eaten that day. Michaels called moments like this "us making it up as we went along." He said, "That part was the sacred part." Eager for more such moments, he lured Marilyn Miller, whom he'd worked with on Tomlin's specials, to move from L.A. and join the writing staff.

Tomlin didn't arrive for her hosting gig as a cozy dear friend, the way Simon had; between her and Michaels there was a slight froideur. But she was eager to put her stamp on the episode by pitching ideas. The combination of Tomlin and Miller, bolstered by Shuster and Beatts, produced more female-centric material than usual, which upended the power balance. Tomlin found the guys' "machoism" overbearing. "O'Donoghue didn't like my style of humor," she said. "He was shooting daggers at me." She pitched a sketch about a class to teach female hardhats how to catcall at men ("Hey, studmuffins, wanna make bouncy-bouncy?"). None of the guys wanted to play the humiliated beefcake. Finally, Michaels persuaded Aykroyd, who did the role justice in short-shorts and a tank top.

Feminism was in the air, but it wasn't a dominant theme at *Saturday Night*. The Equal Rights Amendment had just been derailed, and the women on staff were demoralized. ("I couldn't stop crying," Curtin said, calling the vote "the end of dignity.") The cast's three women shared a dressing room; the men each had their own. Belushi sometimes said that he wouldn't do pieces "written by girls." The writers liked to cast Garrett Morris as a woman, which annoyed the actual women in the cast, not to mention Morris, who got sick of playing mammies and wearing dresses, when it fell to him to impersonate Ella Fitzgerald, Tina Turner, Diana Ross, and Pearl Bailey.

Shuster was in a tricky position. When a Canadian newspaper reporter wrote about the show, he treated Michaels and Shuster as a couple; it was simpler (and easier on the parents back home, perhaps) to play along. Her growing autonomy was marked by her changing credits: in the early shows she was listed as Rosie Michaels, then the nom de plume Rosie Apple, and finally as Rosie Shuster. In her sketches, she sometimes named characters after Florence Lipowitz's friends, "like Mrs. Kelman," she said. "It would make Lorne cringe. It was like chalk on a blackboard to him. It was me just going, 'You can't make me go away.'" (Looking at what has been written about the show over the years, she believes that there's been "a severe excision" of her contribution.)

Michaels didn't indulge what Shuster called the show's "testosterone energy," but he also didn't intervene much. He was like a parent who lets the children sort out their squabbles themselves. Newman calls the notion that the women were sidelined "bullshit"; Michaels's experience writing for Joan Rivers, Diller, and Tomlin, she felt, made him appreciate female perspectives. Shuster worried that the women writers could easily get stuck in a female ghetto, "like in magazines, when you have to write the baking column." Marilyn Miller saw this as an opportunity, not a limitation. "I wrote this very sensitive and observant stuff about how life actually is—female-feeling pieces," she said—sketches about preteens comparing notes on making babies, or Radner's Judy Miller character, a bravura solo turn as a little girl putting on shows for her stuffed animals and jumping up and down on her bed, emoting. (This was based in part on Radner's own stories of being fed Dexedrine and sent to her room as a kid.) "Lorne was interested in inner life," Miller said.

Getting "female-feeling pieces" on the air was a priority for Michaels, but one of his regular put-downs was to say that a sketch was "too Carol Burnett." That could mean that it had a pat ending, but it also referred to tone. "'Carol Burnett' was Broadway. We were rock and roll," Michaels said. "Their sketches were about alcoholism, divorce, life in the suburbs, middle-aged stuff. I wanted us writing about *our* stuff."

To that end, *Saturday Night* reveled in jokes about Belushi's doctor cutting off his drug supply, or about Radner's food issues. (Bulimia, like alcoholism, hadn't been medicalized yet, and both were seen as prime comedy fodder.) "It's all we girls talked about," Miller recalled. "What we ate and whether we put cigarettes out in our food to keep from eating it. We couldn't compete with all the models that would come and hang out, so we just thought, 'At least we'll be thin.'" (Newman once wrote a note to Michaels on an NBC memo form. Under SUBJECT, it said, "My weight problem." MESSAGE: "I've gained 5 pounds! 3 more and I will weigh 90 pounds.") Radner said that she'd thrown up in every toilet in Rockefeller Center. So they put it on the air; in a sketch set in ancient Greece, Newman played a character named "Anorexia."

As the season went on, "real life" for Michaels and his people was swallowed by the life of the show. They spent all their time together; even on Sundays, their only day off, they'd gather at the Russian Tea Room and then watch *60 Minutes* at Michaels's apartment. "I have no personal life at all anymore," he told a reporter that season, adding that he worried about "losing touch." Miller said, "You only went home to take a shower and change and get two hours' sleep." She organized a seder in the office, with food from Pastrami 'n Things, so that the work wouldn't be interrupted. Aykroyd never unpacked his bags. Newman never bought furniture. Chase's apartment held only a mattress. "You didn't mix with the world or with other people because you were locked in that building," Shuster said. "The sketches became completely self-referential. It became a bubble."

It was the seventies, and relationships were fluid and fleeting. Shuster at some point started seeing Dan Aykroyd, and the relationship was an open secret. Aykroyd had also been involved with Newman, and, back in Toronto, with Radner, who was also with Gary Weis at one point. In the second season, Shuster based the character of Fred Garvin, male prostitute, on a bit Aykroyd did lounging around her apartment. Radner had a crush on Paul Simon and was hurt when he took up with Carrie Fisher, who was also briefly engaged to Aykroyd. Fisher also dated O'Donoghue, who had a dalliance with Paul Simon's ex Edie Baskin, who was also briefly involved with Tom Davis. A bit later, when Radner got together with Bill Murray, their chemistry shone through in the teen nerd couple they played, Lisa Loopner and Todd DiLaMuca. (Another example of the show's extreme insularity: Anne Beatts got the idea for the Nerds sketch after Elvis Costello, a poster boy for geek chic, was a musical guest.)

The intertwined intimacies spilled into the sketches; the togetherness produced material, and it forged a tendency to push boundaries. Radner used to say that the cast wasn't afraid to cry in front of each other or to yell at each other; the group's "ocean of neurotic energy," as she termed it, fueled the creative process.

By the time Tomlin hosted, the press was behind the show. Even the *Times*'s O'Connor backpedaled and visited the office to interview Michaels. He singled out Chevy Chase for minting Update jokes out of news that was hours old, and his piece ended on an unintentionally ominous note: "Mr. Chase is already wondering if the 'Weekend Update' has run its course."

WHEN RICHARD PRYOR, THE NAME ON WHICH MICHAELS HAD STAKED THE integrity of his show, came to host in December, the week did not go smoothly. Michaels had already secretly agreed to NBC's demand that there be a tape delay, so that if Pryor let loose with a string of "motherfuckers," they could be bleeped. The network proposed a ten-second delay, and eventually settled on five. Years later, Pryor wrote, "If I'd known, I never would've shown up."

Getting NBC on board was only half of it. Confirming the booking with Pryor was just as hard. In November, on his first Saturday off, Michaels flew to Miami with John Head and Craig Kellem to finalize the details. They met Pryor in a ratty greenroom between sets he was doing at a jai alai fronton. Pryor had a slew of conditions: he insisted on bringing his own writer, Paul Mooney, who was also at the meeting; he wanted the spoken-word performer Gil Scott-Heron as the musical guest; he asked for enough comp tickets to fill most of the audience; and he insisted that his friend Thalmus Rasulala; his girlfriend, Kathy McKee; and his ex-wife Shelley perform in the show.

The demands, which Michaels agreed to, would effectively integrate, for a night, what had been an almost entirely white show. It was a lot to accommodate, but the disenfranchised characters that Pryor would bring into the tame arena of television, like news from the future, were what made him so necessary for Michaels. As they headed back to New York, he told Kellem, "He'd better be funny."

The week started out tense and stayed that way. Pryor was angry that, in the Miami jai alai greenroom, Michaels had subjected Mooney to what he considered an interrogation about his comedy credentials; he compared it to a parole board hearing. The *Saturday Night* staff was disappointed that the comedian refused to come to the office until rehearsals began. Michaels sent Herb Sargent, the television veteran, over to Pryor's Park Avenue hotel to brief him. Pryor, grumbly, asked to see the script. There was no script; the writers would stay up Tuesday night writing the sketches for read-through. Pryor became agitated. When it looked like he was about to pull out, Sargent devised an exit strategy: he said he was heading back to the office to get a copy of "the script."

Worried by Sargent's report, Michaels dropped by with Belushi to pitch Pryor a piece involving his Samurai character. Pryor liked it (apparently he collected Samurai swords), and Michaels was relieved to be able to put one sketch on the board.

When Pryor showed up to rehearse, midweek, the show came together. He played the priest to Laraine Newman's possessed teen in an *Exorcist* parody ("Your mother sews socks that smell!"). Belushi manned a hotel concierge desk and faced off against Pryor as a Samurai bellhop. The best thing in the show is a sketch in which Chase plays a man interviewing Pryor for a job. Mooney, in his memoir, said that he based the sketch on "the fucking cross-examination Lorne subject[ed] me to" in Miami. The piece ends with Chase subjecting

Pryor to a seemingly benign word-association test. "Dog," says Chase. "Tree," Pryor answers. Chase ups the ante, forcing Pryor, ultimately, to turn the tables and reverse the power dynamic:

CHASE: Negro.

PRYOR: Whitey.

CHASE: Tarbaby.

PRYOR: What'd you say?

CHASE: Tarbaby.

PRYOR: Ofay.

CHASE: Colored.

PRYOR: Redneck.

CHASE: Junglebunny.

PRYOR: Peckerwood!

CHASE: Burrhead.

PRYOR: Cracker.

CHASE: Spearchucker.

PRYOR: White trash.

CHASE: Junglebunny.

PRYOR: Honky.

CHASE: Spade.

PRYOR: Honky honky!

CHASE: N———!

PRYOR: *Dead honky!*

The interview concludes with Pryor in a quivering rage, and a whimpering Chase offering him the job at an elevated salary, making him "the highest-paid janitor in America."

The sketch was a sensation; Mooney called it "an H-bomb that Richard and I toss into America's consciousness." Chase's memory was that he and Mooney wrote it together; he remembered "asking Richard for as many slang words for white people as he could come up with." Michaels said, "Paul Mooney was taking credit for writing the show till the day he died." Mooney disdained Chase. "Chevy Chase was the doll-baby," he said, "the darling of the discotheque with straight teeth, and Richard wanted to knock them out." (To get an idea of what Pryor was up against, a *Rolling Stone* piece about the show complained about the comedian's need "to lard the evening with his now tiresome ethnicity.") As for the tape delay, after NBC's engineers painstakingly MacGyvered an apparatus involving a peg board and spools to meet the need, Davy Wilson's crew couldn't figure out how to work it.

Down on the executive floor, Herb Schlosser considered the word-association sketch a "tour de force," and the show did a 7.3 rating, a new high. When the episode was repeated, in March, it got a 9 rating; in July, it ran a third time, with an 11 rating. Based on that, NBC signed Pryor to a prime-time series. "That's American culture, the part I love the most," Michaels said. "It's like, 'You absolutely can't have him!' And then he's president of the United States."

FOXHOLE WRITING

MICHAELS AND HIS PEOPLE KNEW THAT THE SHOW WAS BECOMING A PHE-
nomenon, but they didn't quite grasp how big a phenomenon. Shuster recalled how "freaky" it was to emerge from the cocoon on Sunday,
go to a bodega to buy milk, and hear someone talking about one of her
sketches.

One person heard it more than the rest. Chase started noticing
that, as he walked down the street, he would hear "*ch-ch*" as people
passed. "They were quietly saying, '*Chevy Chase, Chevy Chase,*'" he
said. "It had never occurred to me that this late-night show would be
watched by so many people. And I became fucking huge. Not that I
didn't deserve it." Sometimes, for read-through, Chase would turn in
a sheet of paper on which he'd written only the words "Me being
funny." Buck Henry said, "Lorne had a soft spot for Chevy, partly for
his Waspiness, but mainly it was about Chevy being hilariously, scar-
ily funny."

Having a star was good for the show but bad for morale. "The
byproduct of the show was that the cast became famous," Michaels
said. "That had not been the intent. Certainly, it was not the intent
that one person would emerge as the star." Belushi, who took Chase's
overnight fame the hardest, required the most solicitude. "There's a
certain kind of person who, if they're not famous by twenty-six, they
are going to burst into flames," Michaels said. Belushi was the first of

many. Michaels counseled patience and explained to Belushi that, since Chase said his name on the air every week, people knew him. He said, "It's just going to take longer for them to know you."

Belushi devised ways of dodging Chase's shadow. Under Carswell's budget, the network rented one limousine to ferry the host around each week. "John would walk the host out of the party, and get in the car with the person," Michaels said. "Then he'd drop the host at the hotel and stay in the limo. He'd lean out the window with one hand on the roof and get driven around the city in hopes of being recognized." Faced with the limo bills, Michaels would tell him, "John, you can't return the limousine at six in the morning."

The tension heated up in late December, when *New York* magazine put Chase on the cover, under the line "And heeeere's TV's hottest new comedy star!" In the article, Jeff Greenfield said that five million households (twice as many as had watched the Carson reruns) were tuning in to *Saturday Night,* mainly because of Chase, whom he called "heir apparent to Johnny Carson" and "on the road to bigger things. In prime time." Michaels threw gasoline on the fire by expounding on Chase's "likability." Greenfield picked up on Chase's sharp elbows, quoting an unnamed colleague calling him a "two-faced" opportunist.

It annoyed the cast and writers when Chase compared the show to "playing at the top of the minors." (Michaels put the irritation on the air: in a subsequent cold open, Garrett Morris sticks a pin into a Chevy voodoo doll.) Chase offended Carson when he scoffed at the heir-apparent suggestion: "I'd never be tied down for five years interviewing TV personalities." A couple of years later, after Chase tanked a gig guest-hosting *Tonight,* Carson told a reporter, "He couldn't ad-lib a fart after a baked bean dinner."

Despite the good press, as the first season's Christmas break approached, Michaels was feeling anxious. Candice Bergen's second time hosting had been a little too full of holiday coziness. Gary Weis's short film "Homeward Bound" paired the Simon and Garfunkel track with footage of air passengers being reunited with loved ones at the gate (back when loved ones could wait at the gate); carols were sung; and the cast skidded around the Rockefeller Center skating rink in their bee suits. Michaels considered the episode soft. The sharpest thing in it was a fake commercial—Aykroyd as the proprietor of Mel's Char Palace, a DIY steakhouse with live cows on the menu: "You stun it, you cut it, you charbroil it!"

After a grueling eight shows, the staff was looking forward to a holiday breather. Miller, Radner, and Zweibel tagged along on a trip to the Bahamas with Michaels's Uncle Pep and Aunt Joyce. Belushi and Aykroyd lined up a drive-away Oldsmobile and took off across the country. Michaels holed up to write in the RCA Building with Chase and O'Donoghue, determined to bring the next episode up to par. It would air on January 10, with Elliott Gould as host.

He decided to go back to the strongest characters the cast had done in the screen tests: Newman's Valley Girl and, in a piece that prefigured *The Sopranos,* Belushi's Brando, as a mafia boss in group therapy. The Bees returned too, as a killer swarm, with Gould as the leader of their revolutionary hive. Suddenly, in the middle of the sketch, the only things in the frame are the actors' knees. Breaking the fourth wall, Chase yells, "Hold it!" He drops to the floor and into the shot, and calls out, *"Lorne! Lorne Michaels!"* Michaels's khaki pant legs appear. "What's the problem?" he asks. He gets down on his knees too, and says into the camera, "I'm Lorne Michaels. I'm the producer of this show." He promises to take care of the "minor technical problem." Cut to Michaels, striding purposefully out of the studio, fuming, his hands in fists. In the control room, Davy Wilson is slumped over his console, surrounded by empty liquor bottles. Michaels slaps him around and takes command. Onstage, Belushi in his bee suit says, "Lorne Michaels has the biggest heart in show business," and explains that he'd hired the director despite his drinking problem. "But he knows we've got a show to do. And if he has to fire him, he will. Because he's *that* kind of producer." The pulpy drama ratcheted up, Belushi concludes, "I wouldn't be in Lorne's shoes for all the money in the world, because right now, he's probably in there firing his own father!" The audience roared.

The sketch was the first instance of what Michaels calls "the show itself speaking." It had multiple resonances. The idea of him angrily berating an employee, and even firing one, was funny because it was so unlikely. (He did not fire anyone during the show's first five years.) A Freudian might also note that his first on-camera moment is a confrontation with a fake father—a histrionic reenactment, played for laughs, of the scene that occurred right before Henry Lipowitz's collapse. But this time, the son is ready for his new responsibilities. In the end credits, the fired director Davy Wilson's name is crudely X'd out.

BUOYED BY THE RESULTS OF HIS CHRISTMAS-BREAK WRITING MARATHON, Michaels tried to rev the metabolism of the rest of the group. He was finding that it was a struggle for the writers even to turn out enough pieces for read-through. O'Donoghue referred to their process as "foxhole writing," with no time for overthinking. Michaels was a deft editor. "A sketch would come in at fifteen pages, and Lorne would cut to the quick," Chase said. "He'd figure out what it was really about."

To Michaels's way of thinking, precision in comedy is as unequivocal as a surgeon's cut. Miss your mark by a millimeter, and the joke dies. He subscribed to Twain's observation that the difference between the almost right word and the right word is the difference between the lightning bug and the lightning. When going over writers' scripts, he'd tell them, somewhat cryptically, to remember to leave something for the audience to do. That meant, don't go too fast or overexplain; make sure to give viewers space to make connections. He'd quote Billy Wilder: "Give the audience two plus two and let them make four."

Paul Pape, Michaels's boyhood friend from Toronto, visited the studio that first year, and to his lawyerly mind, the show-making process looked like chaos. "They'd have meetings that weren't meetings," he said. "Nothing seemed to get accomplished." But on Saturday night, he saw his friend switch into another gear. The ninety minutes between dress and air have always been the crucible that creates the finished product. "On Saturday, all the talk stops," Michaels says. "Now we have to put on a show."

The drill has stayed the same for fifty years. During dress rehearsal, done before a full audience, Michaels sits in a makeshift booth tucked under the bleachers on the studio floor, watching the action on a monitor and dictating rapid-fire notes. After the dress rehearsal, he learned, early on, to use the seconds it took to walk up the interior stairs from 8H to his office to sort through the torrent of competing priorities. "Will so-and-so come up in performance? Do I want to bet on this piece, which didn't play? Does this lineup make the host look good? This music cue was off, that camera cut was late," he said. "You're fixing a thousand things, but the amount that you can *really* fix in a few seconds is finite." He keeps all the interlocking parts in his head.

In the ninety minutes between dress and air, his office over the studio on the ninth floor turns into an emergency room. Deciding what sketches will go on the air is triage. At that point, the show is no longer an egalitarian enterprise. After all the waffling in editing rooms on his previous projects, he found the need for decisiveness liberating. "I figured out that I'm good under fire," he said. With the whole staff crammed into his office, he runs through the notes he dictated during dress. At the end of that tense half hour, with many meticulously reworked sketches summarily ditched, he concludes with a low-energy version of a coach's pep talk, an ironic statement along the lines of "This is going to be the best show we've ever done."

At that, the whirlwind picks up: cue cards are re-lettered in a frenzy, unneeded flats and scenery are hustled out of the studio, the cast races to get into costume and makeup. Out on home base, the warm-up act—usually a few cast members singing R&B—is stoking the studio audience. "Everything is leading to those final three minutes," he said. As a stage manager counts down—twenty seconds, ten seconds—the energy level is off the charts; the ordeal is about to begin. There is one pool of stillness. Michaels strolls out from his under-the-bleachers lair and sips a glass of wine, having done all he can do.

As his show gained momentum, its doppelgänger cratered. In January, ABC canceled *Saturday Night Live with Howard Cosell,* after eighteen episodes. *People* magazine suggested that it was "an insult to the American intelligence and an abomination to the American eye." Roone Arledge blamed the time slot, saying, "You could have Elizabeth Taylor doing a striptease and it wouldn't get a 15 share." Michaels sent Arledge a note asking if he could have his show's original name back. The answer was yes, although, for technical reasons, *Saturday Night* wouldn't become *Saturday Night Live* until its third season.

MICHAELS HAD PROMISED SCHLOSSER THAT *SATURDAY NIGHT* WOULD FIGure itself out by the tenth episode. He'd beaten that estimate, but the tenth show marked a milestone. It was hosted by Buck Henry, who would come back to host nine more times. Michaels considers Henry "a founder" of the show and an enormous personal influence. (He speaks of the founders the way Supreme Court scholars speak of "the framers.") Like Michaels, Henry grew up in a family that gossiped about show business around the kitchen table, although Henry's version was far more glamorous. He was born Henry Zuckerman in the Bronx; his mother was a silent film actress (a Mack Sennett Bathing Beauty), and his father was a stockbroker. They were Stork Club habitués, along with Hemingway and Bogart and Bacall.

Henry's first encounter with *Saturday Night* was at a Hollywood party; he was mystified when the music and chatter stopped dead and a TV set was turned on. "I thought, 'Good God, they're going to stop drinking and doing drugs so they can watch *a television show?*'" he recalled. When he came to host, he was a natural. Henry had written on *The Garry Moore Show,* and this both helped and hurt. His first week, he suggested a punchline to end a sketch and got a side-eye from one of the writers. "Too Carol Burnett," he was told. "I like a button on everything," Henry explained. But he got on board. He loved Belushi's Samurai character, and he told Michaels that they should do it again. Repeating characters hadn't been part of the plan, and to some staff members it felt hacky. But to Michaels, who had to fill his bulletin board with cards every week, it sounded like a great idea.

The first time Henry hosted, Michaels asked him to come into his office and watch something that Michael O'Donoghue was pitching. O'Donoghue started in on a routine, an imitation of the talk-show host Mike Douglas plunging 15-inch steel needles into his eyes. The impersonation consisted of O'Donoghue shrieking and rolling around on the floor. "It was pure Dada," Henry said. He fell over laughing, and gave the piece his blessing. (Mike Douglas, like sea monkeys, was a regular motif for O'Donoghue. The NBC censor once cut an Update joke he'd written about a revised Catholic liturgy, in which the host would be supplemented with a co-host, representing the body of Mike Douglas.)

Michaels's preferences ran toward sunnier comedy, while O'Donoghue favored what the *Lampoon* crowd called slash-and-burn humor. O'Donoghue would taunt Michaels for his "Canadian schoolteacher taste," and called him by the nickname Mouse Mittens. But Michaels was open to edginess, and Henry pushed him in that direction. (Henry had his own dark streak, and was always trying to get Michaels to go with him to Show World over on Eighth Avenue, where a stripper named Monica Kennedy had an act shooting a hot dog out of her vagina.)

Henry was the host who would do the taste-free sketches that other hosts rejected—the ones that were intended to be "dangerous" but were often just crude. For instance, a piece called "Stunt Baby" milked the shock value of showing a baby doll (purporting to be a real infant) hurled around the set and bounced off walls. Or Henry's "Uncle Roy" character, the pedophile babysitter who hides candies in his pockets and says to his young charges, "Find the treasure!"

AFTER REVIEWING A DRAFT *SATURDAY NIGHT* SCRIPT LATE IN THE WEEK, AN editor with NBC's Broadcast Standards department would fill out a "Script Acceptability Report," which stipulated that "the acceptabil-

ity of program material covered by this report is subject to the incor-
poration of the requests made herein"; final approval would not be
given "until a rough cut is viewed by a member of this department."
Since there was no rough cut to view on a live show, the Standards
editor—or censor, to use the staff's term—would sit in the 8H control room during dress rehearsal, scribbling on a pad. The first person
assigned to the show was Jay Ottley, an easygoing man who was in
sync with Michaels. If a problem came up, the matter would be referred to his boss, Herminio Traviesas, a middle-aged suburbanite
known as "Travie." His other nickname was "Mr. Clean." Once, when
Barbara Eden, from *I Dream of Jeannie,* was scheduled to reveal her
belly button for the first time ever, on *Laugh-In,* Traviesas vetoed it.

"Lorne was good at handling Travie," Schlosser said. But the show
didn't spur all that much outrage. The complaints about Carlin's God
monologue, Schlosser said, were nothing compared to the reaction
in 1969 when Bill Cosby, on *The Tonight Show,* had referred to com-
munion wafers as "individual pizzas." Buck Henry never forgot an impasse with the censor over a nonverbal joke: making a circle with
the thumb and index finger of one hand, then poking the forefinger
of the other hand through it—the adolescent-boy semaphore for sex.
The censor asked for a demonstration, then told him, "We have to
have a meeting about this upstairs."

Michaels wasn't too concerned about cranky viewers. He always
had the example of the Smothers Brothers in the back of his mind,
and took a businesslike approach. Of the Standards people, he said,
"They're not Oxford dons trying to uphold a moral bar. What it's really
all about is: Will an advertiser object?" Representatives from ad agen-
cies sat in the control room's "client booth" during dress rehearsal. If
a Toyota ad, say, was slated to air too close to a World War II sketch,
the running order might be tweaked.

The writer whose material inflamed the censors most often was
O'Donoghue. One of his rallying cries was: "Comedy is a baby seal
hunt." He liked to say, "We're doing this instead of hitting you in the
face." Sometimes a sketch could be written so that a censor, reading
a script, would miss the main point. One such item was a sportscast

on the "Claudine Longet Invitational" ski tournament. Longet, the ex-wife of Andy Williams, was facing homicide charges after accidentally shooting her lover, the Olympic skier Vladimir "Spider" Sabich. The bit featured stock footage of skiers speeding downhill. As each one wipes out, the crack of a bullet is heard (Chase: "Uh-oh, it looks like he has been accidentally shot by Claudine Longet!"). Traviesas had okayed the script, but the gunshots over the images of the falling skiers had a powerfully disturbing effect. The next week, Michaels was compelled to have Don Pardo read an apology on the air; it wouldn't be the last time the show had to backtrack on a taste issue.

If Standards had a problem with a script, Michaels would buy time by reasoning that it was impossible to tell if something was offensive until he could see how it did at dress rehearsal, and whether it "chilled" the audience. George Schlatter, the *Laugh-In* creator, always liked to say, "You can con people about drama, you can con people about music, but you can't con people about comedy because if it gets a laugh, it's good." Michaels could also appeal to fiscal responsibility, telling a censor that a lot of money had already been spent on a set and costumes. In these moments, Zweibel said, "The poise thing was off the charts."

Occasionally, a performer would comply with a directive from the censor at dress rehearsal, and then, on air, with a wink from Michaels, revert to the original. This is how viewers were able to enjoy the sight of Aykroyd, playing a refrigerator repairman, kneeling down and placing a pencil in his "plumber's crack" in a Nerds sketch. Ottley had ordered him not to do it. But Aykroyd had asked Tom Davis to stand next to Ottley during the air show, and to hand him a diversionary shot of whiskey at the crucial pencil moment.

Early on, Ottley was replaced by Jane Crowley, a Margaret Dumont–ish figure whom Johnny Carson used to refer to, on air, as "Priscilla Goodbody." The writers liked to goad her, salting pieces with references—"Hershey Highway," "golden showers"—that they thought would go over her head. (The former did; the latter didn't.) Once, Crowley objected to an Update piece in which Belushi, as a ranting weatherman, suggested alternatives to the phrase "Don't rain on my parade." The line that Crowley nixed was "Don't take a dump on my parade." O'Donoghue wanted revenge. The fix that he came up with, which Crowley approved, was "Don't drain your boils on my parade."

Generally, the writers mediated with the censors themselves, and they continued to do so for fifty years. *A Very Punchable Face,* a memoir by Colin Jost, who joined the show as a writer in 2005, contains a chapter called "Notes from the Censor," which reprints, without context, requests that the Standards people passed along:

—Please Revise "You piece of <u>shit</u>" and let's talk over the term "cuck."

—Please delete "Jesus comes from sperm."

—Lose the line: "<u>I'm gonna sit on your dick so hard that you die</u>."

—Let's discuss the "wheelchair" riff.

—Delete "God lives for <u>Puss</u>" and let's discuss options that are not centered on female/male genitalia.

—Let's lose the "balls" and make the "penis" a rocket.

—Also, have an alt for "Cowboys and Indians."

—In the "O.J./<u>Grease</u> Mash-Up Musical"—revise the last beat of the song: "<u>He killed Ron Goldman</u>/like a stabby stabby slashy slashy stabbady-slashy-do/And then his ex-wife/like a jabby jabby knifey knifey jabbady-stabby-do."

—Let's soften the line "I got banged twice." Delete "his <u>fingers</u>."

—Caution on "double fisting" beat.

—In "New Medication Ad," what do you envision during the "offensive" Asian impression beat?

—Please revise "<u>1-800-Pubes for Kids</u>" which does not fall within our pre-approved range of phone numbers.

The censors didn't get involved in the issue of whether the show could take shots at the network. The lameness of television was always in Michaels's sights, and he considered NBC a perfectly fine target. (It embarrassed him when the network ran cringey ads for the show, like one urging viewers to "Stay in, stay up, and *dig*.") O'Donoghue wrote a sketch, one of his best, about an NBC executive (Elliott Gould) coming aboard the Starship *Enterprise* and canceling *Star Trek,* as its crew (Belushi as Captain Kirk, Chase as Spock) regard the interloper as an alien life form and try to kill him with their phasers, which have been deactivated by the network. The executive removes Spock's pointy ears to return them to the props department and has the set carried out piece by piece. Kirk dictates the final entry in his Starlog. "We have tried," he says, "to boldly go where no man has gone before. And except for one television network, we have found intelligence everywhere in the galaxy."

Unless ad revenue was affected, network executives didn't seem to mind what the show did. It surprised Michaels a bit that the censors weren't much bothered by references to drugs in sketches, part of the show's mandate to put "real life" on the air. Curtin recalled, "All the sketches about drug use, it was totally in the network's face. There were drug dealers in the hallway." On Update, Chase once gave a report on a strain of pot that the FBI was calling Killer Dope: "In order to aid the FBI in their investigation, Weekend Update is undertaking its own analysis of marijuana sent to us anonymously by any viewers who may be worried." A mailing address appeared on-screen.

Cocaine helped fuel the all-nighters, but pot was the day-to-day workhorse drug. Shuster said that it helped you to "see things sideways." Monty Python's Eric Idle, after hosting the show, remarked on the writers being "whacked out of their skulls." A few suppliers were fixtures in the office. One regular dealer, a man named Merlin David, would roam the halls peddling hand-tooled leather bags and knapsacks. (He kept the drugs inside.) Aykroyd bought a briefcase with a shoulder strap, which he held up during the Goodnights once, Merlin David himself milling onstage. "I hated this guy so much," Curtin recalled. "I just wanted him gone, but he had free rein."

Another dealer, a Connecticut man who went by "Captain Jack," specialized in a strain of weed known as Gulzar Afghanica, which was dubbed "the smell of SNL." Captain Jack was the grandson of a bootlegger for Dutch Schultz, and he distributed plants of his special indica all around the seventeenth floor. Aykroyd recalled, "You could fly an F-16 on it, or judge a murder trial. It was just what we needed to stay at it through three, four, five in the morning." Captain Jack was a regular on seventeen, even attending read-throughs. "Lorne always tolerated my presence," he said. "You could pretty much get away with murder."

FIFTEEN

TALK OF THE TOWN

"THE HISTORY OF NEW YORK IS WRITTEN BY OUT-OF-TOWNERS" IS A LINE that Michaels likes to throw around, attributing it to Harold Ross, the Colorado-born founding editor of *The New Yorker*. There is no record of Ross saying such a thing, but the point is that Michaels identifies with Ross, as a person from Nowheresville who created one of New York's defining institutions. "It's very rare that it's a local who does that," Michaels said. "Whether it's Rupert Murdoch coming from Australia, or Ross, or myself." As a reader and a status seeker, it was a big deal for him when, halfway through *Saturday Night*'s first season, he made the acquaintance of William Shawn, Ross's (Chicago-born) successor at *The New Yorker,* and Shawn's companion, the writer Lillian Ross (no relation to Harold).

When Lillian Ross showed up in Studio 8H one day, notebook in hand, Michaels didn't know who she was. Buck Henry filled him in, explaining that she had written a famous and controversial profile of Ernest Hemingway, and a book called *Picture,* a close-up saga of the making of John Huston's *The Red Badge of Courage*. Michaels, a student of show business, promptly read the book. *Picture* was a story he could relate to; it showed how the work of an idealistic maverick could be messed with by a soulless studio.

Soon he found himself sitting in a red velvet banquette, the guest of Shawn and Ross, at La Caravelle, their regular spot, on West Fifty-fifth Street. A little table lamp illuminated flecks of chives in the champagne cream of his Poularde Maison Blanche, the braised chicken dish that his hosts insisted he order. President Kennedy, they told him, used to get it to go, to eat on *Air Force One*. Ross was voluble and lively, but Michaels had to lean in to hear Shawn. The heady talk was studded with references to William Maxwell and their friend "Jerry" Salinger. (It was in connection with the latter, Michaels remembered, that he learned the meaning of the word "recluse.")

Shawn had a reputation for seriousness, but he and Ross were comedy fans, and they would usher Michaels into another precinct of New York cultural life. "I was so innocent," Michaels said. "Lillian came into my life; suddenly there was Bill Shawn, and those restaurants, and advice, and a million other things. They were two of the people who began to color stuff in." It was important to Michaels that these literary people, close in age to his parents' generation, liked and respected him. He learned from them the finer gradations of metropolitan manners, such as reverse snobbery. Ross and Shawn didn't like *The New York Times*, which they considered highfalutin and dull. They claimed that they only read the *Daily News*, the unpretentious paper of the people. Ross appealed to Michaels's love of blue-chip Old Hollywood—she'd gone sailing with Bogart and played tennis with Chaplin. Huston's producer, Gottfried Reinhardt, once said, "I watched Louis B. Mayer kiss all five of her fingers."

It wasn't long before Ross declared her intention to write about Michaels in *The New Yorker*. Being profiled by the writer whose subjects included not just Hemingway, but Chaplin, Truffaut, Godard, and Fellini was another dose of affirmation. Ross didn't conduct direct interviews so much as just hang around. Michaels called it "that foot-in-the-door quality." For the next decade, Ross planted herself in the show's offices and at Michaels's homes, sometimes with her son Erik in tow. When Michaels got a house in Amagansett, Long Island, Ross could reliably be found on the tennis court. The notebook was not much in evidence; James Thurber had called Ross "the girl with the built-in tape recorder."

A lot of the dinner conversations with Shawn had to do with the tension inherent in hiring creative people, then being patient while they find their voices. Shawn expended a lot of emotional energy worrying about his writers, who vied for his favor in a neurotic way. He teased Michaels about what he called his "pseudo-egalitarian" approach to *Saturday Night*—his notion that everyone was equally necessary. "Bill meant that I hadn't learned yet that some were more talented than others," he said. "And that it could never be 'fair.'"

Michaels had read Orwell's *Homage to Catalonia,* and he related to its description of fighting alongside anarchists in the Spanish Civil War. "When they fight, they have roles—and ranks," he said. "And when they're not fighting, they're all equal." He liked the sound of that: if only he could be a general on Saturday night and everyone's pal during the week. Shawn made him think about how his staff viewed him as all-powerful, and it felt a little lonely.

Like Aunt Joyce and Uncle Pep, Ross and Shawn offered a steadiness that he'd learned not to expect from his mother. He felt valued by them. When Florence Lipowitz addressed her son, she could be sarcastic, an unspoken "Mr. Big Shot" at the end of every sentence. When she talked to him on the phone on Sundays about the previous night's show, she wanted to know what "the brass" thought. It was hard for her to trust that things were going well. He explained to her that the higher-ups only looked at the numbers. "At some point I finally figured out that she was overwhelmingly on my side," he said. "But she never wanted to seem like a pushover about it." O'Donoghue, not the mildest of colleagues, went out to dinner with Michaels and Florence once. The next day, he asked a colleague, "How did he survive her?" He suddenly understood why Michaels had developed such a deep reservoir of resilience. (A lot of comedians are the sons of unimpressible mothers. When Johnny Carson gave his mother a mink coat for her birthday, she sent it back with a note: "Too fancy for Nebraska.") In Florence's later years, however, an Emmy sat atop her television.

It was as if Michaels was making his way around a Monopoly board of Manhattan cultural hubs. If Park Place was *The New Yorker,* then Boardwalk was Woody Allen. Now, a decade after the flat session in which they'd tried to write a lobster joke, Michaels opened his mailbox to find an invitation on heavy Cartier card stock to Allen's New Year's Eve party. The invitation threw him, and he didn't know what to wear. At the party, Allen made a point of introducing him to a woman named Jean Doumanian, who'd been a talent coordinator for Dick Cavett's show. Maybe, Allen suggested, there was a spot for her in *Saturday Night*'s talent department? "The moment he asked—of course I was hiring her," Michaels said. Doumanian, with her designer clothes and beauty salon hair, was more polished than most *Saturday Night* employees. Several times a day, a call for her would come in from "Mo Golden," whom everyone knew was Woody Allen.

The *Saturday Night* crowd had become sought-after guests all over town—in the art-world avant-garde, the music business. Hal Willner, the show's longtime music supervisor, who met Michaels at Elaine's that year, said, "Everyone had to have their SNL person at their parties." The show's own weekly post-show party was becoming a hot ticket, too; it was held at One Fifth, a restaurant near Washington Square that was furnished with castoffs from an old ocean liner. The maître d', a smart, raffish Brit from East London named Keith McNally, endeared himself to Michaels immediately. "He had one foot in the theater," Michaels said (a line he often used to describe himself). In London, McNally had operated the spotlight in *The Rocky Horror Show,* a job that explained his knack for flattering lighting. The restaurants he later created exuded a tarnished nostalgia for an indistinct past, framed by cloudy mirrors and pressed-tin ceilings—urban decay with excellent french fries and martinis. Like Michaels, McNally had a talent for confecting a scene that made participants feel lucky to be there.

WHEN MICHAELS HIRED JEAN DOUMANIAN, HE HOPED THAT SHE WOULD BE able to help book bigger stars to host. But even with her on staff, he never landed Woody Allen, who was at the top of his wish list: others included Donald Sutherland, Michael Caine, Richard Nixon, Jack Nicholson, Johnny Carson, and Warren Beatty. He deputized Chase to woo Leonard Bernstein when the two were seated together at Kurt Vonnegut's fiftieth birthday party; Bernstein made a pass, Chase rebuffed it, and that was the end of it.

Although Michaels was barely thirty, he had become a master at handling stars, instinctually deploying a matter-of-fact authority. Celebrities are used to having control; on SNL's turf, they had none, and Michaels had learned how to turn their destabilization to his advantage. When a host pushed back on a script, he'd calmly say, "These are jokes. This is what we do." Most hosts started the week in panic. Eric Idle described hosting as "this thing that was being done to you." Some showed up not even understanding that the show was live; as Saturday approached, they'd ask, "When do we tape?" When hosts didn't seem to be getting it, Michaels would bounce them over to Howard Shore, who had a windowless rehearsal room with a piano. Shore would ask, "What can you do? Can you dance? Can you sing? Can you juggle?" This could backfire, as when Madeline Kahn showed up to host wearing gigantic clown shoes. Shore recalled, "We looked at each other on Monday and said, 'What are we possibly going to do for ninety minutes on Saturday?' We weren't cutting sketches in the early days." When Raquel Welch hosted, Shore sat through her entire Vegas act, which started with "Let Me Entertain You." Welch had told Michaels ahead of time that she was fine doing a few jokes about her bustline, but he nixed a dumb gag the writers pitched in which the camera kept repeatedly dropping from Welch's face to her chest. She vetoed a few too, including a witless O'Donoghue conceit about her zeppelins bursting into flame when docking at Lakehurst.

If hosts didn't connect with the writers, Michaels intervened. Ruth Gordon, the eighty-year-old star of *Rosemary's Baby*, rejected most of the ideas pitched, including a Franken sketch in which she was to fall over dead. (Michaels won her over with two flower deliveries.) Some hosts were drunk all week. When Kris Kristofferson hosted, sozzled, Michaels dispatched Neil Levy to get vats of coffee. Louise Lasser, the star of the satirical soap opera *Mary Hartman, Mary Hartman*, behaved erratically all week when she hosted. A few months earlier, she'd been arrested in L.A. with cocaine in her purse (police were called after a kerfuffle when her credit card was declined at a toy store where she was trying to buy a $150 dollhouse). On the show, she was adamant about doing a monologue with her dog. Michaels tried to talk her out of it, explaining, "When you put a dog under lights, its tongue comes out and it looks like it's being tortured." Between dress and air, Lasser locked herself in her dressing room. Uncharacteristic shouting ensued. (Staff members were shocked to hear the boss use the word "cunt.") The show went on, shakily; Michaels remembers the panting dog as "painful." The episode, which has an amateurish art-film energy, has never been rerun.

With his reverence for the TV greats from the past, Michaels was keen on booking elder statesmen, which didn't always pan out. He invited Desi Arnaz to host in the first season as a tribute to *I Love Lucy.* Arnaz insisted on being put up at the Waldorf instead of the Berkshire Place Hotel, where other hosts stayed, and Michaels accommodated him. He later learned that in the thirties, when Arnaz played with Xavier Cugat and his Waldorf-Astoria Orchestra, he'd had to use the service entrance. For once, he wanted to walk in the front door. On the air, Arnaz was game, playing "Babalu" on the congas, white hair flying so wildly that observers thought he'd keel over. John Head referred to him as "Old Blue Lips."

Other hosts whose shows were never rerun include Milton Berle; his was an especially tortured episode for Michaels, given his stature as "Mr. Television." Besides being a notorious joke stealer (known to fellow comics as "the thief of bad gags"), he had a reputation for being difficult. When he hosted the show, he tried to take over. His monologue was a string of jokes that even viewers in 1979 found offensive. (A news headline: "Forty-Four Puerto Ricans in a Crash: The Bed Broke." "I've got so much gas I'm being followed by Arabs.") When Michaels patiently explained that ad-libbing in sketches wasn't allowed, Berle patronized him, putting a hand on his shoulder and saying, "I know—*satire.*"

SIXTEEN

THE SHOW ITSELF SPEAKING

IN MARCH 1976, A SAUL STEINBERG ILLUSTRATION CALLED "VIEW OF THE World from 9th Avenue" appeared on the cover of *The New Yorker*. It showed the blocks west to the Hudson River in minute detail, with the rest of the country, and the world beyond, condensed into a few strokes. The joke, about the city's self-absorption, could have applied to the hothouse atmosphere in the *Saturday Night* offices as the first season wound down. The staff, working around the clock, was only dimly aware of the show's wide popularity. They knew that Chase had caught on and that they were sought-after party guests, but they didn't know that their catchphrases—"Never mind" (Radner's Emily Litella), "But *noooooo*" (Belushi's weatherman)—were ricocheting around dorm rooms and high school cafeterias all over the country. Nor did they know that they were not particularly beloved within NBC.

The press was mostly on board, and the network was overrun with ticket requests. But the show was only an underground hit, and the ratings, because they were in late night, didn't impress the executive floor. NBC was down across the board, and a power shuffle was taking place among the networks. Fred Silverman, who had turned CBS around in the early seventies by implementing a "rural purge" of hayseed shows like *Petticoat Junction* and *Green Acres,* jumped to ABC in 1975, and his new slate (*Laverne & Shirley* and *Welcome Back, Kot-*

ter) put ABC ahead of NBC and, soon, CBS. NBC wasn't used to being in last place. Some affiliates in the South had started complaining that *Saturday Night* was offensive. The research department conducted a survey concluding that people found the sketches confusing, and suggested that Michaels let his performers ad-lib. The show went way over budget every week. But the young demographics—and Herb Schlosser—kept it safe.

Another boost came from an unlikely source—Mr. Talent, Dave Tebet. He offered Chevy Chase as entertainment to the 1976 annual Radio and Television Correspondents' Dinner, to be held in Washington, D.C., in March, with President Ford in attendance. Ron Nessen, Ford's press secretary, liked the idea. It would help smooth a side deal Nessen had already made with *Saturday Night*. Nessen had met Al Franken in New Hampshire that year, during the presidential primaries. Franken was tagging along with his news-photographer brother and ended up getting thrown off the press bus for asking Ronald Reagan a trick question about the decriminalization of marijuana and motorcycle helmet laws. Nessen told Franken that, despite the way Chevy Chase was making fun of his boss every week, he was a devoted viewer of *Saturday Night*. Michaels telephoned Nessen the following week, and soon NBC announced that the host for the April 17 show would be the president's press secretary.

Nessen didn't say yes just because he was a fan. He was hoping to effect some damage control by demonstrating that the Ford administration was in on the joke. As Nixon's handlers learned after his *Laugh-In* appearance, throwing in with the hip comedy crowd could provide an image refresh. Michaels knew that having Nessen host would make news, but he was determined not to let it look like the show was being used. He told the writers to pull no punches.

The Correspondents' Dinner, occurring a few weeks before the Nessen show, functioned as an icebreaker. On the day before the dinner, Michaels flew down to Washington with Chase and his fiancée, Jacqueline Carlin, along with Belushi and Aykroyd, who—in a preview of their future Blues Brothers personae—were posing as members of the Secret Service. Nessen had promised a tour of the

White House. After a snafu at the security gate (Belushi forgot his ID), they waited inside, Aykroyd amusing his friends by discreetly dropping a few coins in a White House ashtray. "Leaving a little tip as thanks for the tour," Chase recalled, with admiration. "You cannot touch Danny. He was the resident genius."

At the dinner itself, Chase was seated on the dais with the president, and he opened the festivities by standing at the podium and running through his full array of Fordisms. He took several spectacular tumbles, caught each time by Belushi and Aykroyd in their dark suits. "I have asked the Secret Service to remove the salad fork embedded in my left hand," he said. The president laughed, and so did the assembled dignitaries. After a performance by Up with People, it was Ford's turn to speak. He got some laughs too, addressing Chase as "a very funny suburb."

A few days before the Nessen episode, Michaels returned to the White House to film the president doing some bits to use in the show. He waited in the Cabinet Room while Ford did a photo op with the East Grand Rapids High School Band and met with his chief of staff, Dick Cheney. When Ford arrived for the taping, he greeted Michaels warmly but addressed him as "Chevy." Ford had three lines: "I'm Gerald Ford and you're not," "Ladies and Gentlemen, the press secretary to the president of the United States," and "Live from New York, it's Saturday Night." His delivery was stiff and uncomprehending, and when Michaels tried to loosen him up with a joke—"Mr. President, if this works out, who knows where it could lead"—Ford didn't get it.

On the Friday night before Nessen's show, an entry on President Ford's official White House schedule read: "5:35–6:16 PM The president practised his golf swing." At the same hour, in New York, Nessen was rehearsing a sketch in which, playing himself, he tells Tom Snyder (Aykroyd) about how the president gives milk and cookies to the White House staff at bedtime and reads them ghost stories. If Nessen thought that doing the show was going to burnish the president's image, he was mistaken. The episode was raunchy, containing an unusual amount of scatological material, and Emily Litella, Radner's malaprop-prone character, riffed about "the presidential erection." There was a feminine hygiene ad parody, in which Radner shills for "Autumn Fizz, the carbonated douche" (in strawberry, lemon, and egg cream). O'Donoghue contributed a piece about "Flucker's" jam ("With a name like Flucker's, it's got to be good") that included suggestions of other promising jam names, such as Nose Hair Jam, Death Camp Jam, Dog Vomit Jam, Painful Rectal Itch Jam, and Ten-Thousand-Nuns-and-Orphans-All-Eaten-by-Rats Jam.

The sketches featuring Nessen were straighter, and he looked delighted to be there. In one, he played himself, and sits by as the president (Chase) staples his own ear and cracks jokes about his power to pardon. After the show, at the party, Nessen seemed ecstatic. At an after-after-party at Paul Simon's apartment, he even got high with his new friends.

His elation didn't last. On Monday, his career was in jeopardy. Ford's previous press secretary, Jerald terHorst, called Nessen's appearance "a gross error of judgment." The first lady, Betty Ford, told reporters that she and her husband had laughed at the Ford-related sketches, but added that she thought the president's pre-recorded cut-ins made it look as though he had officially endorsed the show, including the "distasteful" parts. The president's twenty-five-year-old son, Jack, sent Nessen a note on White House stationery: "If you get a min., I'd be happy to explain to you that your job is to further the Pres. interests, not yours or your family's."

Nessen realized that he'd made a mistake. He'd thought the SNL people were on his side; he would have been shocked to know that Chase would hang the framed official White House photo of himself with Ford on his office wall having defaced it with a fake autograph—"Gerald Fuck/Fart/Ford."

The show, a disaster for Nessen, brought *Saturday Night* out of the college common room and into a bigger public sphere. *Saturday Night* had flipped off the president's press secretary, and the president, too. It was not the way network television usually worked, and it was an exhilarating feat of producing. In the *Times*, John J. O'Connor waffled about who had used whom, and called the episode a "cosmic co-opting."

The next episode blasted standard TV protocol again, by putting a new, enduring character in the spotlight—the Producer, Lorne Michaels.

For months, the press had been reporting a bidding war among promoters to entice the Beatles into doing a reunion concert, the price going as high as $230 million. Michaels decided to go on the air himself, to invite the Beatles to perform on *Saturday Night:* Seated at a desk decorated with a framed photo of Nixon and one of himself with Chase and President Ford, he stares straight into the camera. The mother-duck pin on his lapel is the only thing that pierces the seriousness of the scene. He begins by asking the audience's permission to allow him to address himself to "four very special people— John, Paul, George, and Ringo." He then makes the pitch: "Now, we've heard and read a lot about personality and legal conflicts that might prevent you guys from reuniting. That's something which is none of my business. You guys will have to handle that. But it's also been said that no one has yet to come up with enough money to satisfy you. Well, if it's money you want, there's no problem here. The National Broadcasting Company has authorized me to offer you a certified check for *three thousand dollars.*" He holds up a check as the camera zooms in, and the audience laughs crazily. "You divide it any way you want," he continues. "You want to give Ringo less, that's up to you."

Four years later, John Lennon famously told a *Playboy* writer that he was watching the show that night in his apartment in the Dakota with Paul McCartney, who'd dropped by. "We were watching it and almost went down to the studio, just as a gag," he said. Comedy can be a close confederate of exaggeration, and it turns out that the oft-told story of Lennon and McCartney almost dashing down to the studio that night is too good to be true. In 2020, McCartney clarified the details on a podcast: the Saturday he visited Lennon, he said, was the week *after* Michaels had made the pitch on the air. "As with all of these stories, it's kind of true, but it's not," McCartney said. "Lorne came on the telly the week *before*, and John told me, 'Saturday Night Live! . . . You know, we should go down there. It's live!' And so, for five minutes we were like 'Yeah, let's go down. That'd be great, what a hoot!' And then we went, 'No, let's not.'" (If they had in fact taken a cab to Fiftieth Street that night, they would have found an empty studio. *Saturday Night* was on a week's hiatus, its time slot filled by a pre-taped newsmagazine show featuring the mothers-in-law of the presidential candidates.)

The Beatles-check piece hit a lot of marks—the ludicrous calculus of the showbiz "get," eternal Beatlemania, NBC's lame pay scale ($3,000 was indeed the sum that the network had authorized Michaels to offer). Mostly, though, it solidified a signature tone. "It was the show speaking," said Michaels, who'd come up with the bit. Of his deadpan producer role, he said, "That played."

The more the show spoke in its own language, the stronger the hold on its viewers. So when Michaels showed up behind the desk again, the next season, to say that the host, Eric Idle, had taken the $3,000 and promised to bring the Beatles with him to New York, it was like the Samurai or Roseanne Roseannadanna (or, later, Church Lady or Stefon) appearing. (He told the viewers that Idle did not in fact bring the band, but a film of the band. That would be "The Rutles," a short that Idle made with Neil Innes about the "Pre-Fab Four"—"a musical legend that will last a lunchtime.") The following year, Michaels appeared at the desk a third time to address the Beatles, saying that he'd been "able to convince NBC to sweeten the pot." He holds up a check for three thousand, two hundred dollars, as Don Pardo's Wurlitzer voice describes the accommodations awaiting the lads at the Crosstown Motor Inn, where water glasses are sanitized for their protection, and checkout time is a lordly 10:00 A.M.

After the huge success of the first Beatles-check piece, the writers wanted more Lorne. "Producer Lorne Michaels" was written into a prologue to one of Franken and Davis's most memorable political sketches, "Final Days," which they'd completed with the help of a few tabs of acid. The prologue (and Michaels's lines) ended up getting cut, and the piece opened with Madeline Kahn, as a drunk Pat Nixon, writing in her diary, while her husband (Aykroyd) fulminates about "Jewboy" Henry Kissinger. "Dick wasn't anti-Semitic," Pat writes. "He hated *all* minorities." In the same episode, Chase happens on the disconsolate, fired Muppets, packed up in trunks backstage, and Scred begs him to persuade Michaels to keep them on the show. Chase isn't encouraging. "Now the show's a hit, it's a pretty big success, and I think it might have kind of gone to Lorne's head," he says, presciently. "Right now he's not even here. I think he's out having dinner with Lee Radziwill."

ON A WARM DAY IN THE MIDDLE OF MAY 1976, MICHAELS STEPPED OUT OF A car onto the red-carpeted entrance to the Beverly Hills Hotel. A lot had changed in the fifteen months since he'd shown up to meet the NBC elder statesmen, Marvin Antonowsky and Dave Tebet. This time, Michaels was checking in, preparing to attend the 28th Emmy Awards. *Saturday Night* had been nominated for five—for writing, best comedy-variety and music series, directing, graphic design, and best supporting player, Chevy Chase. Michaels also got a nomination that year for writing on the Lily Tomlin special. This was a homecoming for him, the long-awaited payoff for nearly a decade of second-guessing himself and wondering whether he should have gone to law school.

At the Emmy ceremony at the Shubert Theatre, the award for writing was the first of the show's four wins. The second winner was Davy Wilson, for directing. The third was for supporting player (Chase beat Harvey Korman and Tim Conway from *The Carol Burnett Show*, who, between them, had won five times). Chase charmed the audience by falling on his face at the podium. Michaels was already having a very good night, so when he heard his name read out as a winner for best writing in a comedy-variety or music special, for *Lily Tomlin*, he looked startled. Tomlin popped up and grinned at Michaels, Captain Kangaroo visible in the row behind them, and the two of them strode up to the stage, his fat bow tie askew. Leaning way over to get his mouth near the mic, like a man unaccustomed to such a circumstance, he said, "Lily was the first person to go to a network and suggest that I could produce, and I thank her for that. I think I'm being spoiled."

At the podium for the third time, collecting the award for best variety series from Milton Berle, Michaels channeled his Producer character. He acknowledged Berle for "warming up the studio" decades earlier, and he thanked NBC for reopening it; he thanked Dick Ebersol "who was there at the beginning." He thanked the writers and Bernie Brillstein, and also New York City, for providing the "rejection and alienation which keeps the comedy spirit alive." And he thanked the old-timers on the crew "who worked in live television and neglected to mention what it was like."

Ebersol was registered at the Beverly Hills Hotel that night, but he wasn't at the Shubert Theatre. There had been a commotion the day before the ceremony, when Brillstein and Michaels realized that the Television Academy had Ebersol listed as *Saturday Night*'s executive producer, based on the early errant credits. It appeared that, if the show won, Ebersol's name would be read out along with Michaels's. NBC quickly got Ebersol to sign a document expunging his name from the official credits. Michaels's thank-you, while gracious, was careful to define the time limits of Ebersol's involvement.

The *Saturday Night* group celebrated in a private room at Mr. Chow, the chic Beverly Hills place that served celebrities chow mein with forks and was memorialized in a Steely Dan song ("Meet me at midnight / At Mr. Chow's / Szechuan dumplings / Now that the deal has been done"). Embracing the glitz, O'Donoghue and Beatts threw an after-party in one of the Beverly Hills Hotel's bungalows. As the champagne corks piled up, Michaels found himself thinking, in his slightly precautious way, *It's not going to get better than this. Is there a way I can get out of here?*

He had just been through what he called his "championship season"; but it was difficult to enjoy. After the Emmys, he kept being asked what he was doing next. The implication was that the situation wasn't permanent: "A miracle happened, and now they're making you think it's not enough," he said. Still, when the group returned to New York, they briefly had a renewed sense of solidarity. Michaels called it "a state of grace." On show nights, the cast and writers all wore personalized SATURDAY NIGHT retro bowling shirts that Franne Lee, their costume designer, had made them. After the Emmys, the show attracted around two million more viewers a week. NBC took out an ad in *Variety* congratulating the "crazies" at *Saturday Night*. "We loathed them for that," said Marilyn Miller, who was urged by her colleagues to write a letter of protest to the PR department. For comedians, the word "crazy" is in the same distasteful category as "wacky" and "zany." Michaels and his staff thought of themselves as practicing something closer to social criticism than clowning.

Still, the Emmys had legitimized the show in the network's eyes, and NBC increased the budget and upgraded the offices. Brillstein renegotiated Michaels's deal. His salary for a second and third season was to have been $145,000 and $175,000, respectively; under the new deal, he'd get $300,000 and $350,000; the cast and writers got large increases as well. But the love from the corporate floor felt like too little too late, and the *Saturday Night* crowd still had the sense of being an alien culture within the building. As NBC's chairman Julian Goodman put it, "This was not a group that you'd have at your daughter's wedding."

AFTER THE EMMYS, TOWARD THE END OF SEASON ONE, THE CAST WAS REGU-larly being called "the Beatles of comedy," not the most auspicious predictor of longevity. In January, Peter Cook and Dudley Moore had hosted, and Michaels noticed how bitter Cook seemed at the success that Moore, his former Beyond the Fringe partner, was having in Hollywood. Despite the morale boost of the Emmys, competition was souring his staff, too, with Chase the main irritant. When Chase had accepted his award, his opening line got a big laugh: "Needless to say, this was totally expected on my part." Then he thanked Michaels and the cast. "It's been great working with them," he said, in an odd, valedictory tone. By then, he'd privately decided to leave the show. Because he'd never signed a contract as a performer, NBC had no hold on him. Ever since the *New York* cover, the network was eager to get him signed so that it could use him in prime time. Dave Tebet was especially anxious, referring to Chase as "the only white Gentile comedian around today," and adding, "Think what that means when Johnny leaves."

Belushi had always found Chase overbearing, and he chafed at the way the NBC publicity department favored him. "Once we bend to a fucking star system here," Belushi told a reporter, "everything changes." Chase was drifting into a haze of cocaine and fame, spending a lot of time doing press. It didn't help relations that he joked to reporters that his jobs at the show included teaching Belushi how to eat with a fork and shaving his back.

As the season wound down, Michaels could see the surrogate family he'd created for himself beginning to break apart, and in an unusual pep talk that spring (given in the company of a journalist), he told his people, "I have to decide whether to keep the show changing for the needs of those who've originally created it, or just let those people leave to do other things. The show is only valuable as long as the people here get off on it, get out what they have to say. As soon as anybody starts staying because of loyalty, or some similar fucked reason . . ." It sounded like he was trying to talk himself into something, and also making a coded plea for his staff to appreciate what they had created.

The final weeks of the season Michaels recalls as "a torturing, tortured thing." Chase would walk out of meetings to take long calls from L.A. Then he'd come back and say, "Warren Beatty just called and said, 'I really admire your work.'" He started talking about himself in the third person. One day, Aykroyd confronted Michaels in a fury: Chase was giving him notes on a Scottish accent. Michaels views this period as the commencement of his becoming "the world expert on people getting famous." He urged the others to cultivate sympathy toward Chase, despite how annoying he could be. "It was the first time through," he said. "Nobody had been here before."

Brillstein, Chase's manager as well as Michaels's, negotiated a raise, but Chase didn't think it was big enough, so he hired a Harvard Law School friend of his brother. The new lawyer brought in an agent from William Morris and fired Brillstein. They cut a $2 million deal with NBC for Chase to make three prime-time comedy specials for the network. It wasn't clear where that left *Saturday Night*.

Michaels was gutted when he heard the news. But the deal hadn't been made public, and he hoped that Chase might have a change of heart, or figure out a way to do the specials and *Saturday Night*. One night after dinner at Elaine's, Michaels poured his heart out to Buck Henry as they walked down Park Avenue. "I don't know what to do," he moaned, feeling like a spurned lover. Chase had been there from the beginning. A veteran analysand, Henry offered a psychological take. "Chevy doesn't want to be the kind of person who would leave a friend in the lurch," he said. "So he has to do something provocative and obnoxious. It's like in a breakup: you pick a fight, and then you feel justified in walking away. It makes the separation bearable— because he loves you." (Forty-five years later, Henry said, of Chase leaving, "It was the stupidest mistake I ever saw a performer make.") Michaels decided that he wouldn't fight with Chase, or beg him to stay. His public stance would be: "The show would take a hit but we'd still be okay." He took another walk, up Sixth Avenue, with Marilyn Miller one afternoon. "I remember Lorne repeatedly telling me, every block, that *he wasn't mad at Chevy, he wasn't mad at Chevy,*" she said, but she could tell that he was devastated. "The only reason anyone knew Chevy was alive is that Lorne let him write and perform on the show."

Chase's exit was traumatic, but it would be the first of dozens, and Michaels would come to see turnover as the natural order of things. He remembered how, when he was in high school and his grandmother was dying of cancer, he asked if her estranged husband could visit her. "I have no use for him," she'd said, without rancor. "It was like a door slamming," Michaels recalled. "The idea that you could feel things for somebody, and then you run out of it. I realized: so people *burn out* in relationships." Reflecting on that during the Chase drama, he tried to learn what twelve-step programs call "detaching with love."

It pained Michaels to see his colleagues bad-mouth Chase. They were mad at the way he dumped on the show in the press, bragging about movie offers and cutting an album. Chase insisted that his fiancée had given him an ultimatum: Move to L.A. or else. (He'd tried to persuade Michaels to relocate the show there, and to air every other week.) But he found Michaels's businesslike pose confounding. "I knew Lorne wanted me to stay, but he didn't make a big deal of it, which I needed him to do," he said. "I was his best friend. I expected him to say, 'If you go, the show won't be the same.' But he holds himself back. Never said it. So I left." Unable to let the topic go, he continued, "It wouldn't have fucking taken much! All he had to do is tell me he loved me, basically. But his nature is to be above it in some fashion." He attributed Michaels's reluctance to insecurity. "Frankly, I always felt back then that I was smarter than him, that I was really the guy who got the show going, not Lorne. Having had this stardom thing, it got in the way of—gosh—of caring more."

The rockiness continued as the season lurched toward a close. Chase's deal had not been announced, and there was an air of ambiguity. Might he be back? Might the show cease to exist without him? Michaels, fried from working hundred-hour weeks, was too exhausted to contemplate it. But the last show in May ended on a warm note, with Elliott Gould hosting for a second time, leading the cast singing the Roy Rogers classic: "Happy trails to you, until we meet again."

SEVENTEEN

BICENTENNIAL

THE SOUND THAT AWAKENED MICHAELS IN THE DRY JUNE DAWN WAS SOME-thing between a thump and a twang. Hungover, he opened the door of his cinder-block room in the Joshua Tree Inn and peered out at the pool area. Belushi, who had not been to bed, was jumping up and down on the diving board, doing a series of thunderous cannonballs. Michaels watched him spring high into the air, above the desert horizon line traced by the Little San Bernardino Mountains in the distance, and then bang his coccyx against the board on the way back down, before flopping into the water, unharmed. Aykroyd, who was watching from the doorway to the room next door, glanced over at Michaels and nodded toward Belushi. "Albanian oak," he said.

They had survived the first season. It was just before the Bicentennial, when most Americans were busy painting fire hydrants red-white-and-blue and gearing up to watch parades of tall ships or tune in to *Bob Hope's Bicentennial Star Spangled Spectacular*. Michaels was worlds away from the patriotic hubbub; he had brought a group of his comrades out to the Mojave Desert. It was a site of inspiration and revelation for him, and after the crushing workload of the past eighteen months, he wanted to make a pilgrimage with his closest colleagues. They felt like army buddies. Aykroyd, padding around the pool deck with his webbed toes exposed, was entranced by the landscape and the promise of UFOs in the black sky. Belushi and some of the others had taken the "when in Joshua Tree" route and eaten some mushrooms; pot, quaaludes, and tequila were also on hand. Chase had come along too, still in *Saturday Night* limbo, and the hard-partying night before the cannonball session had begun with him grilling burgers on the motel's patio.

A summer getaway wasn't always in the cards. NBC had initially balked at the idea of putting on reruns over the summer, but Michaels insisted on it. He needed a break.

For him, the trip was a way to dip back into his old California life, only this time with proper funding. NBC was paying Michaels to produce a prime-time special about a Beach Boys comeback concert in L.A., which, if it wasn't *The Graduate,* was at least a foray into film-making. The special marked Brian Wilson's first appearance with the band since 1964, when he'd had a nervous breakdown. The week after the Joshua Tree stay, Michaels got the Malibu gang back together to make the film: Gary Weis directed; John Head and Joe Boyd helped out around the edges. Aykroyd and Belushi appeared in a comedy bit, as highway patrolmen arresting the zonked-out Wilson for violating a local statute ("failing to surf") and dragging him out of his bed and into the Pacific Ocean. Officer Belushi: "Let's go surfing now." Officer Aykroyd: "Everybody's learning how."

The Beach Boys: It's OK was an amiable and aimless assemblage of concert footage, vérité snippets shot at the Beach Boys' cavernous houses, and a few comedy sketches like the surf-police one. (Playing a cop delighted Aykroyd, who had a double preoccupation with law enforcement and lawlessness; friends used to say that his fantasy would be to commit a robbery and then arrest himself.) One scene shows Brian Wilson's thirty-fourth birthday party, with Paul McCartney seated next to the birthday boy as Brian opens gifts in a catatonic stupor.

McCartney had turned thirty-four two days earlier, and he combined his own birthday bash with the wrap party for his Wings Over America tour. He had admired Belushi's impersonation of Joe Cocker singing "With a Little Help from My Friends" on *Saturday Night,* and had arranged for Belushi to perform it at a Wings show that week in L.A., celebrating the band's roadies. Onstage, Aykroyd joined in, doing his pitchman character shilling for an outfit called "I.R.M.S.—International Road Management School," offering a complete course in "loading, unloading, loading, unloading, loading, unloading." Michaels was in the audience, along with Cher and Elton John.

The next night, Thursday, June 24, McCartney's celebration continued, with an opulent party at Greenacres, the Harold Lloyd estate in Benedict Canyon. Michaels was on the guest list, and ascending the cypress-studded hilltop as a string quartet played Wings tunes felt like another waypost. The invitation had asked guests to "Please wear white"; a Hawaiian graffiti artist named Star Rainbow had been hired to decorate guests' pristine garb with spray paint. The L.A. City Ballet performed on the pool deck, the pool itself having been drained and converted into a dance floor, where partygoers—Warren Beatty, David Cassidy, Bob Dylan, Alice Cooper, and such representatives of Old Hollywood as Henry Fonda and Steve McQueen—flounced around to Nelson Riddle's orchestra. Every Beach Boy attended except Brian, who, a society columnist noted, was "going quietly nuts in Bel Air."

McCartney made a toast about Wings, referencing the mixed reviews of his earlier solo outings. "This tour has convinced me that we *are* a group!" he said. Years later, he recalled the party as "basically a way to spend the entire profits from the tour in a complete wipeout." He also recalled meeting Michaels there. Their friendship would later blossom on the East End of Long Island, where McCartney's Eastman in-laws had roots.

After the L.A. trip, Michaels spent a few weeks with Paul Simon, out in Bridgehampton. He'd become worldlier since his visit the previous summer, when he'd been surprised to see the ocean. Down the street from Simon that Bicentennial summer, a young Texan woman named Susan Forristal had a basement rental. Forristal, a successful model, had been at the Ron Nessen show back in April with a friend. She had stayed till dawn at the after-party at Paul Simon's apartment, where Forristal first saw Michaels. But the person who caught her attention that night was Aykroyd. "I got this wild crush on Danny," she said. A while later, she found herself at Elaine's—a planned fix-up between Simon and Shelley Duvall. Michaels was at the table. After the gluey spaghetti, Forristal joined Simon and Michaels as they walked the forty blocks down to the Osborne, where they did some lines of coke. Simon quickly slipped out, and Michaels set to work trying to persuade Forristal that Aykroyd already had a serious girl-friend back in Toronto. He was persistent, and by late summer, when he showed up in Bridgehampton, he had won her over.

The Bicentennial hoopla was still going on, and he was fascinated by the Hamptons WASP gentry, who were doing elaborate reenact-ments while dressed in Revolutionary War gear. For the son of a first-generation furrier, the lineage made an impression. He'd been developing an appreciation of the East Coast as a "deeper culture" than anything he'd sniffed out in California, where the Chateau Mar-mont felt like the caves of Lascaux. The month before, in Malibu, he'd attended Dick Ebersol's wedding on the beach, a very L.A. affair. The bride, whom Ebersol had met weeks earlier, was a co-host of *Wheel of Fortune*. The minister told the guests, "The only celebrity at this wedding is Jesus Christ, our Lord." Michaels's thoughts were firmly on New York as he stood on the sand with his friends—including Chevy Chase, who, after the vows, picked up the bride and tossed her into the surf.

STARMAKING

Don't be timid.
Don't be nondescript.
Be assholes.

—LILY TOMLIN, ON AN INDEX CARD PINNED
TO MICHAELS'S BULLETIN BOARD, 1976

THE PRODUCER MIKE TODD USED TO SAY, "WHEN A SHOW IS A HIT, DON'T even change the ushers." As Michaels headed into his second season, the press was calling *Saturday Night* NBC's "fair-haired program" and "the network's sole smash hit." The show had the best demographics in the history of television; the price of a thirty-second commercial had jumped from $7,500 to $60,000. But change was going to be forced on the show: NBC's news division was temporarily taking over Studio 8H for its fall election coverage, and Chevy Chase, it was finally announced, was leaving the show, although he'd remain in the cast until the end of October.

His last few appearances have a half-hearted, walking-through-it feel, as if he were a divorced father awkwardly stopping in for Christmas dinner. NBC had shifted the show to a soundstage in Midwood, Brooklyn. (Michaels hated being in an outer borough; he'd pitched the idea of doing some shows live from college campuses instead, but it was too costly.) During the season premiere, hosted by Lily Tomlin, Chase injured his testicles in a Gerald Ford sketch by falling onto a podium that the props department had forgotten to pad with foam rubber. "I peed blood that night and went to the hospital," he said. On the fourth episode, still healing, he returned in a wheelchair pushed by Belushi, who dumped him out of it onto the floor. On the fifth, he appeared in a futuristic "Jeopardy 1999" sketch, in which one of the answers is "Comedian whose career fizzled after leaving NBC's Sat-Nite."

Belushi compounded the strange energy of Chase's final show, the sixth of the season. In a "Samurai Stockbroker" sketch, Belushi, wired on coke, swung his katana sword with extra verve and struck Buck Henry, the host. "He took a half-inch piece out of my forehead," Henry recalled. "There was a lot of blood on the set." Michaels combed the audience for Belushi's doctor, who patched Henry up; a telegram was sent to his mother saying he was okay. Weekend Update followed, and Chase led the segment with the news of Henry's injury, recounting how "drugged-out John Belushi hits him with a sword." In solidarity, Chase had put a Band-Aid on his own forehead. Backstage, Michaels ordered the rest of the cast to slap on Band-Aids too.

There was no farewell party for Chase, but during the Goodnights, the cast engulfed him in a group hug, and then fell down together in slow motion, making a Twister pile of splayed limbs on the stage, an impromptu homage to the master pratfaller.

Chase married Jackie Carlin in December in L.A., and Michaels and the cast flew out. There was the usual misbehavior; Belushi got drunk and made a pass at Chase's mother. But despite the show of solidarity, Michaels found the wedding hard to sit through. On top of losing Chase, whom he considered a brother, he felt that his own network had conspired against him by luring his star away. But one kind of pressure was off. At least NBC wouldn't be leaning on him to turn *Saturday Night* into the Chevy Chase Show, which he had no intention of doing. The marriage was brief; within months Chase's new wife threw a hot iron at him during an argument.

The loss of Chase as an anchor in Michaels's life was to some degree softened by the addition of a steady girlfriend, Susan Forristal. Though they were both busy, they had dinner every night. Even on Tuesdays, Forristal would tag along for the host dinner. Then Michaels would go back to the office for the writing all-nighter. "After a show, he stayed in bed all day Sunday through to Monday morning, talking to Bernie on the phone and smoking his joints," Forristal said. "Then he'd slowly walk to the office." After Aykroyd took up with

Rosie Shuster, the two couples socialized. Cherie Fortis, Michaels's new assistant, remembers thinking, "Wow, this is very modern."

With Chase off the show, Michaels's role shifted; he felt more like management. For one thing, he was writing less. (By the end of the first season, he said, he'd written everything he'd ever wanted to write twice over.) By Season Two, the writers, cast, and staff knew what they were doing in terms of getting the show on each week. People started coming to Michaels for help with personality conflicts. Camaraderie was trickier now that everyone in the cast was entertaining the notion of stardom. Belushi doubled down on his own ambition. He made sure that there were plenty of moments in the show when he identified himself by name; he worried that they were leaning too much on repeated characters and catchphrases. "We're just jerking off over and over," he told *Rolling Stone*. After the Emmys had certified the show's primacy, he didn't see the need for the guest hosts or musical acts; why not just have the cast take turns hosting and singing?

Addled by pot and cocaine, Belushi was pissed off at the parts he got; he felt that he was always typecast as a wild man. At the same time, he wrote less, showed up late, and missed rehearsals. When Paul Simon hosted again, Belushi skirmished with him, arguing over who would play "Billy Jack" (the vigilante vet hero of a hit movie) in a sketch. (Simon recalled saying to himself, "No fight, no fight, no fight, no fight." Then, "Too late, now we're in it.") Ebersol, who dropped by the studio occasionally, brought Belushi home with him to L.A. one week to get him away from his dealer. He set Ebersol's mattress on fire, something he did again at Michaels's apartment, when he'd shown up after a fight with his girlfriend. (Michaels called her and said, "Can I send him home now?") Michaels's response was to turn it all into material. On the Christmas show, Candice Bergen, the host, announced an Adopt Belushi for Christmas contest. "I'm not fussy," Belushi tells viewers, sitting cheerily beside Bergen. "I like some candied yams, some plum pudding, a roast goose stuffed with drugs."

Michaels generally used loose reins with talent, but Belushi made that difficult. "John always liked the boss to be the boss," Michaels said. "He didn't want a friend." Belushi ran hot and cold: when he needed something, he'd wander into Michaels's office and give him a shoulder massage, or call him "the best producer in TV" on a talk show; other times, he'd incite screaming matches and storm out of the office. Michaels hated scenes, and although he tried to get Brillstein to handle Belushi's outbursts, he ended up firing and rehiring Belushi several times.

"Loving the show is like loving humanity and yet not liking people," Michaels told a reporter around that time, paraphrasing Dostoyevsky. With Belushi on the rampage, staff problems multiplied. Curtin stopped speaking to Michaels, angry that he didn't intervene with Belushi, whom she once found rifling through her purse in search of money or pills. "I confronted Lorne," she recalled. "I said, 'Are you going to do anything about this?' And he'd say, 'Yeah, well, he's an adult.'" Aykroyd, who had a party-proof work ethic, got frustrated at Belushi's behavior, but when he could not rein in his friend, he acted out himself, once smashing the glass in the pictures on the office wall. "I'd rather be psychotic than quietly neurotic if my psychosis comes out on breakable objects," he said. O'Donoghue, who often disagreed with Michaels's sketch picks, took out his aggressions on telephones, ripping them out of the walls and smashing the receivers. "He'd always be bleeding a little bit himself," Tom Davis said. Like Florence Lipowitz at her kitchen table, Michaels often found himself with people crying in his office.

He had neither the time nor the inclination to micromanage these flare-ups. Garrett Morris was so zonked from freebasing cocaine at one point that he hallucinated invisible robots trying to control him, and got aggressive with a production assistant. Michaels, told about the incident, conveyed the sentiment "I don't want to know about it. Work it out."

At the bottom of the tension within the cast was a fight for airtime: first, the performers had to get writers to cast them in sketches. Radner had her cookie-baking gambit. Laraine Newman felt helpless. "I realized it was always a meritocracy," she said. "I just didn't know how to be my own advocate. I had so many expectations of Lorne, and rather than being empathic about the demands that were being made on him, I just expected him to take care of me in some ways. I know that he tried."

But Michaels made the final picks of which sketches got on the air. "He's the dad," Penelope Spheeris observed. "And the cast and writers are the children. And he makes them compete with each other. And out of that competition comes two things. Brilliant writing. And dislike for the other person." The dynamic was natural for Radner. "Gilda had been a daddy's girl, and so that's the way she approached situations," Curtin said. "She chummed up to Dad." When she had an idea, she'd run into his office "to dance it out for him, like showing your dad your new party dress," Zweibel said. Radner told friends that she once went through Michaels's desk in hopes of finding a note saying "I really do like Gilda."

For many on the show, trying to get Michaels's approval was like twisting a dry sponge. "Lorne is repelled by the sight of needy people," Newman said. "He senses weakness, or lack of confidence, and he wants to get as far away from it as fast as he can."

Another part of Michaels's evolving manager persona was being impervious to refusals. Paul Simon's second episode included a bit in which Michaels cajoles him into wearing a ridiculous turkey costume. "By that point, my role in the show was talking people into doing things they didn't want to do," Michaels said. One sketch had him haggling with George Harrison, the musical guest, about the $3,000 he'd offered for a Beatles reunion. Harrison tries to claim it ("I've come all this way!"), but Michaels tells him, "I thought that you would understand, you know, that it was $3,000 for *four* people." Michaels recalled, "The audience loved that kind of stuff because it seemed like backstage reality. It was the start of the myth-making."

HAVING A BEATLE ON THE SHOW DID A LOT TO CALM MICHAELS'S SECOND-season jitters. The show had picked up thirty-five new affiliate stations, and ad slots were selling well. *The Washington Post's* Tom Shales, who was becoming the show's self-appointed Boswell, weighed in with a story headlined "Chevy's Gone But Saturday Night Lives."

Two people entered the *Saturday Night* orbit that year who decidedly shaped the direction of the show. Even before Season One, Brillstein had urged Michaels to consider Steve Martin as a potential cast member, but Michaels didn't see it. He'd known Martin a bit as a member of the Smothers Brothers' writing staff, but his stand-up act—fake arrow through the head, balloon animals—seemed like old-timey prop comedy, with what Michaels called "a Disney element." He hadn't understood that Martin was doing something more ambitious, a gloss on variety conventions, with an existential twist. "It's about individuals and how distorted their thoughts can get just being alive in the world," Martin said, "and how you have to become crazy in order to survive." Both Martin and Michaels had viewed the political tenor of the times—Vietnam and Watergate—as a touchstone: For Michaels, it was a call to arms, banishing big dumb comedy. For Martin, it was a chance to poke at the pieties of the counterculture. He cut his hair and put on a suit. "The country was angry, and so was comedy, which was addressed to insiders," he wrote in his memoir, *Born Standing Up*. He thought it was time for some silliness, and he put together an act that he considered simultaneously smart and stupid. Michaels didn't see past the stupid. "I was completely off about Steve," he recalled. "You forget that there have to be jokes. His work, I began to see, had a joyousness. And we were deadly serious."

Martin was selling out the same stadiums as Led Zeppelin. Kids all over the country were saying his tag line "Well excuuuuuse *me!*" After Jean Doumanian started pushing Martin too, Michaels finally booked him to host. Martin would alter the show forever, adding a flavor of comedy that was goofy and sophisticated at the same time.

Like other hosts, Martin was nervous when he arrived on the seventeenth floor. He expected Michaels to be more of a suit and was relieved to find a guy with a gift for putting others at ease. After working solo for a decade, Martin enjoyed collaborating. "It was like a great escape from my solipsism," he said, like "being dropped off at a playground." Martin would host eight times in the first five years. After every show, before heading to the party, he and Michaels and some others would watch the episode on tape in the office. "We just loved ourselves," he said.

Martin came across as a part of the cast, not a visiting dignitary who needed propping up. "Danny had this idea about two Czech guys that I didn't quite understand," he said. "And I had this thing, 'Wild and crazy guy!' that I was doing in my show." They merged them and put on over-the-top accents, along with plaid bell-bottoms and gold medallions, two foreigners on the prowl. The first time they tried it on the air, Martin said, "it was killing us with laughter." The live audience was a bit cooler. By the second time the Czech brothers, Yortuk and Georg Festrunk, appeared on the show ("Bring on the foxes with their big American breasts!"), he said, "somehow it got in their brains." Martin called the sketch "my second ticket into catchphrase heaven." He brought to the show his love of what he called "unbridled nonsense," but there was a meta element, too: in his monologue he complained about being typecast as a comedian.

Michaels was starting to see that, like the city that was its home, his show would exist in a permanent state of flux, and that this was both a burden and an asset. "Whenever it was getting to the point where smugness was about to creep in," he said, "I tried to kick it around a little." Embracing Martin was an example. With Chase gone and Belushi MIA, Michaels decided to expand the writing staff.

Doug Kenney, the *National Lampoon* founder, had a name to suggest. Kenney was working on a script called *Animal House* with Harold Ramis and Chris Miller, while a younger *Harvard Lampoon* friend, Jim Downey, crashed on his couch in the Village, throwing in the occasional joke. In college, Downey had distinguished himself by persuading John Wayne to parade through the anti-war crowds of Harvard Square in a tank. Michaels liked a list of raw ideas that Downey sent (one of them was "Pet Peeves: Don't you hate it when . . . "), and invited him to the studio for an interview.

They sat in the bleachers and talked, Downey in a jacket and tie, trying to hide his astonishment at seeing The Band rehearse "Life Is a Carnival" twenty feet away. He found Michaels inscrutable; rather than asking questions, Michaels kept saying things like: "You'll find, in writing sketches, that . . ." There was no way of knowing whether he was talking about comedy writing in general, or about Downey writing comedy on his show.

Like thousands of interviewees to come, Downey left confused. Michaels had made the offhanded suggestion that he start hanging out in the office, so he did. At some point, he figured that he was hired.

If Steve Martin broadened the show's range into sillier (but still smart) territory, Downey tipped it in the direction of smart (but also silly). At Harvard, he'd majored in folklore and mythology and studied Russian, a curriculum that would seep into the show as wonky detail about the Vikings, or medieval doctors, or nineteenth-century seafaring life shot through with absurdity.

In Michael Arlen's *Saturday Night* review, describing the work of Monty Python and Spike Milligan, he used the term "a comedy of surplus education." Nichols and May, with their parodies of Pirandello and psychoanalysis, were an American version. *The Harvard Lampoon* was another. The *Lampoon,* which produced its magazine (the oldest humor publication in the country) from a miniature Flemish-style castle a block from Harvard Yard, was for years not dissimilar to the college's male final clubs, with regular boozy black-tie banquets and competitive admissions protocols. *Lampoon* dinners often ended with members ceremonially smashing plates and flinging lobster shells around the castle's Great Hall. But unlike the more legacy-oriented clubs, the *Lampoon* attracted more middle-class members who bought their tuxes from a local used-clothing warehouse called Keezer's, often hemming the trousers with a stapler in their dorms. (Women began being admitted in the seventies.) John Updike, George Plimpton, and William Gaddis were members, and the organization funneled graduates into the literary scene. Doug Kenney and Henry Beard changed that in 1970 when they founded *National Lampoon,* which eight years later would surprise Hollywood by producing *Animal House,* which was then the highest-grossing comedy of all time. Kenney, who a few years later would die in a mysterious fall off a cliff in Hawaii, opened the door between *The Harvard Lampoon* and the professional comedy world; it would be Jim Downey who personally shepherded many dozens of young writers through it, by hiring them. In the process, the *Lampoon* ended up filling the writing and producing ranks of a good portion of the best TV comedy shows, including *The Simpsons, Seinfeld,* Garry Shandling's two sitcoms, *Late Night with David Letterman, Parks and Recreation, 30 Rock,* and *The Office.*

WHEN MICHAELS REPLACED CHASE, HE WANTED SOMEONE WHO DISTINCTLY lacked a golden-boy aura. He hired Bill Murray, who'd been on his short list from the start. Murray, an Irish Catholic from the Chicago suburb of Wilmette, grew up in a big working-class family. He started the same week as Jim Downey, an Irish Catholic from a town south of Chicago called Joliet. Michaels put the two new kids in an office together. They weren't immediately compatible. "They were both altar boys," Michaels said. "But Jim was in a seersucker jacket and Bill was an unmade bed. So you had this quiet guy thrown together in an office with a guy who's making daiquiris in a blender and inviting everybody in."

The office mates embodied a principle that became part of Michaels's staff recipe. *Harvard Lampoon* writers, he thought, tended to bring an "intellectual rigor" to sketches, and shared a mischievous rebellious streak—a reaction to Ivy League fustiness. And he believed that Chicago writers, many the product of Second City, were generally more blue-collar and went for harder, earthier laughs. The writerly *Lampoon* style and the more physical Chicago style was like peanut butter meeting chocolate.

The NBC publicity department wasn't enthusiastic about Murray. (Neither were viewers, who sent in letters when he first arrived complaining that he was no Chevy Chase.) He had a rougher vibe than Chase did—acne scars, a droopy head-shop mustache, and the prickly energy of a guy who liked to party. Gary Weis compared him to "an Irish pirate." After an okay first show, Murray went into a slump. When he blew a line on air, O'Donoghue declared, "I'm not ever writing for him again." Murray was miserable, angry that he was only getting second-cop parts.

Five shows in, Michaels had an idea: Murray would appeal directly to the audience. It would be "the show speaking." Together they wrote a monologue called "The New Guy." Murray sat at a desk with a name plaque on it, and looked into the camera. "Hello, I'm Bill Murray," he said. "I'd like to thank the producer, Lorne Michaels, for urging me to speak with you directly. You see, I'm a little bit concerned. I don't think I'm making it on the show. I'm a funny guy, but I haven't been so funny on the show." He talked about his eight siblings and his dead father, and concluded that, if people started laughing at him, he'd be able to stand on the stage in Rockefeller Center in New York "and say, 'Dad, I did it.' He'd like that."

The bit worked. "It ended all the conversations about Billy," Michaels said. "It's the Checkers speech." Murray quickly found his place. (He did not fall under Michaels's paternal spell, however. "Because I was the new guy I was less susceptible to that father stuff," Murray said. "I decided to stick with the father I had, who had already died.") Soon, goofing around with a soap-on-a-rope, Murray devised a premise that involved conducting interviews in the shower. The "Shower Mike" sketch aired on the season finale, hosted by Buck Henry. Murray starts out alone in the stall, crooning into his soap "mic." Radner, as his wife, joins him, and Murray interviews her in the gushy tones of an entertainment reporter. He introduces a surprise guest, Henry, as Radner's lover, all three of them squeezed under the streaming showerhead: "Now tell me, kids," Murray asks, "You kids must spend a lot of time in the shower together when I'm not here, huh?"

Hiring Downey and Murray brought another abiding quality to the show: Irishness. (There would be many more Irish Catholics, including Chris Farley and Molly Shannon, both of whom prayed before every show; and Amy Poehler, who credits her "Irish Catholic mouth" and work ethic with endearing her to the boss. There would also be an unusual number of assistants named Erin.) As a student of Yeats and James Cagney movies, Michaels was attracted to a certain Irish sentimentality—"all these Irish people in show business who would get moist talking about their families," as he put it.

The comedy of Downey and Murray had a sunniness that helped balance the sinister contributions of their fellow Irishman, O'Donoghue, whose deepening cynicism was starting to worry Michaels. *The Village Voice*'s twenty-four-year-old critic James Wolcott criticized the show's "Grand Guignol scumminess." The tone of O'Donoghue's regular segment "Mr. Mike's Least-Loved Bedtime Tales" got even more corrosive: an Uncle Remus story featured Br'er Rabbit getting skinned alive and eaten, his feet sold as good luck charms. Garrett Morris, as Uncle Remus, asks Mr. Mike what the moral of the story is, and Mr. Mike replies, "There's no moral, Uncle Remus, just random acts of meaningless violence."

THE NETWORK WAS EAGER FOR MICHAELS TO CLONE SOME OF THE SHOW'S hip allure by developing programs for prime time, and even considered moving *Saturday Night* to 10:00 P.M. But prime time, with its canned laughs and police dramas, held no interest for him. Late night was like the Chateau Marmont, a protected corner of hip nonconformism. There was even talk of Michaels taking over all of late-night programming. Right after the Emmys, over dinner at Dan Tana's in L.A., Richard Pryor had also dangled an offer: Universal had signed him to a three-picture deal, and he wanted Michaels to work with him on the films. Saying no to his comedy hero and to a career in the movies made Michaels realize that he was, astonishingly, right where he wanted to be.

But the network did get Michaels to produce one show in prime time—almost by accident. His idea of doing shows live from colleges had been scuttled, but he was still determined to take his show on the road. He had a grand idea of broadcasting live "against real architecture—so that, in a sense, the city became the sets." John Head suggested New Orleans, and a plan was made to broadcast the show live from Mardi Gras. A city defined by spontaneity and mis-rule, it seemed an ideal setting for Michaels to demonstrate that his show had held on to its outlaw bona fides.

He had wanted to do the New Orleans show in *Saturday Night*'s regular 11:30 P.M. slot, but his projected budget was too high for late night. Fortuitously, NBC had ninety minutes to fill in prime time; the network had planned to air a special celebrating Jerry Lewis's Broad-way revival of (again!) *Hellzapoppin'*, but it closed during previews. Michaels's cast and writers were stoked to be heading south during a slushy New York winter, especially Garrett Morris, who'd grown up in New Orleans and wanted to show his colleagues the town. But the tech crew was wary; Davy Wilson had filmed a special there with (again!) Perry Como, and he'd found the city to be mayhem.

Michaels brushed off these concerns, and, to round out his ex-travaganza, he invited along Penny Marshall and Cindy Williams, the stars of *Laverne & Shirley*; Eric Idle; Buck Henry; Henry "the Fonz" Winkler; and Randy Newman, an old New Orleans hand. Newman gave Michaels a warning. The city was pure disorder, he said, not a place "to have a timetable that goes off on time." But Michaels said he thrived on chaos.

The *Saturday Night* gang, plus Susan Forristal, settled into a faded grand hotel, the Maison Dupuy. There were 112 people in all—more, Michaels told the *Hattiesburg American,* than NBC employed to cover the Super Bowl. He had a ceremonial meeting with the mayor, who assured him that New Orleans could be brought to heel and promised special police escorts for the cast. The crew had to set up lighting and sound equipment in fifteen locations across the city. There would be several mission control vans, and Michaels would sit in one to oversee the live show. The telephone company had to string Telco lines to get power to the sets. Belushi and Aykroyd rented Harley-Davidsons and zoomed around barhopping, and used up their thirty-dollar per diem partying with Hunter S. Thompson, who was covering Mardi Gras for *Rolling Stone.*

Being at large, together, in a distant American city gave the Not Ready for Prime Time Players a sharper sense of how famous they were. Signing autographs at a mall, they were mobbed by fans, one brandishing a toilet seat to be signed. Well-wishers scored them coke; a brewery sent a carload of beer. Michaels was getting unnerved, but he projected his usual calm.

Rehearsing sketches at scattershot locations was near impossible, as was getting accurate time readings on them. Curtin and Henry were to preside over the Bacchus Parade, giving color commentary from atop a purpose-built reviewing stand on Canal Street. Michaels kept saying that if anything went awry, he could just cut to the parade.

A few months earlier, Michaels had described to a journalist what he liked about live television. "It is terrifying, but I live on it," he said. "When you think of the vastness of what can go wrong." More went wrong in New Orleans than he could ever have imagined. The evening began with Michaels addressing a crowd before the show began at the city's Performing Arts Center, where Randy Newman sat behind a piano. Michaels came onstage in a huge white baseball cap that, the *South Mississippi Sun* reported, made him look like a Peanuts character. The crowd, already reeking of what the paper called "Mardi Grass," didn't need much warming up. "Get to know the person next to you, because if we have technical problems, it might be a long wait and at least you'll have something to say," he advised, to a chorus of rebel yells.

The show opened with Aykroyd, as President Jimmy Carter, straddling Andrew Jackson's horse on the statue in Jackson Square. He likened Mardi Gras to "fifteen thousand Datsun salesmen dressed up as pickles" and yelled "Live from Mardi Gras, it's Saturday Night!" Cut to Randy Newman performing his hit "Louisiana 1927." Then a couple of the remote television vans lost power, and Michaels had no way of communicating with them. In his own van, Michaels got a call from the mayor, who told him that one of the parade vehicles had struck a pedestrian, halting the procession. It was said to be a fatality. Michaels managed to roll out a mixture of taped segments and live sketches, often drowned out by the shrieking crowd: Belushi as Brando in a *Streetcar* send-up; Aykroyd as Tom Snyder interrogating a strip club proprietor (Bill Murray, debuting his Honker character); Radner as "Baba Wawa" interviewing "Henwy Winkwa."

Two million people were in the streets, and the revelers turned into a churlish mob. As the cast tried to reach their locations, drunks pelted them with bottles. Radner, dressed as Emily Litella, was groped on her way to set. Doubloons and beer cans rained on O'Donoghue as he stood on an iron balcony in front of plastered Tulane students and did "the Antler Dance," an inane jig he'd devised.

The first time Michaels cut to Curtin and Henry in the reviewing stand, twenty feet above street level, a superball bounced hard off of Curtin's head. "We had nothing to report on, so we just started making things up," she said. Henry ad-libbed, "Hundreds of thousands of Americans have traveled thousands of miles, just to come here to New Orleans to visit Bourbon Street and to throw up." Michaels, who threw up himself during the evening, continued cutting to the nonexistent parade. Belligerent onlookers yelled at Curtin to take her shirt off. Henry recalled people "screaming obscenities and vomiting in our direction." Revelers climbed the swaying scaffolding. Curtin recalled, "A poor little production assistant is stepping on people's fingers, trying to keep them from coming up on the platform." Curtin concluded the ninety minutes of non-parade commentary by telling viewers, "Mardi Gras is just a French word that means 'no parade.'" After she and Henry clambered down into the swarm, a pair of retired cops grabbed them in fireman's holds and ran them to a waiting police sedan.

The collision of *Saturday Night* and Fat Tuesday made for mediocre television, but it was a bonding experience for the group. Henry recalled, "Every minute of it was weirder than every other minute." The after-party at Antoine's turned out to be "more of a wake," according to Randy Newman, who said that the New Orleans show was "the only time I've ever seen Lorne shaken. He said he just had to go to bed for a while."

When everyone was safely back in New York, the set designer Eugene Lee made Michaels a plaque reading YOU CAN ALWAYS CUT TO THE PARADE. But the Mardi Gras show was a black mark with NBC, way over budget and soundly beaten in the ratings by *Secrets,* an ABC made-for-TV movie starring Susan Blakely as a nymphomaniac home-maker. The network tabled its hopes that Michaels might swoop in and sprinkle his pixie dust over the rest of the prime-time schedule. That was fine with Michaels, who was happy to stay in the safety of late night and who never thought of venturing from his home turf, Studio 8H, ever again.

The prime-time fiasco aside, his second season had already pro-duced a number of indelible characters. Besides Murray's lounge singer Nick (who played venues like the Powder Room of the Meat-loaf Mountain Ski Lodge), and Aykroyd's Irwin Mainway (a purveyor of dangerous toys, like "Bag O' Glass"), there was a family of extrater-restrials trying to fit into suburban America, who tell neighbors that they're "from France." The germ of the Coneheads had surfaced in a cast improv session and sprouted when, during Christmas break, Davis and Aykroyd traveled to Easter Island and had a blissed-out drug experience communing with the Moai, the big-headed ancient stone statues. (Davis also had an idea for a TV show about a character called Dippy the Hippie, who could make a bong out of any two ob-jects.) The first iteration of the Coneheads involved two aliens pick-ing up a couple of Earth girls in a car. Michaels suggested making the aliens into a family, a send-up of classic family sitcoms, and also a trippy commentary on suburban life. The Coneheads—Aykroyd as Beldar, the father; Curtin as his wife, Prymaat; and Newman as the teen daughter, Connie—like to "consume mass quantities," stuffing their faces with bags of chips and draining six-packs at one go. The first of the show's characters to require elaborate prostheses, Cone-head pieces were scheduled early in the show, since the latex domes took so long to apply.

When the *Saturday Night* group headed to the Emmys that sea-son, they won only in the writing category. The rookie allure that had helped them sweep the awards their first year had dwindled, but this time Michaels and his people pretended not to care. Marilyn Miller went onstage to collect the writing award with her colleagues wearing a dress she'd bought for $39.99 at a mall store called Strawberry's. "That's how we treated the Emmys," she said.

NINETEEN

AVANT-GARDE V. GARDE

MICHAELS ALWAYS WANTED HIS SHOW TO BE PERCEIVED AS A SCRAPPY UN-
derdog. (Losing Emmys helped.) On his own time, he was running
more and more with overdogs. In January 1977, Jann Wenner and his
wife, Jane, moved to New York from San Francisco, bringing the offices of *Rolling Stone* with them. Like Michaels, Wenner had seen it
as his mission to upend establishment media and infuse it with his
generation's values. It was inevitable that the two men would become
friends.

The Wenners lived in a duplex on East Sixty-sixth Street, a block
from Richard Nixon. They were from a part of New York that Michaels didn't know. "They were East Side," he said. "They had the
apartment with the white walls, and a big mirror leaning against the
wall." They had a park bench indoors. Wenner, the son of an Air
Force veteran who ran a baby formula company, was more openly
ambitious than Michaels. "It mattered more to Jann than to most
people to be rich and successful," he said. Michaels wanted to be
rich and successful too, but he didn't want it to show. "Jann was all
appetite," he said. Michaels, in contrast, views himself as having
been "dragged kicking and screaming into almost everything I've ever
done, because I can always think of all the reasons it won't go well."
He had a laid-back facade, striving but without breaking a sweat, and
adding plenty of Jack Benny pauses. Not putting himself on the line,

he knew, gave him plausible deniability. Wenner's obtrusive neediness was a lesson in how not to be.

Like Michaels, Wenner collected celebrity friends like baseball cards. Jean "Johnny" Pigozzi, an Italian playboy and photographer, and a friend of both men, observed that they both hit it off with stars whose backgrounds were similar to theirs—middle-class guys like Mick Jagger, who got rich and famous young. "They weren't stupid," he said. "They didn't go out and buy Ferraris and crash them."

Wenner saw Michaels and his crew of SNL cool kids as his magazine's television counterpart, and he assigned dozens of articles on the show and its stars. "We were all the same age and all rebellious and breaking through the establishment," Wenner told his biographer, Joe Hagan. When he commissioned the first *Rolling Stone* piece on the show, Wenner dangled the notion to Michaels that *he* would be on the cover. That didn't happen, and Michaels made a mental note of the way Wenner's gushing masked pragmatic wiles. But SNL and *Rolling Stone* fed one another. Hosting Michaels's show and appearing on the cover of Wenner's magazine were rites of passage for hip actors and musicians. Wenner got Belushi and Aykroyd to write up a Southern road trip they took for the magazine. He sent a note to Michaels apologizing when they missed rehearsal, ending with "P.S.: New York *is* big enough for the both of us."

Wenner acted as if he viewed Michaels, two years older, as a role model—a novelty for Michaels, who'd spent years accumulating father figures. For *Rolling Stone*'s New York headquarters, Wenner rented four floors in an Art Deco skyscraper, just up Fifth Avenue from the Art Deco skyscraper that housed *Saturday Night Live*. He rented an old house on Further Lane in Amagansett, a short walk from a bungalow that Michaels rented and would eventually buy. A few years later, he told *Architectural Digest*, "Between Lorne Michaels and all his guests and us and all our guests, the [tennis] court is constantly booked every weekend." He made sure the reporter knew that the lawn was big, too: "It takes one person on a big machine one full day to cut this greensward."

Anne Beatts used to say that you can only be avant-garde for so long before you become garde. Maintaining their insurrectionist cachet after they became successful was a conundrum for both Wenner and Michaels. Wenner threw himself at journalists, then was outraged when the profiles they wrote made him look foolish. Noticing that dynamic renewed Michaels's conviction that keeping a low profile with the press was the wiser approach. When Wenner finally managed to fulfill his dream of collaborating with SNL, he pulled off a networking trifecta. He collected all of *Rolling Stone*'s articles about his new friend Lorne's show into a book, and he persuaded another new friend, Jacqueline Onassis, who was an editor at Doubleday, to publish it. (At the lunch where Wenner pitched her the idea, he got a cocaine-induced nosebleed; back at his office, he told a colleague, "I just bled all over Jackie—just like Jack!")

The summer after the second season, Michaels and Forristal rented a ten-bedroom turreted mansion near the beach in East Hampton. Chase and O'Donoghue took a huge place across the street; the two of them were collaborating on a screenplay called *Saturday Matinee* for United Artists. Belushi would ride over from the Wenners' house on a moped to bring Michaels the Sunday *Times* (the 1978 sketch "The Thing That Wouldn't Leave," a horror-movie parody about a guest who overstays his welcome, was based on Belushi). Then he'd raid the refrigerator and make some long-distance calls. "The initial gesture allowed him carte blanche for the rest of his visit," Michaels said.

On Labor Day, Michaels teamed up with O'Donoghue, Chase, and Paul Simon to throw a lawn party. "It was the first flush of success and the first time there was any money," he recalled. Copying McCartney's Wings Over America bash, the hosts asked their guests to wear white. To O'Donoghue, the party was the apotheosis of a highly aestheticized worldview. Michaels had a more complex take: Was he throwing a parody of a party that Jay Gatsby would throw? Or was it the real thing, the ostentatious yet elegant exhibition of a talented out-of-towner's rapid ascent? Michaels, in his white trousers and open-necked shirt, stood somewhat apart, idly fiddling with a badminton racquet. The Wenners were there, along with Shelley Duvall, Jerry Wexler, Lillian Ross, and Eric Idle. A harpist plinked melodies on the lawn; the guests, in white poplin and garden-party hats, ate watercress sandwiches and sipped a special cocktail invented by O'Donoghue, called the Soiled Kimono: two parts champagne and one part Japanese plum wine. One guest told a local newspaper reporter that the party was "just like an Antonioni movie." There was "the same languor, the same insouciance. It was incredibly weird." The White Party became an annual tradition, the guest list growing richer and more famous each year. At the 1979 party, O'Donoghue would make his entrance in an ambulance, dressed in a Panama hat, wifebeater T-shirt, and white boxers, accompanied by two nurses in white underpants and bullet bras.

AS *SATURDAY NIGHT LIVE* BEGAN ITS THIRD SEASON (THE FIRST UNDER ITS intended name), Michaels began his second American decade. In a curtain-raiser for *The Washington Post,* Shales called him "the latenight Orson Welles of latter-day television," and referred to the show as a "trend-setting satirical theater of the air." Around the office, the atmosphere underwent a subtle key change. If the White Party had had an air about it of playing dress-up—like putting on a show at Camp Timberlane—by the fall, the sense of being at the center of the smart set was entirely real.

Everything about SNL was now A-list. Even the office Passover seder that Marilyn Miller organized was clogged with stars. (Zweibel complained, "I don't want to daven in front of Mike Nichols!") For the first two years, writers and cast got six tickets each per show, with orders not to give them to industry people; Michaels wanted real fans in the seats. By the third year, the allotment was two tickets, and Michaels, Tom Davis wrote in his memoir, "filled the audience with show business royalty." There was a feeling among the staff that Michaels was spending more time hanging with his celebrity pals than at the show. Belushi referred to the boss's fancy friends as "the dead."

At SNL, there was a sense that although they had all started at the same place, Michaels was moving into a different realm. "He spent a lot of time talking about where he was going to eat," Curtin said. Of Michaels and his constant companion Paul Simon, she said, "Where was the joy? They outlived the joy." Michaels seemed to be forgetting how to speak Earthling.

He kept in touch with old Toronto friends, but they were jangled by his rarefied new scene. Paul Pape and his wife, Karen, who were living in the U.K., accompanied Michaels and Forristal to a London art gallery with Anjelica Huston and Jack Nicholson, who was filming *The Shining* at Elstree Studios. "I may as well have been a shadow on the wall," Pape said. Side projects diverted his attention, too. He produced an NBC special for Paul Simon, and with Gary Weis he teamed up with Eric Idle and Neil Innes to make a feature-length special on the Rutles (*All You Need Is Cash*), which was shot mainly in England, with input from George Harrison. Michaels had a role in it as a merchandising maven.

Michaels wore the silver mother-duck brooch in his lapel less and less often, and the cast members inched toward greater independence. Radner told a reporter, "We're all saying, 'Wait a minute, I'm a team player, but I'm not. I'm an individual!'" Curtin, the most level-headed one, was drafted to negotiate the cast's salaries with the network; they were wary of leaving their fates to Brillstein and Michaels. (Radner sometimes went over to Curtin's apartment so she could observe her and her husband being regular married people.) With Chase gone, the cast members started fixating on their own next acts. Radner set her sights on Broadway. Belushi eyed the movies. He had been cast in *Animal House,* which required him to miss some SNL episodes. John Landis, the director, had wanted Chase and Aykroyd in the movie too, but Michaels discouraged them. "Bluto was a great part for John, but the Chevy part and the Danny part weren't really anything," he said. "Landis just wanted them in it for marketing. They wanted an SNL movie, and I didn't think there should be one." He felt that he was protecting the show.

Aykroyd remembers Michaels soft-pedaling his misgivings. "Lorne is not a warden of talent," he said. He turned the movie down, he said, "because, with Johnny gone, I thought Lorne would be short another writer and actor. I felt good about walking into his office and saying, 'Boss, I'm staying.'"

The movie was a huge disruption anyway. "*Animal House* changed everything," Michaels said. *Newsweek* put Belushi on the cover, which was just as distracting as when Chevy Chase made the cover of *New York.* "Suddenly, with the others, it was 'What about me?'" Michaels shared the feeling.

After *Animal House,* Belushi came to work with a new hauteur. Once, he treated a reporter to his impersonation of Michaels keeping a guest waiting while he made some calls: "Nicholson, can you hold just a second? I have Mike Nichols on the other line. Mike, can you hold for a second? I've got Mick Jagger on the other line. Mick, I'll be with you in a second . . ." When Michaels read about it, O'Donoghue recalled, "He went nuts."

The seventeenth floor was still the site of elevator-bank handball games and Merlin the leather-tooling pot dealer; Cherie Fortis, Michaels's assistant, was still greeted in the morning by writers trudging down the hall with their toothbrushes. But there was a new level of backbiting, of jockeying for position. Doors were closed more often, and people kept to themselves. Writers refined strategies to get their pieces on the air: making the set ultra-simple could work; so could writing parts for Laraine Newman or Garrett Morris, who were both often light in the show. (Morris did have a solid hit with his recurring Update role in "News for the Hard of Hearing"—another segment that wouldn't cut it today—in which he simply repeated news items as Chevy Chase spoke them, but yelling). Sketches featuring beloved characters, like the Coneheads or the Nerds, were generally a shoo-in. "It was survival of the fittest," Zweibel said. "Figure out a way to pair up. Figure out a way to get so-and-so to be in your sketch. Figure it out."

They would do three or four shows in a row without a break, which took a toll, and everyone burned out. The all-night Tuesday writing sessions set a tone of dysfunction that permeated the week, and after read-through, Michaels often didn't post a lineup until the wee hours. The set, props, costume, and music staffs waited, killing time with

ping-pong, griping, eating takeout food, and getting high. Michaels
hid out in his office, away from the cast, who always seemed to want
more—airtime, money, attention. In the meeting between dress and
air, people took the boss's list of cuts as personal slights, and they
sulked. "I began to be more removed, I think because the consequences of my actions began to have greater weight," he said. "We
were a team and we had to stay together and fight for each other. At
the same time, I had more power than everyone else."

Newman said, "It became difficult to adjust to having less time
with Dad." Marilyn Miller told a magazine reporter that she saw a
family therapist to vent about the office dynamic. Some colleagues
felt that although Michaels expected them to work out their scuffles
themselves, "he orchestrated some of the conflicts," according to one,
if only by benign neglect. Newman and Garrett Morris both thought
about quitting. Morris had to put up with a narrow and degrading
range of roles—he was cast as a flying monkey in an "Oz" sketch, and
was regularly cast in racist pieces like a fake ad for a toothpaste called
Tarbrush, designed to dull African Americans' supposedly too-bright
teeth. Michaels killed the Tarbrush ad before air; he saw that it was
offensive, and two Black crew members had walked off the set after
seeing it at dress. The white writing staff didn't know how to write
material for Morris, and he was reluctant to advocate for himself.
Once, when he did push an idea of his own—a viewer write-in campaign to nominate Sammy Davis Jr. to be the new pope—it got no
traction. He pitched the idea to Michaels in his office, an approach
he later regretted. "If you want to sell an idea to a producer, you go in
with your boy or your girl who will laugh at your jokes," he said.

The Not Ready for Prime Time Players found that their small talk
now centered on the industry. Newman recalled a day of camera
blocking, "and we were all talking about what we were naming our
corporations." Hers was Init Productions, "because I'm *in it*. I'm *in*
show business, you know?" Aykroyd's was Applied Action Research
Corp. O'Donoghue had Ghost Fox, Inc.; Downey, A Brighter Tomorrow, Inc. Michaels formed one called, with Canadian diffidence,

Above Average Productions. (Shuster came up with the name.) Radner stopped, mid-blocking, and said, "What's happened? We've joined the establishment."

THE NEW FOCUS ON MONEY AND CAREER CAME TO A HEAD ON THE EVENING of November 17, 1977, Michaels's thirty-third birthday. That afternoon, the staff had thrown him a surprise party, crouching in the conference room outside his office until Buck Henry brought him in. Fifty-odd people yelled, "Live from New York, it's Lorne's birthday!" A writer from *Viva* magazine was there, reporting a story, and he recounted the scene in his piece: "Love exudes from every person in the room."

Hours later, when he had gone out to a celebratory dinner with Forristal at the Box Tree in Turtle Bay, Aykroyd corralled the writing staff for an urgent confab. According to Hill and Weingrad, Aykroyd had seen some budget papers relating to the writers' salaries on Michaels's desk, and the figures made him question whether funds that were earmarked for writers were being diverted to other parts of the show. The discrepancy was only around $10,000 a week, but it was enough to agitate people. Everyone felt exhausted and depressed, as Marilyn Miller put it, "because you had no life." There was a motion to provoke a confrontation.

The next day, Friday, Aykroyd and a group of writers gathered again outside Michaels's office; he was inside with the door closed. Down on the studio floor, a Samurai Psychiatrist sketch was being rehearsed, with Buck Henry as the patient, despairing over his "father problem." Upstairs, Aykroyd readied his comrades in the greenroom next to Michaels's office, ticking off the collective grievances with oratorical flourish. At the height of his rant, he kicked a hole in the wall. Hearing the commotion, Michaels opened the door, took in the scene, and asked, "What's up?"

Aykroyd unspooled his critique, complaining that the writers were overworked, and accusing Michaels of holing up in his office and going to restaurants when he could be righting the ship. Michaels listened in silence, then walked back into his office and closed the door.

Aykroyd remembers kicking the wall and rallying the writers, but he doesn't remember the focus being money. In his memory, the key issue was the way the show's chronic lateness was hard on the cue card department. "Scripts were coming in minutes before air," he said. He wanted a hard deadline for changes. "The cue card guys are your tanker refuelers, man," he said. "They've gotta get that nozzle right in the hole, and they gotta do it in time."

The idea of a mutiny offended Michaels. "The trouble with a thankless job," he used to say, "is that no one thanks you." The first season, when Franken and Davis had given him a birthday gift of an old Shriner's fez that they'd found in Franken's grandparents' closet, seemed like a distant Eden. (Michaels had given Davis, for his twenty-fourth birthday, twenty-four cases of Heineken.) Michaels preferred solving problems with staff members one-on-one. "Danny I had known since he was nineteen, so it was more complicated," he said. Internally, the insurrection took on the name Black Friday. "That was the only time I gave the ship a little trouble," Aykroyd said later, conceding that Michaels's management style was "sane and firm." "Lorne's not a Gurdjieffian," he said, referencing the philosophy of the Greek Armenian mystic George Gurdjieff, who espoused conflict as a path to enlightenment. After Michaels's father vanished into the hospital the night they argued, confrontation became too risky; Michaels always walked away. As Paul Simon put it, "That's why Lorne doesn't get into fights with anyone."

Jim Downey, the new writer, steered clear of Black Friday. So did O'Donoghue, who socialized regularly with Michaels and Forristal, once sending a Mailgram to them in East Hampton reading "Help, I'm trapped on a planet of assholes." Shuster also hung back. "Not about to get in a confrontation that pitched my then boyfriend versus my erstwhile husband/current boss," she said. "Shit was fraught enough."

As Michaels nursed his hurt feelings, some of the insurgents came to apologize individually. Tom Schiller gave Michaels a little sketch he'd made of his face in alarmed profile. The caption read: "Producer under strain. Hang in there. Black Saturday '77." The mood on the floor was glum and vaguely adversarial. "It was easy to portray it as if all I did was drink champagne from slippers," Michaels said. "But the work had gotten harder."

After Black Friday, Michaels retreated further, locking his office door at night for the first time. He also had a new private bathroom built. (Davis believed this was the result of a prank he played one day, when he spied, beneath a stall in the men's room, a pair of sleek cowboy boots that Forristal had given Michaels. Winking at a colleague, Davis started bitching about the boss: "Maybe he's starting to lose it" and "He's turning into an asshole.")

That it was the writers who'd ganged up on him was especially painful. "I was creating a culture where the writers were more important than the stars," he said. He always defended them from other staffers, who considered them coddled. For example, the third time Michael Palin hosted, Jim Downey reprised a Dickensian waif that Palin had played earlier, a poor lad named Miles Cowperthwaite who is forced to empty his benefactor's drool bucket. In Part II, Miles is put on a schooner, the *Raging Queen,* helmed by Captain Ned (Belushi) and a squad of randy seamen, including a first mate named Spunk and a soon-to-be-amputee sailor played by James Taylor, the musical guest. Downey didn't finish his draft by read-through, but Eugene Lee got started building the ship, which would cost $25,000. "So now it's Thursday," Michaels said. "Work is progressing on the boat, the actors are here, but not the script." Pages of dialogue made their way to the studio floor one-by-one. "If I hadn't started building the boat, we would never have gotten the piece. It was entirely boat before the horse."

It was a brilliant, if overlong, sketch, which Michaels felt took the cast to a new level. (By today's standards, the gay jokes would grate: "Captain Ned, I learned from my shipmates, was a very manly, virile, manful person, and a firm believer in strict discipline, corporal punishment, and nude apartment wrestling.") "But I knew what I know,"

Michaels said. "Which is that there was no way Jim was going to do it faster. So you're patient with it, because you know there's value there."

Michaels's contract with NBC was for three years. A few weeks after Black Friday, he let it be known that he might not stick around for Season Four. In the *Viva* piece he complained that his writers were whining over how much more they'd earn on a prime-time sit-com. "It *is* a family," he said. "I don't want to see it ripped apart." He added that he also was ready to earn more money, and he was getting tired of working eighteen-hour days. After professing his devotion to the show, he said, in the tones of an underappreciated dad, "But when it takes every ounce of my strength to get it on, and there's nothing but resistance, and nobody seems to give a fuck, then I want out. Because you can only give up your life for something greater than you. So far, it's been worth it."

The family feud got stirred up anew in February 1978, when the cast was doing a sketch called "Celebrity Crackup" at dress. Michaels had asked Chevy Chase to host, a sweeps-week strategy that some of the cast resented. Chase arrived in the building like a returning hero, telling tales of Hollywood. Murray remembered a feeling of "general animosity." The real celebrity crack-up happened just before air. Murray and Chase had been circling each other warily, with Belushi ratcheting up the tension, badmouthing his old rival. Minutes before Chase was to step onstage to play Gerald Ford in the cold open, it exploded. Schoolyard-level insults were traded: taunts about Chase's failing marriage (Murray: "Go fuck your wife. I hear she needs it"), jeers about Murray's acne scars (Chase: "I'm gonna land Neil Armstrong on your face if you don't shut up"). Chase remembers getting into "a boxing pose" in a dressing room, and the two started throwing punches. Murray said, "This is *my* show now!" and called Chase a "medium talent." Curtin said, "There were these two bull mooses going at each other. Testosterone was surging." So was cocaine, in the case of Chase.

"It was really a Hollywood fight, a 'Don't touch my face!' kind of thing," Murray later said. "It was an Oedipal thing, a rupture. Because we all felt mad he had left us, and somehow I was the anointed avenging angel who had to speak for everyone." He wasn't speaking for Michaels, who was disheartened when he learned about the fracas. "It tore at the fabric of the show," Michaels said, and the episode didn't deliver.

O'Donoghue was one of the few who welcomed Chase's return. He still expected the screenplay the two were writing to be his big break. For a while he'd been trashing SNL to reporters, complaining that his best stuff was censored (e.g., the Tarbrush ad and a sketch about the censor Herminio Traviesas called "Dead Censor"). Michaels, he felt, had stopped supporting his ambitious sketch ideas, such as "Attack of the Atomic Lobsters," a baroque sci-fi parody that required elaborate special effects. He also pushed for live gunfire in the studio. "I got tired of being lectured by Lorne 'The Rabbi' Michaels," he said.

Michaels, having got through the pain of Chase leaving, had to cope with the congenital scorn of Belushi, and now O'Donoghue. "Lorne loved Michael, worshipped Michael, envied Michael, snubbed Michael," Tom Davis said. "Michael was jealous of Lorne's wealth and power." O'Donoghue's moods were becoming ever darker, worsened by the painkillers he took for chronic migraines.

Percodan rage was on display when Michaels, to mollify O'Donoghue, found a way to get the Atomic Lobsters piece on the air. The premise, that radioactive-waste-eating lobsters had grown to the size of Cadillacs, was threaded through the episode, culminating in the crustaceans climbing the RCA Building, demolishing the studio, and killing anyone in their path. Glitches during dress provoked an O'Donoghue tantrum; he kicked chairs amid pools of fake blood and yelled, as frightened audience members made their way through smoke for the exits. He had finally found a way, figuratively at least, to express his wish to burn the show down.

While Chase was in L.A., O'Donoghue's screenplay draft had ballooned into an unmanageable opus, hundreds of pages long. The idea had been to create a whole movie-theater experience: a fake newsreel, a cartoon, a bouncing-ball song, coming attractions, and two features, with Chase playing thirteen different roles. A concession stand promo ended with "After the show, why not drop by and say hello to our projectionist? He will be glad to give you a tour of the projection room and show you his cock—The Management." Chase knew that the script needed to be cut radically, but he was scared to risk an explosion from O'Donoghue. So he just dropped it, accepting an offer to star opposite Goldie Hawn in a movie called *Foul Play*. O'Donoghue framed the story as Chase double-crossing him to make Hollywood crap for a lot of money. Michaels said that in O'Donoghue's mind, "Chevy was going to be a movie star, so he should be able to get anything he wants," including a green light for a weird four-hour movie. "Not true. Chevy just listened to his agent."

O'Donoghue quit SNL at the end of the season, griping to the press ("I wanted to bail out of the plane before it crashed into the mud"). Nonetheless, Michaels stepped in and engineered a deal whereby O'Donoghue could make specials for NBC, with Michaels as executive producer. The network, in last place, was hungry for any programming that smelled like an SNL spin-off. "All Lorne did was give Michael second chances," Marilyn Miller said. "And all Michael did was raise the bar for how horrible he could be to Lorne."

The result was *Mr. Mike's Mondo Video*, with O'Donoghue directing. NBC approved the shooting script, but, when a cut was screened, Traviesas declared that the special would run "over my dead body." (O'Donoghue said that he'd agree to those terms.) The show was a hodgepodge of inventive and sour: a segment called "Cat Swimming School," in which an instructor throws cats in a pool; a report about "gals who love creeps" (one gal says, "When I reach down and feel a firm colostomy bag, I know I'm with a real man"); a report on a cult that worshipped *Hawaii-Five-O*'s Jack Lord; an ad for a military weapon called Laser Bra 2000; all capped by a scene of O'Donoghue himself wishing viewers goodnight from a blood-stained beach. Edits were ordered, then more edits, until the enterprise became like peeling an onion. O'Donoghue was apoplectic, believing that Michaels, who had invested around $250,000 of his own money in the project, had failed to back him with the network. ("What were they expecting from me, *Porky Pig Takes a Trip?*" O'Donoghue raged.) Realizing that *Mr. Mike's Mondo Video* would never be shown on NBC, the network programming producer, Paul Klein, bought the rights and planned to release it in theaters as "the TV show that can't be shown on TV."

At the premiere, in a scuzzy Times Square movie house, Michaels sat between Klein and O'Donoghue. People walked out in droves, and Klein kept nudging Michaels and whispering, "We're going to lose all the money!" Critics hated it, too. (*People:* "Tasteless, raunchy and, worse yet, only intermittently funny.") But Hollywood, drawn by the SNL brand, didn't seem to care. Paramount offered O'Donoghue a three-picture deal. O'Donoghue considered the film a breakthrough, but to Michaels it cemented another lesson. It was what CBS had told Lily Tomlin five years earlier: "Remember Podunk!" Michaels's version of the sentiment would become one of his mantras: "You've got audience in all fifty states. You've got to hold the audience. Then you get to do another show."

TWENTY

RESPECTABLE

ON A SUNDAY IN OCTOBER 1978, MICHAELS FOUND HIMSELF BACK HOME IN Toronto, trying to find a tailor shop that was open. He had flown in after a bumpy episode of SNL hosted by Frank Zappa. Mick Jagger had arranged a private plane; he'd asked Michaels to come to Toronto to testify as a character witness in Keith Richards's heroin trial. The year before, Canadian Mounties had busted Richards as he nodded out in the presidential suite of Toronto's Harbour Castle Hilton; they'd found twenty-two grams of heroin, enough to charge Richards with intent to traffic, a crime that could carry a life sentence. When Michaels landed, he went into producer mode, helping to get Richards out of his pirate getup and into a tan three-piece suit, so that on Monday he would look presentable when the matter of *Her Majesty the Queen, and Keith Richards* commenced.

Richards arrived at the courthouse through a back entrance, wobbly in his new duds, which he wore with white socks and a loud tie. The Canadian prosecutor wanted a tough sentence (the minimum was seven years), arguing that the Rolling Stones' lyrics promoted drug use. Richards's lawyer portrayed his client as a troubled artist, comparing him to Vincent van Gogh and Sylvia Plath. In the courtroom, he quoted from a biography of Baudelaire, maintaining that true art comes from "pieces of the shattered self."

Michaels, a local boy made good, was an ideal character witness.

The week before, in New York, he'd been jumpy; he was pleased to be asked to do a favor for his close friend Mick, but what if he had to perjure himself? He knew that Richards wasn't clean. (In a back room at the courthouse, Richards took a quick snort from a bag of coke he had in his pocket.) Seated in the Toronto courtroom, Michaels fixed on the portrait of the queen looking down at him and Richards. He said to himself, "I'm Canadian. I'm not going to lie."

He didn't have to. When he took the stand, he was asked only about the defendant's creative role in the Stones; he responded that Richards was "the catalyst of the band." He said that he chose the Rolling Stones over Muhammad Ali to host his show's fourth-season opener, because the Stones were "the number one rock and roll band in the world." In a decision that surprised many jurists, Richards got off with a suspended sentence and an order to play a benefit concert for the blind.

"Canadians would not want to put a real artist in jail," Michaels said later. Whether the outcome was due to his testimony, or to the intercession of a blind teenage superfan who had made a private appeal to the judge, is impossible to know. Within hours of the verdict, members of the press corps were making "blind justice" jokes.

Michaels came to view the episode as an example of How Things Work, as opposed to what they look like on the surface: he believes that the Mounties who arrested Richards weren't in the hotel that night to make a bust, but to keep an eye on Margaret Trudeau, the fifty-seven-year-old prime minister's twenty-eight-year-old wife, who was in another hotel room with Stones guitarist Ronnie Wood. The bust happened almost by accident. He refers to that kind of larger perspective as "having a wide shot" on a situation. Richards sent Michaels a thank-you note, on stationery from a Jamaica hotel.

Two weeks before the trial, Richards had been at the RCA Building preparing to act as host, with the rest of the Stones, on SNL's season premiere. A memo had circulated beforehand, about recruiting the audience: "No sophisticated 'Elaine's' upper east siders, no moms and pops, no showbiz folks, just young rock and roll fans." The directive came from the Stones. Like Michaels, the band wanted to maintain its nonconformist cred, even though its members were verging on gentility. (Days before the band showed up, Michaels arrived home from a trip to Paris and ordered a lightning-fast sprucing up of the dressing rooms that the band would use; furniture was cadged from executive offices all over the building.) In the end, the concern about a glut of society types rattling their jewelry was misplaced. Tickets were so closely guarded and security so tight that there were empty seats just before air, and NBC pages scrambled to fill them. (Henry Kissinger had a secretary call to request tickets for his teenage son, David; Franken happened to pick up the phone and explained that the former secretary of state "could have had the tickets if he hadn't bombed Cambodia.") The band appeared in sketches—Jagger interviewed by Aykroyd as Tom Snyder, and Charlie Watts and Wood as customers in the Olympia Cafe "cheeseburger cheeseburger" sketch. Richards was scheduled to be in two pieces, but his parts were cut when, in rehearsal, he didn't appear to know where he was. The censor had waged a failed campaign to get the costume people to ask Jagger to wear underpants beneath his tight, stretchy orange trousers. (The male cast members needed prodding in this regard, too. Franne Lee, whose staff helped with quick costume changes, once posted a sign reading ALL CAST MEMBERS MUST WEAR UNDERWEAR ON SATURDAY.) The censor did not have the foresight to request that Jagger refrain from licking Ron Wood on the mouth during the song "Respectable."

Michaels regarded the Stones' hosting as a visit from royalty; their new album, *Some Girls,* was number one. After the show, before everyone went up to a party in the Rainbow Room, Michaels brought a few guests (Steven Spielberg, Paul Simon, Ahmet Ertegun) back to his office to watch a cassette of the Stones' three-song set. Jagger squeezed on a sofa next to Mayor Ed Koch, who had done a cameo. "Maybe this wasn't such a good show," Jagger said in a croaky whisper. His voice was shot from days of over-rehearsing and partying with the cast, and the band's performance had been ragged. Bedraggled or not, the world's best rock and roll band had played its first TV performance in a decade on Michaels's show, and the comedy—

including Murray's first appearance as the co-anchor of Weekend Update—was solid.

It almost didn't happen. Despite the speculation that Michaels's third-season waffling was a contract ploy, he really had been close to leaving the show. People kept asking him what his next move would be after his three-year contract was up. "You begin to think, 'Jesus, I'm an asshole for still being here,'" he said. "'What about my other ambitions and dreams? And didn't I want to direct a movie?'" Herb Schlosser, his protector, had been kicked upstairs by then and replaced by Fred Silverman, the former president of ABC, who, years before, had tried to kill Tomlin's Juke and Opal sketch. Silverman was known as "the Man with the Golden Gut," famous for slick packaging, creating the "jiggle show" genre (showcases for busty actresses, like *Charlie's Angels*) and making an art of the spin-off (*Mary Tyler Moore* begat *Rhoda*; *Happy Days* begat *Laverne & Shirley*). When Silverman took over, Michaels gave an interview to *Us* magazine preemptively declaring his independence. He speculated, in his flat way, about the new boss trying to raid SNL for spin-offs, joking, "The Coneheads are a touch away from being the new Munsters." He didn't have faith that NBC understood what it had with SNL, and he waffled in the press about whether or not he would stay on.

Exhausting as it was, the third season had been the strongest so far; one episode is often cited as the best of all time. Steve Martin was the host, and he appeared in a Festrunk Brothers sketch ("The two most swinging foxes had the hots on for us and are coming here tonight to let us hold onto their big American breasts!") and as Theodoric of York, his medieval barber character, who treats patients by bleeding and applying leeches; when he muses about chucking his old methods and ushering in a new age of science, he takes a long pause, then says, *"Naaaaaaah."* He also debuted his original song "King Tut" ("Buried with a donkey! He's my favorite honky!"), which Michaels mounted with lavish production values. The King Tut single promptly sold more than a million copies. The season also introduced Aykroyd's Update retort to his co-anchor, "Jane, you ignorant slut"; Radner's Roseanne Roseannadanna; and Father Guido Sarducci, the rock critic and gossip columnist for the Vatican newspaper (the creation of a new writer, Don Novello).

Torn over whether to sign on for the fourth season, Michaels found clarity, as he often did, while taking a walk. Strolling on the beach with Howard Shore, he confessed that he was leaning toward leaving. Shore said, "It's too bad, because we're just learning how to do it." That gave him pause.

With most conundrums, he'd ask himself, *What would Uncle Pep do?* He remembered a time when, wiped out from doing seven shows in a row, he'd looked forward to a rare week off. He had circled the programs he wanted to watch in *TV Guide,* and he knew what movies he was going to see and which sandwiches he was going to order from the Carnegie Deli. Between dress and air, Pep called to tell him that his grandfather had died; he'd booked his nephew a seat on a Sunday morning flight to Toronto for the funeral. Michaels protested that he was too exhausted. "Pep said, 'It's your mother's *father.* I'll pick you up at the airport,'" he recalled. "No one had said 'no' to me in a long time. Because, you know, I was 'changing American culture.'" He made the flight and the funeral. Showing up mattered.

Returning for Season Four was a version of showing up. Not using his success to run off and pursue the old Hollywood dream seemed like the adult decision. Another show business tenet that Michaels often spouts off is "The quickest way to kill off somebody talented is to let him do everything he wants." The movies could wait.

Dragging out the decision paid off. For the fourth season, Brillstein negotiated a contract that gave him a minimum salary of $750,000 and a fund to develop other projects. SNL was the highest-rated late-night program in history, and its young demographic kept growing, generating annual revenues for NBC of $30 to $40 million. And so the network acceded to every demand. It upgraded and expanded the offices again: a multi-nozzled shower was added to Michaels's private bathroom; and Beatts requested, and received, a hospital bed in her office for the all-nighters.

The new contract made it possible for Michaels to live like a truly rich man. He now had a car and driver. He started wearing better-cut blazers and Italian suits, and traded his sneakers and desert boots for loafers. Having decided to stay in New York, he bought a property that he had been renting near the beach in Amagansett, paying $165,000 for a clapboard house on 1.3 acres with a pool. Then he purchased a large apartment in the building where Paul Simon lived, a stately 1910 edifice of beige brick on Central Park West, which had what uptown real estate agents call "Snoopy-eye views," a reference to the Macy's Thanksgiving Day Parade. On the recommendations of friends (Jagger, Martin, Caroline Kennedy), he would engage a series of British interior designers—Geoffrey Bennison, Ian Odsoll, and Kathryn Ireland—who specialized in sumptuous, be-swagged rooms anchored by English antiques.

Paul Simon and Carrie Fisher lived in the apartment next door. The two kitchens each had a door that opened onto a common landing for the service elevator, so that the friends could wander in and out of each other's apartments like Ricky Ricardo and Fred Mertz. Simon remembers there being an ongoing argument about who were the Mertzes and who were the Ricardos. For years, Michaels used Simon's gym room to work out with a trainer.

The strangeness of Michaels's new life hit him one night as he was pulling up to his apartment building in his limo. It was 3:00 A.M., after the host dinner and the marathon writing session. A light snow was falling, and a couple was walking slowly up the sidewalk. They leaned over to look in the limo window, figuring, Michaels suspected, that someone important must be inside. He was startled to see that it was John Lennon and Yoko Ono. He said nothing. "It was one of those moments," he recalled. "I thought, 'No, it should be *me* looking in.'"

Outside the show, his life changed too. He and Forristal traveled a lot. They stayed at the Savoy in London on theater trips, and they went with his wild old London friend Melissa North and her husband to Kenya, where they were put up at the jewel-like Peponi Hotel on the island of Lamu. When Paul Simon chartered a yacht (one that Aristotle Onassis gave to Princess Grace as a wedding present), Michaels went along, braving an unglamorous bout of seasickness as they cruised the Greek isles and dropped in on Melissa North in Lindos. He and Forristal traveled to Barbados with Simon, Eric Idle, and David Geffen. On the recommendation of Edie Baskin, they started renting a house on St. Barts, years before the oligarchs showed up, sometimes with their friend John Head along. In the beginning, Michaels was paying $350 a week. "There was nothing there then," Forristal said. "One person on the road made roast chickens, and an old lady sold baguettes." At one point, the Eden Rock Hotel, where Greta Garbo and Howard Hughes had stayed, went on the market, and Michaels toyed with the idea of buying it and turning it into a clubhouse.

In Paris, on a trip to celebrate the Wenners' tenth anniversary, they'd attended a Bob Dylan concert at the Pavillon de Paris; Johnny Pigozzi remembers Michaels and Wenner being "completely gone," holding up their gold Dupont lighters during the encore, as Dylan sang, "May you build a ladder to the stars / And climb on every rung / And may you stay forever young."

After the show, Martin Scorsese and Robbie Robertson joined the group for dinner at a grand penthouse that Pigozzi's mother owned in Neuilly. They were on the film festival circuit with *The Last Waltz*, and had flown in from Italy with two models. "Then this guy arrives who looks like every poster in every post office of a junkie heroin addict," Michaels recalled. The man, whom he pegged as a dealer connected to Scorsese and Robertson, laid out lines of powder. "Everybody thought it was cocaine," he said. Pigozzi remembers all of his guests snorting the lines, which turned out to be heroin, and then vomiting out of his mother's window into the courtyard of the German ambassador's residence next door. Michaels said he didn't partake, but he remembers that "people started retching." Not long afterward, Scorsese was hospitalized for addiction. Pigozzi took a photo on the trip of the Wenners with Michaels (wearing a white suit over a Hawaiian shirt) and Forristal, who was grinning and holding up a copy of *France-Soir* with a huge headline: "Record Battu a Roissy: 40 kg de cocaine saisis" ("Record Broken at Roissy: 40 kg of cocaine seized").

Back in New York, Andy Warhol invited Michaels to the Factory for lunch. He was hoping that Warhol would agree to host the show, but the artist, resolutely uncharmable, wanted to take over a whole episode, swapping in his own actors. Michaels wouldn't hear of it. His own cast were stars now. When the fourth season began, he had even instructed Don Pardo, when he read SNL's opening credits, to stop introducing the cast as the Not Ready for Prime Time Players. In their scant free time, their social lives were buzzing; they all got good tables at Elaine's, hobnobbing with Mikhail Baryshnikov or Norman Mailer. The cast found themselves besieged by crowds, and the nature of their followers got them down. "We were the TV literati," Shuster said. But the fans, increasingly, were drunken metalheads, Bluto fanboys who threw toga parties in their frat houses. Michaels began to refer to this new group of viewers as "the undeserved audience," because they arrived in the slipstream of *Animal House*. Reacting to the fan brouhaha, NBC had started paying for town cars to ferry the cast around, and a burly guard was stationed in the elevator bank on the seventeenth floor. Most SNL employees thought the guard was there to protect them from a potential drug raid.

The cast needed a hideout. Aykroyd, looking for a place to store a couple of new Harleys, rented an old saloon by the Holland Tunnel, on the corner of Dominick and Hudson, for $400 a month. In Toronto he had run a speakeasy called the 505, and now, with Belushi, he set up the new place as a private clubhouse, the Blues Bar. Drinks were free, so they didn't need a liquor license; Keith Richards and Francis Ford Coppola tended bar. The regular SNL party had gotten too posh, full of scenesters and agents. The Blues Bar was a refuge. Belushi would play guitar with whatever indulgent pro he could cajole onstage—Richards, the Allman Brothers, Bowie, ZZ Top. (Belushi called his group "the Stink Band.") Michaels usually made an appearance on Saturday nights, to reassure people that it had been a good show, but he preferred holding court in the relative civility of the official party, in a banquette at One Fifth.

Having re-upped his contract, Michaels wanted his people to stick around, and he rewarded those who'd stayed. After seeing Belushi sing one night in 1978 at the rock club Trax, he'd asked him to warm up the SNL audience with the act that he and Aykroyd had been developing. By the fourth season the duo, which Howard Shore christened "the Blues Brothers," was opening arena shows for the Grateful Dead and Steve Martin. At Martin's L.A. show, backed by a roster of blues greats, they recorded an LP called *Briefcase Full of Blues*. On his thirtieth birthday, Belushi found himself a star of the hottest show on TV, with a number one album and a number one movie. He ran into Chase in the men's room at One Fifth. "You know," he said, zipping up, "I make more money in movies than you, *boy*."

Everybody started to get what they wanted. Belushi and Aykroyd got to be rock stars. And with Michaels's help, Radner got to be on Broadway, which was her dream. Michaels and she had both been theater nerds as kids. He once teased Laraine Newman for moping about an errant boyfriend and surprised her by bursting into a song from *West Side Story*: "A boy like that—will bring you sorrow!" He had been working with Radner on an album of funny songs (like "Let's Talk Dirty to the Animals"), and had the idea to put it onstage at the Winter Garden Theatre as "a new form of vaudeville."

Fred Silverman wanted Radner to star in a prime-time spin-off show; NBC gave her a development deal and a secretary. Murray, who had filmed *Meatballs* during the summer, had a secretary too, and the joke went around that now everyone's assistants had assistants. So far, Michaels's talent-retention plan seemed to be working. Radner told Tom Snyder, on *Tomorrow*, that leaving the show at this point would be like slapping a parent in the face.

The cast's contracts were just for five years, and everyone was in demand. Brillstein represented almost all of them, which complicated things for Michaels. With the new-project fund that Brillstein had negotiated for him, he made thirteen *"Best of"* SNL specials, to run on a weekday at 10:00 P.M. He had set up his own production company, Broadway Video, in a rented space two blocks away in the Brill Building, at 1619 Broadway. There was a business logic to the arrangement; besides earning Michaels a producer's fee, the *"Best of"* shows provided a nice payday for Broadway Video, who edited them.

Broadway Video also represented an escape route for Michaels, a landing pad for whatever might come next.

He had a good feeling about video. Friends had already been telling him that they often taped SNL on their Betamax machines and watched it on Sunday. In the same way that television liberated the movies, Michaels believed that video and cable would liberate television. "Suddenly there will be more freedom," he told *Rolling Stone:* "The networks will remain financing organizations, but there will be enormous fragmentation in terms of viewing audiences. With fifty or more stations to choose from, a certain segment of the public will be able to tune into a certain horticulture show, and other very esoteric programs."

Around Times Square, video stores were already proliferating. They sold mostly porn, but Michaels realized that porn got people to buy the hardware, and that soon people would be watching movies and TV shows on cassettes. "Why should Steve Martin hassle with network censors . . . when he can simply do a new video disc show and ship it directly to the record stores? It's going to happen," he said. "Just wait and see how quickly all of this becomes commonplace."

This was prescient, but the specter of people watching movies on their little Zenith sets unsettled traditionalists. Woody Allen was one such skeptic. Right after O'Donoghue had marched out of SNL, Allen, fresh off the success of *Annie Hall,* cast him in *Manhattan* as a twit named Dennis who holds forth on orgasms and death at a party in the Museum of Modern Art's sculpture garden. Dennis also had a scene, which was cut, in which he proclaims, "Video is where it's at! When big screens get perfected and the cable is developed, you can sit home and watch sixty channels—once that happens it means movies are dead, like when films came in, theater was dead."

Michaels and Allen were on different sides of the video question, but they seemed to be in a kind of cultural lockstep, inhabiting adjacent comedy universes. In *Manhattan,* Allen's character, Isaac, quits his comedy-writing job at a live sketch show that he thinks is garbage. Isaac complains that viewers "sit in front of their sets and the gamma rays eat the white cells of their brains out." A few years later, Allen used a similar live sketch show as a setting in *Hannah and Her Sisters,* with offices situated in an Art Deco tower whose hallways are decorated with framed production stills and a rainbow logo, just like the ones outside 8H. The cast is always high on quaaludes, and Allen, who plays the producer (the Lorne part), battles with a censor in a suit over a sketch about child molesters.

"Woody was having dinner every night then with Jean Doumanian," Michaels said; it was clear where he got his details. But he was content to view Allen's mimicry as more homage than hostility. "There's always been this parallel thing," he said. "Woody is the intellectual basis for a lot of New York Jewish comedy, but SNL wasn't that."

If Allen was disparaging the show, he wasn't alone. In a pattern that would continue for decades, as quickly as critics valorized *Saturday Night Live,* they turned on it. The mega-success of *Animal House* made the show popular with the wrong kind of viewers; success made it seem mainstream. In August 1979, just before the fifth season, *TV Guide* published a story called "Saturday Night Moribund," saying that the show wasn't funny anymore. Brillstein sent a telegram to the editors: "It's unfortunately true that whenever a star makes it to the top there are always little men with dull hatchets determined to cut him or her down." Journalists used to roam the office freely; now the cast regarded reporters as vultures, and NBC publicists trailed them even into the restroom.

Publicists also shielded the staff from negative feedback. A PR memo to Michaels after the Rolling Stones' appearance said that they'd been "holding aside" critical letters. The memo contained the following breakdown:

Feedback on the Stones:

Obscene—7 (about half were older parent types)

Catholics upset about Pope & Cardinal jokes—4

"Who are Devo?"—3

Scotch Tape Store- sensitively done—1

Franken & Davis—always disgusting –1

Lorne with his father, Henry "Lefty" Lipowitz, in Toronto

Lorne and Mark Lipowitz, mid-1940s

Lorne, thirteen years old, front row center,
at Camp Timberlane, 1958

Lorne and his girlfriend Rosie Shuster, at a
friend's sweet sixteen party, Toronto, 1964

Lorne directing *Bye Bye Birdie* at
Camp Timberlane, 1964

From the opening credits of *The Hart and
Lorne Terrific Hour*, which ran on the CBC
in the early 1970s

Michaels interviewing Hart
Pomerantz as the Canadian Beaver,
on *The Hart and Lorne Terrific Hour*

Michaels on his first visit to Studio 8H, 1975

Chevy Chase, Dan Aykroyd, John Belushi, and Michaels in the kitchen at Elaine's, 1975. *Photograph by Jonathan Becker*

Michaels, Paul Simon, and Buck Henry, back in Elaine's kitchen, 1978. *Photograph by Jonathan Becker*

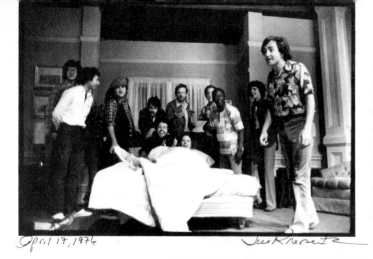

Rehearsing a Supreme Court sketch with, from left, Tom Davis, Tom Schiller, John Belushi, Dan Aykroyd, Chevy Chase, Michael O'Donoghue, Jane Curtin, Alan Zweibel, Garrett Morris, and Neil Levy, in 1976

April 17, 1974

Michaels giving notes on a sketch about host Ralph Nader inspecting blow-up dolls, with Garrett Morris and costume designer Franne Lee, 1977. *Photograph by Jonathan Becker*

Michaels "consuming mass quantities" with Aykroyd as Beldar Conehead, 1977. *Photograph by Jonathan Becker*

With Susan Forristal at the first White Party, East Hampton, 1977. *Photograph by Jonathan Becker*

Michaels and his manager Bernie Brillstein

The only known photo of Michaels dancing: with Susan Forristal and Lauren Hutton at the opening of a Richard Avedon exhibition, MoMA, 1978

Backstage at SNL with musical guest Ray Charles, 1977

The Malibu "four musketeers," around Michaels's pool in Amagansett: Gary Weis, Michaels, Joe Boyd, and John Head, late 1970s

In the SNL green room with the Rolling Stones (and Alan Zweibel), 1978

Buck Henry, Michaels, Jean Pagliuso, Gilda Radner, François de Menil, and Susan Forristal, 1978

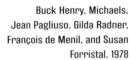

In Paris, with Susan Forristal and Jann and Jane Wenner, 1978. (Headline translation: "Record broken at Roissy: 40 kg of cocaine seized.")

With Susan Forristal in Paris, 1978

At the Hawaii Kai, in New York City, during the filming of *Nothing Lasts Forever*, with Howard Shore, Tom Schiller, and musical arranger Cheryl Hardwick, 1982

SNL 1985-6 writers room. Top row: Don Novello, John Swartzwelder, Mark McKinney, Jack Handey, Tom Davis. Second row: Bruce McCulloch, Robert Smigel, Carole Leifer, George Meyer. Front: A. Whitney Brown, Lanier Laney, Terry Sweeney, Michaels, Al Franken, Jim Downey

Camping with
Jonathan Becker,
Peter Maas, and their
sons in Connecticut, 1998.
*Photograph by
Jonathan Becker*

Michaels's
portrait painted
by Eric Fischl,
2002.
*©Eric Fischl/
Artists Rights
Society (ARS), NY*

Michaels on Ajax Mountain, Aspen, 2002.
Photograph by Jonathan Becker

With Conan O'Brien and news anchor Brian Williams at a MoMA gala, 2004

Michaels with his wife Alice celebrating their son Henry's graduation from the Buckley School, 2007.
Photograph by Jonathan Becker

Ice sculpture of Lorne Michaels's head crafted by Mark Mckenzie, on display at the book party for Tom Davis's *Thirty-Nine Years of Short-Term Memory Loss*

Homer: "Here comes Lorne Michaels. Pretend you don't see him." Michaels in an episode of *The Simpsons*, written by John Swartzwelder, 1999

Dinner poster for a celebration honoring Michaels and SNL at the *Harvard Lampoon* castle, 1998

Backstage with Jim Downey, 2006

From "The Anatominals," an episode of Robert Smigel's "TV Funhouse" on SNL, 2001

Michaels with his wife Alice, and Anne Stringfield and Steve Martin, at the renaming ceremony for Lincoln Center's Geffen Hall, 2015

In the audience for SNL's fortieth anniversary show, 2015. Michaels is flanked by (clockwise from left) Jason Sudeikis, Sophie Michaels, Randy Newman, Alice Michaels, Jack Nicholson, Eddie Michaels, Henry Michaels, Tom Hanks, Paul McCartney, Nancy Shevell.

Afloat in St. Barts with David Geffen, one of Michaels's first agents, on Jean Pigozzi's yacht, *Amazon Express*, New Year's Day, 2011

With Leslie Jones, in a sketch called "Leslie Wants to Play Trump," 2017

Rehearsing "Weekend Update," with Amy Poehler, Seth Meyers, Fred Armisen, and New York governor David Paterson, 2010

Backstage with Senator John McCain, Tina Fey, and Seth Meyers, 2008

Alaska governor Sarah Palin with Michaels, watching Tina Fey as Palin on a monitor, 2008

Michaels giving notes on a sketch with Kate McKinnon as Hillary Clinton, and Clinton as a bartender, 2015

In the studio with
Justin Timberlake,
Jimmy Fallon, and
Chris Rock, 2015

Sophie, Henry, Lorne, and Eddie Michaels at the Tony Awards, 2018

Under the bleachers with
Paul Simon and Bill Hader,
as Stefon, 2012

With New York City police commissioner Bernard Kerik and Paul Simon, before he sang "The Boxer" on the first SNL episode after 9/11

Michaels in the bleachers with Paul McCartney, 2015

The Kids in the Hall (Bruce McCulloch, Scott Thompson, Dave Foley, Mark McKinney, and Kevin McDonald) with Michaels at the *Tonight Show with Jimmy Fallon*, 2022, the year he produced a reboot of their series

With Mick Jagger, Sabrina Guinness, and Tom Stoppard, at the opening night of Stoppard's play *Leopoldstadt* on Broadway, 2022

Michaels with host Pete Davidson at read-through in 8H, part of the new post-Covid protocol, 2023

Sid Vicious—"unforgiveable" —2- from parent and relative of
   Nancy Spungen

Where is Chevy?—3

Mongoloid joke—offensive –1

When it came time to renew his contract, Michaels again felt conflicted. The show was almost too popular with the public, the critics were gunning for him, and the work was a grind. He wasn't laughing that much. Jim Downey said, "When you first get there you have a lifetime's worth of ideas. Then, the next season, you have a summer's worth." Audiences loved the repeating characters, but they would laugh at them no matter what; those sketches were becoming rote. From time to time Michaels would announce that he wanted to banish them. Of the gush of catchphrases he'd spawned, he said, "Like everything else, brilliant people do it, then everyone does it and you get tired of it."

One example of success gone sour concerned Mr. Bill, the little Play-Doh character who'd become a huge star. Mr. Bill was the creation of a viewer named Walter Williams, who'd sent in a Super-8 film when the show put out a call for home movies. Michaels gave Williams a contract, and at the end of every film Mr. Bill would squeal, "Ohh, nooo!" as he was squashed or mangled by his two adversaries, Mr. Hands and Sluggo. All sorts of unlicensed Mr. Bill merchandise flooded the market, without earning a dime for the show or for Williams. Then a former collaborator of Williams sued him for half the profits. The hearing became a media circus, and the coverage introduced the idea that the Mr. Bill films were tainted by what Michaels called "a certain kind of racial tension." The title character was sculpted of white Play-Doh, and the evil Sluggo of dark Play-Doh. Williams was aghast at the accusation that he was perpetuating racial stereotypes. "The only color of Play-Doh I had left was dark blue, so that's what I used for Sluggo," he said.

The hearing made Michaels sicker than ever of repeating characters. The judge was an SNL fan, and he'd placed on his bench a nameplate that read JUDGE SLUGGO next to a (pirated) Mr. Bill doll.

After he read his decision, he raised his gavel as if to pulverize Mr. Bill; instead he picked up a pair of scissors and snipped the toy man into pieces. The people in the courtroom screamed, *"Ohh, nooo! Mr. Bill!"* The spectacle made Michaels's heart sink.

He struggled, mostly in vain, to keep control of the show's cultural reach. The success of *Animal House,* which had happened under his nose but without his involvement, had caught him off guard. Assuming that Michaels's show could throw off similar revenues, people were pitching him SNL merchandise of all kinds and tie-ins with McDonald's. He routinely said no. Walter Williams had no such hesitation, licensing Mr. Bill to appear in ads for Burger King, Ramada Inn, Pringles, and MasterCard.

Brillstein was fielding movie offers for Michaels, too. Paramount, headed by his old *Lily* bosses, Diller and Eisner, pushed hard. They sent a telegram promising to give Michaels "six 'go' pictures," but Brillstein was wary of Barry Diller. Brillstein always told Michaels that there were two kinds of managers, the ones who walk through kitchens at the dumps their clients play, and the ones who don't. Brillstein was the first kind—he knew the guys with the hairnets— but he wasn't so sure about Diller, who seemed slick. Michaels ended up signing with Warner Bros., whose charismatic production chief, John Calley, was close to Candice Bergen and Mike Nichols. Brillstein negotiated a deal for Michaels to write, direct, and produce three films at the studio.

BELUSHI LIKED TO SAY THAT PEOPLE TAKE DRUGS OR DRINK "TO MAKE things harder when they get too easy." At the end of the fourth season, things around the SNL offices didn't seem easy at all. Given the show's schedule, and the rising salaries, it was perhaps inevitable that cocaine, or "the devil's dandruff," as Radner called it, became a staple for many. Morris was freebasing it, and Radner suffered from severe anorexia, which cocaine didn't help. Some weeks, people snorted heroin. Belushi was using more than ever. After *Animal House,* his movie price jumped from $35,000 to $350,000, which is what Brillstein got him to star in Steven Spielberg's unlikely Second World War comedy, *1941*. He was commuting to the West Coast for the movie—a troubled production—and was a sorehead around the studio. Perpetually strung out, hungover, and jet-lagged, he bitched about the sketches he was given, muttering, "I go where I'm kicked." O'Donoghue, who still hovered around the office, had buttons printed up reading JOHN BELUSHI: 1949–1941.

Michaels's stock advice to colleagues was to "rotate your drugs." The line "Cocaine is God's way of telling you you have too much money" was invoked around the show, but as a joke. The prevailing belief, which Michaels shared, was that you were weak if you couldn't control it. "Between *Arthur* and *Arthur 2,* alcoholism became a disease, and no one wanted to laugh at drunks anymore," he said.

One Saturday, Belushi was in such bad shape that he said he couldn't do the show. He'd been up for three nights partying with Keith Richards, and the constant air travel, he claimed, had caused a bad ear infection. Michaels conferred with a doctor who was evaluating Belushi in his dressing room. The doctor said that if Belushi performed that week, his chances for survival were fifty-fifty. Michaels, fed up and unsure of whether the doctor was on the level, said, with a grim smirk, "I'll accept those odds." Belushi did the show, bloated and perspiring. In the cold open, he played the new network president, Fred Silverman, as a double agent paid by ABC, aiming to destroy the competition. When Belushi said, "Live, from New York" in a raspy croak, he could barely get the words out.

One of Michaels's axioms about celebrity is "People don't like to collaborate past the point of fame." Belushi felt that he'd become bigger than the show, and his resentment centered on Michaels, whom he referred to as the "Canadian Jewish intellectual." One Wednesday in April, a telegram was delivered to the seventeenth floor. "Sorry I can't be on the show this week . . . A lot of doctor's orders." Instead, Belushi sent a video that he'd made, poolside at Spielberg's house. It got no laughs at dress, and Michaels cut it.

PART FOUR

THURSDAY

On Thursdays, as the elephantine process of producing ten or so brand-new comedy sketches begins in earnest, SNL's nerve center relocates from the seventeenth floor down to nine, just upstairs from Studio 8H. The studio is two stories tall, and a warren of offices snakes along behind the bleachers on the ninth-floor mezzanine. Michaels's satellite office is one of them. It's a smallish space, around fifteen by twenty feet; one wall is a big glass window overlooking the studio, usually covered by a brocade curtain. A door in the office opens into a small conference room, where the assistants sit around a Mission-style table; another door opens into a hallway (for discreet getaways). In the conference room, a couch and a couple of armchairs flank a coffee table, and two huge flat monitors hang on the walls, broadcasting a feed of what is going on in the studio below. On Saturday night, this is where a couple dozen guests of the show gather, watching on a monitor and drinking. Two refrigerators are tucked under a counter that holds a kitschy carved-wooden Polynesian figure of a naked woman made into a lamp. Someone had stuck a neon green Post-it over her crotch. More important guests watch the show on a screen in Michaels's adjoining office.

For most of Thursday, Michaels was at home, putting out fires, returning calls. There was the museum gala (Cecily Strong took Che's place under the whale), some details to sort regarding his goat cheese operation in Maine, and the dozen other shows he executive produces. He would walk down to the office after five.

Maggie Rogers's music rehearsal, on Stage 2, was called for 2:00 P.M. When Rogers, wearing a white T-shirt and baggy leather pants, ran through her songs, five camera operators shot it from different angles, while the director watched on a bank of monitors in the control room. He stabbed a pencil in the air as he called shots.

The writers and performers rolled in around two o'clock as well, having caught up on their sleep. At 2:45, Rogers would join Jonah Hill to tape promos: short spots that air during the week and go out on social media. In the first decades of the show, Michaels oversaw the promos himself, and used the sessions as opportunities to observe the hosts, to see how to light them. "That was my road test," he said. "I could figure out how to make them charming." After the promos, Hill and Rogers would each have a session with Mary Ellen Matthews, the show's photographer, for images to air as bumpers during the show. And, at 5:30, Hill would report to the makeup lab to have a plaster face-cast made. This helps the hair and makeup people in fitting wigs and prosthetics for him. When Jeff Daniels hosted, in 1995, a chemical mishap resulted in hardened plaster ripping hunks of flesh from his face; it took a hammer and an X-Acto knife to get the mask off.

Blocking would be done that afternoon for three or four sketches on stages outfitted with a few folding chairs. One of the unusual things about SNL is that the writers are in charge of producing their own pieces—they dictate what the set and costumes should look like, what music or sound effects are needed, and direct the actors in rehearsal. This is why SNL's writers' room produces so many future showrunners. John Mulaney said, "For five minutes, NBC is yours."

On Thursday, two rewrite tables start in the early afternoon. Michaels doesn't involve himself in the rewrite process. If there's a major change in a sketch, one of the head writers will give him a heads-up, and he might weigh in with some course-correcting. But he prefers to see the material with fresh eyes, the way the audience does, on Saturday.

In the ninth-floor writers' office, down a zigzagging hallway, eight writers were trimming and punching up the Political Musical pretape that would be shot the next day in Studio 8G, where Seth Meyers tapes *Late Night*. Most of the space in the room, which gets no daylight, is taken up by a long table. On the walls hang framed headshots of SNL writers from the past: Bob Odenkirk, Larry David (who lasted one season), Jim Belushi, Jack Handey, and Sarah Silverman among them. Many of the writers started as comics and made their way to SNL by auditioning to be in the cast, so when they toss out lines at the table, they perform them, trying to crack each other up. Political Musical would be shot like a TV ad, fast-cutting between audience testimonials and snatches of the play itself. The writers at the table were former theater geeks, kids who had memorized the score to *Rent*.

The play in the sketch was supposed to be dreadful, the work of pretentious theater students. A writer suggested making Melissa Villaseñor a sexpot Statue of Liberty, in a skimpy outfit. Someone tried out the line "You'll love her in the number 'Sexy for No Reason'!" They worried whether it was clear that this show was *way* off Broadway. The script put the theater on Thirteenth Avenue, a nonexistent street. Maybe "Lincoln Tunnel Service Road" would be funnier? Then they worked on quotes from news outlets. "A show that asks the question 'Whose parents paid for it?'" someone yelled, and the table erupted in laughter. Someone wrote it down.

After Wednesday, all script changes are made on paper; the writers don't use their computers. (Another quaint and, to some, pointless holdover.) When a rewrite session is finished, an assistant quickly types the marked-up pages into a new draft.

The group turned to KCR News, the piece where Jonah Hill bothers his weather-girl fiancée at work. In the sketch, the anchors, played by Leslie Jones and Kenan Thompson, discover a drawing of a penis on the anchor desk. Bowen Yang, a new hire, suggested, "How about adding veins to the penis?" (The next season, having had a terrific year as a writer, he would become the show's first Chinese American cast member.) His colleagues cackled, and they tried out endings for the line "We'll be right back with more coverage of . . ." Some of the suggestions: "more coverage of right-wing extremist hate crimes!"; "a barrelful of dead kittens!"; and "Holocaust survivor found dead."

The show's writers have all imbibed Michaels's fundamentals of comedy writing, which he has drilled into his staff over five decades. When Bill Hader was on the show, he came to realize how unusual it was to have a producer who was a comedy writer rather than a business-school type. He recalled, "Lorne would take your sketches and note them up and kind of tell you, 'You can't do this. I'd be careful with that. Shouldn't the joke belong *here*?' Structural things." Michaels has a lot of precepts designed to make sketch comedy important. For instance, you don't want "funny" sets or costumes because they compete with the writing. Michaels says, "My job now is walking around with a ruler and slapping designers or costumers on the knuckles, saying, 'No. You can't contribute to the comedy. You have to *serve* the comedy.'" When there are too many things going on in a scene, he says, "You're putting a hat on a hat." (Another term for this is "premise overload.") Anything that will take viewers out of the moment is to be avoided. For instance, if the characters are on a date, Michaels will say, have the man bring chocolates, not flowers. (If he brings flowers, the viewer will worry, *Isn't she going to put them in a vase?*) "When the details are accurate, your brain goes, 'Somebody's taken care of this,'" Steve Higgins told me. "It's the difference between trying to sleep in the back seat of a taxi when a strange cab driver is at the wheel, and sleeping in the back seat, as a kid, when your dad was driving. Someone's in charge."

Making sketch comedy important is not the same thing as making "important" comedy—which Michaels discourages. He likes to point out that many of the "serious" writers who went to Hollywood in the last century, like Herman Mankiewicz, didn't take the movies too seriously, and that's why Mankiewicz's work is remarkable. One of Michaels's rules is "Do it in sunshine," which means, don't forget that comedy is an entertainment. Colors should be bright, costumes flattering. He likes hard laughs, he says, because "I search for anything that makes me feel free." People watch TV, he believes, as if they're huddled around a fire at night. You don't want "dark" in comedy: "You can just look out the window for dark." He has no patience for the pretentious grittiness that makes independent filmmakers want to shoot in black and white. ("You can do that in improv class," he says.) Facial hair falls into the same category. A Michaels cri de coeur is: "You can't hide behind art."

In 2002, Tina Fey brought Michaels a book by a well-known sociologist about teen cliques called *Queen Bees and Wannabes*. She wanted to turn it into a movie about "relational aggression," as she put it. He said sure, she recalled, "as long as you do it in sunshine." He told her, "You have to be prepared to draw people in." She promised that the characters would have cool cars and cool clothes. *Mean Girls* was the result.

Fred Armisen remembers Michaels telling the writers, "There's enough misery in the world." Michaels counsels writers to avoid writing anger: "It's really difficult to make anger funny." Idiots, he always says, play better than assholes. Michaels always wants his actors to give a drop of something appealing to even the worst villain. Without a spark of humanity, a bad guy will be a two-dimensional caricature who can't engage an audience. "What the English know is that if you're playing the greatest villain, make him charming," he says. Newcomers to the show are often surprised to hear him talk about wanting "sweetness" in sketches—the interior, emotional shadings that Gilda Radner and Marilyn Miller specialized in, back in the seventies. (New writers are often told that Michaels dislikes what Jim Downey calls "pee-pee doo-doo jokes," but the show airs lots of them, often written by Michaels's pets. When John Mulaney hosted in 2017, he got a sketch on called Toilet Death Ejector.)

"Do it in sunshine" is not to be confused with another Lorneism, "Sunlight is the best disinfectant." That line, about transparency, is a quote from Supreme Court Justice Louis Brandeis, and Michaels uses it to promote the idea that it's good to show your work to others and get their input. It's the principle behind the read-through, the rewrite table, and using the dress audience as a gauge.

"To this day, I think about these proofs Lorne's passed down," Chris Rock told me. Michaels hired Rock and Adam Sandler in 1990 after seeing them at a showcase where other comics got bigger laughs. He later told Rock that he appreciated what he called his "original thought." Of the other guys, he said, "Yes, they're killing, but I've heard versions of every joke they're killing with."

"It's like mixing chemicals," Rock said. "Too much of this or too little of that and you've got a disaster. Comedy is a precision instrument." He ranks Michaels, as a producer, with Quincy Jones: both focus on fundamentals. "Comedy is no different than music," he said. "There's scales and there's keys and there's notes to hit. There's no prolonged success if you're not grounded in the fundamentals. When I write a bit, it's got a verse, it's got a chorus that repeats itself, and occasionally it has a bridge. Stand-up comedy is on the four—just like pop music. The laughs are almost every fifteen or sixteen seconds, on the four." Sometimes a sketch lives or dies because of some rhythmic alchemy. The famous Blue Öyster Cult sketch didn't get on SNL the first week it was rehearsed, with Norm Macdonald as the lead, but when Christopher Walken played the producer yelling "More cowbell!" in his very particular cadence, it exploded. Twenty-five years later, when Walken does a play on Broadway, fans wait outside the stage door and ask him to sign their cowbells.

Jon Hamm—a student of the show since he was six, when his divorced dad let him stay up and watch Belushi—learns something every time he hosts. He remembers Michaels explaining how sometimes he'll pick one sketch over another not because it's funnier, but because it will be powerful *live*. Hamm had a monologue once that involved showing pretend "clips" of his pre–*Mad Men* acting jobs; the show could have pre-taped the bits of him selling jewelry on QVC, or doing stand-up on *Def Comedy Jam* (the joke: he sounds and looks just like Don Draper in all of them), but Michaels knew that it would be more exciting for the studio audience to see him running around making quick changes and popping onto different stages for the "clips." This is the essence of producing.

MICHAELS ARRIVED AT 30 ROCK A LITTLE BEFORE 5:00 P.M. HE TOOK THE studio elevator up to six, where Jimmy Fallon tapes his show in 6B, the studio where Carson did *The Tonight Show* until 1972. He stops in on most weekdays, listening to Fallon practice his monologue to a dress rehearsal audience, then offering comments and edits. Justin Timberlake and his wife, Jessica Biel, were the guests, and the first thing Michaels said when he saw the singer, who had bruised vocal cords, was "Don't talk!" After some jolly miming of *hello and good luck* with the two stars, Michaels joined Steve Higgins in a tiny green-room. As Higgins stood shooting the breeze with Michaels, a wardrobe woman knelt down and tied the laces of Higgins's polished oxfords. Fallon dashed in—in contrast to Higgins, a bundle of manic energy and elfin agreeableness—and gave his boss a squeeze. Michaels briefed Fallon on the Five Timers Club idea. "We're trying to lean on Melissa to come from Chicago," he said. "We got Tina."

Amid the bustle of *The Tonight Show*'s backstage, Michaels's almost languorous comportment stood out. All of his movements were slow. It's the same up in 8H: as stagehands and cue card people dash around the floor, he calmly saunters. Or, more often, he stands still, leaning fractionally backward on his heels, hands in his pockets, surveying his dominion. He is careful to project an image of a man who doesn't have many of what Henry James called "uncomfortable hours," but an inner pilot light is always on. Producing, whether an SNL episode, a Broadway show, or the seating plan at the host dinner, is a full-time job. The trick is making it look invisible. "If you're any good at it," he's said, "you leave no fingerprints."

Fallon rushed off, and Higgins held up his iPhone to show Michaels something. "Tina sent me this," he said. On the screen was a YouTube video of a toddler and a little boy reenacting the Chippendales audition sketch done by Chris Farley and Patrick Swayze in 1990, the two gyrating in only spandex tights and bow ties. The toddler, all rolls of jiggly baby fat, played the Farley part perfectly, lurching off, unsteady and wide-eyed, toward the camera. Michaels smiled. "I'd bet my life that we could not do that sketch today," he said. "It'd be called fat-shaming."

A minute later, Higgins was in Studio 6B, screaming at the audience: "Are you *ready* to start the show? Thirty seconds! Twenty seconds! *Get ready!*" A cymbal crashed and he said, "And now, here's your host, Jimmy *Faaalllon!*" The audience shrieked, and Fallon, in a sleek dark suit, ran out through a tall blue curtain. Michaels watched the monologue from a dim side area. Fallon started with some stories in the news. Then: "Did you hear that KFC gave a family eleven thousand dollars for naming their baby after Colonel Sanders?" Beat. "The money will help with his siblings P. F. Chang and Long John Silver."

The ritual completed, Michaels took the elevator up to eight. In the studio, he said hello to Jonah Hill, who was blocking the KCR News sketch. On the studio floor, crew members milled, along with a woman in a lab coat—the NBC nurse, who was there to give Michaels a shingles vaccine. All seemed to be going smoothly, so he walked up an interior staircase to the ninth floor. Willa Slaughter greeted him with his messages and fiddled with his new phone's ringtone settings, which were bothering him. Other assistants were buying gifts over the phone, ordering dinner, making sure tickets for the dress and air shows were getting organized. Like most show-business assistants, Slaughter listens in on Michaels's business calls, to keep track of details and take notes. (Years ago, whenever Brillstein phoned, Michaels would cringe knowing that an assistant on the call would hear the older man describe business associates as "cunts" or call a project "as cold as whale shit.") A deliveryman wheeled in a cart laden with tubs of pink roses, to replenish the vases in the office.

Around 5:30, Michaels asked Slaughter to round up his producers so that they could have their cold-open meeting. While he waited, he gave some quick closed-door pep talks to performers who needed a boost. ("Everyone is given a certain number of grains of salt, according to what they need," Mike Shoemaker, a longtime SNL staffer who now produces *Late Night*, said.) Pete Davidson spent fifteen minutes with him discussing ways to make an Update feature out of his Ariana Grande mess; he also met with Cecily Strong, who had been struggling with self-doubt. Physical affection doesn't come naturally to Michaels, so the constraints dictated by the #MeToo era relieve the pressure of having to offer a hug when someone cries in his office.

Different personalities require different approaches. To some, Michaels will bark, "Don't fuck it up." Bill Hader, who was prone to anxiety attacks, remembers Michaels coming to his dressing room and snapping, "Calm the fuck down. Just have fun. Jesus Christ." But Molly Shannon treasures the memory of how, when she was nervous just before going onstage, Michaels would "reassure me with his eyes."

When Michaels is getting to know a new employee, he'll latch on to a single trait: *this* one went to Yale; *that* one is from San Diego; another one's mother works for Chrysler; Robert Smigel is the son of a celebrity dentist. In keeping with his all-fifty-states fixation, he tries to hire people from the wide open spaces of America, and he fancies himself a student of regional traits. Employees often repeat baffling statements he makes, along the lines of "Ted is from Tennessee, so he eats a bigger breakfast than you or I," or "Nick is from Cleveland, so you know he can change a tire fast." A writer told me, "Sometimes you think he doesn't know who you are, and sometimes you think he knows everything about you." He likes to have the sense, as Tolstoy put it, that he knows "whose shoe pinched on which foot."

AFTER CECILY STRONG LEFT MICHAELS'S OFFICE, SLAUGHTER POPPED IN TO show him a few news clips. One of the assistants' jobs is to scour the media for mentions of him and his friends, so he is never caught out unawares. "It's very important that he be prepped," Mark McKinney, who joined the show in 1995, said. "He always has to feel like he's a step ahead." Consequently, there is practically no piece of information one can tell Michaels that does not prompt a rapid-fire "No-no-no-no, I know" or a languorous *"Right."* There used to be a writers' room bit about this compulsion: one version has Lorne strolling on the beach in St. Barts with one of his young children. The toddler points at the rising moon and says, full of wonder, "Look, Daddy!" Lorne shoots back: "*No-no-no-no,* I know. We had the moon in the seventies."

Some Thursday nights, Michaels will pop across the street to Christie's auction house with a mentee in tow, on a mini art-appreciation trip; he scrutinizes the wall labels, noting the names of rich friends who are deaccessioning. Adam Sandler accompanied him, a few years back, to look at S.I. Newhouse's Cezanne still life and his Jeff Koons rabbit, part of a twentieth-century sale. (Michaels isn't much of an art buyer; however, he has a couple of Léger water-colors in his kitchen, a Hockney print in a kid's room, and a small Matisse. A flirtation with one of Francis Bacon's Screaming Pope canvases was shut down by his wife, Alice, who didn't want it around the children.) Bob Odenkirk once went with him to see a Monet show in Chicago. Most of his people don't have what he calls "an NPR upbringing," and he expects them to elevate themselves cultur-ally, to read the newspaper and go to the theater.

By 6:00 P.M., his deputies were in his ninth-floor office, ready to discuss news stories that could work as a cold open. The upper walls of this office, just below the ceiling, are lined with framed tickets to the premiere of each of the show's forty-plus seasons; below them are framed *Times* crossword puzzles with answers related to the show ("It never gets old," he said, of that institutional honor); a scrawled note from Belushi ("Lorne, Stay kool!"); a photo of Michaels and Jim Downey on a dock at Mohonk Mountain House, upstate. A large basket of popcorn sits on a side table. Another is piled with awards and a couple of joke glamour headshots, signed—one from the writer Paula Pell, a Michaels favorite. As on seventeen, an index-card-covered bulletin board dominates one wall.

Michaels sat in a leather club chair, his cashmere sweater flecked with popcorn. The updates: Michael Che hadn't heard from Jordan Peele about playing Obama. Maybe, someone suggested, a cold open about Trump ordering soldiers to build decoy Chipotles and Taco Bells to waylay the caravan of migrants? Jost had the latest details on the Whitey Bulger story: the lock-in-sock beating had reportedly dis-lodged Bulger's eyeballs. And he was still alive when prison guards found him. Michaels mimicked a prison guard in an old movie: *"Whitey! Who did this to you?"* Someone suggested Kate McKinnon doing her impression of Laura Ingraham, whose Fox show had lost advertisers after she made fun of a survivor of the Parkland school shooting. Oprah Winfrey had been in the news campaigning for Sta-cey Abrams in Georgia. Michaels mentioned that Winfrey had stumped for Obama in 2008, but it had resulted in bad blood because she didn't feel that the Obamas had been appropriately grateful. "Like Sinatra and JFK," he said.

Talk turned to the opening monologue—Hill in the Five Timers Club. It turned out that Melissa McCarthy couldn't get back from visiting her family in Chicago, even though NBC had offered to fly her and her parents in. Michaels suggested that Lindsay Shookus look into whether McCarthy's family could be driven to New York by a chauffeur. (Michaels relishes meeting parents. One Saturday in the eighties, he delayed the start of the high-stakes meeting between dress and air by ten minutes because he'd heard that Jim Downey's father was in the studio, and he wanted to visit with him.)

When Michaels is trying to persuade a good friend to appear on the show, he will pick up the phone himself. He once called Martin Short, a very old pal, to ask him to play Trump's kooky long-haired doctor, Harold Bornstein, in a cold open. Short declined; he was doing a show at the Beacon Theatre that night. Michaels sweetened the offer: "We can send a police escort." Too tight, Short said. Finally, he added: "Can I up the ante? Stormy Daniels will be doing it with you." Short caved. "That's Lorne's way," he said. "You end up doing exactly what he wanted." Short had no regrets. On the Saturday he played Dr. Bornstein, he sat under the bleachers with Michaels and Stormy Daniels, and Michaels offered them drinks. Short said, "It was worth it just to hear Lorne say the words, 'Stormy—rosé?'"

On this Thursday evening, with no resolution on the cold-open idea, Michaels decided to call it a night. He knew that drawing out the process of settling on an idea made it harder on everyone, but it's the way he likes to do it. "Decisions lead to stability, decisions lead to calm," he said. "But snap decisions get you into trouble. My nature is, I tend to do *rolling* decisions." He headed over to Orso, the Theater-District Italian place he likes, for dinner. There were, after all, still forty-eight hours until showtime.

TWENTY-ONE

THE FIFTH YEAR OF COLLEGE

Bears are gnawing on the carpets.
Bones are tumbling into tarpits.
Nolde's gone and so is Arp. It's
Later than you think.

—FROM "THE BEARS," A POEM BY MICHAEL O'DONOGHUE,
IN A VOLUME INSCRIBED TO MICHAELS

ONE OF THE STORIES THAT MICHAELS TELLS ON REPEAT GOES LIKE THIS: "I
was on a boat once, and there was a man on the boat. He was from
the audience"—meaning, he was a normal human being. "The man
was being funny in the way that Bill Murray is funny, and I thought
to myself, 'I *know* Bill Murray.' You know what I mean?"

When he told this story to Bill Hader, who joined the cast in 2005,
Hader had nodded yes. "But I had no idea what he was talking about,"
he said.

What Michaels was talking about was that, at a certain point, the
show got away from him. By the fifth season, it had become an institution. Now there was a feeling of needing to be responsible to "the
audience." And the members of the audience had sucked up what he
and the show were selling so avidly that the language of SNL had
rewired their brains. People inserted SNL catchphrases into their
wedding vows and talked in robotic Conehead voices around the
water cooler. The show had become collective cultural property.

The American public had taken ownership of the show, and it
would never relinquish its grip. This is what every TV showrunner
longs for—but it also presented Michaels with a problem. The cast
members all had five-year contracts. As their sense of themselves,
and their possibilities, changed, it didn't feel like Eden anymore. Michaels noted a "psychic panic" overtaking his people, who suddenly

worried that they needed to seize the moment. Things at the show began to fragment and implode.

For one thing, if the world was going to treat the show as a commodity, the former rebels behind it wanted to be compensated accordingly. Raises were secured for the cast, and heading into Season Five, Michaels's new contract gave him a base salary of around $1.5 million, plus 50 percent of any future syndication deals. Frustrated that he'd had no part of the movies SNL had spawned, he was determined to change that. But then Brillstein put together a movie deal that not only excluded Michaels, but made producing the fifth season of SNL particularly challenging for him: Brillstein sold a Blues Brothers film, starring Belushi and Aykroyd, to Universal. Although it looked like a clear-cut conflict, pitting the best interest of one client against another's, Michaels insisted that he wasn't angry. ("That's a Hollywood thing," he tends to say, about business prerogatives.) Belushi had already made it known that he would be leaving with a year left on his contract. Staying on felt redundant, he said, "sort of like the fifth year of college, you know?"

Michaels knew that in a year, with the cast's contracts up, he might have to start from scratch, and it had made him question whether he wanted to keep running SNL. "Many observers believe that the show has been going downhill," a story in *The Washington Post* read, "succumbing slowly to success and ennui." There was talk of the show simply ending. The network was eager to cash in before the clock ran out, airing the *"Best of"* SNL specials while the show was still on the air, and getting ready to sell its five seasons into syndication.

All of the cast, except Garrett Morris, had movie deals, and most were millionaires. Commuting from the RCA Building to film sets had become the norm. Michaels was nostalgic for the early years. "Back then, nothing mattered in anyone's life as much as the show," he said. "You could work for sixteen or seventeen hours, then go back to someone's house and smoke a joint and talk for two or three more hours."

He was fine with letting Belushi out of his contract. "After *Animal*

House and the cover of *Newsweek,* it was just a nightmare because he didn't know who he was anymore," he said. But Aykroyd, who planned to commute from the *Blues Brothers* set in Chicago, had promised Michaels that he would not abandon ship. Aykroyd would be carrying the show on his shoulders, and his promise went a long way toward making Michaels himself decide to stay on for the fifth season.

Then, during the summer before Season Five, Brillstein called Michaels and said that Aykroyd wanted to come out to Amagansett and talk to him: The *Blues Brothers* shooting schedule had changed. Michaels's stomach lurched. He said, "Bernie, he gave me his word."

When Aykroyd arrived, he and Michaels headed out to the beach for a walk. Aykroyd broke the news that he wouldn't be able to come back for the fifth season. Put in a position to choose between the show and the movie—between Michaels and Belushi—Aykroyd chose Belushi. Michaels was hurt. "But Hollywood is Hollywood," he said. "Few are summoned but almost everyone answers the call." There was no shouting or drama. It was just business. The absence of sentiment was becoming familiar; he connected it with fame and success. He remembered having Ray Charles on the show; Michaels had walked him into a rehearsal room where he would be reunited with his original octet after many years. "I said, 'Are you excited to see these guys?'" Michaels recalled. Charles flatly replied, "Most of them owe me money."

Losing Aykroyd was a big problem. He had more range than anyone in the cast; Michaels called him the Alec Guinness of the show. And he was steady and reliable, having what Michaels thought of as "the virtues of the old youth novels." Besides needing to keep up the show without two of his stars, Michaels had the old feeling of being stuck in a cul-de-sac. He was supposed to be making *The Graduate,* and now his protégés were off doing movies without him—movies based on characters that had sprung from his show, with his own manager executive producing. Suddenly Brillstein, who'd started out as a Broadway Danny Rose with a cardboard briefcase, was having a rock and roll moment. After so many years of midwifing talent, now he was wearing silk jackets and sunglasses and doing coke. "This was his shot," Michaels said. "There's only so much parental love you can give somebody else if you thought you should be *the guy*. It's Mama Rose." (It was becoming automatic for Michaels to repress his own inner Mama Rose.) He added, "Or as they say in Monopoly, bank error in your favor."

Most of the SNL crowd had never taken the Blues Brothers seriously. They thought it was just a cute comedy bit and started referring to the movie as *1942*. But with stars like Aretha Franklin and James Brown joining the cast, it was a hit, and the soundtrack sold more than a million copies.

THE SIDE PROJECT THAT MICHAELS WAS WORKING ON DIDN'T PAN OUT THAT well. He had thrown himself into *Gilda Radner: Live from New York*, which was going to be an album, a Broadway show, and possibly his first movie. When the show opened at the Winter Garden, in August 1979, Gilda fans filled the seats and found it a pleasant evening in the theater, but critics weren't convinced, and many compared it unfavorably to SNL.

That left the potential movie—finally Michaels's Mike Nichols moment, although not at all the way he'd imagined it. When he had been deciding which movie deal to take, a meeting with Warner's John Calley tipped the balance. Michaels told Calley about a movie idea he'd been nurturing, a contemporary version of *Pride and Prejudice*, one of his favorite books. "It takes place in Ohio, on a movie set," he said. Mr. Darcy is the aloof and distant director, in the mold of Stanley Kubrick, and the slippery Mr. Wickham is the movie star playing the lead. "These local girls can't believe the movie is being shot in their town," Michaels said. "And they hear all these terrible stories about how the director has mistreated this actor, who's so charming." If Calley detected a personal note in Michaels's story about a misunderstood genius ill-treated by an ungrateful jerk of an actor, he didn't say so. The day after the meeting, Calley had a package hand-delivered to Michaels's apartment. It was a first edition of *Pride and Prejudice*.

Seduced, Michaels set up an outfit he called Broadway Pictures, with temporary offices across the ice rink at 75 Rockefeller Plaza. He recruited Joe Boyd, his old Malibu housemate, to be in charge of developing scripts. "I was one of the original foursome in L.A. when Lorne was scuffling," Boyd said. "His godfather instinct was to bring me in." Boyd, who was at loose ends in London, was happy to be flown over to meet Michaels and Brillstein for dinner. Michaels was excited about his *Pride and Prejudice* notion, but the main idea behind Broadway Pictures was to mine assets of SNL for films. After Michaels had a few more conversations with Calley, it looked as if the first project could be, not the Jane Austen adaptation, but a filmed version of *Gilda Live*.

Michaels was eager to direct, and he wasn't certain that the Gilda project, a stage show, made sense as his first movie. But Calley was high on it, and over dinner on the night of Radner's Broadway opening, he surprised Michaels by coming out with the suggestion that their mutual friend Mike Nichols direct it. Michaels found himself in a situation both surreal and uncomfortable. Nichols was his hero. But was it a good fit? It would have to be done fast, and he knew that Nichols didn't work fast. He hedged. When Brillstein called the next day and said "It's a go. Mike's directing," Michaels didn't know how to react. He thought, *Oh, fuck,* and called Nichols. "Well, they gave me my price," the director said, of the studio. "And fifty hours on the [Warners] plane."

By the time Michaels filled in Joe Boyd about the deal, he had spun it to himself. "I've got great news," he told Boyd. "Mike Nichols is going to direct *Gilda Live*." Boyd took a breath and said, "Lorne, that's a terrible idea." Nichols had no experience shooting live performances. Having him direct this, Boyd said, "was like using a sledgehammer to swat a fly." But it was a done deal. Boyd had no inkling of Michaels's complicated ambivalence.

Because of union technicalities, the film was shot not at the Winter Garden, but over two days in August at a Boston theater. "Nichols directed it with his little finger," Boyd recalled. Radner said that the director hardly spoke to her. It wasn't an auspicious start to Michaels's long-awaited film career.

DURING THE GILDA SHOOT, AT THE END OF THE SUMMER OF 1979, MICHAELS was commuting four hours by limousine from the set in Boston to the Shawangunk Mountains, in upstate New York, where he was holding a pre-season retreat for his SNL cast and writers at Mohonk Mountain House, a funky old Quaker family resort a couple of hours north of the city. When Aykroyd quit, Michaels had gone into hiring mode, trying desperately to prevent the show from falling apart. On Franken's advice, he'd brought on Harry Shearer, a former child actor who was an early member of the L.A. troupe the Credibility Gap. The cast still didn't have enough men, so Michaels designated a bunch of writers (including Downey, Zweibel, Franken, and Davis) as featured players, to act in sketches. He hired some new writers, too: Matt Neuman (from *Lily*), Sarah Paley, and two of Downey's pals from *The Harvard Lampoon,* Tom Gammill and Max Pross. Pross's previous job had been with the Suffolk County Sanitation Department.

When Michaels interviewed young prospective writers that season, he started by wearily saying, "So I suppose you want to know what John Belushi is *really* like." Gammill and Pross couldn't tell whether or not they were hired, and Tom Davis told them, "Just show up until someone asks you to leave." If Michaels ran into the new youngsters in the hall, he would stick his hand in his pocket and ask, "Uh, are you okay for money?"

By gathering his new group at Mohonk for a retreat (Michaels had gone there once with O'Donoghue and judged it "astringently Canadian, a sensible holiday"), he hoped to summon the spirit of Camp Timberlane and give his new hires a chance to get to know the old guard (although most of the old guard, busy with their movie commitments, didn't show up). Those who attended canoed and hiked, convening for occasional pep talks and brainstorming sessions. Michaels dropped in and out, and at one session he made a plea: "Please don't use cocaine. It doesn't make you funnier. It only makes you think you're funnier." Downey raised his hand and asked, in mock concern, "What about Merlin?" Everyone laughed at the mention of the leather-tooling dope peddler, and chants of "We love Merlin!" filled the room.

A couple of weeks later, when the season got underway and everyone was settled into their offices on the seventeenth floor, Michaels seemed to be studying the young people, as if they might hold the key to the future. At their first Monday writers' meeting, Gammill and Pross pitched a sketch about a spy who was a former cha-cha instructor. Pross recalled, "I remember Lorne looking at us as if he were thinking, 'So, the kids are into cha-cha now.'"

He knew by now that maintaining a hit was almost harder than creating one, and he struggled to keep his standards high. The best he could say of the fifth-season premiere, which featured Steve Martin and Blondie, was: "Not a great show, but a great ticket." It embarrassed him when the ratings for the fifth season came in as the highest so far. He felt like he was being rewarded for work he'd done five years earlier.

The whole outfit had been gradually professionalized, and Michaels behaved more like a chief executive. Every day, one of his assistants gave him an 11:30 A.M. wake-up call from the office. When he phoned to say he was leaving his apartment, another assistant would grind the coffee beans so his coffee would be ready when he arrived. "Lorne was starting to become the emperor of New York City," Curtin said. This was reflected in the kind of stars he could book. Bob Dylan was on the fifth season's second show, and he performed his song "Gotta Serve Somebody." Around the office, people were singing an alternate lyric: "It may be the devil, or it may be the *Lorne*, but you're gonna have to serve somebody."

That week, Dylan's producer, Jerry Wexler, threw a dinner party for the singer. Michaels was there, seated "below the salt," as he put it. He craned his neck to hear what Dylan was saying at the far end of the table, but a white-haired guy next to him, an SNL fan, kept asking him questions about the show. Michaels brushed him off. On the way out, Wexler asked him how he'd liked talking to Elia Kazan, the legendary director of *On the Waterfront* and *A Streetcar Named Desire*. "Oh no," he said, cursing his own arrogance.

The new SNL staffers sensed that they'd arrived at a transitional time, as Lorne the wunderkind was transforming into Lorne the legend. He was constantly on the phone, the calls placed by assistants who, in those pre-autodial days, had to memorize the numbers of his friends. In his office, he'd tell his young aides, "Talk faster."

THE ONGOING RISE AND FALL OF SNL HAS ALWAYS TURNED ON HOW SMOOTHLY the transitions between casts are made, older players overlapping with new ones as the guard gradually shifts. By the fifth season, there was a sense of two generations colliding—the founders and the new kids. Michaels tried to show the young people the ropes. "You can't just love the *show* part of show business," he'd tell his people, urging them to pay careful attention to how deals were done. "If you don't love the *business* part, you're not going to make it." Downey, a relative elder, mentored the newbies too, during wasabi-eating contests at Chin-Ya, or over Eggs Bobby Goldman at Farmfood, an ancient vegetarian joint. Sometimes the culture-clashing got strange: for Christmas, middle-aged Garrett Morris gave young Sarah Paley a negligee.

Michaels once overheard Paley joshing backstage with Laraine Newman, who was anxious about a sketch she was about to do. Paley had cracked, "Don't worry—only thousands of people are going to see it." Michaels took Paley aside and chastised her. "Don't ever do that," he said. He explained that handling the talent—knowing just what to say to each particular performer to get a good performance—was his domain on show nights.

But he found no traction with his new hire Harry Shearer. Shuster described the relationship as "oil and water." Shearer, who took pride in being a showbiz lifer, found SNL's protocols bizarre. He told Hill and Weingrad, "It was a highly political hierarchical organization masquerading as a college dorm." Michaels's opaque management style contributed to the bad blood. Shearer said that he was hired as a writer *and* a cast member, with the understanding that his performing duties would be officially announced later in the season. The others on staff, he said, were not informed of this plan and therefore considered Shearer pushy when he kept writing himself into sketches. Michaels's take: "We didn't find out until too late that Harry wasn't a good team player."

SNL's next star, he knew, would be Bill Murray, who'd pumped a lot of energy into the show since his arrival in Season Two, thanks to what Michaels called "his athletic grace." Murray had spent the summer driving the boss's red VW from L.A., finally dropping the car in Amagansett, equipped with a new cassette player he'd had installed and one tape, the Eagles' *Greatest Hits*. Michaels was optimistic about their relationship. But once back in the studio, Murray had a chip on his shoulder. "Billy was the alpha," Michaels said. "He felt at some level that he'd made a mistake staying, because John and Danny were now movie stars." Fresh from the set of *Where the Buffalo Roam,* a film in which he played a version of Hunter S. Thompson, Murray would show up at the office in character, wearing shades and clutching a cigarette holder. He complained that he was carrying the whole show; he yelled at the new people. Sometimes he brought Thompson along. Under Thompson's influence, Murray waved scripts around and complained about how flabby they were. "Let's get rid of all of those fucking *the*'s and *and*'s!" he said, editing the lines into diction more suitable for a cave man. As Belushi had, he took out his animosity on Michaels, negotiating over which parts he would play and which he wouldn't. Hill and Weingrad quoted a colleague saying, "Billy had Lorne by the balls, and he yanked."

Murray and Shearer took a dig at Michaels in a script they co-wrote with one of the new writers. There was an asshole character in it named Lipowitz, a reference lost on the new writer, whose initials were on the script at read-through. Michaels flinched when the piece was read at the table. "It was a real fifth-grade prank, a really stupid, mean-boy thing," the victimized novice said.

The NBC Standards people were hassling Michaels, too, after a period of hanging back. The censor tried to kill a Nerds sketch in which Lisa and Todd play Mary and Joseph in a Nativity pageant. Among the objections, which were painstakingly adjudicated all week: using the word "ass" for a donkey; Todd telling Lisa, "I happen to know that you're one of the few girls at Gus Grissom High who is, uh, *physically correct* for this part"; and, in the censor's words, "You can't give noogies to the Virgin Mary!"

In March, Michaels celebrated the hundredth episode of the show, with an episode featuring New York senator Daniel Patrick Moynihan, who read a leprechaun story. Belushi and O'Donoghue made cameos, their heads appearing in a crystal ball (part of a séance sketch) to make cracks about the show's decline; the spectral O'Donoghue said, "Did I mention that since I left, the show really sucks rubber donkey lungs?"

Michaels was just trying to make it to the end of the season. The movie of *Gilda Live* opened right after the hundredth show, and it was a flop. (After a few days in the editing room it had become clear that Mike Nichols didn't have the camera shots he needed.) Over at Broadway Pictures, Joe Boyd started counting down the days until his contract was up. He'd figured out that Michaels wasn't going to turn over any control when it came to his deal with Warner Bros. After the Gilda film wrapped, Michaels sent him a Franken and Davis sketch that had been cut from SNL, with instructions to develop it as a feature. Boyd read the pages and found them uninspiring and expensive to produce ("Rockets and shit, special effects—big budget," Boyd recalled). But Michaels insisted, and his working relationship with Boyd stalled. "That was kind of it," Boyd said. He and Michaels never discussed that their arrangement had petered out.

Michaels felt that Warners never got behind the Gilda movie, despite Calley's early ardor. The studio had released a print ad for it that was a crude—and worse, "zany"—cartoon of a movie-popcorn tub, crammed with Radner's SNL characters. "The ad made Gilda cry," Michaels said. So he personally hired the designer who'd done the campaign for *Rosemary's Baby* to redo it. "I went uptown with it," he said of the new, elegant image, a photo of a spotlit Radner in front of a stage curtain, with the tagline "Things like this happen only in the movies." The studio complained that the ad made the film look like a stage show, which would limit box office. Michaels pointed out that it *was* a stage show.

Michaels's movie dream seemed to be sputtering. After the Gilda washout, Brillstein met with Calley's boss at Warners, Frank Wells, who told him that the studio would pay off the deal terms, but that Michaels was "too much of a maverick" for the studio, which was focusing on bigger projects. Michaels was off the lot. He'd thought Calley shared his vision, but *Pride and Prejudice* had dropped off the radar. "What they wanted was big dumb comedy," he said.

Joe Boyd felt that the convoluted structure of the movie business didn't play to Michaels's strengths. "All of the qualities that are problematic in Lorne—like when he doesn't have a deadline—are solved by the SNL format," he said. "It's got to go on air at eleven-thirty. It's perfect for him. Otherwise, he wants everyone to be happy, and he wants to maintain his power over everybody."

HIS HOLLYWOOD DREAMS DAMPENED, HE TRIED TO MANAGE HIS EXHAUSTED staff, who plodded through the final months of the fifth season. One day, Michaels gathered Franken and Davis and Downey in his office to discuss the possibility of pulling the plug on the whole thing. Maybe, he was thinking, he should follow the cast out the door when their contracts were up. "We were tired," Franken said. Downey agreed: "We'd done everything we wanted to do." Although the decision wasn't final, Michaels invited his top people, as a sort of graduation gift, to choose a favorite artist as a host or musical guest for the final stretch. "It was like your dad taking you to FAO Schwarz and letting you pick out one special toy," Downey said. He chose the character actor Strother Martin, who hosted in April. Bill Murray picked the Amazing Rhythm Aces, a Memphis band. Franken and Davis got Michaels to rebook the Grateful Dead. Some old favorite sketches that the censors had repeatedly blocked got on, too. One, which would become a classic, was a history piece that utilized the whole cast. Set in the eighteenth century, it features elaborately costumed and bewigged characters who are named after new inventions: Lord Worcestershire, Lord Salisbury, the Earl of Sandwich, and finally— making a grand entrance, announced by footman Garrett Morris in a booming voice—Lord and Lady Douchebag.

As Michaels brooded about his next move and the fate of his show, Lillian Ross suggested that he talk to William Shawn, who, at seventy-two, was wrestling with his own succession dramas at *The New Yorker*. Michaels went to see Shawn in his office on West Forty-fourth Street. "I always called him Bill, because Lillian did," he said. "Then I learned that everyone called him Mr. Shawn." As Shawn, hunched and barely audible, talked about legacy, Michaels realized what their roles had in common: they were both good at developing talent, at "giving people confidence who aren't born with it," he said. "Nothing happens unless there's *that* person." But Shawn had waffled about picking a successor, and he felt depleted by managing his staff's infighting and expectations. As the meeting ended, Michaels thought to himself, *I don't want to end up like this. And if I stay at the show, I may end up like this.*

The time for new contract negotiations was drawing near, but Michaels was in a strained period with Brillstein, who'd been instrumental in the creation of a rival sketch show on ABC called *Fridays,* which *Variety* referred to as a "direct copy" of SNL. Tom Shales, usually SNL's booster, began his piece on *Fridays* by saying, "Cheap wisdom has it that *Saturday Night Live* is past its palmy days and into the winter of discombobulation." Other networks and, eventually, cable channels, rushed in with their own imitations. At the same time, Michaels's increasing friction with NBC's president, Fred Silverman, made the idea of staying on tough to imagine. Silverman was a different kind of executive than Herb Schlosser, the elegant Princetonian who deferred to talent. A fireplug of a man with beetle-brows and few social graces, Silverman liked to mess with the product. Michaels never forgot a story that Brillstein had told him, about the day Peter Finch had a fatal heart attack in the lobby of the Beverly Hills

Hotel. Most patrons detoured to a different exit as doctors attended to the fallen actor, but Silverman, in a rush to get to the valet, stepped over Finch's body.

The tension had ratcheted up the previous fall, when Michaels was abruptly summoned to Silverman's office on Election Day, to find a roomful of executives studying a big scheduling board. In the Wednesday 9:00 P.M. slot was the word "Gilda." Pointing to the board, Michaels turned to Silverman and said, "No-no-no-no. Gilda passed on that." He had relayed this to Silverman earlier (the workload would be too great, on top of SNL), but it evidently hadn't stuck. Silverman was enraged. He was the spin-off king, and he had pegged Radner as the next Lucille Ball. "Fred used some foul language about Gilda," Michaels recalled. "And I said, 'You can't talk about her that way.' It got ugly."

Radner was the only one left at SNL whom Michaels considered true-blue; he always remembered the time she'd pinned a card on the bulletin board that said, "Lorne, I'm happy—Gilda." He didn't want to share her, even with a series that he'd produce.

After the Gilda dustup, Silverman crossed Michaels off his list of team players. He was already angry that NBC had lost control of the Blues Brothers, which he considered the network's intellectual property. But SNL, a hit, was the least of his problems. Silverman had been counting on a revenue bump from the Summer Olympics in Moscow, but then Jimmy Carter decided to boycott the games after the Soviets invaded Afghanistan. NBC was not only in third place, it was on the verge of bankruptcy.

"At ABC, Fred Silverman had been like A-Rod," Herb Schlosser told me. "But then he flamed out completely at NBC." One Silverman fiasco, *Supertrain,* about a nuclear-powered luxury train that contains a disco and a hospital—a *Love Boat* on rails—was at the time the most expensive TV show ever made.

Things at SNL had gone south the way Hemingway said people go broke—gradually, then all at once. The fifth-season ratings started dropping. Doing the show every week, Michaels said, had cost him "a chunk of my intestines and a large part of my brain." After a five-year crash course in managing prickly egos, he realized that, if he were to stay, he would have to do a complete overhaul. His compulsion about avoiding conflict meant that he hadn't let a single person go in five years. Would he be able to stomach cleaning house? To give himself time to decompress and find new blood, Michaels proposed that the network let him delay the start of his sixth season by a few months. Silverman wasn't sympathetic; NBC had already sold the show's October ad slots.

Michaels also hoped, if he returned, to transition into more of an executive producer role, leaving the day-to-day showrunning to Franken, Davis, and Downey. Brillstein presented these demands to NBC, and a meeting was arranged with Silverman and his lieutenants to discuss them. At the last minute, Silverman canceled, and Michaels felt slighted, particularly when it became obvious that the other executives who'd shown up had not even looked at his proposal. One of them hit Michaels up for tickets to a Rolling Stones concert for his kids. Brillstein lost his temper, and after some shouting, he took Michaels and left.

They went to Wally's, a restaurant down the block from Broadway Video, and talked until closing time. Brillstein advised Michaels to walk. "They won't understand until you're not here," he said.

Silverman called to apologize the next day and said that he was prepared to come up with whatever was necessary—money, development opportunities, TV movies—if Michaels would stay. The two men would never be friends, but Silverman recognized that SNL was one of the only sure bets NBC had. The meeting was rescheduled for the following Monday. Before it could happen, however, a Franken sketch dissolved whatever remaining goodwill Silverman had.

The show had always made jokes about NBC's failures and fuck-ups, including taking shots at Silverman. On the episode two days before the rescheduled Silverman meeting, Franken did an Update spiel pitching the 1980s as "the Al Franken decade," and asserted that he should have a limo, given that the president of the network got one. And Silverman, he said, was "a total, unequivocal failure," a "lame-o" who, in his two years as president, "hasn't done diddly-squat." Franken went on, "I like to call it a limo for a lame-o." He urged viewers to mail postcards to Silverman demanding a limo for Franken.

"It was classic Al," Michaels said. "He's putting himself in a category with someone big and powerful. But it was a more complicated issue than he knew."

In the studio that night were Barbara Gallagher, the former SNL producer who was now on Silverman's staff, and Brandon Tartikoff, the new president of network entertainment. In the minutes before dress, Tartikoff walked over to Michaels with the Franken script in his hand and said, "Are you going to put that on?" Michaels recalled, "And I said, 'Well, we'll certainly take it to dress and then we'll see." The segment got huge laughs from the dress audience. Gallagher told Michaels she was concerned, and he sent her over to Franken to discuss it. "Barbara came to me and said, 'You can't do that,'" Franken recalled. "And I went, 'It's funny.' That's what we're doing here."

Michaels told the executives not to worry, that Franken would probably tone it down. "I can't kill that piece, because it played," he said. And he had a suggestion: "I told them to call Fred and tell him not to watch tonight." (This had become the protocol whenever friends of the network or of Michaels himself were going to be ridiculed on the air.) But no call was made. "Neither of them wanted to get the wrath of Fred," he said.

During the air show, Franken didn't tone it down. As soon as Update ended, an NBC page found Tartikoff in the audience and said that Silverman was on the phone. Tartikoff wriggled out of taking the call.

"Silverman exploded," Michaels said. Their Monday meeting was canceled. Thousands of postcards poured into the mail room calling Silverman a lame-o. "Fred was flailing," Michaels said, referring to NBC's overall situation. "I was the least of it, but here I was, all trouble."

On Monday, at Michaels's prompting, Franken sent Silverman an apology, explaining that the commentary was just a version of the healthy American tradition of knocking the boss. "I also understand that you were hurt that Lorne allowed the segment on the air," he wrote. "It's difficult to explain to someone who has not worked within Lorne's system, but he really had little choice in the matter. Lorne's system is based on allowing different comic sensibilities to be expressed within the show's style, craft, and taste criteria. These criteria are established by a consensus of Lorne and trusted members of his staff, of which I am, believe it or not, one. It was the overwhelming consensus of the group that my piece was funny. Besides, Lorne lets us satirize everything, except, of course, himself and his family." Silverman did not respond.

Franken had no idea that his bit would tank the negotiations about the show's future. Michaels wasn't surprised by the fallout. Franken, he said, "was always touching the third rail." As for Silverman, Michaels said, "The show was making too much money for him to give me the time off I needed. It was a business decision."

The negotiations sputtered along with no resolution. Nothing had been decided by May 24, the day of the season finale, hosted, as had become customary, by Buck Henry. Michaels and his team made a point of acting like they were driving the bus, controlling the message. The show was studded with clues that Michaels considered the show his property to dispose of. Going into one commercial, a bumper slide read: COMING UP NEXT: *SATURDAY NIGHT LIVE* GARAGE SALE. When the cast gathered onstage at the end, Henry gave a somber wave and said, "Good night—and goodbye." The final shot was the ON AIR light outside the studio doors, flickering and then going dark. When the staff members returned to their offices that night, each found a gift from Michaels—an engraved cigarette lighter in the shape of the RCA Building. The inscription read: "Nice working with you 1975–1980."

There had been no official announcement that the show was finished, and some felt a peculiar sense of déjà vu: the uncertainty about whether they still had a job was just like the uncertainty they had felt over whether they'd gotten the job to begin with.

But Michaels still held out hope that a deal could be struck. He loved the show, and he fretted that leaving might just be running away, which is what his tough-minded mother, Florence, thought.

The week after the finale, he met with Tartikoff and Gallagher and reiterated his proposal: he would stay nominally involved and leave the showrunning to deputies. "I told Brandon, 'All that matters is the writing. You need Downey and you need Franken and Davis,'" he recalled. "'That's the core group.'" Tartikoff told him that Franken was out of the question. He asked Michaels's opinion of Jean Doumanian, the talent coordinator. She was great as a booker, Michaels said, but she didn't have producing chops; more important, she lacked any experience writing or working with writers, who were, after all, the soul of the show. At an impasse, Michaels figured that there'd be one of two outcomes: the network would cave and let him pick a day-to-day producer, or NBC would take the show off the air.

A WEEK LATER, MICHAELS FOUND HIMSELF IN A CROWDED SEDAN ON A HOT Texas highway, being pulled over by a state trooper. Michael Klenfner, a record executive, was driving, and squeezed in with him were the music promoter Ron Delsener and a few others. Susan Forristal recalled, "It was me, and a car full of Jewish guys." The cop let the group, a bit rattled, drive on. As Michaels always did after the season finale, he had left town. He had flown to Houston, Forristal's hometown, in the private plane of their Hamptons neighbor François de Menil. They were heading to the premiere of the John Travolta–Debra Winger movie *Urban Cowboy*. The party was at a club called Gilley's, whose centerpiece was a huge mechanical bull. Diane von Furstenberg wore a sheriff's star reading DISCO SUCKS. The party was packed with Houston socialites and Hollywood people in spangly ten-gallon hats. (Andy Warhol, who'd stuck with his wig, wrote in his diary that night about Winger trying to sell him on colonic irrigation.) Through the scrum, Michaels spied von Furstenberg's date, Barry Diller, who was done up like a half-bald buckaroo. Michaels had been discussing a possible movie deal with Diller and Eisner again, at Paramount. Now Diller took him aside and passed on some news: he'd just heard that NBC had appointed a new producer to take over *Saturday Night Live,* and it was Jean Doumanian.

Michaels was blindsided. He hated nothing more than surprises, and the idea that the network would take his show away from him and put someone else in charge had never occurred to him. It seemed to Michaels like classic bad faith, what he calls "straight out of the handbook of small time." Reeling, he soon had a nervous call from Tartikoff, who told him that NBC was going to announce Doumanian's hiring the following day. Doumanian called next, apologetically explaining that Tartikoff had sworn her to secrecy about the negotiations. This was a more painful breach. Over the past months, as Michaels had been pondering a Paramount deal, he'd asked Doumanian to join him there, and she'd played along. SNL would be going on without him.

He gradually pieced together what happened. Tartikoff, new in his job, was dealing with a boss who was barely hanging on; the network wanted a link to SNL's first season. "The talent department is the outward-facing person," Michaels said. "So the industry *knows* that person. The meeting with the host, arranging the car for the movie stars—that's a very visible thing. But it's what happens *here*—in the office, with the writers, at two A.M., which is invisible—that is the most important thing." Doumanian had never been in the roomful of monkeys.

"Jean was not the right person," Franken said, and most of the staff agreed. They viewed her as a "fashion person," according to Downey. She embodied the highfalutin side of Michaels's life that they always made fun of.

Shales, in *The Washington Post*, quoted Michaels calling his exit "a painful experience" and saying that his summer plans included "writing and taking long walks." Tartikoff offered a lot of gold-watch remarks, calling Michaels "the first television pioneer of the television generation." Doumanian thanked Michaels for "the terrific legacy" and said that she hoped to keep the show "as outrageous as ever." The departing SNL staffers were given twenty-four hours to clean out their offices. In an interview with the *Associated Press*, Michaels said that the show was dead.

TWENTY-TWO

IN THE WILDERNESS

ON NOVEMBER 15, 1980, MICHAELS WAS SOUND ASLEEP UNDER A FLUFFY duvet at the Plaza Athénée, in Paris, when Jean Doumanian's first episode of SNL aired. He and Forristal had taken the trip with some friends to celebrate his thirty-sixth birthday. He felt a little stab of regret when he heard that Elliott Gould was hosting, but he didn't watch. "A big piece of my life was missing," he said, but he was looking forward to "a fallow period."

NBC had signed Michaels to a loose development deal that prevented him from going to work for another network, and he'd gotten the band back together—O'Donoghue included—in August, to make a special about the 1980 presidential election. But Silverman killed the special at the last minute, cementing the rancor. The network suggested airing it after the election, an idea that O'Donoghue compared to looking at pictures of naked women after you'd come.

Michaels told everyone that his plan was to start watching TV again until he got angry enough at what he saw to come up with another idea for a show. Mainly, he wanted to take a break from dealing with talent, and he turned his attention toward home and family. For Michaels, one of the legacies of losing his father early was that, as an adult, he liked to have someone to mentor. Now he invited Susan Forristal's seventeen-year-old brother, Joe (one of nine siblings), to move to New York and help out at Broadway Video. "Lorne literally took me off a soybean farm when I was driving a tractor," Joe Forristal said. "I was a fucking hillbilly." He traveled everywhere with Michaels— regular trips to Europe and to St. Barts. "I was like his puppy," he said. "Paul McCartney would call me by my fucking name!" Then Michaels gave Joe $2,000 and packed him off to Europe, just as Uncle Pep had done for him. When the money ran out, Michaels brought him home and sent him to Hunter College.

The Forristals, like the Levys and the Shusters, became an alternative family, warmer and livelier than the Lipowitzes. Michaels and Susan would visit Florence Lipowitz in Toronto, checking into the Windsor Arms, the hotel that Michaels had always dreamed of staying at as a kid. Once, on a trip timed to his birthday, Florence stood at one end of her living room and held out a large, wrapped box. When Michaels didn't move forward, his mother tossed it on the floor, halfway between them. He poked the gift with his foot and finally unwrapped it—a bathrobe—but there was no display of affection, physical or otherwise.

After tending to home and family matters for a few months, mainly in Amagansett, he decided that it was time for the motion picture portion of his career to begin. He made a deal with MGM, a studio whose leadership was in financial disarray, headed by Freddie Fields and David Begelman. Michaels gathered his core support people: Cherie Fortis, Cristina McGinniss (a former nurse who'd been hired as an assistant in Season Five), his old Malibu friend John Head, and Jane Bonham-Carter, a posh British girl he'd met through Melissa North. They set up camp on the ninth and tenth floors of the Brill Building, employees of Broadway Video. "We were all happy to be under his umbrella," said Franken, who, along with Davis, Schiller, Downey, Paley, and Gammill and Pross, was given office space to work on screenplays as part of the MGM deal. John Head fiddled with the *Pride and Prejudice* adaptation. Franken's wife, Franni, ran the business side.

The Brill Building, on the corner of Forty-ninth and Broadway, fit right into Michaels's Rolodex of culturally significant addresses. A. J. Liebling profiled the place in 1941, in a three-part *New Yorker* article, describing a den of rakish show-business types, song-pluggers, and "heels." In the fifties and sixties, the building became the center of the pop music world, as a bevy of songwriters—Carole King and Gerry Goffin, Burt Bacharach and Hal David, Doc Pomus—churned out hits, and music publishers held court behind wavy glass doors. The entrance, although not as grand as the lobby of Rockefeller Center, was gilded and mirrored, a tin-pot Versailles. When Michaels met with his young screenwriters in his new corner office, he would lean back in his chair and say, in the voice of a Tin Pan Alley veteran, "Did I mention that they all have to be hits?" He'd also spout the old Lubitsch line: "I've been to Paris, France, and I've been to Paris, Paramount, and Paris, Paramount, is better."

Brillstein had negotiated for him to receive half the money from syndicating SNL; NBC sold the first five seasons to Filmways for around $10 million. Broadway Video got paid to edit the episodes into hour-long segments. At first Michaels sat with an editor and supervised as the SNL shows were cut down, but without his accustomed 11:30 P.M. cutoff, the sessions dragged on. John Fortenberry, a young Broadway Video editor, recut the first season three times. "Lorne's indecisiveness became kind of a joke, but he recognized it," Fortenberry said. Broadway Video produced other projects, including concert films with Neil Young, Randy Newman, and Simon and Garfunkel, and videos for the Stones, directed by Michael Lindsay-Hogg. The projects piled up, and Broadway Video expanded, regularly adding new state-of-the-art equipment.

They were happy in the Brill Building, in what Shales dubbed "Saturday Night Exile." Michaels had always told his staff that the show was a family, and that they'd always have a place in it. "Lorne said to me, 'Write a Tom Schiller film,'" Schiller recalled. "So I took my legal pad, and started. I had no idea how . . . I just wrote this homemade film, the way Grandma Moses picked up the brush and started painting." His script, called *Nothing Lasts Forever*, was a futuristic fantasia spoofing old sci-fi movies. Michaels wasn't much interested in hearing a pitch, and when Schiller finished the screenplay, Michaels didn't read it. "Lorne often does not attend your creativity, your work," Schiller said. "He had other people listen to me read it." Over the years, many writers have heard him say, only half joking, "If I have to read it, the answer is no." This served him in two ways: it's consistent with his "You pick the horse, you let it run the race" philosophy. And it gives him an out in case the project is a bust.

After the Doumanian humiliation, the old SNL crowd rallied around Michaels. Belushi came back that fall to appear in a Steve Martin special that Broadway Video produced. In lieu of payment, Belushi suggested a barter arrangement, giving him free access to Broadway Video's resources. Among his list of demands: "2) General use of everything I can have fun with and people to give assistance when I need it; . . . 4) Unlimited access to refrigerator; 5) Every time I come by the office, I would like people to be nice to me and make me feel at home; 6) All the above free for one year." Michaels recalled, "Beneath my signature, John requested the phrase 'Hire the Skinhead' be entered."

SNL was behind him, but Michaels remained in father mode. He gave the young people advice about finances and real estate, and Gammill created a goofy weekly newspaper on the office copy machine called *10,* about the doings on the tenth floor. On page one was the "Editor's Prayer." It went: "Dear Lord, Watch over Us and All Our Friends / On the Tenth Floor / May Broadway Video Prosper / May the Broadway Pictures Succeed / May Lorne and All Employees / Find Happiness and Peace. / Amen." One issue carried Susan Forristal's recipe for veal scallopini, with the intro "Here's a meal with little fuss to cheer Lorne when he's a grumpy Gus." There was a pool table in the office, and a movie-theater-grade popcorn machine. Michaels was trying to quit smoking, and eating popcorn gave him something to do with his hands. When Sarah Silverman encountered the popcorn basket a decade later, it threw her. "For such a fancy, Hamptons-y man, I will never comprehend the big bowl of popcorn in his office," she said. "So many filthy writers' hands in there—the amount of fecal matter and dried semen in that bowl I cannot fathom."

One part of Broadway Video's office culture centered on a secret: employees whispered to each other about an old half-inch videotape that was supposedly on the premises, a recording of Lorne Lipowitz's bar mitzvah. Closely guarded, it held the last known images of Lorne's father. "We knew that his dad's death was a huge emotional loss," a colleague recalled. "Not looking at the tape was a boundary to be respected by his employees." The employees found it, of course, and watched it after-hours, searching for clues.

Another legacy of Henry Lipowitz's death was his son's need to create beautiful and comfortable environments, a result of spending a dismal year in a rented house with little furniture. He lavished time and money on the Broadway Video space, hiring an interior designer named Nord "Missy" Haggerty, who was dating John Head and had done work for Keith McNally and his brother Brian, who'd opened the Odeon, which was an unofficial SNL canteen. She filled the space with Mission furniture, vintage light fixtures, and old oak doors. Michaels's clubby office was furnished with green leather wing chairs, and the windows were screened with wooden blinds evoking Dashiell Hammett. When the mother of Michaels's friend Penny Marshall died, Marshall came to his office with a baggie of ashes in her purse and scattered them out his window, over "the Great White Way," as Michaels called it, with only a little irony.

The SNL writer A. Whitney Brown remembers visiting Michaels in Amagansett and hearing him hold forth about his re-upholstery plans "like an old lady, with his swatches and shit." He treasures a chair from his old suite at the Marmont. He wanted interiors that felt exclusive, but conducive to a creative ruckus. "Places that made you say, 'Yeah, I'd like to hang out here,'" said Paul Simon, who also rented space in the Brill Building. "Lorne loves a clubhouse, and it was always one of his fantasies that we would create a club." To achieve that effect, Michaels rented out spare offices at Broadway Video to cool-kid tenants like Martin Scorsese and Paul Schrader; George Harrison had his film business in the building, and Woody Allen and Warren Beatty edited movies there. In 1983, Mike Nichols tried to interest Michaels in going halfsies on a French chateau and vineyard—no less than Haut-Brion, which was for sale. That went nowhere, but the following year, Michaels enlisted Nichols, Paul

Simon, and Steve Martin to join him in putting up funds to help his old pal Melissa North and her husband Tchaik Chassay open the Groucho Club in London.

The Central Park West apartment became a high-thread-count crash pad. "Lorne was like the dream parent to everybody," said Melissa North, who stayed there when visiting from London. "People would break up, or they'd lose all their money, and then they'd be living in Lorne's place. People moaned, people collapsed, people went mad and Lorne just always took care of them." Once, when North arrived, her usual room was occupied by Gary Weis, who'd had some kind of crisis. Michaels told her, "This time we've put you over with Paul, through the kitchen."

The Mertz-Ricardo groove continued out east. Simon was building a new house in Montauk then, and he sent his architect over to look at Michaels's pool with orders to replicate it exactly—but to make it two inches longer. In Amagansett, Michaels was using his new freedom to put in a pond and a fountain, so that he could hear the sound of water. He drew up a long list of improvements. ("That was the summer I smoked too much pot," he would later tell visitors, showing them around.) He had a favorite maple tree—a totem of his homeland—and he planned to expand the house around it. He moved trees and read gardening books. "A garden is like a show that doesn't talk back," he'd say. It was satisfying to revel in the production values of ten thousand daffodils.

The Central Park West apartment had long been the setting for holiday meals and chic parties. Abbie Hoffman, on the lam, showed up at one with his model girlfriend, and Mike Nichols brought a new discovery, Whoopi Goldberg, who hid behind the curtains, intimidated. The Amagansett house became a social scene, with Forristal throwing big dinners, extending what North called her "Y'all come on over" brand of hospitality. Jack Nicholson became a frequent summer lodger, eventually taking over a room (later a guesthouse) for weeks. Lillian Ross and her son, Erik, were regulars. Early one August morning, Forristal blearily watched from a bedroom window as mother and son trampled a stretch of newly laid sod en route to the tennis court.

"We were living hard then," Forristal said. "Getting up at nine in the morning to play tennis wasn't happening." Ross later said, "I was so stupid. I'd see everyone sniffing, and I'd think, 'Gee, I guess they all have colds.'"

After years of separation, Michaels secured a divorce from Rosie Shuster, and in September 1981, he and Forristal were married. All the SNL people turned out for the wedding in the backyard in Amagansett, and Franken and Davis hired a small plane to fly by trailing a sign that read MAZEL TOV, LORNE AND SUSAN. Art Garfunkel was the cantor, and Paul Simon the best man, although Radner and Buck Henry gave the official best man's toast. Belushi came directly from an all-night photo shoot after a two-day binge; Simon grabbed him and helped him shave. Gammill and Pross gave the newlyweds a toaster.

Some old Canadian friends made the trip south. Paul Pape's wife, Karen, described the scene as "the prince of New York is having a wedding." She'd only met the bride a few days earlier, and approved; she decided that Forristal "had the greatest self-esteem of any human I'd ever met," because her ten bridesmaids included Lauren Hutton, Cheryl Tiegs, and Forristal's five stunning sisters. At one point Nicholson approached the Toronto table. "You're all looking at me!" he said, in a rascally voice. Karen Pape replied, "Wearing a red suit with a pink tie and pink socks means that you *want* us to look at you." Later, when he wandered into the bushes with a production assistant, the red suit didn't provide much camouflage.

The society bandleader Peter Duchin supplied the music; given all the rock and roll professionals in the tent, Duchin had been advised that it would be better to stick to the American Songbook. (One Texas relative requested "Anchors Aweigh.") By that time, Belushi had passed out on a chaise longue. Brillstein dragged the chair and its occupant behind a hedge. Duchin kept the dance floor crowded all night, Buck Henry frugging wildly with all the ladies. The only person not dancing much was the groom, who watched from the sidelines. It was a producer's prerogative.

———

JEAN DOUMANIAN WAS NOT AT THE WEDDING. HER SNL TENURE HAD ALREADY flamed out, after just twelve episodes. She had ordered a deluxe over-haul of Michaels's old office and, like him, she kept visitors waiting. But for all the gloss, the show she produced was vulgar. Shales opened his review, called "From Yuk to Yeccch," with "Vile from New York—it's Saturday Night." There were a lot of "shock value" sketches, pieces about S&M (a "leather weather report" given by a dominatrix torturing a man tied to a map) and racial issues, including a tone-deaf one about the Klan. Advertisers dropped out in droves, and in March 1981, after the cast member Charles Rocket said "fuck" on the air, Doumanian was fired. Some felt that she wasn't given a fair shot, and that too many people in the media were gunning for her, although her own staff nicknamed her Ayatollah Doumanian. The one bright spot in the season was the debut of nineteen-year-old Eddie Murphy, a discovery of Michaels's cousin Neil Levy, who'd stayed on as a talent booker after clearing it with Michaels.

Silverman was frantic over the collapse of his one solid franchise; revenues were down $10 million. Michaels hadn't watched the show; however painful its decline was for him, he did feel some vindication. Paul Simon sent him postcards from his travels to cheer him up. One, from Tokyo, read " 'Saturday Nite Dead.' Lorne, hate to say it, but it's true. Show's lost its zip." (Simon added "Everything great here! Open-ing up Tall man–Big man shop!")

The person NBC hired to take over from Doumanian was Dick Ebersol, who'd never believed that he got enough credit for SNL. Tartikoff had been wooing him for weeks before he fired Doumanian, and when Ebersol agreed, he said that he'd need a bit of time to regroup—precisely what Michaels had requested earlier and been denied. Ebersol asked NBC to hold off on announcing the news. He wanted to get Michaels's blessing. He made a pilgrimage to the Brill Building to speak to his old partner, and they continued the conversa-tion over a long dinner at the Odeon. It was an inversion of the mara-thon session at Nibblers, this time Ebersol trying to get back into the good graces of the Canadian he'd raised up to the network.

Michaels gave his benediction, and he sealed it with a token: the silver mother-duck pin that he used to wear on his corduroy lapel. The 8H crew, he knew, would recognize it.

Clearing the way for Ebersol put Michaels in a position to ask a favor himself. But he framed it so that Ebersol thought that Michaels was doing a favor *for* him. He suggested that Ebersol hire Michael O'Donoghue. He'd had a visit from O'Donoghue's manager, who'd said that his client was broke and needed help. Michaels told Ebersol that O'Donoghue could be just the link to the glory days that he needed, an ideal right arm. Ebersol promptly made O'Donoghue head writer.

It surprised no one when the first thing O'Donoghue did in his new job was to announce his intention, as Michaels put it, "to destroy everything Lorne Michaels ever stood for." (Carol Caldwell, O'Donoghue's girlfriend, said that, in private, "he was always very, very ugly about Lorne.") O'Donoghue had told Ebersol that he thought SNL needed "a decent Viking funeral" and that he wanted, instead of "head writer," one of two titles: Reichsmarschall or Godhead. Human resources countered with "Chief of Staff."

O'Donoghue ordered a case of spray paint, and, on day one, he gathered the troops and bellowed that the show had been "dog shit." What it was lacking, he said, was—and here he grabbed a can and started spraying on the wall. Laboriously, he graffitied a *D,* then sputtered out an *A,* then an *N.* The puzzled staffers wondered if he was bringing back Dan Aykroyd. Finally, after a series of awkward exertions and pauses to shake the can, he spelled out *DANGER.*

He ordered each person to take a can and deface the walls, pronto. One writer compared the scene to a Weather Underground ritual. Catherine O'Hara, whom Ebersol had hired away from Second City, took the next plane home to Toronto. She didn't think it was scary; she thought it was dopey.

Shortly before Ebersol's debut, in April 1981, Michaels stopped by to show his support. Ebersol jumped up from behind Michaels's old desk in his old ninth-floor office and signaled for his guest to take his rightful seat. Word went out that Michaels was in the studio, which did as much as the duck pin to legitimize the new era.

Chevy Chase was hosting, and the episode opens with him in a backstage storeroom, chatting with Mr. Bill among dusty mementos—the foam Land Shark head, Coneheads prosthetics. He does his fall. At the Update desk, he reads a bunch of headlines that O'Donoghue had never been able to get on the air, including the one about the Catholic Church and co-host Mike Douglas. He introduces Franken, who drones on about how terrible the show has become, commanding viewers to send in postcards with the message "Put SNL to sleep." He sarcastically refers to Ebersol as "Mr. Humor," a guy who "doesn't know *dick*," and plugs the following week's show, to be hosted by Franken and Davis.

But that show, which would have been Ebersol's second, never happened, scuttled by a Writers Guild strike, which also scuttled the remainder of the season and made it seem quite likely that Ebersol's first episode of SNL could be the series's last. That night, O'Donoghue threw a party at the Winter Palace with the theme The Day the Laughter Died.

Everyone involved with SNL was surprised when, in May, Tartikoff put SNL on the fall schedule. The network was sticking with the show, and the strike ended up giving Ebersol six months to refine his new vision. O'Donoghue lasted until January. He'd tested Ebersol's patience by getting rid of Don Pardo (his original idea was to have Pardo learn of his termination when Pardo himself read it off cue cards live on the air); and he'd hired a friend, the screenwriter Terry Southern, who installed a wet bar in his office. Southern wrote a sketch (never aired) called "Sex with Brookie," in which two guys compare graphic notes about getting it on with sixteen-year-old Brooke Shields. O'Donoghue also berated the staff, and he and Ebersol communicated largely by yelling. The breaking point came after O'Donoghue insisted on doing a twenty-minute sketch called "The Last Ten Days in Silverman's Bunker." In June, Silverman had been ousted, and O'Donoghue's sketch depicted him as a boobs-obsessed führer, presiding over the "Nazional Broadcasting Company," whose gold-peacock logo is a dead ringer for the Nazi eagle. A voiceover describes Silverman thusly: "A twisted genius whose strange experi-

ments lobotomized his helpless victims; a power-mad tyrant who reduced a proud nation to a vast wasteland." The network quite
reasonably ordered the piece killed before Saturday. O'Donoghue
went into retaliation mode, mailing copies of the script to journalists,
who didn't rush to defend him. A month later, he was fired. He left a
parting note to the staff, saying that he was getting out of show business, and that if anyone at NBC tried to make it sound as if he had
resigned, "he is, to steal a phrase from Louisa May Alcott, a 'lying
cunt.'"

FAKING VIRGINITY

> There are no bad ideas, Lemon. Only good ideas that
> go horribly wrong.
>
> —JACK DONAGHY (PLAYED BY ALEC BALDWIN), 30 ROCK

WHILE MICHAELS WAS OFF THE PREMISES THAT YEAR, TWO FLOORS DOWN
in the RCA Building another comedy experiment was underway. It
wouldn't have existed without SNL or Ernie Kovacs, and it gave off a
whiff of Michaels's early notion about the grown-ups leaving and letting the kids take over. On the first episode of *Late Night with David
Letterman,* in February 1982, the boyish Midwestern host gave viewers a tour of his studio. He stopped in the greenroom, which was
kitted out like a greenhouse, full of plants. "These are some of the
few vegetables here at NBC not in programming," he said. He poked
at the network, but with a mischievous twinkle and none of the bile
that marked the salvos of O'Donoghue and Franken. Letterman's first
guest was Bill Murray, who walked out with mussed hair in a ratty
cardigan and made fond banter with Dave. This was not Carson, and
it was not SNL. It was something new: genial, amused, low key. The
music was changing again.

Michaels was spending a lot of time in L.A. that year, for meetings
with MGM, staying in his old suite at the Chateau Marmont. One
night in February, Buck Henry invited him to the Playboy Mansion,
where Hugh Hefner was having a movie night, screening the Armand
Assante film *I, the Jury.* Belushi was there; he greeted Michaels
warmly and told him about *Noble Rot,* a script set in the wine business that he was writing with Don Novello. But he was manic and

couldn't sit still. He tried to get Michaels to eat some opium and snort some coke. Mostly Belushi played video games with a dealer friend, but he'd pop into the wood-paneled screening room and creep up to where Hef sat, in his robe, beside his own personal bowl of popcorn. Then Belushi would grab a handful of Hef's popcorn and slip away. Michaels watched as the bowl was steadily and stealthily depleted. "It was a nice visual," he said.

As Michaels was leaving, Belushi went into a nostalgic reverie, reminiscing about how good, how important, SNL had been, and how all of them now were "playing it safe—all agent stuff." He finished with an observation that Michaels was beginning to agree with: "The movie business is shit."

Less than a month later, in the first week of March, Belushi was found dead in a bungalow at the Chateau Marmont. The cause of death was an overdose—heroin and cocaine. Brillstein became a focus in the aftermath, because he'd given Belushi cash at a time when loved ones were doing anything to prevent him from buying drugs. People who knew Belushi were shocked but not shocked. He'd been so difficult for so long that being wasted seemed like part of the package. He was Albanian oak. It would be a few days before the coroner announced his findings. Carrie Fisher said, "We were all sitting there waiting to find out what killed him and hoping it wasn't our drug of choice."

Michaels was in his office at the Brill Building when he heard about the death, and his first reaction was anger: Belushi always left a mess, and he'd done it again. Also, the circumstances of his death "couldn't have been more low," Michaels said. The next morning, he climbed onto his never-used exercise bicycle and put on a tape of the Stones record *Tattoo You*; he lasted thirty minutes before he started to cry. "It was so much easier to be mad at him than it was to be moved," he said, "because it was impossible to comprehend." In his shock and distress, he began to question his old practice of staying out of other people's private business. "Part of the problem of my generation was a morality that said you don't tell people how to live," he said. "That was garbage." Belushi's death shook him. He'd always believed that the show's rigid schedule helped keep people in line, but clearly there was more that he could have done.

The Albanian Orthodox funeral, in Martha's Vineyard, where Belushi and his wife owned a house, served as an unwished-for reunion. Michaels went into producer mode, chartering planes to help get everyone back to civilization with a snowstorm coming. He was terrified of the open casket, but when he filed by and looked at his friend, laid out in a tweed jacket, army pants, and high-tops, he murmured, "I've seen him look worse." And it was true. "I thought for a moment as he was lying there that he was like Christ and had died for our sins." Grief didn't prevent many of the mourners from snorting lines of coke in the chilly backseats of limos. Belushi's mother, Agnes, broke down, screaming and throwing herself on the coffin.

To Michaels, Belushi's death—and O'Donoghue's flameout—signaled the true end of the original outlaw era. He was supposed to be starting over, with a movie career, but he felt like he was free-falling, in a kind of limbo. His new chapter wasn't going the way he'd pictured it. Although he hadn't performed since the CBC show with Pomerantz, the director Sydney Pollack tried to persuade him to play the part of Dustin Hoffman's sidekick in *Tootsie*. (He declined, and the role went to Bill Murray.) Franken, Davis, and Downey were going on two years without finishing the screenplay that Michaels was planning to produce for MGM, an Orwell spoof called *Nineteen Eighty-Five,* a date that, in real time, crept ever closer, threatening to kill the joke. To keep his MGM deal alive, he had to have a film in production by a certain date. Schiller's script for *Nothing Lasts Forever* was ready, and the film got a start date to shoot at an old studio uptown, along the FDR Drive.

Belushi had been cast in the film, and his death hung over the kickoff party held at Trader Vic's. Schiller had put together a high-powered and eccentric cast, including Bill Murray, Imogene Coca, Eddie Fisher, Mort Sahl, Zach Galligan, and Dan Aykroyd. Michaels had told MGM's Freddie Fields that Schiller was a genius and that the studio should just stay out of his way; Michaels envisioned a film with a modest budget of half a million dollars. But because Aykroyd and Murray were in the cast, MGM was expecting a blockbuster SNL movie; they upped the budget to $2.5 million. Tensions emerged the first week of shooting, when Schiller rebuffed a couple of Michaels's suggestions about line readings. After that, Michaels didn't spend much time at the set.

The frostiness between first-time producer and first-time director invited meddling from the studio. Fields gave notes directly to Schiller and cut Michaels out of the discussion. When a finished cut was screened for Fields and some other executives, Michaels didn't attend, but afterward Schiller called Michaels with a full report. "Tom was on a manic high," Michaels recalled. "He said that Freddie Fields had turned to him as the lights came up and said, 'It's an art film.'" Schiller was ecstatic. It was left to Michaels to explain that Fields hadn't meant it as a compliment. "I told Tom I thought it meant that he wasn't going to release the movie, which is what happened."

Nothing Lasts Forever is a moody and dreamy film, full of retro touches and obscure references. Adam, the young protagonist, fails the official "artist qualifying exam" at the Port Authority, and goes to work for Dan Aykroyd at the Holland Tunnel. He eventually boards the "Lunarcruiser," a bus to the moon, where Bill Murray is a steward and Eddie Fisher sings his hit "Oh! My Pa-pa." Dr. Bronner, of hippie-soap fame, makes a cameo.

But Schiller was a member of the SNL family, and Michaels invited a group of his own friends to see the film at the Broadway Screening Room in the Brill Building. Sitting up front with Michaels were Candice Bergen and her husband, Louis Malle; Mike Nichols; Paul Simon; and Lillian Ross. No laughs were heard while the film played, and the spectators were quiet as they filed out. Malle did have one suggestion. "Cut it to the bone," he told Schiller, as he passed. Nichols offered a diplomatic "Good for you!"

"Nothing would have delighted me more than everybody rising to their feet and applauding at the end, but that's not what happened," Michaels said. Although he considered the film charming and original, he felt that it should never have been saddled with commercial expectations. MGM didn't release it, and when the Cannes Film Festival invited Schiller to show it, Fields said no. He'd already decided that the movie would be impossible to market. (It turned out that MGM wasn't contractually allowed to use Aykroyd's or Murray's names in promotional materials.) MGM's financial disappointment over *Pennies from Heaven,* the Steve Martin musical that the studio released in 1981, was still fresh. The studio had spent $22 million on it, expecting a follow-up to *The Jerk;* but Martin singing and dancing in a Depression drama was the opposite of boffo. *Nothing Lasts Forever* was, similarly, a victim of misguided expectations. Michaels decided that, going forward, any movie he made would be small enough that, if it failed, it couldn't hurt the studio.

Nineteen Eighty-Five was the next Michaels project to get the Freddie Fields treatment. Set in a post-apocalyptic world under a dome, whose inhabitants are named for old New York City phone exchanges, like Butterfield 6-9546, or Endicott 8 1698, Michaels believed in it. Although it was conceived as a vehicle for Aykroyd and Murray—an *actual* SNL movie—it went nowhere. Fields sat in a conference room one day at Broadway Video and listened to Downey, Susan Forristal, Franken, and Davis read the script aloud. He didn't laugh once. He did give Michaels some notes—including an order to lose the phone-exchange names, which he thought would confuse the *Animal House* demographic—but a green light never came.

Like the Warners deal, the MGM deal seemed more and more like an illusion. But Michaels enjoyed getting to know an East Coast MGM executive named Boaty Boatwright. She hosted parties in her apartment in the Apthorp for British friends like Michael Caine and Sean Connery, which appealed to Michaels's Anglophile side. One night at Boatwright's he was seated next to Sue Mengers, the schmoozy Hollywood agent. (She had famously calmed her client Barbra Streisand, in the wake of Sharon Tate's murder, by saying, "Don't worry, honey, stars aren't being murdered, only featured players.") The next day, he sent Boatwright flowers with a card reading "I could have danced all night with Sue." Mengers became a regular name on his call list. Like him, she had lost her father when she was an adolescent—a suicide—and had an overbearing mother. She was

powerful, full of salty Hollywood gossip and wisdom. Rolling her eyes
at a misstep by some big shot, she'd mutter, "God didn't send his best
Jews to Hollywood." Boatwright said, "Sue had the kind of wit that
Lorne liked. And they both liked their grass."

They also both liked being in a roomful of celebrities, whom
Mengers called her "sparklies." Her homey dinner parties mixed stars
like Elizabeth Taylor and Mikhail Baryshnikov with Princess Margaret and David Geffen. "Lorne loved the people that Sue could bring
to his dinners," Boatwright said. "And she loved the people that he
could bring to hers." They used the phrase "a good draw" to describe
an especially desirable guest of honor.

Michaels was a restaurant maven, and so, when he started musing
about writing his own coming-of-age screenplay, his version of *The
Graduate,* he hit on the title *Women, Money, and Restaurants.* He
wanted to direct the film, a romantic comedy that would describe, as
he put it, "the transitional moment before I came to New York."
Broadway Video employees got used to hearing the title thrown
around, but no one ever saw an actual script. *Women, Money, and
Restaurants* became shorthand around the office for Michaels's phantom movie career.

But by now the idea of directing had lost some luster. "Standing
around at seven A.M. and waiting for the actors to be ready—not for
me," he said. No friend to the alarm clock, he'd only want to direct a
movie, he said, if he could work "French hours"—short shooting days
without meal breaks. He started telling himself that directing movies
might be more of a grind than an artistic pursuit. The small screen,
familiar to him, began to beckon again. Sandy Wernick picked up his
phone one day and it was Michaels, with an idea: He wondered if
NBC would be interested in a special called *Two Pauls,* starring his
two famous friends. Wernick got a quick yes from the network and
called Michaels right back. There was a pause on the line, and Michaels said that maybe he should ask McCartney and Simon first.
"Typical of Lorne," Wernick said, figuring that it was just "a middle-
of-the-night idea."

The CAPTAIN'S WORD IS LAW plaque hung on the wall of Michaels's new office, but it wasn't clear what he was the captain of. "Lorne used to tell me how the phone stopped ringing when he gave up SNL," Joe Forristal said. "That was a surprise for him. He told it to me as a cautionary tale." Broadway Video's editing rooms were bustling, but the SNL writers who'd followed Michaels to the Brill Building were getting antsy. MGM had blinked at their scripts, and SNL was receding into the past. Jim Downey took a walk on the beach with Michaels to tell him that Merrill Markoe, the head writer for *Late Night with David Letterman,* had recruited him to take over her job. Gammill and Pross went to *Letterman* too, and Michaels wished them well. Some in the SNL crowd weren't shy about saying that they found *Letterman* kind of cornball, although Bill Murray and Steve Martin were regular guests, and Paul Shaffer became Dave's bandleader sidekick. Building on Markoe's foundation, Downey would define the voice of the show, creating magnificent segments of deadpan silliness like "Camping with Barry White" (Dave sucks snake-bite venom from the singer's leg).

The relationship between Letterman and Michaels was, from the start, cordial but formal. They were NBC's two princes of late night, but while Letterman was on the way up, Michaels was coasting. Letterman is a guy from nowhere (Indiana) who decided to milk the aw-shucks style of his roots. Michaels is a guy from nowhere (Canada) who worked very hard to blend in with the cultural gentry. Steve Martin said, "Dave is genuinely self-deprecating. He genuinely doesn't think he's any good. Those issues don't come up for Lorne."

TARTIKOFF HAD TAKEN OVER NBC'S ENTERTAINMENT DIVISION, DESPERATE to get out of last place. When he called Michaels in the middle of 1983 to ask him to come back to the network, perhaps to take over SNL, he didn't get a hard no. "I told him that I could never do that to Dick," Michaels said. "It was his show now." Tartikoff had another idea: What about creating a brand-new show in prime time?

Michaels was torn, but after the terrible few years in the wilderness, it felt good to be wanted. "He'd been in a King Lear period,"

Susan Forristal said. "He'd given up the kingdom." A throwaway line of Steve Martin's haunted him: "You're out of the business five years before anyone will tell you." He mulled it for a while, and then let Tartikoff know that he would do an hour-long program for 10:00 P.M. Friday night, to begin in January 1984. What it would be, Michaels didn't know. And Tartikoff, who promised him thirteen episodes, didn't seem to care.

"What I learned from experience is that it all rests on conception," Michaels had told *Rolling Stone* a few years earlier. "Because if you're wrong at point A, it never gets any better." *The New Show,* as the program was coyly titled, had a murky conception and an indeterminate point A. Much of Michaels's old SNL staff was reconvened, but no one quite understood what the show was. He tossed a few crumbs to a reporter: he wanted to remedy the way "shocking has replaced funny" in comedy, and he was excited about covering Ronald Reagan's reelection campaign. His default self-deprecation intact, he joked about the likely "public humiliation" just ahead.

At thirty-nine, he was no longer an outsider. His hair was graying, and he was on his second marriage. He knew that he was competing against himself and that a big part of what had made SNL a success was novelty. "You can't fake virginity," he told reporter after reporter, hedging.

The New Show had three regular hosts and three guest stars each week, plus a music act. The hosts were Buck Henry and two mild Canadians, the SCTV stars Dave Thomas (half of Bob and Doug McKenzie, the ski-cap-wearing brothers who call each other "Hoser") and Valri Bromfield. The guests were Michaels's friends—including Steve Martin, Gilda Radner, and the newlyweds Paul Simon and Carrie Fisher. Live television was what Michaels knew, but the only NBC studio that could handle a live show was 8H, and Ebersol was using it for SNL. So *The New Show* was taped on a soundstage rented from CBS on West Fifty-seventh Street. The idea was to tape in real time on Thursday evening, and air the show on Friday night, with any big flubs edited out over at Broadway Video. Jim Downey returned to be head writer and assembled a stellar writers' room, bringing back Gammill and Pross and hiring another *Harvard Lampoon* alum, George Meyer, and a Texas-born writer recommended by Steve Martin: Jack Handey.

Unsure of their mission, the writers set to work, shuttling between the Brill Building office and CBS. The day of the first taping was January 5, 1984. Steve Martin showed off his dance skills with a choreographed parody of Michael Jackson's "Billie Jean" video, a staple of a weird new cable network, MTV, which had "video jockeys" as hosts.

Lillian Ross had kept showing up at the Brill Building with her notebook (staffers called her "Zelig"). Her conviction that SNL had merely been Michaels's first act encouraged him at a time when he wasn't so sure. After the first dress rehearsal, he stood before his troops, prepared to go into field-marshal mode as he had on so many Saturday nights. This time, something was off. Instead of listening to the boss's notes, people were snickering, distracted by a persistent crinkling noise. Ross, seated behind Michaels, was fiddling with the cellophane wrapping on a congratulatory fruit basket. "Lorne was trying so hard to make things work," Max Pross said. "I've never laughed so hard. Lillian Ross trying to get at that apple—it crystalized all the frustrations of *The New Show*."

Working on tape brought out Michaels's weakness for second-guessing. He would yell "Cut!" in the middle of a sketch, and then start again from the top. As the taping dragged on, audience members began to leave. The show included bleacher shots, so the next week the doors were locked, the audience literally held captive, sometimes till two or three in the morning. "The length of the tapings wore out the audience," Downey said. "And a dead audience is bad for comedy, and horrible for performers."

The first show got a terrible rating, and Michaels decided that the CBS soundstage was the problem. He'd noticed that there were stools by all the cameras. "Those cameras were locked in position," he said, "whereas our cameras at 8H were always in motion." He got Ebersol to let him tape *The New Show* in 8H on Thursdays, on the SNL set. But the tapings continued to be marathons. After each one, the hours of videotape were rushed over to Broadway Video, where

John Fortenberry, with Downey and Michaels, stayed up all night cobbling together different takes. It was an entirely new rhythm. When a live show wrapped, everyone could go get drunk; after a *New Show* taping, the hard work was just beginning. A finished cut on cassette was supposed to be delivered to NBC by 6:30 P.M. Friday, to air at 10:00. More than once, two NBC guys in suits showed up at Broadway Video after the deadline on Friday night. "Give us the tape now," they said.

"It was the worst of both worlds," Downey said. "All the imperfections and the crudeness of live television, with all the staleness of tape." The sketches were so sliced-and-diced that canned laughter had to be added. "Lorne is like a guy who is great at taking exams and bad at writing term papers," Downey said. "He needs someone to take away the blue book."

Neither Michaels nor his people were used to working on a dud. Among the staff, consensus grew that the show had not been properly thought out. Some speculated that Michaels did *The New Show* mainly because it provided billable hours for Broadway Video.

A big problem was that the three hosts—Henry, Thomas, and Bromfield—were middle-aged and on the bland side. "We weren't an interesting enough nucleus," Henry said. The show put a strain on Henry's relationship with Michaels. At SNL, he had always been treated as an honored, if familial, guest. At *The New Show* he was in the trenches, and it aggravated him that Michaels seemed to be phoning it in. "Lorne never communicated a vision, if he had one," Henry said. Staffers referred to him as "Lord Michaels." ("Lorne was really into *bathing*," a colleague from that time recalled. "'The bath' came up in conversation a lot.")

Dave Thomas was unhappy, too. One night he confronted Michaels in his office. "I said, 'Jesus Christ, you told me you were going to be behind this, but you're cruising around late at night in a limo with your friends like some kind of New York vampire, and you're not putting any effort into this show.'" Michaels's reply disarmed him. "You know, it's true," he said. "Instead of thinking about what great comedy ideas I can come up with, these days, when I wake up, I think about what I want to eat that day." Thomas burst out laughing. "I realized that Lorne is an expert at diffusing the rage of artists," he said. "It's one of his great skills as a producer: he knows how to handle people, and it makes him bulletproof."

The writers felt pressure from Michaels to make his friends look good when they hosted. One kerfuffle involved the question of who would play Abe Lincoln in a sketch—Jeff Goldblum (the writers' choice) or Paul Simon. Simon was something of a sore point to the writers. In October, a few months before the show premiered, Michaels hadn't been available to help brainstorm and map things out. Instead, he had tagged along on Simon's honeymoon with Carrie Fisher, a lavish cruise up the Nile to Luxor, a gift from Mo Ostin. On the boat, he posed for snapshots horsing around in a droopy kaffiyeh, like Lawrence of Arabia. The twenty-six-year-old bride, who'd brought a Murine bottle full of LSD, pranced around tossing glitter on everyone. The staff felt that if Michaels had been in the office and not on the Nile, *The New Show* might have been better.

The show ended after nine episodes, just as the high-end redecoration of the Brill Building offices was finished. *The New Show* was the lowest-rated of ninety-four programs that aired during the 1983–84 season. Failure on this scale was entirely new for Michaels, and he was knocked off-balance. Downey called the experience "soul-punishing." At a wrap party, Michaels confided to a guest, "My mistake was calling it *The New Show*. Because I do *one kind* of show."

Besides being Michaels's first public failure, *The New Show* was a personal financial setback. His company, Broadway Video, had produced the show, spending vastly more money on it than NBC was paying for it. "I was losing two hundred thousand dollars an episode," he said. When it was over, he'd lost a couple million dollars. Brillstein advised him to take out a mortgage on his Central Park West apartment to raise cash. Randy Newman never understood *The New Show*'s business plan. "You don't put money *in* show business," he said. "You take it out."

The staff, crankiness notwithstanding, rallied around the boss. Downey wrote him a note saying that he'd never seen such grace under fire, and that he appreciated how, with the show hemorrhaging money, Michaels had never asked anyone to take a pay cut. "When it was over, all that washed up was debts," Michaels said. "I'd been in a bubble since 1975. I'd think, '*You* were the guy who invented SNL.' But no one even remembered that. And you had the vague sense that you might be out of the business now."

FOR THE FIRST TIME IN YEARS, MICHAELS WAS WORRIED ABOUT MONEY. IN his old L.A. life, he could just bump down to a smaller room at the Marmont. Now he was living beyond his means, with a mortgaged apartment, an expanding place in the country to maintain, and a business with salaried employees, including a number (John Head, assorted young Brits) with the flimsiest of job descriptions. He'd also bankrolled an art gallery downtown for Forristal to run. Broadway Video had plenty of work, but the company was spending heavily on equipment upgrades. Having Michaels's rock-star friends (Jagger, Bowie) edit their videos there was more glamorous than lucrative; the invoices, if they were paid at all, reflected deep house discounts.

Michaels had become used to regarding money the way his wealthier friends did. Under the influence of Steve Martin, who collected art, he nosed into the art world. Egged on by Nichols, who bred Arabian horses, he and Paul Simon invested in an expensive mare together. On a lark, the two men also bought a local radio station in Hampton Bays, WWHB-FM, and let Simon's brother Eddie program it.

Bills were piling up for the Amagansett renovations, and Michaels's marriage was fraying. He and Forristal clashed over the scale and character of the remodeling. The prospect of starting a family caused stress between them. Michaels continued to mentor his brother-in-law Joe, and, one by one, the other Forristal siblings had been moving north. Friends thought that having so much of his wife's family around made Michaels feel sidelined, no longer the center of attention. Once, when Mick Jagger and his wife, Jerry Hall, were visiting, Jagger had commiserated with him. "That's what happens when you marry a Texan," he'd said. "The whole family comes to live with you." There were also tensions about Forristal's gallery work and her independent social life on the nights when Michaels was at the office late. "In my village, the women stayed home," he would tell her.

They decided to get a divorce. Michaels felt as low as he had the day on the beach in Malibu a decade earlier, when he'd done the stress quiz in the *L.A. Times.* Forristal moved down to her gallery space, and Michaels threw himself back into the family he'd created at the office. But with the MGM deal kaput and *The New Show* a washout, there wasn't much for his team of loyalists to do. Gammill and Pross went back to *Letterman,* then wrote for Garry Shandling's show, before taking jobs with a new sitcom created by Jerry Seinfeld. Downey moved over to Ebersol's SNL, being careful to get Michaels's blessing first.

Feeling lost once again, Michaels swiveled back to the movies. Brillstein had made him a new deal with Orion, and he got excited about the young Canadian director of a romantic comedy called *Almost You.* Adam Brooks had grown up near Forest Hill, the son of a Hart and Lorne fan. When Michaels summoned him to the Brill Building for a meeting, the "Jewish geography," as Brooks called it, was irresistible. Right off, Michaels told him, "I'd like to make an Adam Brooks movie." Twenty minutes later they were in a stretch limo, stopping to pick up Art Garfunkel, then Jack Nicholson, and then on to Yankee Stadium and matchless box seats. "That's how the Cinderella story started," Brooks said; he'd entered what he calls "Lorneworld."

Soon Brooks was in L.A. to pitch Orion's Mike Medavoy a romantic comedy that Michaels would produce. He met Michaels at the Beverly Hills Hotel (after Belushi's death, Michaels never returned to the Marmont) for some coaching, pointers on how to behave in the room with Medavoy. "He liked to give you little tidbits," Brooks said. "'Here—I let you into this room. I think you can *be* in this room.'" They walked to the pitch meeting—even Brooks knew that was unheard of in Hollywood—Michaels spouting Hollywood history as they went. They walked by the "storybook"-style Spadena House, and he explained that it was known as the Witch's House, and was built by an art director in 1921.

Medavoy bought the pitch, but the movie stalled. Back at the Brill Building, after a few more dead ends, Brooks started working with John Head on an adaptation of *White Noise*, Don DeLillo's dystopian novel about consumerism and death. It ended up on the unproduced pile with Michaels's other scripts.

Amid the dead ends, a project suddenly turned up that Michaels would come to regard as the one that saved his life. On a trip to St. Barts, Steve Martin showed him a screenplay he'd been fiddling with for years, called *Three Caballeros*. Working at Disneyland demonstrating rope tricks had been Martin's job as a kid, and he had always loved the park's trio of singing birds and their repertoire of silly Mexican songs. Michaels liked the caballeros idea but told Martin to throw out the script, which he considered too broad and punny.

Michaels and Martin began rewriting the script with Randy Newman. The premise was physical comedy done in mariachi costumes, but Michaels thought it needed something more. "What if they're actors?" he asked Martin. "Because I can write actors till the day I die." The story came together quickly. "What if they're silent-movie stars, and their careers are kind of winding down," he said. "A Mexican girl writes to them for help, and they think it's a fan letter. They think they're just going to Mexico to do a show, but it's actually dangerous." Besides knowing how to write actors, Michaels was beginning to know how to write about feeling washed-up. Martin was all in.

Back in L.A., the trio met every afternoon at Martin's house. Martin would type on his IBM Displaywriter, one of the earliest computers, brandishing 8-inch floppy disks like playing cards. He would interrupt mid-brainstorm and say, "Hold on, I have to paginate!"

For Michaels, this was the first experience in the movie business that lived up to his imaginings—his fantasy of laughing and drinking coffee for hours, the way he pictured George S. Kaufman doing it. "I was in that lost period, and I was getting divorced," he said. "Just having a job to go to every day—it was so much fun." He was also being well compensated. Michaels incorporated a bit that Frank Shuster loved from *Modern Times:* Chaplin picks up a red flag that's dropped from the back of a truck and ends up leading a parade of political agitators. They got inane notes from Orion, which was producing the movie as part of Michaels's deal. "They wanted 'an amusing crucifixion' in there," Newman recalled, still puzzled.

At one point Spielberg was slated to direct *Three Amigos* (copyright issues necessitated a title change), with Bill Murray and Robin Williams flanking Martin as the titular amigos. Rick Moranis and John Candy were also floated as Martin's co-stars, but Candy bowed out because he thought he was too heavy to work on horseback. He recommended Martin Short. It was his first starring role. "He called himself the cheap amigo," Steve Martin said.

There had been talk of Michaels directing—finally—but John Landis ended up behind the camera, with Chevy Chase as the third amigo. During post-production, Landis was standing trial for involuntary manslaughter (for the horrific accidental death of three actors on the set of *The Twilight Zone*), and a good amount of material ended up being cut. Among the lost scenes was a Hollywood sequence panning soundstages where different movies are being filmed—including one called *The Dueling Cavalier,* an homage to the accursed film-within-a-film in *Singin' in the Rain*. Like that classic, *Three Amigos* is about one of Michaels's hobbyhorses: the struggle to stay relevant as the culture moves on.

Three Amigos disappointed at the box office (years later, it would develop a cult following). If working on it had fulfilled Michaels's vision of old-fashioned Hollywood magic, the romance was short-lived. There were too many people's fingerprints on the movie. It was becoming clearer to him that his true calling was television. He'd begun to realize, as he would tell generations of employees, "You can't make an entrance if you never leave."

TWENTY-FOUR

THE RESTORATION

WHEN DICK EBERSOL RETURNED TO NBC TO CLEAN UP THE JEAN DOUMANIAN derailment, in 1981, Michaels told Tom Shales that he was "tired of repeatedly attending 'the funeral' for *Saturday Night Live.*" Back then, he had wanted Tartikoff to cancel the show, which was his baby, after all. Now, four years later, Tartikoff called Michaels and told him that he was going to do just that—unless Michaels would come back and take the reins.

By 1985, grappling with a second broken marriage, movie dreams that had mostly come to nothing, and his first professional failure, Michaels was on the lookout for the next chapter. Losing so much money on *The New Show*—more than two million in all—had spooked him, reminding him of the economic uncertainty after his father died. When he talked of that time to colleagues, he told them that he was determined never to be poor again. Buck Henry had sent Michaels a telegram on his fortieth birthday that hit close to home. It read: "Dear Lorne, Rest assured that I and your many more experienced friends will help you to get through these last few difficult twilight years sympathetically."

But when Tartikoff asked him to take over for Ebersol, who'd recently given notice, he said no. He hadn't watched SNL since he'd left. "It was too raw," he said. "Like seeing your widow marry and somebody else bringing up your children." But Ebersol had bolstered

SNL in its tenth season by hiring a team of comedy superstars—Billy Crystal, Martin Short, Christopher Guest, and Harry Shearer. People called the season the "Steinbrenner year." (He also hired, as a writer, Larry David, who got nothing on the air and quit, then, thinking better of it, came back the next week and pretended that he hadn't.) Despite a rickety start, Ebersol's strategy had worked, and a number of funny characters came out of it. There was Short's high-strung nerd, Ed Grimley ("I must say!"); Crystal and Guest as whiny cops ("I hate when that happens"); Shearer and Short as synchronized swimmers; and Crystal's unctuous talk-show host, Fernando ("You look mahvelous!"). Now Ebersol wanted to leave the show to spend more time with his family.

The only leverage Tartikoff had over Michaels was SNL itself: NBC would cancel it if he didn't return. Wrestling with whether he should rescue his creation, he sounded out a couple of close advisers. The first was David Geffen, who counseled against going back. He said, "Somebody who *wants to be you* should do it." Michaels's initial reaction to that: "Well, I kind of enjoyed being me." The second mentor was Mo Ostin, who ran Warner Bros. Records; he offered a more practical analysis. "Well, you want to live in New York," he told Michaels. "And producing SNL is a great job in New York. It's a power base. And you're *good at it*." Michaels took the advice of the older man, who calmed his fears that it would look like he was going back with his tail between his legs.

The comeback was announced in early August. Michaels had the CAPTAIN'S WORD IS LAW plaque nailed up in his old office, which he had redone just as he'd left it. The press loved the "restoration" angle. Michaels told the *Times* that he'd exited five years earlier because he'd run out of steam. "I wanted to do my real life," he said coolly. "Have lunch with friends, get married. Now I have that out of the way." Tartikoff strongly urged him to take a more detached management approach this time.

The team Michaels ended up with was the one he'd envisioned in 1980: he would be executive producer, Franken and Davis were co-producers, and Jim Downey was head writer. (Michaels would continue to take a writing credit.) A new cast had to be found immediately, and he asked Franken and Davis to scout comedy clubs for young talent. Ebersol's all-stars weren't returning.

One day in August, Franken, Davis, and Downey drove out to Amagansett to discuss the new season. Michaels greeted them in his driveway with a young woman named Laila Nabulsi, who'd assisted Schiller on his SNL short films. Michaels had hired her as an associate producer to help with talent. Downey, Franken, and Davis were surprised to hear that she and Michaels had already signed several cast members, including Anthony Michael Hall, a blond seventeen-year-old; and Robert Downey Jr., a long-lashed twenty-year-old. Both had just hit it big starring in John Hughes's teen sexbot comedy, *Weird Science*. Having turned forty, Michaels had decided that the show had to skew younger. "Dick had hired Baby Boom people," he said. "I decided to drop down a generation."

Seeing the ashen looks on the faces of his three lieutenants, Michaels said, "Trust me." He thought the young movie stars would get more women watching the show. As the three friends drove the bumpy length of the Long Island Expressway back into town, they were glum. The new world order that they'd envisioned, with Michaels more hands-off, turned out to be somewhat notional. Around Ronkonkoma, Davis started venting. "Lorne said he'd just be 'overseeing' things," he said. "I know what that means. He'll be spending all his time in restaurants and then show up after all the work is done and screw stuff up."

Nonetheless, Franken and Davis scouted dozens of performers. On a tip from Charles Grodin, they found Jon Lovitz at the Groundlings. "I told Lorne, 'He's everything we don't want all in one person," Franken said. They dismissed Jim Carrey as "too broad, not our style," Franken said. "That was a real stupid thing." The cast was filled out with Randy Quaid; Joan Cusack, who'd acted with Hall in Hughes's *Sixteen Candles;* Nora Dunn, a Chicago comedian; Dennis Miller, whom Michaels saw at The Comedy Store; Danitra Vance, a Black theater actress; and Terry Sweeney, an openly gay actor who did an uncanny Nancy Reagan impersonation.

Michaels called back his old tech people, including Eugene Lee, who again commuted from Providence, sleeping some nights on a yacht at the 79th Street Boat Basin. Downey put together a strong team of writers. Handey and Meyer came on, as did Don Novello. Then there was John Swartzwelder (a future *Simpsons* stalwart), Carol Leifer (a future *Larry Sanders* and *Seinfeld* writer), A. Whitney Brown, and Robert Smigel, whom they found in a Chicago improv troupe. A New York comedy kid, Smigel remembers the day that year when he picked up *TV Guide* and read, "on the first non-glossy page, that Lorne Michaels was coming back to SNL. I felt that I was floating."

On a tip from Dave Thomas's wife, Pam, Michaels sent Downey and Franken to Toronto to check out a young comedy troupe called Kids in the Hall. They brought back two of the five members, Mark McKinney and Bruce McCulloch, to audition. The two Canadians had been warned that Michaels rarely laughed during tryouts. ("It doesn't help the performer, and it doesn't help the people waiting," he'd tell his people.) After he watched McKinney and McCulloch, he mumbled to them, "So are you busy in September?" The two went back to Toronto and spent weeks puzzling over what that meant. "It was like a koan," McKinney said. The pair finally learned that they were hired as writers, and Michaels put them up in the Berkshire Place; because they didn't have visas, they weren't listed in the credits and got paid in cash.

McKinney was intrigued by another Michaels koan: "You always go back to your last hit." It was intended to encourage writers to break away from their old, safe moves, but it applied equally to Michaels as he set out to reboot the show. Most of his talking points about it concerned restoring its pre-Doumanian luster, with more political humor and fewer pre-tapes. With all the videos Ebersol had been airing, Michaels said, "it lost what is magic about it. I think 'Saturday Night Live' is about a contact with another group of humans coming through this tube."

Operationally, the show did get some tweaks. Downey instituted group rewrite tables, and the writers were expected to keep more regular hours. (Franken had two small children at home.) When Davis lit a joint in the writers' room that fall, everyone gasped. "You can't do that anymore, Tom," Downey told him, laughing. After that, Davis walked around the office carrying a mug, contents unknown. He was annoyed by the new temperance, and took to saying, "Hung-over people are people too."

One of the biggest changes was in the kind of musical guests the show booked. Before, Michaels and Howard Shore had picked musicians they listened to, offbeat acts that passed the John Head coolness test. Now Michaels wanted Top 40 hitmakers, even if he'd never heard of them. Exceptions were made for friends of the family. One time, Elliot Roberts, David Geffen's partner in Asylum Records, called to pitch a new artist named Tracy Chapman. The SNL bookers were lukewarm about her demo, but Michaels scheduled her on the show as a personal favor. Her booking ended up being postponed by a WGA strike, during which her album came out and rocketed to number one. Michaels recalled, "Then she gives an interview and says something like, 'I would never do TV except for SNL because Lorne Michaels believed in me from the beginning.'" The takeaway: "For every time you get blamed for something that you didn't deserve, there's a time when you get credit for something that you didn't deserve."

BY THE WEEK OF THE PREMIERE, MICHAELS HAD SLIPPED RIGHT BACK INTO his unflappable SNL stance. "Bruce, do you know Madonna?" he said, introducing the host of the comeback show to one of his new young Canadian writers. Bruce McCulloch was thrown by the question ("Of course I didn't fucking *know* Madonna"), but grateful for the inclusive gesture. Getting her to host was a coup. That year, she'd starred in *Desperately Seeking Susan,* completed her Virgin Tour, weathered the publication of old nude photos in *Penthouse,* and married Sean Penn in a ceremony that was buzzed by press helicopters.

In the first five years, Michaels had grown accustomed to hosts using the show to demonstrate their underappreciated talents. The

Wednesday read-through with Madonna showed that little had changed. One sketch was about the singer sleeping with a paper boy—Anthony Michael Hall. In rehearsal, Madonna, instead of playing the part as her "boy toy" self, put on an arch Katharine Hepburn accent, "like a peppy forties girl—really bad," recalled McCulloch, who co-wrote the piece. Michaels hated it. McKinney, out of nervousness, gave a loud courtesy laugh. "It was one of the only times I ever saw Lorne mad," McCulloch said. "He asked me, 'What the fuck was Mark doing?'" The sketch didn't make it anyway; Anthony Michael Hall, who was seventeen, announced that he didn't want to play teenagers anymore.

The day before the premiere, Buck Henry sent one of his telegrams: "Dear Lorne and Tom and Al etcetera, Keep doing it until you get it right." Madonna was game and professional, sparkling in one sketch as the host of *Sábado Noche,* a Latin variety show, but she couldn't rescue the episode. Right from the cold open—about the new cast members submitting urine tests, a nod to the show's druggy origins—it all felt slightly lurid. "We actually showed Brandon Tartikoff holding plastic cups full of urine," Smigel said, still appalled years later.

The *Times* called the episode "tasteless and witless." One sketch posited that the Kennedys murdered Marilyn Monroe, showing Randy Quaid as JFK smothering Madonna (as Monroe) with a pillow. (The NBC switchboard logged 140 complaints about that one.) Another, responding to the recent death of Rock Hudson, was an extended AIDS joke. "Fold up the tent and let the series die," one critic wrote.

Downey, who hated the urine-test opening, said, "The press was lying in wait for us already. We played right into their hands." But Michaels held the line, telling the *Times*'s Leslie Bennetts, "I lived through it for five years, all that 'Saturday Night Dead' stuff. Everything new tends to look ugly before it looks beautiful, and the critics were expecting what they had gotten comfortable with." ("Saturday Night Dead," an irresistible formulation to lazy headline writers, would haunt Michaels for decades.)

Morale sank. Restoring the show's political humor had been one of Michaels's aims, but his young cast, quickly dubbed a "brat pack," didn't have the range to pull it off. "You couldn't do a Senate-hearing sketch with this cast," Franken said. (Years later, when Franken was elected to the U.S. Senate, Marco Rubio, a keen SNL fan, would approach him on the Senate floor and ask, "What happened that season?") Michaels's casting strategy had backfired. "After five years away, I was off my game," he said. "I couldn't make it jell. I went too young."

He also found that the censors were tougher than they'd ever been. They cut from the broadcast a five-minute drug riff by Sam Kinison before it could air on the West Coast. (They never got to see a bit that Kinison had demonstrated on the floor of Michaels's office about gay necrophilia.) They forbade Downey to call a talk show *Pussy-Whipped,* even though, a decade earlier, the show had gotten away with the line "sponsored by Pussy Whip, the dessert topping for cats." But Tartikoff, knowing that advertisers wanted younger viewers, and that younger viewers wanted what was then called "edginess," remained supportive. "I'm thirty-six years old, and I'm at least sixteen years too old to judge this show," he said. "What is one critic's most unfavorite sketch is probably a teenager's favorite sketch."

Chevy Chase was lined up to host the second show; Michaels hoped that a dose of the original magic might help. Rather incredibly, he had rehired Michael O'Donoghue, to generate ideas for film segments (none were ever shot). The day Chase arrived, O'Donoghue, still mad over the aborted script the two had collaborated on, came to the office early and distributed copies of a host monologue that he'd written for his old friend.

> Good evening. Right after I stopped doing cocaine, I turned into a giant garden slug and, for the life of me, I don't know why. Hi, I'm Chevy Chase. Have you noticed that, in the years since I left *Saturday Night Live,* my eyes have actually gotten smaller and closer together so they now look like little pig eyes? Why? Again, I don't have a clue. As I was saying

to Alan King the other day at the Alan King Celebrity Tennis Tournament, "Alan, I need more money. What I can't fit in my wallet, I'll eat or I'll shove up my ass, but I must have more!" And when I looked in the mirror, my eyes were the size of Roosevelt dimes and had moved another inch closer to my nose. "What is going on here?!?" I exclaimed to my new wife, who looks like my old wife except she's new. Still, the fans showed up for my last movie—*The Giant Garden Slug's European Vacation*—a movie any man would be proud of, particularly if that man was Cantinflas. There's much more I can say but I have a twenty lodged in my lower colon and it's just driving me crazy. My next film is called *The Giant Garden Slug Blows Eddie Murphy While John Candy Watches* and it opens tomorrow at Red Carpet Theaters everywhere. Don't miss it.

Chase laughed when he read the monologue and wanted to do it on the air, but Michaels vetoed it. In-jokes could only go so far. In the *Times* O'Donoghue was quoted comparing SNL to Union Carbide and saying that the show was "like watching old men die." That week, he was fired for the last time. Michaels found himself ruing his vow from a decade earlier that he would never become one of the people on O'Donoghue's enemies list. "I didn't understand the inevitability of it," he said. "That he was going to make that narrative come true, because that's just who he is."

The eviscerating headlines kept coming: "SNL Hit Rock Bottom," "Slippery Slide." "The press were beating the shit out of me, talking about 'the Golden Years,'" Michaels said. "I was like, 'No, I was *there* for the Golden Years. Trust me—they were not that golden.'" George Meyer, a writer known for his cerebral bent, walked around the studio on Saturday nights holding his head, murmuring, "Show dying. Show dying."

Michaels blamed schadenfreude. "The show had been beaten about the ears for so many years with how great it would be if the original people were there," he said. "Well, now the original people were there, and we were old and annoying." He resisted the idea that the show had become an institution. Mason Williams, a former Smothers Brothers writer, had written during the Doumanian season, and even then he'd described the show as "like a head shop at Sears."

Being cool was almost as important to Michaels as being funny. It pained him to hear that his show was out of sync. He disliked feeling edged out by Letterman, with his anti-hip, gee-whiz approach. The season forced Michaels to ask himself, "Is this a seventies show that came of age as an expression of the counterculture movement, or is this a form that any generation could find a use for?" He realized that when Franken and Davis had dismissed Jim Carrey as "too sweaty," their benchmark was the first five years. "It was as if we were still in our Robert Bolt period—the classical era of SNL," he said.

By 1985, New York had changed too. The city had become prosperous. Hal Willner, the longtime music supervisor, viewed the history of SNL as naturally aligned with the history of the city. "New York is always going to attract the most interesting and creative smart people," he said. "But in 1975, you didn't move to New York to make money. You left New York to make money. It was avant-garde and dangerous, and so was the show. It's not any less creative now, but the people on it are thinking about their careers." (As the city got richer and shinier, Michaels had Eugene Lee update SNL's home base accordingly; chandeliers appeared.) But navigating the cultural currents was a delicate business. In 1985, Jann Wenner launched an ad campaign to update *Rolling Stone*'s crunchy image. Under the headings PERCEPTION and REALITY, the ads paired photos of pot brownies and Häagen-Dazs, or a psychedelically painted VW van and a sleek sports car. In response, Hunter S. Thompson declared that the magazine, once a weapon, had become a tool. Michaels worried that the same might be said of his enterprise.

THE CAST WASN'T COHERING, BUT THE WRITERS' ROOM WAS STOCKED WITH proven talent. Trying to get the show back on track, Michaels and his writers looked hard at what kinds of sketches seemed to be working.

A successful SNL episode always had a balance of what Smigel calls "crowd-pleasing and strange." Madonna's *Sábado Noche* was low-concept—straightforward crowd-pleasing, with hard laughs. High-concept sketches—hinging on a weird, sideways premise—are more admired by writers, but tougher to sell to an audience, and sometimes to Michaels, who, in desperation, had started to lean toward broader material with harder laughs.

Smigel, unsure of whether he should be pleasing Michaels or Downey, felt that he was failing at first. He wrote a pre-tape piece called "It's a Wild Wild Wild Wild Kingdom!" about a show that played practical jokes on animals. "Look! We told a turtle he's gonna get a limo ride with Burt Reynolds! Watch his face when he finds out it's just a Burt Reynolds impersonator!" Snap-zoom to an expressionless turtle. "Downey was in heaven," Smigel said. "But that one ate it. Crickets."

Jack Handey was a hero to the writers' room; he wrote sketches that had a childlike purity. Although Michaels recognized his genius, his pieces, full of cowboys and cavemen and Martians, were short on the topical references that Michaels wanted at the top of the show. It took several years for Michaels to get behind "Deep Thoughts by Jack Handey," which had appeared in a mimeographed-and-stapled publication called *Army Man* that George Meyer started in 1988, as a break from the high stakes of network television. Part of Michaels's reluctance was wanting to avoid branding a piece with a writer's by-line; also, "Deep Thoughts" consisted of absurdist trifles, without hard jokes. He finally aired the first one in 1991: "To me, clowns aren't funny. In fact, they're kinda scary. I've wondered where this started, and I think it goes back to the time I went to the circus and a clown killed my dad." Handey, with his penchant for "little-boy stuff," recalled, "I owned that twelve-forty-five slot."

Michaels would check in with the writers about what they were working on after the host dinner on Tuesday night, roaming the office, a little drunk. Some from the original group felt that, after five years away, he was half-consciously playing himself—the role of producer Lorne Michaels. Delegating to his three deputies when it suited him could create collateral damage, allowing him to keep himself at a remove. Carol Leifer, a writer who'd been recruited by Franken and Downey, never felt recognized by Michaels. "It felt like being asked to play on a Beatles album by Ringo," she wrote in her 2014 memoir. She got little feedback from Michaels on her sketches, which he rarely picked, so she gave up trying to connect with him. "He had clear favorites among the performers and writers, the ones whom he invited to dinner and events." She only lasted for that season.

Lots of new hires had the experience of trying to be "on" around Michaels, only to hear him say, "You can stop auditioning. You're here." With his favorites, he was generous with attention. Smigel wrote a sketch once in which Tom Hanks played a stand-up who talks like Jerry Seinfeld—in an overly emphatic way, starting every line with, "I mean, hey!" "No one had imitated Seinfeld yet," Smigel said, "and I wanted to show how that Seinfeld manner of talking had seeped into so many wannabe comedians." He had Hanks, as the comic, interacting with people at a drugstore in that honking voice. ("Hey! Did you ever read the ingredients on the Tums bottle?") Michaels suggested that it would be funnier to set the piece backstage at a comedy club and have a bunch of comedians talking to each other in Seinfeld-speak. "As young writers, you notice that Lorne doesn't write a lot himself, so it's easy to be a hotshot and think, 'What's *this* guy telling me?'" Smigel recalled. "But he was right." He didn't strong-arm the writers, though, and his suggestions were never commands.

At some point, the show's critical freefall had the effect of liberating Michaels and the writers: Why not try anything? Michaels had the novel idea of asking Francis Ford Coppola to appear as a "guest director" one week. The cold open is Michaels talking to the cast in a locker room, explaining that bringing in Coppola was the network's decision. "I'll still be here in a supervisory role," he says, "before I move full-time into wrestling." Coppola, in a beret, pulls out all the auteur clichés, yelling "Cut!" during the monologue. He stops in the middle of a sketch in which Danitra Vance plays That Black Girl, spoofing the old Marlo Thomas sitcom. Insisting that it needs to reflect more of "the Black experience," he calls for the writers, and three blond preppy guys in tweed jackets, one smoking a pipe, appear: a Harvard joke. "There was nothing funny in that show," McKinney said. "But it was great television."

In his new hands-off mode, Michaels tended to avoid situations in which he might be told no, and writers sometimes felt that he used them as cannon fodder. Once, he dispatched Bruce McCulloch to sell the host, Oprah Winfrey, on a sketch that contained an abortion reference. Flashing his pirate smile, Michaels told him, "You're good with people." McCulloch pitched Winfrey in her dressing room, surrounded by people from the NAACP, who were there to vet material. "I got fucking thrown out of there," he said. In the end, a cold open was devised about racial stereotypes: Michaels visits Winfrey's dressing room and urges her to try on her Aunt Jemima costume. (Downey had unsuccessfully pitched a piece in which Oprah, as Aunt Jemima, is let go by the owners of the pancake-mix empire, which is looking to update its image, and then offers herself as a potential mascot to other corporations, like IBM.) She informs Michaels that she won't play Aunt Jemima, a maid, Br'er Rabbit, or Refrigerator Perry, and slams the door. Then Danitra Vance appears, in slave garb, holding a tray, and serves coffee to "Mister Lorne." Michaels asks her what he should do to make Oprah cooperate. Vance says, "Beat her." He enters the dressing room, and a bang-up brawl can be heard from behind the door. It opens, and Winfrey emerges with Michaels, bloodied, in a headlock.

Although Vance made a mark with That Black Girl, she often felt invisible on the show, as Garrett Morris had, playing stereotypes conceived by the white writing staff. The Black comedian Damon Wayans, who was a featured player that season, got so frustrated that he basically provoked Michaels into firing him: In one show, Wayans had only a small service role as a cop. On the air, he decided to bust out and deliver his few lines in a swishy accent. Under the bleachers, Michaels turned to the writer of the piece, Andy Breckman, and glumly said, "I have to fire him." And he did—although he invited

Wayans back to do a stand-up set on the season finale. Terry Sweeney also complained of having to play too many gay clichés.

Sweeney and Vance each only lasted that one season, but the same fate befell most of their colleagues. What had been intended as a return to glory was "a fantastically grim reversal," as McKinney put it. In a piece about SNL that appeared that year in *The New Republic,* called "Samurai Snobs," Frank Rich painted Michaels as a decadent has-been who had sold out his show's original mission and allowed it to be "bought, packaged, tamed, and sold during the 1970s—thus making the country safe for the return of the complacent, business-as-usual ethic of the 1980s."

By the end of the comeback season, Michaels resorted to booking multiple hosts to try to keep the show afloat. The season finale was hosted by Anjelica Huston and the Yankees manager Billy Martin, who gets "fired" mid-episode by Michaels for being drunk. Martin, enraged, sets the studio on fire. Michaels takes this in; then, with a gleam in his eye, he runs into the flames and returns with only Jon Lovitz, leaving the rest of the cast to their doom. "Don't ask any questions, Jon," he says. "Just go downstairs to my limousine and wait for me there."

Smigel and McCulloch wrote the piece, a parody of the season-ending cliffhangers on *Dallas* and *Dynasty,* and it was a tour de force. Rumors had been circulating that if the show somehow escaped cancellation, there'd be a major housecleaning. Lovitz was the breakout star, so Lovitz was the one Michaels rescued from the fire. Smigel said, "Was anybody angry? Just anybody who wasn't Lovitz."

Instead of "Who shot J.R.?" the question hanging in the smoky air of Studio 8H was "Who will perish?" On the end credits, every single name had a question mark after it, starting with "Lorne Michaels?"

TWENTY-FIVE

HANDS OFF, HANDS ON

LATE ONE NIGHT IN AUGUST 1986, IN THE HIGH-CEILINGED LIVING ROOM OF his Amagansett house, Lorne Michaels was ruminating on his second divorce. He looked over at Dana Carvey, his houseguest and brand-new employee, and said, "Marriage is a prison that everyone is trying to escape *into*." Carvey nodded dutifully and thought, *Maybe it's Shakespeare?*

As Michaels had done at the conclusion of the bruising fifth season, after the comeback year—Season Eleven—he retreated into the expensively simulated pastoral life that he was building on the East End of Long Island. With Susan Forristal out of the house, Michaels had moved the show into it, creating a kind of SNL Camp David. Joe Forristal, his ex-wife's brother, was still a regular, along with the SNL writer A. Whitney Brown, the pair acting as unofficial majordomos. They tended the vegetable garden, tinkered with the cars, and, unbeknownst to Michaels, hunted rabbits with BB guns. "Joe and I were very useful," Brown said. "We could supply things, whether it be provisions from Lorne's own house that he didn't know he had, or exotic substances from our seedier connections." Brown also regularly handed off loose joints to Michaels's friend Paul McCartney, who was nervous about getting busted.

Carvey was to be in the new cast Michaels had assembled for Season Twelve; having no place to live, he took Michaels up on his offer to move in with him at the beach. It had been a busy summer of hiring. Toward the end of the disastrous comeback year, Brandon Tartikoff had told Brillstein that he was pulling the plug. Brillstein told Michaels to get on a plane to L.A., so they could both sit down with Tartikoff and plead their case. At the meeting, Brillstein bristled like a grizzly. "You begged him to come back, and now you're *canceling*?" he shouted. Michaels recalled, "Brandon was just shamed into keeping us on the air." However, for the first time, NBC agreed only to a thirteen-week commitment. Brillstein made the network issue a press release to show support. It quoted Tartikoff being euphemistic— "This has been a rebuilding season for 'Saturday Night Live'"—and Michaels deflecting, as usual: "I'd forgotten how to do the show but I just found my old notes in the basement and I think it's going to make a big difference next year."

This time he knew what *not* to do—pick young, attractive people with no connection to one another. Many of the new performers he hired knew each other, helping the ensemble cohere. Carvey had been recommended by Brad Grey, a Brillstein partner who repped Dennis Miller. Michaels went to see him open for Rosie O'Donnell at a small L.A. club called Igby's. He brought along Tartikoff and, for a reason he cannot recall, Cher. Carvey felt that his set (it included his "Choppin' Broccoli" song, Church Lady, and impressions of Casey Kasem and Jimmy Stewart) was lame—a C-plus. But the next day he was invited to meet Michaels; his memory of the meeting is Michaels just murmuring the phrase "You just never know, putting a show together." He left confused.

Yet Carvey soon found himself employed and flying in a twin-prop plane to East Hampton, on his way to bunk with his new boss. When he walked in, he felt like he was "in outer space," he said. There was a giant refrigerator just for beverages. He was further discombobulated when Michaels said, "You can be in Jack's room." Carvey woke up the next morning to find his host naked, draped across a massage table on the lawn. In his flawless Lorne voice, Carvey imitated the boss's greeting: "You get the massage, the muscles are light, you're ready for the day."

It was a glamorous scene for a guy who had been living over a friend's garage in the Bay Area just a week earlier. In Amagansett, Chevy Chase would stop by with pizza, and one night Michaels announced, "Paul's coming over." A lifelong Beatles fan, Carvey spent the afternoon in Jack's room, using Jack's phone to call friends from home and whisper the news about who he was about to meet. At 10:00 P.M. the bell rang, and Michaels had Carvey answer the door. "Your face, it's gone a bit *foony*," McCartney said to him in greeting. Carvey was inwardly flipping out, but, once seated on a couch, he had the presence of mind to ask McCartney about his solo album *Tug of War*. Relieved not to have to answer Beatles questions, McCartney relaxed. A joint was passed; Carvey, a novice, tried a hit. (Years later, Carvey incorporated the evening into his stand-up, where he has McCartney declining a beer, saying, in perfect Scouse, "I don't think I'll have any sudsy-wudsy. Staying with the hempy doobies.") He had McCartney in stitches with a riff about a show-business horse that wouldn't shit on cue. Then McCartney put on a demo of a new song that he had brought along and said to Carvey, "You know, Dana, sometimes when you're writing, you try so hard to live up to whatever, that you end up ruining the fucker." Carvey found this observation profound. Michaels doubtless did as well.

In Amagansett, Michaels applied his producer's skills to planning dinners and organizing beach walks. He'd grab a piece of driftwood to use as a staff and lead his flock, holding forth about the dune vegetation or the history of potato farming in the East End. Back at the house, it would be "Whitney, pick some heirloom tomatoes" and "Dana, set the table." (Carvey stayed a month.) Michaels has always liked putting his very famous friends together with his SNL staff and watching the result. The employees, funny people (but mostly regular Joes), function as court jesters (who doesn't want to make a Beatle laugh?), while trying to keep their cool. Those who didn't get to experience the all-access pass that an Amagansett or St. Barts visit offered were jealous. Colleagues in the writers' room scoffed, "Whitney is so far up Lorne's ass that he has a three-bedroom condo in there."

A few years later, when Mike Myers was the rookie invited out to

Amagansett, he too was put on a little plane ("very much Buddy Holly Airways"), and he marveled at the glass-fronted refrigerators while Michaels got a massage. Michaels put him in "Mick's room"—the guest room spiel already shtick. One night Michaels threw a dinner party packed with captains of industry. ("All elemental-things people," Myers recalled. "Like, 'Meet Tandalia—she invented the question mark.'") After three days, Paul Simon offered to drive Myers back to Manhattan in his sports car. Myers declined and took the bus, which, he learned, was called "the jitney." "I was too scared," he said. "There's a sense, when you're starting out and you're seeing very famous people, like you're in trouble, like you shouldn't be seeing them."

Over time, the new hires figured out that the boss enjoyed raw, awkward people who, as Smigel put it, "didn't know how to make the effort to be charming." In the city, a few of the Kids in the Hall once went to Michaels's apartment to watch football. They marveled that the bathroom contained a urinal. For Michaels, they were all clay to be molded. Also, he was a little lonely.

The following spring, Carvey joined Michaels out at the beach again, less startled by then that the boss lit a joint in the limo. They went to the movies (medium popcorn, no butter), watched *The Godfather* on video, and drove around in a Mustang, Michaels pointing out the sights. After dinner, he would talk for so long that Carvey had trouble staying awake. "There was no Chevy or somebody on cocaine to stay up with him and listen," he said. "I'd finally say, 'I have to go to sleep, Lorne.' And he'd keep going—'You know, Danny was there . . . the network didn't want it'—as I'd be slowly backing into Jack's room. I'd close the door and he'd still be talking. I'd be under the covers and I'd hear 'Memllmmbrmm . . .'"

Michaels curated his arcadian life with the same attention to detail that he brought to the show. Part of his ideal mise-en-scène included hearing what he called "an orchestra of frogs." He had had his pond lined with expensive Bentonite clay he'd imported from Canada, to create an amphibian-friendly ecosystem. When the pond remained silent, he asked Forristal and Brown, his resident country boys, "I wonder why I don't have any frogs?" The pair exchanged a look and said nothing. They'd been hitting the local fishing holes, including one on the golf course of the Maidstone Club. The club pond was full of five-pound lunker bass, and Brown and Forristal had been catching them all summer, using pet-store mice for bait. The pesticide runoff from the golf course made the fish inedible, but, wanting a trophy, they brought them home and tossed them into Michaels's new pond, where, unbeknownst to him, the fish made short work of any frogs.

If the frogs wouldn't come on their own, Michaels decided, he would order them, as if from a casting agency. He sent away for a truckload from a facility that supplied science labs. Michaels and his two stoned helpers stood on the pond's bank and watched workmen pry open a large plastic tank. With a mighty splash, its wriggling contents were dumped in the water. Instead of an orchestra of tranquil croaking, Michaels got a frantic flurry of wet carnage. "There were pieces of frog flesh flying through the air," Brown recalled. "A feeding frenzy." Forristal and Brown slunk away without a word.

AS SNL'S TWELFTH SEASON GOT UNDERWAY, FRANKEN AND DAVIS AND Downey could have sympathized with the frogs. Tartikoff had given the show a reprieve, under one condition. He'd told Michaels that he would pick up the show for another season only if he went back to doing it the way he had in the first five years, being more fully at the wheel. Hearing this from Michaels, Downey understood it to mean one thing. "The network wanted bodies on the ice rink," he said. He and Franken and Davis felt like the fall guys. Michaels said that he would save their jobs, but that Tartikoff insisted that he be more hands-on.

The so-called "hands-off" season, many felt, had created a template that allowed Michaels to blame others when things went wrong. That was the year that *Three Amigos* bombed at the box office; people at the show exchanged looks when Michaels, who co-wrote and co-produced the film, said, "Well, it's not a movie *I* would have made."

Around this time a bit took root in the writers' offices. Someone would say, "This is Lorne sleeping" and close his eyes. Then he'd pantomime waking with a start, and muttering, "It's not my fault!"

Franken and Davis and Downey came back with a new attitude. "There wasn't quite as much awe of Lorne," Downey said; they didn't entirely trust his taste and pushed back on hiring cast members just because someone he knew said they were sexy. Michaels got sniffy with them, saying, "Apparently I don't run the show anymore."

Besides Jon Lovitz, Nora Dunn and Dennis Miller had been saved from the fire. (The first two had popular recurring characters—Lovitz: the Pathological Liar, the Master Thespian; Dunn: Pat Stevens, Ashley Ashley; and Miller was the Update anchor.) They signed thirty-eight-year-old Phil Hartman, from the Groundlings and *Pee-wee's Playhouse*; Victoria Jackson; and Jan Hooks. Michaels wanted somebody tall (the Chevy slot), so Carvey suggested Kevin Nealon, who had been the bartender at the Improv, and who was also dating Hooks. Michaels also added to the mix Buster Poindexter, the blues-singer alter ego of David Johansen, the former New York Dolls frontman; he'd do fun novelty numbers with the band. "We were an assortment pack," Carvey said of the cast. "Lorne's always looking for chemistry—a group that would all fit together, like the Beatles."

On the premiere of Season Twelve, Madonna came back for the cold open. "NBC has asked me to read the following statement concerning last year's entire season," she announced. " 'It was all a dream, a horrible, horrible dream.' " It was a reference to *Dallas*, which had used the ploy in order to bring back a character who had been killed off. Hopes high, an extra-splashy premiere party was held at Gotham Bar and Grill down in the Village. But no one was sure how it would go. Carvey recalled, "I thought my legacy would be that I was in the last cast."

Now that Michaels was a generation older than his cast, his father-figure status veered more prominently in a Henry Higgins direction. He advised them on how to live. He told them to pony up for a nicer apartment than they thought they could afford; "then you come home and think, 'Someone important lives here.' " (He also told them, "You know what's better than ten-foot ceilings? Twelve-foot ceilings.") The eight members of that cast would remain on the show together for four years, a kind of continuity that Michaels hadn't had before. The ratings weren't great, but the fact that not too many people were watching, Nealon said, "freed us up a bit."

Most of the writers had been kept on. Smigel didn't know that he'd been rehired until a few days before production started on the new season—a lapse that became standard procedure, making for a lot of fun-free summers for performers and writers alike. For the writing staff, Michaels brought in Bonnie and Terry Turner, a married couple from Atlanta who had been writing for Jan Hooks. They were uncharacteristically adult in that group, and their office contained a cozy rocking chair, which Bonnie had used to nurse their daughter. Rosie Shuster was back, helping with Carvey's Church Lady sketches. A year later, Downey brought on Smigel's friend Bob Odenkirk, from Chicago, and a youngster right out of *The Harvard Lampoon* who came equipped with a comedy name, Conan O'Brien. O'Brien had a *Lampoon* partner, Greg Daniels, and together with Odenkirk and Smigel, the four were christened "the nerds." (Tom Hanks, by then a regular host, called them "the boiler room boys.") Smigel said, "When I met Conan I was like, 'Wow, Preppie Preppington.' But he turned out to be a complete freak and a goofball."

Many of the new cast brought characters to the show—Carvey's brittle but randy Church Lady; Carvey and Nealon as the dim-bulb bodybuilders Hans and Franz; and Dunn and Hooks as the treacly big-haired Sweeney Sisters, who played such rooms as the Baycrest Jewish Retirement Home, belting "Bang, bang, bang went the trolley!" Unlike the previous year's actors, many of them wrote as well as performed. When Victoria Jackson complained to Michaels that she wasn't written into enough sketches, he passed on Gilda Radner's technique: "Well, do you bring the writers food?"

As in the first five years, competition for airtime was fierce, and the women often felt sidelined. Dunn came up with a shorthand for the Monday writers' meeting. "I used to call that meeting 'It's about a guy who . . .'" she said. "Because they never came up with any ideas for the women." Jackson could feel thwarted by Hooks and Dunn, who seemed to get a lot of her sketches on, and who liked to hint that she had an especially close relationship with Michaels. Despite the hands-on directive from Tartikoff, Michaels didn't bother himself with this level of diplomacy and left it to Downey, who called a meeting for the staff to discuss the mounting tension and clear the air. "Victoria just came to pieces," Bonnie Turner recalled. She stood on a sofa, pointed at Hooks and Dunn, and said, "You're a bitch. And you're the devil." (Jackson, a devout Christian, always stood somewhat apart in the group; one Christmas she gave Michaels and her fellow cast members the audiobook of Charlton Heston reading the New Testament.)

Nealon compared the atmosphere to *Lord of the Flies*. "Everybody's kind of figuring out who to work with. Trying to not get fired. Trying to come up with a catchphrase," he said. He described Michaels's approach this way: "Let the stew cook itself. I'll stir it a little bit, but that's all." Hooks used to call the show "a star-making machine" that "aged you in dog years."

Michaels kept the new hires on tenterhooks. Conan O'Brien remembers being thrown, and later amused, by Michaels walking by in the hallway and idly asking, "Still with the show?" ("It's a barb that has a hint of brown sugar in it," O'Brien said.) McCulloch once went into Michaels's office to tell him about an Update bit he'd written with Smigel. The cheerless response: "So it takes two men to write a joke now?"

Michaels knew that he pushed people hard and that his sink-or-swim approach was tough on the new hires. "The only thing that justified that level of abuse is the exhilaration of it working," he once said. (Alec Baldwin, who would make his first appearance as host a couple of years later, sized up Michaels's management approach as "Darwinian." "Lorne just stands back and lets them cannibalize each other," he said.) But even veteran writers sometimes felt that Michaels was messing with them. Downey wrote an ancient Rome sketch for Bill Murray when he hosted; he played an over-the-hill Hercules struggling to lift a boulder. The sketch was framed as a sword-and-sandals parody, "Il Returno de Hercules," dubbed into En-glish with sloppily aligned voiceovers. After rehearsal, Michaels sug-gested losing the overdubbing; it wasn't fair, he said, to take away an actor's voice. Downey argued and argued: the bad dubbing *was* the joke. On Saturday night the dubbing remained, with hilariously stilted voiceovers done live by Downey, Tom Davis, and Jan Hooks. Eddie Murphy, a movie star by then, called in to say that it was the best sketch he'd ever seen on the show. In a meeting the next week, Michaels said, apparently serious, "Jim, aren't you glad you listened to me about adding the dubbed voices?"

A few years later, Chris Farley, a new cast member, went to Bob Odenkirk with tears in his eyes. He said that every time he messed up, Michaels told him he hit it out of the park. And every time he killed, Michaels chastised him for not making enough of an effort. "He was mindfucked," Odenkirk said. "Lorne clearly felt that if you kept people off-balance they'd try harder." Michaels would regularly call Farley in to lecture him about his drinking and drug use; Farley would be thrilled just to be one-on-one with the boss in his office.

By this time, trying to figure out what made Michaels tick, most of the new recruits pored over Hill and Weingrad's 1986 book, *A Backstage History of Saturday Night Live.* (Michaels said that although he's only glanced at an excerpt of the book, his reaction to it, as to most things he reads about the show, was "Well, that didn't happen.")

Looking for survival tips, they read about the father figure dy-namic, and about how Michaels fostered competition. They knew that he was stingy with compliments, and that even if you killed as the lead in a big sketch, at the next Monday's meeting he was more likely to single out a small supporting performance, as in: "Nora, your exit as the meter maid was breathtaking."

"I shouldn't need a father figure, because I have a dad," O'Brien said. "But a lot of us, we all make Lorne the mentor that we want to impress. It's like we've all been imprinted with a chip." Freud-readers on staff talked about how he enacted a classic transference: he be-came a father figure to his underlings, then withheld his love, re-creating in them the loss that he experienced as a boy.

New recruits didn't know whether the remote management style was a demonstration of ambivalence or technique. Jan Hooks, who gave stellar performances, was going through a hard time dealing with the death of her mother. Michaels adored Hooks and considered her a star. But when Nealon asked Michaels if he might give her a pat on the back, he responded, "I understand what you're saying, but you'll find that it's never enough." He often compares doling out praise to feeding a stray cat. Or, using a different metaphor, he once said, "A baby looks at the mother and thinks 'Why do you only have two breasts, why do you not have three breasts?' It's an insatiable demand, and you see it in performers, and you see it in writers."

Odenkirk described the atmosphere at SNL, as the show tried to regain its footing, as one of "nauseating tension," a "no-fun, we're-already-fucked vibe," not the best recipe for being funny, and not conducive to the kind of creativity that made the early show feel handmade and original. Odenkirk recalled how if you were joking around with the host, "Lorne might wander by, killing the laughter." People were afraid of him. For Odenkirk, walking through the shiny doors of 30 Rockefeller Plaza didn't provide uplift; it was a trudge through "the lobby with its nightmare murals featuring gods working menial jobs. Poor saps."

Failing to get the attention and instruction they craved from Michaels, the writers looked to Jim Downey, who set the bar high; he always liked to evaluate sketches according to "degree of difficulty." He'd cite the old line about country music—that it was made up of "three chords and the truth," and say that a good sketch needed five or six jokes around an interesting and original idea. He taught generations of sketch writers that, among other things, there are three essentials—a character to root for, an arc, and a payoff—but he specialized in pieces in which a character painstakingly explains something that is crushingly obvious. He called this technique "deliberately wasting the audience's time." A prime example is "Change Bank," a room-temperature piece in which Downey plays a bank employee, earnestly explaining the First Citiwide Change Bank's mission. "We will work with the customer to give that customer the change that he or she needs. If you come to us with a twenty-dollar bill, we can give you two tens, we can give you four fives—we can give you a ten and two fives. We will work *with* you."

Having a sketch kill in read-through didn't guarantee its success. The writing staff had a phrase, "Wednesday's hero, Saturday's goat," for pieces that lost steam by the time they got into 8H. Writers were frustrated with the culling process. "You'd think that you'd say, 'We're gonna pick the best sketches and then we're gonna shine 'em up as best we can,'" Odenkirk said. But the way the show runs, "the focus is on just getting it to happen, and not on the quality level." Many thought that more rewriting could be done in advance, or during the down week, but neither Downey nor Michaels was inclined to mess with the formula.

The one time writers were guaranteed to hear Michaels's feedback was during dress rehearsal on Saturday nights, when they observed him in laser-focus mode, in his cubby under the bleachers. Even today, during those two hours, he watches what the audience watches, but he sees more: lighting, music cues, wigs, accents, entrances. "If you were to read a year's worth of his notes from dress rehearsal, you'd have a master class in TV production that is unparalleled," Whitney Brown said.

Lots of writers have sat beside him in the dim space, watching their sketches die, only to have him turn and say, with stony sarcasm, "You must be very proud." If he hates what he sees, he might yank off his headphones and toss them on the console. If the host monologue is flat, he'll moan, "Can we get *any* charm out of him?" If a piece is too erudite, he might look at the writer and say, "You know the show is on in all fifty states, right?" Or, with heavier irony: "Alert the Peabody Committee." Sometimes he'll be straightforward, turning to a writer and saying, "Really good." Or: "It's just bad sketch-writing."

Often the notes are related to a production issue: "That dress is dowdy." "The curtains are co-starring in the sketch." "The shot is too wide." He'll often change a sketch's blocking to eliminate a character's entrance, lest it look like the actor is expecting applause. As a Canadian, he can be tetchy about hockey jokes. He hates it when characters speak in unison. ("Chanting is never my thing," he's said.) If a sketch bombs completely, he might show empathy and just sigh, blowing the air out of his cheeks in a way that suggests "Who knows?" Aware of how crucial the reaction of the dress audience is, writers sometimes drafted friends to stand under the mics on the studio floor and laugh hard; others would clap at their own sketches, to get some applause going. Andy Breckman calls this "comedy helper."

Smigel started out being terrified by the triage atmosphere under the bleachers, but he grew to love it. In his second year, he wrote a *Star Trek* sketch in which William Shatner, the host, excoriates a roomful of nerds at a Trekkie convention. "Lorne was excited about it," he recalled. "I'm standing right next to him, and when Shatner says, *'Get a life, people!'* there's a gigantic explosion of laughter. We just looked at each other and smiled. He was enjoying it for the show, and he was enjoying it for me." Nealon had the same feeling when, seconds before he stepped onstage to do his first sketch ever ("Mr. Subliminal"), Michaels put a hand on his shoulder and dryly asked, "Are you sure this is what you want?" Nealon said, "He knew how to make you feel relaxed and be funny at the same time."

"He couldn't always afford to care," McKinney said. "Because he can't get into the agonies of generation after generation of broken little toys who show up to write comedy for him. But he could be very classy."

Will Ferrell thinks that being a writer on the show is ten times harder than being in the cast. Not only do writers have to oversee all aspects of their sketches, but they can't enjoy them while they're being performed, he said, "because you are under the bleachers with Lorne during dress, listening to notes about the furniture." John Mulaney said, "May the cast members go to their graves never knowing the things I heard under the bleachers."

THE INVITATION TO THE SEASON TWELVE FINALE PARTY INCLUDED AN RSVP card, with instructions to check one: *Will attend___ Will not* *attend____ No longer in the business____*. The gallows humor signaled a newfound cockiness. Michaels's anxiety about getting canceled had faded as the show "found itself again," as he put it. The reviews and the ratings had stabilized. Colleagues noticed that he was walking around the office murmuring, only partly in jest, one of his favorite lines: "The show's a hit." (A close second: "We have a new star.")

Carvey was indisputably a star, and a significant factor in saving the show. He had an innate sense of how to connect with the audience. "In the clubs I was trained to kill—like James Bond," he said. He always pushed the design team to put his sketches at home base, rather than in a corner, or the dreaded Shitcan Alley. "At home base you can hear the laughs," he said. "The audience doesn't have to watch on monitors. It's more intimate." He thought like a producer.

Rosie Shuster came up with the idea of making Carvey's Church Lady a talk-show host. Michaels thought that, for emotional verisimilitude, Church Lady should have a name, so they christened her Enid Strict—a near-violation of the no-funny-names policy. He personally selected Church Lady's mannish purple dress; Church Lady was not a drag act. "Lorne's instincts were to make sure it stayed real," Carvey said. The character hit a nerve not just because of her prurient prudery, but because the scandals in the news involving evangelical Christians gave her a bonanza of talk-show guests: Jimmy Swaggart (Hartman) and Jim and Tammy Faye Bakker (Hartman and Hooks). At the end of each episode, she would do her "superior dance," a hip-jerking version of the moonwalk. Carvey and Michaels disagreed only once about the character; Michaels thought that Church Lady getting frisky with the pro football players Joe Montana and Walter Payton was too dirty. ("I try to penetrate any opening I can find," Payton, the running back, explains, as Church Lady wriggles.) Annoyed, Michaels moved the sketch to late in the show. Carvey surprised himself by pushing back. "I can't believe I did this," he recalled, "but I snapped at Lorne and said, 'I'm just trying to *make the show a hit again.*'" The result was that Carvey gave the piece everything he had, and despite its Siberian time slot, it destroyed. "This old sound guy came up afterward and said, 'I never seen the needles peak like that, kid,'" Carvey said.

But Carvey generally appreciated Michaels's input, as when he discouraged him from wearing prosthetic ears for his impersonation of Ross Perot. "There are two competing ideas," Carvey recalled him saying. "You've got to pick your poison. Is he a real character, or is he just big ears?" Without that restraining influence, Carvey said, "the show could turn into *Hee-Haw* in a minute." Carvey bonded with Michaels and Downey over a love of pure silliness—Church Lady getting possessed by Satan and doing a blistering drum solo, Carvey as the pop star George Michael, declaiming on the superpowers of his ass: "Put a wilted flower near my butt—it blooms!"

Jon Lovitz played Michael Dukakis in the 1988 election season, and a line Franken wrote for him in a debate sketch—"I can't believe I'm losing to this guy"—was made funnier by Carvey's epic George H. W. Bush impersonation, which nailed the president's lazy syntax and frathouse way of speaking. Downey and Franken wrote Bush speeches as stripped-down word dumps, like this one about the Berlin Wall: "Before Bush, Wall; with Bush, no Wall." Carvey had the audience howling simply by making the president's chopping hand motion, or saying, *"Na ga da,"* a crazed elision of the Bush phrase "Not gonna do it." Watching Carvey, Michaels would stand under the bleachers and shake his head in admiration. "He's a fucking show pony," he'd say. Carvey got five Emmy nominations and one win.

After an uncertain period of following demographic breadcrumbs, Michaels had begun trusting his gut again. "We were quietly pleased with ourselves," he said. More proof that he was officially back on track: in 1988, he was asked to produce the fortieth anniversary broadcast of the Emmy Awards. He agreed in part because a WGA strike had scotched the TV season, and he wanted to get his people some paid work. He wasn't allowed to mess much with the show's staid formula, but he opened with the Sweeney Sisters singing a batty medley of TV theme songs. They began with "Hey, hey, we're the Monkees!" and segued into the *Magilla Gorilla* theme, then crooned "Who can turn the world on with her smile?" to a delighted Mary

Tyler Moore. It was a skewed love letter to the television generation. One touch was pure SNL: Michaels designated one actor to come up and accept the award anytime a winner wasn't in the house; eight such Emmys were collected by the sitcom star Tony Danza, a human sight gag.

TWENTY-SIX

MENTORS, MENTEES

NBC, LIKE MANY MEDIA COMPANIES, EMPLOYED A CLIPPING SERVICE TO gather news stories related to its business. In the spring of 1986, among the items in the SNL file was a clip from the *Calgary Herald* with the headline "Arms Dealer Faces Charges." The article described the indictment for conspiracy in U.S. federal court of Levy Auto Parts, whose owners were identified as the Levy family of Toronto and the television producer Lorne Michaels. Morris P. Levy—Michaels's uncle Pep—faced a potential five years in prison. Along with a partner, Al Raskin, he'd been charged with attempting to illegally export thirty million dollars' worth of M60 tank engines to Iran, conspiring with a Pakistani citizen named Saeed Zakaria to violate the Arms Export Control Act. After intercepting suspicious cables, Customs officials had detained Zakaria at Dulles Airport, where they found an incriminating file in his briefcase, part of a Reagan-era crackdown called Operation Exodus.

A *Washington Post* article on the case made it sound more like a ham-handed caper than the work of sophisticated criminals. The indictment alleged that at one point Levy berated Zakaria on the phone for being so dumb as to send a telex naming Iran as the interested buyer in the all-cash deal for tank engines; Levy ordered him "never to list Iran as the customer again but that all future correspondence should reflect Pakistan as the buyer." Canadian papers further reported that the Levys were suspended from doing business with the Pentagon after being charged with bribing inspectors from the Canadian Department of National Defence.

United States of America v. Morris P. Levy was scheduled to go to trial on April 10, 1986, the same day that Joe Jackson was rehearsing a number called "Right and Wrong" in Studio 8H. By that time, Michaels had moved to prop up Uncle Pep financially by buying 100,000 shares in the family business, which explained why the papers listed Michaels as an owner.

When I asked Michaels about the indictment, one day in his office, he said that he didn't know what I was talking about. He is used to manifesting the reality that he wants, and he only acknowledged the case when presented with printouts of relevant newspaper stories. He then said that he believed his uncle had been drawn into something that he didn't fully understand, at the hands of a Levy relation who was in the process of selling the company. "Pep was out of it by this point. And they sold engines; they didn't sell guns," he said. In the end, Pep Levy and Al Raskin resigned, Levy Auto Parts paid a fine, and the company was placed in receivership and sold. Around Toronto, the Levy saga was referred to as the Fall of the House of Atreus.

The following year, Michaels came to the aid of another father figure who had gotten knocked off a pedestal. In early 1987, William Shawn was fired by S.I. Newhouse Jr., the owner of Condé Nast publications, which had purchased *The New Yorker*. Michaels immediately called Shawn and offered him the use of his own office in the Brill Building. The publishing house Farrar, Straus and Giroux had given Shawn a job as a consulting editor-at-large, and so, on most weekdays, Shawn would shuffle in to 1619 Broadway (averting his eyes as he passed the marquee of the Ramrod Theatre, touting *Plug That Plumber* and the Stud Room) and settle into the stylish gloom of the ninth floor. He edited a nursery school application that Michaels's executive assistant had to submit for her son, and he and Lillian Ross collaborated on a screenplay called *Info,* a farce about a vulgar billionaire destroying a venerated weekly magazine. (Ross hoped that Michaels might produce.)

The firing shook Michaels. From their talks, he knew that Shawn had anointed and then rejected various heirs, and at nearly eighty, with no one in the wings, he had left himself vulnerable. Michaels had believed for a period that Shawn wanted him to leave SNL and become the successor—the third editor of *The New Yorker.* Michaels talked to several people about the possibility. Although he had no publishing experience, he and Shawn both had romantic ideas about the city, and they shared managerial attributes; they were each elliptical, secretive, and, when it came to tactics, quietly steely. Both were figures of fascination bordering on obsession to their employees. People who knew both men noticed Michaels adopting some of Shawn's mannerisms—his underpowered speaking voice, and the way he folded his hands as a prelude to discussion. Employees whispered about Michaels's highly implausible idea that he would one day be asked to step into Shawn's shoes.

Michaels doesn't deny that the notion was circulating. "The problem with the idea of being the editor of *The New Yorker* was that I have a need for action," he said. He added, "I'm not just a comedy person. I'd like to think I was always funny, but I also didn't think I couldn't be prime minister of Canada or whatever."

Shawn's ouster put an end to the prospect of Michaels's long-awaited *New Yorker* profile. Lillian Ross had resigned in protest, and the following year she turned her years of reporting into a short article about Michaels for *Interview.* But she continued to haunt the show, wearing an SNL lanyard with a permanent all-access pass, and she pitched Michaels the occasional sketch idea, including one about Korean and American car salesmen competing for customers while dressed as hockey players. He liked having her around.

THE BRILL BUILDING OFFICE THAT SHAWN SQUATTED IN WAS OTHERWISE being used by Eric Ellenbogen, a young Harvard grad with an MBA from UCLA, whom Michaels had brought in to help shore up the finances of Broadway Video. Seeing both Uncle Pep and William Shawn brought low, and losing so much money on *The New Show*, had spurred him to ask for business advice from Mo Ostin, another trusted adviser. Ellenbogen had come to him through Ostin, and part of his brief as president of Broadway Video Entertainment was to make sense out of the company's bloated payroll. Assorted children of friends, and English girls who only knew the metric system, milled around the office collecting salaries. As Michaels's success and influence had grown, so had the number of people who benefited from his patronage. He propped up Gary Weis, who had hit some hard times. John Head had stayed on salary, quietly nodding out in his office without a defined purpose other than tinkering on video projects. "By then, John was reduced basically to being people's drug connection," a Broadway Video employee named Jim Biederman said. "But he was still Lorne's main taste guy."

On the roster of mentors whom Michaels kept close, Mike Nichols was the smooth and smart one, Mo Ostin was the menschy one, Brillstein was the shrewd one, and Head was the cool one, almost a Rosebud figure. Joe Forristal said, "Except for lacking a Harvard degree, John was everything Lorne imagined himself to be—a well-connected, tasteful English gentleman." His sense of humor was sweetly acerbic; he had grace and class; he was an expert vacationer. "Lorne seemed like a loudmouth next to John," Forristal said.

Michaels never stopped trying to find projects for John Head. In 1988, Ellenbogen and Michaels, inspired by Herb Schlosser's "time-of-day" shows, created a new music program called *Sunday Night* and put Head in charge. It featured surprising combinations of musicians—Sonny Rollins jamming with Leonard Cohen; or Conway Twitty with the Residents. Hal Willner, a shaggy young genius from Philadelphia who'd been producing incidental music on SNL, helped program it. Taped on a shabby-chic set created by Eugene Lee, it was the anti-MTV. Head was great at picking the musicians, but he butted heads with the show's sponsors.

Like early SNL, *Sunday Night* was radical and smart, but it was too rarefied. Many affiliates didn't pick it up, complaining that the guests were obscure and that the British co-host, Jools Holland, was too sarcastic. Head responded to executives' notes by sulking, and Holland was sent back to London, where he started a copycat BBC show, *Later . . . with Jools Holland,* that is still on the air. NBC retitled the show *Michelob Presents Night Music.*

One day Michaels dropped by a taping because his friend Eric Clapton was on. He looked up at the monitor and saw a ninety-two-year-old woman playing the Kaddish on a theremin. Hal Willner remembered the look on his face: "I could just see cartoon stacks of dollars with little wings flying out of his head," he said. When the show was canceled, after two seasons, Willner said, "Lorne told me that I wouldn't get another opportunity to do anything that cool for at least twenty-five years."

Some of the projects taken on by Broadway Video (and executive produced by Michaels) seemed to exist mainly to disburse money to friends of the family. *Coca-Cola Presents Live: The Hard Rock* was an hour of music and (for some reason) Roman-themed comedy written by Tom Davis and Dan Aykroyd, with John Candy as an overripe emperor, and performances by INXS, Paul Simon, and Aykroyd, trying out his post-Belushi solo act, the Elwood Blues Revue. Broadcast from Spartacus Square, the set on Universal's back lot that had been built for Stanley Kubrick's 1960 epic (and kitted out with truckloads of expensive dirt, per Eugene Lee's design, which then had to be carted away when a sandstorm threatened), the special was a financial setback.

Ellenbogen judged the *Hard Rock* adventure "the *Heaven's Gate* of TV specials," and he hoped to right the fiscal ship. Before Broadway Video, Ellenbogen had worked in independent-film distribution; he had a glossy charisma and a quiet Ivy League confidence that Michaels liked. He also liked that Ellenbogen had experience with intellectual property acquisitions. When NBC kept SNL on the air without Michaels, in 1980, Buck Henry had asked his friend what his cut of the ongoing profits was. The answer was zero. Michaels knew that Paul Simon held his own copyrights, but he himself owned nothing of the show he'd created. Copyrights, Simon told him, are like children; they'll take care of you in your old age, in the form of passive royalty income. Paul McCartney had been buying up catalogs of other musicians, like Frank Loesser and Buddy Holly. John Eastman, McCartney's lawyer brother-in-law, walked Michaels through the details. Michaels liked the idea of owning IP; it was a way of using his taste to make money.

Until then, his network deals had largely been brokered by his lawyer Elliot Hoffman, guided by Brillstein. Ellenbogen, with input from Michaels's other advisers, began a series of negotiations that, over the next ten years, chipped away at various rights held by NBC— SNL home entertainment rights, merchandising rights, distribution rights. First, he created an in-house agency to represent those rights, which NBC had never capitalized on, with the proceeds to be split fifty-fifty between Michaels and the network; Broadway Video also got a distribution fee. The strategy in "clawing back" these rights, as Ellenbogen put it, was to renegotiate during the years when the show was performing best, bringing in the most ad revenue for NBC. "We wound up owning stuff at NBC that no one's ever owned before," Sandy Wernick recalled.

If Michaels was old-school show business, with his focus on talent (and Brillstein was older-school show business, focused, as Bob Odenkirk put it, on lunches and valet parking), Ellenbogen was new-school, part of a movement that Michael Ovitz started at CAA, which saw power shift to dealmakers and away from stars. The contracts with Broadway Video, which had been created in part to edit SNL episodes for syndication, were also retooled in ways to cover more overhead and create more revenue. By the time Ellenbogen was through, Broadway Video had its own international distribution operation that sold SNL episodes to markets around the world.

Ellenbogen also saw a chance to turn Broadway Video into a major entertainment company that could help push the talent Michaels had discovered to the next level. But Michaels was wary. *The New Show* had cured him of feeling infallible. He worried that, if a project didn't succeed, he'd be seen as the source of the failure. Ellenbogen recalled, "I'd say to him, 'Why couldn't we be like Act III, the company that Norman Lear created, or like Jim Brooks's company?' Lorne would say that actors all want to kill their father." If his protégés worked for a production company that he owned, he thought, it would remind them that he'd helped create them. Michaels often says, of the talent he fosters, "They have to believe they did it themselves."

It was an injustice, Ellenbogen felt, that so many of Michaels's protégés went off and did their own thing without him having a piece of it. When Bonnie and Terry Turner created the sitcom *3rd Rock from the Sun,* in 1996, Ellenbogen told Michaels, "Lorne, this should be *your* show." (SNL's writers were more prone to competitive grudges: Tom Davis, Michaels recalled, "always thought that *3rd Rock from the Sun* was Coneheads. And Mike Myers always thought *That '70s Show* was *Wayne's World.*")

Ellenbogen did persuade Michaels to soften his stance against merchandising. For SNL's first years, there had been no Killer Bee beach towels, no Roseanne Roseannadanna lunchboxes. Michaels considered such items crass, selling out. Then Ellenbogen told Michaels about a radio ad in which Mick Jagger himself hawked Rolling Stones jean jackets. Creating a licensing business around SNL, he explained, was an easy way to build wealth. Some in the company were snooty about what they saw as Ellenbogen's mercenary streak, but Michaels gave him enormous freedom to pursue business opportunities. Nowadays, the show's studio audience exits through the NBC store in the 30 Rock concourse, stocked with SNL socks, baby onesies, and Christmas ornaments.

Jim Biederman, who worked his way up at Broadway Video, has a theory that Michaels's career has a lot in common with Andy Warhol's. "Both were outsiders who got inside and changed everything," he said. "Yet they never stopped worrying that they weren't really inside." Ellenbogen was like Paul Morrissey, who arrived at Warhol's Factory and professionalized it, getting rid of the partiers and wastrels, and helping to transform the place into a profit center that churned out what Warhol called "business art," including portraits commissioned by socialites.

Ellenbogen started shopping for intellectual property that would throw off royalty income for Michaels. "Lorne loved that," he said. "It didn't involve any of his relationships or any of the talent. It was as if we'd gone into the real estate business." Best of all, Brillstein couldn't commission any of it. Among the unlikely assets that Ellenbogen bought were the back catalogs of *Lassie, The Lone Ranger, Felix the Cat,* and the pre-1974 library of Rankin/Bass, the company behind a slew of "Animagic" stop-motion animation Christmas specials, including *Rudolph the Red-Nosed Reindeer.* These kiddie properties provoked a lot of tittering around Broadway Video, but they appealed to Michaels's "television generation" mindset, and there was something auspicious about the fact that Johnny Marks had written *Rudolph* in the Brill Building. Under Ellenbogen, Broadway Video distributed these shows domestically and internationally, syndicated them, merchandised them, and even produced sequels.

Ellenbogen had brought in outside private equity and arranged lines of credit from banks to finance some of the library acquisitions. He had also negotiated equity for himself. Every time a big deal closed, Michaels gave him an eye-popping gift, like a silk Sulka bathrobe. "I learned everything from Lorne about how to reward talent," he said. "And when these deals happened, he treated me like talent."

The shopping project overseen by Ellenbogen ultimately paid off big. In 1996, he sold the whole of Broadway Video's family-video library to Golden Books for $91 million. Golden Books envisioned a multimedia empire in which Rudolph and Frosty and Lassie would join the publisher's topliners, like the Saggy Baggy Elephant and the Poky Little Puppy, in big-ticket Hollywood deals. Michaels was well-compensated by NBC, especially with his retooled contracts, but the Golden Books sale represented a colossal windfall.

TWENTY-SEVEN

HEAD-CRUSHING

AS MICHAELS WAS FENDING OFF COMPARISONS TO THE MYTHICAL GOLDEN years of SNL, he stumbled on a way to recapture some of the old experimental energy. It had nothing to do with 8H, or with the dreamy, druggy nights around the pool in Joshua Tree. The source of renewal was in Toronto. After the horrible comeback year, he'd sent the writers Mark McKinney and Bruce McCulloch back to Canada, where they happily rejoined their comedy troupe, the Kids in the Hall. Michaels had never seen the group perform, and when he saw them at the Rivoli, on a trip back home in 1986, he was impressed. Afterward, he told them that they were "of a piece"—another koan. Their nervy outsider spirit was the first new voice he'd heard since the birth of SNL. "They were very much their own thing," he said. (Michaels was likely the only one in the audience who recognized the group's name as a Jack Benny reference; when Benny used a joke tossed to him by one of the acolytes who waited outside his radio studio, he'd tell his listeners, "That one's from the kids in the hall, folks.")

The Kids had a way of playing women that felt naturalistic, nothing like a drag show. Michaels liked McCulloch as "Cabbage Head," a churlish mutant who rationalizes his behavior by saying, "I had a *baaaad* childhood"; a frontiersman balladeer bit called "Running Faggot," an ahead-of-its-time sketch that used homophobic language to laugh at homophobia; and McKinney as "Chicken Lady," the horny menopausal offspring of a farmer and his fowl. Compared to the observational comedy of Jerry Seinfeld, the Kids in the Hall embodied a kind of alt-philosophical program. Kurt Cobain was a fan.

Michaels signed the troupe to a contract with Broadway Video and paid to set them up in New York for a few months of seasoning. They'd perform in clubs and work up a TV pilot. He wanted to acclimatize them to "professional show business." "That was done with inside knowledge as a Canadian," McKinney said. "It kicked the Canadian out of us."

The troupe knew the hometown lore about its new patron, including the father-figure stuff. That chimed with them; Kevin McDonald, the curly-headed troupe member, felt that the Kids were on a group quest for authority figures. "Our fathers were violent or drunks or both," Scott Thompson, the one gay member of the troupe, said. "If you wanted to work with the Kids, you had to play the Daddy card. Very primitive."

Michaels cut a deal with the CBC and HBO for a pilot special of the Kids in the Hall's sketches. The Kids would come to his office for marching orders; he'd give them each a cash allowance in an envelope, like a dad. When they signed the pilot deal, he advised them that this was the last time in their lives that $100,000 would seem like a large sum. He told them never to be photographed mugging or doing anything "funny." McDonald, trying to lose some weight before the filming, went on a crash diet that limited his food intake to one deli muffin a day. He quickly dropped sixty pounds, and loose skin hung from him in folds. "Lorne was freaked out because Kevin looked like a basset hound," said Joe Forristal, whom Michaels had assigned to shepherd the troupe.

Forristal found New York apartments for the Kids and booked them into clubs—a comedy boot camp for them and for him. "Lorne wanted me to know how the money works," he said. "Understanding who you get it from, where it goes, how to do the budgets and salaries, getting loans. That's what Uncle Pep had taught him." Eventually, the Kids-minding duties were shared by two other young Broadway Video employees, Jim Biederman and Jeff Ross. Biederman remembers Michaels telling him, "Here's your shot. Don't fuck it up."

The Kids felt that he thought of them as his art project, more fulfilling than dealing with the suits at NBC. "SNL was the thing that brought fame and money," Thompson said. "We were something he fiddled around with in the garage."

The Kids struggled to decode his notes and to get him on board with their weirder notions. Michaels initially hated one of McKinney's signature characters, a man who peers through the space created by pinching his thumb and forefinger together and says, in a low screech, "I'm crushing your head!" "At the first read-through, Lorne went, 'Really? This is going to be a funny-voice thing?'" McKinney recalled. Later, when Michaels grasped that the camera angle would show the fingers "crushing" the tiny head of a person in the distance, he couldn't get enough of it.

Michaels flew to Toronto for the taping of the Kids pilot, and that afternoon he personally re-blocked all the sketches and camera shots. Brillstein told the troupe that he hadn't seen him work that hard in years. In contrast to their barebones stage act, he wanted hard-wall reality, like at SNL. He'd imported Eugene Lee, his exacting New York set designer, who, faced with indolent CBC crew members, ended up throwing a sink at one. The Kids picked up on the stagehands' hometown hostility toward Michaels—typical Canadian resentment of a countryman who became famous south of the border. The runaway lobster had become an American citizen on April Fool's Day of 1987.

He insisted that the pilot be taped on the SNL model, with a dress rehearsal followed by an "air" show. In the break between the two, he gave the Kids a set of harsh notes, delivered with piercing sarcasm: "I take this to mean that you're not interested in having a TV show." Dave Foley, the twinkliest troupe member, recalled, "He kicked our asses. He said we were terrible." "It was right out of a sports movie," Thompson said. "Like, 'After everything I've given you, you let me down.'" McCulloch was ordered to put on some eye makeup. "Audiences don't like people with such small eyes," he remembers Michaels telling him.

After the talking-to, McDonald, Thompson, and Foley locked themselves in a dressing room and trashed it. Crew members heard chairs being smashed, but Michaels told them not to intervene. He let the Kids have their Belushi moment. Then they came out and did a terrific show. "Lorne was such a proud daddy," Thompson said. "He knew what we needed." The pilot aired on HBO in October 1988 and *The New York Times* called it "some of the freshest and most disarming material the comedy scene has been able to claim in a long while." Michaels was briefly transported back to 1975. He felt relevant again.

By contrast, the same month, back at the SNL offices, Michaels was dealing with corporate blowback over a ridiculous baiting-the-censor sketch titled "Nude Beach," known around the office as "The Penis Sketch." Smigel had the idea for the piece, about a bunch of naked guys comparing notes on each other's penises, which are tastefully obscured by a tiki bar. The word "penis" is spoken sixty times.

JACK: Hey, pretty small penis there, Doug.

DOUG: Huh?

TED: Yeah. You could pick a lock with that penis.

The sketch culminates with a bouncy sea chantey called "The Penis Song":

CARVEY: I once had a penis sing to me his Penis Penis song! And when that Penis Penis sang, here was the Penis's song. He'd sing me . . .

ALL: Penis, penis, penis, penis! Penis, penis song. Penis, penis, penis, penis! Penis all day long! Penis, penis, penis, penis . . .

After the penis sketch, the Reverend Donald Wildmon, of the American Family Association, orchestrated a letter-writing campaign that flooded NBC with 46,000 complaints and resulted in Domino's

Pizza, Ralston Purina, and General Mills pulling their ads from the show—a headache for Michaels, but one he shrugged off.

The Kids in the Hall skirted that kind of drama, protected by their insiderish obscurity and the freedom afforded by cable. (One of HBO's few notes: "Hitler can fuck the donkey, but the donkey has to be alive.") Michaels had Joe Forristal relocate to Toronto for the series, which was taped in the same CBC studio that had been home to the Hart and Lorne show. "I based everything I did on shit Lorne taught me," Forristal said. "Lorne told me that it's much better that they hate *you* than each other. If you pick the material, you're the bad guy. It's healthier that way."

HBO canceled the Kids' show after one season, despite its fervent following. Then McKinney was nominated for a CableACE Award in a Best Actor category and won, beating Garry Shandling (*It's Garry Shandling's Show*). He forgot to thank Michaels in his acceptance speech ("You might want to find a phone," Brad Grey urgently told McKinney as he came offstage). After the win, Michaels made some calls, and HBO restored *The Kids in the Hall* to the schedule; it ran for five years.

At the end of the second season, to reward the Kids for their hard work, Michaels took them out for a boozy dinner at Orso and announced that he was going to buy each one of them a car. This was a jump from the previous gift—five sterling silver bowls—and, at dinner, they all elaborately thanked him. But four out of five of the Kids wanted cash instead of a car and discreetly arranged with Joe Forristal to get a disbursement of $20,000 each instead. McCulloch used his money to buy a painting of a fish; Foley wanted to keep the car out of politeness and argued about it with his wife, who ultimately convinced him to use the twenty grand as a down payment on a house. ("That house is worth four million now," Foley, who is divorced, said. "And I'm not allowed on the property.") "We were such assholes," Thompson said. "We sold the cars and didn't want Lorne to know." The only one who took the actual car was Kevin McDonald, who doesn't drive.

———

ONE OF THE KIDS' BIGGEST FANS WAS MIKE MYERS. WHEN HE WATCHED their pilot on the CBC as a young comic in Canada, he reacted just like Steve Martin did after seeing SNL in 1975: "You did it!" he said to the TV screen. "You did what everyone wants to do." Myers was such a comedy geek that when he was in the eighth grade he did a school project about Lorne Michaels. He'd grown up watching *The Hart and Lorne Terrific Hour,* and the Puck Crisis film had made him proud to be Canadian. "It made me feel like I was from somewhere," he said. He tried to copy what he called Michaels's "fantastic low gear as a comedian," and at the age of eleven he got a role in a commercial as Gilda Radner's son. Then he saw her on SNL and announced to his family that one day, he'd be on that show.

By 1988, he was part of Toronto's Second City troupe, where he regularly did a bit about a loser teen named Wayne with a van. Pam Thomas, Martin Short, and Dave Foley all saw it and called Michaels, telling him he had to get this guy. A tape was sent to Michaels, and he summoned Myers to New York.

"Is that the Empire State Building behind your head?" Myers said, sitting across the desk from Michaels in his office. "Last time I looked" was the drawled reply. There had been an awkward phone call (Myers babbled about the school project) and eight hours waiting, and here he was, trying not to stare at the cards on the bulletin board. After a while, Michaels asked, "Is this something you'd like to do?"

Despite yelping "Yes, please!" Myers left baffled. There had been no audition. He returned home and fretted through Christmas before hearing that he'd been hired as a writer and featured player in the middle of Season Fourteen. He found a sublet; the rent shocked him. "Everybody told me, if you're super, super broke, Lorne will lend you money," he said. By May, out of funds, he got a $5,000 advance on future earnings. That fall, he went to cash the season's first paycheck and the bank teller laughed in his face when he presented a check for zero dollars. It would be weeks before he worked off the loan and his paycheck contained any actual money.

Myers was twenty-five. Michaels, energized by the Kids' success, wanted youth again. Soon after Myers arrived, Michaels hired Ben Stiller, who lasted only six episodes. (Carvey said, "We had a murderers' row of people who were going to dominate for a long time. Ben realized, this is gonna be a long wait.") Jon Lovitz left after five strong seasons, and so did Nora Dunn, who exited after an embarrassing public squabble over Michaels's decision to have the comedian Andrew Dice Clay host the show. Dunn had issued a statement to the Associated Press announcing that she would not share the stage with Clay, whose stand-up persona was a misogynist Flatbush lout in studded leather. Clay, she told the *Times,* says "that a man has a right to have sex with his daughter because he pays her tuition, and Lorne is going to make him look like he's the Fonz." Things got so heated that Michaels went on *Nightline* to defend himself. When a moderator compared Andrew Dice Clay to Hitler, Michaels, exasperated, said, "Whoa, just a minute. How did we just jump to the Holocaust?" Although he always appreciated outspoken women, he was more annoyed about Dunn's preemptive press maneuver than about her walkout. "It would have been nice if she'd called me," he said. The other women on the staff felt that Dunn had unfairly positioned them as collaborators. "You don't go outside the family," Terry Turner said. Dunn said that the reason she didn't give Michaels a heads-up before going to the press was that she simply couldn't reach him. "He was never accessible," she said.

Clay regarded his "Diceman" persona as character comedy in the tradition of Andy Kaufman's alter ego Tony Clifton, a performative scumbag designed to make audiences uncomfortable. Michaels argued that, in the context of SNL—a thoroughly written show—Clay would be harmless, "the comedy equivalent of heavy metal" and "a phenomenon worth examining." Dunn countered that the show's brief wasn't to examine the host, but to make the host look good. The Clay show introduced a debate that would come up in 2015, when Donald Trump hosted: Is having an apparent cretin on the show a de facto endorsement?

On the night of the Clay show, metal detectors were set up to screen guests, and security removed chanting protesters from the studio: "Racist, sexist, anti-gay. *Clay*, go away!" Michaels managed to own the controversy by transforming it into material. On air, Jan Hooks and Kevin Nealon delivered their own fake "protest speeches." In hers, Hooks sorrowfully admitted that she "didn't have the guts" to boycott the Clay show but had decided "to protest tonight in a different way, by giving a lackluster performance." Looking off-camera, she yelled, in pretend defiance, "Do you hear me, Lorne?"

MICHAELS HAD FIGURED OUT THAT HE NEEDED TO KEEP THE SHOW YOUTHful, but there was a distinctly adult feel to the fifteenth anniversary special that he mounted in September 1989—a blowout packed with celebrities and statesmen in black tie. (Jane Curtin hated it: "All of us onstage were basically there to acknowledge all the famous people in the audience.") The RCA Building had recently been rechristened the GE Building, the $6 billion merger of the two companies a boom-time signifier. Michaels, feeling surefooted, told the *Times,* "For the first time, we're not afraid to look back at the first five years." But there was a somber note: just before the anniversary, Gilda Radner had died of ovarian cancer, making the show's early days feel even more remote. Michaels's hair had gone gray. He nodded to the passing years by showing forty-five-year-old Chase signing legal liability forms before taking his signature fall in the anniversary show's cold open.

At the time of the anniversary, every one of the top-ten-grossing movie comedies of all time starred SNL alums. Michaels had learned by then to avoid letting a single cast member's departure upset the show's equilibrium; as the success of the Kids in the Hall proved, he needed to continually replenish the ranks. In the 1990–91 season he brought on seven new cast members. Tim Meadows and Chris Farley were from Second City, Julia Sweeney from the Groundlings. The other four, Adam Sandler, Rob Schneider, David Spade, and Chris Rock, were brash young stand-ups. Sam Kinison had brought Rock by, on the night when Kinison did his routine about Jesus's last words ("Ow! Ow! Ow!"). Michaels held another pre-season retreat at

Mohonk, where the new staffers could bond with the older ones while hiking the Shawangunk Ridge or engaging in rocking-chair races on the veranda. At Mohonk, Farley, who was desperately eager to please, sidled up to Downey by the campfire and whispered, "Jim? Do you think it would help the show if I got even fatter?"

Always attuned to the hinges between eras, Michaels opened the first show of 1990 addressing the audience as himself, the Producer. "We plan to keep right in step with this fantastic new decade," he announced, "and all the changes it is bringing." He listed a few: Cast members would be issued jetpacks to move between stages and would gradually be replaced by automatons. And if you missed a show, you could simply pop a *Saturday Night Live* rerun pill. Michaels swallowed one and said, "Mmmmm. Tony Danza."

Danza was an eighties joke. The new cast members were a distinctly nineties group—laddish, with more silliness and snideness between them than the Nealon-Carvey-Hartman cohort. And Farley was a hard partier who modeled himself on Belushi. The Generation X influx pushed the show forward, away from the Baby Boomer generation and toward a younger sensibility that celebrated sarcastic man-boys. Michaels saw that the transition wouldn't be seamless.

Bob Odenkirk, for one, couldn't figure out where he fit in, generation-wise. When he was hired as a writer in the late eighties, at twenty-five, he said, "classic rock had just hit radio, and I remember thinking, 'That defines our situation right now. My generation doesn't have a voice.'" SNL was straitjacketed, he thought, by playing to fifty-year-olds. "I thought, fuck this guy for being in charge. Why does he get to sit there and judge what's funny?" he said. "Shouldn't SNL be for each generation?" (In hindsight, Odenkirk said, "I was a dick. How did they tolerate me?")

Adam Sandler struggled to figure out how to work in the ensemble. Michaels at first viewed him as a leading man type and tried to put him in sport jackets rather than sweatshirts when he did Update features. He had pacing issues. "I peaked at dress because I thought that no one was gonna see it except that audience," he said. "But then, when it made it on the show, and I knew that all my family and friends were watching, I'd come out of my body and go at it too hard." In the dress rehearsal for a sketch in which a young wife (Kirstie Alley) is groped and kissed by exuberantly amorous workers at an Italian restaurant, Sandler had the audience screaming as the waiter who comes out in black bikini underpants and frantically rubs his face around in her cleavage. Just before the air show, Michaels had some words of caution. "I know you like to do a little *worse* on air," he told Sandler. "So let's not do that this time." Michaels also warned Sandler about becoming too one-note—just a clueless overgrown kid who talks in weird voices. "Don't just become *that guy,*" Sandler recalls him saying.

Chris Rock kept a strategic distance from Michaels and the tutelage he had to offer. "I was of the mind 'I got the best thing I can get from this guy. I got on SNL,'" he said. "I thought, 'All I can do is fuck this up.' My talent as a kid was the ability to blend in around powerful people. I had a really good quiet game, sucking in knowledge." Rock had mopped floors before getting SNL; he was impatient with the people who moped if their sketches got cut. "I learned everything I know from that show. You got to shoot your shot that week," he said. "Killing onstage isn't subjective. When people talk about fair and unfair, I'm like, shut up. It's like, get bigger laughs."

EMERSON DEFINED AN INSTITUTION AS "THE LENGTHENED SHADOW OF ONE man," and Michaels, by 1990, felt confident that he cast a long shadow. The show won a Peabody Award that year (its subliterate citation read: "For fifteen years *Saturday Night Live* has provided millions of persons with a fun-filled late Saturday night. The humor, often incisive, coupled with the other entertainment factors has made *Saturday Night Live* truly a national institution.")

With business going smoothly, Michaels had turned his attention to his personal life and the project of starting a real family. After splitting from Forristal in the mid-eighties, he had lived a bachelor life for a while. He dated a friend of one of his assistants, and at one point he lived with Miranda Guinness, a British heiress who'd worked for

Mick Jagger. His eligibility became joke fodder in an SNL episode with Rosanna Arquette; in the cold open, she fends off a potential "neck with the producer" sketch. Bachelorhood seemed to suit Michaels; colleagues always felt that, really, he was married to the show. The producer Julia Phillips, in her prickly 1991 Hollywood memoir, *You'll Never Eat Lunch in This Town Again,* wrote of chatting with Michaels at the Polo Lounge about his search for the perfect woman. His ideal mate, she recalled him saying, was someone in her mid-twenties, whom he could mold. Phillips's response: What happens "once they were molded"?

One night in the mid-nineties, at the after-show party, Michaels was sitting with a newish cast member named Jay Mohr, and offered some unsolicited romantic advice. Mohr wrote a book about his short, troubled SNL tenure, *Gasping for Airtime.* In the book, he relates Michaels telling him that every man should have three wives: "One in his twenties, one in his thirties and forties, and one in his fifties, when he knows what he really wants." It's what Michaels had done. In 1991, he'd married Alice Barry, one of his former assistants.

Michaels had met Barry, a bright, fresh-faced young woman with a sleek preppy tilt, when she was an assistant at Broadway Video. Soon she was transferred to Michaels's desk, and after she accompanied him on several work trips to the West Coast, they became a couple. (With the long hours and the hermetic atmosphere, people pairing off at SNL had continued to be nothing unusual.) He was protective of their privacy and got angry when he learned that there was whispering in the writers' room about the boss-assistant relationship and their eighteen-year age gap. They got engaged within a matter of months and planned a small wedding in Paris. With producer-ish dispatch, Michaels called his friend Pamela Harriman, soon to be the U.S. ambassador to France, to ask for help in sidestepping the complicated Parisian marital bureaucracy. With a few friends as witnesses, they were married in the city hall in the Place Saint-Sulpice, across from the famously beautiful church where Victor Hugo was married and the Marquis de Sade baptized. Keith McNally's two chil-

dren acted as ring bearer and flower girl. Back home, the couple celebrated with a party in Amagansett.

Michaels didn't like his private life gossiped about, but he had no
difficulty tolerating more general ridicule. He enjoyed playing his
Lorne character—what Carvey calls "the kinda Jack Benny Lorne
thing, above-it-all and unflappable." He teased underlings who rode
in "those yellow limousines" or joked about riding "that train I've
heard about that runs under the ground."

One of the most celebrated cold opens in the show's history mined
this emerging mandarin profile—Lorne, the effete fat cat. Robert
Smigel (with Christine Zander and Franken and Davis) wrote the
piece, which was in a 1991 episode hosted by Steve Martin. It begins
with Martin slumped in his dressing room, jaded and world-weary, as
young Chris Farley comes in and eagerly asks him to sign the old King
Tut costume that Martin wore in the seventies. Jolted out of his
ennui, Martin breaks into song, dancing through the hallways and
into 8H as if in a scene from *The Music Man:*

> *Not gonna phone it in tonight!*
> *Not gonna go through the motions tonight!*
> *This time I'm really gonna do the best I can!*

Backstage, the usual costumed extras that telegraph "showbiz" are
loitering—Santa Claus, a big-headed alien, Elvis. Another stock character is there, too: Lorne. As Martin belts "For some reason, tonight I
care!" he comes upon Michaels in his command post under the
bleachers, getting a manicure while an artist paints his portrait.

"Steve, what's going on?" Lorne drawls. "The show's on automatic
pilot. I don't even come in until Saturday."

Martin sings, "Lorne, don't you see? That's not the way it was in
the seventies! Back in the seventies, people cared. They believed in
something!"

A flicker of recognition registers in Michaels's eyes; he stands,
turns to camera, and, in a voice dubbed by an operatic baritone, bel-
lows, "Then go, Steve, go-o-o. And do a great *sho-o-o-o-o-o-owwww!!*"

Lorne, the self-satisfied pasha, is as much a character on the show as Church Lady. The character is funny and feels real because it draws on aspects of who Michaels really is—the boss who languidly answers the door in a robe while his bath is being drawn, the mogul who maintains a poise that teeters on the edge of prissiness. Ten years after the "Not gonna phone it in" opening, the real Michaels sat for a portrait by his Hamptons neighbor Eric Fischl, the celebrated painter of the creative-capitalist set whose previous subjects included Mike Nichols and Steve Martin. Michaels has never tried to conceal his appetite for the things that money can buy. People, he has said, like to imagine that "I'm on my way into a hot tub with seventy-two virgins or whatever. Fine. I'd much rather my life be perceived as glamorous or stylish than as one of an enormous amount of work that is unceasing."

For non-performing or -writing roles, he always sought out sophisticated, connected types—children of stars and bigwigs. In 1989, he hired Calvin Klein's daughter, Marci (whose de facto godfather is David Geffen), for the talent department. As Mark McKinney put it, "Lorne had the genius of putting the one person who can't be impressed by anyone in charge of talent." That approach could backfire. One assistant, the granddaughter of a governor, would balk when Michaels told her to place a call while riding in a limo with him. "You're right by the phone," she'd tell him.

Known around the show as Lornettes, the assistants were a formidable battalion, adept at slipping in and out of the boss's office and giving the staff sotto voce reports on his mood. Usually there was one at Broadway Video, one in L.A., one at home, and a couple in the SNL office. On Saturday nights several were in the lobby, shepherding VIP guests (a practice that continues). Marci Klein, in talent, made sure the assistants looked correctly cosmopolitan. Once, a new assistant from the South showed up in a pink skirt and flowered blouse; Klein soon had her in head-to-toe black.

The Lornettes were the inspiration for one of David Spade's recurring characters, the snooty male receptionist at Dick Clark Productions: when big stars came in for a meeting, he would ask, "And you

are . . . ?" "This is in regard to . . . ?" Some felt that Michaels's assistants and special pets kept tabs on people. (Colleagues recall Klein
saying, "I'm telling Lorne!") Chevy Chase offered a Freudian analysis:
"Every woman around him is his mom in some fashion," he said. "So
many of them are pushy or fierce, but with a pleasant side for dealing
with Lorne." Another colleague views Michaels's tumultuous adolescence as "part of the reason he became such a controlled and controlling person, and why he thinks he needs to have three secretaries."
The Lornettes learned to intercept prank calls to Michaels from
Sandler and Farley, who did a flawless Brandon Tartikoff impression.
One remembered being reduced to tears after botching an assignment and having Michaels tell her, while riding in a limo, "I teach by
humiliation. But after you leave me, you'll be able to work anywhere."
The job often led to a producing career, particularly as the outside
shows Michaels produced multiplied. He seeded his empire with
loyal retainers.

The writers chafed at the outsize influence these young women
had. "It did bother me how many of Lorne's assistants were in there,
piping up about their favorite comedy sketches," Bob Odenkirk wrote
in his memoir. The assistants spent more time with Michaels than
anyone; they often ate three meals a day at their desks, although popping out for a therapy appointment was encouraged.

For Michaels, hiring relatives of the powerful also accrued capital
in the favor bank. Over the years, famous names have routinely
scrolled by in the closing credits—kin to Joe Biden, Woody Allen, Al
Gore, Mo Ostin, Jeff Zucker, and Lew Wasserman. Giving a tribute
to Michaels at a Writers Guild awards ceremony, Jim Downey ge-
nially spoke of "Lorne's outreach program for the children of celebrities."

TWENTY-EIGHT

SPINNING OFF

"MAYBE BABIES BRING LUCK," MICHAELS SAID TO A REPORTER IN THE spring of 1992. Bonnie Turner, the show's only writer who was also a mother, compared Alice Barry to "a quiet calm wave that came into Lorne's life," and in April, Alice gave birth to a son, named Henry after Lorne's father. When Florence Lipowitz, the new grandmother, visited her son at work, carefully coiffed and holding court in the conference room on nine, she declared that they should have named the baby Lefty. Michaels was elated by being a father. "Having a baby is the single best thing that has ever happened to me," he said. And he was on a roll. That year, he was named broadcaster of the year by the International Radio and Television Society. Bruce Springsteen, famous for never doing television, appeared on SNL as a musical guest. Soon, Paul McCartney did too, and Michaels got to reprise the Beatles check bit with him. Perhaps the most surprising development, however, was that, after all the years of dreaming about the movie business, Michaels had a number one picture out, *Wayne's World,* with a number one soundtrack as well.

He finally had his own parking space on the Paramount lot. In 1990, he had signed a producing deal with the studio, and, on his weeks off from SNL, had settled into an office on the lot, beyond the Bronson Gate. The history of the place frequently made him stop in his tracks, remembering the chatter around his grandmother's table.

He loved the way he could turn a corner and come upon two Kling-ons having a smoke, or find himself on the spot "where Francis shot the scene in *The Godfather* where Robert Duvall says, 'Mr. Corleone is a man who insists on hearing bad news *immediately*.'"

Mike Myers had pitched him the idea of turning "Wayne's World" into a movie during a visit to Amagansett. When he'd first submitted a sketch featuring his Wayne character for an SNL read-through, back in 1989, the other writers were skeptical; the loser-teen thing felt stale. Michaels put the piece in the ten-to-one slot. But it clicked, in part because he had suggested that Myers give Wayne a sidekick, a sweet goofus named Garth, played by the cast's biggest star, Dana Carvey. Myers had also taken Wayne out of his van and situated him in his basement, as the host of a public-access cable show. The sketch took off, and "Schwing!" "Party on!" and "We're not worthy!" entered the lexicon.

Michaels had notes on the first draft of Myers's *Wayne's World* screenplay: originally, Myers had envisioned Wayne getting his own country, the first "heavy metal state." Michaels nixed that, telling Myers that the film shouldn't be a delivery system for politics. "There's movies, there's films, and then there's confections," he said. "We're making a confection." The plot was retooled to focus on Wayne's struggle to keep creative control of his cable show. "I thought that was ironic," Myers said, "because Lorne wanted to change everything I was doing."

If Myers pushed back, Michaels would bring out one of his koans: "It knows what it is," he'd say, sphinxlike. He discouraged overreach-ing, having seen movies like Spielberg's *1941* implode from grandios-ity. "It was like university," Myers recalled. "Lorne explained that there are two horses you have to keep your feet on. One is plot and the other is comedy momentum—when did we have the last big laugh?" Michaels pointed out that the Hope-and-Crosby road pic-tures had the thinnest of plots, which allowed them to easily edit out anything that wasn't working without affecting the storyline. If Myers lobbied to put in more backstory, Michaels shot back, "Nobody ever cared about the country of Freedonia."

The Marx Brothers were a constant touchstone: Michaels felt that for Myers and Carvey, having performed their "Wayne's World" characters on SNL so many times gave them the same limberness that the Marx Brothers got by touring their movies as live shows on the vaudeville circuit before filming them. "Like the Beatles after Hamburg, where they played six shows a day," he said.

After revising his script, Myers was pleased to see that the big comedy set pieces from his original draft still worked with the rejiggered plot. The most famous of these is the scene in Garth's Mirthmobile, an AMC Pacer, in which Wayne and Garth and two buddies sing along to Queen's "Bohemian Rhapsody," furiously bobbing their heads. The headbanging sequence required dozens of takes and quantities of Advil; Carvey and Myers suffered stiff necks bordering on whiplash. Paramount and Michaels had pushed to instead use a song by Guns N' Roses, which had a number one hit, but—to Myers's thinking—no comedy cred. When Myers dug in, Michaels came around and got the studio to accept the sixteen-year-old Queen song.

Michaels brought in Bonnie and Terry Turner from SNL to work on the script. They were the show's high-functioning adults, the writers who had fresh flowers in their office instead of a Nerf basketball hoop. Barnaby Thompson, a suave young Englishman whom Michaels had hired to oversee his Paramount operation, offered the movie to a string of directors, all of whom declined; he finally hired Penelope Spheeris, from Michaels's Malibu period. She'd made a pair of well-regarded documentaries about punk and heavy metal, called *The Decline of Western Civilization,* and the Paramount executives worried that she'd make *Wayne's World* too dark and arty—what Michaels, quoting Jack Warner, calls a "fog on the lake" movie. Michaels promised that she'd direct *Wayne's World* in primary colors, "in sunshine" as he likes to say. Spheeris figures that the only reason Paramount okayed her was "because it was a fourteen-million-dollar movie in an age of sixty-three-million-dollar movies."

Old Hollywood joke: Guy asks, "What did you think of that screenplay?" Other guy says, "I don't know. I'm the only one who's read it." Although Michaels had put script beats on index cards on a bulletin board, as at SNL, he didn't offer much feedback on the screenplay itself. "None of us had actually made a movie," Thompson said. "We didn't know what we were doing." The Turners wrote thirteen drafts.

Michaels, in talent-management mode, did take care to ensure that the material Carvey contributed to the script stayed in and he cautioned that the female characters not be depicted as victims. Terry Turner recalled that when Wayne's stalkerish ex (Lara Flynn Boyle) crashes on her bike, "Lorne insisted that she get up and say, 'I'm okay!'"

He wasn't very involved with the shoot, but he watched dailies the way he'd watch an SNL dress rehearsal. "If he didn't like a scene, he would want a reshoot—probably costing tens of thousands of dollars," Bonnie Turner said, adding that she sometimes felt like whacking him with a bat.

Michaels hoped to cast Dennis Hopper as Wayne's father, but they ran out of shooting days, and the role was folded into the character of Benjamin Oliver, the oily TV producer played by Rob Lowe. It was Michaels's idea to approach Lowe, who'd just barely weathered a sex-tape scandal, and Myers was skeptical. Michaels pointed out that Lowe would work cheap. (Michaels once told Steve Martin that he likes to hire "people who've just had a flop, because they work twice as hard.") Tutored by Carvey and Myers, Lowe gave the character a sprinkling of Michaels's mannerisms, including the verbal tic, "It's like . . ." He did a "very subtle Lorne," Carvey said. The role jumpstarted Lowe's comedy career.

Paramount's publicity push for the film revolved around the slogan "One World. One Party," but the atmosphere on set was fractious. The shoot was a tight thirty-four days, to allow the stars to return to SNL for the premiere of Season Seventeen. Myers's father, an encyclopedia salesman, was dying during the filming, and Myers was on edge. His father died the week of a key test screening in Westwood, which scored phenomenally well. Myers didn't attend, and when he saw the first cut, at a screening held, cutely, in Wayne, New Jersey, he was addled by grief, and he hated it. He wrote up eleven pages of suggested cuts. Michaels looked at the notes and let Spheeris know that Myers was insisting on a massive re-edit. The two agreed that the revisions could wreck the movie. "Lorne hates confrontation," Spheeris said. "He told me, 'Penelope, I really need Mike to come back to the show. So I can't be the one to tell him.'" Spheeris battled over the notes one-by-one with Myers, holding the line, but killing any goodwill that was left between them.

Wayne's World grossed $183 million worldwide, and Michaels finally was a player in Hollywood. It still rankles him that Janet Maslin panned the movie in *The New York Times* ("H. L. Mencken may have noted that no one ever went broke underestimating the intelligence of the American people, but not even he could have anticipated this," she wrote), only to change her tune, in a subsequent piece, after her colleague Vincent Canby cheered the film as "sweetly mad." Michaels has no patience for the high seriousness of critics: "No one, especially at the *Times*, ever wants to just say, 'It's fun.'"

Fans of *Wayne's World* could also shell out for a *Wayne's World* book, a hat, six different T-shirts, greeting cards, a mug, and Wayne and Garth action figures. "I was a bit of a snob about merchandising in the 1970s," Michaels said. "I thought it was in conflict with doing a satirical show. Then, a few years ago, I was in Greece buying a Beatles T-shirt, and I thought, Would it have been so bad if there had been Coneheads lunch boxes?"

Paramount wasted no time making plans for *Wayne's World 2*. Spheeris wasn't invited back. "Lorne was honest enough to have told me that that's what would happen if I didn't take Mike's cuts," she said. Michaels resisted the sequel at first, but Paramount was on board, and so were Myers and Carvey, who would each take home a reported $3 million this time—a huge bump. Although Myers was happy to keep riding the wave, he told *Entertainment Weekly*, "I hope to God I'm not doing this at forty. That'd be a little sad." Around thirty years later, Wayne and Garth reunited to film a Super Bowl commercial for Uber Eats.

When Barnaby Thompson had started working for Michaels, in

1990, the unproduced *White Noise* script was on his desk. But Michaels took a hard swerve away from that type of story; the success of *Wayne's World* made Hollywood frantic, once again, for SNL movies. Michaels was happy to deliver, and in the next several years he'd produce six such confections for Paramount. A Coneheads movie was already in production—a nostalgia piece by then—written by Tom Davis, Dan Aykroyd, and the Turners.

But making the *Wayne's World* sequel was fraught. Trouble started when Sherry Lansing, Paramount's chairman, discovered, ten weeks before filming, that Myers had based the script on a 1949 British movie called *Passport to Pimlico* but had not secured the rights. (According to Michaels, Myers thought that the studio had dealt with the rights issue and that he was free to draw from the movie in writing his script.) Thompson accompanied Myers to a tense meeting in Lansing's office. With a fierce Francis Bacon canvas glowering from the wall, Lansing ordered Myers to "go to Lorne's office right now and stay there until you come up with a new script. We'll slide food under the door." If he didn't, she said, the studio would sue him for $200 million. "We'll take your fucking house," she said.

The new script, bashed out during a series of all-nighters, centered on Waynestock, a blighted music festival. A stern five-page memo from Howard Koch, an executive producer, lamented how drastically the late changes would affect the budget. ("There was $50,000 spent for the Mirth Limo. As of now, the Mirth Limo is not in the film.") Myers got mad when Michaels told them that Kim Basinger wanted to be involved and floated the idea that she play Garth's love interest, Honey Horneé. The plan, Myers said, had been to have no movie stars. "Then I dug my heels in," Carvey recalled. "Like, 'You can't tell *me* who my love interest is!'" Myers countered by signing up Drew Barrymore to play Bjergen Kjergen, a sexy secretary. Another time, Myers complained about a design decision, and Michaels snapped. "Lorne sort of lurched at him, like 'You fucker!'" Carvey said. "It was just one flash, but I'd never seen Lorne angry like that." Carvey worried that Myers, a former hockey player, was going to head-butt the boss. After episodes like that, Michaels remembered why he'd rebuffed Eric Ellenbogen's grand idea for him to run his own entertainment conglomerate.

The sequel did well, but it wasn't a blockbuster. "It didn't have the same innocence as the first one," Carvey said. The set was vastly more expensive, and even though Carvey was only two years older—he was thirty-eight now—the makeup people had to spackle his face with thick pancake. "I was bright orange," he said. "They aged me ten years by trying to cover up my stubble." Michaels had become an old pro at watching innocence fade; he made a mental note to keep his eyes on the generation coming up.

A DIRECTIVE FROM JOHNNY CARSON IS WHAT FIRST SET MICHAELS ON THE path to creating a live comedy show at 11:30 P.M. More than fifteen years later, another decision by *The Tonight Show*'s star prompted a new late-night opportunity. In May 1991, Carson startled NBC's executives when he announced that he would retire the following January. Michaels immediately understood that the *Tonight Show* succession could upset the power balance in NBC's late-night world.

He had always respected Carson as the steward of the longest-running entertainment program in history. Even though SNL had taken shots at Carson—chiefly, Carvey's brilliant Carsenio character (Johnny trying to court youngsters by mimicking Arsenio Hall, with a flattop wig and big-shouldered suits)—Michaels admired his skill at navigating the changing times. A baroque tug-of-war played out in the press and in network offices over whether Carson's successor would be Jay Leno, who'd become the show's permanent guest host, or David Letterman, whose show had followed *Tonight* for a decade and whom Carson considered his natural heir. NBC executives in L.A. favored Leno, whose easy-listening style went over well in the middle of the country. In New York, Letterman was the pick. His comedy was sharper and smarter, his mischievous silliness more modern.

Besides preferring Letterman's sensibility, Michaels liked that Letterman was a true broadcaster and not merely a guy who went out and told jokes. Michaels has a reverence for broadcast, which he thinks of as a historic force that unified the nation, the way the railroads did in the nineteenth century. When General Electric acquired NBC in 1986, Bob Wright had come over as president. Derided in some network corridors as the "GE Plastics guy," who had no entertainment experience, Wright hit it off with Michaels, and Michaels told him that Letterman, without question, would be the stronger host.

The network went with Leno. Letterman, stung, instructed his agent Mike Ovitz to find him another network. He ended up with a princely deal at CBS for an 11:30 show that would go head-to-head with Leno's *Tonight*. Realizing too late that NBC was about to lose an irreplaceable talent, Wright tried everything he could think of to keep Letterman—even unseating Leno from his new perch at *Tonight*. After an opera buffa–esque series of machinations, which included Leno listening in on network executives' conference calls while hiding in a Burbank closet, NBC stuck with Leno, causing the world of late-night television to shift on its axis. (People close to the proceedings have always believed that the closet story was a fabrication, something fed to the *Times* to protect the insider who leaked the information about the calls to Leno.) "It's simple plate tectonics," Conan O'Brien said, of what happened next.

Letterman left for CBS, and NBC had a big gap-toothed hole to fill. To appease the affiliates, the network made a splashy announcement that Lorne Michaels had been charged with finding a new host for *Late Night*. "Lorne has a very basic skill," Warren Littlefield, a Tartikoff protégé at NBC, told the *Times*. "He knows what's funny." As the network's chief developer of comic talent, Michaels had a lot of possible candidates at hand. Dennis Miller had pitched himself immediately. The writers Robert Smigel and Bob Odenkirk were mentioned, as were comedians Drew Carey, Paul Provenza, Allan Havey, and Jon Stewart.

Michaels decided to look for a producer first. He offered the job to a former SNL writer who had gone on to distinguish himself at *The Simpsons,* Conan O'Brien. (He'd written an especially funny episode called "Marge vs. the Monorail.") Michaels told O'Brien that if he came to *Late Night*, he'd have carte blanche to reinvent the show. O'Brien dithered. "No one can replace Letterman," he remembers thinking. "So I wanted nothing to do with finding that guy. Who wants the headache?"

While Michaels was casting around for a producer, NBC was antsy for a new host, so a showcase for executives to check out possible talent was arranged in L.A., where Michaels was dropping in on the set of the Coneheads movie. One day, he got a call from Gavin Polone, a brash young agent at UTA, who repped O'Brien. Michaels hung up and, with a startled look, told his colleagues, "Conan wants to be the host."

O'Brien hadn't spent much time onstage, and Polone knew he was aiming high when he made his pitch. O'Brien happened to be on the Paramount lot that day, filming a bit part in *Coneheads* (it got cut). Michaels sent an assistant to find him, "to see if Gavin was agenting me or telling the truth." O'Brien, seated in a makeup chair with a latex cone adding a foot to his own seventy-six inches, confirmed that he was indeed interested.

Michaels doesn't like being turned down, and he'd been unnerved by O'Brien's indifference to his earlier offer to be the mind *behind* the new show. But the notion of Conan in front of the camera started growing on him. He knew that O'Brien was always the funniest guy in the writers' room, and the SNL assistants all adored him. O'Brien also wasn't burdened with the light hostility that club comics have; he was a pleasant conversationalist. Michaels also liked the Harvard pedigree.

O'Brien didn't participate in the showcase that NBC held at the Improv, and his name had not been mentioned to NBC as a potential host. Right after the showcase, Michaels and his people joined some executives for a drink at a bar across the street, to discuss what they'd seen. Among the NBC group were Warren Littlefield, Rick Ludwin, and Don Ohlmeyer, Ebersol's old colleague from ABC Sports, who was now the president of NBC's West Coast division. Jon Stewart seemed to be the leading candidate, but there was no consensus, so

Ohlmeyer tabled the discussion and ordered the group to reconvene the next day in Burbank.

The following morning, Michaels kicked things off. "When I discovered Chevy—" he began, but Ohlmeyer, a gruff man who favored the turtleneck-and-Brylcreem look of a sportscaster, cut him off. "Yeah, we know," he said. "Let's talk about what we just saw."

Michaels, carrying on, said that he had a new name to throw into the mix: Conan O'Brien. Ohlmeyer and his men exchanged looks. Littlefield wrinkled his brow and asked, "Red hair? Tall Conan? You mean the *Simpsons* guy?" Jim Biederman, part of Michaels's Broadway Video team, spoke up in support of the idea. He told Ohlmeyer, "If Letterman was your generation, Conan is mine." The executives considered the O'Brien idea far-fetched; they were interested in finding out if Garry Shandling was interested.

After the meeting, Michaels had an assistant get O'Brien on the phone and asked if he would tape an audition show, being careful not to promise anything. To produce, he had in mind Jeff Ross, who had done well with the Kids in the Hall. Ross had never met O'Brien, but Michaels suggested they get together and hash it out. Within days, Conan showed up at a Burbank studio for the tryout. Jeff Ross handed him some index cards with research notes about Jason Alexander and Mimi Rogers, who'd been recruited to be pretend guests. O'Brien didn't own a suit jacket, so his friend Lisa Kudrow had taken him shopping and helped him pick out a floppy off-white blazer that made his Irish complexion even more washed-out. Michaels watched the audition show on a feed from New York, and he called just before the taping to wish O'Brien well and to help manage his expectations. At that point, Shandling was the network's clear favorite and word was that a contract for $5 million a year was being discussed. (Stewart had signed a deal with MTV for a syndicated talk show.)

O'Brien did a strong fake show. In his monologue he talked about how the Irish don't age well; their faces get bigger and bigger until everyone looks like Ted Kennedy. The high point was an exchange with Mimi Rogers, who talked about how modeling is hard work. "No," O'Brien ad-libbed. "Modeling's not a hard job. Turning a big crank is a hard job." During a break, Ross dropped a sheet of paper onto O'Brien's desk reading "You're killing." Afterward, Michaels called and said that Bob Wright and his wife had loved it. (Conan didn't know who they were.) But, Michaels cautiously added, the odds were still in Shandling's favor.

O'Brien was surprised, then, when he was called to Burbank so that he could talk through his vision for *Late Night* to a group of NBC executives. The leader was Ohlmeyer, whom O'Brien described as a tough guy: "Imagine Babe Ruth at forty-five years old." But he was ready, having mapped out some ideas with Robert Smigel, whom he hoped to bring in as head writer. "I told them that Letterman had done ironic detachment—the meta thing," he recalled. "The show I wanted to do would be more silly. There would be surreal elements. It would use puppets, it would use animation."

He couldn't tell if he was winning them over. "It seemed like none of them knew what the fuck to do," he said. "They had a piece of tape with a goofy guy on camera who's not throwing up." Mainly he felt relieved that he hadn't embarrassed Michaels in the audition. He'd been credible, and he knew that Michaels was putting his own credibility on the line. But he was anxious; what if NBC actually wanted him to step into Letterman's shoes? "That week, George Meyer cornered me at the *Simpsons* offices," O'Brien said. "And he told me, 'Man, don't do it. It's feeding the dragon, man. Every day, feeding the dragon.'"

The network people had regarded the tryout show as just okay, but Michaels prevailed, in part by letting the clock run out. The O'Brien idea now felt just right to him. O'Brien had intelligence and originality, and, like SNL at the start, he was coming out of nowhere; he had no "ratings history." Shandling had removed his name from consideration, wanting to keep doing *The Larry Sanders Show,* at HBO, and one morning in May, just after O'Brien's thirtieth birthday, NBC held a press conference in the Rainbow Room to name him as Letterman's successor. The press office didn't even have a headshot to hand out. O'Brien, wearing a brand-new Armani suit, met Michaels at his apartment beforehand, and they walked together through Central Park, down to Rockefeller Center. As the event was getting underway, Ohl-meyer stood by the bar holding a Scotch. "Here goes nothing," he said.

Before O'Brien came out onstage, Michaels was introduced as "a great discoverer." Casting unknowns had worked for him at SNL, and he loved putting his homegrown talent out in the world.

Every article about the Cinderella story at *Late Night* identified Michaels as the all-powerful fairy godfather. O'Brien was determined to prove him right. "It was a crazy Hail Mary," he said. Michaels spent a lot of time that summer with Jeff Ross, O'Brien, and Smigel, tossing around ideas and talking about comedy. O'Brien said, "The problem was, none of us had ever done one of these shows, including Lorne." At Smigel's suggestion, O'Brien proposed that his show get a new title, *Nighty Night with Conan O'Brien*. It captured the *Pee-wee's Playhouse* tone he was going for, and he thought it might ward off unfavorable comparisons with Letterman. NBC didn't go for it.

The SNL design team created a new set for O'Brien, inspired by Michaels's clubby office. (One difference: the view of the Empire State Building behind the host's desk was a painted backdrop.) Al-though Michaels was the executive producer, he didn't get involved in the day-to-day. "A lot of people, myself included, think that Lorne has the Secret," O'Brien said. "And Lorne has made a career out of letting people think he has the Secret." He went on, "I think Lorne's real Secret, with me, was to communicate to me, 'You have to figure out this show.'" He recalled feeling like Dorothy in Oz, when the wizard tells her that she'd always had the power to return to Kansas, but she had to find it herself.

LATE NIGHT WITH CONAN O'BRIEN DEBUTED IN SEPTEMBER 1993. O'BRIEN nervously chatted with his first guest, John Goodman, whom he then persuaded to leg wrestle George Wendt—a grudge match, as he put it, between the lovable burly guys of TV. He closed the show by sing-ing "Edelweiss," a lullaby for his viewers, while in the audience a nun and a man in a Nazi uniform wept. Reviewers were puzzled. Shales,

The Washington Post's Lorne watcher, called it "a protracted wheeze" and described O'Brien as "a walking shambles," who should be "the head writer of the show, not the star." The network was perplexed, too. "Lorne and I were both on wobbly ground," O'Brien said about his first weeks. "There were many moments when I could tell that I was scaring him. And he doesn't like to be scared." Some of the show's abstract, aggressively strange bits—like showcasing "the Lenny Bruce of China," the Gaseous Weiner (a farting hot dog), and, later, the Masturbating Bear and the Horny Manatee—pushed boundaries even for late night. O'Brien yodeled; he wore a bikini. He sensed that Michaels wished the show had less of his crazy comedy and more of him just talking to the guests: "I've always thought of Lorne as having this very thin, strong pipelike core of brilliance and amazing taste, which is surrounded by layers of insulation—layers of insecurity. We all have it. A Jewish kid who started out with a furrier for a father, and he somehow makes it to *this* place? Our insecurities, our defense mechanisms, are what we use to survive, and they build up, like plaque. When my show started, I think Lorne felt, 'I don't have control over this thing. Conan's getting the shit kicked out of him.' He could make suggestions to me here and there, but that's it. He still had to do SNL."

O'Brien had an especially bad experience on *Charlie Rose* in late 1993, and it helped him understand why Michaels is so determined to avoid being surprised. Seated at Rose's round table, he had to endure hearing the host talk about Shales's second evisceration of *Late Night,* in that day's paper ("Hey you, Conan O'Brien! Get the heck off TV!"). "I pretended that I had seen the piece," O'Brien recalled. "I said, 'Yeah, no, I know.'" After the taping he went back to his office and crawled under his desk until Ross could coax him out.

After especially harsh reviews, Michaels would call O'Brien to commiserate, but it often had the opposite effect. "Well, I think it's terrible what so-and-so wrote about you," O'Brien recalled him saying. "I mean, you don't deserve to *die.*" Then he'd turn back into the reassuring dad, signing off with one of his showbiz bromides, such as "The longer you're on, the longer you're on."

But Michaels wasn't worried. The audience, he often says, is more patient than the industry. Years of putting novices on camera at SNL had shown him that "you have to live through that thing of people not being good." It's a corollary to another of his favorite sayings: "All babies are ugly unless they're your baby." (Three months later, he says, everyone goes "Oh, what a cute baby!") The network, however, was shaken. In a baffling gesture, Ohlmeyer had treadmills sent to the *Late Night* office, which were interpreted as a mafia-esque message either to get in shape or to work harder. Littlefield called Gavin Polone and, referring to O'Brien's sidekick, Andy Richter, barked, "And get that fat fucking dildo off the couch." By the summer, with affiliates complaining, NBC announced that it would renew *Late Night* only on a week-to-week basis.

Michaels and O'Brien huddled over dinner. "Lorne looked right into my eyes," O'Brien recalled. "And he said, 'You do not want to get canceled. I've been canceled. You do not want to get canceled.'" The *New Show* debacle, O'Brien realized, had been "real trauma for him. It was like someone who had survived a Great White attack and was missing a piece of their torso, saying, 'You do not want to ever meet up with a Great White.'"

Everyone in the business assumed that NBC was about to pull the plug. "The show was basically gone," Eric Ellenbogen said. "But Lorne acted as a human shield." Michaels had dinner with Ohlmeyer in L.A., at Morton's, whose banquettes were crammed with Hollywood players, and he made a direct appeal. He tried talking Ohlmeyer's language, deploying a boxing metaphor: "Conan's been in there—it's the eighth round—taking body blow after body blow. He's given everything he has to this."

To his surprise, Ohlmeyer replied, "What are you talking about? Conan's our guy." This was the side of Ohlmeyer that made employees admire him, even when he was making their lives complicated. "Don was like a football coach who beats you within an inch of your life, but he isn't going to cut you," Michaels said. A reprieve was granted: NBC would commit to thirteen episodes at a time, with a caveat: the ratings had to improve.

Two years later, Shales officially recanted what he called his "excessively mean" reviews and described O'Brien's show as "one of the most amazing transformations in television history." He finally twigged to what the show was offering—an unironic sense of play. O'Brien, he said, is "his own secret ingredient, and his show an inspired absurdist romp." Letterman lent support by calling to ask if he could be a guest on the show. O'Brien at first thought it was a prank.

TWENTY-NINE

THE MAKE-FUN-OF-LORNE SHOW

BERNIE BRILLSTEIN USED TO CALL MICHAELS "A RELUCTANT MOGUL." HE EN-
joyed being a power player—the friend Jagger or Geffen calls when
they need a quick joke for a public appearance (for example, from
Jagger's speech inducting Jann Wenner into the Rock & Roll Hall of
Fame: "This is a wonderful, heartfelt occasion and I will treasure it,
the memory of it, all the way to the airport"). But, even with his multiple residences, army of assistants, and Gucci loafers, he shrinks
from the crassness associated with moguldom. His cultivated nonchalance about living a grandee's life—the rarefied social circle and
swish vacation calendar—have long made him ripe for razzing.

For the people in the SNL writers' room, the most reliable source
of comedy has long been Michaels himself. Turning the boss's tics
into elaborate private comic scenarios about him provides distraction
during the long, exhausting writing nights. The goofing-around de-
fuses tension in what can be a gladiatorial atmosphere. "It was a way
for us to laugh and not be so afraid of Lorne," Paula Pell said. It's also
a salve for what Smigel called "the hilarious schizophrenia of the writing process: 'I hate myself!' 'I'm the best!' 'I'm a fucking idiot!' 'I'm on
a roll!'" He said, "If there had been a spin-off show—*The Make-Fun-
of-Lorne Show*—the writers would have been so productive."

Although Michaels isn't present when this is going on, he is aware of it. He views his employees' making sport of him as "a defense against feeling"—taking control of their anxiety. "It's the most American thing there is," he said. Canadians don't do it as much, "because nobody in Canada is that successful." "Everyone does Lorne," Chevy Chase said. "I read that as fear. He's the big man. He is the king of comedy." In Norm Macdonald's magic realism–tinged memoir, *Based on a True Story,* he writes: "The boss is always a big joke, just dumb and lucky, and nobody's afraid of him at all and everybody has a good laugh at him. Until he walks into the room, that is. It's a different story then."

Michaels may have edged out Jimmy Stewart as the most impersonated man in show business. The Lorne impressions started with Dana Carvey, who is credited with being the da Vinci of Lorne impersonators. He was initially inspired by watching Michaels standing in front of his bulletin board. "The first hook I saw was him saying, 'I still have no fucking first act.' Then I started growing the impression. Phrases like 'Riiiiight.' Or, 'That thing of, like . . .'" Carvey did it in private, for the writers, in fifteen-minute arias. "It was a pressure valve," he said.

Mark McKinney had been developing his own impression, which was studied and precise. ("Dead-on Lorne," Conan O'Brien called it.) Then Smigel started doing one. "I would cartoonify mine," he said. "Neither me or Dana was interested in doing the McKinney version, with all these beautiful observational excerpts from Lorne's library of Lorneisms." They had phone calls to each other as dueling Lornes. "It was all free-form, not about the content, which was just nonsense," Carvey said.

Carvey began embellishing his Lorne with some self-satisfied lip smacking, and Smigel focused on the word "show," which he pronounced in a quasi-British accent. Smigel went further, coming up with a character he called Little Lorne Fauntleroy. He'd do the bit in the writers' room, pretending to be Lorne dancing around his index cards like a madman. "Whom shall I *make,* and whom shall I *break?*" he'd prattle to the bulletin board, adding, in Punch-and-Judy delirium, "I get to put on a *shoooow!*" The Smigel Lorne line that had everyone laughing the hardest was "Show's a *hit!*" (Especially when it wasn't.)

By the nineties, the impressions had become increasingly baroque. Carvey noticed that Michaels bit his nails in meetings, "so I started doing the pinky thing, where he held his pinky up to the corner of his mouth," he said. The pinky gesture would become a cause for contention a few years later.

When Bonnie and Terry Turner joined the staff, Michaels had asked them, "Has everyone done their Lorne impression for you?" Terry Turner had already perfected his own, which he reckons is "closer to George Sanders." The most-often imitated Lorne is laconic, name-dropping Lorne, the one whose conversation can sound like a private-jet manifest. Or Lorne dispensing nuggets of show-business wisdom or tips on vacationing. Once, at a dinner party, Michaels started in on one of his oft-told tales: "I was on a boat once in Egypt," he began. Steve Martin cut him off, saying, "I was on a plane once in Des Moines."

For their private amusement, the writers devised a character who was supposed to be Lorne's fictional, less-successful brother. This fake brother was friends with lamer celebrities than the ones Lorne hangs with, but he would name-drop them just as much. For instance, "You know, we were with Weird Al and Tony Danza, and we were at a minor league ball game . . ."

The actual name-dropping amuses as much as it exasperates. Although it's curious that a man as successful and powerful as Michaels feels the need to trumpet that he has celebrity friends, there's something vulnerable about him having remained unabashedly starstruck. (He saves his voicemails from Paul McCartney.) "It's a funny weakness to have," Randy Newman says. "But he never apologizes for it. He likes that stuff, and I like that he does."

He's not the only celebrity delighted by celebrities. Michaels has been a guest on David Geffen's eighty-two-room yacht, *Rising Sun,* which routinely accommodates a squad of the ultra-famous. On one voyage, Martin Short got Warren Beatty and Annette Bening, Nick Pileggi and Nora Ephron, Tom Hanks and Rita Wilson, Mike Nichols and Diane Sawyer, Steve Martin and his wife, Anne Stringfield, to play a party game called "Who's Met *Blank*?" The idea was to come up with a celebrity whom no one on board had met. "You couldn't come up with a name!" Short said. "One night, I said, 'Okay. Did anyone meet Eleanor Roosevelt?'" Beatty piped up that he had. After a beat, Nichols asked, "Did you fuck her?"

By the time Smigel made Michaels a regular character in his animated SNL segment "TV Funhouse," the high-handed caricature was set. Smigel's animated Lorne is a silver-haired avatar, sauntering with one hand in his pocket; his signature bit is blowing his top at a terrier who tries to make off with the stage curtain. Giving a tug-of-war yank, he yells, "Come back here with my *shoooow*!" The cartoons were so mind-bendingly funny and fresh that Michaels gave Smigel carte blanche. Whether it was "The Ambiguously Gay Duo" of Ace and Gary (Batman and Robin stand-ins) or "Christmas for the Jews" (done in ersatz Rankin/Bass claymation)—Michaels was happy to wait until Saturday to watch.

One episode of Funhouse's "Anatominals"—a Yogi Bear parody about critters with big boobs and bulgy genitals encased in tight clothes—cuts away to cartoon Lorne watching on a monitor under the bleachers. Cartoon Lorne shakes his head, muttering, "This is what it's come to. It's not fucking worth it." He summons Satan and tells him that their deal is off: "You never said it would get *this* bad." Satan replies, "You say that after every SNL movie." The devil snaps his fingers and restores Lorne to the place his life would have taken him had he not made a Faustian bargain in 1975: a forlorn Peace Corps relief station in Africa, where earnest Lorne has a gray ponytail. The vision appalls him, and the devil zaps him back to 8H in exchange for possession of his soul for "double eternity." Chastened, cartoon Lorne leans toward the Anatominals screen and purrs, "I smell a new hit."

Colleagues tell a story about being with Michaels at a Yankees game, in his box seats behind home plate. Among his guests was a potential partner in a business venture. After a couple of innings of listening to Michaels's patter—"This is where Jack likes to sit," etc.— the guest made a gently mocking remark: "Gee, do you only know famous people?" Michaels's cutting reply: "I know *you*."

PART FIVE

FRIDAY

"We have nothing" is a sentence that staffers are used to hearing Michaels say on Friday. He'll be staring at the cards on his bulletin board, tense. Employees a quarter of his age are amazed that, after fifty years, he can still seem scared.

Friday is the day when the pace picks up on the eighth and ninth floors. Pre-taped pieces get filmed; rewrites continue; sets are constructed and wheeled out for more blocking. On the Friday of the Jonah Hill week, things were on schedule overall, and Michaels felt secure in the lineup. Neither Jordan Peele nor Dave Chappelle had been persuaded to play Obama, so Colin Jost was in his office writing a cold open about Fox News and the caravan. A rewrite table was punching up Hill's Five Timers monologue, and Tina Fey was heading in to help. The plan to drive Melissa McCarthy and family from Chicago to New York had been scuttled, and Scarlett Johansson was unavailable, so the club members would be Barrymore, Bergen, and Fey. Pete Davidson was dispirited about his Ariana Grande idea getting killed, but he'd shot a promo with Maggie Rogers that covered the same ground (in the promo, he introduces himself to Rogers and immediately proposes marriage). It was doing well on social media. Leslie Jones was unhappy that the Weezer dinner-party sketch had been cut. Movie Theater had been rewritten according to Hill's notes—with more gags about pretentious menu items. There were voiceovers to be recorded for pre-tapes. In Seth Meyers's studio, dozens of extras sat scrolling their phones. The Montreal Motorcycle Club sketch was scheduled for blocking at three, so five huge Yamahas clogged the hallway outside 8H.

In the conference room on nine, an assistant was on the phone, sorting out who would be seated with Michaels in his special command station under the bleachers during the live show. Donna Langley, the head of Universal Pictures, NBC's sister company, had invited

Daniel Katz, from A24, the studio that produced Jonah Hill's film, and his family. "Will it be okay to move the aunt and uncle to regular seats?" the assistant was asking. "We want to do whatever Donna will want." (Michaels had recently ended his nearly thirty-year-long producing deal with Paramount Pictures and moved his movie operation to Universal, synergistically keeping all his projects under one umbrella.)

Around 11:30, when Michaels was waking up on Central Park West, he got a text from Alec Baldwin. For the past few years, Tina Fey and Robert Carlock, who had developed the sitcom *30 Rock* with her, had been working on a *30 Rock* spin-off, following Jack Donaghy's post-GE political career. It had taken some doing to talk Baldwin into it. Michaels, who was to executive produce, had just read the pilot script, and NBC was on board. Michaels texted Baldwin back and said that he'd call later. "I wanted to tell him the good news," he said.

He never got a chance. Two hours later, Baldwin's agent called Michaels to relay that Baldwin had just been arrested for punching a man in a dispute over a parking space in the Village. He was being booked down at the Sixth Precinct. The story was all over the internet. On Twitter, Donald Trump Jr. called Baldwin "a piece of garbage." (When Don Jr. tweeted about the show, he used to misspell it "S&L.") The news sped through the eighth, ninth, and seventeenth floors of 30 Rock. People received it with a mixture of amusement and concern. "That's *so* Alec," one said. A few were annoyed; the reason Baldwin couldn't play Trump in that week's show, supposedly, was that he had obligations in the Hamptons. "He blew his own alibi," someone said. Baldwin had hosted SNL seventeen times; he was family. Some at the show regarded him the way you would an incorrigible relative, with affectionate exasperation. The internet was buzzing with speculation about how SNL would deal with the incident on the show.

In midafternoon, Tina Fey walked into the ninth-floor conference room, like someone returning to her parents' kitchen after a semester at college. She had on jeans, a black blazer, and flat boots. After greeting the young women around the table, she got right to Baldwin. "The stuff he pulls off on the streets of New York!" she said. "He'd get killed in my old neighborhood in Philly." She laughed and went up to seventeen for the Five Timers rewrite.

Michaels arrived at the office at around five, in a downpour. He'd let himself be driven. He looked nettled over the Baldwin news. "There's no one faster at getting in his own way," he said. Baldwin was supposed to have signed on to the *30 Rock* spin-off that day, with the expectation of a thirteen-episode commitment. On the White House lawn, a reporter asked Trump if he'd heard about Baldwin's arrest. The president gave a crooked smile and said, "I wish him luck." "It was a pure showbiz thing," Michaels said. "Trump knew exactly what to do."

After venting a bit about Baldwin, Michaels had a meeting with three of his music bookers, Rebecca Schwartz, Keri Powers, and Brian Siedlecki. He knows that young musical acts are one way to keep the eighteen- to twenty-four-year-olds watching, and he regularly uses his three twenty-something children as sounding boards. (One Direction had been on the show multiple times when his daughter, Sophie, was a teenager.) These days, it's not uncommon for a musical guest or host (the rapper Jack Harlow, Seth Rogen) to tell him that their SNL-loving mother and father were crying with happiness in the dressing room. "It's the parents' dream," he said.

Siedlecki floated some ideas for potential musical guests: "The new names are Bazzi"—a Lebanese American singer-songwriter— "and a person named Jorja Smith."

"More elevated than Maggie Rogers?" Michaels asked. He didn't hide his ambivalence about this week's guest.

Schwartz tried to sell him: "Jorja's English, half Black, twenty-one, sounds like Amy Winehouse. Drake put her on a record. She's definitely not a big name, but if we're not getting a name, she's quality."

Michaels wanted someone splashier. "Unless you think she's the nineteen-year-old Adele," he said.

The bookers backed down. "Feels a little early," Siedlecki said.

"When they haven't done a lot of live shows, and it's just a girl in front of a mic, and no one knows the song yet . . . ," he said, a veiled reference to Rogers. "Is this the voice of the future?"

He asked what Lana Del Rey was up to. Recommended by Fred Armisen, in 2012 she had made a rocky SNL debut, drawing scathing reactions because she was audibly shaking when she sang. But her record ended up going to number one. The talent people said that Del Rey had new music, but they weren't sure she was "ready to nail it."

"It would be a moment, though," Powers said. Michaels liked the idea of a moment, and this brought him back to his uncertainty about Rogers.

"Well, Jorja is definitely buzzier than Maggie, and sexier," one of the bookers said.

"And yet we have Maggie this week," Michaels said. The talent trio laughed uncomfortably.

Powers mentioned that people on social media had been asking for more female artists. Michaels looked frustrated. "I'm not opposed to Jorja being a girl," he said. "My question is, can she hold the audience? If we're too early, and it becomes a smudge, you're not really helping them." Thinking ahead two weeks, when Steve Carell was booked to host, he asked if any of them had seen Carell's movie with Timothée Chalamet, *Beautiful Boy*. Chalamet, he said, might only have an audience in L.A. and New York—a phenomenon he calls having "coastal love"—and something he steers clear of when booking hosts. He told the talent people the story about putting ABBA on the *Titanic* in Season One, making them laugh. "So, should we book ABBA?" Schwartz said. "Are they still alive?"

Michaels was back on Carell, who had another movie opening soon, *Welcome to Marwen,* about a reclusive cross-dressing victim of bullying who lives his life through his collection of dolls. "That *Marwen* trailer—whoa," he said. "Steve Carell being beaten by neo-Nazis may not be that interesting. And he makes little dolls." He took a beat and added, in a Dr. Evil voice, "How do I invest?"

Scheduling SNL hosts can be a byzantine process. ("Do you know how many funny people there are in the world?" Michaels often says. "There are about nine. They know who they are.") The talent department draws up lists of happening stars whose reps have confirmed that their client has the entire week free. The names are presented to Michaels "like a menu at a restaurant," one booker said, and he makes a selection, not always quickly. Sometimes a talent coordinator will make the confirmation call to the rep so late that the star is no longer available. Other hosts-in-waiting get offended; they thought they'd agreed to host, but it turns out they were only on a short list. In rare cases, hosts cancel at the last minute (Gary Oldman, Roseanne Barr), and that's when the short list comes in handy. So does the network of rabbits' feet (Jon Hamm, John Goodman, Kristen Wiig, Alec Baldwin, John Mulaney). Michaels rarely makes a call himself. "He's great at convincing people," Tina Fey says. "But if it's a definite no, he knows you shouldn't squander your capital that way."

In the music meeting, Michaels asked if any of the bookers had watched the blocking on the Beavis and Butt-Head sketch. Schwartz said it had been hard to tell if it worked, because the big prosthetic cartoon heads weren't ready yet. "Like Coneheads with no cones," Michaels mused, connecting dots across the years. Asked if Baldwin would be back next week, he said, "I don't think so, but it won't be my not wanting him. It's the shame thing. He'll be in hiding." Michaels thinks that Baldwin habitually "guards against enjoyment"; it exasperates him to hear, for instance, that Baldwin is driving a carful of children out to East Hampton in traffic rather than hire a driver, or a plane. Michaels himself rolls his eyes at billionaires who say they fly commercial so as not to lose touch with "regular people."

What a thousand websites now call "work-life balance" is something Michaels was on to decades ago. He designed the show's schedule with plenty of time off, and made sure it aligned with the dates of New York's private-school vacation weeks. In Amagansett, he is part of a yoga class with Alec Baldwin and Paul McCartney, who named the group "the Yoga Boys." Fey observed, "He has just enough of the seventies in him that he didn't catch that eighties epidemic, becoming one of those people who need to prove themselves by working way too much and being tired all the time."

Employees are used to him quizzing them about their vacation plans, counseling them to take ample time off in acceptably swanky locales. (Fey does a riff in Lorne's voice about buying a vacation home on the planet Naboo, from *Star Wars: The Phantom Menace,* and how chic and undiscovered it is.) The summer London trips he takes with Jimmy Fallon are sacrosanct; they walk Hyde Park, see plays, watch the tennis at Wimbledon, and Michaels is feted at an annual chicken-salad-and-martinis party. One of their regular stops is Budd Shirtmakers, a century-old establishment in Piccadilly Arcade. The longtime manager, a man with brushed-back white hair, talks linen pajamas with a poetic hint of mortality: "They're never softer than the last time you wear them." He once asked his client, Mr. Michaels, how he manages everything. Michaels's answer: "I take time off."

MICHAELS POPPED DOWN TO THE STUDIO, WHERE BLOCKING HAD STARTED on Hill's monologue in the Five Timers Lounge. He wanted to make sure that the set was big enough to feel empty now that the men had been banished. He worried that the Movie Theater piece, with its hulking rows of seats, took up too much space. Then he headed back to nine, where his team had gathered to brainstorm about the cold open. With the current sketch lineup, the show was way over ninety minutes. The dress rehearsal, which starts at 8:00 P.M., usually runs a half hour longer than the air show. This is by design. After days of almost Talmudic debates over which pieces to run, the three hundred civilians at the dress rehearsal often have the deciding votes. Everyone involved in the show has faith in laughter; it's the only real proof that something is funny. It's why guest hosts sometimes give back their allotment of tickets, to be distributed to diehard fans in the stand-by line. Every performer has a story about looking up at the balcony and seeing a row of agents and their dates, asleep.

"Who's in the cold open?" Michaels asked. With twenty-four

hours to go, this was the top priority. It was to be Laura Ingraham's Fox show, *The Ingraham Angle,* with Kate McKinnon interviewing right-wing guests about the threat of the caravan. Jost told him that they had Cecily Strong as Judge Jeanine Pirro, Kenan Thompson as former Milwaukee sheriff David Clarke, and Jonah Hill as Steven Seagal.

"Is it worth having Jonah in the cold open?" Michaels asked, looking for ways to cut minutes. The door opened and Tina Fey walked in. "Some day!" Jost said.

"You've been saving a parking space for Alec?" Erik Kenward asked her.

Michaels couldn't resist joining in. "Some confusion between Tenth Street and Tenth Boulevard, I guess," he said, a stab at an outer-borough joke.

Fey said, "I'm like, 'Buy yourself a milk crate, buddy! Do it Philly style!'" She told them that Baldwin had checked in with Carlock, but didn't mention his arrest: "He called Robert from jail, pretending that he was not in jail, to discuss the script we sent him. He said he didn't think he could possibly do it. And Robert said, 'I agree!'" Everyone laughed. There was sympathy and exasperation in their tones, and the kind of queasy satisfaction that comes with having your worst expectations met.

"That was him pretending he could still be in charge," Michaels said.

"It was, 'You can't fire me—I quit!'" Fey said. "It was, 'I'm dealing with some personal stuff.'"

Michaels added, "It was like, 'As soon as I get these cuffs off . . .'"

They could have riffed on Baldwin all evening, but there was a cold open to sort out. Jost wanted to keep Hill in as Seagal, who is a big supporter of Vladimir Putin.

"Seagal's a Russian citizen now," Michaels said. "Is there a tax advantage to that? He always had a really good business manager." He returned to the president's comments on the caravan. "I think there's something funny in taking the caravan seriously," he said. "Like it's a real military invasion."

Fey lobbed a Canada joke: "Canada should just come pick those caravan people up. They're just trying to get to Canada."

"If they walk forty miles a day, they'll get there in six weeks," Michaels said, laughing.

"You sent them all Fitbits, right?" Fey asked him, scoring the most raucous laugh of the meeting. Michaels digressed into a recitation of factoids about the diet of the average Central American, and how that part of the world has been deforested. (Trees are one of his interests.) He was interrupted by the arrival of Steve Higgins, from the studio.

"Do you have a waiter in the Five Timers Lounge?" Michaels asked him.

"Kenan is the bartender," Higgins answered. "And we have the three women."

Michaels still wasn't quite grasping the #MeToo ladies-only angle. "And John Goodman is out?"

Fey re-explained the concept: "Jonah will say, 'Where are all the guys?' And we'll go, 'Oh, no. Time's up!' Then, something like 'You're not gonna believe this, but Steve Martin? You actually *want* his hands occupied by a banjo.'" Everyone laughed. Then Fey furrowed her brow and asked whether any of the real Five Timers men had been caught up in the #MeToo storm. "Louis was close to five, right?" she asked, meaning Louis C.K.

"Louis hosted four times," Kenward said.

Jost said, "How many was James Franco? Three? Four?" (Four.) All of the Five Timers had clean records, so far.

Fey tried out a line. "And Justin Timberlake—he ripped a lady's top off at the Super Bowl. Time's up!" As everyone giggled, Willa Slaughter stuck her head in and mouthed to Michaels that Lance, his barber, was waiting downstairs.

Michaels seemed satisfied. "And Jonah has a bolero jacket on?"

Kenward nodded: "It can't miss."

Ignoring the waiting barber, Michaels suggested that, in the cold open, they show some news clips of Trump. "That way the audience also won't be waiting for Alec to appear," he said.

Jost said, "And you know, we *have* to have some Alec joke in the show."

"We could put an announcement at the top of the show," Michaels said. "'Alec Baldwin will not be here tonight. You know why.'"

They laughed, and Fey added, "Due to reasons completely within his control, Alec Baldwin will not be appearing."

Before adjourning, Michaels asked if anyone had ideas about cutting a sketch. "It's a little cramped timewise," he said. "How was Craigslist in blocking?"

Kenward said, "It's hard to tell because there's no van yet. I hope it works, but it's vulnerable."

Michaels left the office to watch the blocking before going to dinner at Orso with Steve Martin. In the conference room, the NBC nurse was waiting to give him a shingles vaccine. Takeout containers, the assistants' meals, covered the table. "I've never been able to tell whether Lorne is driven by a managerial philosophy or a lifestyle philosophy," Robert Carlock told me. "He'll let everyone fight things out while he's at Orso, and he'll come back after a nice dinner and make the decision."

By ten, Michaels had returned from dinner. He was itching to see the cold-open script; Jost had promised ten pages soon. Before he could call it a night he had two tasks: to check that Jonah Hill was in good spirits, and to sequence the lineup, making sure that the sketches flowed in a way that worked with the location of the sets. The day had been grueling. Besides the Baldwin mess (Twitter had been demanding NBC fire him for his "toxic masculinity"), there had been another Pete Davidson incident. Michaels hadn't been told about the promo he did proposing marriage to Maggie Rogers. Within hours of it airing, Ariana Grande had decided that she'd been disrespected. She angrily tweeted about it a bunch of times ("for somebody who claims to hate relevancy u sure love clinging to it huh. thank u, next"), deleted the tweets, then promised to release a new single addressing her insensitive ex-fiancé on Saturday. Suddenly Davidson had even more haters than he'd had the day before.

"Ariana is furious," Michaels said. "She feels like he trivialized their relationship." He called the promo a "mindless mistake" and blamed Lindsay Shookus, the talent coordinator, who'd overseen the promos and had been in the doghouse for a few months. She'd recently broken up with Ben Affleck, whom she'd met when he hosted. "She's going through this *fame* period," a colleague said, using one of the boss's lines.

Out in the conference room, Erin Doyle typed on her laptop and quietly sang a few verses of a song from *Brigadoon:* "What a day this has been / What a rare mood I'm in . . ." The first line was the point. Someone asked how the Leslie Jones drama was shaping up, and Doyle made a face. Hill arrived and went into Michaels's office for a check-in. All week, Michaels makes a point of asking everyone around him for their opinions—William Shawn's pseudo-egalitarian observation. By the time of the Friday night meeting, he is still polling people, but it is partly pantomime. He is starting to make up his own mind, a process that culminates after dress rehearsal, at 10:00 P.M. Saturday. The dynamic between him and the host evolves all week.

Now, when he asked Hill which sketches he favored, instead of listening and nodding, Michaels felt free to disagree in an almost breezy way. The producers and head writers joined them in the office, and Michaels asked Hill whether there was anything he particularly liked or disliked. His *Late90s* trailer had been nixed in the first round, but Hill spoke up for his Movie Theater idea, which he had been defending all week against the writers' interventions. "I don't think the writers quite understand that the joke is in the foodie-arty thing, like, with a Michelin chef," he said. "They keep putting in fajitas."

Michaels nodded, ignoring Hill's note. "It's a big set. That's the problem."

"I have no personal connection to it," Hill shot back, not wanting to look like a diva. "And I love Montreal Motorcycle. It'll be fun to see if it tanks or is the funniest fucking thing ever."

They discussed how the Beavis and Butt-Head headpieces were coming along. Louie Zakarian, the show's master prosthetist, was still building them. The cropped, girly version of the Five Timer jacket—an important sight gag—wasn't ready yet. And the Craigslist van had not yet arrived.

"We're not buying the *real* van, are we?" Michaels said, making the room laugh at the extravagant lengths the show goes to in the service of verisimilitude.

Hill was still mulling his dream lineup. "I would say that KCR News isn't my absolute favorite," he said.

"It's generic, but the performances should be good," Michaels said, shutting him down.

Hill retreated: "It turned out *really* funny."

Michaels said that the show was still twenty minutes too long, which meant that three pieces would likely have to go. He signaled that the host-coddling part of the meeting was over. "I think it's going to be really good," he said in the direction of the door, as Hill walked out.

The producers and senior writers stayed, and the tech people came in. They all looked at the bulletin board. Michaels was happy with the "power of the first act": it was the Cold Open, Monologue (Five Timers), America's Got Talent, Benihana, Political Musical, and Beavis and Butt-Head. "America's Got Talent should destroy," he said, given the strength of Kenan Thompson and Leslie Jones singing together, and Cecily Strong as the Sondheim-spouting wild child. And he felt good about Political Musical, which checked a few boxes. "It's bad showbiz, but *smart* bad showbiz," he said. "And politically, it's not a screed."

Consulting with Janine DeVito about the length of each sketch, they discussed rejiggering the order to allow time for costume changes. (In the hallway outside the studio doors is a row of curtained changing stalls, one for each cast member.)

"Streeter, you're a hundred percent that Movie Theater is gonna work?" he asked the writer Streeter Seidell.

Seidell bristled. "I want to be clear: I didn't order up those giant chairs," he said. "The set doesn't *need* to be that big. We could lop it off, but that would be a lot of rebuilding tonight."

"Maybe if we used smaller people . . . ," Higgins said.

Seidell tried to stick up for the sketch, which he sensed was on the bubble. "We now have the chef talking about a clam foam that's been *starred* and *bursted*," he said. The others laughed.

"I don't like starting an act with Teacher Fell Down," Michaels said, referring to the quiet piece by the new writer Alison Gates. Cards shuffled.

"Okay," Michaels said. "We'll find out tomorrow whether Craigslist freaks people out or not." He paused. "Is Kate on Update?" He was disappointed that she hadn't been persuaded to do Angela Merkel. "She's got three more years as chancellor!" he said.

With only Higgins and Doyle left, Michaels worried aloud about the pug sketch. "It felt a little thrown together," he said. "Like the writers laughing behind the camera." He meant that the idea was purely silly, an indulgence. "Do we have professional pugs?" he asked. He retold the story about Louise Lasser and her panting dog under the hot lights in 1976. Kenward went down the hall to check on the pre-tapes in Seth Meyers's studio. It was after eleven, and the cast and crew would be working until two or three.

As Michaels got ready to go home, he brooded about Alec Baldwin and "his shame spiral." The aborted pilot rankled. "With him it's that thing of having to be in charge—'I'm the boss,'" he said, scooping a handful of popcorn. "And you go, 'No-no-no-no. It's so much better *not* to be. Just be the guy with the great part and the good writers and producers.'" Having spent so many decades running the show, he knows the territory. The problem with making it look easy, he likes to say, is that then people think it's easy.

THIRTY

SATURDAY NIGHT DEAD

THE BEGINNINGS AND THE ENDS OF THINGS ARE OFTEN GREAT, LORNE MI-
chaels likes to observe. It's the middles that are tricky, if not downright bad. That's how he looks at SNL in the mid-nineties. The show
was coming off a high. In December 1992, *Entertainment Weekly* put
the cast on the cover as "Entertainers of the Year," announcing that
SNL had "reclaimed its status as the show of the moment," turning
newsmakers into pop culture artifacts. Clinton, Bush, Ross Perot,
and Dan Quayle became the same kind of comic characters as Wayne
and Garth and Hans and Franz. Carvey's Bush and Perot impersonations had driven the conversation during the 1992 election season.
Phil Hartman hit a high point with his performance of President
Clinton stopping by a McDonald's while jogging with the Secret Service: "Let me tell you something. There's gonna be a *whole bunch of
things* we don't tell Mrs. Clinton," he says to the worried agent. (The
First Marriage, as it happens, was precisely as old as SNL; Bill and
Hillary were married on the day that *Saturday Night* debuted, in
1975.)

The show had become more of a celebrity hangout than ever, with
DeNiro and Scorsese popping by to do cameos when Joe Pesci hosted,
and Barbra Streisand and Madonna stealing onto the set of "Coffee
Talk," Mike Myers's Jewish-housewife chat-show sketch. Both Christopher Walken and Alec Baldwin had hosted for the first time in

1990, each achieving show-pony status. When Baldwin played a scout leader making lecherous advances to young Sandler in a sketch called "Canteen Boy," Michaels stood under the bleachers and murmured, in admiration, "Alec will do *anything*."

Michaels knew from experience that being on top means that there's nowhere to go but down. He was wary. "My hope is we'll get through this little period of success," he told *The New York Times*. As if on cue, the paper weighed in with a sour reassessment, John O'Connor declaring that SNL was showing "the electronic equivalent of wrinkles." His characterization of an appearance by Mick Jagger, whose "craggy face is increasingly out of sync with his boyishly gyrating torso," suggested a metaphor for the whole enterprise.

Other critics started piling on, too. To some extent, the show was getting pummeled for being too popular. But even if the sketches were flat, Michaels had engineered an experience for the members of the 8H audience that made them feel like they had entered the ultimate VIP room. A great "Chris Farley Show" sketch in which Farley gushes over his guest, Paul McCartney, stands out not only because of McCartney's patient deadpan in the face of idiotic non-questions like "Uh, you remember when you were with the Beatles? That was *awesome!*" but also because it replicated the way so many of Michaels's employees were reduced to stammering when Michaels would casually bring McCartney by. O'Connor wrote, disdainfully, of Michaels's cameos on the show as himself, "Hip? Not terribly. Chic? You bet."

The season after a presidential election is known around SNL as a hangover year. Having paid a lot of attention to how the show spoofed the political players, the media moves on, and 1993 was no exception. In *The New Yorker,* James Wolcott complained about the ballooning size of the "oddly starless" cast, which seemed shaped "by megadoses of MTV": "The opening credits seem to take forever, as the cast's hopeful young faces flip past like a pack of Actors' Equity playing cards." Adam Sandler, "with his baseball cap worn backward and his acorn head, is a Gap ad gone wrong." He called Chris Farley "the most over-indulged one-note," and the women in the cast, he suggested, "could stage a work stoppage and who would know?" This was undeniable. Julia Sweeney, commenting to a reporter about the show's reputation as a boys' club, said, "It's everything you think it is, times a hundred."

Michaels didn't focus on diversity when hiring cast members; he always maintained that he just hired the funniest people he found. But race became a focus of the critics. ("Blacks are not abundant," O'Connor wrote in the *Times*.) Chris Rock carried the burden of being the first Black cast member in five years and was known to be Eddie Murphy's protégé ("Talk about a fucking albatross!" Rock said), but he was a bright spot, and helped tip the show's racial balance fractionally with such successful pieces as "I'm Chillin," a parody of *Def Comedy Jam*, HBO's Black-targeted competitor to SNL. Rock, who was on the show for three seasons, didn't have complaints. "Nobody ever asked me to play Hattie McDaniel," he said. He didn't expect the show to be something it wasn't. "Culturally, SNL is really white," he said. "I don't say that in a bad way. It's white like Boston is white." He noted that even when the show had Black musical acts, it got them too late. "SNL would have the white bands on the way up. Like, Nirvana was on when 'Teen Spirit' was big, whereas MC Hammer is on when he's doing the *Addams Family* song." It was the same deal with Black hosts; "They had Sinbad on the way down."

Michaels knew he had to keep bringing on rookies to refresh the ranks, but the show was awkwardly divided between veterans and youngsters, and the two groups didn't always jell. There were people in their fifties and people in their twenties, millionaires and kids just scraping by. And Sandler and the other "Bad Boys," as the media branded them, were funny in a different way than Hartman or Lovitz. Sandler would walk into Michaels's office with a hammer clenched between his butt cheeks, or he'd pee in a plant in the writers' room, horrifying Bonnie and Terry Turner. Farley would moon the office window-washers or stroll into the writers' room naked. Franken remembered being frustrated that Sandler had never heard of Helmut Kohl.

The phrase "anal probe" turned up in a lot of sketches, and naysayers complained that the show was getting too sophomoric (a designation that Michael O'Donoghue always defined as "the liberal word for funny"). Farley was a talented physical comedian, but the writing for him could get repetitive. A joke diagram circulated in the office labeled "Sketches for Chris Farley." It had three different dials. The first one was labeled "Chris is: Dry. Moist. Soaking Wet." The second was: "Chris is: Quiet. Talking Loud. Screaming at the Top of His Lungs." The third: "Chris is saying: 'Gosh!' 'Oh no!' or 'Oh, sweet mother of God!'" Each dial was turned to the third choice. Odenkirk would counsel Farley, before going on, "Whatever you do, don't start at *the end.*" In other words, don't start a sketch by smashing something. "You need some *build* in there."

The middle-aged men who ran NBC had given Conan O'Brien his own show because they saw him as the voice of a new generation. But they didn't view the young blood at SNL in the same way, particularly once the critics (also middle-aged) had started dumping on the show. By the time that O'Brien was on his feet at *Late Night,* having weathered NBC's doubts and dings, SNL was the problem child. O'Brien recalled, "That began the period of me feeling like I was maybe a ray of light for a while in Lorne's life."

Michaels had always rolled his eyes when his mother asked, in a worried voice, what "the brass" thought. Now, for the first time, the brass was encroaching. They were paying attention to what the critics said. In 1994, *Entertainment Weekly,* barely a year after its "Entertainers of the Year" cover, asked, "Is 'Saturday Night' Dead?" and offered a twenty-point plan on how to solve "the SNL crisis."

Number one on the magazine's list was getting rid of Kevin Nealon as the Weekend Update anchor. The network felt the same way, and they were ready to meddle. Nealon was a superb sketch player, but there was a sense that, on Update, he was a mushmouth, his delivery not crisp enough. Nealon had been feeling a chill from Michaels for a few seasons: "Whatever I was doing, it was annoying Lorne," he said. Weekend Update also suffered because Herb Sargent, by then in his seventies, clung to it as his fiefdom. The writers found Sargent's jokes soft, but Michaels would tell them, "Be nice to Herb. He gave me my first break." And when Michaels was persuaded to bring in some young reinforcements to write on Update, Sargent basically ignored them. More than a hundred good jokes came in under the radar from Steve Koren, an NBC page who slept in the dressing rooms and submitted anonymously through Sargent's assistant. Koren was eventually hired as a receptionist, and finally as a writer.

Michaels generally reacted to network interference like a driver who turns the wheel in the direction of a skid. He brushed off NBC's directives and stalled, hoping that the issue would go away. But Season Nineteen (1993–94) was a debacle. The ratings, boosted the year before by the election and the success of *Wayne's World,* dropped precipitously. "It had started to fragment," Michaels said. Key cast members were leaving: Lovitz, Carvey, and Hooks had gone, and now Michaels lost Hartman and Julia Sweeney.

The writers' room had been gutted too, as Smigel, Jack Handey, and the Turners left. Jim Downey, the longtime head writer, who had also been made a producer of the show back in 1987, tried to hold things together. He compared the early SNL years to "a children's crusade; people would camp out here and not think about anything but the show," he told a reporter around that time. "Nowadays, anyone coming here knows what the formula is: a couple of hit characters, then you get a movie." Michaels pulled writers off the show to work on scripts for Paramount. Having enough sketches for readthrough was a challenge.

In the writers' room, a new game called "Hands Off, Hands On" was born. It targeted Michaels's tendency to take credit when things worked out, and to skedaddle when they didn't. If a sketch succeeded, they felt, he would say he'd been "hands on" with it; if it bombed, he was retroactively "hands off." This turned into silly sessions of writers talking in a Lorne voice, saying "Battle of Hastings? Hands on!" "Soviet invasion of Hungary? Hands off!" "Invention of penicillin? Hands on!"

As the ratings kept falling, the network executives focused their disapproval on Downey, and what they saw as his loose management style. They ordered Michaels to fire him. Downey's producer duties made it tough for him to focus as much as he used to on his own writing, a palpable loss for the show. The writers viewed themselves as "Jim's guys," as opposed to part of what one called "Lorne and his 'room of people.'" David Mandel, a writer who was a *Harvard Lampoon* alum, said, "Jim Downey is the funniest person on the planet Earth and the known galaxy. We idolized him, and we writers often felt that we and Jim were being blamed by Lorne for whatever was going wrong."

But Michaels and Downey were close confederates who had been through a lot together; staffers thought of them as an old married couple. Downey had what Michaels called "that Chicago integrity." ("In L.A. and New York it's about the career," he said. "In Chicago and Toronto, it's about the work itself.") Downey was the kind of writer who pulled delightful premises out of the air: "Discount babysitters—why pay more?"; "Experienced prostitutes"; *Women's Problems*—a talk show on which guys complain about women. Michaels considered him irreplaceable. "Jim is a truly original comedy thinker," he said. "With the network, I always made a case for him; I wasn't just saying 'Leave me alone.'" When executives pressed him to fire Downey, he tried explaining the infinite monkey theorem to them—the idea that trying to impose order in a comedy writers' room is impossible. "It looks like they're not doing anything, because they're just throwing jokes around and laughing," he said. "But you create a culture, with walls around them, where they can be funny. It can't be regimented."

At the end of the season, Michaels and Downey were summoned to a meeting in Burbank with NBC executives. Downey, figuring that he was being scapegoated, guessed that he was expected to beg for his job. It was easier for NBC to blame the number two guy. "The network loved the show from '91 to '93, but they had no idea what I did," he said. "It was only when they *didn't* like the show that I became known as the producer." He was miserable and exhausted; his father had just died. If they wanted to fire him, he felt, let them.

The meeting took place in Ohlmeyer's office; he chain-smoked Marlboros, sitting at a desk on a raised platform in front of an illuminated trophy case crammed with Emmys and other awards. "The effect was not quite Il Duce, but close," Michaels said. Ohlmeyer handed Michaels a copy of a list of SNL writers and cast, annotated with their salaries, and read them off one by one, assessing whether each was worth the money. When he got to Norm Macdonald, the Canadian stand-up who'd come on as a featured player the previous season, Rick Ludwin, one of the NBC guys, dumped on Macdonald's recent impression of Andy Rooney. Macdonald had played the white-haired *60 Minutes* commentator nattering while holding up letters from viewers, a dazzling display of deliberate tedium, and Downey interrupted Ludwin to defend it. Downey remembers Ludwin being so surprised that he waggled his head back and forth like a cartoon dog shaking its jowls and asked, *"Wha-wha-wha-what?"*

Ohlmeyer broached the Weekend Update situation. Michaels, in his pristine white sneakers and sport coat, had come armed with a few names of potential replacements for Nealon. Al Franken had always wanted to host Update and was making a forceful push. Littlefield and Ludwin were pro-Franken, but Brillstein had some other suggestions, including his client Bill Maher, who hosted *Politically Incorrect* on Comedy Central. Downey quietly threw out another name: What about Norm Macdonald? Ludwin made his cartoon wobble-face again: *"Wha-wha-wha-what?"* he said. "Please tell me that was a joke."

Macdonald had an anchorman's good looks and a mischievous deadpan that recalled Chevy Chase. "Norm was perfect for it," Downey said. "He was about words and language, with a low-key, dry attitude." Michaels admired Macdonald's way with a pause, and he found Downey's suggestion interesting.

Before anything could be settled, the meeting abruptly ended. An aide had come in and whispered in Ohlmeyer's ear that it was time for his daily visit to his close friend O. J. Simpson, who was being held in an L.A. jail on suspicion of murdering his wife, Nicole Brown, and her friend Ron Goldman.

When Downey buckled into his seat on the red-eye back to New York, the Update matter wasn't resolved, but his job, for the moment, felt safe. Ohlmeyer had been impressed by his willingness to speak his mind, and Michaels had supported him. Macdonald got the Update job, and Downey was put in charge of the material. The first week, the new anchor began: "I'm Norm Macdonald, and now, the fake news." His first joke was about the O. J. Simpson trial.

Michaels had taken another of *Entertainment Weekly's* suggestions (Number 12: "Sign up the brilliant cast of Fox's failed *Ben Stiller Show*") by hiring Janeane Garofalo, whose Gen-X bona fides included the movie *Reality Bites*. The sprawling, jumbly new cast he put together—an unwieldy seventeen people—included an unusual number who were already famous; besides Garofalo, there was Michael McKean (*This Is Spinal Tap*), Chris Elliott (from *Letterman*), and Mark McKinney (the Kids in the Hall's series had ended after five seasons).

Although the network had backed off, the press did not. *Newsweek's* next review of the show, headlined "Dear 'Saturday Night Live': It's Over. Please Die," called the program "now almost 100 percent humor-free," and skewered Michaels as "a mogul now, spreading himself thin over a comedy conglomerate of bad movie spin-offs, CD-ROMs, and 'Richmeister' mugs." John Podhoretz, in the *New York Post,* said that the show was less entertaining than being "smashed over the head with a hammer for 90 minutes." The *Times* ran a piece quoting Ohlmeyer saying that he'd given Michaels his marching orders and calling Downey "bedraggled." Even Judge Lance Ito, who was presiding over the O. J. Simpson trial, weighed in, declaring that the show "hasn't been funny for 10 years."

Morale in the office was at a low, as the writers struggled to turn out sketches for the too-large cast. "There was a stench of desperation to it," Mandel said. The stress set the scene for clashes between friends, as when Norm Macdonald decked the writer Ian Maxtone-Graham for extinguishing his cigarette with a squirt from a water bottle. Michaels wasn't around; he was spending more time in L.A. producing movies (*Stuart Saves His Family, Tommy Boy*). Ohlmeyer kept making cracks to reporters about him being distracted, running around with his high-profile friends, spending too much time in St.

Barts. Stories popped up in the paper about Michaels's side projects—a country inn he wanted to build in Amagansett with François de Menil; or producing a theatrical version of Randy Newman's album *Faust,* whose storyline weirdly echoed Michaels's own public-relations problem. Describing the plot, Michaels said, "The character of God is sort of like Bing Crosby. He's golfing all the time, on heaven's endless fairways. He's tuned out, not really involved in Earth much anymore."

When a *New York Times* writer interviewed him, Michaels brushed aside questions about the network's attempted incursions; he felt that he was still paying a political price for having backed Letterman over Leno in 1992. The fallout from that bungled transition, he believed, had led to "a much more activist management at NBC." The executives, emboldened by the success of *Seinfeld* and *Friends* (a show that Michaels referred to as a "warmedy," because it lacked hard jokes), wanted to fiddle with SNL, despite the fact that it pulled in significant revenue even when the ratings were down. "The network is feeling its oats right now," he said.

He took the unusual step of publicly addressing the issue of his own survival. "Rebuilding is tough to live through and tough to do, but I think that the show will be here in five years," he told the *Times.* "And it's my expectation that I will be here as well." Downey's longevity was less certain; he'd begun comparing himself to Admiral Dönitz, the German officer stuck with surrendering to the Allies after Hitler killed himself.

ON A MONDAY NIGHT IN NOVEMBER 1994, MICHAEL O'DONOGHUE SAT UP IN bed, yelled "Oh my God!" and fell back on the pillow, unconscious. Hours later, he died of a cerebral hemorrhage at St. Vincent's Hospital in the Village. That Wednesday afternoon, Alice Barry delivered her second son, Eddie, in the same hospital. "I thought, 'Michael is floating around in here somewhere,'" Michaels said. He made it up to the office in time for read-through with the host, Sarah Jessica Parker, and four days later, in the wee hours of Sunday morning, friends packed into the Winter Palace, where O'Donoghue had still been living, for a wake; Michaels had told Cheryl Hardwick, O'Donoghue's widow and the show's former music director, that he would foot the bill. The apartment was decked out in black tulle, the gold baby grand piano topped with a flower arrangement that paid homage to O'Donoghue's signature gift bouquet: a dozen white roses and one red, which he called "Blood in the Snow." On the wall was a framed photograph of the deceased holding a large handgun, and two contact sheets showing O'Donoghue's postmortem brainscan, a jagged mark indicating the hemorrhage that did him in, at the age of fifty-four.

In the cosmic frame of mind that experiencing death and birth in close proximity can produce, Michaels arrived at the wake with Chevy Chase in tow, despite the fact that Chase and O'Donoghue had never patched up their feud. "No one could have been more out of style around Michaels's friends than Chevy," he said. Guests noticed, on a side table, a stack of videocassettes labeled THE CHEVY CHASE SHOW. Chase had done a quickly canceled talk show for Fox the previous year; O'Donoghue had lustily hate-watched every episode. O'Donoghue and Michaels hadn't patched things up either. Yet, for Michaels, showing up was automatic.

The apartment was jammed—young writers and old, Penny Marshall, James Taylor, Susan Forristal, Carol Kane, Bob Guccione Jr., Stephen Colbert, Farley, Downey, assorted acolytes. "Michael had become a kind of martyr," Michaels said. Laila Nabulsi was there, and Mitch Glazer, who'd co-written the 1988 comedy *Scrooged* with O'Donoghue. (In one scene, Bill Murray's Scrooge, an ice-hearted TV executive, goes through his Christmas gift list with an assistant, deciding who gets a bath towel with the company's logo and who gets a VCR. One of Michaels's go-to staff gifts has long been a logo-printed sweatshirt.)

"Can you imagine this house, filled with people, filled with dope, filled with grief?" Marilyn Miller recalled. At some point Bill Murray climbed onto a chair to speak. Earlier that night, he'd made a cameo on SNL to eulogize O'Donoghue. ("He was a writer that the writers, actors—and even the producer—feared. And in this business, it's better sometimes to be feared than loved. But we're not afraid of him anymore—because he's dead.") At the wake, Murray described how O'Donoghue "taught you how to hate." "He hated the horrible things in life, and the horrible people in life," he said. "He hated them *so good.*"

When Chase climbed on the chair, he said how much he loved O'Donoghue's impression of Merv Griffin having needles jammed in his eyes. A heckler shouted that it was Mike Douglas, not Griffin. Michaels spoke next. "He was an incredibly important person in my life," he said. "I loved him deeply. And it would embarrass him, as it embarrasses me, to say so."

Then Buck Henry got up on the chair. "Thank you, Lorne. Thank you, Chevy. I think we all know how much Michael loved *you,*" he said. Laughter, cathartic and mean, filled the room.

"It was a hideous, hurtful thing," Chase recalled, of his reception at the wake. "Part of who Michael was was that he could love and hate a person in the same weekend." Michaels felt that the others at the wake had treated him as if he'd "defiled the temple."

Despite the newborn baby at home, he felt that he was losing his equilibrium. The network was all over him, and he was still mourning Uncle Pep, who'd died the previous winter, at seventy-two, of cancer. The roster of rabbis—of people who had been there at the beginning—was being depleted.

AS MICHAELS STRUGGLED TO FEND OFF THE NETWORK'S TAMPERING, A PO-tential escape route appeared. Howard Stringer, the president of CBS, tried to lure him away from NBC to re-create SNL at his network, as he'd lured Letterman, going so far as to present Michaels with a 3D mock-up of the Lorne Michaels Theater, to be built in Columbus Circle. The offer was flattering, but Michaels declined. He remembered how hard it was to do *The New Show* in a CBS studio, where the camera operators sat on stools affixed to the floor. A live show like SNL only worked at NBC, he felt. "There's

an old quote from Mr. Bulova: 'If it's ticking, don't open the back,'"
he said.

But SNL wasn't ticking. Johnny Carson used to say that fixing a
TV show while it is in production is like trying to change a tire on a
moving car. In January 1995, in the middle of Season Twenty, Michaels met with Ohlmeyer and reassured him that he was doing just
that—adding Molly Shannon, a fizzy NYU friend of Sandler's, who'd
created a painfully awkward Catholic schoolgirl character called
Mary Katherine Gallagher; and Darrell Hammond, a master impressionist. But Ohlmeyer wanted more drastic change; specifically, he
wanted Chris Farley and Adam Sandler fired.

"All the Baby Boomers, Don foremost among them, thought they
knew the difference between good SNL and bad SNL," Michaels
recalled. "I said, 'Don, it's generational. For you, a good show is Bill
Murray as the lounge singer.'" The critics trashing the show were
Baby Boomers too. Michaels knew by now that anytime you ask people to name their favorite SNL cast, they'll say it's the one that was on
when they were in high school. Determined to keep pace with the
times, he'd long ago internalized a line from Lenny Bruce: "There's
nothing sadder than an aging hipster."

Sandler didn't know that he was a hot topic in Burbank. "Lorne
shielded us," he said. "He knew it would affect your performance." If
someone brought up the bad press, Sandler recalled, Michaels reassured them: "Don't worry about that," he'd say. "I like you, and I make
the decisions and that's it."

In March 1995, the situation with NBC reached a crisis point.
New York magazine published a story about SNL with the banner
headline "Comedy Isn't Funny: The Inside Story of the Decline and
Fall of Saturday Night Live," the cover showing a photo of a scowling
Farley with his head crammed inside a tiny TV set. The writer, Chris
Smith, had unprecedented access to the studio for four weeks and
depicted the show as in "a deep spiritual funk," as bloated as "late-
period Elvis," "a rare portrait of institutional decay—the gargantuan
exertion of sweat, blood, fried food, and bluff self-denial that yields,

for example, a mind-bendingly awful sketch about space aliens and rectal probes."

Hanging around the office, Smith had witnessed the internal politics close-up, including tussles over who sat where in meetings, writers wolfing down Quarter Pounders at midnight, and Chris Farley farting into a phone while making a prank call. Janeane Garofalo was the article's heroine, a visitor from the new generation, too smart and hip for the room and deeply unhappy. She compared her SNL experience to "fraternity hazing." Smith quoted former and current employees being critical: Julia Sweeney (she couldn't bear the Lornettes), Rosie Shuster ("Talking to Lorne is like talking to tundra"), the cast member Ellen Cleghorne ("There's no Black writers on the show—this is 1995, and I feel like I'm in a really bad sci-fi movie where all the Black people already got killed, and I'm next"). Dozens of nasty unattributed quotes completed the picture. One anonymous staffer described Michaels's management style as "the same techniques cults use—they keep you up for hours, they never let you know that you're okay, and they always make you think that your spot could be taken at any moment by someone else."

In conversation with Smith, Michaels kept his cool. "If your angle is going to be that the show is decadent and out of touch, we have that reduced to a press release to save time," he told the writer. He proffered his theory that critics resent SNL because it forces them to stay up late; they can't watch the show on an advance cassette. (John Mulaney later developed another theory about how critics view SNL: "It's never reviewed like something that's thrown together in a week, but like it's the next Eagles album.")

Terrible press had been the norm for a couple of years, but the *New York* story struck a nerve. Michaels thought that he came off as "some sort of Howard Hughes figure." He still refers to the piece as "the death knell," the article "that killed everything," "the piece where I was disemboweled." He regretted giving Smith—"that weasel"—so much access. "Wherever he is, I hope his teeth hurt," he said, thirty years later. (The teeth line was one of Dave Tebet's, he said.) He'd always counseled his protégés to talk to reporters as little as possible; there's no upside. One of Michaels's axioms is that people like to root for your failure—they define their own success by your failure—so it's better to keep a low profile.

The article made Farley cry. (For years, he worried that by posing for the cover photo, he'd "ruined the show.") And it spurred the executives in L.A. to get on the phone with reporters to try to contain the damage. The headline on Bill Carter's *Times* story told the next chapter: "*Saturday Night* Lives, for Now, but Then What?" The first sentence described Warren Littlefield's conviction that the show "needs a creative overhaul that may include everything except the show's live format and its location in New York City." What made this moment more perilous, Michaels realized, was that it was the first time in twenty years that the critical community and the network were on the same side. "I was the odd man out," he said. It was also the first time that NBC had publicly hinted that it might fire him.

He was in St. Barts when the *Times* piece was being reported, and did not comment. But he was furious about what Littlefield had suggested. A few weeks later Michaels took Littlefield on in another piece by Carter, headlined "Lorne Michaels Vows to Stay With His Show." "I was surprised and angered again at Warren's comments," he told Carter. "A very conscious decision was made to sidestep support for me, and that to me is infuriating." He went on, "In one sense this is about defending yourself for being 50. I'm 50 and successful and I have two small children. But there is certainly no lack of commitment to the show. We'll fight back."

He insisted that he refused to be told what's funny by a bunch of suits. For years, he'd managed the corporate types by training what Carvey calls his "charm beam" on them, or by staying quiet and going about his business, but Ohlmeyer was different. Although he had made his bones in TV sports, he considered himself as having an artistic side. He'd once aspired to write the great American novel, and in his spare time he painted dark, abstract canvases. (He drank like an artist, too. At SNL's twentieth anniversary bash, the Lornette who'd been tasked with shepherding Ohlmeyer had to call for help;

he got hammered, and handsy. Michaels had him escorted out by security.)

"Don believed that he did what *I* did," Michaels recalled. After the *New York* cover story, Michaels was summoned to Burbank, where he sat in front of the Il Duce desk and listened to the litany of defects one more time.

Ohlmeyer had also invited a programming executive, Gary Considine, a muscular man with a ruddy complexion and spiky MTV hair, who had spent years as an associate athletic director at UCLA before coming to NBC. He brandished pages of data about viewer reactions, "like a McKinsey analysis," Michaels remembered. "He said, 'Farley has to go, and Sandler.' But those network guys never know that they're just choosing on personal taste. It was a culture clash."

Michaels explained, again, that he was implementing "a generational change," and talked about how his young cast members were funny in a different way than the original Baby Boomer cast. Ohlmeyer thought he was being stubborn. He found Michaels impervious to his demands. "Lorne would be calm during an earthquake," he told Tom Shales, calling it "one of his strengths as a producer."

Continuing his crusade for drastic change, Ohlmeyer would sit behind a double cheeseburger in Morton's with Michaels ("I'd have something green on my plate"), and say, "You think you *need* those people, but you could stand in the middle of Times Square holding a sign that said 'SNL,' and just rebuild the show by yourself." Michaels reminded him of the disaster in 1985, when he'd started from scratch. If you do that, he observed, "it's like saying, 'Come to a dinner party; there will be twelve people you haven't met.' No one's dying to run to that dinner party." Ohlmeyer, after five or six drinks, would segue to critiquing Michaels's extracurricular pursuits: his movies and his social life. Michaels said, "And I'd go, 'Don, I *am* paying attention. Honest. Live TV is complicated.'"

"Don't tell *me* about live," Ohlmeyer shot back. "I did *Monday Night Football!*"

Wearily, Michaels explained that the game was going to happen anyway: "We have to *write* the game every week." (Exchanges like this one are what Michaels is referring to when he reminds staffers who view him as all-powerful that, "in my job, you're always a supplicant.") The job, Michaels told him, wasn't like playing third base: "It's all about getting the best out of people. Your system is, you do it through terror."

FACED WITH OHLMEYER'S INTRANSIGENCE, CONSIDINE'S CLIPBOARD, AND the battering of the press, Michaels gave in. There would be an SNL purge. In some ways, letting go was a relief. He was now the age his father was when he died. All the years ahead were years that Henry Lipowitz never had. At home were two young sons and an over-whelmed young wife. "The birth of my kids was the biggest thing that had ever happened to me and the only thing in my life that I wanted one hundred percent to get right," he said. The shift from father fig-ure to actual biological father was profound. "I had to reinvent my game," he said. Regarding his family, he said, "I'd decided: I'm going to be there. I'm not going to be there at school drop-off, but I will be there at pickup, and I will go to every game." Because his son Henry loved the Seven Dwarfs, every time Michaels came back from a trip to L.A., he'd bring home a different dwarf toy. He'd tell the boy, "I went to a lunch at Morton's, and I saw Dopey at another table." From then on, SNL's off-weeks aligned with the vacation schedule of New York's private schools; later, father-son trips to Mohonk were on regu-lar rotation. Even with his schedule adjustments, he worried about whether he was present enough; Henry once asked him, "Why do I have to have a nocturnal dad?"

Being a father helped erase the tinge of uncertainty and guilt that had stayed with him since his own father died. "I finally figured out, by the way I feel about my own sons, that there's no question that he was crazy about me," he said. He tells his protégés, "If you're on your deathbed, and your kids are next to you, you've done it right."

Family sentiment aside, there was a pragmatic reason to give in to Ohlmeyer. Speaking of SNL, Michaels said, "I realized how I would feel if it stopped."

Ohlmeyer's clean sweep left few performers and writers standing.

Sandy Wernick, who represented Sandler, heard rumbles of what was coming and called Michaels. "Adam will stay if you want him to," Wernick told him carefully. "But if it's all the same, he'd like to leave, because it's going to be tough sledding there." Michaels was grateful; he could offer up Sandler as a sacrifice to the network without having to deal the blow himself. The same happened with Farley. Mike Shoemaker, a young producer on the show, called their exits "nebulous leavings." The details were kept close. "Lorne and I conspired not to tell Adam or Chris what had gone down," Wernick said. "I knew that Lorne would be embarrassed if the staff knew that he didn't have that kind of control." Wernick spun it as an opportunity for Sandler to finish the screenplay for *Happy Gilmore,* which he was writing with SNL's Tim Herlihy. Farley had just wrapped *Tommy Boy,* produced by Michaels. Also not returning were Jay Mohr, Morwenna Banks, Michael McKean, Chris Elliott, Nealon, Franken, Garofalo, and Mike Myers (the last two had left midseason). Some were relieved. "It wasn't just a boys' club," McKean said. "It was a depressed boys' club." Remaining were Mark McKinney, Norm Macdonald, David Spade, Molly Shannon, and Tim Meadows.

Most of the writers left too, reading the tea leaves. "If there was an ax, it was a very passive-aggressive ax, which is *Saturday Night Live* in a nutshell," said Mandel, who took a job at *Seinfeld.* Tom Schiller and Herb Sargent, both with the show since 1975, came to the office to find an assistant packing their belongings into boxes. Jim Downey got a call from his agent: this time, he hadn't been spared. That same day, he was served with divorce papers.

Downey would be a mammoth loss. He'd done more than anyone to shape the show's comedy personality, and he had deep institutional memory. Conan O'Brien said, "Downey was the only person left who would get in Lorne's face and say, 'What the fuck, Lorne?'" He wasn't afraid to push back against a kind of warm and fuzzy comedy that Michaels liked—like hosts making winking, self-referential jokes in the monologue—which Downey derisively called "adorable."

The network signaled its new tough approach in smaller ways, too. The office fridge was no longer stocked with soda. The bounteous spread of Chinese food from Shun Lee that was delivered every Friday night was reduced. Even the popcorn budget was cut. So that Michaels could keep his focus on the show, SNL spin-off movies, such as one based on Smigel's "Da Bears" sketch and a musical called *Hans and Franz: The Girlyman Dilemma,* were shelved. That summer, a series of new protocols went into effect: NBC would approve all new cast members; every Thursday, the executives gathered in Burbank to discuss the show.

In August, Michaels gave a stiff-upper-lip interview about the network's encroachment to Tom Shales ("Barely Alive, It's Saturday Night!"), who went so far as to suggest that Hollywood was calling Michaels a has-been. "I know that I will not wear my baseball hat backwards and I am probably not going to get an earring," Michaels told him, but he believed that he knew how to make SNL work. He admitted to being in the hot seat. "Can I be fired? Of course I can be fired," he said calmly. "Yes, I am mortal."

For years he'd told NBC that his plan was to seed the cast with talented young people, and develop them. The network decided to try the same thing with producing. Around the time of his firing, Downey had received a phone call from the twenty-seven-year-old comedy writer Judd Apatow. The two had met ten years earlier, when teenage Apatow arrived at *The New Show*'s offices with a bulky tape recorder to interview Downey and John Candy, purportedly for Syosset High School's 125-watt radio station. Apatow was such an SNL nerd as a kid that he recorded the show on his VCR and transcribed it. Working at SNL was his dream. When his roommate Adam Sandler was hired, Apatow would get on the phone and pitch in jokes for Update bits, and once Sandler slipped an Apatow sketch (about a family who dotes on its daughter's ex-boyfriend) into the read-through packet, and it made it on the air.

Apatow had recently been the head writer and co-creator of Fox's *The Ben Stiller Show,* which had been speedily canceled despite being widely admired. Now he wanted to ask Downey some questions about SNL's day-to-day operations. Warren Littlefield had reached out to him to discuss the idea of his working at SNL in a producer capacity, intimating that he could be in line to take over the show. "I investigated it for a moment," Apatow said. "They gave me the budget to look at, and I called a few people and asked what they were spending money on." He even met with Michaels a couple of times. But there was a vagueness to the discussions. Littlefield never explicitly addressed the job responsibilities—or NBC's SNL succession plans.

Apatow was at a loss. SNL was his dream. But the show was getting rid of all the people he admired most. He was unsettled by the evident back-channel interference. "I think they thought Lorne was on his last legs, that he was getting stale," he said.

In Burbank, rumors were making the rounds. Conan O'Brien said, "We were hearing all these crazy things about NBC wanting to get in there and fix SNL, and that maybe Lorne was out." Another name whispered as a possible replacement was NBC's Gary Considine, the bodybuilding statistics buff. In a counteroffensive, Michaels himself courted Adam Resnick, a former *Letterman* writer whom Downey admired. Michaels invited Resnick to watch the show with him under the bleachers, to eat the Shun Lee, to attend the Monday writers' meeting. Resnick could see that Michaels was under pressure to make changes. Suddenly Resnick's agent heard from Littlefield and Ohlmeyer. They flew him out to Burbank for a meeting, and he was taken aback to find that Michaels hadn't been invited. "That's how scummy they were," Resnick said. "They had it out for him." Ohlmeyer struck Resnick as a "cufflinks and cocktail guy who could've been a prick high school principal." Resnick let his agent know that he had no interest in taking the job, whatever it was.

One of Michaels's pet sayings is "There are no heirs apparent in show business." He did not want to lose control the way William Shawn had at *The New Yorker.* So he played along, poker-faced, and did nothing. He intended to wait out the storm. Ten years later, on *30 Rock,* the NBC sitcom that Tina Fey created, the character of the GE boss played by Alec Baldwin (and modeled, in part, on Michaels) espouses a management theory called "the Fabian strategy." Robert Carlock, who developed the show with Fey, remembered a high-school Latin lesson about General Fabius Maximus, who avoids battle and seeks to win by attrition. "His strategy was retreat, retreat, retreat, and wear the enemy out," Carlock said. He and Fey had seen Lorne Michaels triumph with NBC again and again by simply deflecting, letting time go by.

Michaels didn't think much of Warren Littlefield (who once underwhelmed Michaels by telling him that he brought his lunch from home, to be more efficient). But Michaels had been polite during his chats with Judd Apatow and didn't betray any apprehension. He might have remembered the line from *King Lear* that he'd steeled himself with as a young producer at the CBC: "Even a dog's obeyed in office." But he was getting worn down.

THIRTY-ONE

"IS HE *DOING* ME?"

BY THE END OF 1995, IT LOOKED AS IF MICHAELS HAD SURVIVED WHAT HE called "Ohlmeyer's pounce," and he set about rebuilding the show yet again. Judd Apatow had instructed his agent to give Warren Little-field a firm no. "I realized that I probably wouldn't have any power to make decisions at the show," Apatow said. There were issues of re-spect and karma, too. "One of the biggest reasons I went into comedy was watching SNL," he said. "I thought, this is Lorne's show, and I don't want to be a part of anything that disrespects his captaining of his ship. At some point, I realized that Lorne is a master strategist. Whatever's happening, Lorne is going to win. It was clear that he wasn't going to step back, and that he was playing some game of judo with the network."

Conan O'Brien never doubted that Michaels would outsmart Bur-bank. "If there were a *Game of Thrones* of show business, Lorne would be the last person standing," he said. Vindication came from various directions. Buck Henry wrote Michaels a letter apologizing for the cheap shot he'd taken at O'Donoghue's wake. "A pack of dogs was barking at your heels, and I joined the pack," the letter read. "For that I'll always be sorry." And Ohlmeyer admitted that he'd been wrong about Adam Sandler; when *Happy Gilmore* came out, he called Michaels and asked if he could get him a print of the movie to show at his son's birthday party.

By fall, Michaels had quietly brought back Jim Downey to continue overseeing Macdonald's Weekend Update. He also hired, as a writing supervisor, Apatow's friend Steve Higgins, who'd been writing for Jon Stewart; Adam McKay, a young Chicago improv guy came aboard, and would be promoted to head writer the following year. Consciously trying to shed the show's reputation as a boys' club, Michaels looked at a lot of tapes of women, and flew Paula Pell up from Orlando, where she was a performer at theme parks. "Lorne has a way, when you sit down with him, where you think, 'Did we already have part one of the conversation?'" she recalled. When he offered her a job on the spot, she was so scared that she tried to talk him out of it. ("Like, is this a pyramid scheme?") He hooked her with a speech promising that the show would "rise from the ashes again."

The hire who would contribute more than anyone to the show's eventual rebound was Will Ferrell, who created a roster of ineradicable characters, including Janet Reno (of "Janet Reno's Dance Party"); the middle-school music teacher Marty Culp (partnered with Ana Gasteyer's Bobbi Mohan-Culp); the Spartan Cheerleader (with Cheri Oteri); one of the Roxbury disco guys (with Chris Kattan); and Alex Trebek, the fed-up host of Celebrity Jeopardy, a regular "impression parade" sketch that allowed the cast to show off their specialties. (Norm Macdonald distinguished himself as Burt Reynolds, who insisted on being addressed as Turd Ferguson.) Michaels had leaned this time toward improvisers, finding Ferrell, Oteri, Gasteyer, and Kattan at the Groundlings. Other standout characters included Molly Shannon's Mary Katherine Gallagher, Alec Baldwin's Pete Schweddy (of Schweddy Balls), and Tracy Morgan's Brian Fellow, the unaccredited zoologist.

After the purge and the press barrage, the bar was low. "People would go out of their way to hate this show then," Pell said, recalling cabdrivers who, when dropping her off at the GE Building, would say, "Man, that show used to be funny." Coming out of the bad year, the cast and writers felt wobbly at first. Ferrell tried to dissipate anxiety around the office by dressing up and pretending to be different characters. He had one named Chip Kudrow, Lisa Kudrow's fake brother, a "guest writer" who gave unhelpful notes. Once he and Adam McKay ran into the writers' room brandishing Downey's Emmy Awards and yelling, "It's *our* time!" Downey chuckled and kept on working.

BY THE FALL OF 1996, SEASON TWENTY-TWO, THE SHOW HAD STABILIZED, being steadily revived by the latest infusion of new blood, and Michaels once again found himself able to enjoy the West Coast part of his life. His office on the Paramount lot was a minimalist all-white zone, a contrast to the dark, knickknack-filled spaces he had at NBC. And he was largely left alone by the studio. Michaels had dedicated a movie to Uncle Pep: 1995's *Tommy Boy,* the latest in a string of goofball buddy comedies, had had a uniquely personal origin story. Michaels had pitched Sherry Lansing an idea about the charismatic head of an automotive business, who dies and leaves his inept son— played by Chris Farley—in charge. In the Uncle Pep role Michaels envisioned Brian Dennehy, a casting coup that came about after a chance meeting between Farley and Dennehy at the Rochester Big & Tall store in Beverly Hills. "*Tommy Boy* was a rough version of my life," Michaels said. "Killing the father at the end of the first act—it's what happened to me." He related to the story of the bereft son "being stuck at the loading dock and having to figure it out."

Most of the critics viewed *Tommy Boy* as sketch material stretched thin (Roger Ebert put it on his "Most Hated" list), but it did strong box office and would, like a number of panned SNL movies, accrue a kind of cult status. Dana Carvey likes to say that, over time, these movies "get shinier and brighter"—a phrase that Paul McCartney taught him, describing how various innovations in audio technology have kept the Beatles recordings ever-fresh.

Sherry Lansing had initially been dismissive of the SNL vehicles. Even though *Wayne's World* had been a whopping hit three years earlier, Michaels felt that Paramount stinted on marketing his projects. But after Lansing's stepson told her that *Tommy Boy* was his favorite movie, she came around. An artist in the Paramount marketing department had designed the *Wayne's World* poster, showing the two stars against a blue sky dotted with puffy white clouds. It worked so well that Michaels stuck with the formula; the goal, he says, is to make someone say, "That looks like fun." Consequently, the posters for almost all of the films he's produced since then feature blue sky and clouds.

Michaels had his own shingle at a major studio, but some colleagues felt that his Paramount operation was "underpowered"—staffed with former employees and friends rather than by experienced development executives. Barnaby Thompson believed that some part of Michaels wished he worked with tonier directors. "It's not what Lorne got into show business for," he said, "to make films with the guy who directed the second *Naked Gun* sequel. He wanted chic and smart." But the scripts were rarely chic and smart, and at the start of every project he'd tell his crew, "I want to make sure everyone's clear that we're not making an art picture."

For every collaborator who praised Michaels for giving filmmakers space, there's one who complained that he only ever visited the set to have his picture taken with the stars. He was impatient with how long movies took and would talk about how agonizing it was that six years went by making *Enigma,* a 2001 thriller he co-produced with his friend Mick Jagger, from a script by his friend Tom Stoppard. "Lorne doesn't feel like a Hollywood guy to me," Randy Newman said, intending a compliment. "He's in it like a guy going to the track. He's a creative guy." Producing movies played to his avocation of rounding up amusing people, as if for a dinner party. It didn't bother him much if they bombed. Critics rarely like his films, he said, "because they use another kind of standard, and anything that looks dumb will be reviewed as dumb. But dumb is a very important part of American culture and comedy."

After the Kids in the Hall TV series wound down, Michaels offered the troupe a movie deal at Paramount. They wrote *Brain Candy,* about an evil corporation peddling a Prozac-like miracle drug, Glee-MONEX. The Kids argued with the studio people, who were expecting something involving the troupe's popular TV characters (perhaps Chicken Lady or Cabbage Head), not a dark satire on Big Pharma.

Michaels coached them through the process, telling them, "You want it to be successful enough that you get to make another one."

A character in the script called Cancer Boy, played by McCulloch with a bald wig and a wheelchair, provoked a showdown. (Sherry Lansing was a leader in the cancer-charity world.) Michaels told the Kids to work it out. They got on the phone with the studio and then triumphantly reported back to Michaels that they'd won the Cancer Boy fight. "And Lorne went, '*Riiiight*,'" McKinney recalled. Cancer Boy stayed in the film, but its marketing budget dried up. "Lorne let us make our own mistakes," McCulloch said.

When Michaels first read the *Brain Candy* script, he thought Cancer Boy was a funny, if risky, subplot. But he didn't see anything touchy about a character named Don Roritor, the villainous pharmaceutical CEO. When the cameras rolled in Toronto, however, McKinney played Roritor with an unnervingly blank affect, wearing a wig of swept-back silver hair. His delivery was so languid that the character barely registered a pulse. It was clear to everyone on the set that Roritor was McKinney's Lorne impression, with an extra shade of nonchalant menace and acid wit.

Roritor's dialogue is all circular logic and verbal jujitsu. Trying to prevent a scientist from leaking the company's venal intentions, he says, "You know, Chris, the thing about being upset is that, besides it sometimes being a turn-on to women, is that it's not a state that you really want to be in when you make an important decision, like, say, going to the press. Wouldn't you agree?" The scientist does not, and Roritor continues, "But Chris, you would agree that Paris is the capital of France? Wouldn't you agree to that? Good. Then we're back in agreement." (Lorne watchers recognized an unsettling truth about Michaels in that exchange. Jim Biederman, at Broadway Video, likened it to "that classic mind-fucky thing that Lorne does. No matter how strongly you feel about something, he knows how to throw you off your game, so you go, 'Of course, you're right.'")

The *Brain Candy* impersonation reaches its peak in a speech that Roritor gives to the scientist in his office. "Can I get you anything else?" he asks, his face a mask of patrician contempt. "Grappa? Wine?

Cappuccino? Tickets to a Lakers game? . . . What about cheesecake? Double-A batteries? Land in Montana?" Bruce McCulloch wrote the lines based on years of close study. "Lorne's got that seductive speech pattern," he said.

Barnaby Thompson sent the *Brain Candy* dailies to Michaels in New York. Employees at Broadway Video panicked when they realized what McKinney was doing. Nobody wanted the boss to see it cold in a screening room. (Rule number one: Lorne hates surprises.) A diplomatic explanation was prepared: Don Roritor was supposed to be one of the most powerful people in the world, and the only such person that Mark McKinney knew personally was Lorne Michaels. McKinney was anxious, too, remembering how he'd once displeased Michaels by describing him as "loquacious" in a magazine profile; "I didn't know what the word meant!" McKinney said. "I thought I was calling him eloquent."

The anxiety turned out to be misplaced. "With Lorne, it's always: 'If it's funny, it's OK,'" Scott Thompson said. "He has a clean line." Later, Brillstein told the Kids that he'd watched the Roritor scenes alone in a screening room with Michaels, who had leaned over in the dark to whisper, "Is Mark *doing* me?" Brillstein replied, "Of course he's doing you!" Michaels asked, "What should I do about it?" Brillstein's reply: "You should shut the fuck up and applaud! You're the executive producer!" But when the film was screened at the Brill Building, staffers were discreetly advised not to laugh too loud at the Roritor parts.

THE FOLLOWING YEAR, MICHAELS GOT ANOTHER SURPRISE IN A DARK screening room. *Wayne's World 2* had been his last project with Mike Myers, and the relationship between the two had cooled. But he unwittingly made a big contribution to Myers's 1997 blockbuster, *Austin Powers: International Man of Mystery.* Some SNL writers felt that the script contained echoes of two old sketches—"Tightwad 007," in which Steve Martin, as a cheapskate James Bond, tries to stuff his pockets with free casino pretzels; and a talk show on which the docile trio of Auric Goldfinger (host Jimmy Breslin), Ernst Blofeld (Lovitz), and Emilio Largo (Randy Quaid) discuss bungling their many ornate schemes to kill James Bond. (Consensus: they should have just shot him.) "Mike mined all of that for *Austin Powers*," one writer said. (Jack Handey, who co-wrote the talk-show sketch with Downey and George Meyer, got a "special thanks" in the credits.)

More notably, Myers mined Michaels himself. Dr. Evil, Austin Powers's bald Blofeldian nemesis, often says *"Riiiiiight"* with parched sarcasm, and repeats favorite Lorne words like "breathtaking." With his jittery hauteur and his circle of eye-rolling henchmen, Dr. Evil is a caricature of Lorne Michaels. Myers plays him as a man who has a lot of power, but whose deliberately casual—even singsongy—way of speaking suggests a wish to come off as a regular guy. Dr. Evil also raises a pinky to his mouth when he's scheming.

That was the detail that got Dana Carvey's attention. If Michaels was surprised to hear his speech cadences on-screen, Carvey was even more surprised to see his own hand gestures. When Carvey first took in Dr. Evil in *Austin Powers,* "the hair stood up on the back of my neck," he said. The character was, beat for beat, Carvey's Lorne. Besides the vocal tics, there was the visual: Carvey had honed his Lorne while wearing a bald cap backstage at SNL, waiting for his George Bush wig. The cueball head and the pinky gesture clinched it. "Then I had everyone calling me—Sandler and the rest," Carvey recalled. "They said, 'What's going on?' I thought, 'Wow, clever guy.'"

Carvey was shocked not only that Myers had appropriated the impression, but also that he had put on-screen, for millions, a bit intended as a private joke. "It wasn't mean, but I didn't think I could ever do it publicly, like Mike ended up doing," Carvey said. "That would be cruel to the guy who gave you your break." If Myers had asked him for permission, he said, he probably would have granted it: "I guess you could look at it as a collaboration." Carvey has discussed Dr. Evil with his therapist, but not with Myers, who publicly said that the character is an amalgam of Michaels and Donald Pleasence, the actor who once played Blofeld. Relations are restored enough that, for SNL's *40th Anniversary Special,* Wayne and Garth closed the show.

Being the inspiration for Dr. Evil didn't bother Michaels. (He did note that, in regard to the finger-mouth gesture, "I might be more thumb.") The press loved the connection, and it enlarged Michaels's public profile beyond SNL. He ended up being depicted on *The Simpsons* three times, voiced by Harry Shearer. He was a Hollywood character now.

Critics continued to make digs about him strip-mining SNL sketches for no-account movies, but he reveled in his West Coast persona. The Lornettes had perfected a system by which a driver was sent to Nate'n Al's, the Jewish deli on North Beverly, to pick up pastrami sandwiches for the private jet ride home to New York. He liked showing people his deluxe room at the Beverly Hills Hotel. He'd also charted a regular walking route through the suburban streets around the hotel, pointing out landmarks to his companions. (Years later, he'd note the corner of Rodeo and Elevado, where Pete Davidson crashed his Mercedes into a house.)

Also a short stroll from the Beverly Hills Hotel was the house of his old friend and confidante Sue Mengers. By the nineties, she was in her sixties, doing more hostessing than agenting, but she loved nothing more than putting together evenings of above-the-line talent with Michaels. She didn't often leave her orchid-filled house on Lexington Road; on a rare outing to an industry party, she summed up the throng as "Schindler's B-list." Instead she would preside, in a silk muumuu and rose-colored glasses, from a low easy chair in her living room, commanding two sofas' worth of movie stars on either side. (She liked to serve mugs of soup and cheesecake from Costco.) The guests—Warren, Barbra, Elton, Jack, Bette, Anjelica—would lean down to kiss her or shake the hand that wasn't holding a joint. Two highlights cherished by Michaels: attending a dinner for Billy Wilder, at which Mengers served his favorite brisket and horseradish sauce; and hearing Gore Vidal reminisce about lunching with Eleanor Roosevelt. "You weren't going to get that anyplace else," he said.

Mengers was out of the business, but she threw a dinner for Michaels whenever he was in town. (As she dressed in the next room, she'd coquettishly say, "You can come in if you want.") She used to talk about writing a memoir about her career peaks, to be called *When I Was Alive*. As devoted as Michaels was to her, Mengers was something of a cautionary tale. She'd burned too many bridges. He had been careful to do what was necessary to stay in the game.

THIRTY-TWO

INTERFERENCE

Let your enemy bury himself.

—BERNIE BRILLSTEIN

MICHAELS BELIEVED THAT, AFTER THE PURGE OF 1995 AND THE HIRING OF A hot new cast, he was in the clear with Don Ohlmeyer. But by 1997, Ohlmeyer was on a new high, having dragged NBC from third place into first, and he turned his attention back to SNL—more specifically, to Norm Macdonald, who had continued to tell O. J. Simpson jokes on Weekend Update, under the gleeful supervision of Jim Downey. "The O.J. jokes were a good illustration of Joseph Stalin's observation 'Quantity has a quality all its own,'" Downey said. During the first season the jokes concerned the aftermath of the murders and the criminal trial; in the second season they were about the acquittal; in the third season they were about the civil lawsuit for wrongful death. The jokes were illustrated mainly by the same photo of Simpson with a simpering smile. With topical material like the Simpson case, Downey and Macdonald took a stripped-down approach that they compared to punk rock. "We weren't going to do easy political jokes, letting the audience know we were all on the same side," Downey said. "We were going to be mean and, to an extent, anarchists." Macdonald didn't care if the audience got his jokes; after telling one, he would just hold to camera, grinning, letting the laughter not happen. He certainly didn't care whether Don Ohlmeyer, Simpson's close friend, liked his jokes.

"They were good jokes," Michaels said. "So I put them on the air."

When Simpson was acquitted, Macdonald had opened the newscast by saying, "Well, it's finally official. Murder is legal in the state of California." On the night of the acquittal, Ohlmeyer attended a lavish victory party at Simpson's house on Rockingham Drive in Brentwood.

Michaels had thought that Ohlmeyer was out of his hair, but since the purge he had been keeping tabs on the show through back channels. Gary Considine was stationed in the control room. Littlefield used to call writers and pump them for inside dope. Ohlmeyer offered an East Coast job at NBC to James Miller, a journalist who was compiling an oral history of the show with Tom Shales, and who had written a script that he hoped Broadway Video would produce; when Miller realized that the job was mainly to spy on Michaels, he turned it down.

In the summer of 1997, when Michaels had his regular pre-season meeting with Ohlmeyer in L.A., he brought along the two producers who'd taken over Downey's role, Mike Shoemaker and Steve Higgins. "We had to go out there and have him berate us in a room," Higgins said. "It was a charade, to try to show who was boss," Shoemaker recalled. "It was just to embarrass Lorne."

Ohlmeyer had one order: Get rid of Jim Downey and Norm Macdonald. O. J. Simpson wasn't mentioned.

"Well, I think it's working," Michaels responded. He had the numbers on his side again; ratings were up. "Let's give it one more season."

Six months into the following season, Ohlmeyer thought he'd won. For the first eight shows, Weekend Update was entirely O.J.-free. This had nothing to do with Ohlmeyer's wishes. "O.J. simply wasn't in the news," Downey said. Then, in December, Simpson made headlines again: he had been asked to leave a restaurant because he made other diners uncomfortable. After doing no O.J. jokes since May, on the Christmas show Macdonald made two. Within days, Downey got a call from Shoemaker passing on two pieces of information. The first was that, on Ohlmeyer's order, he and Macdonald were fired. The second was that Chris Farley was dead.

Michaels was in Aspen when he heard the Farley news. He had

brought Henry and Eddie out for a ski trip over the holiday break; Alice, eight months pregnant, stayed behind in New York. He had just skied down Buttermilk Mountain with the boys when his phone rang. He pulled off a mitten and heard Alice's voice on the line telling him that Farley had been found dead in his apartment in Chicago. The funeral, in Madison, Wisconsin, was scheduled for a few days later, on December 23. That was the night Michaels was slated to have dinner with Ohlmeyer, in Aspen, to try to talk him out of firing Macdonald and Downey.

The last time Michaels had been in Aspen, in March, Farley had been there too, joining a big group for an SNL-reunion panel at the U.S. Comedy Arts Festival. Farley had been a drugged-out wreck on-stage with his heroes Steve Martin, Aykroyd, Chase, and a couple dozen others. Mid-discussion, Dana Carvey had stood up and quietly walked Farley off into the wings.

But the last time Michaels saw Farley was just before Halloween, when he'd hosted SNL. He was in terrible shape then, too—drinking, taking drugs, even bringing a couple of prostitutes up to the office. Farley had struggled with heroin while he was on the show; after getting clean once and relapsing, he'd been suspended by Michaels, who sent him to a tough-love rehab facility in Alabama. Michaels knew that the show was what Farley liked best, so taking it away from him, he hoped, would make an impression. Since Belushi's squalid death, Michaels had rethought his approach to employees' drug problems. His former value system, he said, was "As long as people showed up on time and did their job, it was nobody's business what they did in their bedroom or in their house. That value system turned out to be wrong." He'd tried much harder with Farley, but it wasn't enough.

The cold open of the show Farley hosted was Tim Meadows persuading Michaels that Farley was sober enough to go on. Out of the side of his mouth, he adds, "Fatty falls down, ratings go up," a joke that was uncomfortably close to reality. When Farley appears, he's sweating and gulping for air. Marci Klein worried that he would have a heart attack on the air.

Some criticized Michaels for letting him perform in that condition. Farley's manager, Marc Gurvitz, had asked for the hosting gig as a favor: he thought that, for Farley, being back at 8H might have a stabilizing effect. Michaels agreed. The discipline and rigor of SNL, he always believed, helped keep people straight. "It's a small point of pride that nobody has ever died *doing* the show," Michaels told Marc Maron on his podcast. "It generally happens a couple of years after they leave."

When Farley died, Michaels's staff in New York made frantic arrangements to get him to the funeral in the middle of the Christmas rush. A private jet was located in Aspen, and on the twenty-third, Michaels dropped off Henry and Eddie at Powder Pandas, a kiddie ski-program, and drove to the Aspen airport. Tim Meadows met him on the tarmac in Madison with a blue suit in a bag. The funeral mass had already started when they arrived at the church, so Michaels was spared having to view the body in the coffin. In the jammed pews, Chris Rock and Adam Sandler were sobbing. Afterward, with helicopters of paparazzi overhead, he went to the cemetery for the burial, paid his respects to Farley's parents, and jetted back to Aspen for dinner with Ohlmeyer; he'd asked earlier if they might reschedule, but the answer was no.

After picking up his boys and giving them an early dinner, he met Ohlmeyer at a steakhouse. He'd hoped that, given the Farley ordeal, he might catch a break. But Ohlmeyer started right in with his Update tirade. "Downey's got to go," he said. "Macdonald's got to go." He did not mention O. J. Simpson. Instead, he cited a memo from Gary Considine, full of complaints from executives that Michaels always ended up getting his way. "Those guys were just sucking up to Don," Michaels said later. "It was really all about O.J."

Michaels put his fork down and interrupted. "I just buried this kid," he said. "He's thirty-three years old. He's somebody I loved." Ohlmeyer wouldn't move off his agenda.

Talking Ohlmeyer down was something Michaels had done before. "Don, don't do this in the middle of a season," he pleaded. Norm Macdonald had a following; firing him would incite the press. "SNL is deep within the culture, like the Dallas Cowboys are," he went on. "People have a sense of owning it. They have some notion of meritocracy, and if a network comes in and makes changes, they won't like it." He added a warning: "You do not want to pick a fight with a bunch of comedians. Pettiness knows no bounds. They will keep taking shots at you forever."

He'd saved Downey's job before by stressing that he was part of the show's core identity. He'd always kept going by telling himself that this or that executive was just someone he had to outlive. But this time, depleted by sorrow and stress, with a new baby about to be born, he couldn't pull it off. And he was not prepared to quit and let the show collapse. Ohlmeyer prevailed.

Ohlmeyer granted one concession: Macdonald could stay at the Update desk, but only without Downey. Macdonald wouldn't hear of it.

Two weeks later, on January 7, David Letterman brought out Norm Macdonald as the first guest on *The Late Show*. Michaels's warnings came true. Letterman had his own bad blood with NBC, and he started right in. "Did you get your ass fired?" he asked Macdonald. "I know Don Ohlmeyer, and between you and me, he's an idiot." Outraged, Letterman called Ohlmeyer a weasel, a pinhead, "Mr. Bigshot-cologne-and-cufflinks," and, referencing Ohlmeyer's recent stint at Betty Ford, "Happy Hour Don."

Doing his fake-clueless thing, Macdonald explained that Ohlmeyer just didn't think he was funny on Weekend Update. "It's just a matter of opinion," he said, and added, "He also thinks that O.J. is innocent."

Letterman also went hard at Michaels, who, through the dustup, had lived to fight another day. "It's *his* show!" Letterman said, disgusted. "Mr. Bigshot, Mr. Table-at-Orso's—*Lorne Michaels*! Why doesn't he step in? Why doesn't he throw himself in front of this gorilla to save your job? What's going on there? It sounds to me as if he's a quisling."

Macdonald asked for a dictionary. A stagehand brought one, and Macdonald read out the definition of "quisling": "a traitor who serves as the puppet of the enemy occupying his country." After a beat to let the audience laugh, he defended Michaels: "He's a good man and he has always been very supportive of me."

Letterman had the last word: "Well, I guess *not!*"

When Michaels saw the "quisling" segment, he was thrown. "Really?" he said to the screen. "That's your take?" Letterman had lumped him with the network suits. Back in 1992, when he was trying to get Bob Wright to keep Letterman at NBC, Michaels had gone to see Letterman, and the two had an unusually long talk. Michaels believed that *Late Night* had borrowed a lot from SNL, and he thought Letterman and he, if not close, were at least on the same wavelength. "It's how the Romans felt about the Greeks," he said. "They took their same gods, but called them different names."

The public and the press shared Letterman's anger. Readers of *Time* found a "Save Norm" postcard in the magazine to mail in to Ohlmeyer at NBC, a campaign hatched by a young *Time* writer named Joel Stein. Ohlmeyer and his executives were lambasted as nitwits. Even Warren Littlefield piled on, if belatedly. In his 2012 memoir he wrote, "Don was first a drunk bully and then a sober bully, but always a bully." In 1998, months after firing Macdonald, Ohlmeyer blocked NBC from running an ad for his movie *Dirty Work* on SNL, and he tried to have Macdonald banned from appearing on Conan O'Brien's show.

Those were the last swipes that Ohlmeyer ever took at Michaels and his show. In June of 1999, Ohlmeyer, at fifty-four, retired from NBC. (He'd later return to ABC's *Monday Night Football*.) The lusterless honor of replacing Macdonald on Update had gone to a new-ish cast member named Colin Quinn, and he did a yeoman's job until he left the show a year later. Michaels hated that Ohlmeyer had made him switch horses midseason, but even without Macdonald doing the news, the show's numbers kept improving.

By the time SNL celebrated its twenty-fifth anniversary, in the fall of 1999, the network troubles were in the rearview mirror. Michaels again quietly brought back Downey, who would take the show's political satire to a new level. A month before the anniversary show, Michaels received a star on the Hollywood Walk of Fame, an honor that would have astonished his movie-loving grandparents. Weeks after the anniversary, Norm Macdonald was back in 8H, hosting SNL. Michaels's survival instinct, the quality that Higgins compares to "playing a five-dimensional chess game," had prevailed.

Judd Apatow never regretted saying no to Littlefield. "History has shown those network guys to be more wrong than you ever could imagine," he said. "Because right after that, Lorne picked one of the best casts in the history of the show." Michaels continued hiring mainly improv people—Maya Rudolph, Amy Poehler, Rachel Dratch, Chris Parnell, Fred Armisen, and Horatio Sanz. (Sanz was the result of Michaels's never-ending search for a new Belushi. "Lorne was like Ahab looking for the great white whale," Downey said. He was always alert to "anyone who was pudgy, and ethnic, with a slight air of menace.") Tina Fey had come on in 1997 as a writer, recruited by her former Second City chum Adam McKay, whom she would replace as head writer. "The women came out like gangbusters," Paula Pell said. With Fey in charge, it became easier to see that, as the writer Emily Spivey put it, "Lorne really, really, really loves funny ladies and he really goes to bat for that."

IN SEPTEMBER 1999, NBC AIRED A TWO-AND-A-HALF-HOUR SPECIAL TO mark SNL's twenty-fifth anniversary, gathering writers and cast from all the years of the show's history. The week before, Alan Zweibel paid a visit to the ninth floor. The elevator doors opened, and Anne Beatts, who was writing on the episode, was standing there. "Fucking Lorne," she said. A quarter century hadn't made the SNL process any less stressful.

Comedy people tend to be unsentimental; the ruthlessness required rules it out. But milestones soften Michaels up. He had hired Beatts to help with the anniversary show because she'd called to tell him that she was in financial trouble. By this time in her life, she'd confessed, she thought she'd be on Norman Lear's yacht. Like many others who started at the show, Beatts, Michaels said, "didn't understand heat. They didn't understand that you're hot for about two or three years, and if nothing else happens, you go to the back of the line again."

When graduates of the show reunite for anniversaries, they feel a kinship across the decades. They are an elite tribe, like astronauts. "It's like Lorne had a hundred children with nine wives," Paula Pell said. "It blows your mind, the amount of connective tissue he's created in the world of comedy." Fred Armisen describes a "secret feeling, like ESP," between everyone who's ever been in the cast. "And there's something you can hear in people's voices that makes you go, '*That's* an SNL person.'"

Former cast members will say that, no matter how successful they are after leaving SNL, nothing ever replaces the feeling of being at the center of the universe that performing live in Studio 8H gave them. (Darrell Hammond describes life after the show this way: "You're talking about living on the moon and then not living on the moon.") Anytime that Pell hears the opening theme, she feels an adrenaline surge; "It's like hearing a baby crying and lactating," she said. "But Lorne does love that family dynamic, as fucked-up as it is sometimes." Kristen Wiig, who likes to visit, compares the show to "an ex-boyfriend who I can't get over."

But many, having moved on to directing or producing, belatedly apologize to Michaels for not having had the capacity to understand how hard his job is. After stopping by the show in later years, Bob Odenkirk said, "My resentment has mutated into respect—respect at his ability to keep pursuing quality despite the chaos of simply making that beast of a show happen every week."

When the alums come together at a big anniversary, feelings are mixed. Chris Rock likes to say that he hasn't been broke a day in his life since he met Michaels. Others describe the letdown of a school reunion, the sheepish pang of trying to measure up to their glory days. One vet described feeling like a fossil compared with Michaels's glossy new cast, with him projecting an attitude "like, 'I dated you in high school, but I'm dating supermodels now.'"

A centerpiece of the twenty-fifth anniversary show was a Smigel cartoon featuring Michaels addressing his black-tie audience, which he controls with a TV remote (a button marked BOTTOM SHOCK ensures an ovation). He tells the crowd of VIPs, "*Saturday Night Live* is not just about glitzy guests and fabulous outfits and glamorous parties. It's also about merchandising," then plugs a VHS tape of the future forty-fifth anniversary show, twenty years hence, featuring a grizzled Paul Simon croaking "Still crazy after all these years." Then 1999 Lorne breaks into song, and scampers around the bleachers organizing the celebrity seating, sticking headshots on chairs. The big finish has him strutting in the footlights, tossing a bowler hat in the air, belting *"For it's . . . my . . .* [a falsetto high note] *shoooooow!"* At the moment when cartoon Lorne holds the note on *"shoooooow,"* the real audience in the studio rose to its feet.

THIRTY-THREE

THE RULES OF COMING AND GOING

BY THE TIME THE SHOW HAD BEEN AROUND FOR A QUARTER OF A CENTURY, a folklore developed among SNL aspirants around the way Michaels hires people. (The protocols have remained consistent during the second twenty-five years.) There were the laugh-free auditions, the under-the-breath asides, the sphinxlike questions to interviewees who had sat on the couch in the outer office for hours, listening as assistants booked helicopters to the Hamptons. (Paula Pell compared it to waiting to get your teeth cleaned; Odenkirk called it "Head Games 101.") "You're right outside his office," said Chris Rock, who waited six hours for his interview with Michaels. "You hear him. Occasionally he walks out to do something." Through the years, careful students knew that if Michaels asked how you felt about wigs, that was a good sign.

When Michaels is watching people audition, he's looking for a few different things—sparkle, utility, originality, likability. But the post-audition meeting in his office is a personality check, a chance for him to make sure people aren't excessively annoying or crazy. "It's like you're being adopted into a family," Kristen Wiig said. Potential hires spend hours, days—and in the case of Marc Maron, years—puzzling over what Michaels could have meant by a certain phrase or tilt of the head. Every time Maron interviews an SNL alum on his *WTF* podcast, he recounts the agony of a meeting in Michaels's office in the nineties, for what he thought was an opportunity to anchor Weekend Update. He was sure that he'd blown it. When Michaels started in on his story comparing comedians to monkeys, Maron came back with a line about monkeys throwing feces. Michaels just stared, and finally said, "You can tell a lot by looking into someone's eyes." Maron anxiously took a Jolly Rancher from a bowl on the desk. Meeting over; no job offer. "I thought I failed the candy test," he said. For years afterward, he obsessed over Michaels as "an evil wizard."

Two decades later, on his podcast, Maron interviewed Michaels, who did his best to demystify the situation. He handled Maron gently, like a dog with a hurt bird in its mouth. He said he'd brought him in, all those years ago, just because he'd heard he was funny. Also, Maron remembered the candy wrong; they were Tootsie Rolls.

Conan O'Brien and his writing partner Greg Daniels were sure that they had failed a test, too. The first time they met Michaels, in L.A., in the eighties, he kept his sunglasses on and asked them to name their favorite cast members. "I said I loved Kevin Nealon, because he was so dry and cerebral," O'Brien recalled. "I could tell that was the wrong answer." Later, they were summoned to New York with hours' notice. They found Michaels in his office drinking red wine with Jim Downey. Offered a glass, they declined. Later, they worried that the wine had been a test. Jason Sudeikis was also sure that he'd messed up—by admitting he hated Cirque du Soleil.

Will Ferrell thought that the popcorn was a test: Was he supposed to eat it? ("It's like going to Buckingham Palace for dessert," he said. "Which fork do I use?") Asked back for a second audition, he was thrown when he learned that he was supposed to do all new material (he came up with a bit about a man who plays with cat toys). He'd heard that Adam Sandler had made Michaels laugh at the post-audition meeting in his office by pretending to hump a chair, so he devised an elaborate bit that involved carrying with him a briefcase full of fake money and piling stacks of bills on Michaels's desk. On the meeting day, he was too nervous to open the briefcase. Worse, as he was leaving, Higgins smirked and said, "Nice briefcase." After this story made the rounds, agents began telling clients not to do anything "big" or goofy during their Michaels meeting. Fred Armisen just stared at him the first time they met and said, "My God. You knew George Harrison."

Michaels does most of the talking in these interviews, parceling out his showbiz stories (hanging in Prague with Neil Young) or comically bewildering koans ("There are two kinds of people in the world: people who build the house, and people who buy the house"), gauging how well the person listens. He might mention what he's reading, or refer to the summer he got through all of E. M. Forster ("Only connect," he'll murmur), or *Middlemarch,* or Chekhov's stories. Hilary Mantel's *Wolf Hall,* with its narrative of Tudor palace intrigue, is a favorite conversational touchstone, and he gave copies of the novel to underlings. One young producer, who ended up being forced out, came to view the gift as a coded message; Thomas Cromwell, the protagonist, ends up without his head.

Michaels generally avoids the emotional expenditure of telling people that they're hired. "It's an amazing sense of discipline, almost Puritan in its restraint, how he doesn't give himself the pleasure of hiring people," Amy Poehler said, particularly because his job involves saying no so often. Steve Higgins is the one who told her she was hired. (Higgins does most of the face-to-face firing as well.) Tina Fey said, "After fifty years, there's only a certain amount of people's gratitude that you can absorb." Michaels knows that, as happy as the initial moment is, he might have to fire the person a year later. Ferrell thinks it's part of his baseball-derived management style. "Baseball players keep the highs not too high and the lows not too low," he said. "Lorne knows that it's a long season." (Michaels is fond of a quote that Fellini gave to Lillian Ross, about how actors believe that they're your children: "They will eat you.") The emotional-energy efficiency takes many forms. The writer Carol Leifer ran into Michaels in a loud restaurant once, and after a few volleys of shouted pleasantries, he amiably mouthed the words *Conversation over* and returned to his meal.

When Ferrell finally realized that he was hired, he asked to shake his new boss's hand. "Do whatever you need to do," Michaels said.

Higgins thinks that he outsources the good-news-giving because it empowers the actual giver: "The new hire will remember for the rest of his life, *this* person told me I got the job." It's related to one of Michaels's core teachings, which is telling people to spread credit around. Credit, he likes to say, is the easiest thing to give away.

He's aware that for most of his people, SNL is their first job, and that they arrive unformed. "The most difficult thing is the first rung in show business," he often says. "That's where you overthink everything." Working for him is a finishing school. Fey said, "He likes to show people how to run their lives. And he does live well."

"When you begin at the show, there's a bit of 'Come join us, and you'll get your teeth fixed and learn how to talk to the rich and famous!'" Amy Poehler said. (Michaels paid for her veneers.) "The read-through table is like the dinner table, and where you sit changes over time. I remember thinking, 'I want to do a good job, not just because I want to feel good about the comedy I'm producing, but because I want more access.' By osmosis, you get lessons in how to deal with people in power." She added, "and eventually you get to the room where everyone gets to badmouth everybody."

The cryptic hiring protocols extend to staying hired. Cast and writers are supposed to be notified by July about whether they are being asked back. (Michaels has a rule about not making big decisions in June, when he is sick of everyone, and exhausted.) That date often slips by, with people not knowing their fates until Labor Day, a month before the season premiere. Odenkirk said, "Would it have hurt to hire a person whose job it was to sit down with the writer and go, 'Here's how you'll get paid; here's the hours we expect you to work; we'd like you to come back next season'?"

"At SNL, it takes three weeks for a writer to go from grateful to indignant," Conan O'Brien likes to say. It's common for performers to abruptly shift from worrying about being fired to worrying that they'll never escape the show's golden handcuffs.

After six seasons, Ferrell told Michaels that he thought it might be time to go; Michaels took him to dinner at Pastis to try to get another year. "Right now you're riding high," he told Ferrell. "You really want to start to dip a little bit, and *then* you should leave the show." (Ferrell's reaction: "Wait, what?") When he did leave, in 2002, Michaels told him that he considered him one of the "top three" cast members ever. ("Am I third?" Ferrell asked.) Carvey left in the middle of his seventh season; he'd found it too difficult to tell Michaels. "We were together at the party till like four in the morning," Michaels recalled. "And then he just didn't come back. It was like he slipped out in the dead of night." After you leave, Molly Shannon told Kristen Wiig, you can live like a normal person: you can go to the dentist; you can go to friends' weddings. Amy Poehler counseled Fred Armisen, "Don't worry. When you go, Lorne still stays in your life. He's always looking for a tribe."

Michaels warns his people that their agents, thinking of commissions, might want them to leave the show too soon. "Agents are about chess moves," he says. "And they're all morons." He tells his charges, "You'll know when it's time to leave. But don't do it because of some strategy, because you may never get *this* again. A hit is very rare. Some people get two, so enjoy this and do it until you can't bear it." The summation: "Build a bridge to the next thing, and when it's solid enough to walk across it, walk across."

There's genuine warmth, too. Wiig's final show, in 2012, had her dancing with Mick Jagger as he serenaded her with "She's a Rainbow," and ending up in Michaels's arms. Fred Armisen, on his last show, wore a guitar strap printed with TY LM I♥U. As a parting gift, Michaels gave Kevin Nealon a Cartier watch with a message engraved on the back; he also apologized for the rough patches they'd had. By the time Pete Davidson left, he had spent a quarter of his life on the show; now he wears a necklace that dangles a tiny charm with Michaels's image inside, like a reliquary, and he fondly teases the boss about "Blabbagansett." The night of the first show without Will Forte, Michaels emailed him, "It's not the same without you."

Employees who said no to him or pulled away have accrued a kind of spookily legendary status in his world. A few later sent him letters of apology or regret, which underlings intercepted and mirthfully read aloud at meetings. John Fortenberry, the early Broadway Video editor and a favorite mentee, left under a cloud in the mid-nineties, when he declined Michaels's offer of directing SNL after Davy Wilson retired. Directing SNL was mostly moving cameras around, like directing a sporting event, and Fortenberry had wider ambitions. "I think Lorne felt 'I trained you; I own you,'" Fortenberry said. "It was a hard decision." If a parting doesn't go the way Michaels wants it to, a "cut-off psychology," as one staffer calls it, kicks in. You're out: off the Broadway Video T-shirt list, off the birthday and Christmas gift lists. "If you say no to the emperor," the staffer went on, "you're banned from the kingdom."

Jim Biederman started as an assistant at Broadway Video in 1989; by the time he was producing the Kids in the Hall show, he was a Michaels pet, regarded as a resident Lorneologist, an expert at unraveling the boss's deeply coded conversation for confused colleagues. While on staff, he developed a talk-show pilot called *Wake Up, America* that involved life-size puppets. On Broadway Video's behalf, he sold the show to Fox. When he called Michaels from L.A. with the good news about the deal, he got a flat response that didn't make sense. "'Great,'" he recalled Michaels saying. "'So you're using my name to sell stuff?'" Biederman was flummoxed. "I had been so good at slaloming my way between the poles of his psyche," he said. A chill set in.

"Sometimes I think he's Henry Kissinger, and sometimes I just think he's Chauncey Gardiner in *Being There*," Biederman said. "One bombs Cambodia, and the other didn't know that we bombed Cambodia." At an uncomfortable impasse, some time later Biederman accepted a job with Howard Stern and called Michaels to tell him he was leaving. In a clipped tone, Michaels responded, "Right. Have a nice life." Biederman recalls the exchange as "like kissing Fredo on both cheeks."

Michaels strongly prefers to keep his people in the family. He asked Bruce McCulloch, the Kids in the Hall alum, to direct *Superstar,* Molly Shannon's Mary Katherine Gallagher movie. He wanted Penelope Spheeris to direct *The Ladies Man,* the 2000 Tim Meadows film, but she didn't like the script. "He called me three or four times about it," she said. "You just don't say no to Lorne four times. Because he has hardly spoken to me since."

In Michaels's suzerainty, loyalty is a tortured concept. One of his regular sardonic asides is "You'll find that your most loyal employees are your least valuable employees." There's a sense among people who know him that he doesn't really respect people until they leave. When someone quits to do another TV show, he has a regular exit zinger. "Let me know when it's on," he says, with a smirk.

THIRTY-FOUR

"CAN WE BE FUNNY?"

ON SEPTEMBER 18, 2001, A WEEK AFTER TERRORISTS TURNED FOUR COM-
mercial airliners into bombs that killed nearly three thousand people,
Graydon Carter, the editor of *Vanity Fair*, declared, "It's the end of the
age of irony." And it actually felt as if he might be right. Late-night
comedy shows stopped broadcasting. In the SNL offices a paralysis
set in, as everyone wondered what role comedy could play in the new,
smashed-up world.

The day of the attacks, there was to have been a preliminary read-
through of commercial parodies for SNL's twenty-seventh season,
due to premiere on September 29. But after Michaels saw the planes
hit on his television screen at home, he put his three-year-old daughter, Sophie, in a stroller and walked around the neighborhood, trying
to maintain a feeling of normalcy.

As the premiere date approached, he thought about how to respond. His staff was rattled, anxious about it being too soon to make
jokes. Less than a week after the attacks, Bill Maher said, on his ABC
show *Politically Incorrect,* that it wasn't the terrorists who were cow-
ards; the USA was the coward, for lobbing missiles targeting Al Qaeda
from thousands of miles away. His show was speedily canceled. Letterman returned to the air on September 17, winning over viewers
with somber, statesmanlike remarks. Looking for guidance, Michaels
called the mayor, Rudolph Giuliani (at the peak of his hero phase),

who urged that SNL go ahead with its premiere. Somewhere along the way, Graydon Carter amended his prediction. What he'd meant to say, he explained, was that it was the end of the age of *ironing*.

Reese Witherspoon, who'd been set to host the season opener, was still on board. On Monday the twenty-fourth, people warily filed into the writers' meeting, and Michaels gave a low-key speech. Among the new hires in the room were cast members Seth Meyers, Amy Poehler, and the writer Emily Spivey. "One thing I respect about Lorne is that there's not a lot of overpromising," Poehler recalled. "So the speech wasn't like, 'It's gonna be great! And we're gonna do it together!' It was a very elegant version of 'Let's get back to work.'" He emphasized that the way they could help people feel stable again was simply to show up.

They discussed whether to address the atrocity head-on or to stick with un-topical comedy bits. Making fun of politicians was out. Viewers didn't want to see Will Ferrell do his idiotic President Bush. Was there anything that wouldn't chill the audience? At read-through, a sketch about Cat Stevens, a convert to Islam, retooling his hits along 9/11 themes did okay, but it got cut before Saturday. Among the pieces that made it to air was one about a farting baby and another with Witherspoon as a lascivious mermaid. Weekend Update had Darrell Hammond in blackface as Jesse Jackson, volunteering to negotiate with the Taliban. (Within a few years, everyone involved regretted the bit.) Update concluded with information about where viewers could send donations, but the segment avoided anything emotional. "No one wants to see your existential crisis," Michaels had told the staff beforehand.

What most people remember about the show is the cold open. Michaels knew that it shouldn't feel like an entertainment, but he didn't want anything mawkish either. He asked Giuliani to come to the studio on the night of the show and to bring with him the police commissioner, the fire commissioner, and a group of first responders. The mayor, standing onstage beside his chiefs, the cops and firemen behind him, said, "Good evening. Since September eleventh, many people have called New York a city of heroes." He gestured at the people behind him. "Well, these are the heroes." The camera panned to Paul Simon standing on the music stage wearing an FDNY cap. He started to play, not "Bridge Over Troubled Water," which is what many at the show had expected, but "The Boxer." Michaels had chosen it because it is an anthem of resilience: "The fighter still remains."

While Simon sang, the camera slowly panned the faces of the first responders with their thousand-yard stares, many of them still dusty with rubble and debris from Ground Zero. After Simon finished, the mayor made a short speech. "*Saturday Night Live* is one of our great New York City institutions," he said, then turned to Michaels. "And that's why it's important for you to do your show tonight." Michaels looked at Giuliani and said, "Can we be funny?" The mayor took a beat, then responded, "Why start now?" A huge, pressure-relieving laugh filled the studio. Giuliani paused for the applause, looked into the camera, and said, "Live from New York, it's Saturday Night!" The line meant more than it usually did: New York had survived.

Michaels had written the bit, which, in the show's best tradition, was both self-referential and self-deprecating. He played his habitual straight-man role and, in rehearsal, had to drill the mayor in not smiling before his punchline. "You are tipping the joke," he'd told Giuliani. On air, Michaels grimly stared the mayor down, to remind him to stay serious. "In the midst of this overwhelming tragedy, there was also cuing, and how you pace a moment, and how you connect to an audience," he recalled.

The season lurched along, the writers finding ways to deal with the new reality. On the second show, Will Ferrell played a guy at a business meeting showing his amped-up patriotism by wearing tight, tiny shorts imprinted with the Stars and Stripes. The following week, anthrax was discovered on the third floor of the building. Fey, hearing this on the TV news in her dressing room, picked up her things and walked straight home. Michaels calmed those who stayed, reasoning that they were five floors above where the anthrax was detected. "When you go into the elevator, don't press three," he told them. That evening, he called Fey at home and invited her back. "We're all here," he said, adding that they were ordering dinner. She cautiously returned.

THE SEASON AFTER 9/11 WAS FERRELL'S LAST; WILL FORTE, A NEW CAST member, would take over as President Bush. The year before, in 2000, the show had become more politically relevant than it had ever been, but for several years after the terrorist attacks, SNL was unusually light on politics, as Michaels tried to gauge what the public wanted. The whole country was caught up in the wave of patriotism that had rechristened french fries "Freedom Fries," protesting France's opposition to Bush's invasion of Iraq. Liberal institutions of all sorts were waving the flag. *Vanity Fair* put an Annie Leibovitz glamour shot of President Bush and his brain trust on the cover.

During the 2000 election, SNL had been a powerhouse of political humor, and the show was credited with affecting the outcome of the election that put Bush back in office. The show's political satire was Downey's domain, and Michaels was gratified that he'd brought him back. Downey's cold opens lampooning the debates between Ferrell's goofball Bush and Al Gore, played by Darrell Hammond as an overbearing know-it-all, were riveting and hilarious, and they helped set the agenda for the national political discussion. Downey dreamed up a one-word slogan for each candidate to sum up his campaign: for Bush, "Strategery." And for Gore, "Lockbox." Gore's handlers made him study a tape of the SNL piece so he could try to avoid being so robotic in his next outing. He admitted to learning from the exercise. "I think I'll sigh a little bit less," he said.

Michaels was reluctant to take credit for Bush's victory, but he felt that "the combination of Jim's writing and Will's performance gave George W. a slight edge over Gore" in the historically close election, because there was "something charming" about the character. "We all know a guy like that," he said. "Whereas Gore—we didn't know a guy like that." The election opened up a debate about whether SNL had an obligation to express a political opinion. Ten years earlier, during the Gulf War, Downey had written a sketch about a Pentagon press briefing at which reporters demand absurdly sensitive information. One asks an officer, for instance: "Sir, knowing what you know, where would you say our forces are most vulnerable to attack and how could the Iraqis best exploit those weaknesses?" Several staffers viewed the sketch as pro-military, and therefore, unacceptably conservative. Over time, some colleagues regarded Downey as tilting the show toward the right. (Adam McKay has branded Downey a right-winger, and Horatio Sanz once referred to him as "the Karl Rove of SNL.") But Downey, a registered Democrat, always considered his approach nonpartisan. He counsels writers not to stick with "first idea" premises, and to push past easy liberal pieties. "I like to grab live wires and see what happens," he said. He, like Michaels, saw it as his role to jab at power and idiocy of every kind. As Michaels says, "You go where the laughs are."

Ever since *The Daily Show* had debuted on Comedy Central in 1996, Michaels and his people had noticed that audiences were responding to political comedy in a new way, reacting not because a joke was funny, but because they agreed with its political sentiment. Seth Meyers coined a name for this response: "clapter." Comedy purists look down on clapter. "Comedy is a disruptive thing," Michaels says. "People don't plan to laugh. They're taught when to applaud, but they're not taught when to laugh." Clapping for a political leaning is like patting yourself on the back for your own discernment. Clapter, Michaels believes, is why *The Daily Show,* which was unapologetically liberal, beat out SNL for an Emmy seven times. "It was about politics," he said.

For months after the 2000 election, Michaels steered the cold open toward politics. So when he pulled back on political satire after 9/11, he filled the void with celebrity culture. Impersonations of stars had always been a staple, from Gilda Radner's Baba Wawa to impression-parade sketches like *Celebrity Jeopardy.* Now the show started to feel like a live-action *Us Weekly,* packed with sketches about scandal-racked celebs. Even Smigel's TV Funhouse cartoons skewed in that direction; one, about Michael Jackson's child molestation trial, showed the singer aiming to snatch a tyke from a window-sill as if he were a pie set out to cool.

Although the cast did deliriously funny work with the material—Poehler as Anna Nicole Smith and Britney Spears; Maya Rudolph as Diana Ross, Whitney Houston, Oprah, Beyoncé, and Donatella Versace—some SNL stalwarts felt that the show had abandoned its mission. Adam McKay, who left in 2001, complained about the tabloid focus, calling it "such a safe, wishy-washy target, as opposed to going after the powers that be." Michaels defended the shift as simply fun, and continued to book media-bait hosts like Lindsay Lohan and Paris Hilton. "I've always been, when in doubt, go young," he told the *Times*. "Because lots of things are much more forgivable when it's someone young trying it."

For the Paris Hilton show, in February 2005, Downey wrote a cold open making fun of the show's complicity in the scandal-culture glut. It opens on Michaels pacing in his office, brandishing a videocassette at Hilton. "I just looked at it, and frankly, I'm still reeling," he says. "It's a *sex tape,* Paris. A sex tape, and you're in it! Don't bother to deny it, I know it's you. I've watched it eight times, just to make sure." Hilton expresses surprise that he hadn't heard about the tape, which had surfaced the previous year.

"Paris, I'm afraid I can't let you host tonight," Michaels says. He gestures at a plaque on the wall. "Do you see the phrase there? It's Latin: *Praeter Lucrum, Honor.* Do you know what it means?"

She says, "Of course. 'Honor before profit.'"

"It's the motto of the show," he says. "Paris, throughout its thirty-year history, this show has had a watchword. That watchword is 'excellence.' If I were to let you walk out on that stage tonight, it might somehow create the impression, however erroneous, that the show was attempting, even if only in a slight way, to trade on, or exploit, or profit from, or milk, or cash in on the notoriety of that tape. In order, I suppose they would say, to get a rating. And if even only one person thought that, it would destroy everything this show has stood for."

She says, "But that's crazy! Who would think that?"

She finally hears him, and leaves. As she goes, a Lornette comes in and says, "Mr. Buttafuoco's here." The real Joey Buttafuoco appears and chest bumps Michaels. "Joey, thanks for filling in," he says. "You're a lifesaver!" Buttafuoco replies, "Hey! Fuggetaboutit. Lorne's got a problem, Joey Buttafuoco's got his back."

Hilton did the piece at read-through but categorically refused to let it in the lineup. The cast found her standoffish, and during her week at the show they made a bet among themselves: the first person Hilton engaged with a personal question would get a hundred dollars. No one collected.

BY 2008, AN ELECTION YEAR THAT PROVIDED AN UNPRECEDENTED ARRAY OF characters tailor-made for comedy, SNL was fully back in its political groove. That year, *The Washington Post*'s media columnist, Howard Kurtz, coined the term "the SNL Effect" to describe the show's new influence. The show had marked the lackluster election of 2004 with a lackluster debate special pitting John Kerry (Seth Meyers) against Bush (Forte), but four years later, Barack Obama faced Hillary Clinton in the Democratic primary and then ran against John McCain, who gave a gift to comedy writers everywhere in the form of his running mate, Sarah Palin. Michaels managed to convince each of the major candidates to do cameos on the show that year. When the debates got underway before the primaries, Downey noticed how the press seemed to be fawning over Obama, the sexy newcomer. By contrast, reporters often treated Hillary Clinton as damaged goods, deriding her for everything from old Whitewater rumors to her headbands to her decision to stand by her wayward husband. Downey wrote a piece showing starstruck debate moderators fawning over Obama and asking him softball questions.

The press, not Obama, was Downey's target, but critics complained of pro-Clinton bias. During the next actual debate, Clinton herself complained that she was being treated more harshly than her rival, and said, "If anybody saw *Saturday Night Live*, maybe we should ask Barack if he's comfortable and needs another pillow." In fact, the top producers of SNL were not Clinton partisans; Downey told Kurtz that he'd vote for Obama if he got the nomination, and Michaels had given money to McCain.

In the summer of 2007, Clinton's people had put out a feeler to Michaels about her appearing on the season premiere. (Evidently the hard feelings about the 1992 show, in which Wayne and Garth made fun of twelve-year-old Chelsea Clinton as a "babe in waiting," had faded.) Michaels eagerly agreed. Having presidential candidates on the show made headlines, and it flattered Michaels's sense of himself as a player; he liked to tell staffers that he'd had his picture taken with every president since Ford.

To Michaels's great annoyance, days before the show, Clinton canceled without explanation. The Obama campaign had reached out too, so Michaels promptly put him on in the fourth show. Often, when people who've been impersonated on SNL appear themselves, they do what's called a "sneaker-upper," creeping up behind the performer who is playing them, and acting irritated. (Writers don't love these cameos, viewing them as an easy laugh—*adorable!*—and an easy way for a politician to look like a good sport.) Obama appeared as a guest wearing an Obama mask ("I have nothing to hide," he says) at a Halloween party hosted by the Clintons (Darrell Hammond and Amy Poehler). Michaels took the opportunity of having Obama in his office to ask the candidate's advice on whether to air a TV Funhouse by Smigel that the dress audience had loved but the censors wanted to cut. It was a fake airline safety video, a satire of racial profiling. The questionable line showed Arab passengers being told, "Please, do not blow up the airplane." Obama's call: "It's funny, but no, I don't think so." Michaels took the future president's note.

In March, Clinton had her turn saying "Live from New York!" when she did a reverse sneaker-upper, with Poehler playing Clinton. (She joined the real candidate onstage wearing an identical jacket, and each says, "I love your jacket.") But the most striking sneaker-upper of the year happened that fall. Shortly after McCain announced that the governor of Alaska, a former beauty queen named Sarah Palin, would be his running mate, Michaels was stopped by his doorman Frank Smith. "What a gift!" Smith exclaimed, and told Michaels that Tina Fey was a dead ringer for Palin. Robert De Niro, a neighbor, said the same thing when he bumped into Michaels on the sidewalk. Normally, Michaels ignores casting suggestions from civilians. But a couple of weeks later, when SNL's season was about to start, he checked in with Fey, who was then starring in 30 Rock. No go. That Saturday, she told him, she had a shoot with Oprah Winfrey, who was guesting on 30 Rock, and Sunday was her daughter's Peter Pan–themed birthday party. On Thursday, Michaels tried again, suggesting that she come over Friday to rehearse a Palin piece that Meyers had written. Fey again rattled off the reasons she couldn't do it (Oprah, Kristen Wiig would be better, her worries about performing a political bit that she didn't herself write). Michaels listened patiently. On Friday, she showed up for rehearsal.

"Lorne will manifest the reality he wants—a lot," John Mulaney said. He's mastered the art of slow, unpushy persuasion. "He uses it on all of us all the time," Fey said. "He gets you to *want* to be a part of it. You want to be a good family member."

That Saturday's show opened with Fey as Palin and Poehler as Clinton, jointly addressing the nation about sexism. Clinton asks the media to stop writing that she has "cankles," and Palin begs reporters to stop referring to her as a "MILF." Meyers wrote the piece with the two actresses. Mike Shoemaker contributed Fey's line "I can see Russia from my house," which became as big as "strategery." The electrifying pairing was a high point for women on the show. Poehler and the rest of the cast were stoked to be doing meaningful political parody again, after the Paris Hilton years. Poehler especially liked it when, six months pregnant and dressed as Clinton, she'd pass Michaels on the way to the stage, and he'd quietly say, "Shall we do a show tonight?" "It made you feel adult," she said. "I enjoyed the quiet, out-of-the-side-of-his-mouth stuff where you felt like a peer."

The next month, Palin herself made a cameo on the show. Fey refused to do a bit on camera with her, concerned that it would look like an endorsement. So a cold open was devised in which Michaels and the real Palin stand in the hall, watching Fey impersonating Palin on a monitor. Alec Baldwin walks up and, mistaking the governor for Fey, makes some disparaging comments about Palin ("Caribou Barbie," etc.). Realizing his error, Baldwin tells Palin that she's "way hotter in person" and leads her out onto home base, where she briefly crosses paths with her doppelgänger, Fey, before taking the podium to say, "Live from New York, it's Saturday Night!"

Rounding out the election-year bonanza, McCain and his wife, Cindy, appeared on the last show before the election, as QVC hosts hawking "John McCain's complete set of pork knives—they cut the pork out." SNL, McCain said later, "has as much impact on younger Americans as any other aspect of a political campaign."

The 2008 election episodes attracted the largest audience in more than a decade. On the night of the season's finale, between dress and air, Michaels told his staff how special the year had been. Meyers called it a "goosebump moment." Fey won a best guest actress Emmy, and Palin reportedly dressed up as Tina Fey for Halloween. A couple of years later, Fey thanked Palin in the speech she gave accepting the Mark Twain Prize for American Humor, bestowed by the Kennedy Center in Washington. "My partial resemblance and her crazy voice are the two luckiest things that have ever happened to me," she said. She thanked Michaels, too, and spoke about how she'd been the first female head writer at SNL, the second woman to be pregnant while working at the show, the third woman to win the Twain award, but was stopping short of becoming the fourth woman to do something, because "I just don't see myself married to Lorne."

Michaels had won the Twain prize in 2004, the only Canadian yet to receive it. In his short acceptance speech, he played his aloof dilettante Producer character: He mentioned the dozens of people who work hard to create SNL. "And yet *I'm* the one getting on the plane . . . with my tuxedo," he said. "And I thought, 'Yes, that's the way it should be. When it comes to being honored, I work alone.'" But the speech had a few unironic moments. He invoked *Huckleberry Finn*. "I realized that *Saturday Night Live* has always been stuck in adolescence, that time of life when you first begin to question authority, declare your independence—a time of risk and adventure, and occasionally bad behavior." He paused and concluded, "I've had the coolest job in New York City."

The format he'd created guaranteed the show's perpetual adolescence. Anne Beatts used to describe Michaels as "the leader of the Lost Boys." In *Peter Pan,* the boys never grow up; at SNL, they are rotated out and replaced, with Michaels presiding in a role that's part Wendy, part Captain Hook. He didn't escape aging, but the company he's kept has prevented him from becoming a dinosaur, or worse, an unhip dinosaur. Sticking to the formula—his Snickers bar concept— sustained him, and it sustained his show.

A BURST OF ADOLESCENT ENERGY HAD ENLIVENED THE STUDIO WITH THE arrival, in 2005, of Andy Samberg and his two old friends from Berkeley, Jorma Taccone and Akiva Schaffer. Jimmy Fallon had met them when he hosted that year's MTV Movie Awards, where they were writers. They called themselves the Lonely Island, and they brought with them expertise in a new technology. The Lonely Island made Digital Shorts, cheaply produced videos that recalled the quirky little films that Tom Schiller and Gary Weis had made in SNL's early seasons. The first one that the show aired, "Lettuce," was just Samberg and Will Forte sitting on a stoop talking about a dead friend while chomping on heads of lettuce. It cost twenty dollars to make. The next one, "Lazy Sunday," was Chris Parnell and Samberg rapping about going to see *The Chronicles of Narnia,* and stopping for cupcakes at Magnolia Bakery. A fan posted it to YouTube, then brand-new, and it racked up two million views in a few days; then NBC's lawyers threatened to sue YouTube and demanded that the video be taken down. Michaels thought this was an idiotic response; he knew that having a piece of the show go viral (a phrase that still felt awkward to say, the way "dot com" had ten years earlier) would only be helpful. He started lobbying the network to create SNL.com, so that the show could have its own platform, one likelier to draw comedy fans than would a sprawling NBC.com, which is what the network wanted. Soon, some SNL sketches could be viewed on Apple's iTunes for $1.99 a pop. Sounding a bit like a granddad talking about kids and their gizmos, Michaels told a reporter, "The audience of the show has always been young and I think they're more likely to be aware of the new technology."

At the start, the Lonely Island videos cost next to nothing, an attractive feature in an era of budget cuts. NBC's prime-time ratings had plummeted, along with ad revenues. In 2006, although Michaels's show was holding steady, the network gave him a choice between losing cast members or episodes, cutting back from the customary twenty per year. He chose to slash the cast, from sixteen to eleven, and, over the next years, some of the show's long-serving (and high-salaried) employees—Horatio Sanz, Chris Parnell, Robert Smigel, Rachel Dratch, and Fey—made their exits. (The latter two left to do *30 Rock.*)

The economical nature of the Digital Shorts appealed to Michaels, as did their speed. He viewed them as a surefire way to keep young people paying attention. (He was beginning to realize that his competition was not so much other television shows as it was video games like Guitar Hero.) When the Lonely Island came up with an idea for a Justin Timberlake show—two guys rapping about the gift boxes they held in front of their crotches, positioned so that when a girl lifts the lid, she gets a stiff surprise—they worried that Michaels might find it too crude. But he was delighted by "Dick in a Box," and he surprised Schaffer, Taccone, and Samberg by enthusiastically greenlighting another, unrelated short called "Jizz in My Pants." Over time, the budgets of the Digital Shorts expanded with their popularity, and soon Schaffer was doing shoots so elaborate that one required getting the city to close down an East River bridge.

One time, in 2007, the Lonely Island guys asked Michaels to use his formidable powers of persuasion to get Kanye West, the week's musical guest, to make a cameo in one of their shorts. It revolved around a love song to Mahmoud Ahmadinejad, the Iranian president who'd recently declared that there were no homosexuals in Iran. In the song "Iran (So Far Away)," Samberg serenades Ahmadinejad (Fred

Armisen) about his "butter-pecan thighs," crooning, "You can deny the Holocaust all you want, but you can't deny that there's something between us." Michaels got on the phone with West, prepared to gently cajole him into agreeing. "We have this really funny Digital Short," he began. "It's about Mahmoud Ahmadinejad." Silence on the line. Michaels tried a joke: "Look, the worst that could happen is that there'll be a fatwa against you." West shot back: "Yeeeah—not doing that." Adam Levine, from Maroon 5, did the cameo.

With the mainstreaming of the internet, it wasn't long before the cast and writers started scrolling social media on Saturdays at 10:00 P.M., to see how the dress audience had liked particular sketches—undermining, in their heads at least, the triage notes that Michaels was about to give in the meeting before air. Yet at the same time, digital technology propelled the show forward, allowing Michaels to keep pace with the changing culture. When SNL was about to turn forty, Amy Poehler offered a wry characterization of the institution that had made her a star, calling it "the show your parents used to have sex to that you now watch from your computer in the middle of the day."

THIRTY-FIVE

THE BIG TENT

ERIC FISCHL BEGAN THE PROCESS OF PAINTING MICHAELS'S PORTRAIT, IN 2002, by taking dozens of reference photographs as his subject chattered to him about show business. After Fischl developed the film, he was surprised. "What I was seeing was someone not as buoyant or confident as he'd come off," he said. He painted what was on the film. When Michaels came to the artist's studio to see the finished portrait, he stared at it in uncomfortable silence for a long time. Finally, without taking his eyes off the picture, he asked Fischl, "How did you know?" "Lorne said it captured something that he was feeling that he didn't think he was conveying," Fischl said. "He talked about approaching a certain age—success, the question of what comes next. A world-weariness. He couldn't believe that he had projected a truth rather than a story, or a character."

Michaels was accustomed by then to having a public persona, and one that people liked to mimic. Within a few years, takeoffs of SNL itself had become common—a new kind of tribute.

On a Saturday night in May 2006—two days before the Upfronts, at which NBC was to announce its new sitcom *30 Rock*—the president of NBC television, Jeff Zucker, was standing in Michaels's ninth-floor office yelling at him. Zucker's face was red. Michaels was *30 Rock*'s executive producer, and Alec Baldwin, its star, had not signed a contract for more episodes beyond the pilot. The program, a behind-the-scenes take on a variety show much like SNL, was created by and co-starred Tina Fey, one of Michaels's protégés, who'd quietly studied his management style for years. She was in the room when Zucker lost his temper; she recalled the dynamic as "appalling." "In that moment I had no idea how crazy it was that we were asking NBC to announce the show without having the lead actor locked up," she said. "But Lorne was so calm. He just went, 'Hmmmm.'"

It was a replay of the night in October 1975 when, just before air, John Belushi alarmed NBC by refusing to sign his contract. Michaels was playing a Fabius Maximus game with Baldwin, who he felt confident would sign. He was happy to wait it out. Pushing talent and being a scold, he believes, are the wrong ways to deal with creative people; it makes them dig in. "Alec will get there," he told Zucker. "He'll sign up for more. You'll see." Baldwin did eventually sign (and he won a couple of Emmys for his role), but Zucker never warmed to the show. A critical favorite, it failed to get big ratings and always hovered near cancellation.

Fey had originally set 30 Rock in a cable TV newsroom, but NBC had urged her to write what she knew, which was SNL, and the show's enigmatically unflappable leader. When she began writing, she had no idea that NBC was developing another pilot set behind the scenes at a show like SNL. This was Aaron Sorkin's Studio 60 on the Sunset Strip, his follow-up to The West Wing, which had been a prestige hit for the network.

The idea that Michaels's show had become an institution worthy of fictionalizing wasn't a complete surprise to him. Around this time, as The Apprentice was becoming a big hit on NBC, the network tried to persuade Michaels to host his own reality show, broadcasting the competitive scrum behind the scenes at SNL. "They wanted me to do a Trump thing," he said. "I would have liked the money, but I didn't want to be that." And he would never let a film crew regularly shoot his fulminations between dress and air.

Ordering pilots for 30 Rock and Studio 60, NBC had created a bizarre horse race, and it seemed unlikely that the network would pick up two different shows about one of its other shows. Fey's was the dark horse, and she and her showrunner Robert Carlock got queasy every time they walked by the huge *Studio 60* billboard looming over Times Square. Their project felt dinkier. The fuss about the Sorkin show didn't worry Michaels, who always preferred setting low expectations. Still, when Sorkin called Michaels and asked if he could spend a week at SNL observing how the show worked, the answer was no.

Studio 60 debuted a few weeks before *30 Rock* and was a disappointment, despite its starry cast—Matthew Perry, Bradley Whitford, Amanda Peet. The show focused on fights with the evil, meddling network; it was worthy rather than funny, more interested in First Amendment speechifying than laughs. It was "sweaty," to use a Michaels word. "The reality is that the network isn't that powerful anymore," he said. "Talent is." That's why he felt confident that, the night that Zucker was yelling, he would do just fine staying in Baldwin's corner. Sorkin's *Studio 60* was canceled after one season.

Although Fey's show didn't do much better in the ratings, it was cheaper to produce and the critics loved it. She got the last laugh, slipping jabs at Sorkin's turkey into her show. In *30 Rock*'s fifth season, Sorkin made a cameo as himself, prickly about his *Studio 60* failure and barking his *West Wing* catchphrase "Walk with me."

The character Alec Baldwin plays—Fey's boss, the bluff GE executive Jack Donaghy, "VP of East Coast television and microwave oven programming"—has more than a passing resemblance to Lorne Michaels. A good chunk of Donaghy's character—the Catholic guilt, the Republicanism, the Princeton football background—has nothing to do with Michaels. "But Jack's mentorship—the idea that you can live a better life, that you should take better care of yourself," Fey said, "those things are inspired by Lorne, for sure." Writing the character, Fey and Carlock would ask themselves: What would Lorne do? Some of Donaghy's precepts are Michaels-esque in the extreme: "Never go with a hippie to a second location." Also: Donaghy often appears in black tie ("It's after six. What am I, a farmer?"). Baldwin likes to say that Michaels keeps a tuxedo in his glove compartment.

Michaels didn't involve himself much in *30 Rock,* although he relished having Fey and Baldwin and other SNL alums under his big tent. "He wisely knows what he didn't like, which is sitting in the edit room," Fey said. But his imprint was everywhere. Her 2011 book, *Bossypants,* contains a section called "Things I Learned from Lorne Michaels." Among them: don't overthink the comedy, "never cut to a closed door," "don't hire anyone you wouldn't want to run into in the hallway at three in the morning." She appreciated the Fabius Maximus strategy—management by deflection—but considers herself more direct, a quality that makes some colleagues say that Michaels can be afraid of her. Like Florence Lipowitz, Fey didn't rely on coded conversation to make herself understood, and at SNL she was fearless about pushing an idea through. Michaels's own take is that he is "susceptible to strong women, because they're more apt to fight and stand up for themselves than I am. I think women see more clearly." (Fey observed, "He probably likes me and David Spade best. There, I said it.")

In the guise of management advice, Michaels would talk to Fey about the James Garner pool-hustler character in the late-fifties TV series *Maverick:* "The guy's a coward—but he realizes that he's a genius for being a coward," Fey said. "It's a natural instinct for self-preservation." He avoids confrontation and rides things out. She compared it to the way, when Michaels's daughter wanted to get her ears pierced, he never forbade her outright, but strung out the negotiation with a series of stall tactics ("You have to have it done by a doctor," etc.). Fey said, "After a year of this, I asked, 'Why don't you just tell her no?' He said, 'You'll notice, she still doesn't have her ears pierced.'"

30 Rock became a new iteration of the SNL family, a house party to which all of the show's special friends and showbiz heroes were invited to appear: Jon Hamm, Elaine Stritch, Carrie Fisher, Jim Carrey, Steve Martin, Betty White, Jason Sudeikis, Fred Armisen, Alan Alda, Will Forte, Tom Hanks, and Andy Samberg. Hamm met Michaels through the *30 Rock* gang during the run of *Mad Men,* when both were winning every year at the Emmys. "It was a cool kids' club," he said. Increasingly, spinning projects off of SNL became a gratifying way for Michaels to lasso his favorite talent into side projects. When he turned "MacGruber," SNL's note-perfect *MacGyver* send-up, starring Will Forte, into a Pepsi commercial for the 2009 Super Bowl, the ostensible reason was to placate NBC Entertainment's new co-chair, Ben Silverman, who was pushing that kind of dubious revenue-enhancing partnership; but really, it was just fun for Michaels to work with Forte and Kristen Wiig and the rest of the tribe— which is also why he then turned *MacGruber* into a movie (like *Brain Candy* and others, it followed the flop-to-cult-classic trajectory) and, in 2021, a TV reboot for Peacock.

KEEPING THE SNL DIASPORA CLOSE INFORMS A LOT OF MICHAELS'S BUSINESS decisions—and personal ones. He believes in marking milestones. Like many men who become fathers later in life, he proselytizes about the joys of starting a family. The first hug that Hader got from Michaels occurred after Hader's first child was born. Michaels said, "A new chamber of your heart will open." (He inquired to make sure they had one of the good corner rooms at New York Hospital.)

"He's really there when you have kids or get divorced," Mark McKinney said. "But not, oddly, when you get married." Because SNL people tend to have their weddings during the show's hiatus weeks, Michaels sometimes sends regrets; his time off is sacred. But he is ready with pointers on prenups and honeymoons; Kristen Wiig recalled walks on the beach in which he would "go really deep" with advice on boyfriends and how to handle her sudden fame.

"Lorne was a big help when I was going through a divorce," Paul McCartney told me, referencing his split from Heather Mills, which filled the tabloids in 2008 (in court, Mills dumped a pitcher of water on McCartney's barrister). "We could talk quite intimately about things like that, and at a time like that you need to have a close friend," he went on. "He said to me that he'd had three marriages, and he never wanted to get divorced again. He didn't want to be known as a serial divorcé." Chris Rock had the same take: "Lorne's great in a divorce." Barnaby Thompson said, "Not a day's gone by in the past thirty-five years when I haven't thought, 'What would Lorne do?'"

He did make it to Adam Sandler's wedding, in 2003, and he gave the groom a piece of advice. "Lorne said, 'Don't feel like you have to be responsible for everybody,'" recalled Sandler, who is known for doling out jobs to friends and family. "He was trying to tell me, 'You're allowed to enjoy some of this yourself.'" (David Spade once joked that the call sheet for a Sandler movie looks like a page from Ancestry .com.)

Events Michaels always shows up for include memorial services, bar mitzvahs of friends' kids, and big birthdays. He was there for Paul Simon's final concert, in Queens, in 2018; he played air drums and cried a little during "Still Crazy." When Tom Davis, a stalwart from the early years, published a memoir, *Thirty-Nine Years of Short-Term Memory Loss,* in 2009, Michaels's assistant almost neglected to tell him about the book party, lumping it in with the many missable events he gets invited to. He dashed over just in time to find that the centerpiece on the bar was a life-size ice sculpture of his own head.

In 2001, when Florence Lipowitz died, Michaels was touched to see, among the mourners at the funeral in Toronto, Jimmy Fallon and Mike Shoemaker. "My group," he likes to say, "we measure people on whether or not they show up." Florence had been hospitalized with intestinal issues, and Michaels got on the phone, from the Beverly Hills Hotel, with a nurse in Toronto. There was a surgery that could be done, but, since Florence was in her eighties, the nurse said, "Maybe, Mr. Michaels, it's time to let her go." He was infuriated by the Canadian-ness of the attitude, all actuarial tables and practicality. The operation went forward at his insistence; his mother hung on a few more days, and he was able to fly to Toronto in time to visit with her before she died. She was cranky with him for pulling strings on her behalf; she didn't like jumping the queue.

Too many of Michaels's SNL compatriots had untimely deaths, including Belushi, Radner, O'Donoghue, Farley, and Hartman, whose wife shot him in bed. Tom Davis was diagnosed with throat and neck cancer in 2009. Michaels told Davis that he knew he'd have a hard time visiting him "when it's all the tubes and stuff," so he proposed organizing a big dinner with guests of Davis's choosing, "so we can all spend a night talking." He booked a private room at Lattanzi, and everyone made toasts. Paul Simon sang "Feeling Groovy," and Paul Shaffer accompanied Bill Murray as Nick the lounge singer. Davis cracked his friends up when he said, "Don't be surprised if I'm not the first person in this room to die." He lived for two more years, which, he joked toward the end, was embarrassing, because he'd already told everyone goodbye.

Michaels hosted a memorial service in 8H. In his brief remarks, he said that he'd always trusted Davis's laugh. Bill Murray, who had kept a distance from Michaels in the years since he'd left, gave a eulogy that had a slightly mystical tone, in the spirit of healing old wounds. "I think that something really good is coming, for all of us," he said. When Franken, by then a U.S. senator, spoke, he said, "Tom wanted you all to know that he loved every person he worked with at SNL. Except Harry Shearer." Franken also gave a eulogy on the Senate floor, in which he read from an essay that Davis had written called "The Dark Side of Death." In it, Davis said that he was still buying green bananas and quoted his local grocer, who "recently asked if I had heard that there are two stages in life: 'Youth,' and 'You look great.'" Davis concluded, "Wish I'd thought of that."

THIRTY-SIX

NOT TONIGHT

Answer: "Sis boom bah."
Question: Describe the sound made when a sheep explodes.
—JOHNNY CARSON AS *THE TONIGHT SHOW*'S CARNAC THE MAGNIFICENT, 1981

JOHN MULANEY AUDITIONED FOR SNL ON AN AUGUST DAY IN 2008. SETH Meyers and Amy Poehler had recommended him after seeing him at the Upright Citizens Brigade. He remembered that, when he was ten, there were jokes about Lorne Michaels on *The Simpsons*. "But I didn't get why it was funny that Homer is reading a *Playdude* magazine interview with Lorne Michaels," he said. He knew that he'd be auditioning to a cold room, with no laughs. But as he waited in the hallway to go on, he was rattled to see Michaels repeatedly walk in and out of the studio, a phone pressed to his ear, talking intensely.

When Mulaney got back to his hotel that night, he opened his laptop and learned what the phone calls were about: Bernie Brillstein had died that day. Although Brillstein's influence on SNL had waned, he'd been there at the beginning, and being in Michaels's slipstream, he'd spawned an empire of his own; his firm, Brillstein Grey, managed the bulk of the comedy world. ("Whatever debt Lorne owed to Bernie, he definitely fucking paid it back by flinging every cast member that way," Chris Rock said.)

On the phone in the studio, Michaels had been hashing out funeral arrangements with Brillstein's former business partner, Brad Grey, and after a lot of velvet-gloved pressure, he'd managed to get the Hillside Memorial Park in L.A. to bump a dead guy from Encino so that Brillstein could be interred on Sunday. Michaels would produce the memorial at UCLA's Royce Hall. Alan Zweibel flew west with Michaels and Martin Short, who emceed. They compared eulogy notes on the plane. At the memorial, Zweibel talked about how, when he became Brillstein's client, he'd asked about signing a contract; Brillstein put out his hand and told him to shove his contract up his ass. "I have here," Zweibel said, "a partial list of other things Bernie requested that I shove up my ass. The internet, Sepulveda, Mike Ovitz." Michaels brought the service to a close by having Kermit the Frog sing "The Rainbow Connection."

The other thing that happened on that August afternoon was that when Mulaney auditioned, Michaels laughed, loudly. He hired Mulaney as a writer. Mulaney and another newcomer, Simon Rich, quickly figured out that a surefire way to get material on the air was to write the host's opening monologues, a job nobody wanted.

The pair mastered decoding what Mulaney calls "the macro lessons" of Michaels's stories. Every December, on the day that the Rockefeller Center Christmas tree is lit, Michaels hosts a bagel and lox buffet in his office. That first year, Mulaney, holding a paper plate, asked the boss when Johnny Carson had moved *The Tonight Show* from New York to L.A. Michaels unspooled a long story about the move, which happened in 1972. The gist: Ed McMahon, Carson's longtime announcer, didn't want to relocate his family from their home in Avalon, New Jersey, and he instructed his reps to use the move as leverage for a raise and a new title. Carson, on hearing these demands from an agent, responded that he'd find a new announcer. The agent had to scramble to get McMahon to personally patch things up with Carson. Mulaney recalls Michaels concluding: "Because, it's that thing of, if you have a personal relationship and you get agents involved, nobody likes that."

After Michaels walked away, Simon Rich said to Mulaney, "That's not a story about Johnny Carson."

The subtext of the story was loyalty, the personal touch, staying within the family, and Mulaney never forgot it. Two years later, in early 2010, he thought of the Ed McMahon story when he noticed that Michaels seemed to be a wreck in the office; Sigourney Weaver was the host. While Michaels went through his paces in 8H, out on the West Coast his onetime protégé Conan O'Brien was in the final days of his tenure as host of *The Tonight Show*. Having succeeded Jay Leno, O'Brien had had the gig, his dream job, for just under eight months.

The latest transfer of power at *The Tonight Show*, the most golden franchise in television, had played out like a boardroom déjà vu. In 2004, when O'Brien had successfully been hosting *Late Night* for eleven years, his manager, Gavin Polone, had made an unprecedented, if not downright strange, deal with NBC. O'Brien's *Late Night* contract would be up soon, and he was being courted by other networks. To keep him in the fold, NBC agreed that, in five years' time, Leno would retire and O'Brien would become the fifth host of *The Tonight Show*. Leno went on record as approving the deal, saying that he hoped it would prevent a succession drama like the one that had pitted him against Letterman. O'Brien carried on with *Late Night*, which had staked out a new sensibility of silly comedy. (Bill Hader and Mulaney each mentioned their love of the show to Michaels when he interviewed them for SNL. He responded, like a proud father, "Yes, that's mine.") Of the delayed-gratification deal that NBC and Polone devised, Michaels later said, "It was very muscular. I wouldn't have done it that way." Even Carson made a crack about the layaway arrangement when he called Conan to congratulate him on the deal: "It does seem like a long engagement before the marriage," he said.

When the five years had elapsed, the deal began to resemble a pixelated version of *Rumpelstiltskin*. O'Brien was ready to claim his prize, but Leno decided that he wasn't ready to retire. ABC and Fox were wooing him, so he had NBC over a barrel. And his *Tonight Show* had been killing in the ratings, beating Letterman at CBS.

Even so, as dictated by his contract, O'Brien took over *Tonight* in June 2009, doing the show out of a new $50 million studio in L.A. NBC, wanting to keep Leno, and his good ratings, gave Leno a new show of his own at 10:00 P.M. But after seven months, the network made an abrupt turnabout: it announced that the new *Jay Leno Show* would move back into the 11:35 slot, pushing O'Brien's *Tonight Show* to just after midnight. It was a makeshift compromise that would turn into a conflagration.

The trouble started even before O'Brien took over *Tonight*. In the months leading up to the switchover, there was a widespread assumption that Lorne Michaels would be O'Brien's executive producer at *Tonight,* as he'd been at O'Brien's *Late Night. Variety* even said so. But that didn't happen. On O'Brien's *Tonight Show* premiere, two executive producer credits appeared on the crawl: Conan O'Brien and Jeff Ross.

O'Brien claimed to be clueless about the perceived slight. "It never occurred to me in a million years that Lorne would executive produce this show in Los Angeles, when he was in New York," he said. "So, stupid me. I thought *The Tonight Show* was not a Lorne-produced show. But NBC made it clear from the beginning that they didn't think it was a Lorne-produced show either." That's what an NBC executive had told Jeff Ross earlier, asking him to keep the information to himself and not let Michaels know. "We were uneasy, but we really didn't want to jump in front of the truck," Ross said. "I'm not saying we did the right thing, but it's what we did." Ross eventually had to tell Michaels, who took the news in his unperturbed way. His colleagues, however, believe he was hurt.

NBC put out a story that the Conan camp didn't want Michaels in the mix, which infuriated O'Brien. "If NBC wants to pay Lorne a million dollars a year or whatever to have a credit on *The Tonight Show,* what does that have to do with me?" he said. "But they didn't want to do that, and then, what really bothered me later on was NBC saying, 'Well, Conan didn't want him.' I was, like, 'You fuckers.'"

From an operational standpoint, keeping Michaels on board didn't seem obvious. He hadn't spent much time at Conan's *Late Night,* which taped just down the hall from 8H. And O'Brien didn't always take Michaels's notes anyway, including one early suggestion about losing a signature Conan move—the hip-swiveling "string dance," which ended with the host licking a finger and rubbing his nipple while making a sizzling sound.

Whether the decision was made by intention or inertia, Michaels considered the EP issue largely symbolic. Steve Higgins said, "Everyone else was more offended than Lorne was"; after all, Michaels had been there with Conan from the beginning. On a trip to L.A., Michaels had shown the flag by dropping by the elaborate new *Tonight* set being built for O'Brien on a soundstage at Universal, and suggested—too late, it turned out—that it looked excessively large, almost like those cyclorama-wall sets for old variety shows. "It's nighttime," he said. "It has to look cozy, like you're huddled together by a fire."

O'Brien's *Tonight* reign may have been snakebit from its inception. When the baton was finally passed, Leno's new 10:00 P.M. show was an immediate ratings washout, which created a domino effect: it was a bad lead-in for the eleven o'clock news, which was a bad lead-in for O'Brien's *Tonight Show.* Worried, O'Brien called Michaels for advice. Both agreed that the Leno prime-time show needed to go. It had never made any sense to Michaels: Leno was a late-night guy. Michaels had dinner with Jeff Zucker in New York and told him that NBC should just let Leno go to another network; he came away believing that O'Brien would be protected. Michaels's philosophy has always been: you pick the horse, you let him run the race.

After four months, NBC finally decided that Leno's prime-time show wasn't working, initiating a strange period of uncertainty. Was Leno leaving the network? Or was NBC going to pull O'Brien off the air and reinstall Leno at *Tonight*? O'Brien took pains to calm his staff's jitters, but he was nervous. Suddenly he was having a hard time getting Michaels on the phone, despite the fact that he had recently written a letter of recommendation to bolster the Harvard application of one of Michaels's sons. The vague chill from New York seemed very different from the support O'Brien had felt during the shaky early days of *Late Night.*

When NBC finally told the Conan camp that the network had decided to put Leno back on at 11:35, and push Conan's *Tonight Show* to 12:05, O'Brien felt blindsided. He and Jeff Ross had been the last to know, and it stung to learn that Michaels had heard the news before them. The network expected that O'Brien would comply.

Instead, over the next week, he held a series of intense meetings at his house with his wife, Liza; Ross; and a few colleagues. A litigator was brought in to determine whether NBC's plan violated O'Brien's contract. But his next move was radically at odds with the protocols of backroom contract discussions. On January 12, 2010, O'Brien released a statement to the press. His wife had typed it on a typewriter while he dictated. It was addressed not to Jeff Zucker or NBC, but to "People of Earth."

The main point: "I sincerely believe that delaying *The Tonight Show* into the next day to accommodate another comedy program will seriously damage what I consider to be the greatest franchise in the history of broadcasting," he wrote. "*The Tonight Show* at 12:05 simply isn't *The Tonight Show.*" O'Brien refused to go along with NBC's plan. Suddenly, the succession drama turned into a culture war.

As Michaels had told Don Ohlmeyer in Aspen years earlier, making enemies of comedians can be dangerous. Fans reacted to O'Brien's manifesto, as it came to be called, with a tidal wave of support on social media. O'Brien rode it expertly, corralling his followers into "Team Coco." Celebrities flocked to the "I'm with Coco" movement, and other late-night hosts joined in, battering NBC and Leno, who was viewed as a bully who wouldn't get off the stage. Letterman joked about a fake show called *Law and Order: Leno Victims Unit.* O'Brien didn't shy away from the topic on *Tonight.* "Hosting *The Tonight Show* has been the fulfillment of a lifelong dream," he said in one bit. He added, to all the kids out there, "You can do anything you want in life. Yeah, yeah—unless Jay Leno wants to do it, too."

As NBC negotiated an exit package with O'Brien's representatives, the public side of the squabble got uglier. Zucker threatened to force O'Brien to stay off the air for three and a half years without pay. Throughout the media storm, Michaels kept his head down. He neither advised O'Brien nor made any statements in support of him.

During the weeks of chaos and negotiation, the two men, on opposite coasts, enacted an agonized silent standoff. Each seemed to be waiting for an overture from the other. "I felt like Lorne couldn't say how excruciating it was to watch one of his kids go through this,"

Mulaney said. At the same time, Michaels was frustrated with O'Brien. The I'M WITH COCO T-shirts, the fan frenzy—it went against his instincts. It reminded him of all the cant around the Smothers Brothers, who had let themselves become martyrs. They positioned themselves as free-speech crusaders, only to be heckled by a drunk John Lennon. "*That's* who you sacrificed for," he remembered thinking, back at the Troubadour. The Smothers Brothers had lost sight of the long game, and so, he thought, had O'Brien.

In the early-morning hours after the Sigourney Weaver show, Michaels and Mulaney flew on a private plane to L.A. for some meetings. At forty thousand feet, Michaels talked about "the gods of show business" and how O'Brien had forgotten the main thing: Stay on the air. Don't die on mole hills. Don't die on *any* hill. ("Jews do not celebrate martyrdom," he has said.) O'Brien's self-immolation obscured a plain business fact. "If you don't get ratings, they take you off the air," he told Mulaney on the plane. "It happened to me, and it'll happen to you."

Had they talked, Michaels would have advised O'Brien to sleep on it before hitting SEND on the "People of Earth" statement. He would have told him to take the 12:05 slot and ride it out. Besides, time slots didn't mean anything anymore. Plenty of people, he knew, watched SNL online the next day. But he felt that O'Brien was "post-listening," and Michaels isn't by nature a rescuer. Bill Hader described Michaels's damage-control instinct this way: "If you start drowning, he's not like, 'Here's a life jacket.' He's like, 'Oooh, look at that guy drowning in my pool. That's disgusting; let's go over here and hang with Alec Baldwin.'"

O'Brien felt abandoned. "Lorne could have said, 'You know what? They didn't really give Conan a chance. Conan's proven he can do this.' He could've said some positive things about me, and he wouldn't have lost anything," he said. "He's Lorne fucking Michaels. That's what bothered me."

During the *Late Night* years, O'Brien and Michaels had bonded over the sting of each being repeatedly beaten, at the Emmys, by Jon Stewart's *Daily Show.* But the closeness was precarious; Michaels always held his emotions in reserve. O'Brien remembered how, one night several years earlier, at a party in Michaels's honor, Dan Aykroyd opened the floor for speeches. O'Brien, who'd had a couple of drinks, made an extemporaneous toast. He said that everything good in his life—Liza, whom he'd met through *Late Night,* and, by extension, his kids—had come about because of Lorne Michaels. He ended by saying, "And that's why I love him."

"I saw Lorne visibly blanch when I said it," he recalled. "In that millisecond, I said to myself, 'Fuck. I fucked up.'" He went on, "It took me a long time, as I grew up more and got therapy, to realize, he's a really scared person. A lot of brilliant people are."

When the exit negotiations were finished, NBC agreed to pay Conan's operation $45 million—$32.5 million to O'Brien himself and $12 million to settle the contracts of others connected to his show. He used his final days on the air to stick it to NBC, which he was leaving after nineteen years. He wanted, he said, a "Viking funeral." Norm Macdonald came on the show bearing a gift basket, with a belated card reading "Congratulations Conan on finally securing your place as permanent host of *The Tonight Show.* That's something they can never take away from you." The parade of parting guests—Will Ferrell (doing "More cowbell!" with the band), Sandler, and others—were all members of the Lorne Michaels family.

Whether Michaels could have saved O'Brien if he'd been an EP on *Tonight* is an open question. He felt that O'Brien had lost some fundamental control by doing the show in L.A., as NBC had wanted. "That was Conan's mistake," he said. "For me, it was always a New York show." A view holds in the comedy world that not keeping Michaels close was a misstep. Or, as Jeff Ross said, "We didn't throw ourselves in front of the truck for him, so why should he throw himself in front of the truck for us?"

After things settled, Leno placed a courtesy call to Michaels, who, if by no means a fan, did appreciate Leno as a practitioner of professional show business. O'Brien reached out to Michaels as well, with a note thanking him for betting on him in the very beginning. He was launching a new late-night show, *Conan,* on TBS, and he wanted the air to be clear. When the letter arrived, Michaels asked someone else to read it first. Relieved by its friendliness, he called O'Brien and wished him luck. But Conan was off the network, and off the gift list. Five years later, when SNL celebrated its fortieth anniversary with a three-and-a-half-hour-long alumni-packed show, O'Brien was taping his own show, in Cuba.

With the passage of time, O'Brien has a wider shot on the situation. "I understand now that NBC and SNL had been Lorne's bread and butter since 1975—I was an ancillary thing," he said. "In retrospect, I get why he was torn and wanted to lay low. I've made my peace with it. We're friends, and I love the guy."

As children, Michaels and O'Brien were both in awe of *The Tonight Show*. Before the decade was over, Michaels, too, would get his shot at the show.

THE PROCESS THAT LED TO JIMMY FALLON BECOMING THE SIXTH HOST OF *Tonight* began in 2000, when he was regularly "breaking" on SNL, giggling through sketches with Horatio Sanz. Colin Quinn had anchored Weekend Update for a season and a half, and Michaels decided a change was needed. "I wanted to go back to what my original impulse had been in the seventies with Update," he said. "Charm."

Fallon had been hired at SNL in 1998. He grew up in upstate New York, obsessed with the show; when he came in for his first interview, he'd snapped photos of the peacock-patterned carpet in the elevators with an Instamatic camera. One night in 2000, sitting together in the office, Fallon told Michaels that, after three years, he thought it was time to leave the show. Hearing this, Michaels just said, "Yeah, no." He told Fallon that he was going to be the new star of Weekend Update. Fallon resisted. "Uh, man, I'm the worst person for that," he said. "I don't really read the papers or anything."

But Michaels had a particular hold on him. In Fallon's first season, Marci Klein, the talent coordinator, would nudge him after every show to thank Michaels at the party. "After maybe the sixth show, Lorne goes, 'Jimmy, we're good. Just have a seat,'" Fallon said. He sat at Michaels's table from then on. Fallon, newly flush and "first-generation famous" (a Michaels term), always asked Michaels all the questions he couldn't ask his middle-class father, like what kind of car to lease. (The answer: "A Lexus, because they're unassuming but they're a great ride.")

When Fallon pushed back against the Update idea, Michaels told him, "Just do the test." Others auditioned, including Tina Fey, who was then head writer. She wowed everyone in the room, and Michaels decided to team her with Fallon. Not everyone saw it immediately: Fey was an egghead, and Fallon didn't follow the news. Michaels was implementing what he calls the Fred Astaire–Ginger Rogers strategy, in reverse: He would give her sex appeal, and she would give him class. "He's the cute boy and she's the smart girl," he said. "It's a chemistry thing."

After a few years of Update seeming like an auteur's parody of a newscast, Fey and Fallon created a loose, convivial format, playful banter mixed with political commentary. Critics compared them to Nichols and May, Hepburn and Tracy. Fallon hosted the 2002 MTV Awards, and *People* included him on its list of the fifty most beautiful people.

A couple of years later, in 2004, Fallon decided again to leave the show. He wanted to move west and become a movie star, as Bill Murray and Eddie Murphy had done. Michaels didn't try to stop him this time, but he did ask Fallon if he'd ever want to host a talk show. He explained about O'Brien's deferred *Tonight Show* deal, and that his *Late Night* job would be up for grabs in 2009. Fallon wasn't much interested, but Michaels got NBC to give him a holding deal.

A few years later, after Fallon had made several bruising Hollywood bombs (*Taxi* and *Fever Pitch*), Michaels lured him back east, dangling the *Late Night* offer. Fallon had flatlined, and he was drinking too much. He'd gotten married in the interim, and after securing his wife's buy-in, he told Michaels that he was ready to come back. But Jeff Zucker wasn't so sure a failed movie star filled the bill. Michaels arranged a dinner for the two so that Fallon could present himself as a level-headed hard worker; Michaels also told Zucker that if the network didn't want Fallon on *Late Night,* they'd have to find a new executive producer. Zucker came around, and Michaels sent Fallon on a stand-up tour of colleges to hone his solo skills.

Fallon's *Late Night,* which launched in March 2009, was a closer satellite of SNL than O'Brien's had been. Michaels installed Mike Shoemaker from SNL as producer (he knew all the shorthand) and told him to start wearing a suit. O'Brien had brought his house band, the Max Weinberg 7, with him to *Tonight,* so Fallon hired the Roots, the Philadelphia hip-hop group led by Ahmir "Questlove" Thompson. That music is a shortcut to coolness is one of Michaels's core beliefs, and Fallon's own musical chops made his show unique. His affectionate parody of early Neil Young prompted Bruce Springsteen to come on the show and join "Neil" in a duet as *Born to Run–*era Bruce. Michelle Obama felt comfortable enough with Fallon to do a "Mom dance" demonstration on the show (the "Sprinkler," the "Driving the Station Wagon"); her husband came on, too, doing a "Slow Jam the News" bit. Michaels dropped in every day, offering monologue edits and suggestions about camera angles.

Up on seventeen, the Update situation had been shuffled and reshuffled. When Fallon had moved west, Michaels gave Fey the option of anchoring the segment on her own. She came close to saying yes, but ultimately asked Amy Poehler to join her, making it the first time that two women held down the desk. Poehler had been trained in improv but not in stand-up, and Michaels coached her on how to perform as herself, rather than as a character. He told her that everything would change once she looked into the camera and said, "I'm Amy Poehler." She and Fey were co-anchors for two seasons. "With Tina and Amy, and then later with Amy and Seth, you got the feeling these people are best friends," Robert Smigel said. "The show became more loose and clubby, like the old-fashioned comedy that Lorne loves."

PEOPLE WHO WORK WITH MICHAELS SAY THAT A CONVERSATION WITH HIM often feels like a follow-up to a conversation that never happened. In the spring of 2013, Seth Meyers got this sort of phone call from Michaels, when he was on the road doing stand-up. Jay Leno had just announced that he'd be retiring from *The Tonight Show,* this time for real. The management at Comcast, which had recently completed its takeover of NBC, wanted to avoid a third bungled transition and was eager to anoint Jimmy Fallon as Leno's replacement. The *New York Post* had printed a rumor that Seth Meyers was in the running for Fallon's old job. Meyers didn't think anything of it.

The first thing Michaels said when Meyers picked up his phone call was "So, look, I think you'll figure it out. You'll make it your own." Meyers was perplexed. "It took me a second to realize, 'Oh, that rumor was a real thing,'" he said. "And this is Lorne telling me I can do it."

The in medias res conversational gambit makes Michaels hard to argue with. Meyers signed on, keeping Shoemaker as producer. Michaels, as executive producer, stepped in as a go-between with the network when needed. Steve Higgins said, "You can have as much of Lorne as you want. Either he is a fire hose that you keep behind glass you can break when you need it. Or he can be there all the time as a fire safety system."

With Fallon hosting *Tonight,* there was no question that Michaels would be executive producer. Fallon said, "I was, like, obviously, 'Lorne, do you want to produce the show?'" Now he would control the network's whole late-night operation: SNL, *Late Night,* and *Tonight.* Michaels set about re-creating the *Tonight Show* of his dreams: it broadcast from New York City, in a luxe yet intimate studio, where Jack Paar and then Carson had done the show. "You want to connect to the best of what came before you," he told Fallon.

He had considered O'Brien's pieties about *Tonight* overblown, yet he believed in the cultural largeness of the gig. When Fallon took it over, Michaels told him, "There is *no* job after this. You don't go play the third lead in a movie." With SNL, Michaels had invented a lifelong position for himself; hosting *Tonight* was in the same category: more than a job, it was a reign.

The new set that Eugene Lee designed was a Proustian callback to the bus trip that Michaels had taken to New York City as a teen-ager: blond wood, a sweeping curtain sewn from seventy thousand dollars' worth of velvet. ("I want your curtain *bigger*," Michaels told Fallon.) He also advised him that, if he wanted to keep the Roots as his band, they'd have to add a horn section. "Anytime you're announc-ing a king or a queen," he said, "there are horns."

With Comcast behind them, the budgets were generous. As a cor-porate owner, GE had been driven more by industrial profits than by cultural excellence. (Mike Schur, a former SNL writer, had a funny riff imagining the GE leadership assessing its various divisions: "Why is our laser-guided mission department doing so much better than our fart-joke division?")

Michaels's presence hovers over *Tonight* even when he's not in the studio. Fallon has a pre-show ritual of going into his private bathroom to wash his hands and gargle. He's been known to pretend that Mi-chaels is hiding in the shower stall. "Now, Lorne, come out of there," he'll say. He switches to a petulant Lorne voice: *"Fuck you, Jimmy!"* It's funny because it's preposterous; Michaels would never be in a vulnerable position like that. But Michaels's fingerprints are every-where on the show, and Fallon can present like a Lorne Mini-Me. His office anteroom is decorated with framed tickets to his show, like the ones on Michaels's walls, and a fish tank and a popcorn maker hum in the corners. The gifting routine is the same, too: Fallon doles out T. Anthony luggage, and he tells his own staff the old-timey stories that Michaels told him. Now a new generation of comedy writers can recite the one about Flip Wilson and the layer cake.

IN THE VOLLEYBALL-STYLE ROTATION BETWEEN MICHAELS'S SHOWS, SETH Meyers took Fey's place alongside Poehler when Fey left to start *30 Rock*. When Meyers left the show, in 2014, there was an opening again. John Mulaney, a writer who'd always wanted to perform, enter-tained private fantasies about being offered the Update slot, but he never considered making a bid for it. (After so many years, Franken didn't want it anymore, having been elected a U.S. senator from Minnesota; Jack Handey said, "I'm sure he's a fine senator, but he's such a great comedy writer, it's almost like . . . Mark Twain deciding to be a florist.") Like Fallon, Fey, Poehler, and Meyers, Mulaney was one of Michaels's favorites. So he was crestfallen when he heard that Michaels had told someone, "If Mulaney thinks he's guaranteed Update, he's got another thing coming." Colin Jost got the gig, sharing the duties with Cecily Strong; Michaels asked Mulaney to contribute by writing some Update features.

Upset and hurt, Mulaney did the thing that Michaels hates the most: he sulked. Michaels noticed, and asked him to come in and talk. During their sitdown, Mulaney blurted that he'd never be so presumptuous as to expect to be a cast member, and he knew that there were no heirs apparent in show business. Michaels listened. Then he said, in a paternal tone, "John, I know everything about you." They put aside the issue and moved on.

The next year, after Mulaney left the show, he created a sitcom, *Mulaney,* for Fox, which Michaels produced. Despite having the gang's-all-here feeling of a Michaels family project (Elliott Gould, Martin Short, Nasim Pedrad, Penny Marshall, and Nora Dunn), the show failed. The buzz was bad even before it debuted (there had been an executive shuffle), and Michaels took Mulaney to dinner to prepare him for the worst. He said, "Listen, this is going to be really, really hard, but you're going to get through it."

Even so, when Fox shut down production with no warning, Mulaney was devastated. Michaels was furious, too. Universal Television, NBC's sister company, was the production company, and Universal had neglected to tell him they were scrapping his show. When Mulaney gave him the news, he crisply asked, "Who at Universal?" He had a lunch scheduled with the Comcast leadership, and this procedural slight would be Topic A. It was a *Do you know who you're dealing with?* situation. (Colleagues have mentally linked Michaels to the line in *The Godfather,* spoken by the movie producer Jack Woltz: "A man in my position can't afford to be made to look ridiculous!") Mulaney said, "In that moment, he was like a hit man."

———

DURING THE HALF CENTURY THAT MICHAELS HAS BEEN AT NBC, THE NET-work has had more than a dozen entertainment-division presidents and three changes of ownership. He has prevailed by quietly going about his work. "Lorne is able to navigate those waters," Fey said, "because he knows that you never get the long run by being the guy who says, 'I told *them!*'" He sees the show, which is an island inside NBC, as a microcosm of all of show business: if you learn how to stay afloat, and if you don't expect that the show will always be great, if you know that it will go up and down, you'll survive. Business tycoons ranging from David Zaslav to Brian Roberts to Jeff Bezos consult him when they need a take from "a wise owl," as Martin Short calls him. One strand of the writers' room *Make Fun of Lorne Show* clowning is a postapocalyptic bit about how, after Earth is ravaged by nuclear war and the cockroaches evolve and take over, they'll turn around and Lorne Michaels will be standing there, feeding the fish in his office. He'll say, "Okay, so. I see you as kind of a Chevy cockroach."

Survival has created a sense of stability. Aside from the sleep de-privation, the SNL process is machine-like. The schedule that Mi-chaels devised in 1975 was no accident. As Cherie Fortis, from the early days, put it, "Because he liked to stay up all night and sleep late, he set up an environment that was tailored to his needs—an entire organism that suited his biorhythm and strengths and weaknesses." And when a show happens twenty times a year, people get good at it. The sketches are written, the index cards shuffled, the tables at Orso booked, the flowers replenished, the Yankees seats distributed. July is Wimbledon with Fallon. Sunday dinner is fajitas at home, Christmas is in Jamaica. Michaels is a creature of habit. If his lunch date arrives before he does at the Grill, in Beverly Hills, a maître d' advises the guest, "Mr. Michaels sits on *this* side of the booth."

In the dozen years after 9/11, an overlapping group of mightily talented cast members brought the show into a period of unusual and sustained equilibrium. The intelligence and cracked originality of Bill Hader and Jason Sudeikis, Fred Armisen's music parodies and off-center kooks (the punk rocker Ian Rubbish), Kenan Thompson (ebullient host of such TV parodies as *Black Jeopardy* and *What's Up with That?*), and Kristen Wiig's way of creating huge laughs with underplayed, quiet moves and indeterminate accents (Vanda the "Super Showcase" model, Target Lady)—all coupled with strong political pieces, produced a run of solidly funny and un-neurotic seasons. Michaels's decision, in 2013, to hold a special audition to add a Black woman to the show's main cast (only the fourth in its history), marked another change of course. Up till then, he'd defended the show's weak record on race by saying that he'd followed a cardinal rule: hire the funniest people and put on the funniest material. "If it's not funny," he said, "it doesn't matter if it's well-intentioned." Assessing talent using a lens of diversity, he said, was "a weird sort of way of looking at it because you don't judge comedy that way. Versatility is what we look for." But over time, prodded by critics and the evolving expectations of his viewers, he became open to putting extra effort into finding writers and cast members who better reflect all fifty states.

During SNL's second quarter-century, the office atmosphere gradually grew less cutthroat. Surviving the Ohlmeyer years was part of it, but some people date the shift to Michaels's becoming a father. "You begin to realize that people are affected by what you do," Seth Meyers said. "Especially when you have authority over them, the way a parent does." People who read the books about the early years absorbed them as cautionary tales; Mulaney said, "I went into the job thinking, 'This is going to be a cold atmosphere—it's okay if you get fired; people here are not that nice.'" He was surprised to find it pleasantly collaborative.

But with so few slots available in the air show, a certain amount of tension and disappointment is built in. Michaels's lieutenants have absorbed his habit of smoothing conflict with a bit of soft soap. "You'd never tell somebody that something's not funny," Higgins said. "You'd just go 'Mmmm. Okay, let me think about that.'" Michaels might disguise a critique as a riddle. Poehler recalled, "He'd say, 'Do *you* think it's working?'" When he was an SNL producer, Shoemaker made a point of passing on information humanely—letting someone know that he'd been cut from a sketch, trying to shoehorn him in somewhere in a "service part." ("The worst thing that can happen to you on a Saturday was not to need hair and makeup," Meyers said.) Cast members think of it as a numbers game. Hader advised Taran Killam, when he started in the cast, that if you do two great sketches per season and stay on for seven seasons, that's enough for a *"Best of"* DVD. (There are currently almost thirty of them.) If a performer is on a roll, killing in several shows in a row, Michaels takes advantage of the arc. "Momentum is everything," he says. Giving someone else a turn is the way things were done in Canada.

The lighter mood was evident even under the bleachers. Instead of cowering before Michaels, writers started to parry with him. Once, around 2000, he directed a favorite putdown, "Alert the Peabody Committee," to Adam McKay, and McKay replied, "Should we?" Others jumped in: "Why not?" "Let's call them now!" "It was really healthy," Shoemaker said. As Paula Pell found her bearings, if she heard Michaels eviscerate a sketch, she'd turn and say, "Lorne! My God! You are going to *hell* for saying that!" He'd laugh. Pell has a special power over him, once stuffing her bra with oranges and leaning over him to go through notes. "He'd laugh harder than I'd ever seen," Poehler said. Pell is one of the few people who can get away with invading his personal space. She'd say, "I think you need a hug" and jump in his lap.

"In my later years there, something flipped in me," Pell said. "It was like when you see your parents as whole people." People called Pell a "Lorne whisperer." She developed a bit she'd do when friends called her at home, pretending that Michaels had spent the night and was blow-drying his hair. She'd yell, with a hand over the receiver, "Lorne! *Can you turn that off?*" Like the writers playing the Which Paul? game, or Hands Off, Hands On, it was a way of defusing tension. Non-staffers play, too: Martin Short appeared on the show in 2005 as Jiminy Glick, his triple-chinned showbiz reporter character, and showed a "vintage" clip of Glick interviewing young Lorne Michaels (played by Will Forte). "Why are you so *boring*?" Glick asks, as

"Lorne" stares, unruffled. "But isn't blandness your *strength*?" Forte was so nervous playing the boss that Michaels considerately left the studio during the taping.

New employees are still routinely terrified of him; when the office feels too friendly, whispers circulate that Michaels doesn't like "the treehouse vibe." He recognizes the supercharged dynamic. "The people that I can be closest to, like Steve [Martin]—they came in under their own steam," he said. "They don't have any paternal confusion. Their happiness is not in my hands."

Employees talk about Michaels haunting their dreams. Paula Pell used to have one about making him climb on her back at a party, "and I would carry him around." This, she said, was "working out my need to be familiar with him, and not so formal." Speculation about his retiring routinely makes headlines. "Nobody can ever replace him, because he has *love*," Molly Shannon said. "Underneath that depth and intelligence is deep love. It's only him, it's his show." Some of his people find themselves preoccupied with his funeral. "The entertainment business will just shut down," Hader said. "Because everyone will go to it." Talking about the way people constantly analyze Michaels's mindset and moods, Mulaney said, "Sometimes my friends and I would think, 'Maybe he's just having bridgework done.'"

A FEW YEARS BACK, A GROUP OF SNL ALUMS WERE OUT TO DINNER AND THE talk turned, as it always does, to Michaels. Discussing him is no longer a fear-based thing, one of the group, the writer Mike O'Brien, said: "It's affectionate and teasing—it's how you talk about a fun parent." Someone asked, "How many years do you think it'll be before we don't automatically do a Lorne chunk of our evening?" O'Brien answered, "I was thinking it might not be ever. It might just be a forever thing."

THIRTY-SEVEN

THE TRUMP BUMP, THE PLAGUE YEAR

"THANK GOD LEONARD COHEN DIED." THAT'S WHAT MICHAELS SAID TO HIM-self two days after the presidential election in 2016. Donald Trump had won, shocking the world, much of the American electorate, and the cast and writers of SNL. By dying during election week, Cohen, a fellow Canadian, saved Michaels from a cold open that he would have found hard to live with. The writers' plan had been for Kate McKinnon, dressed as Hillary Clinton, to sit at a piano and sing John Lennon's "Imagine," with female cast members chiming in with glum testimonials about what Clinton's historic candidacy had meant to them. With Cohen freshly dead, Michaels suggested his song "Hal-lelujah" instead, a famous ballad of resignation and loss. It was also a less hackneyed anthem than "Imagine," which gets hauled out, like a tonier "Kumbaya," whenever global tragedy strikes. The Cohen song was the hipper choice.

On Saturday, November 12, the show opened on McKinnon at a piano in a white pantsuit. She sang "Hallelujah" like a dirge. When she finished, she turned to the camera and said, "I'm not giving up and neither should you. And live from New York . . ."

Around New York City and L.A., the phones of former SNL writ-ers started ringing. "What was *that*?" many asked each other. "I thought, 'Was Lorne absent this week?'" one alum recalled. To old-timers, the mawkish righteousness of the bit palled. Michaels didn't much like it either ("I can't do emotion, and I can't do bias," he recalled thinking), but he preferred "Hallelujah" to the alternative. The younger writers had pushed hard for their longer version of the cold open, featuring "Imagine" and the women's testimonials. Later, describing the back-and-forth to an SNL veteran, Michaels said, "The writers have lost their minds."

Dave Chappelle had long been Michaels's choice to host the post-election show, and he'd laid the groundwork over the summer, wooing the elusive comedian by giving him the run of his Amagansett guesthouse. "It was a blessing," Michaels said, "because I needed someone to tell the truth right after that election." Chappelle's friend Chris Rock hung around the studio that week, to help out with the writing and make a cameo. Watching McKinnon rehearsing "Imagine" early in the week, Rock turned to Michaels and said, "Where are the jokes?"

Michaels would have preferred some comedy. Even after 9/11, the show had managed a joke. The only other time a cold open had been comedy-free was after the Sandy Hook massacre, in 2012. "I knew it couldn't be *entertainment*," Michaels said. That time, he decided to ask the children's choir that had been booked to accompany Paul McCartney, the musical guest, to open the show by performing "Silent Night." Then, after the kids sing "slee-eep in heavenly peace," he faded to black, and cut back to the children, who smile and yell, "Live from New York!" "Lorne is very good in situations like that," McCartney said. "We morphed it back to a lighter moment."

On the show after Trump's election, Michaels knew he had to let his people strike a somber note—bidding Hillary farewell. "Do I want to fight?" he remembers thinking. "I understood that they needed to be giving that message." The cast and writers, like most of the liberal establishment, had expected to be celebrating America's first woman president that night. Besides disappointment, they felt shame and anger. Many of them believed that SNL bore some responsibility for Trump's win: a year earlier, Michaels had invited Trump to host, over the objections of some staffers. Had Trump's appearance on the show contributed to normalizing him?

At read-through the day after the election, one of the sketches in the packet was a self-referential bit of self-loathing: Beck Bennett gets a call backstage with word that President-elect Trump is canceling SNL and replacing it with a reality show called *Body Shamers.* Aidy Bryant protests, "But we helped him get elected!" Bennett gives a Trumpy pep talk. "We're still *one* country, from whites to guys. From Christians to Catholics!" he says, finishing with "Live from Jew York, it's Saturday Night!" The piece didn't make it onto the bulletin board.

When Michaels had booked Trump to host in 2015, he, like most people, considered the candidacy a big joke. But it was a lucrative joke. Trump was a ratings magnet: people liked to watch him, either in spite of or because of his noxiousness. Trump had hosted SNL in 2004, when he was doing *The Apprentice,* and Michaels knew that he'd deliver again; he was all ham. As for Trump's politics, having the GOP candidate on the show wasn't new; John McCain had hosted when he was a senator, and had made cameos when he ran for president. "It's the hardest thing for me to explain to this generation that the show is nonpartisan," Michaels said, two weeks before the election. "We have our biases, we have our people we like better than others, but you can't be Samantha Bee." He meant one-sided and strident.

Staffers felt that having Trump on before the election had been a kind of endorsement. NBC, which had aired fifteen seasons of *The Apprentice,* cut business ties with Trump early in his campaign, after he called Mexican immigrants rapists. A Hispanic coalition urged the SNL cast to boycott the episode he hosted. "It's where I get my back up," Michaels said, just before the episode. "I don't mind any reaction to a show we *do.* I really mind it *before* we've done it." Chatter circulated that Michaels was just helping one of his billionaire friends, a charge that would resurface in 2021, when Elon Musk hosted.

When Trump got to 30 Rock, he alienated the cast and writers by taking a call on his cell phone during read-through. (After he hung up, he told the group, "My book just went to number one!") Wafting up from the street below, the angry chants of activists protesting Trump's booking could be heard. The writers noted that Trump stumbled over the words in the scripts with great difficulty, challenged by the punctuation. Many on the staff felt that they'd been too soft on him all along. One night earlier that season, word came back to the writers' room that Michaels wanted them to tone down a harsh Trump sketch. (He wanted them to give the character "some charm," like Alan Rickman in *Die Hard.*) Tim Robinson smacked the table and said, "Lorne has lost his fucking mind and someone needs to shoot him in the back of the head."

Michaels remembers Trump's pre-election appearance on the show going just fine. He recalled, "By the end of the party, Larry David and Kate"—McKinnon—"both said, 'I really like the guy.'"

IN JUNE 2016, MICHAELS HAD CALLED ALEC BALDWIN TO ASK IF HE'D PLAY Trump in the show's forty-second season. It was Fey's idea. "It'll be three episodes and out," he assured Baldwin. "There's no way he's going to win." (Michaels felt that, after the pussy-grabbing tape, Trump had moved into "just craziness—like Eugene McCarthy at the end.") Baldwin said no at first, because of a movie commitment, but he came around to yes. The fact that he shared a few traits with Trump—bluster, pugilism, stubbornness—gave the impersonation a visceral feel.

Not long afterward, Michaels spoke to Trump himself on the phone. SNL was planning to have both him and Hillary Clinton on the show in the months before the election. Trump was tickled to hear that Baldwin would be playing him, and he told Michaels a story about meeting the actor twenty years earlier, when Baldwin was shooting a movie at the Trump International Hotel: on set, he recalled, Baldwin told him that if there were ever a Trump biopic, he wanted to star. Michaels loved the kismet. (Baldwin has a different memory of the encounter on the movie set: Trump, he said, asked him if there was a role for him in the film, because "Every movie I appear in is a hit!")

It didn't take long for Trump to change his mind about Baldwin, who played him as an unstable bully; as Baldwin put it, "like a manic-depressive in his speaking pattern." On the *Today* show, Trump called the impression "really mean-spirited and not very good." Of the show itself, he tweeted: "Not funny, cast is terrible, always a complete hit job. Really bad television!" Trump never appeared on the show again, and neither did Clinton. "I bailed on both candidates because it got too ugly," Michaels said.

Election night itself came as a jolt to Michaels and his staff. He'd told Higgins to take Chappelle down to the MSNBC studio on four to watch the returns. Unsettled by what they were seeing, they went back up to seventeen to write. It was Tuesday night, after all. McKinnon and some writers had gone to the Javits Center, where they'd been expecting to attend the Clinton victory party. Around midnight, a few of them arrived back at the writers' room, sobbing. Writers slumped in front of their laptops, stealing glances at the TV screen as they waited for Trump to appear among the American flags at the Hilton and give an acceptance speech. "Are we finishing our stupid sketches now?" one muttered. There was talk of riots in the streets.

Higgins, who'd been at the show during 9/11, was exasperated by the bathos. "You don't have time to cry," he remembered thinking. "It's selfish of you to cry. Your job here is to make other people feel better." Chappelle wandered around the floor with an I-told-you-so smirk. "Y'all really betted against the rich white guy," he said. "That's like betting against the Harlem Globetrotters."

On Wednesday afternoon, Michaels walked into the writers' room for read-through. He surveyed the table and saw his staff looking crushed, the usual post-writing-night exhaustion magnified by fear and disgust. A number were weeping. Usually he starts right in with the stage directions on the first script. This time, he raised his chin and addressed the group. He knew he needed to shift the emphasis away from "Saint Hillary," as he put it, and focus on the task at hand. "It was jarring," a writer said, "because he never, ever speaks at read-through."

"In 1968, when I was working on *Laugh-In,* they shot Bobby Kennedy, they shot Martin Luther King, the Tet Offensive happened, Vietnam was peaking, and Hubert Humphrey was defeated by Richard Nixon," he said. "I didn't know anyone who would have voted for Richard Nixon, so it came as a complete surprise. But the republic is strong. There is a permanent government, not a deep state. It will withstand this. We have a job to do, and we have to get on with it. Whoever is in power, we're supposed to, in some way, challenge. So let's just do the job."

He reminded the group that half of the country voted for Trump, and added that SNL is for those people as well. Those who felt that the show had been criminally soft on Trump were confused and annoyed to hear him add, "We did our best."

Chappelle, sitting beside Michaels, advised the group to use the moment for comedy. He read a quote from Toni Morrison: "This is *precisely* the time when artists go to work. There is no time for despair, no place for self-pity, no need for silence, no room for fear. We speak, we write, we do language. That is how civilizations heal."

On Saturday night, Chappelle's monologue did just what Michaels had hoped. He began by chiding white people for being shocked at Trump's victory and he lambasted white rioters in Portland as "amateurs." He ended with an uplifting story about attending a recent party at the Obama White House, and how seeing the gilded rooms full of Black people (except for Bradley Cooper) had made him hopeful.

The Hillary/"Hallelujah" requiem had opened the show, but the first sketch was Chappelle and Chris Rock in a living room with naive millennials watching the election returns together. The young white people are shocked, while their two Black friends aren't surprised at all.

CECILY STRONG: Oh my God. I think America is *racist*!

DAVE CHAPPELLE: Oh my God. You know, I remember my great-grandfather told me something like that. He was, like, a slave.

The piece ends with Beck Bennett declaring, "This is the most shameful thing America has ever done." Chappelle and Rock give each other a look and burst out laughing.

The show's young head writers hated the sketch, but Michaels liked that it was a corrective to the earnestness of "Hallelujah."

A year after the election, Michaels was leaving an L.A. restaurant after a dinner with his son Henry, Owen Wilson, and the filmmakers Peter and Bobby Farrelly. Peter Farrelly took him aside. "You think the reason you were put on this Earth was to do a great comedy show, but that wasn't why you were put here," Farrelly whispered. "You were put here for *this*." He was talking about the show's response to Trump. Alec Baldwin's impersonation of the president had been causing a ratings sensation, which was boosted by the appearance of other stars as members of the Trump entourage: Melissa McCarthy as Sean Spicer, with a rolling podium; Ben Stiller as jittery Michael Cohen; Bill Murray as Steve Bannon, blotchy and bloated; Scarlett Johansson as an ice-queen Ivanka Trump (in an ad for a fragrance called Complicit). But even with the glowing notices and internet memes, some members of the staff continued to feel that they were responsible for the national disaster.

The "Trump season" earned twenty-two Emmy nominations, and scores of adulatory pieces in the press. When Michaels accepted the Emmy for best comedy-variety series, he talked about SNL winning the first time, in 1976, and thinking that "there would never be another season as crazy, as unpredictable, as frightening, as exhausting, or as exhilarating. Turns out I was wrong." But the fuss and the praise made him anxious. "I can't hear it," he said, "because I know in six months everyone's going to be saying, 'SNL—it's just awful.' I've lived through it too many times."

TWO YEARS EARLIER, HE'D CELEBRATED THE SHOW'S FORTIETH ANNIVER-sary with a special even longer and more VIP-packed than the twenty-fifth had been. Chevy Chase was put out that he wasn't featured more, and he didn't like his seat. ("I wanted to sit in the section with Walken and De Niro," he complained.) The yearlong hoopla included a feature documentary, a six-pound coffee table book, a traveling exhibition called "SNL: The Experience," and a bash at the Plaza that culminated in a jam session that included, by turns, Prince, McCartney, Taylor Swift (who stumbled over the words to "I Saw Her Standing There"), Bill Murray, Debbie Harry, Elvis Costello, the B-52's, Maya Rudolph, and Chris Rock. Jimmy Fallon jumped onstage with a gin and tonic to emcee. A framed seating chart of the starry audience hangs on a wall on seventeen.

Cast members from four decades came back to take part in the show, including Laraine Newman, who was delighted to deploy her Valley Girl accent in a "Californians" sketch, and Jane Curtin, who sat in the bleachers during rehearsals and chatted with Amy Poehler. Both were experiencing a new mellowness toward the show. "I feel that my blood is carbonated," Curtin said; Poehler felt it too, and they agreed that, with time, all the bad feelings, the battle scars, had been smoothed over. "It was all just disappearing," Curtin said. "All of a sudden I felt a connection again."

As the decades went by, it became tougher for Michaels to showcase many of SNL's greatest hits on anniversary shows without ruffling cultural feathers. "There's almost nothing we did in the seventies that we would do now," he said. "We couldn't do 'News for the Hard of Hearing,' the Samurai, Uncle Roy." Wayne and Garth aged perfectly well, and on the three-and-a-half-hour fortieth show, Carvey and Myers did a "Wayne's World" sketch featuring an "SNL Top Ten" list. Number two on the list is "Lorne Michaels." Myers, as Wayne, brandishes a big glass of white wine, like the one Michaels was known to hold on show nights, and says, "The man is a genius. For forty years he would say things like"—switches to Lorne voice—"It got a laugh but did it get the right laugh?" Carvey adds, "You know, it becomes that thing of, like, you're really glad it's Thursday." Myers: "Mick liked it. Paul hated it. Marci didn't see it. The Stings laughed." He ends with, "Lorne, we love you." Carvey goofily adds, "One day I hope to *meet* him."

A few days after the celebration, Michaels said, "My emotions tend to be in another room, which is locked." But surveying the domain he'd built and populated over four decades—a perpetual motion machine of comedy—had moved him greatly.

He'd also come into some serious money. Just before the anniversary, Steve Burke, NBCUniversal's CEO, told Michaels that the company wanted to buy back his half of SNL, and offered him several hundred million dollars. Michaels knew that the show's value would likely be higher at the fiftieth anniversary, but he asked himself, "Do I want to have the money to spend, or do I want my kids to have the money to spend?" He made the deal and used some of the money to buy a place in St. Barts, after decades of renting.

THE FORTIETH ANNIVERSARY, IN 2015, PRODUCED PLENTY OF HUBBUB, BUT it was nothing compared to the frenzy brought on by the Trump bump. The accolades and attention almost embarrassed Michaels. "People are constantly coming up to me saying, 'Thank you so much,' like this is an act of patriotism," he said. "And I go, 'No, no. I'm in *comedy.*'" Friends started comparing him to a man who beat cancer, a man who'd fallen in love again late in life, a man struck by (nonlethal) lightning. Like everyone in show business, Michaels loves being relevant. Of Trump's presidency, Candice Bergen said, "It's a curse for the country but it's a gift for the show."

The fandom wasn't universal. As the presidency slogged on, many of the cold opens were basically beat-for-beat transcripts of idiotic things Trump had said the previous week. Old SNL hands called it "no-value-added" comedy, or comedy "by the numbers." The pieces lacked a conceptual spin, like the one underpinning a classic piece based on an idea by Smigel, "Mastermind," from 1986. (In the sketch, Phil Hartman plays President Ronald Reagan, who, far from being the benign dolt known to the public, is actually a knife-sharp strategist in conference with his staff.) Among the more innovative Trump pieces was a recurring sketch called "Melania Moments," written by Julio Torres. He wrote the First Lady as a dazed damsel, held captive in Trump Tower, staring out the window at Fifth Avenue and wondering if a Sixth Avenue exists.

Jim Downey was no Trump supporter, but, watching from home, he sometimes felt that the show's political material seemed like a product of "the comedy division of the DNC," something that Michaels generally took pains to avoid. ("Lorne's got a real old-fashioned, 1930s hard-boiled antenna for that kind of liberal bullshit," Randy Newman told me.) An overused go-to move was nailing a disliked GOP politician by casting a woman to play him. Issues of "tonnage" also burdened the show. Trump did or said something preposterous almost every day. Will Ferrell found the quantity of Trump material "almost oppressive."

The show was hotter than it had been in years, but it was an uneasy buzz. The writers worried that something they put on the air might provoke Trump to blow up the world (or make the IRS audit them). The success raised the stakes, making office life more stressful. One staffer's therapist compared the SNL environment to the Trump administration: both hinged on trying to please a fickle, ratings-obsessed boss; both fostered paranoia about who's in and who's out; both cared about appearances and were stingy with praise.

The show got under Trump's skin, and his Twitter rants escalated as he repeatedly commanded the FCC to initiate a probe: "There must be Collusion with the Democrats and, of course, Russia!" "I once hosted Saturday Night Live, and the ratings were HUUUGE! Now, however . . . L.M. is angry and exhausted . . . it is over for SNL—A great thing for America!" Bizarre as the outbursts were, they were satisfying. From a ratings standpoint, the show had regenerated again, like a hydra. For the first time, *The New York Times* began running recaps of the show every week. And the president of the United States, it seemed, was paying more attention to SNL than to ISIS, immigration, the opioid crisis, or gun deaths. Michaels, presented with the proposition that maybe satire works, couldn't help but agree—with one qualification: "As long as it's not called satire."

WHEN THE CORONAVIRUS PUT MOST OF THE WORLD IN LOCKDOWN IN MARCH 2020, silver-lining seekers started reminding people that Shakespeare wrote *King Lear* while sheltering at home from the bubonic plague. Michaels was in St. Barts when Covid hit. The government closed the island's borders ("When the French shut down Hermès, you know it's serious," he said), and he ended up enjoying an extended visit with his daughter, Sophie, who had been on spring break from Yale.

A reader of biographies, Michaels keeps a running mental list of historical figures whose careers remind him somehow of his own. There's Thomas Edison ("He didn't think he *invented* anything; he thought he *perfected* things, and that all the ideas he perfected were already in the air") and William Shawn (he corralled a gang of talented, needy egos into producing a fine weekly publication), but the one who haunts his conversation the most is Shakespeare. He views Shakespeare as "the ultimate problem-solver," for the way he saw to it that, despite any obstacle, the show would go on. Shakespeare first had to get a play approved by the Lord Chamberlain and the monarch. Then he scrambled to cast it and get it on the boards—not unlike a week at SNL, hurtling toward Saturday. Instead of 11:30 P.M., Shakespeare's deadline was sunset; Michaels talks of him shaving twenty minutes from *Hamlet* to get the play over before dark. Shakespeare also wrote expressly for the actors in his company. ("I know he had a Belushi," Michaels told me. "That's why Falstaff appears in three plays.") But the biggest challenge was getting productions on while the plague raged. If there were more than thirty deaths in a week, the London authorities closed the theaters. "So Shakespeare had to have the carts and horses ready to go to tour the provinces," Michaels said. "Because he had all the actors to pay."

When the 2020 plague hit, SNL couldn't pack up its wigs and actors and take the show to the provinces. It remade itself as a Zoom vehicle, *Saturday Night Live at Home,* beaming the show from the bedrooms and kitchens of its cast, from Tampa to East Hampton.

Michaels had never missed a show in his decades at SNL (he's produced almost nine hundred episodes), and he was the last person to accept that the March 28, 2020, episode could not be broadcast from 30 Rock. The March 7 show, the last one before everything shut down, played the looming coronavirus for laughs: a soap opera parody incorporated awkward social-distancing protocols, and Rachel Dratch made a Debbie Downer cameo as a Covid-obsessed wedding guest in a gas mask. On March 16, NBC announced that SNL wouldn't resume production "until further notice." Locked down in St. Barts, Michaels kept in close touch with his lieutenants. He hated the idea of his season being cut short. A man of steady habits, he kept up his daily walks, despite the beaches being closed; residents were permitted to walk the cobbled streets of Gustavia for ninety minutes a day, gendarmes monitoring the situation in their flat-topped Claude Rains hats.

He decided that they should try producing the show remotely, entirely on tape, to air on April 11. He wasn't sure it would work, but his team, he thought, was good at solving problems. NBC asked to have the finished show on a Tuesday; everyone knew that wouldn't happen.

Sophie Michaels was taking her Yale classes on Zoom, but Michaels wasn't interested in learning a new technology. The telephone was more his speed, and he sat through cacophonous conference calls with his people. The thing they missed the most was the constant flow in and out of Michaels's office, bouncing ideas around. "You *hear* stuff, and no number of emails or texts can replace it," he said. "It's tribal."

The SNL "Quarantine Edition" was experimental, closer to the 1977 Mardi Gras show than anything since. At first Michaels thought they'd pull together thirty minutes of new material, then cut to a regular rerun. The cast was asked to come up with ideas that they could film themselves at home, using their webcams. NBC mailed out microphones and simple lighting kits. McKinnon decided to do her Ruth Bader Ginsburg impersonation, showcasing RBG's home workout. Pete Davidson wanted to shoot a parody of a Drake song in his mom's basement. A read-through over Zoom, including some group sketches, was called for Wednesday. The session would be recorded, in hopes that a couple of the raw pieces might be used on the air. In an email, Erin Doyle cautioned against "re-submits"—pieces that had been read at the table before—since the only laughs would be whatever noise the cast members made from their Zoom squares. She added, "Bring your own snacks!"

The next day, Michaels's phone rang in his kitchen in St. Barts. It was his supervising producer, Ken Aymong, in a shattered state, calling with the news that Hal Willner, the show's legendary music supervisor, had died that morning in his apartment, from the coronavirus. He'd had a fever; a doctor had made a house call. It had all seemed okay, until it wasn't. Like a lot of New Yorkers in April of 2020, Michaels felt the disease closing in. Also, Willner had a teenage son.

That day, dozens of people emailed and called him, wanting to talk about Willner. "Hal was the person who, when you were new and nobody was that interested in you, Hal had time and was encouraging," Michaels said. He'd find the perfect music for their sketches, "but he was always careful to let it be theirs." Kate McKinnon started writing an appreciation. Michaels decided that she should read it as an intro to a longer tribute. He called Tina Fey and asked her to be a point person in putting together something with former cast members. (It ended up being her and Maya Rudolph, Amy Poehler, Ana Gasteyer, Rachel Dratch, Molly Shannon, Emily Spivey, and Paula Pell singing "Perfect Day," a song by Willner's friend Lou Reed, in a Zoom grid.) He also spent time on the phone comforting Michael Che, whose grandmother had died from Covid. Colin Jost, his co-anchor, was quarantined in Montauk, just down the road from Alec Baldwin in East Hampton. Michaels wondered if they could somehow safely get together to tape a Trump Update segment.

When the cast logged on the next day for the Zoom read-through, they looked like people reuniting with long-lost family members. They waved frantically, exclaiming about new quarantine facial hair. (On the air, Michaels always wants the men clean-shaven, like the New York Yankees.) Zoom meetings were new enough that people were still making jokes about *The Brady Bunch* and *Hollywood Squares*. "Gallery View" had to be explained. Averse to Zoom, Michaels wasn't in the grid, and Jost read the stage directions. Thirteen sketches were read. The best were those that dealt with the new reality of quarantine. An Aidy Bryant line: "I used my license as toilet paper and now I don't know my birthday!" Davidson at one point says,

"I've been quarantined with my mom so long, she's starting to look hot."

In St. Barts, Michaels was working the phone. From the start, he wanted Tom Hanks to "host." Hanks, besides being a founding member of the Five Timers Club, was the first celebrity to go public with a diagnosis of Covid-19. He agreed, and planned to film himself doing an opening monologue at his house in L.A. on Friday afternoon. An early version had Bryan Cranston standing in the Hanks kitchen holding cue cards from six feet away. Michaels wanted it simpler. "I was looking for: 'I'm here. I was Patient Zero, and it's going to be all right.'"

A Zoom version of Update was recorded on Friday, too, with Jost in his Montauk living room and Che in Manhattan. Baldwin phoned in as Trump, offering alternative names for the virus: Hong Kong Flu-ey; Crouching Tiger, Hidden Symptoms; and General Tso's Revenge. (In an earlier Update Zoom meeting, which didn't go to air, Baldwin offered some lockdown life advice as himself: "I haven't had a drink in thirty-five years, but I hope you're drinking your fucking balls off.") There were some shots at Rudy Giuliani, the president's lawyer, that Michaels ordered cut, not wanting the show to feel bitter. "It has to be fun," he said.

Just like a regular week, as Friday turned to Saturday, dozens of decisions were up in the air. "It was like mercury on a mirror," Michaels said. NBC's ad sales people were pestering to make sure that, to honor a deal made with Walmart, someone would thank essential workers on air, before the store's patriotic commercial ran. Chris Martin, the Coldplay frontman, had volunteered to tape a song from his home in Australia, but he wasn't sure what to sing. Michaels suggested Dylan's "Shelter from the Storm." Late Friday, Michaels's deputies sent him a very long rough assemblage; he dictated cuts, and he re-sequenced everything. In the wee hours, instead of dissecting the first act in his office, he sat reading a Sicilian murder mystery in St. Barts, frangipani rather than popcorn scenting the air.

At 11:30 P.M. on April 11, *Saturday Night Live at Home* opened on the Zoom grid of the cast greeting one another. A new opening montage began with the bandleader, Lenny Pickett, playing the first notes of the show's theme on his saxophone at home, adding shots of band members playing their parts alone. The cast, instead of gliding through New York glamour spots, is introduced poking around their houses: Beck Bennett unloading laundry, Heidi Gardner doing curls with cartons of oat milk; many pets appear. (Michaels's little black dog, Lola, died while he was in St. Barts; he Facetimed with her toward the end.) Then Tom Hanks appears in his kitchen. He deploys the show's trademark self-deprecation, echoing Michaels's exchange with Mayor Giuliani from 2001. "It is a strange time to try to be funny," Hanks says. "But trying to be funny is SNL's whole thing, so we thought, what the heck?"

Seven million people tuned in, almost as many as when Eddie Murphy had hosted earlier that season. Michaels was not one of them. NBC isn't on in St. Barts. He had signed off at 5:00 P.M., and that was it. While the show played, he was watching an episode of *Fauda,* an Israeli TV drama. He was very happy with his team's work, and he hadn't micromanaged. The *At Home* edition reminded him of SNL's early days, when the show felt like something homemade. Working on this episode, and on the later ones done with various degrees of PPE, brought him closer to his staff. SNL had shown up. He said, "It's like my grandmother always said: In a situation like this, what's in you comes out."

PART SIX

SATURDAY

On Saturday the pugs arrived. They were sequestered in a make-shift dressing room in Seth Meyers's studio among a squad of extras. The five dogs waited in baby strollers, tended by several seen-it-all matrons who guarded their charges' privacy as though they were the Redgraves. If a sketch calls for an animal, SNL always uses the same agency. A llama named Pierre appears on the show nearly as often as Alec Baldwin does.

Since the seventies, when a sketch features a moment backstage, there is usually visible, milling in the hallway, a showgirl in a feathered headpiece, a man dressed as Abe Lincoln, and a llama. The tableau first appeared on SNL in a 1978 episode hosted by Eric Idle; thirty years later the trio started appearing again as a regular sight gag. It's a winking reminder that SNL is just show business, even when the world wants it to be something else—an anarchist collective, a settler of political scores, a cultural institution. (Michaels gets frustrated by the way the show is regarded as a public utility—*"You let us down."*) Pierre's handlers know the drill, and they regularly bring him up to eight on the same Art Deco elevators that the audience uses. One recent December, a sketch called for a live camel, which seemed like an easy get; camels are regulars in the Radio City Christmas Spectacular across the street. ("Every camel works at Christmas," Michaels says.) But the camel's hump was too tall to go through an archway in the 8H hallway and it got wedged there, like a truck stuck in a low underpass. Carpenters had to remove a portion of the ceiling to get the animal out. Pierre took over the part.

The revised schedule for Saturday, the longest twenty-four hours in the week, is printed on pink paper and has two columns. On the left is the DRESS RUNDOWN, which lists the order of the sketches during dress rehearsal, the crew's copies annotated with running times, down to the second. On the right is the RUNTHRU ORDER. At 1:00 P.M., the sketches are performed, for the first time in costume and on sets that are mostly completed. The studio swarms with people, as carpenters and set designers run around applying finishing touches.

The Craigslist sketch was first. The design department had bought a used Chevy van in Brooklyn for $5,000 and then spent another five thousand having it disassembled and covered with hate-speech graphics. "We take it to the junk shop," Eugene Lee said. "They take the engine out. Anything that they can to make it lighter. Then they cut it into two pieces, because that's the only way it will fit in the elevators." The studio was built for radio, so the 1930s elevators weren't designed to carry scenery, and although they are big enough for an average llama, they can't fit a van. "All the scenery has to come in in small pieces and be put back together," Lee continued. "A car just fits by sometimes half an inch."

The French Canadian Motorcycle piece was magically transformed now that all of its design trappings were in place. The sight of Bennett, Moffat, Hill, Mooney, and Thompson walking into the studio, zipped into black leather and capped with scraggly metalhead wigs, cracked up the crew. *"Alors!"* the actors crowed, delighted by the autumnal road footage that showed up behind them on the monitors, courtesy of a green screen.

Most of the writers had been called for 1:00 P.M. rewrite tables, to punch up the monologue. Jost was working upstairs on the cold open. All week, the writers and support staff come to work in jeans and sweatshirts. On show days, per tradition, everyone dresses up. The men wear jackets and ties and recall little boys being forced to go to church; the women come in cocktail dresses and tug at their tights through the day. In the ninth-floor writers' room, Fran Gillespie called the meeting to order. The bit where Tina Fey implants a computer chip in Jonah Hill's neck had been cut because Michaels thought it felt too violent. And they needed to find a funnier reason for why Kenan Thompson is in the Five Timers Club. It would be a bad look for him to be there as a servant.

Someone said: "What if every four seasons in the cast counts as one year of being a host? Like dog years."

Another suggested: "Kenan says, 'Four generations of Thompsons have tended this bar'—and we show four shots of Kenan through the ages."

Still another: "Kenan says, 'This is where I come to take dumps.'"

Scatological jokes wake everyone up; something about material too gross to use gets comedians going. Gillespie said, "Maybe it's something positive for Kenan, like 'I come here to relax because I'm tired of carrying the whole cast.'"

Another writer ran with the idea: "Kenan goes: 'This is *my* show, and I let *y'all* come here sometimes.'"

Everyone laughed: that line did it. On a monitor, they could see the Benihana sketch being rehearsed down in the studio. They noticed that Jonah Hill's arms, revealed for the first time that week, were covered with sinister-looking tattoos. Moving on with the monologue, Steve Higgins said that the part where Tina Fey prank-calls Kyle Mooney as Lorne could be funnier. He put on a Lorne voice: "Kyle, let's talk about how you're doing on the show this year." The energy level spiked. The chance to imitate Michaels, a staple activity, is a treat.

"Hi, Kyle. Any *family matters* to discuss?" (Michaels likes to have sage heart-to-hearts.)

"Let's talk *Animaniacs*—does that wet your whistle?"

"Kyle, you know they're making a reboot of *ALF,* in case you're interested."

Amid the laughter, someone suggested Mooney do a running-in-place move like a character in a Hanna-Barbera cartoon, and sprint right out of his clothes in his eagerness to meet with the boss.

An NBC page brought in a platter of fancy sandwiches, courtesy of Hill. Keeping the writers well-fed is a time-honored way to get them on your side. Down the hall, in Michaels's conference room, each assistant had a phone pressed to her ear. It was 2:30, and he was expected around 5:00. Erin Doyle was shopping for blackout shades online. (Sleeping all day Sunday is the norm.) A fresh vat of roses was wheeled in, and a young man brought in tubs of ice to hold beer and wine for later, when Michaels's guests would gather in his office to watch the show on the monitors.

In the studio, the pug wig infomercial was rehearsing. A sleek boutique set was squeezed into a corner, with shelves full of miniature wig stands shaped like pugs' heads. The professional dog minders passed the wriggling pups to the actors, who struggled to keep them facing the camera. Across the studio, the massive set for Movie Theater was wheeled out. The last piece to be rehearsed before the cold open and the monologue was Teacher Fell Down. As the first sketch of a new writer, it was handled with extra care. Down the hall, the sets completed, Eugene Lee napped in a chair in his office.

Michaels arrived at five, spiffy in a dark suit. He went directly to the studio floor, where the Five Timers monologue was starting, to greet Drew Barrymore, who made her first appearance on SNL in 1982, at the age of seven; and Candice Bergen, who won Michaels's loyalty by appearing on the fourth show ever. Both women wore Five Timers Club smoking jackets. Michaels had a huddle with Bergen, the warmth between them evident.

The run-through satisfactory, Michaels retreated to his office. He was conferring with Higgins and Fey when Steve Burke, the CEO of NBCUniversal (and Michaels's boss), walked into the conference room with his teenage daughter to say hello. Michaels's assistant, Willa Slaughter, gestured toward the closed office door, so the Burkes took a seat and waited. A few minutes after they had their audience, Brian Roberts, the CEO of Comcast, popped in as well. Michaels's relationship with the Comcast leadership is as cozy as any since the days of Herb Schlosser. The executives revere his longevity, and his attunement to business realities. A few years ago, the show aired a parody of a feel-good Toyota ad about a father dropping off his daughter, who is shipping out for military service. In the SNL version, the daughter is shipping out to join ISIS. Toyota was an advertiser in the show, and the company complained to the ad-sales department. Michaels offered to call the Toyota executive and extend an invitation to come see the show live, which did the trick.

Dress rehearsal, performed for a live audience at 8:00 P.M., is the do-or-die moment of every SNL week. It is the first time Michaels has heard the sketches since read-through, and the first time they are seen by civilians, as SNL employees call regular people. The dress lineup usually contains twenty or thirty more minutes of material than will fit into the air show. Michaels's foxhole underneath the bleachers, just ten feet by six, is enclosed by tacked-up yards of black cloth. The studio stages are not visible from there, so a large monitor anchors one end of the hideout, surrounded by a handful of tall direc-tor's chairs for his lieutenants. Wineglasses are lined up on a shelf, next to a bin filled with ice and bottles of beer and wine. A pair of swinging doors behind him leads to the control room, a few steps away.

As Michaels settled into his chair with a goblet of mineral water, Kenan Thompson was warming up the audience from home base. A true utility player, he had the audience cheering as he tore into the opening of "Gimme Some Lovin'," a number that the Blues Broth-ers had sung as a warm-up forty years earlier. Strong, McKinnon, and Gardner sang backup, wiggling in sequined sheaths. Pondering the cuts he knew he'd have to make, Michaels told me, "You always have pieces that you'll stick with, even if the audience isn't there immediately." Sometimes he doesn't want to trust three hundred strangers. "We're in a hot period right now," he said. "So the audience loves everything." He put on a pair of large headphones. Flanking him were Kenward, Higgins, Doyle, Che, Maroney, and Jost. As each sketch began, its writers slipped into the command center and stood at the ready, waiting for Michaels's notes. Some of the writers joke that, if under-the-bleachers ever had a corporate sponsor, it would be Imodium.

A stage manager named Chris Kelly, a tall man with mussed gray hair, started a countdown over the PA, always done the same way. "Thirty seconds!" he yells, then "Twenty seconds!" When he gets to the final call, he makes his voice crack, and the "Ten seconds!" comes out as a deranged yodel. The audience laughs every time. The first thing that appeared on the monitor was the logo of Laura Ingraham's

Fox show, *The Ingraham Angle*; then McKinnon, at a news desk in a red dress, greeted viewers "live from the Arizona border." The studio audience cheered. The first big laugh came when she showed a new "official portrait" of the president: Trump as Rambo, glistening with sweat, with a coonskin cap on his head, in front of a sombrero-wearing mob. She narrated: "Thankfully we have a president who actually protects America. All of a sudden the term 'white' is bad, 'nationalist' is bad, 'white nationalist' is bad." The screen cut to Cecily Strong as Judge Jeanine Pirro, Ingraham's guest.

In his booth, Michaels yelled, "Get Tom!" An assistant scurried to fetch Tom Broecker, the costume designer. Seconds later he was there, and Michaels gave him a note about Strong's wig obscuring her face. He also wanted the shot on her to be tighter; Caroline Maroney scribbled on a legal pad. Meanwhile, on-screen, Pirro commented on footage of the caravan (actually film of a Black Friday stampede at Walmart) as the audience roared. The next "caravan" clip was the zombie apocalypse scene from the movie *World War Z,* with Brad Pitt running away in terror. Strong declared that Pitt was now "dating the caravan," which would henceforth be known as "#Bradavan." Michaels gave his first big smile. His first laugh was for Kenan Thompson as Ingraham's guest, "Trump cheerleader, former Milwaukee Sheriff David Clarke." When Ingraham asks how he is, he responds, "Unpopular among my own people." Hill made his first appearance, in a Fu Manchu mustache, against a backdrop of the Kremlin, as "martial arts legend and newly minted Russian citizen Steven Seagal." Michaels winced. "Did he try the glasses?" he asked, unconvinced by the impersonation.

Next, McKinnon cut to footage of Leslie Jones as "poor has-been Oprah Winfrey" stumping for Stacey Abrams.

"She should already be talking when we cut in on her," Michaels said in a quiet voice, as Maroney wrote on her pad. The cold open had been playing for more than seven minutes, and Michaels impatiently said to Erik Kenward, "End on Oprah?" But there was more: Ingraham/McKinnon promised to bring out "a hilarious George Soros impersonator"; on-screen flashed a shot of Beck Bennett as a rabbinical Soros, payos dangling, blood dripping from his mouth, saying "I vant to fund your terrorism!" She wrapped up: "All that, plus an update on disgraced former actor Alec Baldwin, seen here molesting a young Boy Scout." On the monitor flashed a still from the 1994 sketch "Canteen Boy," featuring Baldwin nuzzling a nervous Adam Sandler. "And Live from New York, it's Saturday Night!" The audience overhead thundered its approval.

As the show's opening montage played on the monitor, the monologue's writers filed in, to watch at Michaels's side. There was a note on Hill's opening line: Michaels didn't want him to plug his movie, *Mid90s*. When Fey walked on to welcome Hill to the club, the audience went crazy, and they got noisier when they saw that Barrymore and Bergen were there as well. Hill asked the women where Tom Hanks and the other guys were, and Fey explained, "They're not allowed in right now; turns out they were a bunch of horny perverts. Time's up on that business!" Despite his earlier directive to make the clubhouse look empty, Michaels thought the shot was too wide, with "too much rug." The new Kenan line, "This is *my* show," made the audience whoop. When Fey, doing the prank phone call, lobbed the *ALF* reboot line to Mooney in her prissy Lorne voice, Michaels doubled over laughing.

America's Got Talent played well, but Michaels, speaking quickly and precisely, gave a note about the lighting, and pointed out that the camera missed judge Howie Mandel (Mooney) when he was announced. As predicted, Thompson waking from the coma to sing with Leslie Jones was a marvel. But Michaels noted a "structural problem." The elaborate graphics mimicking actual NBC promos for the show went on too long, and he wanted to get to the action faster. And the title was bad: "America's Got Talent: Wait For It!" might confuse the audience. He wanted it changed.

Before any lines were spoken in the kid-in-Benihana sketch, Michaels barked, "Tom!" He was seeing Hill's bare arms for the first time. "Lose the tattoos," he said. "Also, Jonah's too low in the chair." The divorce line ("Because it's worth it!") got a laugh, but already Michaels was making a resigned expression that suggested he was merely tolerating the sketch. "Anyone remember why we brought this one back?" he asked. Heidi Gardner, as a hibachi chef, flipped a shrimp in the air and the camera missed it.

The audience liked Beavis and Butt-Head, with Bennett as a jumpy murder suspect, but Michaels was bothered by the way Hill kept twisting his neck around. "Why does he keep doing that?" he asked. Someone explained that, in the cartoon, Beavis is always pictured in profile. Pete Davidson flubbed a line. Michaels sighed. As the piece wound down, he said, "Is murder too dark? It's like entry-level comedy. It feels forced." He glanced at the writers and murmured, "No disrespect."

At home base, Hill looked into a camera and introduced Maggie Rogers. She swooped around the stage in a billowing red caftan and no shoes. Michaels looked annoyed. "Barefoot?" he said. "Where is she from? Kansas? A place with roads?" Broecker was summoned and, after a huddle, dispatched with orders to kill the red muumuu.

Next came the dramatic music heralding the start of Weekend Update. The segment opened with a caravan joke ("A second migrant caravan just pulled up to landscape Mar-a-Lago"). A joke about the subway ended with a punchline about a guy "taking a dump in a McDonald's bag." Michaels aimed a weary glance toward Kenward: *Too dark.* He laughed when Che said, "You know how those red states stay so red? By sending all their liberal kids to the coastal cities to study improv."

When Davidson appeared for his Update feature, he was swimming in an enormous orange work shirt, his skinny neck poking out of the collar like a stem from a flowerpot.

"Tom!" Michaels yelled: *The shirt.* Davidson started with an oblique reference to Ariana Grande, mentioning that he'd had to move back home with his mom (the audience loved it), but the bulk of his bit was riffs on the appearance of various political candidates. "Rick Scott," he said, of the bald Florida senator, "looks like you tried to whittle Bruce Willis out of a penis." New York's "Peter King looks like if a cigar came to life." Michaels nodded: "Good." Davidson moved on to Lieutenant Dan Crenshaw, who wears an eye patch. "He is a congressional candidate from Texas and not a hit man in a porno movie," Davidson said. "I know, I know. He lost his eye, in war or whatever. Who cares?" Michaels grimaced, and Davidson moved to Andrew Cuomo: "He looks like the guy who's banging your mom and stays overnight and has breakfast with you in his boxers." Michaels's note: "*Banging*? Let's say 'sleeping with.'"

Davidson closed with an earnest pronouncement about Ariana Grande. "Some of you are curious about the breakup," he began. "I don't have social media, so this is my only outlet—work. The truth is, it's nobody's business. She's a wonderful, strong person and I genuinely wish her happiness, and can we all just, like, move on and be positive and vote on Tuesday?" The audience hollered as he made one final joke, something about Mario Kart and eating mushrooms.

"Lose the mushrooms," Michaels said. "End on Ariana."

Soon it was time for Melissa Villaseñor's Teen Murder Suspect. As she rolled up to the desk, wearing a cowl-necked sweater, Michaels murmured, "She doesn't look like a teen. Get Tom." Villaseñor went through her paces expertly ("I stabbed her with a knife!" she cried. "But Logan took it the wrong way and started bleeding!"), and Michaels gave an order about streamlining the camera work.

Update had run twenty-one minutes. Movie Theater was next. Once the pretentious-food gag was established, the piece unspooled flatly; it was long and listy. Hill delivered his line about the "farm to screen" menu, "a fusion of high-end classic American cuisine and movie munchies." Michaels turned to a writer and said, "Well, he can read."

The Craigslist van sketch was next. Alex Moffat was sinister as the hustler cousin of the pipe bomber trying to close a sale. When he pulled a blue tarp off of the van, revealing hate slogans and images of Hillary Clinton with a target over her face, nervous giggles could be heard from the bleachers, followed by gasps and groans. "That's the MAGA mail-bomber's van!" Hill says, alarmed. As predicted, the moment chilled.

Michaels was looking at composition: "Step *in*! Step *in*!" he said to the unhearing actors. "They need to get closer to the van faster." By staying too tight on Hill and Villaseñor, the camera missed the visual punchline—the placarded van. "We lost them," Michaels said, of the audience. As Moffat continued with the most ick-making lines—"We got a bucket in the back for *human waste!*"—Michaels was stone-faced. The laughs had petered out. "That's disgusting!" Villaseñor, as the wife, snapped, her face registering revulsion.

"Melissa, it's still *comedy,*" Michaels muttered to himself. When Moffat came to the line "Thirty bucks and I'll clean out the piss smell," Michaels scowled and turned to the two young writers of the piece. "Can you take it and make it *longer?*" he asked, icily.

The pre-taped sleep-aid ad for "HuckaPM" played better. The audience loved it every time Aidy Bryant's Sarah Huckabee Sanders swallowed a pill and fell over unconscious, crashing through furniture and banisters, Chris Farley–style. They shrieked when she was pictured in a hot tub with Satan, and when she said, on the phone with Trump, "CNN is just ISIS spelled backwards? Sounds good to me, sir." But Michaels wasn't convinced: "It's one joke: How do you sleep at night?"

Jost asked, "Is it too political, maybe?"

Michaels shook his head. "I like the falls, but let's get to the premise faster," he said.

Alison Gates, the new writer, reported for duty looking terrified, along with Anna Drezen, the seasoned pro assigned as her backup for Teacher Fell Down. The piece opened with a slow pan of McKinnon's prone body on the floor. Someone noted that it was weird that the piece followed one about Huckabee Sanders repeatedly falling over. "How does it feel to see Teacher, who usually lords over you, on the ground?" McKinnon asks pensively. Michaels gave a quiet laugh. His only note: "Should you *see* her fall?"

Kenward looked up from his pad and reported, "We're twenty-one long now." Maggie Rogers had started her second song and had changed into jeans, a white shirt, and shoes.

"Better," Michaels said, watching her on the monitor. "Let the lens come to *her.* The other thing was just too overthought. You can tell that she's not a seasoned performer."

KCR News started, and Michaels noted that it took two minutes before the first joke landed. He called for Broecker: "Would normal hair be better?" Hill was wearing a man bun: "The wig is starring in the sketch."

There were two pieces left. As expected, Pug Wigs killed. The new celebrity wigs that had been added in rewrite did well—Troye Sivan's peroxided tousle, and Larry David's side tufts. Michaels noted that the two pugs wearing the Wolf Blitzer and ZZ Top beards came out in the wrong order. Maroney wrote it down. Also, he asked, straining to identify the hosts' accents, "Are they from New Jersey?"

The technically challenging Montreal Motorcycle Club sketch was last. "Is there a title on this?" he asked. "Or are you just supposed to figure it out?" The audience had been watching the dress rehearsal for almost two hours, and they found the motorcycle piece, beloved since read-through, appealing. The Montreal Chaos Dragons, as the bikers call themselves, trade lofty observations about the beauty of nature ("The leaves—they dance, no?" "It is God slipping out of her summer dress, no?"). A running joke is that Hill keeps encountering obstacles—dripping sap, a hungry timber wolf—but there were prop snafus. On the monitor, Michaels watched as Hill awkwardly pressed a wad of dead leaves to his face. The audience laughed at the screw-up. "He puts them on himself?" Michaels asked, irritated. "Should happen off-camera." Hill rhapsodizes that the smell "reminds me of my first girlfriend, Jeanine—we made love at the maple refinery!"

"It's a maple *syrup* refinery, not a maple refinery," Michaels snapped. On the monitor, a floppy stuffed wolf the size of a Great Dane appeared on Hill's lap, placed there by a stagehand way too early. Hill looked confused and the audience laughed; seeing mistakes is part of the thrill, which is why audiences love it when actors "break," as they now began to do.

Michaels got up and walked out of the studio before the sketch ended. He usually goes up to his office at ten, even if dress hasn't finished. If there is anything important left, he'll watch it upstairs on the monitor. As the descending piano chords of Howard Shore's "Waltz in A" were heard, along with a stage manager's voice saying,

"Cast to the floor for Goodnights," he was checking the messages on his phone.

The ninety seconds or so that it takes him to walk from his encampment under the bleachers, along the short hallway to the cinderblock service stairwell, and up the one flight to his office, are the most intensely focused moments of Michaels's week. "Generally I know where I'm going with the final lineup," he told me. "And then I start hearing stuff." People whisper in his ear, sometimes even during the walk upstairs. Among the swirling considerations: *If this sketch is cut, does one cast member not have a show anymore? Can we put him in something else? A certain piece got hurt because it played too early. Who's fixing the monologue? Is the cold opening working?*

A few minutes later, his key lieutenants convened in his ninth-floor office. This is the moment in which Michaels displays his superpower. He is definite and direct in a way that he is not during the rest of the week, a mode he describes as "being on knifepoint." His aversion to confrontation is outweighed by the urgent need for triage. He issues orders quickly. There is less of the usual joshing-around, and when it occurs, Michaels can lash out. Everyone there has heard about a night, in the 1990s, when he turned to Bob Odenkirk, who was whispering to his neighbor as the minutes to airtime were slipping past, and said, evenly, "Odenkirk, if you speak again I'll break your fucking legs."

Watching Michaels make these lightning-fast decisions reminds John Mulaney of a line from Sondheim's *Sunday in the Park with George*: "The choice might have been mistaken, but choosing was not." Michaels's choosing is the zenith of the week. He loves this part of the job; he likes not having time to obsess over details. It's all from the gut. In the final winnowing, the order is reshuffled and whole sketches are ditched, but also, new endings are added, the cold open might be replaced wholesale, costumes and props and graphics are switched out. Paul McCartney relishes sitting in on this meeting. "I like to see him in action because I know him just as a mate," he said.

And if he makes a mistake, there's always next week.

As Michaels and his deputies went through the lineup, a few

more people, including the tech heads, came in and settled into their regular seats. Michaels began with a direct command: "Get the *Mid90s* reference out of Jonah's monologue," he said. "It's crazy. As if we give out the hosting gigs for *directing*." He moved on to the cold open. He needed to find twenty minutes' worth of cuts overall. Should they get rid of Leslie Jones as Oprah? "I just worry that it's not a good enough impression," he said. "Also, it's not a *fun* moment." (When Ingraham plays footage of Oprah backward, the audio has her saying "I eat white baby parts!" Not sunny.)

Jost, who likes to have arcane references in the show, was hoping to keep his George Soros vampire joke. "I thought if you lift out Steven Seagal, you can still do Soros," he said.

"I wish those things had played, but it feels like you've already won, and now you're just doing a lap," Michaels said. "The piece is nine minutes, and I'd prefer it at six and a half." Also, Soros as a vampire in payos is something that might play on the coasts but could confuse the rest of the country.

Jost kept pushing: "We cut all of Seagal, and it would just be rolling out with the George Soros impersonator and the update on Alec Baldwin."

"I'd rather *not* do Alec," Michaels said, a bit of jujitsu designed to divert Jost's focus.

"Does it feel weird to not address the Alec thing, though?" Jost said, alarmed. "Doesn't it feel like we're too much on his side if we don't do it?"

"It does feel weird, and we *are* on his side," Michaels said. "Why don't you ask Tina."

"I'll ask her," Jost said. He didn't mention Soros again.

When Jost was gone, Michaels said, "I think the Soros thing will chill. It's just such a clear antisemitic trope; even Fox News doesn't do that. Colin wants to make a point, but I don't think so."

He turned to the bulletin board and started at the top, with America's Got Talent. "Beck's Simon Cowell is good, and there's a lot of good beats in it," Michaels said. "But you want to get to the contestants' songs with a minimal amount of texture. Less getting them in and out." He wanted it later in the show. Moving on, he asked, "Should we cut Movie Theater?"

Kenward snickered and said, "Can we leave the set in the studio anyway?" Everyone laughed again at the monstrous size of the theater seats.

"I don't think it's going to work," Michaels said, plucking the card from the board. The Craigslist Van card had already been removed. "I'm assuming that Jonah will get it with Benihana, because he has the other times," he said. "He hit it so hostile at the start."

Someone said that Hill had had "a meltdown" because the dress audience was quiet. Michaels raised his eyebrows. "Because there was no recognition for his *signature* piece," he said archly. "Anyway, we're doing it. If he has long sleeves over the tattoos, he'll find it," he said, pinning the Benihana card in the Act One column. "But he's got to play *charm*. The question is, what to open with. I would almost trust KCR News. It's dumb and—"

Kenward jumped in: "And it's presentational."

Jost made a plea for Beavis and Butt-Head, which he said was being rewritten, with the murder stuff taken out.

"I think we play it later and be safe," Michaels said.

Shookus noted that Hill didn't want to do Pug Wigs. "It makes him uncomfortable," she said.

"On the *dog* level?" Jost asked in a voice full of scorn. "Like, the dogs are uncomfortable? Shit!"

"The dogs are fine," Michaels said. "I think his discomfort is all displaced." (Translation: Hill didn't like the sketch because he wasn't the star of it.) He stared at the cards, trying to find a first act. "Should we move Kate's Teacher earlier?" he asked. "You need either the *sound* of a fall or a title card, like 'Teacher Fell Down.' Because it's so theatrical." He worried that the dress audience had started out confused. Maybe cut to the startled students before Teacher begins talking? Che added that the slow pan of McKinnon's body looked almost sexy, which was weird.

"Who's on it?" Michaels asked. Doyle sent Slaughter to find the writers, Alison Gates and Anna Drezen.

Shookus asked Michaels whether he wanted to flip the order of Maggie Rogers's songs.

He nodded. "She just came out so crazy, so intense," he said. "And is she going to wear that red dress?"

Shookus nodded. "She's going to wear the dress. She had a white lab coat on before," she told him, suggesting that the red dress was not the worst option.

"Well, she doesn't know who she is," Michaels said and moved on. "How long is Update?" It was twenty-one minutes, and he decided to keep all three features for now. "Pete's thing started weird," he said. "No need to make him dislikable at the top. And him having to apologize is crazy. Apologizing for a *promo*."

Doyle agreed. "When he says 'Can we just move on?' I think that's kind of cringey." Shookus reminded them that Ariana Grande was releasing her new single that night at eleven, "to address Pete."

"We're not in a war," Michaels said.

Higgins said, "I wouldn't do it if I were Pete."

"Who's on it?" Michaels asked. The Davidson debate was interrupted by the arrival of Gates and Drezen to discuss the Teacher sketch. Michaels turned to Gates: "Don't be frightened," he told her. This was her first time at this rodeo—being expected to retool a sketch with less than an hour before air. He gave them notes on a redraft. "Give us more of a fall, and then the kids laughing, and then cutting to her. The pan looks like it's going to be some erotic thing, as opposed to just an offstage *thud*, a graphic, then a laugh."

The women listened as though they were getting instructions on how to defuse a bomb. Drezen said, "We also talked about Kate giving a little 'whoops.'"

"Be my guest," Michaels said.

Higgins said, "Having the kids laugh might be weird."

Doyle said, "Maybe a gasp?"

"How do you orchestrate nine gasps?" Michaels asked.

Higgins: "It's a fun challenge."

"Okay, will you assign a gasp leader?" Michaels said, with a twinkle. He turned to Drezen and Gates. "Any other cuts? Because this is going to go up earlier."

The two realized that their piece, which they'd considered a ten-to-one contender, was out of third-act danger. Drezen said "Cool!" and they rushed out.

"There's a little Bette Davis in that character, no?" Higgins said, of Teacher.

"And the kids *love* Bette Davis," Michaels shot back.

"If you want to get the tweens," Higgins said, "it's *Now, Voyager.*"

Michaels moved some cards around, considering who was in what pieces and calculating how much time they had for costume changes.

"Jesus, it's late," Michaels said, looking up at the clock: 10:50. Hill came in toting his water jug and took in what was left on the board. He saw that Movie Theater was out and so was Craigslist. The expensive movie seats and the $10,000 van would be in a dumpster by morning. Michaels told him that his Benihana piece was going to lead the show and instructed him to sit up straighter. "And you'll have to make it more comedy than insult-comic," he said. Hill looked confused.

"The six-year-old seemed very angry," Higgins explained.

Doyle came in, after a quick chat with Davidson, downcast. "Pete wants to do the Ariana stuff," she said.

Michaels looked exasperated. "About a *promo*?" Doyle had persuaded him to cut it way back. Looking for reinforcements, Michaels said "Get Dennis in." Dennis McNicholas supervises the Update scripts. "And the cold opening—it's *nine minutes*—is still too long."

"I'm in agreeance," Kenward said. Jost had gone back to his office to rewrite, which was beginning to feel like stalling. McNicholas, a man with long hair and a tweedy air, walked in, and Michaels told him that Update was seventeen and a half minutes. The show overall was now sixteen and a half minutes too long, without the expected cuts from Motorcycle, Teacher, and the cold open.

McNicholas slumped, his hands in his pockets, and asked how many minutes he should cut. "I'll give you whatever you want," he said. "Pete is gonna be real brisk."

"Is the Bruce Willis penis line in?" Michaels asked.

"I like the joke," McNicholas said. "Is it the whittling that's a problem?"

"We're not talking about individual jokes here," Michaels said impatiently. "I want to talk about how he starts it off."

Doyle raised a new concern. "What about the eye patch line? Does anyone feel—"

Shookus jumped in. "Yeah, he *is* a vet," she said. Dan Crenshaw, a former Navy SEAL, had lost an eye when an IED detonated near him during his third deployment in Afghanistan.

McNicholas replied, "We'll adjust that, for sure. That wasn't how it was scripted."

"Yeah," Michaels said, then mimicked Davidson: "He lost his eye—*so what*?" He shoveled popcorn into his mouth.

"Not a winning strategy," Higgins said.

"Especially coming out of the mouth of a twenty-four-year-old," Michaels said. He looked at his watch. "I've got to start in two minutes," he said, referring to the final meeting with the rest of the staff. He turned to Janine DeVito. "Where are we?"

"Sixteen and a half," she said. He told McNicholas that he could have sixteen minutes for Update. "Now we're at fourteen and a half," he said. "I think the rest of the cuts will be in the cold opening and in the monologue. Get Jost. I've got to move." This was the most wound-up he had looked all week.

Hill chose this pause to try to wield the last bits of his influence as host. "Lorne, did you like the dog infomercial sketch?" he asked, hoping to scuttle it.

Michaels was prepared. "I thought it was playing well and the two of you were good together," he said with an air of finality.

"Okay," Hill said.

"Where's Jost?" Michaels asked again, getting testy. Just then, Jost appeared. Michaels told him he had to lose even more from the cold open. As for the rest of the cuts, he said, "I don't mind losing as we go." He meant that they'd tally the minutes as the live show unspooled and then pick which sketch to cut based on the cumulative math. "I just don't want to go in long with everyone being precious about what they've got," he said. "Pieces like Beavis and Butt-Head will be dependent on their cuts. That starts to get scary. Motorcycle becomes vulnerable, and I'd rather keep it, because it's fun." Doyle told him how many seconds had been cut from each piece.

"OK. Get the rest of them in," he said. "I have to start."

The remainder of the group—around a hundred people—streamed in and squeezed onto every inch of the floor, some on their knees so as to take up less space. This is the moment that can be most devastating for cast and writers. Rachel Dratch said, "You look at the board, and you can see if your sketch is on the good side of the board or the bad side. You could be all over the show at dress and not even *in* it on air." Will Ferrell called it "cutthroat."

As the staff fit themselves together like puzzle pieces, Jost quietly detailed the latest beats in the cold open for Michaels: Steven Seagal was out. Michaels nodded and said, "Soros is out too, right?" Jost said yes and added that he was keeping the line about disgraced former actor Alec Baldwin.

"Yeah. I don't mind," Michaels said. Having the Fox network be the one making fun of Baldwin solved the problem for him.

"Fun," Jost said, greatly relieved. Finally everyone was settled on the floor, as they had been at the start of the week, on Monday, once again looking up at their boss.

Michaels stood. "Okay, cold opening," he said, looking at his notes. "Kate, I'd rather take the applause *after* they see you. So, you say 'I'm Laura Ingraham,' then it's applause. Tighten the shot of Cecily. The background behind Kate was shaking a little." Many people scribbled on pads.

"We need to drive this one as fast as possible," Michaels said. Any piece that runs longer than expected affects everything that follows it. Next was Hill's monologue in the Five Timers Club. Kent Sublette said: "Trims throughout and Kyle's prank phone call is gone." Michaels said: "Can we get a single of Candy? Can you not show so much of the rug? We cued Kenan early." The new jacket didn't look quite right. Could it be shorter? More sequins? Michaels's final comment: "And will it be *funnier* on air?" Nervous giggling in the room.

"Benihana," he said. "Jonah's too low in that seat. I need composition on that so we know he's a kid." He mentioned the missed shrimp-flipping shot, then turned fondly to Heidi Gardner: "You were pretty deeply *in* that part."

Turning pages, he ticked through Teacher (the gasping had been sorted), America's Got Talent ("Is Simon Cowell's hair too gray?"), Beavis and Butt-Head ("Jonah, don't get locked up in that profile shot"), Pug Wigs (keep the dogs facing the camera), and KCR News (the man bun was gone; "Jonah, you're too far upstage"). Of KCR News, he added, "I was very moved by that piece. There's a sincerity to it that you don't often see in late night." People snickered, not sure whether he was serious.

Montreal Motorcycle Club was last. Michaels asked, "What are we doing with the leaves? Does Jonah have them in his hand?"

"It was my fault," Hill said. "I stuck them on my helmet at the wrong time." He mentioned the timberwolf fuckup, and everyone laughed: "I didn't know whether to acknowledge it."

"All right," Michaels said, talking over him. "This piece is coming at the end of the show," he told Hill, "so you may be getting some late instructions on it in terms of pace and time. Just pay attention—there will be information coming."

He looked at the clock, which said 11:02. Then he looked at his staff. "This is the show before the election, and so it should be *sort of* inspirational," he said. Everyone, himself included, laughed. "All right, that's it," he said. This was a more optimistic valediction than he often gives, which can be along the lines of "Try not to embarrass yourselves," or "There's a good show in there somewhere. It's your job to find it."

Everyone applauded and jumped up to go get ready; several grabbed a handful of popcorn on the way out for good luck. These minutes are the last chance for the writers to give the scripts what Tina Fey calls "a little turd polish." They'd huddle with the cast and go over final changes, then take the revisions to Wally Feresten and his cue card crew, who would write new cards with lightning speed. Each actor's lines are in a different color Magic Marker. Stage directions—*sit, cross*—have boxes drawn around them, so an actor knows not to speak them aloud. The director, Don Roy King, called his cameramen together, alerting them to shot changes. Production assistants would be doing speed surgery on King's "book"—the binder that holds his script—adding green pages and a multicolored fringe of Post-its. During the live show, as Michaels continually orders seconds shaved from sketches, PAs would update King's book during commercial breaks.

The notes meeting between dress and air suits Michaels's temperament. "The deadline—that's Lorne's cocaine," Barnaby Thompson said. But some writers consider the "fake adrenaline"—generated by waiting till the last minute for Michaels to weigh in—unhelpful. There's a feeling that "baloney-slicing" sketches this way leeches the life from them. In the early decades, Michaels would often hold a sketch for another week rather than slash it beyond recognition. Hurriedly shaving minutes from scripts in the control room while the show is on the air can result in choppy pacing and weird endings. "It's like trying to get more people in a lifeboat by cutting off their arms and legs," one writer said.

As everyone was executing Michaels's last changes, Slaughter and Maroney sat alone in the conference room. The show was going to air almost ten minutes long, twice the usual overage. "They'll definitely lose another piece," Maroney said. They suspected it might be a pretape, which could air in a later week. "And anything in the third act is vulnerable."

At 11:29, Michaels made his way down to the studio and took up his position under the bleachers, alongside Daniel Katz from A24 and his wife. Most ticket holders arrive at ten and, after going through a TSA-level security check, wait in a holding area on the mezzanine. Michaels's guests are spared these maneuvers, and are greeted in the lobby by one of his assistants, who will whisk them upstairs and deliver them to taped-off seats in the bleachers.

In his foxhole, Michaels poured himself a glass of wine. The warm-up music blared, Chris Kelly did his wobbly countdown, the APPLAUSE signs flashed, and the Fox logo for Laura Ingraham's show splashed across the studio monitors. The slimmed-down cold open played well (no vampiric Soros), except that the wrong graphic appeared during the "Voting Tips" bit. This would be fixed before the show was put on the NBC website the next day.

The opening montage played on the monitors, the cast members whirling around Manhattan, looking casually glamorous in still photographs by Mary Ellen Matthews. The audience, still hopped-up from the Baldwin "Canteen Boy" joke, shouted and clapped when Jonah Hill walked onto home base in serious-looking black eyeglasses and a trim black suit. When Fey joined him, in her velvet Five Timer jacket, they screamed, and they screamed more when Bergen and Barrymore showed up. The piece moved briskly: the line about keeping Steve Martin's hands busy with a banjo had been changed to one about how Martin sometimes just starts playing banjo with "like, no consent!" When Thompson brought out the retrofitted Five Timer jacket for Hill, it wasn't quite the spangly bolero that Michaels had asked for. But at least Hill hadn't plugged *Mid90s*.

The rest of the first act went according to plan. Teacher did well, the new whoops-thud-and-gasp opening clarifying the premise. Maggie Rogers was next, so Michaels's guests ventured out from the bunker under the bleachers and watched from the floor. Wearing jeans, and shoes, Rogers did her first number, which began flat. During her performance, Michaels visited the control room, a large, dark NASA-like space with a wall of monitors and two banks of consoles manned by technicians. After each sketch, he gets an update on the time—whether they are ahead or behind, down to the second. When Rogers began, the show had moved from being almost ten minutes over to eight over. Higgins and Kenward huddled with DeVito, feverishly adding up the lengths of the remaining sketches. Sometimes cast members speed-talk their lines to make sure there's room for a sketch in peril. Aykroyd was an expert at this. Once, in the nineties, the writer Steve Koren made the rookie mistake of telling an actor, after dress, to say his lines more slowly on air, prompting Michaels to lose it. "Lorne went, 'If you ever tell an actor to take his time again, I'm gonna break your fucking legs,'" Koren recalled. He hadn't realized that his note had affected the entire show, forcing Michaels to cut a whole sketch.

In the control room, looking at the math, Michaels will order a specific number of minutes or seconds cut from each of the remaining sketches. In the back of the control room, script coordinators stand by a photocopy machine, churning out revised scripts for writers frantic to get new changes circulated and transferred to cue cards.

Also informing these on-the-fly decisions is how the segments fit into the preordained slots for commercials. Ken Aymong had done some calculating during the first act, and he reported to Michaels that if he cut Villaseñor's Teen Murder Suspect, on Update, there would be room for two more sketches. The Teen feature could hold for another week, but Michaels was intent on giving Villaseñor her shot.

Then it was time for Weekend Update, which is often the night's biggest control room challenge, comprising dozens of complicated graphics, videos, and live guests who roll in from offstage on desk chairs. This time it went smoothly. Jost started strong with the "Faithful Patriot" joke, which had a new punchline: "Fun fact: 'Faithful Patriot' is also what Mike Pence yells out during sex." Villaseñor's Teen Murder Suspect made a strong connection with the audience. Broecker had put her in a flowery sweater and given her bangs; she performed the character with a meticulous tautness. As she came offstage, she jumped up and down with some writer friends. From his perch, Michaels looked over and smiled.

The Update feature on which Michaels had lavished the most time and concern, Pete Davidson as himself, seemed to go smoothly. Ariana Grande's new song, "thank u, next," had been released online just before 11:30. (It wasn't the expected Pete slam, but a song expressing gratitude to her assorted exes for what they'd taught her.) Davidson appeared at the Update desk in a different big orange shirt. The audience gave a collective "awww" when he said he'd moved back in with his mother. They laughed hard at the Bruce Willis penis-whittling joke. The photo of Lieutenant Crenshaw in an eye patch flashed on the monitor, and Davidson stuck with what he'd said at dress, with one small change. After likening Crenshaw to a porn-star hit man, he said, "I'm sorry. I know he lost his eye in war, or whatever." At the desk, Che laughed in pained astonishment. Davidson shrugged and repeated, "Whatever." The change was that, this time, he did not finish with a breezy "I don't care." (Backstage, at least one writer was surprised: Hadn't Michaels given a "hard note" to cut the joke about losing an eye?) He signed off with a few sincere sentences about the breakup with Ariana Grande. When the segment was done, there was a palpable sense of relief under the bleachers.

It was nearing 12:30, and the show was still eight minutes over. Death Valley, the ten minutes just before 1:00, was looking particularly lethal. In the control room, Michaels consulted with DeVito, Kenward, and Higgins. Scribbling numbers, they decided to cut Beavis and Butt-Head, the longest sketch in the lineup. But that wouldn't be enough, so either Montreal Motorcycle Club or Pug Infomercial would have to go as well. Motorcycles had had tech issues at dress, and Michaels preferred the pug sketch, which was silly and fun. He killed Motorcycles.

"It's a tough way to get a piece cut," a writer said. The motorcycles sketch had made it through all the hurdles of the week. It was the only piece that the new writer, Bowen Yang, had in the lineup.

The audience ate up the retitled "America's Got Talent: Wait, They're Good?" Then it was time for Maggie Rogers's second song, and even though she was barefoot in the unloved red caftan, her number was musically more together. HuckaPM played well, although a few writers were grousing that it would've been easy to hold it in favor of one of the live sketches that had been cut. Pug Infomercial ended up being the ten-to-one sketch, even though it was rather middle-of-the-road. On air, the pugs faced the camera, and a few of the rewrite adds (Hill and Strong singing "What's pug got to do, got to do with it?") had the audience screaming.

For Goodnights, Hill came onstage, looking happy and tired as he plugged his movie. The stagewide round of hugging went on for longer than usual; there was extra time because so many sketches had been axed.

The show over, the air pressure on the eighth and ninth floors shifted, like an exhalation of breath. Everything slackened. The Lornettes passed out tiny slips of paper printed with the address of the party. The audience streamed toward the elevators. Michaels headed up to his ninth-floor office—now cleared of guests, popcorn basket refilled—to gather himself. The static in the back staircase that links the eighth and ninth floors cleared, as throngs of well-wishers trudged up or down to pay their post-show respects or crack a beer in the conference room. Down on eight, Leslie Jones, looking radiantly happy, stopped Candice Bergen in the hall and asked for a selfie. Jones's week had panned out.

The post-show euphoria can be chaotic. One Saturday in the following fall, on Michaels's seventy-fifth birthday, the host Harry Styles ordered an elaborate cake that was a model of 8H, with a marzipan Lorne in marzipan black tie standing in the middle. It got wheeled into the studio hallway just after Goodnights, but in the mayhem, Michaels didn't even see it. Later, he heard that the crew ate it.

Outside the street door on Forty-ninth Street (the exit that Jost avoids), a fleet of black cars was waiting to ferry the cast and writers to the party at Dos Caminos on lower Park Avenue. A mob of fans and autograph seekers pushed against velvet ropes, as the revolving door deposited the tired stars on the sidewalk and a dispatcher put them in cars. Michaels got in his car with an assistant and headed downtown.

At Dos Caminos, a smaller group of fans clustered in front of the entrance. Inside, two PAs checked names against a list, shouting greetings over loud house music. Michaels always has a table reserved toward the back. He holds court there, sipping Belvedere, flanked by a helper or two. After almost fifty years, people who attend the party still feel like they are in on something special. "It's always the coolest place to be in New York City," Jon Hamm said. "Every time I'm there, I'm like, this is the greatest place to be, in the greatest city, in the greatest country, on the greatest planet." Daniel Katz and his wife sat with Michaels at his corner table, along with Mark Ronson, the record producer. During the evening, cast members stopped by to pay their respects, like a scene from *The Godfather* but with a thumping bass line. It was so dark that guests used their phones' flashlights to read the menu; each table paid its own bill. The corporate coffers are opened every May, though, for a big bash after the season finale, held on the ice rink outside Rockefeller Center. At the previous season's send-off, the cast of *Mean Girls* danced in a circle around Kate McKinnon, and electricians and camera operators did the Hustle with back-office staff. Jerry Seinfeld, Chris Rock, Bradley Cooper, Kanye West, and Fred Armisen watched from the sides. Michaels rarely goes anywhere near the dance floor, although an SNL receptionist who later wrote for *Seinfeld* claims to have modeled Elaine's spastic dance style on him, claiming that he'd once watched as Michaels "heaved and gyrated" to a beat that "only he could feel."

At the party, the younger writers squished together in a booth. They felt that it had been a pretty good night, and that Michaels's interaction with them under the bleachers had been "average to good," one said. Hill had done well, they thought, but his "constant need to be funny," as one put it, took opportunities away from the cast. "He was very supportive of the writers on one level, but was tanking them on another." As for the show overall, some groused that, with the loss of Craigslist and Beavis and Butt-Head—and Weezer, for that matter—Michaels had neutered the episode. (Six years later, Beavis and Butt-Head was resurrected when Ryan Gosling hosted; the sketch went viral, and Gosling delighted a screaming mob at the premiere of his movie *The Fall Guy* when he got out of a limo dressed as Beavis.)

Michaels usually spends the party sitting with his pets and talking show business—recommending Tom Lehrer records, or reciting old bits by Bob and Ray, or Nichols and May. If a performer has had a breakthrough, an assistant will summon him or her to the table. The party also serves as a loose postmortem session. That night, Michaels gave his standard assessment: "I tend to only see the mistakes," he said. "By and large, this one worked. But it wasn't a *hot* show. It didn't have that surprise thing."

He explained how he made the choice to cut the three sketches he did. "I knew that Pugs would get Cecily back out there," he said. "And Beavis and Butt-Head didn't go to Jonah's strengths. Motorcycles would've been a blow for surrealism, but the dog thing was more fun." (Three things accomplished: raising a performer's self-esteem, showcasing the host, and keeping things light.) He called the audience's reaction to Hill "underwhelming," likely because Hill hadn't just starred in a big movie. "There's no *refresh,*" he said. "He's really talented, though." Michaels was satisfied with Davidson's segment—breezy and sweet—and he seemed glad that "he took the high road" with the Grande material.

The part of the show that brought him the most pleasure was Villaseñor's feature on Update. "Finally!" he said. "It took her two years to figure it out." Breaking through, he believes, has to do with learning to read the room. "What you'd do in old show business," he said, "is you'd call someone who'd played that room before and ask, 'What works in that room? What are the acoustics like? How's the audience?'" He went on, "Melissa will wake up different tomorrow. She'll hear from people she hasn't seen in ten years." And with the echo chamber of YouTube, he said, she was on her way to being a star. He predicted that before the party was over, she'd come sit next to him and thank him. (She didn't.)

Over the course of several hours and a few vodka-and-cranberrys, he held forth on a range of subjects: a woman billed as the Hip Hypnotist, who did her act in a club on Sunset Boulevard; the 1970s fad for brass-rubbing; how the Canadian prime minister Lester Pearson used to drive his own car to the airport to pick up heads of state in the sixties. Thinking about his mother, Florence, he bemoaned the phrase "single mother" as patronizing, suggestive of a group that you "should have a telethon for." He wondered what kind of name "Liev Schreiber" is ("Who would name a kid that?"). He said that he had two rules that he expects his children to follow: "No tattoos, and you can't move to Brooklyn."

Aidy Bryant came over and sat down. Michaels congratulated her on her Sarah Huckabee Sanders.

"I definitely have the bruises to prove it," she said. "But it was really fun."

Davidson leaned over from the next table to say hello. "Not now!" Michaels barked, pretending to be bothered: "I'm talking to Aidy!" He turned back to Bryant and said, "I can't believe Lindsay"—Shookus—"let him do that promo." He talked about the "fame bubble." "We are a culture where people can go a bit crazy," he said. "But if you care about someone, you cut them some slack. Penny Marshall used to say that everyone who gets famous has to become an asshole for a while." Michaels likes to quote Ahmet Ertegun, from a *New Yorker* profile by George W. S. Trow. Ertegun is in a car in the South of France, and he leans toward the chauffeur and says, "We are very restless people. Please drive faster." Although he himself has undoubtedly been in a fast car with Ertegun, he recognizes the entitlement that fame brings as an Icarus problem. "You want to get close to the sun, but not get burned by it."

Bryant yielded her seat to Jonah Hill, and Michaels wished her a good day off. His plan for Sunday was to walk the length of Central Park with Ed Schlossberg, Caroline Kennedy's husband. "He knows every block of the West Side," he said. "Those old buildings full of Euro-influenced shrinks. It's a lost world."

Hill sat down. "After three months of being on the road with my movie, this was just joy!" he said.

"The trouble with being in charge is everybody who *isn't* thinks it would be a better way to live their life," Michaels said. "But when you just get to *play*, it's better."

"So true!" Hill said. "Just to give yourself over to the machine and not have to make decisions. I said to the writers: 'I'm here to sell your shit.'"

Michaels made the case that nothing is better than being a movie star. "No one would choose to be the one who *makes* it as opposed to the one that's *in* it," he said. "At the end of the day, anybody west of Doheny only cares about the numbers."

When Maggie Rogers drifted over, wearing a pale blue cowboy hat, Michaels gave her a big smile and a compliment. Next in line was a member of the ensemble in the Broadway production of *Mean Girls*. He had done two shows that day. After Michaels sent him on his way, he said to Hill, "They work so much harder than we do. And they never complain. Our world is filled with people who do nothing but complain."

Hill said, "Nothing fills the hole."

Michaels had more wisdom to impart: he advised Hill to find something in his life that "functions, in the evolutionary scale, like the opposable thumb. You have to find the *other* thing that will satisfy you. Because show business success is never going to be enough. If your movie does 150 million, you'll want 155. It will always leave you with an empty feeling." He went on, "No one is ever going to feel sorry for you, because you won so much bigger than everyone else. But when you find the *other* thing—and if you're lucky, it's a kid— some other part of your heart opens up and you go, 'Oh! I had no idea.'"

It was after three, and Hill got up and said, a final time, how joyous the week had been. "I was so much more present this time," he said. "I finally realized that the journey is the destination."

When Hill had left, Michaels eyed the next table, where Pete Davidson was being fussed over by a brunette woman in a snug dress. Davidson has a tattoo of his father's FDNY badge number on his arm, and Ariana Grande got an identical one on her foot (she has since tattooed over it). "Pete was seven when his dad died," Michaels told me. "I was fourteen when I lost mine, and it was still a calamity."

Workers started stacking chairs, and Michaels looked around for the waiter, whose name he had learned (Cesar), for his check. It was nearly four. Davidson, in his hoodie, came over. "Do you like my new wife?" he asked, with his man-boy grin, gesturing over his shoulder. "She's thirty-seven, has two children, and she's a writer. I've never been more in love in my life."

Michaels laughed.

"Honestly, though, how do you think that came across tonight?" Davidson asked.

Michaels assured him that it had gone well. "Way better than dress," he said.

"I hope this shit calms down," Davidson said.

Michaels nodded, then put on a news announcer's voice: *"Then he walked through the door and was shot four times,"* he joked.

Davidson put on his coat. "I'm gonna go get married," he said.

Michaels's eyes glinted as his young star exited with the mother of two. "He's a good boy," he said. "They don't all like him, but he's a good boy."

THE WEEK HAD BEGUN WITH A DEATH THREAT, AND IT ENDED WITH A DEATH threat. Around the same time that Michaels arrived home, near dawn, Meghan McCain, the daughter of the late senator, tweeted about the Pete Davidson Weekend Update segment, calling the joke about Dan Crenshaw's eye patch "awful and incredibly tone-deaf and offensive to veterans, their families and all who serve." Michaels was close enough to John McCain to have attended his funeral. Meghan McCain's tweet ended, "Come on SNL, do better."

The anti-Davidson tweets had started while the show was still on the air. Just after 1:00, Fox's Greg Gutfeld weighed in: "This is @snl—they address a cast members breakup as if it's of vital importance. but laugh at a vet." At 1:21 A.M., a tweet called the segment "truly abhorrent and rotten to the core. And the fact that so-called 'joke' was approved by an entire staff of writers is horrific." The incident was discussed on the Sunday morning political shows and on Monday's *The View* (a "sucker punch" and a "really crappy joke"). On Sunday, Lieutenant Crenshaw himself tweeted, "I hope @nbcsnl recognizes that vets don't deserve to see their wounds used as punchlines for bad jokes." Sean Spicer upped the ante with "#FireLorneMichaels."

Michaels is a bone-deep contrarian when it comes to weathering criticism. "When people outside the show are most upset, he will be the least upset," a producer on the show said. "If there is a very obvious fuckup, he will stay chill." But as an adoptive American citizen, he respects the U.S. military, and the Crenshaw incident distressed him. It was not what he calls "a clean hit."

Discussing it a week later, he took pains to reconstruct the notes he'd given between dress and air. "I'd told them that we could do the Crenshaw photo, but you can't make fun of a guy who lost an eye in the line of duty," he said. "It just isn't justifiable." The writers, he felt, had been willfully obtuse. "There's a certain amount of spectrum behavior around here," he said, explaining that they must have been "overthinking" his note. "They thought that the line could be fixed just by changing the way Pete said 'Whatever.' But I'd said no, that's a boundary you don't cross."

Dennis McNicholas, the Weekend Update supervisor, bore the brunt of Michaels's anger. "Lorne has the capability to be mad at certain people," a writer said. Pete Davidson is not one of them.

On Sunday, when the internet was calling for both of their heads, Michaels and Davidson texted back and forth. "Pete was defensive at first," Michaels recalled. "He said that assholes on the internet were making fun of his dad being killed on 9/11. But that was just defending against emotion." Michaels told him that he wasn't going to win this one. Then Davidson's mother received a death threat: someone said he was going to kill her son. Michaels recalled, "Finally Pete said, 'Oh my God. It's serious.'"

By Monday, Davidson and Michaels each had a pair of bodyguards, and NBC security was on high alert. The network's PR department drafted an apology, which the writers tweaked, and sent it to Crenshaw's campaign. Davidson was heartsick that he'd created trouble for Michaels, his protector.

On Tuesday, Crenshaw won his election and Michaels invited the congressman-elect to be a guest on Weekend Update the following Saturday. Davidson could apologize in person, and the show would make a generous donation to veterans' causes. Michaels told Crenshaw that he could say whatever he wanted. "And I had a loose idea of a joke he could do," he said. "That he could thank Pete for helping him win." Crenshaw was open to appearing, but he asked if he could delay a few weeks, because he was committed to several Veterans Day events in Texas. "I said to him, 'Let me explain something to you,'" Michaels recounted. "'I'm older than you. You can go through with your plans, make your speech, and a few thousand people will hear it. Or you can come to New York and speak to a national audience.'" The blandishment worked, as it usually does.

Crenshaw flew to New York on Friday, with his wife and his parents. He was wary in the studio at first, but the SNL staff was relieved to find that he had a sense of humor. Michaels had roughed out his joke idea with Jost and Davidson, and Crenshaw added some ideas of his own. Live on air, Davidson sat at the Update desk in a pink hoodie and looked into the camera. "In what I'm sure was a huge shock for people who know me, I made a poor choice last week," he began, and apologized for making fun of Crenshaw. "The man is a war hero, and he deserves all the respect in the world. And if any good came of this, maybe it was that for one day, the Left and the Right finally came together to agree on something. That I'm a dick."

Crenshaw then appeared next to Davidson. "You think?" he said. The audience whooped. The representative-elect accepted the apology, and after some business with his phone (his ringtone was Ariana Grande's hit "breathin") he expertly riffed on a photograph of Davidson ("He looks like a troll doll with a tapeworm"). Then he grew somber. "There's a lot of lessons to learn here," he said. "Americans can forgive one another." He cited Veterans Day, and urged viewers to be "connected together as grateful fellow Americans who will never forget the sacrifices made by veterans past and present. And never forget those we lost on 9/11, heroes like Pete's father."

Davidson was trembling with emotion. After a beat, he looked into the camera and said, "Never forget," and the two men shook hands. It was a stunning moment of television. Funny, sincere, and unexpected. Jim Downey, who'd watched from home, called it "the best five minutes of SNL since Bill Murray sang the theme to *Jaws*" at the fortieth anniversary. Michaels called it "a miracle show."

The Crenshaw truce cleared up other spots of turmoil. The business tycoon Ron Perelman called Michaels and said that he was at dinner with McCain's widow, Cindy; perhaps Lorne could join them? He did, and peace was brokered. The day after the Crenshaw apology, Michaels got many texts and emails from NBC executives. He was surprised that the people whom Florence Lipowitz had called "the brass" had followed the brouhaha. Steve Burke wrote and said, "I knew you'd figure it out." Brian Roberts told him, "This honors our company." Michaels said, "And I went, 'Oh. So they were all really frightened.'" Having written the constitution of SNL, Michaels brings a world of practice to solving the problems it creates. It's supposed to be funny, and when it's not, he said, "You have to demonstrate that there's a decency to the show."

EPILOGUE

"YOU KNOW WHEN PEOPLE LEAVE SHOW BUSINESS?" MICHAELS OFTEN says. "Never. No one ever leaves show business."

One way the cultural-industrial complex traditionally helps shuffle aging worthies offstage is by giving them lifetime achievement awards. Michaels is the rare pooh-bah to survive an onslaught of honors, including the Presidential Medal of Freedom, which he got in 2016, with his career still barreling along. He is aware that no network would ever again greenlight a show as expensive and elaborate as his—which he considers the television equivalent of a David Lean epic—and he's held tight to the franchise he created by knowing how to continually renew it. Like New York City, *Saturday Night Live* lives to obliterate its past. It's a little like what he learned about growing blueberries in Maine: if you want them to be certified organic, you have to burn the bushes to the ground three times and start again. The metaphor works the other way, too. He bought the five thousand acres in Maine because he'd run out of room to build and plant in Amagansett; Paul Simon calls the Maine spread "the nature analog of SNL." Up there, near the Canadian border, he brought in electricity, put in miles of new roads and woodland paths, planted an orchard, and purchased a herd of goats. He also bought a load of old pencil-making machines at auction in hopes of building a pencil factory nearby for Eugene Lee to run; Lee died at eighty-three before that could happen.

As Michaels approached eighty, an age at which the word "event" more often refers to a medical crisis than to a party, he'd become an old hand at producing his friends' memorial services. But his cultural reach persists. Mike Myers says, "It's like he created Yale or NASA." With nearly five decades of SNL behind him, the extracurricular projects on his docket were a funhouse mirror-maze of reboots: Mulaney and Randy Newman collaborating on a Broadway musical of *Three Amigos,* a new Kids in the Hall series, and Fey turning the *Mean Girls* musical that she adapted from her *Mean Girls* movie into a movie musical.

So when Michaels was invited down to Washington in late 2021 to collect a Kennedy Center Honor, he had to squeeze it into his schedule. The third and final day of award-related hoopla began with a brunch in the lobby of the Mandarin Oriental Hotel. Calligraphed signs designated tables reserved for the year's honorees—Bette Midler, Berry Gordy, Justino Díaz, and Joni Mitchell. There was no sign reading LORNE MICHAELS AND GUESTS. Presumably the organizers knew that he wasn't a brunch man. He'd shown up in D.C., though, along with a group of SNL veterans. There had already been a medallion ceremony at the Library of Congress and a reception at the White House with President Biden. "They move you around a lot," Michaels said.

The Honors are a multi-hour extravaganza, later edited down to air on CBS. The production had all the hallmarks of the variety shows that Michaels had tried to put behind him in the seventies—hokey stage scenery, big swags of shiny curtain, many medleys but few intact songs. (Paul Simon told him that, during his own Kennedy Center Honors induction, in 2002, John Cougar Mellencamp performed a brassy medley of "Graceland" and "Mrs. Robinson," and Simon's fellow honoree Elizabeth Taylor had leaned over and whispered, "How's it feel to hear someone fuck up your song?") The Kennedy Center staff is in charge of crafting the presentation for each honoree; even the identities of the celebrities giving testimonials are supposed to be a secret. For Michaels, having no input on the program was a strange predicament to be in.

Compared to his usual social rounds, the evening had a touch of the Kiwanis Club—a lot of sequins and glad-handing. "Being knighted is what he's after," Alec Baldwin told me, barely joking. "Not being British, he's ineligible. But I'm sure they'll change that for him." Michaels also wouldn't mind winning an Oscar, an award rarely bestowed on comedies. "The nature of comedy is you get the audience, you get the money," he says. "Respect is the last thing you get."

Once the two thousand guests had taken their seats, the orchestra played an overture of stitched-together musical themes associated with the medalists. Joni Mitchell's "Coyote" segued into the blues of Howard Shore's "Waltz in A," which was followed, surely for the first time, by an aria from Bizet's *Carmen*. Emceeing the evening was David Letterman, Michaels's longtime opposite number, who had beaten his competitor-slash-friend to a Kennedy Center Honor by nine years; when he first read Michaels's name aloud, he looked up to the Presidential box holding the honorees and said, in mock deference, "Lorne, can I get you anything?"

When Letterman introduced the SNL segment, he couldn't help taking a poke at the honoree's cosmopolitan profile, reading off the teleprompter about Michaels's talent for "capturing the zeitgeist—I've never been sure what that word means—of American culture." He milked the downhill-from-here implications of lifetime achievement awards: "Lorne recently told me that his resolution for the new year is, when he gets in a car, to not make the sound '*Aarrgh*.'"

The other medalists were showered with praise of the most earnest kind—Cameron Crowe speaking about Joni Mitchell's "chords of inquiry," Chita Rivera lauding Díaz's "uncompromising standards." In comparison, Michaels's tributes had the flavor of a roast, a tone that the crowd didn't know quite how to process. Steve Martin called the evening the realization of a childhood dream: "When I was just a little kid I used to get all dressed up and play 'Honoring Lorne Michaels at the Kennedy Center.'" He said that he often was asked just what it is that a producer does. "Turn around and take a look at

Lorne," he said, then gestured up to the President's box, where Michaels sat beside Joni Mitchell. "*That's* what a producer does." Giant laughs.

Kristen Wiig and Kate McKinnon came out dressed as the Blues Brothers. Wiig said, "When I need to be calm, I just picture Lorne in overalls." Then, from behind a Weekend Update desk, Kevin Nealon addressed his old boss: "If it weren't for you letting me go on SNL, I never would have gotten that lucrative blood-thinner commercial." He pretended to take a call from Michaels with a critical note about the Lorne photo on the screen behind him. Another Update duo, Colin Jost and Michael Che, showed a photo from *The Hart and Lorne Terrific Hour* and described it as a kung fu movie from the days when "Lorne was the Canadian Serpico." Jimmy Fallon trotted out to salute his boss. "It's great to be here, speaking in front of the most powerful man in the world," he said. "And also President Biden."

Just when it seemed as if the SNL group was speaking in a private lingo of Friars Club jibes, a few heartfelt sentiments were heard. Seth Meyers: "One of the lifelong gifts he gave us is each other." Wiig: "Without you, Lorne, there's a good chance we would be living in a van down by the river." Paul Simon came out to sing "America" to his friend. Down the row from Biden, Chief Justice John Roberts could be seen tearing up.

Aside from his library of well-thumbed stories, Michaels doesn't go in much for nostalgia. "You can't just spend the last half of your life watching the first half of your life," he once said. But he found much to be moved about. Herbie Hancock had played "Both Sides Now" for Joni Mitchell, and Michaels had remembered looking out at the clouds on his first plane ride. The day before, at the Library of Congress, President Biden had placed the actual medal around his neck, and Fred Armisen gave a short speech. He said that when he was a kid watching SNL, he thought that the sketches were private messages just for him. "But it's all Lorne," he said. He spoke of "indelible sketches and seminal cast members," and how "the collective remembering of them connects us to other people as profoundly as any classic moment in cinema or literature. We pass and trade the language of SNL back and forth like some family heirloom we share with the entire world."

After the gala, Michaels presided over a long table lined with his wife and kids and his SNL offspring, including Jim Downey, at a grand formal dinner in the theater's lobby. He lingered late talking, as he does at SNL afterparties, and when he headed out to the limo waiting in the cold night, behind Joni Mitchell being pushed in a wheelchair, he was one of the last to leave. It had been a very nice night in show business and a fun performance. But he had a few notes.

ACKNOWLEDGMENTS

Lorne Michaels never asked for a biography to be inflicted on him, but when I showed up at 30 Rockefeller Plaza one day in 2015 and told him of my plan to write one, he took a few deep breaths and generously opened the door. Having a subject who is a great talker but who has made a habit of *not* talking to journalists much over the years is a godsend for a biographer. I'm grateful for the many hours he spent with me—asking nothing in return—and for clearing the way for me to interview hundreds of people in his very large life and at *Saturday Night Live,* all of whom made it possible for me to see the show from the inside out. Thanks are also owed to the battalion of SNL employees who helped facilitate things: among them, Willa Slaughter, Grace Godvin, Peyton Nora, Karina Strom, and Asha-Kai Grant.

I would never have written a book, or even ended up in the journalism business, if not for a handful of people who helped turn the lights on for me years and years ago: Adam Liptak, my oldest and smartest friend; our English teacher at Stamford High School, Jerry McWilliams; and Kurt Andersen and Graydon Carter and all of our colleagues at *Spy* magazine who showed me that work and play could be the same thing.

Further back, it was my tenth-grade friend Robin Guarino who, in 1976, took the Metro-North train with me into the city to be in the audience for an episode of SNL hosted by Elliott Gould, having wangled tickets from her cool aunt at NBC. I certainly missed a lot of the references, but I never forgot the insiderish thrill of sitting in the middle of a working television studio, cameras on cranes flying over our heads. Seven years later, I found my way back to Studio 8H, as a not especially helpful assistant to Jim Downey and the writers of *The New Show,* who gave me safe harbor in the bleak months after my mother died. Their kindness (and all the laughing) meant everything to me. I am also indebted to two other people, lost too soon, who helped hone my inner tuning fork: Max Cantor and David Handelman.

My brilliant editor, Andy Ward, who welcomed this book to Random House, remained faithful and keen throughout. He and his team—Julia Harrison, Azraf Khan, Lawrence Krauser, Mark Birkey, Debbie Glasserman, Lucas Heinrich, Matthew Martin, Mark Maguire, Greg Kubie, and Windy Dorresteyn—handled the book with imagination and care and kept things running smoothly during a very tight turnaround. I am grateful to Courtney Hodell for her skill at paring down my original OED-sized manuscript; she wielded a chainsaw as if it were a scalpel. It is true that I cursed my agent (and old friend) David Kuhn many times during this process, but now I can only thank him; without his persistence and his belief in me as a writer, this biography would never have happened.

A biography is as fact-filled as an encyclopedia, and I could not have done it without the enterprising research assistance of Liana Spiro or the fact-checking expertise of Hélène Werner and Jane Bua. Adam Green, a great friend and a very funny man, shared many writing strategies, including one involving a kitchen appliance. Big thanks to Camille Czerkowicz, who took the chaos of photo wrangling off my plate and managed it with dispatch.

An army of hardworking geniuses at *The New Yorker* made it possible for me to complete the book while keeping my day job. Among those who cheerfully propped me up: Zach Helfand, Emma Allen, Lizzie Widdicombe, Tyler Foggatt, Anna Russell, and Pam McCarthy. My sterling colleagues Daniel Zalewski, Nick Paumgarten, Lauren

Collins, and Ian Frazier offered useful counsel and regular pep talks. David Remnick, besides making the magazine a hospitable home for more than twenty-five years, advised and listened and showed support in more ways than I can count. I benefited greatly from the insight of several early readers—Tad Friend, Bruce Handy, and Paul Simms. Without their notes and tweaks, this would have been a lesser book. I'm also fortunate to have had a few legends in my corner, offering steady encouragement: Gay Talese, Louis Begley, Michael Arlen, Billy Persky, and two beloved mentors who died before I crossed the finish line, Jim Atlas and Lillian Ross. I wrote sections of the book in beautiful rooms kindly lent by my friends Amy Briamonte, Mary Rhinelander, Jennifer Bitman, and Barbara Bestor. Thank you, ladies, for everything.

Shelby White and the Leon Levy Center for Biography provided important support for this book, particularly through the wisdom and experience of Kai Bird and Thad Ziolkowski, and an extraordinary class of Levy fellows, the cozy community that brightened the long months of Covid lockdown. Several books about SNL and comedy in general were especially helpful as I began my research: *Saturday Night: A Backstage History of Saturday Night Live,* by Doug Hill and Jeff Weingrad; *Live from New York: The Complete, Uncensored History of Saturday Night Live,* by James Andrew Miller and Tom Shales; and *The Comedians,* by Kliph Nesteroff.

A special thanks, and love, to Loudon Wainwright, who, in addition to demonstrating remarkable forbearance, kept me company with a round-the-clock live-guitar soundtrack. Finally, nothing would be funny—or any fun at all—without the inspiration, conversation, and company of my daughters, Nancy and Helen Handelman. This book is for them.

NOTES

All quotations in the text are from interviews by the author unless cited below.

vii   **"That's showbiz"** *Saturday Night Live in the '80s: Lost & Found,* directed by Kenneth Bowser (New York: Broadway Video, 2005), DVD.

Prologue

3   **When J. D. Salinger died** Lillian Ross to author.

PART 1 | MONDAY

7   **"You don't say yes"** Tina Fey, interview on *Nerdist* (podcast), episode 206, May 14, 2012.

8   **jumping out of an airplane** "The Tina Fey Interview, by David Letterman," *Hollywood Reporter,* December 7, 2016.

8   **serving in the marine corps** Jefferson Graham, "Change of Pace Sits Fairly Well with Jan Hooks," *Gannett News Service,* March 3, 1982.

8   **insisted that he make Trump "likable"** *I Was There Too* (podcast), October 9, 2018.

9   **"an enthusiasm held under restraint"** A. J. Liebling, "A Good Appetite," *The New Yorker,* April 3, 1959.

11   **"I think all comedy shows"** Elizabeth Kolbert, "New Job for NBC's Laugh Master," *New York Times,* February 23, 1993.

12   **The longtime SNL writer Robert Smigel** Bill Hader to author.

13   **A few years later he would** Michael Paulson, "After Bullying Reports, Scott Rudin Says He'll Step Back from Broadway," *New York Times,* April 17, 2021.

14   **He is the Godfather** Bill Carter, "A Comedy Institution Just Keeps Going," *New York Times,* September 19, 1999.

14   **Jay Gatsby** Bernie Brillstein with David Rensin, *Where Did I Go Right?* (New York: Little, Brown and Company, 1999), 125.

14   **Obi-Wan Kenobi** Ariana Bacle, "Tracy Morgan on Comedy Return: 'I'm a Survivor,'" *Entertainment Weekly,* November 24, 2015.

14   **the Great and Powerful Oz** Lorne Michaels, interview on *Fly on the Wall with Dana Carvey and David Spade* (podcast), September 28, 2022; Liam Berry and Mary Green, "Kate McKinnon Looks Back on 'Scary' 'SNL' Audition," *People,* August 23, 2017.

14   **Charles Foster Kane** "Lorne Stories: A WTF Special Presentation," *WTF with Marc Maron* (podcast), November 10, 2016.

14   **a cult leader** *Saturday Night Live in the '80s.*

14   **Machiavelli** Michael Brett, "Does Late Night TV Still Matter? Jimmy Fallon," *PopMatters*, October 8, 2009.

14   **Robert Moses and the Darth Vader** Bruce McCall to author; Bruce McCall, "Of Moose and Men," *Vanity Fair*, December 7, 2012.

14   **"distant, strange Comedy God"** James Andrew Miller and Tom Shales, *Live from New York: An Uncensored History of Saturday Night Live* (New York: Little, Brown and Company, 2014), 313.

16   **"Ape suits are funny"** Jim Downey to author.

Chapter 1: Toronto the Good

22   **Florence as having a "foghorn voice"** Hart Pomerantz to author.

24   **One researcher tsk-tsked the plastic slipcovers** John R. Seeley, R. Alexander Sim, and Elizabeth W. Loosley, *Crestwood Heights: A North American Suburb* (Toronto: University of Toronto Press, 1954), 89.

25   **Lorne blurted out, "She won't fit"** Brian D. Johnson, "Wise Guys: Lorne Michaels Champions Canadian Comedy," *Macleans*, July 26, 1993.

31   **"He'd say that that look"** Lillian Ross, "Saturday Night Lorne," *Interview*, June 1988.

31   **"How to shoot a sketch"** Brian D. Johnson, "A Comic 'Gold Standard,'" *Macleans*, January 28, 2002.

32   **"came from inside my family"** Miller and Shales, *Live from New York*, 16.

33   **"They had the same effect on me"** Christopher Hitchens, "Kings of Comedy," *Vanity Fair*, December 1995.

35   **"Toronto was where you lived when"** Margaret Atwood, "The City Rediscovered," *New York Times*, August 8, 1982.

35   **"People start to be funny early"** Johnson, "Wise Guys."

36   **"I'm the first Lipowitz to"** Paul Pape to author.

Chapter 2: Two-Man Comedy

45   **"We're not sure if it's you guys"** Lorne Michaels, interview on *Here's the Thing with Alec Baldwin* (podcast), January 29, 2012.

46   **Fothergill remembered the two of them** Robert Fothergill, interview at the Ryerson University Graduate Film Preservation Lab, March 18, 2015, reprinted at taketwoexhibition.weebly.com/robert-fothergill.

46   **Also on the bill** Stephen Broomer, *Hamilton Babylon: A History of the McMaster Film Board* (Toronto: University of Toronto Press, 2016), 56.

47   **"I'm going to make movies even"** "Young Movie-Makers Popping Up All Over the Toronto Scene," *Toronto Daily Star*, June 10, 1967, 31.

47   **"mile after mile of caution"** Margaret Atwood, *Cat's Eye* (Toronto: McClelland & Stewart, 1988), 14.

51   **"I was impressed by the quality"** Lorne Michaels, interview on *Late Night with David Letterman*, NBC, February 14, 1983.

52   **"I believed it should be of *use*"** Tom Burke, "'Saturday Night'—Live!," *Rolling Stone*, July 15, 1976.

53   **held at the Holy Blossom Temple** Wendy Darroch, "Shuster's Daughter Is THE Star," *Toronto Daily Star*, November 3, 1967.

53   **"The only man happier than me"** Jon Ruddy, "Pomerantz and Michaels: Whiz Kids Keep Whizzing Along," *TV Guide*, Toronto–Lake Ontario edition, January 29, 1971.

54   **"there was something in terms of a"** Sheila Weller, *Carrie Fisher: A Life on the Edge* (New York: Sarah Crichton Books, 2019), 105.

Chapter 3: On the Assembly Line

58   **"What's brown and has holes"** Timothy White, "Lorne Michaels, Saturday Night Quarterback," *Rolling Stone*, December 27, 1979.

58   **"This was a profound lesson"** Burke, "'Saturday Night'—Live!"

58   **"This was the beginning"** White, "Lorne Michaels, Saturday Night Quarterback."

61   **But then he lit a joint** Miller and Shales, *Live from New York*, 19.

63   **they quickly became known** Hal Erickson, *From Beautiful Downtown Burbank: A Critical History of Rowan and Martin's Laugh-In, 1968–1973* (Jefferson, N.C.: McFarland, 2000), 170.

65   **shoveling coal on an ocean liner** Judy Carne, *Laughing on the Outside, Crying on the Inside: The Bittersweet Saga of the Sock-It-to-Me Girl* (New York: Rawson, 1985), 126–127.

65   **"I felt like I was standing"** White, "Lorne Michaels, Saturday Night Quarterback."

67   **"freedom words," nonsense utterances** Erickson, *From Beautiful Downtown Burbank*, 130.

Chapter 4: Retreat

71 **"Why shouldn't we get this kind"** Sid Adilman, "2 Laugh-In Men to CBC," *Toronto Daily Star,* July 18, 1969.

75 **"It's been our philosophy that"** Hart Pomerantz, interview on *Elwood Glover's Luncheon Date,* CBC, October 30, 1970.

80 **Hormone House** Doug Hill and Jeff Weingrad, *Saturday Night: A Backstage History of Saturday Night Live* (New York: Beech Tree Books, 1986), 56.

PART 2 | TUESDAY

92 **"thirty-five percent more lung capacity"** Ross, "Saturday Night Lorne."

95 **"like he's really put out by"** Bill Hader, *Conan,* TBS, January 24, 2019.

Chapter 5: The Coast

106 **His emotions were so ragged** White, "Lorne Michaels, Saturday Night Quarterback."

106 **"the period of Singers Horsing Around"** Dan Lewis, "Steve Allen Warns NBC About Comedy," *Farmville (Va.) Herald,* April 28, 1980.

106 **CBS had ordered up a show** Ellin Stein, *That's Not Funny, That's Sick: The National Lampoon and the Comedy Insurgents Who Captured the Mainstream* (New York: W. W. Norton & Company, 2013), 222.

113 **he would offer Tomlin critiques** White, "Lorne Michaels, Saturday Night Quarterback."

115 **"the human untidiness" of everyday life** Hilton Als, "A Pryor Love," *The New Yorker,* September 13, 1999.

115 **"essences of people"** Ellen Cohn, "Lily Tomlin: Not Just a Funny Girl," *New York Times,* June 6, 1976.

115 **"The networks feel certain things"** Cohn, "Lily Tomlin."

116 **Irene Pinn, another producer** Yael Kohen, *We Killed: The Rise of Women in American Comedy* (New York: Picador), 54–55.

117 **a "comedian's lib"** Cohn, "Lily Tomlin."

118 **"Remember Podunk!"** Hill and Weingrad, *Saturday Night: A Backstage History,* 38.

118 **a "three-hundred-and-sixty-thousand-dollar jerk-off"** Joey DiGuglielmo, "Lily Tomlin on Why She's Happy She Lost the Emmy This Year," *Washington Blade,* October 11, 2018.

118 **"It failed"** Kohen, *We Killed,* 55.

120 **"She was probably *the* formative"** White, "Lorne Michaels, Saturday Night Quarterback."

Chapter 6: The Music Changed

121 **Shirley MacLaine special** Burke, "'Saturday Night'—Live!"

130 **The license plate read KILLER** Kevin Cook, *Flip: The Inside Story of TV's First Black Superstar* (New York: Viking, 2013), 1.

131 **To regain his grip** Lorne Michaels, interview on *Later with Bob Costas,* NBC, November 28, 1990.

133 **"I discovered that, right under"** Brillstein, *Where Did I Go Right?,* 134.

133 **"Every young person who would"** E. Graydon Carter, "The Leader of the Lost Boys: A Success Story," *Smart,* January–February 1990.

Chapter 7: New Wine in Old Bottles

136 **Schlosser didn't know it** Herb Schlosser to author.

138 **"It has been proven that more"** Steve Martin, *Born Standing Up* (New York: Scribner, 2007), 102.

140 **He'd started as a cigarette-voiced** Hill and Weingrad, *Saturday Night: A Backstage History,* 40–41.

141 **including a Samurai sword** Kenneth Tynan, "Fifteen Years of the Salto Mortale: The World of Johnny Carson," *The New Yorker,* February 20, 1978.

141 **"a talent liaison, in the same"** Dave Itzkoff, "David Letterman Reflects on 33 Years in Late-Night Television," *New York Times,* April 29, 2015.

141 **Cher, frightened, had locked herself** Scott Saul, *Becoming Richard Pryor* (New York: Harper Perennial, 2014), 361.

142 **"Writing was zilch"** *Variety,* September 10, 1974.

143 **bankrolled by ten Long Island dentists** Stein, *That's Not Funny,* 218.

143 **Another Blue Box adept** Phil Lapsley, "The Definitive Story of Steve Wozniak, Steve Jobs, and Phone Phreaking," *Atlantic Monthly,* February 20, 2013.

144 **"WASP Sammy Glick"** Hill and Weingrad, *Saturday Night: A Backstage History,* 44.

144 **"drifting, opulent barge"** Eve Babitz, *Sex and Rage: Advice to Young Ladies Eager for a Good Time* (New York: Knopf, 1979), 38.

145 **"anything that went wrong stayed wrong"** Martin, *Born Standing Up,* 170.

146 **"all your most conservative instincts"** Michaels, interview on *Here's the Thing.*

146 **Brillstein and Wernick negotiated** Hill and Weingrad, *Saturday Night: A Backstage History,* 44.

147 **"We will always be experimenting"** Hill and Weingrad, *Saturday Night: A Backstage History,* 46–47.

Chapter 8: Going on Board the Ark

148 THE ANSWER IS NO Hill and Weingrad, *Saturday Night: A Backstage History,* 91.

148 **Carswell came back with a budget** Hill and Weingrad, *Saturday Night: A Backstage History,* 44–45.

149 **"I felt kind of used"** Joe Hagan, *Sticky Fingers: The Life and Times of Jann Wenner and Rolling Stone Magazine* (New York: Vintage Books), 230.

150 **"hip and slightly dark"** Brian Jay Jones, *Jim Henson* (New York: Ballantine Books, 2016), 82.

151 **"fear of rejection"** Miller and Shales, *Live from New York,* 33.

151 **"not my kind of comedy"** Joseph Brean, "Toronto Lawyer Flirted with Career in Comedy, Thanks to Fateful Call from Lorne Michaels," *National Post,* August 11, 2017.

151 **"You can't get through the glaze of"** Miller and Shales, *Live from New York,* 29.

151 **The message came back: "abundance"** Hill and Weingrad, *Saturday Night: A Backstage History,* 50.

152 **"a sexy woman surrounded by"** Fred A. Bernstein, "A Hotel's Past vs. a City's Future," *New York Times,* July 21, 2009.

155 **He wanted the show to feel** John Blumenthal and Lindsay Maracotta, "The Playboy Interview: The Cast of Saturday Night Live," *Playboy,* May 1977.

156 **"male-ego sweat-socks attitude"** David Rensin, "The Playboy Interview: Lorne Michaels," *Playboy,* March 1992.

156 **"If Ted Kennedy drove"** "The Press: Lampoon's Surrender," *Time,* November 12, 1973.

157 **preferred the unabashed camp of Cher** *Live from New York: The First 5 Years of Saturday Night Live,* directed by Kenneth Bowser (New York: Broadway Video, 2005), DVD.

158 **"like going on board the ark"** "SNL Pro Helps Students Write Humor," *Orange County (Calif.) Register,* December 30, 2013.

159 **flow into the Pacific Ocean** Marilyn Suzanne Miller to author.

162 **"talk the peel off a grape"** Rosie Shuster to author.

164 "**knowing drug references"** Hill and Weingrad, *Saturday Night: A Backstage History,* 17.

164 **"a book and movie audience"** Ross, "Saturday Night Lorne."

Chapter 10: Sketches, Not Skits

169 **"second-bullet theory"** Hill and Weingrad, *Saturday Night: A Backstage History,* 65.

170 **"I became a producer to protect"** Burke, " 'Saturday Night'—Live!"

171 **a bullet being fired from** Dennis Perrin, *Mr. Mike: The Life and Work of Michael O'Donoghue* (New York: Avon Books, 1998), 279–280.

171 **it's hard to know what's uniquely Canadian** Geoffrey Vendeville, "Live from New York, It's U of T Alum and Saturday Night Live Producer Lorne Michaels," *U of T News (Toronto),* March 7, 2017.

173 **" 'the biggest, ugliest leather queen' "** Perrin, *Mr. Mike,* 284.

173 **"Premise overload"** Hill and Weingrad, *Saturday Night: A Backstage History,* 75–76.

173 **"I knew he would whup my ass"** Shawn Prez, *Power Moves with Shawn Prez* (podcast), October 16, 2023.

174 *Stump Love* Perrin, *Mr. Mike,* 282.

174 **Shuster and Schiller moved the cards** Hill and Weingrad, *Saturday Night: A Backstage History,* 9.

174 **pantomimed unzipping his fly** Burke, " 'Saturday Night'—Live!"

Chapter 11: Not Ready for Prime Time

177 DRACULA SUCKS T-shirt Miller and Shales, *Live from New York,* 32.

177 **One of them was Meat Loaf** Stein, *That's Not Funny, That's Sick,* p. 231.

178 **"She had a face built for"** *Live from New York: The First 5 Years.*

180 **"Herb, where's Vietnam"** Marilyn Suzanne Miller to author.

181 **he even took his shirt off** Tom Davis, *Thirty-nine Years of Short-Term Memory Loss: The Early Days of SNL from Someone Who Was There* (New York: Grove Press, 2009), 135.

181 **A man with a military bent** Hill and Weingrad, *Saturday Night: A Backstage History,* 90–91.

182 **"They called it the Infinity Look"** Sandy Keenan, "Making a Scene, Onstage and Off," *New York Times,* April 2, 2014.

182   **"the feeling of an old shoe"** White, "Lorne Michaels, Saturday Night Quarterback."

183   **he wanted everyone assigned** Hill and Weingrad, *Saturday Night: A Backstage History,* 87.

183   **booing could be heard** Hill and Weingrad, *Saturday Night: A Backstage History,* 95–96.

186   **"It was as beautiful a thing"** Bill Zehme, *Lost in the Funhouse: The Life and Mind of Andy Kaufman* (New York: Delta, 1999), 156.

186   **he'd pitched the idea to John** Rustin Dodd, "Lennon and Cosell: 'Monday Night Football,' Tragedy and a New York Friendship," *New York Times,* December 8, 2020.

187   **"one of the greatest disasters in"** Don Mischer, interview with the Television Academy Foundation, November 7, 2008, American Archive of Television.

189   **"He's punctual and he fills out"** Hill and Weingrad, *Saturday Night: A Backstage History,* 97.

189   **"slightly older than us"** Richard Zoglin, *Comedy at the Edge: How Stand-Up in the 1970s Changed America* (New York: Bloomsbury, 2008), 36.

189   **"it's always been a strategy"** Robert Heilbrun, *Paul Simon: The Life* (New York: Simon & Schuster, 2018), 206.

PART 3 | WEDNESDAY

194   **"Now, more than ever, it's important"** Davis, *Thirty-nine Years of Short-Term Memory Loss,* 172.

201   **"That's an honest room"** Michaels, interview on *Fly on the Wall.*

201   **"enough colors to make a rainbow"** White, "Lorne Michaels, Saturday Night Quarterback."

202   **"Sometimes you have to burn"** John Mulaney to author.

203   **"Clever is overrated"** Lorne Michaels, interview on *Oprah's Master Class: The Podcast,* March 28, 2019.

Chapter 12: Live from New York

211   **As chaos swirled** Craig Kellem to author.

212   **Michaels had wanted Stevie Wonder** Memo to Dick Ebersol from Lorne Michaels, August 1975.

212   **Carlin later admitted** George Carlin, interview with the Television Academy Foundation, December 17, 2007, American Archive of Television.

213   **Kaufman had locked himself** Zehme, *Lost in the Funhouse,* 161.

215   **Shitcan Alley** Rachel Dratch, interview on *Late Night with Seth Meyers,* NBC, June 12, 2024.

215   **"He was like a macho man"** Rosie Shuster, *The Neighborhood News Online,* December 21, 2018.

216   **pay for the cases of white** Hill and Weingrad, *Saturday Night: A Backstage History,* 96.

217   **"I guess we're a hit"** *Live from New York: The First 5 Years.*

218   **The only glitch** Hill and Weingrad, *Saturday Night: A Backstage History,* 109.

219   **"You're the most manipulative human being"** Penny Marshall, *My Mother Was Nuts* (New York: New Harvest, 2012), 117.

219   **"against the neediness of performers"** Lynn Hirschberg, "Bill Murray, in All Seriousness," *New York Times,* January 31, 1999.

220   **"Give a warm welcome to my"** White, "Lorne Michaels, Saturday Night Quarterback."

222   **"Brechtian technique of presenting both"** Matt Fotis, "Falling Down: Gerald Ford, Chevy Chase, and the Power of a Pratfall," *Medium,* June 24, 2020.

223   **"I was highly strung"** Alison Castle, *Saturday Night Live: The Book* (Los Angeles: Taschen, 2015), 309.

223   **"explicitly hip, cynical outlook"** Jeff Greenfield, "Live from New York," *New York,* October 27, 1975.

223   **"Dick *was* ABBA"** Miller and Shales, *Live from New York,* 68.

224   **With Michaels absent** Loudon Wainwright III to author.

224   **Brillstein called an NBC vice president** Hill and Weingrad, *Saturday Night: A Backstage History,* 122.

225   **"If it had been a typical fall season"** *Live from New York: The First 5 Years.*

Chapter 13: The Friendship Economy

228   **"He lives the same life we"** Mark Harris, *Mike Nichols: A Life* (New York: Penguin Press, 2021), 313.

228   **a spooky letter arrived** Blumenthal and Maracotta, "The Playboy Interview: The Cast of Saturday Night Live."

229   **"this virus, this foreign thing"** Hill and Weingrad, *Saturday Night: A Backstage History,* 163.

229   **"little hairy facecloths"** Blumenthal and Maracotta, "The Playboy Interview: The Cast of Saturday Night Live."

229   **"The Day of the Muppets"** Perrin, *Mr. Mike,* 288.

229   **result in a career "thunderclap"** *Jim Henson's Red Book,* October 11, 1975.

231   **When a Canadian newspaper reporter** Blaik Kirby, "Have a Laugh on Lorne: He's Taken a Load of Them to American TV," *Globe and Mail,* December 22, 1975.

232   **thrown up in every toilet** Hill and Weingrad, *Saturday Night: A Backstage History,* 368.

232   **"I have no personal life"** Peter Andrews, "'Saturday Night' Never Plays It Safe," *New York Times,* February 29, 1976.

232   **"You didn't mix with the world"** Schuster, *The Neighborhood News Online.*

233   **Anne Beatts got the idea** Hill and Weingrad, *Saturday Night: A Backstage History,* 342.

233   **"ocean of neurotic energy"** Burke, "'Saturday Night'—Live!"

233   **"Mr. Chase is already wondering"** John J. O'Connor, "Sprightly Mix Brightens NBC's 'Saturday Night,'" *New York Times,* November 30, 1975.

233   **"If I'd known"** Saul, *Becoming Richard Pryor,* 375.

234   **"He'd better be funny"** David Henry and Joe Henry, *Furious Cool: Richard Pryor and the World That Made Him* (Chapel Hill, N.C.: Algonquin Books, 2013), 170.

235   **"an H-bomb that Richard"** Paul Mooney, *Black Is the New White: A Memoir* (New York: Simon Spotlight Entertainment, 2009), 164.

236   **"to lard the evening with"** Burke, "'Saturday Night'—Live!"

Chapter 14: Foxhole Writing

238   **"heir apparent to Johnny Carson"** Jeff Greenfield, "He's Chevy Chase and You're Not," *New York,* December 22, 1975.

238   **"He couldn't ad-lib a fart"** Emily Yahr, "40 Years of Sketch Comedy," *Washington Post,* February 14, 2015.

240   **"foxhole writing"** Michael O'Donoghue, interview on *Midday Live with Bill Boggs,* October 9, 1977.

241   **"I'm good under fire"** Ross, "Saturday Night Lorne."

242   **"Elizabeth Taylor doing a striptease"** "A Candid Conversation with Roone Arledge," *Playboy,* October 1976.

242   **"'Good God, they're going to'"** Buck Henry, interview with the Television Academy Foundation, February 26, 2009, American Archive of Television.

243   **"It was pure Dada"** Mike Sacks, *And Here's the Kicker: Conversations with 21 Top Humor Writers on Their Craft* (New York: Writers House, 2014), 19.

244   **scheduled to reveal her belly button** George Schlatter to author.

244   **"Comedy is a baby seal hunt"** Perrin, *Mr. Mike,* 308.

244   **"We're doing this instead of hitting"** Emma Myers, "Outrageous Humor Is an American Tradition," *Atlantic Monthly,* July 7, 2015.

246   **"Please Revise 'You piece of <u>shit</u>'"** Colin Jost, *A Very Punchable Face* (New York: Crown, 2020), 265–266.

247   **"see things sideways"** *Live from New York: The First 5 Years.*

247   **"whacked out of their skulls"** *Live from New York: The First 5 Years.*

248   **"You could fly an F-16"** Chris Taylor, "The Smell of SNL: An Oral History of the Cannabis That Changed Comedy Forever," *Mashable,* August 20, 2020.

Chapter 15: Talk of the Town

250   **"the girl with the built-in"** Penelope Green, "Lillian Ross's (Many) Choice Words," *New York Times,* October 28, 2015.

251   **"Too fancy for Nebraska"** Henry Bushkin, *Johnny Carson* (New York: Mariner Books, 2013), 90.

253   **Bernstein made a pass** Rena Fruchter, *I'm Chevy Chase . . . and You're Not* (London: Virgin Books, 2007), 184.

253   **"this thing that was being done"** *Live from New York: The First 5 Years.*

253   **she'd been arrested in L.A.** "'Mary Hartman' TV Star Charged on Cocaine Count," *New York Times,* May 6, 1976.

254   **"Old Blue Lips"** Tom Schiller to author.

254   **"I know—*satire*"** Miller and Shales, *Live from New York,* 158.

Chapter 16: The Show Itself Speaking

258   **"a gross error of judgment"** Hill and Weingrad, *Saturday Night: A Backstage History,* 216.

258   **"Gerald Fuck/Fart/Ford"** Burke, "'Saturday Night'—Live!"

259   **"As with all of these stories"** Paul McCartney, interview on *The Adam Buxton Podcast,* episode 144, December 11, 2020.

260   **with the help of a few** Hill and Weingrad, *Saturday Night: A Backstage History,* 159.

262   **NBC quickly got Ebersol** Hill and Weingrad, *Saturday Night: A Backstage History*, 232.

262   ***It's not going to get better*** *Live from New York: The First 5 Years*.

263   **His salary for a second** Hill and Weingrad, *Saturday Night: A Backstage History*, 233.

263   **"This was not a group that"** Hill and Weingrad, *Saturday Night: A Backstage History*, 236.

264   **"the only white Gentile comedian"** Hill and Weingrad, *Saturday Night: A Backstage History*, 247.

264   **"Once we bend to a fucking"** Burke, "'Saturday Night'—Live!"

264   **and shaving his back** Hill and Weingrad, *Saturday Night: A Backstage History*, 245.

264   **"I have to decide whether to"** Burke, "'Saturday Night'—Live!"

265   **They cut a $2 million deal** Fruchter, *I'm Chevy Chase*, 59.

Chapter 17: Bicentennial

267   **"Albanian oak"** Bob Woodward, *Wired: The Short Life and Fast Times of John Belushi* (New York: Pocket Books, 1984), 106.

268   **who had a double preoccupation with** Timothy White, "Blues Brothers: Jake and Elwood's Secret Life," *Rolling Stone*, February 22, 1979.

269   **Warren Beatty, David Cassidy, Bob Dylan** Max Bell, "How Paul McCartney Excised the Ghost of the Beatles and Took Flight with Wings," *Classic Rock*, June 2013.

270   **"The only celebrity at this wedding"** Hill and Weingrad, *Saturday Night: A Backstage History*, 312.

Chapter 18: Starmaking

271   **"When a show is a hit"** Ernest Chambers, "Episode 21—Bobby Darin," *50 Years Among the Stars*, May 19, 2022.

271   **"fair-haired program"** Dan Lewis, "He's Chevy Chase and . . . That's Why He's Leaving NBC's 'Saturday Night,'" *Hackensack Record*, September 19, 1976.

271   **"the network's sole smash hit"** Tom Shales, "Chevy Chase: So Long to 'Saturday Night'?," *Washington Post*, August 27, 1976.

271   **the price of a thirty-second** Ross, "Saturday Night Lorne."

272   **"He took a half-inch piece"** Henry, interview with the Television Academy Foundation.

272   **threw a hot iron at him** Fruchter, *I'm Chevy Chase*, 65.

273   **"We're just jerking off"** Burke, "'Saturday Night'—Live!"

273   **"Can I send him home now?"** Miller and Shales, *Live from New York*, 37.

274   **"the best producer in TV"** Belushi, interview on *Midday Live with Bill Boggs*.

274   **"Loving the show is like"** White, "Lorne Michaels, Saturday Night Quarterback."

274   **"I'd rather be psychotic"** David Hirshey, "The Blues Brothers: The Sleazy Comedy of Dan Aykroyd and John Belushi," *Daily News*, January 14, 1979.

274   **"He'd always be bleeding"** Perrin, *Mr. Mike*, 318.

274   **hallucinated invisible robots** Hill and Weingrad, *Saturday Night: A Backstage History*, 411.

275   **"I really do like Gilda"** Miller and Shales, *Live from New York*, 700.

276   **"It's about individuals and how"** Jonathan Takiff, "Who Was That Masked Martin?," *Philadelphia Daily News*, September 30, 1977.

276   **"The country was angry"** Martin, *Born Standing Up*, 110.

276   **"being dropped off at a playground"** Martin, *Born Standing Up*, 175.

277   **"my second ticket into catchphrase heaven"** Martin, *Born Standing Up*, 174.

277   **"smugness was about to creep in"** White, "Lorne Michaels, Saturday Night Quarterback."

280   **"an Irish pirate"** *Live from New York: The First 5 Years*.

281   **There was even talk of Michaels** Hill and Weingrad, *Saturday Night: A Backstage History*, 307.

281   **Richard Pryor had also dangled an offer** Zoglin, *Comedy at the Edge*, 4–5.

281   **"against real architecture"** Andrew Buss and Chris Kopcow, "The Big Uneasy: When *SNL* Went to Mardi Gras," *Vulture*, April 17, 2019.

282   **"to have a timetable"** Buss and Kopcow, "The Big Uneasy."

283   **"It is terrifying, but I live"** Kirby, "Have a Laugh on Lorne."

283   **"Get to know the person next"** Harold Reynolds, "Saturday Night Crew Wows Hyped-Up Mardi Gras Crowd," *Mississippi Sun*, February 22, 1977.

284   **"screaming obscenities and vomiting"** *Live from New York: The First 5 Years*.

284   **"Every minute of it was"** Henry, interview with the Television Academy Foundation.

Chapter 19: Avant-Garde v. Garde

287   **"We were all the same age"** Hagan, *Sticky Fingers*, 28.

287   **"Between Lorne Michaels and all"** Steven M. L. Aronson, "Jann Wenner's Retreat," *Architectural Digest*, July 1990.

288   **before you become garde** Hill and Weingrad, *Saturday Night: A Backstage History,* 353.

288   **"I just bled all over Jackie"** Hagan, *Sticky Fingers,* 341.

288   **"The initial gesture allowed"** Mitchell Glazer and Timothy White, "John Belushi: 1949–1982 Made in America," *Rolling Stone,* April 29, 1982.

288   **"It was the first flush"** Carter, "The Leader of the Lost Boys."

289   **"just like an Antonioni movie"** Jerry Parker, "Who's Who in the Hamptons," *Newsday,* July 2, 1978.

289   **"filled the audience with"** Davis, *Thirty-nine Years of Short-Term Memory Loss,* 145.

289   **fancy friends as "the dead"** Hill and Weingrad, *Saturday Night: A Backstage History,* 272.

290   **"I'm a team player, but"** Burke, " 'Saturday Night'—Live!"

291   **"Nicholson, can you hold"** Judy Jacklin Pisano and Tanner Colby, *Belushi: A Biography* (New York: Rugged Land Books, 2005), 120.

292   **"I began to be more removed"** *Live from New York: The First 5 Years.*

292   **two Black crew members had walked** Hill and Weingrad, *Saturday Night: A Backstage History,* 268.

292   **"If you want to sell an idea"** "My 'SNL': Testimonials from Cast Members Who Lived It," *Grantland,* August 21, 2014.

292   **"and we were all talking"** Miller and Shales, *Live from New York,* 101.

293   **"Love exudes from every person"** James Delson, "Live from New York It's Saturday Night!," *Viva,* April 1978.

293   **"because you had no life"** Delson, "Live from New York It's Saturday Night!"

293   **Upstairs, Aykroyd readied his comrades** Hill and Weingrad, *Saturday Night: A Backstage History,* 332–333.

294   **twenty-four cases of Heineken** Davis, *Thirty-nine Years of Short-Term Memory Loss,* 139.

295   **"He's turning into an asshole"** Davis, *Thirty-nine Years of Short-Term Memory Loss,* 144.

296   **"But when it takes every"** Delson, "Live from New York It's Saturday Night!"

296   **"Go fuck your wife"** Fruchter, *I'm Chevy Chase,* 67–68.

296   **"two bull mooses going at each other"** Jane Curtin, interview on *Watch What Happens Live with Andy Cohen,* Bravo, June 17, 2021.

296   **"It was really a Hollywood fight"** Nick de Semlyen, *Wild and Crazy Guys: How the Comedy Mavericks of the '80s Changed Hollywood Forever* (New York: Crown Archetype, 2019), xiii.

297   **"I got tired of being lectured"** Perrin, *Mr. Mike,* 340.

297   **"Lorne loved Michael"** Perrin, *Mr. Mike,* 341.

298   **"After the show, why not drop"** Perrin, *Mr. Mike,* 347.

298   **"I wanted to bail out"** Hill and Weingrad, *Saturday Night: A Backstage History,* 337.

298   **"over my dead body"** Timothy White, "Michael O'Donoghue: Is America Ready for Mr. Mike?," *Rolling Stone,* July 26, 1979.

299   **"Porky Pig Takes a Trip?"** White, "Michael O'Donoghue."

Chapter 20: Respectable

300   **comparing him to Vincent van Gogh** Chet Flippo, "Keith Richards Guilty—but Free," *Rolling Stone,* November 30, 1978.

301   **"the catalyst of the band"** Flippo, "Keith Richards Guilty."

301   **"No sophisticated 'Elaine's' "** Hill and Weingrad, *Saturday Night: A Backstage History,* 382.

302   **"Maybe this wasn't such a"** Tom Shales, "Cutups and a Coup on 'Saturday Night,' " *Washington Post,* October 8, 1978.

303   **" 'Jesus, I'm an asshole' "** White, "Lorne Michaels, Saturday Night Quarterback."

303   **" 'What about my other ambitions' "** Michaels, interview on *Oprah's Master Class: The Podcast.*

303   **"being the new Munsters"** Hill and Weingrad, *Saturday Night: A Backstage History,* 421.

304   **"just learning how to do it"** White, "Lorne Michaels, Saturday Night Quarterback."

304   **"The quickest way to kill off"** White, "Lorne Michaels, Saturday Night Quarterback."

304   **minimum salary of $750,000** Hill and Weingrad, *Saturday Night: A Backstage History,* 359.

307   **"We were the TV literati"** Hill and Weingrad, *Saturday Night: A Backstage History,* 358.

308   **"I make more money"** Woodward, *Wired,* 198.

308   **"a new form of vaudeville"** White, "Lorne Michaels, Saturday Night Quarterback."

309   **"Suddenly there will be more freedom"** White, "Lorne Michaels, Saturday Night Quarterback."

309   **"Video is where it's at"** Perrin, *Mr. Mike,* 355.

311   **"a lifetime's worth of ideas"** *Live from New York: The First 5 Years.*

311   **"brilliant people do it"** Johnson, "Wise Guys."

311   **"a certain kind of racial tension"** Tom Shales, "Oooh, Nooo! Mr. Bill!" *Washington Post,* January 7, 1980.

312   **picked up a pair of scissors** "Oooooooh noooo! 'Judge Sluggo' Cuts Up 'Mr. Bill,' " *United Press International,* November 10, 1981.

312 **"to make things harder"** Hirshey, "The Blues Brothers."

313 **"I go where I'm kicked"** Pisano and Colby, *Belushi,* 106.

313 **"I'll accept those odds"** Glazer and White, "John Belushi."

313 **"past the point of fame"** David Frost, "Q.&.A. Lorne Michaels," *Panorama,* January 1981.

313 **"Canadian Jewish intellectual"** Woodward, *Wired,* 52.

PART 4 | THURSDAY

318 **ripping hunks of flesh** Chris Smith, "Comedy Isn't Funny," *New York,* March 13, 1995.

322 **when Walken does a play on Broadway** Jordan Hoffman, "*More Cowbell* Ruined Christopher Walken's Life, Will Ferrell Claims" *Vanity Fair,* November 23, 2019.

Chapter 21: The Fifth Year of College

328 **"psychic panic"** Rensin, "The *Playboy Interview: Lorne Michaels.*"

329 **base salary of around $1.5 million** Hill and Weingrad, *Saturday Night: A Backstage History,* 359–360.

329 **"fifth year of college"** William Knoedelseder, Jr., "Has Success Deadened 'Saturday Night Live'?," *Washington Post,* November 25, 1979.

329 **"Back then, nothing mattered"** Knoedelseder, "Has Success Deadened 'Saturday Night Live'?"

330 **"Hollywood is Hollywood**" *Live from New York: The First 5 Years.*

330 **"the virtues of the old youth novels"** David Michaelis, "Dan Aykroyd and John Belushi: The Best of Friends," *Esquire,* December 1982.

334 **"It may be the devil"** Davis, *Thirty-nine Years of Short-Term Memory Loss,* 150.

335 "*oil and water*" *Live from New York: The First 5 Years.*

335 **Shearer said that he was hired** James Hughes, "This Is Harry Shearer: The Former 'SNL' Cast Member's Remarkable Nose for (the Voices of the) News," *Grantland,* August 25, 2014.

336 **"had Lorne by the balls"** Hill and Weingrad, *Saturday Night: A Backstage History,* 408.

337 **"You can't give noogies"** Hill and Weingrad, *Saturday Night: A Backstage History,* 198.

339 **"Cheap wisdom has it"** Tom Shales, "Fridays' Child," *Washington Post,* April 10, 1980.

340 **"Lorne, I'm happy"** Roy Blount, "Gilda," *Rolling Stone,* November 2, 1978.

340 **"a chunk of my intestines"** White, "Lorne Michaels, Saturday Night Quarterback."

342 **"you were hurt that Lorne allowed"** Hill and Weingrad, *Saturday Night: A Backstage History,* 435.

343 **what his tough-minded mother, Florence** Rensin, "*The Playboy Interview: Lorne Michaels.*"

344 **to sell him on colonic irrigation** Andy Warhol, *The Warhol Diaries* (New York: Warner Books, 1989), 291.

345 **"a painful experience"** Tom Shales, "Michaels Leaving 'Saturday Night' Saturday Night Revised," *Washington Post,* June 14, 1980.

345 **the show was dead** Hill and Weingrad, *Saturday Night: A Backstage History,* 446.

Chapter 22: In the Wilderness

346 **"A big piece of my life"** *Saturday Night Live in the '80s.*

346 **looking at pictures of naked women** Hill and Weingrad, *Saturday Night: A Backstage History,* 441.

349 **" 'Hire the Skinhead' "** Glazer and White, "John Belushi."

350 **a baggie of ashes in her purse** Marshall, *My Mother Was Nuts,* 192.

351 **"A garden is like a show"** Rensin, "*The Playboy Interview: Lorne Michaels.*"

354 **"always very, *very* ugly about Lorne"** Perrin, *Mr. Mike,* 376.

354 **she thought it was dopey** Bradford Evans, "Catherine O'Hara Says Michael O'Donoghue Didn't Really Scare Her Away from 'SNL,' " *Vulture,* August 30, 2013.

355 **Pardo learn of his termination** Perrin, *Mr. Mike,* 379.

355 **who installed a wet bar** *Saturday Night Live in the '80s.*

355 **"Sex with Brookie"** Perrin, *Mr. Mike,* 380.

355 **"The Last Ten Days in Silverman's Bunker"** Perrin, *Mr. Mike,* 382–383.

356 **"a 'lying cunt' "** Perrin, *Mr. Mike,* 394.

Chapter 23: Faking Virginity

358 **"It was a nice visual"** Pisano and Colby, *Belushi,* 252.

358 **"The movie business is shit"** Woodward, *Wired,* 310.

358 **"wasn't our drug of choice"** Pisano and Colby, *Belushi,* 262.

358 **"couldn't have been more low"** Rensin, "*The Playboy Interview: Lorne Michaels.*"

358 **"the problem of my generation"** Hill and Weingrad, *Saturday Night: A Backstage History,* 557.

359 **"I've seen him look worse"** Pisano and Colby, *Belushi,* 267.

359 **mourners from snorting lines of coke** Pisano and Colby, *Belushi,* 269.

360 **Schiller rebuffed a couple of Michaels's** Michael Streeter, *Nothing Lost Forever: The Films of Tom Schiller* (Boalsburg, Pa.: BearManor Media, 2006), 98.

360 **"Cut it to the bone"** Streeter, *Nothing Lost Forever,* 149.

361 **expecting a follow-up to *The Jerk*** Streeter, *Nothing Lost Forever,* 154.

361 **"stars aren't being murdered"** Michael Cieply, "Sue Mengers, Hollywood Agent, Dies at 79," *New York Times,* October 16, 2011, 139.

362 **"send his best Jews to Hollywood"** Maureen Dowd, "Sue Mengers, b. 1932," *New York Times Magazine,* December 22, 2011.

364 **"it all rests on conception"** White, "Lorne Michaels, Saturday Night Quarterback."

364 **"shocking has replaced funny"** Sally Bedell Smith, "Lorne Michaels Readies His 'New Show,'" *New York Times,* January 1, 1984.

367 **a Murine bottle full of LSD** Weller, *Carrie Fisher,* 168.

367 **lowest-rated of ninety-four programs** Carter, "Guess What They Call the Man Behind *Saturday Night Live?*"

367 **"My mistake was calling it"** Hal Willner to author.

367 **"I was losing two hundred thousand dollars"** Rensin, *"The Playboy Interview: Lorne Michaels."*

Chapter 24: The Restoration

372 **"'the funeral' for *Saturday Night Live*"** Tom Shales, "Dead or Alive: It's 'Saturday Night'!" *Washington Post,* April 8, 1981.

372 **"It was too raw"** Rich Cohen, "The Godfather of Studio 8H," *Rolling Stone,* September 16, 2010.

373 **"I wanted to do my real life"** Lisa Belkin, "A Decade Old, 'Saturday Night Live' Looks to Fresh Faces," *New York Times,* November 3, 1985.

376 **"You can't do that anymore"** *Saturday Night Live in the '80s.*

377 **"I lived through it for five"** Leslie Bennetts, "Struggles at the New 'Saturday Night,'" *New York Times,* December 12, 1985.

378 **"I'm thirty-six years old"** Bennetts, "Struggles at the New 'Saturday Night.'"

379 **"like watching old men die"** Bennetts, "Struggles at the New 'Saturday Night.'"

379 **"Show dying"** *Saturday Night Live in the '80s.*

380 **"we were old and annoying"** *Saturday Night Live in the '80s.*

380 **"head shop at Sears"** Hill and Weingrad, *Saturday Night: A Backstage History,* 488.

380 **"Is this a seventies show"** Bennetts, "Struggles at the New 'Saturday Night.'"

381 **"I owned that twelve-forty-five slot"** Dan Kois, "Jack Handey Is the Envy of Every Comedy Writer in America," *New York Times,* July 15, 2013.

382 **"on a Beatles album by Ringo"** Carol Leifer, *How to Succeed in Business Without Really Crying: Lesson from a Life in Comedy* (Philadelphia: Quirk Books, 2014), 132.

Chapter 25: Hands Off, Hands On

390 **"I thought my legacy would be"** *Saturday Night Live in the '80s.*

391 **"'Wow, Preppie Preppington'"** *Saturday Night Live in the '80s.*

391 **"do you bring the writers food"** *Saturday Night Live in the '80s.*

391 **"'It's about a guy who'"** Kera Bolonik, "Nora Dunn: 'SNL Is a Traumatic Experience. It's Something You Have to Survive,'" *Salon,* April 7, 2015.

392 **"You're a bitch"** Bonnie Turner to author.

394 **"nauseating tension"** Bob Odenkirk, *Comedy Comedy Comedy Drama: A Memoir* (New York: Random House, 2022), 47.

398 **"quietly pleased with ourselves"** *Saturday Night Live in the '80s.*

Chapter 26: Mentors, Mentees

400 **The article described the indictment** "Arms Dealer Faces Charges," *Calgary Herald,* April 13, 1986.

400 **illegally export thirty million dollars' worth** "Toronto Company Guilty in Arms Conspiracy," *Montreal Gazette,* April 7, 1987.

400 **Reagan-era crackdown called Operation Exodus** Philip Smith, "Attempt to Sell Parts to Iran Hit a Customs Snag," *Washington Post,* December 14, 1982.

400 **"never to list Iran"** Smith, "Attempt to Sell Parts to Iran Hit a Customs Snag."

401 **doing business with the Pentagon** "Arms Charges Can Proceed Against Toronto Company," *Montreal Gazette,* April 14, 1986.

401 **the company was placed in receivership** John Lorine, "Certain Toys Are Us," *Rob Magazine, Globe and Mail*, July 28, 2000.

Chapter 27: Head-Crushing

408 **"very much their own thing"** John Semley, *This Is a Book About the Kids in the Hall* (Toronto: ECW Press, 2016), 95.

411 **Domino's Pizza, Ralston Purina** Eleanor Blau, "Domino's Pulls 'Saturday Night' Ads," *New York Times,* April 11, 1989.

412 **"Hitler can fuck the donkey"** *The Kids in the Hall: Comedy Punks,* directed by Reginald Harkema (Toronto: Blue Ant Media, 2022).

413 **"You did it!"** *The Kids in the Hall.*

414 **"that a man has a right to"** Jeremy Gerard, "Comic Is Protested as 'Saturday Night' Host," *New York Times,* May 11, 1990.

414 **"It would have been nice"** Miller and Shales, *Live from New York,* 334.

414 **"He was never accessible"** Miller and Shales, *Live from New York,* 335.

414 **"the comedy equivalent of heavy metal"** Gerard, "Comic Is Protested as 'Saturday Night' Host."

414 **brief wasn't to examine the host** Bolonik, "Nora Dunn."

415 **"Racist, sexist, anti-gay"** Dennis Perrin, "When Andrew Dice Clay Came to 'SNL' and Controversy Followed," *Vulture,* September 9, 2015.

415 **top-ten-grossing movie comedies** Carter, "Guess What They Call the Man Behind *Saturday Night Live?*"

416 **"if I got even fatter"** Tom Farley and Tanner Colby, *The Chris Farley Show: A Biography in Three Acts* (New York: Viking, 2008), 157.

416 **"classic rock had just hit radio"** David Handelman, "The Ambivalent-About-Prime-Time-Players," *New York Times,* December 19, 1997.

418 **"once they were molded"** Julia Phillips, *You'll Never Eat Lunch in This Town Again* (New York: Random House, 1991), 632.

418 **"One in his twenties"** Jay Mohr, *Gasping for Airtime: Two Years in the Trenches of Saturday Night Live* (New York: Hyperion, 1992), 4.

420 **"hot tub with seventy-two virgins"** Miller and Shales, *Live from New York,* 525.

421 **"It did bother me"** Odenkirk, *Comedy Comedy Comedy Drama,* 63.

Chapter 28: Spinning Off

422 **"Maybe babies bring luck"** Nadine Brozan, "Chronicle," *New York Times,* April 28, 1982.

424 **"fourteen-million-dollar movie"** Derek Lawrence, "*Wayne's World* Director Explains 'Bohemian Rhapsody' Scene, Mike Myers Tension," *Entertainment Weekly,* January 27, 2017.

426 **"I was a bit of a snob"** Mark Harris, "Citizen Wayne: 'Wayne's World' Goes Hollywood," *Entertainment Weekly,* February 28, 1992.

426 **reported $3 million this time** Jeffrey Wells, "'Wayne's World II' War," *Entertainment Weekly,* February 19, 1993.

426 **"I hope to God"** Harris, "Citizen Wayne."

427 **According to Michaels** Stephen Galloway, *Leading Lady: Sherry Lansing and the Making of a Hollywood Groundbreaker* (New York: Crown, 2017), 193.

427 **"go to Lorne's office right now"** Galloway, *Leading Lady,* 193.

429 **while hiding in a Burbank closet** Bill Carter, *The Late Shift: Letterman, Leno, & the Network Battle for the Night* (New York: Hyperion, 1994), 151–153.

429 **"Lorne has a very basic skill"** Kolbert, "New Job for NBC's Laugh Master."

433 **"a great discoverer"** Bill Carter, "A First Bow, This Time to the Press," *New York Times,* May 4, 1993.

435 **"thing of people not being good"** Michaels, interview on *Fly on the Wall.*

435 **"get that fat fucking dildo"** Bill Carter, *The War for Late Night: When Leno Went Early and Television Went Crazy* (New York: Viking, 2010), 81.

436 **"one of the most amazing transformations"** Tom Shales, "The Late-Night Dawning of Conan," *Washington Post,* July 1, 1996.

Chapter 29: *The Make-Fun-of-Lorne Show*

437 **"This is a wonderful, heartfelt occasion"** Hagan, *Sticky Fingers,* 446.

439 **"on a plane once in Des Moines"** Bill Hader to author.

440 **"Who's Met *Blank*?"** Martin Short to author.

PART 5 | FRIDAY

446 **Baldwin had just been arrested** James Barron and Ali Winston, "Alec Baldwin Is Arrested After Dispute over Parking Space in Manhattan," *New York Times,* November 2, 2018.

Chapter 30: Saturday Night Dead

458 **"My hope is we'll get through"** Bill Carter, "At (or on) a TV Show: Free Fun for a Few," *New York Times,* May 8, 1992.

458 **"the electronic equivalent of wrinkles"** John J. O'Connor, "A Prosperous 'Saturday Night' Grows Tame," *New York Times,* March 14, 1993.

459 **"It's everything you think it is"** Julia Sweeney Relieved to Leave 'Saturday Night Live,'" *Chicago Tribune,* August 13, 1994.

460 **" 'sweet mother of God!' "** Farley and Colby, *The Chris Farley Show,* 195.

460 **how to solve "the SNL crisis"** Bruce Fretts, "Is 'Saturday Night' Dead?" *Entertainment Weekly,* March 11, 1994.

461 **"a children's crusade"** Doug Hill, "Can 'Saturday Night Live' Regain Its Bite?," *New York Times,* October 2, 1994.

462 **"that Chicago integrity"** Ross, "Saturday Night Lorne."

464 **"almost 100 percent humor-free"** "Dear 'Saturday Night Live': It's Over. Please Die," *Newsweek,* October 16, 1994.

465 **"more activist management at NBC"** Hill, "Can 'Saturday Night Live' Regain Its Bite?"

465 **Admiral Dönitz** "Dear 'Saturday Night Live': It's Over."

466 **O'Donoghue's postmortem brainscan** Chris Smith, "Mr. Mike's Mondo Muerto," *New York,* November 28, 1994.

467 **heckler shouted that it was Mike Douglas** Anthony Haden Guest, "Exit Laughing," *The New Yorker,* November 20, 1994.

467 **"He was an incredibly important person"** Smith, "Mr. Mike's Mondo Muerto."

468 **"There's nothing sadder than an aging"** Rensin, *"The Playboy Interview: Lorne Michaels."*

468 **"a deep spiritual funk"** Smith, "Comedy Isn't Funny."

473 **"If there was an ax"** Farley and Colby, *The Chris Farley Show,* 210.

Chapter 31: "Is He *Doing* Me?"

480 **"because they use another kind"** Donald Liebenson, "It's So Dumb, and It Just Felt So Right": An Oral History of *MacGruber, Vanity Fair,* May 21, 2020.

481 **"get to make another one"** Semley, *This Is a Book About the Kids in the Hall,* 162.

483 **Carvey has discussed Dr. Evil** *The Howard Stern Show,* Sirius Radio, May 22, 2019.

484 **corner of Rodeo and Elevado** "Pete Davidson Charged with Reckless Driving in Car Crash," *Los Angeles Times,* June 16, 2023.

484 **"Schindler's B-list"** Brian Kellow, *Can I Go Now?: The Life of Sue Mengers, Hollywood's First Superagent* (New York: Viking, 2015), 7.

484 **mugs of soup** Anne Stringfield, "Sue Mengers and Hollywood," *The New Yorker,* October 20, 2011.

485 *When I Was Alive* Kellow, *Can I Go Now?,* 254.

Chapter 32: Interference

486 **"Let your enemy bury himself"** David Rensin, *It's All Lies and That's the Truth: And 49 More Rules from 50 Years of Trying to Make a Living in Hollywood* (New York: Gotham Books, 2004), 83.

486 **"We were going to be mean"** Mike Sacks, "SNL's James Downey on Working with Norm Macdonald and Getting Fired for Making Fun of OJ Simpson," *Vulture,* June 24, 2014.

488 **Mid-discussion, Dana Carvey had stood** Farley and Colby, *The Chris Farley Show,* 264.

488 **"As long as people showed up"** *Live from New York: The First 5 Years.*

493 **"living on the moon"** Miller and Shales, *Live from New York,* 603.

Chapter 33: The Rules of Coming and Going

496 **hated Cirque du Soleil** Jason Sudeikis, interview on *WTF with Marc Maron* (podcast), episode 205, August 29, 2011.

497 **"They will eat you"** Lillian Ross, "10½: A Profile of Federico Fellini," *The New Yorker,* October 22, 1965.

497 *Conversation over* Miller and Shales, *Live from New York,* 722.

497   **"Do whatever you need to do"** Miller and Shales, *Live from New York*, 725.

498   **Michaels paid for her veneers** Amy Poehler, *Yes, Please* (New York: Dey Street, 2014), 144.

499   **"Am I third"** Grayson Carter, quoted in *Inside.com*, November 21, 2022.

Chapter 34: "Can We Be Funny?"

502   **"end of the age of irony"** *Inside.com*, September 18, 2001.

504   **"In the midst of this overwhelming tragedy"** "Paul Simon & Lorne Michaels," *Iconoclasts*, Sundance TV, November 23, 2006.

504   **"We're all here"** Tina Fey, *Bossypants* (New York: Reagan Arthur Books, 2011), 130.

505   **"I think I'll sigh a little bit less"** Richard L. Berke and Kevin Sack, "In Debate 2, Microscope Focuses on Gore," *New York Times*, October 11, 2000.

506   **a right-winger** Ross Luippold, "'SNL' Writer Jim Downey: No 'Conspiracy' Surrounding Rejected Obama Sketch," *Huffington Post*, May 8, 2012.

506   **"the Karl Rove of SNL"** Miller and Shales, *Live from New York*, 81.

507   **"such a safe, wishy-washy target"** Dave Itzkoff, "The All Too Ready for Prime Time Players," *New York Times*, January 2, 2005.

508   **made a bet among themselves** Corinne Heller, "*SNL* Stars Had a Bet About Paris Hilton When She Hosted the Show," *E! News Online*, September 13, 2018.

509   **"babe in waiting"** Susan Baer, "Nobody's Picking on Chelsea Clinton," *Seattle Times*, July 21, 1993.

510   **Peter Pan–themed birthday party** Fey, *Bossypants*, 224.

511   **"has as much impact on younger"** Miller and Shales, *Live from New York*, 95.

513   **"The audience of the show"** Jake Coyle, "Hey Hey, My My," *Associated Press*, March 4, 2006.

513   **losing cast members or episodes** Bill Carter, "Bowing to Budget Cuts at NBC, 'Saturday Night Live' Pares Five Performers," *New York Times*, September 21, 2006.

Chapter 35: The Big Tent

516   **to host his own reality show** Stacey Wilson Hunt, "A Rare Glimpse Inside the Empire of SNL's Lorne Michaels," *Hollywood Reporter*, April 22, 2011.

517   **Sorkin called Michaels and asked** Tad Friend, "Shows About Shows," *The New Yorker*, April 24, 2006.

517   **"the network isn't that powerful"** Friend, "Shows About Shows."

Chapter 36: Not Tonight

524   **Even Carson made a crack** Carter, *The War for Late Night*, 151.

525   **_Variety_ even said so** Michael Schneider, "Lorne Michaels: I've Seen the Enemy, and It's Guitar Hero," *Variety*, May 12, 2008.

526   **it stung to learn that Michaels** Carter, *The War for Late Night*, 292.

528   **"Jews do not celebrate martyrdom"** Carter, *The War for Late Night*, 388.

533   **"There is _no_ job after this"** David Kamp and Jessica Diehl, "Heeeeere's Jimmy," *Vanity Fair*, February 2014.

534   **"better than our fart-joke division"** David Roth, "My Fabulous Vacation Home on Naboo, with Michael Schur," *Defector* (podcast), March 9, 2023.

535   **"Mark Twain deciding to be a florist"** Kois, "Jack Handey Is the Envy of Every Comedy Writer in America."

537   **"If it's not funny"** Bill Carter, "'S.N.L.' to Add Black Female Performer," *New York Times*, December 12, 2013.

PART 6 | SATURDAY

560   **"We take it to the junk shop"** Joanna Robinson, "*Saturday Night Live*: 41 Years of Backstage Secrets from the Man Who Lived Them," *Vanity Fair*, September 1, 2016.

562   **a parody of a feel-good Toyota ad** Saba Hamedy, "'SNL': Fake ISIS Ad with Dakota Johnson Stirs Controversy," *Los Angeles Times*, March 1, 2015.

583   **"heaved and gyrated"** Jennifer Keishin Armstrong, *Seinfeldia* (New York: Simon & Schuster, 2016), 126.

PHOTO CREDITS

INDEX

ABOUT THE AUTHOR

SUSAN MORRISON is the articles editor of *The New Yorker*. She is the former editor in chief of *The New York Observer* and an original editor of *Spy* magazine. She lives in New York City.